LEGACY

LEGACY

A BIOGRAPHY OF

MOSES AND WALTER ANNENBERG

CHRISTOPHER OGDEN

LITTLE, BROWN AND COMPANY

A *Little, Brown* Book

First published in the United States in 1999
by Little, Brown and Company US
First published in Great Britain in 1999
by Little, Brown and Company UK

Copyright © Christopher Ogden 1999

A CIP catalogue record for this book
is available from the British Library.

ISBN 0 316 85363 1

Printed and bound in Great Britain by
Clays Ltd, St Ives plc

Little, Brown and Company (UK)
Brettenham House
Lancaster Place
London WC2E 7EN

T

For Deedy with love

CONTENTS

LEGACY

INTRODUCTION

———

PRINCESS MARGARET and the Earl of Snowdon were the official honorees at the most anticipated party of London's 1969 fall social season, although none of the 435 guests in black tie, floor-length gowns and constellations of gems came to see them. Several were distracted when Snowdon, the photographer husband of the queen's younger sister began trading kisses with ballet star Rudolf Nureyev. Whispers of "an old Russian custom, of course," buzzed, but otherwise failed to shift the attention of the ball-goers from the solidly built, gray-haired man greeting guests, the striking blonde woman at his side, or from the jaw-dropping beauty of the rooms in which they had begun to mingle.

It was 10:40 P.M. on a crisp, clear Tuesday, November 25, and on the crushed-rock driveway of the Georgian mansion in Regent's Park there was Rolls-Royce-, Bentley-, and Daimler-lock as chauffeurs jockeyed to disgorge one past and two future prime ministers, much of the Labour government cabinet, foreign office mandarins, twenty ambassadors and high commissioners, plus sundry princes, dukes and duchesses, marquesses, earls, viscounts, lords, knights, publishers, authors, actors, barristers, business executives and one maharajah — of Jaipur, naturally.

As the majordomo called out each name, Walter Annenberg greeted the arrivals with a penetrating look, a firm handshake, and a hearty welcome to Winfield House, residence of the American ambassador to the Court of St. James's that he had just spent one million of his own dollars fixing up, or as he had famously put it, refurbishing. At his right side, where he cannot hear, stood his wife, Leonore. Wearing an impeccable pale yellow satin dress made by Hardie Amies, the queen's favorite designer, and her $400,000 ruby necklace and earrings, Lee, as she is known, eased guests into the party with the easy smile and warmth of a born hostess.

Neither she nor Walter revealed the slightest hint of the anger, frustration, nervousness and exhaustion that had plagued them since their arrival in Britain seven months earlier, although both knew that their future in London hinged on how this evening was received. Success would go a long way toward relieving the torrent of criticism they had endured from the moment word leaked out in December 1968 that the newly elected Richard Nixon intended to give his friend Walter the juiciest patronage plum that a president can dispense. Failure would mean that they might as well cut their losses and return home to Philadelphia and Sunnylands, their winter retreat near Palm Springs. The latter was so palatial that on his first visit Prince Charles, no stranger to palaces, cracked, "You gave up *this* to move to London?"

Neither Annenberg had ever been a quitter, but by the time of this party, they had already had second thoughts about the posting. Walter had even told Secretary of State William Rogers that he would leave Britain if he were embarrassing the president. Rogers just had to say the word and he and Lee would start packing. Walter's difficulties were so well known that self-designated candidates to replace him had begun lining up. The secretary of state told his novice ambassador that Nixon had no intention of pulling him out and urged him to keep putting one foot in front of the other. This too would pass. Walter knew Rogers was right. He and his family had been under attack for much of his life, a condition he shared with Nixon and which had cemented their friendship. "Life is ninety-nine rounds," he used to tell the then vice president in 1956 when Dwight Eisenhower nearly dropped him as his second-term running mate and in 1960 after Nixon lost the presidency to John F. Kennedy. During and after Watergate, Walter would remind him of the adage again. Now he was repeating the words, mantra-like, to himself.

He had anticipated the reaction to his nomination. When Nixon offered the London embassy to him while visiting Sunnylands soon after the election, Walter initially balked. As publisher of the *Philadelphia Inquirer,* he recognized from his own enthusiastic participation just how bloody political arenas could become. He warned the president-elect that his confirmation hearing could be embarrassing to the new administration. Damaging allegations about his father, Moses, would be dug up and replayed while Walter was left to swing in a fetid breeze, his naturally combative and retaliatory instincts constrained by his very nomination to become a diplomat. When Nixon insisted that he could stand the heat if Walter could, Annenberg accepted.

The Senate Foreign Relations Committee hearing chaired by J. William Fulbright, the anti-war activist and Nixon critic, was acrimonious. A quarter century had passed since his father died, but, as he had expected, Walter was forced to respond to infuriating rumors, complex half-truths and agonizing facts about Moses Annenberg. One of eleven children, Moses had come penniless from East Prussia in 1885 to Chicago, where, at the turn of the century, he was hired by publisher William Randolph Hearst to battle rival newspapers — sometimes with baseball bats and guns — for circulation gains on the streets of the city's tough South Side. Fearless and a brilliant businessman despite a lack of formal education, Moses moved to New York, bought the *Daily Racing Form*, the racetrack bible, and the General News Bureau, which supplied racing data electronically to legitimate news outlets — and most of the nation's illegal bookmakers. With a monopoly on track information, Moses earned millions, but the links of his empire to the underworld tainted his reputation. He became determined to leave a more respectable legacy to his only son, whose character he was trying to mold through such a skewed mix of indulgence and brutality that Walter's own personality would feature dramatic contradictions.

Moses bought the failing *Philadelphia Inquirer*, a bastion of Pennsylvania's conservative Republicanism, and battered into submission the rival *Philadelphia Record*, owned by New Dealer J. David Stern, one of then president Franklin D. Roosevelt's most ardent supporters. The pro- and anti-FDR battle in the City of Brotherly Love in the late 1930s prompted a federal investigation of Moses, who admitted guilt to one count of income tax evasion as part of a plea bargain in which charges against Walter were dropped. Moses was hit with one of the highest U.S. civil fines in history — $9.5 million, or $110 million in current dollars — was jailed and released two years later in 1942 to die. Walter, until then little more than a college dropout and a playboy with a bad stutter, paid the fine, rescued the family business and, battling guilt over his father's sacrifice, began displaying extraordinary talents no one knew he had.

During Word War II, Walter launched *Seventeen* magazine for young women and in 1953 *TV Guide*, the most profitable weekly ever published. Through the *Inquirer* he became, like his father, a political kingmaker in Pennsylvania, backing favorite candidates and projects and leaving little doubt about where his often — but not inflexible — Republican sympathies lay. As the television era boomed, Walter bought and built stations and launched programs as diverse and popular as *American Bandstand* and the *University of the Air*. He and his seven sisters, influenced by their mother, Sadie, who was as generous-spirited as Moses had been ruthless, became prominent philanthropists. Walter and Lee — his second wife and her third husband — became pillars of Philadelphia, activists in the arts and education, although pockets of the Establishment refused to accept Walter, in part because he was Jewish and in greater measure because he was Moe Annenberg's son.

The confirmation hearing proved ultimately a triumph for Walter, but his ambassadorial troubles were just beginning. Not only had Nixon ended the Democrats' two-term hold on the White House, but in London, Walter was replacing David Bruce, one of America's most experienced and respected diplomats. Bruce's wife, Evangeline, had invited Lee to London to examine Winfield House, which had deteriorated badly during the Bruces' eight-year tenure, but then turned on the Annenbergs when she saw that Lee and Walter intended to make major changes. In a furious vendetta against a couple she considered know-nothing arrivistes out to Hollywoodize a gloomy yet genteel residence that had been good enough for the Bruces, the socially connected "Vangie" did her utmost to poison the London well for Lee and Walter. Instead of leaving the capital for a year, a common diplomatic practice to allow newcomers to get established, the Bruces moved to an apartment a mile from Winfield House and set up a rival court where the sport was making fun of their successors.

Then came Walter's dreadful experience presenting his credentials to the queen before the television cameras of the British Broadcasting Corporation, which was filming a special on royal life. Trying to be less formal, the queen had casually asked where he was living. His stilted, polysyllabic response made him the laughingstock of Britain and America when the documentary aired six weeks later in June. Since then, as teams of contractors under the direction of two California designers labored to renovate the residence in Regent's Park, Walter had gone to ground, refusing interview requests and hoping the storm would blow over.

Tonight was the great unveiling, not merely of the house, but of the Annenbergs as well. The Georgian-style building on the corner of one of central London's most beautiful parks had been redone with exquisite care and lovingly refurnished as Walter's gift to the American people and as a mark of his and Lee's respect for Britain. On the repainted celadon-colored walls hung thirty-two of their prized Impressionist paintings they would later give to New York's Metropolitan Museum of Art. Red, white and blue flowers, colors of the Union Jack and Stars and Stripes and grown in the property's reconstructed greenhouses, filled the residence. Twenty-eight guests, including Princess Margaret and Snowdon, arrived for dinner at 8:30 P.M. Another four hundred began arriving two hours later for a buffet supper and dancing until 4 A.M. in an ethereal gold-colored tent to the music of the Dark Blues, "the best band in England!" according to an enthusiastic duchess of Northumberland.[1]

No sooner had the guests staggered home than praise began flooding in. "A magical evening," wrote the countess of Airlie, wife of the future lord chamberlain.[2] "Unforgettable," said Lady Adeane, wife of the queen's private secretary.[3] "The most successful party in ages," added Lady Rupert-Neville, wife of Prince Philip's treasurer,[4] while Tony Wedgwood-Benn, a Labour party star in the House of Commons, labeled the evening "the most dramatic diplomatic debut."[5] "More than a party, it was a grand occasion," wrote Jean Barber, wife of the soon-to-be chancellor of the exchequer, the government's top economic post.[6] "In mod chat, a Happening," chimed in Lady Elworthy, whose husband was governor of Windsor castle.[7]

The house, according to Lady Hartwell, whose husband owned the *Daily Telegraph*, was "dazzlingly beautiful."[8] "You've made a palace of it," wrote *Observer* columnist Kenneth Harris.[9] "The finest residence in London," was the verdict of historian A. L. Rouse.[10] "Everyone was most impressed with the new decor," said Sir Denis Greenhill, permanent undersecretary of the Foreign Office.[11] "It is an amazingly generous thing to do, to take such trouble over a house which is only a temporary home," wrote the duchess of Devonshire. "It is a great compliment to all of us that you have done it."[12] "Anglo-American relations have been firmly cemented by your kind gesture," added Gillian Rees-Mogg, wife of the editor of the *Times* of London.[13] Lady Shawcross, wife of the former attorney general, cut straight to the point: "I do so hope that after the problems of the last six months you were really happy about the success last night. I feel that you have really won through — due to your charm and determination."[14]

The restoration of Winfield House and its public unveiling turned out to be a watershed in Annenberg family history. After the ball,

Walter's fortunes in London and Washington began to turn. The unkind laughter subsided. Jeers turned to cheers. The Bruce influence waned. Lee and Walter, it had become clear, had impeccable taste and their generosity was boundless. The ambassador was reassessed. Instead of inept or pompous, he was newly judged amusing and original. Walter's confidence soared and his style mellowed. The insecure, hard-charging, partisan publisher became an avuncular public figure. Lee and he transformed the U.S. residence into the most convivial embassy in London. Invitations were prized and reciprocal offers took the Annenbergs from paneled boardrooms and inner-city pubs to country estates and royal palaces.

More important, once accepted in Britain, where Walter became the only U.S. ambassador ever knighted by the queen, the Annenbergs found themselves welcomed everywhere. On returning to the United States, he increased the pace of his philanthropy until, by the late 1990s, he had given away more than $2 billion plus a billion-dollar art collection. He had become the world's most generous living philanthropist. Of greater significance, he had far exceeded the limited expectations his father had for him. And all because of this one dance party? Well, not quite. There was much more to the story.

I

EAST PRUSSIA

———

SHEVA ANNENBERG remembered screaming the first two times she gave birth. Moses, though, was her eighth child, scrawnier than the others and so eager to be born that she had scarcely felt the tug of a contraction turn to a convulsion when she saw him, thick black hair smeared with mucus, cradled in her own mother's calloused hands. It was just past 3 P.M. on February 11, 1877, but the sun had already set in Kalvishken, a tiny hamlet in East Prussia, near the border of present day Lithuania. Baltic Sea gales pushing snow across northeast Europe rattled chill and wind through the chinks in the roof and walls of the one-story timber-and-stone house, guttering the two bedside candles and raising wisps of steam from the newborn's mottled shoulders.

In the next room, where he ran the village's sole grocery store, Sheva's husband, Tobias, eased a birch log onto a low fire, as Moses later recounted. Tobias was not worried about the activity beyond the curtain. His widowed mother-in-law, Leah, had delivered each of his and Sheva's five daughters and two sons on the same split-plank bed. His wife was healthy and her mother preternaturally calm. No problem was expected and there would be none when Moses began life. Later that would change.

For nearly a century Tobias's ancestors had lived quietly in East Prussia, but only for the past half-dozen years did the family have a surname. Until 1871, Tobias was known simply as Tobias, son of Israel. That year, King Wilhelm I of Prussia became emperor of a united German empire and his first chancellor, Otto von Bismarck, began consolidating the new state by ordering a census. When the imperial census takers arrived in Kalvishken in late 1871, they found twenty-four residents, half of them illiterate.[1] Four, including Tobias and Sheva, could read and write Plattdeutsch, or low German. Tobias could also speak Swedish, from living in Sweden before marrying, and some Russian. To improve record keeping in what would become that most precise of nations, the German officials assigned formal patronymics. Tobias, son of Israel, became Tobias "of the hill" — *on am berg* in local colloquial German — because his house nestled in the lee of two hills known as Pertebargh and Umerbargh.

The Annenbergs owned their own home, which consisted of half a house and two acres of land for which Tobias had paid the equivalent of $400, according to notes for an unpublished memoir that Moses made a half century later.[2] He earned the money by working his own plot as well as buying and selling produce from neighboring farmers, carrying milk, eggs, chicken and fish to market on a cart and bringing back clothing, rope, tools, thread and salt to sell from his house. The closest town was Insterburg, fourteen miles north by rutted dirt road. Inland from the port of Koenigsberg, capital of East Prussia, Insterburg was small and sleepy yet modestly prosperous, a military garrison town and the center of the region's horse-breeding industry. Eight days after his birth, just as his brothers, Jacob, ten, and Max, three, had been before him, Moses Louis Annenberg was circumcised in the synagogue on Forchestrasse.[3]

Jews were still relatively new to Insterburg; the synagogue was only twelve years old. There had been Jewish settlements in the old German cultural centers farther west along the Rhine, Danube and Elbe from the earliest Middle Ages, but Prussian law in those years prohibited the residence of Jews. In the seventeenth and eighteenth centuries, Jewish tradesmen were allowed into Prussia after paying hefty fees for "ducal protection" but only after promising they would not practice their religion. In 1786, a small group of Jewish goldsmiths and copper engravers was awarded a royal concession to work in Gumbinen, capital of the administrative district which incorporated much of the northern portion of East Prussia. Not until 1812 were Prussian Jews granted citizenship and the right to travel.[4] At that point, there were seven Jewish families in all of Gumbinen, including Tobias's grandfather. At the time Moses underwent his bris, fewer than fifty Jews lived in Insterburg.[5]

Back in Kalvishken after the ceremony, the Annenberg family continued to grow. During the five years after Moses's birth, Sheva bore three more children. Each time, her mother stood by the bedside and helped deliver the newborn. Each time, she prayed for long life for the child, none of whom would live as long as Leah, who helped raise them all and was 104 when she died.

Moses was five when Sheva's last child was born. Most of the children had a nickname. Eldest son Jacob was "Ashmadie," after King Solomon's magic eagle. Because he had a dark complexion and penetrating eyes, Moses was known as "Schwarzer Zigeuner," the black gypsy. Max had no nickname, but as the most eager to please, he was his father's favorite. Almost every time Tobias went to market in Insterburg, he returned with a *"buntetute,"* a small, colorful bag with a surprise, for Max. Rarely did anyone else in the family get a gift, much to the annoyance of Moses, who recalled the affront a half century later in notes for an unpublished memoir.

(These notes, it should be established, comprise forty-one manuscript pages covering the period from the family's life in Kalvishken to 1904, when the account breaks off in mid-sentence. Yellowed, but carefully typed, the document was dictated by Moses in the 1930s, filed away in family records and apparently forgotten. There is little reason to dispute Moses's recollections. For the most part his anecdotes are not self-glorifying. On the contrary, many are painfully honest, self-deprecating and deflating. Yet they reflect the impressions and interpretations of Moses, not those of his parents or siblings.)

SHEVA AND TOBIAS were Orthodox Jews. Every morning, Tobias would pull on a prayer shawl and affix to forehead and left arm his phylacteries, the two small leather boxes which contained strips of parchment inscribed with verses from Scripture. With the prayer ribbons wound around his arm, he stood in the corner of the store facing east and recited his prayers for up to two hours, all the while refusing to speak with anyone. If unknowing neighbors or travelers entered seeking supplies, Tobias looked bizarre — bobbing, chanting and appearing trussed up. There were other oddities. The Annenbergs stocked lard because rendered pig fat was commonly used in Prussian dishes. But no Annenberg could touch it. If a customer wanted lard, Tobias called Frau Murbrey, the lady who occupied the other half of the house, to come weigh it out.

Such unusual habits aroused the attention of the village bully, a blacksmith named Harder, who was inspired repeatedly to offer Max and his sister Eva pork sandwiches, which they wolfed down in ravenous delight. When he discovered what Harder had done, a livid Tobias confronted the blacksmith, who retaliated by dropping a ham hock down the Annenberg well. Tobias was so distressed that he walked to Insterburg to report Harder to the police. From there, he went directly to the synagogue, where the rabbi, after accepting a donation, granted the Annenbergs a special dispensation to drink their well water. When the police fined Harder ten marks, then about $2.50, the blacksmith struck back by building a fence to obstruct the road to the Annenberg home. "Harder became our nemesis," Moses recalled decades later. "He was the recognized menace and we had to contend with him."[6]

The feud was between Harder and Tobias and his then teenage son, Jacob. The younger Annenbergs were not affected, and the hamlet was so small that the families could not avoid one another. When he was five, Moses often visited the Harder house to play with Bertha, the blacksmith's daughter. The atmosphere was far different from the calm he knew at home. Neither Tobias nor Sheva drank alcohol and both tended their marriage and family with care. Moses learned at the Harder house, where the blacksmith drank heavily, that not all parents behaved like his. During one visit, Moses stared in horror as Harder pulled the coffee pot off the fire and poured grounds and hot water over his wife's head. A half century later, Moses could still recite the blacksmith's drunk, idiomatic cackle over the cries of his scalded wife: "Ich taufer dir mit kaffee grund, du sulz sier mir poodle hund." (I christen thee with coffee grounds so thou wilt be my poodle dog.)[7]

Anti-Semitism in Kalvishken was merely the local manifestation of a larger problem growing worse by the day. On March 13, 1881, a month after Moses turned four, an assassin named Sophia Perovskaya, the daughter of an aristocrat, had flung a bomb and blown up Czar Alexander II in St. Petersburg. An enlightened reformer who had freed serfs, eased Jewish taxes, allowed Jews to become military officers and introduced limited local self-rule, though not enough for some revolutionary groups, Alexander II had governed Russia quite benignly for twenty-six years. "The kindliest prince who ever ruled Russia," Disraeli called him.[8] His thirty-six-year-old son who succeeded him was anything but kind and launched a monstrous effort to root out dissension that spilled over into eastern Europe.

No sooner had the gallows trapdoor sprung on the conspirators, hanged before a crowd of eighty thousand, than the new czar issued a manifesto: "The voice of God commands us to rule with faith in the power and the truth of the autocratic authority."[9] A military officer of limited intelligence and education, Alexander III discarded his father's reforms and cracked down hard, rigidly repressing minorities who had fared well under his father. As a senior adviser, he selected Konstantin Pobedonostev, a fanatic who believed in a church-guided police state and whose motto was "Russia for Russians."

There were already some 650 laws in force restricting Jews that had been in place for years before Alexander III took over. That spring the government added more. The May Laws barred Jews from owning or renting land outside cities. Jews could not practice law or vote. New quotas kept Jews from schools and universities. The alcohol industry was later taken over by a government monopoly which halted sales to Jewish proprietors of restaurants and inns and forced thousands out of business.[10]

Vowing to kill a third of Russia's Jews, drive out a third and convert the remainder to orthodox Christianity, Alexander III next launched a series of pogroms, or organized massacres, the impact of which spilled over Russia's borders. Across the Pale of Settlement, from Odessa and Kiev to Minsk and Vilna — the area set aside by the government since 1791 for Jews to live in — troops and police looked the other way or joined in the brutality as shrieking hordes ransacked and burned tens of thousands of Jewish homes and hundreds of synagogues. Mobs chanting "Christ killers" beat Jews to death. On Christmas day in 1881 the pogrom gangs struck the Jews of Warsaw, destroying forty-five hundred homes, shops and synagogues and killing hundreds. Jewish history turned on the barbarous events of that horrible year. Beginning that summer and continuing for thirty years, until the 1914 outbreak of the First World War, millions of Jews — tailors, cobblers, jewelers, traders and their families — poured from the brick ghettos and wooden shtetls of Russia and Eastern Europe and headed west in search of safety and new opportunity.

In 1882, Tobias Annenberg joined the exodus. At market and at synagogue in Insterburg, he had heard about the horrors of the pogroms firsthand from wretchedly poor, homeless Jews fleeing west in long, tattered coats and broad-brimmed hats with their few belongings on pushcarts or on their backs. He had been antagonized enough by the blacksmith Harder to realize that the Annenbergs would never be able to avoid the spreading violence. An intelligent man of action as well as a man of prayer, Tobias reviewed the family's options out of earshot of the children. "Life and strife continued to be hard and soon we realized that there was no real future for us in Kalvishken," Moses wrote later. "About that time I noticed quiet confidential whisperings between my oldest brother Jacob, father, mother and grandmother. Soon after that, my father departed one night for the golden land, America."[11]

The pogroms were not all that Tobias heard about from Russian Jews passing through Insterburg. The image of America as the Golden Land, the Goldeneh Medina, came burnished in letters from the earliest emigrants to those desperate relatives and friends who remained behind. Many were terrified by the prospect of leaving homes where they had lived for generations. Most had never been more than a few miles from their own neighborhood or town. They had little concept of what Moscow or Warsaw would be like, let alone the incomprehensible foreignness of New York.

When a letter arrived from the New World, neighbors packed into the house of the recipient for a public reading. "In America you can say what you feel. You can voice your thoughts in the open streets without fear. Christians and Jews are brothers together," a woman named Anzia Yezierska wrote her Russian cousins in 1882. "There are no high or low in America. Even the President holds hands with [an immigrant named] Gedalyeh Mindel. Plenty for all. Learning flows free like milk and honey."[12] Little wonder that two million Jews would ultimately leave for America and that the U.S. population of fifty-three million would jump 10 percent by the end of the decade.

Tobias went alone, leaving Jacob in charge. Then seventeen, Jacob had been summoned that year by Prussian authorities for compulsory military service, but was rejected for physical deficiencies. His lung capacity was diminished and his hearing was impaired, the latter a problem that would affect later generations of Annenbergs. He spent most of his time fishing in the lake in the center of Kalvishken, catching the family's dinner and, on good days, an extra lake bass or two to sell to neighbors. For the next year and a half, the Annenbergs survived on Jacob's skills and the five dollars Tobias sent each month along with reports about his life in his own Goldeneh Medina of Chicago. "Father told us how people in America throw out the cake and meat which they cannot eat into the alley," Moses recalled. "We actually thought father had lost his mind in writing such unbelievable things."

After living alone and saving as much as he could for eighteen months, Tobias asked Jacob to join him. Happy to spend most days hunting, fishing and being the man around the house, Jacob was strong-willed, self-centered and reluctant to leave Kalvishken. It was only when Tobias insisted and promised him a bright future, possibly as a bookkeeper in a multi-storied building, that Jacob handed down his fish nets and traps. Max, who was ten, did not like the solitude of fishing. So the gear went to Moses, who assumed angling duties for the family in late summer 1883 when he was six and a half years old. The assignment was a major responsibility because the ten remaining children and their mother and grandmother had little to eat except fish, vegetables and potatoes.

Jacob had hunted for meat to sell, but the family ate none because it was not kosher. Kosher meat was available only in Insterburg and Gumbinen. Once a year, for the ten days between Rosh Hashanah and Yom Kippur, Tobias had loaded the entire Annenberg family in a wagon and taken them to one of the other towns for high holy day services. They ate meat on those occasions and a few other times a year when Tobias trudged back with salt beef from his solitary trips to market. Once he left for America, both family trips and the occasional meat supplement ended.

Fishing was never a chore for Moses. He took pride in being depended upon and he loved the solitude, the peace and quiet away from the house, which was crowded with noisy brothers and sisters. Moses set fish traps and, until the lake froze in early November, fished daily with such joy that the pastime would become a lifelong love. The pleasure never extended to saltwater or deep sea fishing. But the combination of a fly rod, with which he later became expert, and a trout, bass or pike-filled stream or lake was as close to heaven as Moses could imagine.

Jacob's regret at having left the lake increased when he arrived in America, close to collapse with fatigue, and discovered there was no bookkeeping job. Norman Stone, a nephew of Tobias, who was in the secondhand furniture business, hired Jacob to clean stoves for five dollars a month and a place to sleep in a corner of the store basement. On occasion, without the knowledge of her husband, Mrs. Stone would slip the seventeen-year-old a sandwich. Desperately unhappy, Jacob begged his father to be allowed to return home, but Tobias had already made plans to send for the rest of the family.

The Annenbergs were barely making ends meet in Kalvishken. With no adult men to farm, almost no income and letters from Tobias planning their move, Sheva sold their half-house and two acres of land and moved the family to Aldumbloken and into the home of her eldest daughter, Augusta, a prosperous dressmaker. The prospect of integrating nine siblings plus her mother and grandmother must have been terrifying for Augusta, or, at the very least, her husband. Moses, however, was unhappy that he had to give up his independence, put away his fishing poles and for the first time attend school, which bored him no end. "My remembrance of school," he said, "is limited to threats of the teacher who kept telling me, 'Were it not for the fact that you are a new pupil, you would be struck with the ruler so you would remember your lessons.'"

In early summer 1885, three years after Tobias emigrated, he sent extra money for tickets to supplement the property sale proceeds and Sheva made final preparations to leave. The family had little to pack: a change of clothes, a few pillows stuffed with goose feathers and several sacks of bread. Emotions were high. "I remember my sister Augusta crying as if her heart would break," Moses recalled. "She was sobbing, 'Mother, Mother, I shall never see you again.'" Augusta was wrong. There would be a reunion in America.

At Insterburg, the eleven Annenbergs boarded a steam-engine train for the twenty-four-hour ride to Berlin. There were no compartments or soft seats. They traveled in freight wagons that looked like American cattle cars with hard plank benches. Soot and dust poured through the open windows. As they chugged across Poland, men, women and children urinated and defecated through a single hole in the corner of the carriage.

By the time the Annenbergs reached Berlin, they were exhausted from tension and excitement as much as lack of sleep. None of the family had ever been on a train. No one knew what problems they might face at border checkpoints, whether they might be separated from one another or stranded on some remote siding. Would they have to bribe anyone? Would sister Rosa's skin rash make the family medically unacceptable? Were there simply too many of them?[13]

Such anxieties were put aside as the train chugged into Berlin. The outskirts hinted at a massive place. The children were amazed at the number of houses and shops along the tracks. The mammoth central station towered over the platforms, and with the cacophony from whooshing steam, shrill whistles, shouts and the heaving of hand and horse carts, not only was it the biggest, noisiest, most confusing experience any of them had ever encountered, but the city was almost unimaginable.

Frantic that a child might rush off and be lost or crushed under a train, Sheva and Leah ordered the children to hold hands, tied the three youngest ones together with the sleeves of their shirts, and anchored themselves on each end of the human chain. They changed trains and, nibbling on the bread they had brought from Augusta's, Sheva and her children pushed on for another twenty-four hours to Hamburg, the great North Sea port bursting with tanners and carpenters, butchers and bakers, cobblers and tinsmiths, all eager to exit the continent for a safer life.

By 1885, steamships had largely replaced sailing vessels on the transatlantic run. The price of passage ranged from $12 to $35, including food for the two-week journey.[14] With so many family members traveling, the Annenbergs could afford only the cheapest accommodation because the total passage price was more than Tobias had been able to save during the previous three years. Sheva understood that no kosher meat would be served. Before boarding, she stopped at a fishmonger's on the wharf and purchased salted herring to augment a ship's diet that would rely heavily on celery or cabbage soup and thin slices of bread.

Moses did not remember the ship's name, but that was all he forgot when he began to record the family experience. Demand for places was so high that ships were loaded from keel to smokestacks. On a typical ship such as the German vessel *Amerika*, 220 upper-class passengers traveled in cabins with four beds and were fed in two seatings in a comfortable dining room. Nearly ten times that number traveled below on three decks of steerage, where the throb of the ship's engines set thin shoes vibrating, homesick hearts pounding, seasick stomachs churning, and shook mess tins clattering onto the metal deck. On the Annenberg vessel, the third-class steerage bunks were three high with sweat-soaked straw mattresses.

There were no pillows, so Sheva was pleased that Tobias had warned her and that they had brought their goose-feather treasures from Kalvishken. There was no dining space below decks. No public rooms to stretch out in. No showers or baths. Low partitions between bunks offered no privacy. For the two thousand steerage passengers there were forty toilets and sixty washbasins. They bathed in cold sea water. Passengers ate food prepared in two twenty-foot-square galleys at their bunks or standing in gangways or on decks open to the elements.[15]

Conditions notwithstanding, "everything went along satisfactory for the first week or so," according to Moses, but their luck would not last. "One day the sea was very calm, as smooth as glass. We were playing on deck and having a good time generally when I overheard a sailor say in German to my older sister that, 'Vert fund hinter blazzen.' Sure enough, that night we ran into a terrible storm."

The steerage passengers were ordered below deck, into the near pitch dark of their living quarters. The storm was ferocious. Adults and children wailed. Gasping sobs mingled with snatches of prayers.

"The ship rocked from side to side and every time it went over on its side, we would think it would be the last, that surely it would turn over," Moses recalled. "The waves were so high that the water poured in through the smokestacks, putting out the fire in the engines. The ship began to drift aimlessly off course. Every time the boat went on its side, there would be pandemonium. The screaming and hysteria was indescribable. Dishes and trunks were thrown from side to side. There was at least three or four feet of water in the ship's hold. My mother went into one faint after another. Every time she revived, she asked for rope so we could all tie ourselves together and be together as a family to the end."

For forty-eight hours the storm raged. Sheva was certain they were doomed. His mother's mumbling frightened Moses until he realized she had not lost her mind but was praying. Then, just as suddenly as it appeared, the storm subsided. Exhausted engineers relit the ship's boilers and the journey resumed. Below deck, spirits began to rise even as the smell of wet wool clothing and unwashed bodies made it difficult to breathe. Eating was another problem. The storm and the water in the hold had destroyed much of the ship's food supply. Crates of meat, bread and vegetables burst, and the supplies rotted in the damp. The crew added vinegar to make the drinking water potable. "Our family suffered terribly because we had been eating so much herring," wrote Moses. "We were parched for water." The last four days at sea, the Annenbergs lived on bread dust washed down with a rationed mouthful of briny water.

When the ship approached New York Harbor, the steerage passengers rushed onto the deck to get the first glimpse of the golden land. On the port side of the ship, the sun reflected off the copper plates of the still unfinished one-hundred-fifty-foot Statue of Liberty, which soared above Bedloe's Island. The dedication of the gift from France was still a year away in 1886. The pedestal would not be inscribed until 1903 with the words of philanthropist Emma Lazarus: "Give me your tired, your poor, / Your huddled masses yearning to breathe free, / The wretched refuse of your teeming shore, / Send these, the homeless, tempest-tost, to me: / I lift my lamp beside the golden door."

As they steamed past the construction site, the Annenbergs and their fellow storm-tossed travelers could have been the models for Lady Liberty's welcome. Clinging to railings, tears streaming down cheeks into thin scarves and great untrimmed beards, fathers wearing broad-brimmed hats and mothers in ankle-length skirts lifted children onto hips and shoulders. Shading their eyes, straining and pointing, they shouted, "Land, land," and "America! We're in America!" Children danced. Strangers embraced. Men and women clutched their babies and fell to their knees in prayer.[16] An excited babble of Russian, Yiddish, German and Polish mixed together in relief and joy. Whatever the language, the sentiment was the same. They had made it.

Moses was on deck barefoot. His only pair of shoes was wooden and had floated away during the storm and could not be found. Later he recalled more about the pain in his stomach than he did his first sight of land. "We were all famished." Sheva had train tickets for the journey on to Chicago, but when the ship docked, she asked Leah and the children to search their pockets. No one had a single penny. Seeing the Annenbergs' distress as they moved toward the gangplank, a passenger with whom they had been friendly during the crossing gave Sheva five dollars. She asked if he had an address, so she could repay him. He did not and told her that when she got to Chicago and joined a synagogue, she could make a donation and consider the debt erased.

Ellis Island, a twenty-seven-acre site southwest of Manhattan, was the primary processing center for immigrants arriving in the United States from 1892 until 1943. When the Annenbergs arrived in 1885, the gateway, as it had been since 1855, was Castle Garden, a former amusement hall and opera house where Jenny Lind sang, in Battery Park on the southern tip of Manhattan. Processing at Ellis Island would become terrifying for nervous arrivals. Jammed in rooms for days and sometimes weeks, wearing the same filthy clothes because baggage was not delivered, the immigrants underwent medical exams, had their travel papers scrutinized and endured a barrage of questions: Where are you coming from? Why? Where are you going? Who are your relatives? How much money do you have? Some days hundreds of new arrivals would be denied entry and in tears of anguish or frustrated fury would be put back on ships and returned to Europe.[17]

The procedures were not as rigorous when the bedraggled Annenbergs entered Castle Garden. Sheva had the answers. The family was hungry, but everyone was healthy. Tobias and Jacob were waiting in Chicago. Their paperwork was in order. At Ellis Island they would have been sent back to Kalvishken because they did not have the $25 apiece that later arrivals would be asked to show they possessed to be allowed entry. Castle Garden had no such requirement. The Annenberg processing was smooth. In less than twenty-four hours, they crossed the Hudson by ferry and boarded the coach train bound for Chicago, the world's fastest-growing city in the 1880s, chaotically vibrant, a metropolitan magnet for people who wanted to see the future.[18]

The Pennsylvania Railroad's elegant Chicago Limited Express was the most comfortable way to traverse the eight hundred miles between New York and Chicago. The trip took twenty-five hours in Pullman Palace Car Company coaches with thick carpets, gilt-framed French mirrors, tufted footstools, frescoed ceilings and velvet curtains. The $28 fare included a sleeping berth, access to smoking and reading rooms, a barbershop, a toilet with full bathing facilities and a world-class restaurant in which waiters in starched white jackets served woodcock and roast beef on tables set with Belgian linen and hand-painted English china.

That was not the way the Annenbergs traveled. Sitting up again all day and all night on hard benches on a "day coach," named because it offered no beds, the family nonetheless had a good view of the sights along the way. Their train traveled at thirty miles an hour and stopped regularly at crowded depots where passengers bought food.[19]

Sheva insisted the children remain in their seats and not wander around or get off the train. Moses tried not to think about his freezing bare feet, but the knot in his stomach was too much to ignore. A row ahead, a man peeled an apple with a penknife and threw the peeling under his seat. Moses could not resist.

"I looked at the peelings with covetous eyes, my mouth watering. The temptation for those peelings became irresistible. I crawled under the seat, retrieved the peelings and began to eat.

"When the man discovered what I had done, he felt sorry for me. He called over a fruit seller and bought me two bananas. I had never seen bananas before in my life and thought they were a species of long, yellow pear. Before he could stop me, I bit into them, peel and all."

The train ran through the farm country of central and western Pennsylvania, through tiny towns where onlookers came out to wave, over the Alleghenies and into the rolling ridges of Ohio, before hitting the flat farmland of Indiana and Illinois. Closing in on the outskirts of Chicago, the boss town of America, as the porters called it, the engine slowed as the engineer's bell clanged faster. His nose against the window, Moses saw grain elevators and iron mills spouting flame and soot, plateaus of slag and coal, factories and slaughterhouses. At railroad crossings, pedestrians and freight wagons pulled by horse teams waited under clouds of bituminous black-and-white smoke. When the engine pulled under the barrel-vaulted steel-and-glass-roofed rail shed of Union Station, Moses could hear over the hiss of released steam and squeal of hot metal brakes the repeated bellow of the conductor, "She-caw-go, She-caw-go."[20]

To service hundreds of trains a day, Chicago had six major railroad stations in the mid-1880s, more than any other city in the United States. Four of the six stations were within a few blocks of one another near the Chicago River. Thirteen rail lines fed into Union Station, the world's busiest terminal. None of the tracks was elevated and the neighborhood was a warren of belching trains, sidings, platforms clogged with handcarts and freight sheds. The cacophony was unending, terrifying and confusing to some visitors, thrilling and energizing to others.

Tobias and Jacob were waiting at Union Station with a horse and wagon. The family piled out of their carriage and Tobias hugged Sheva, Leah and each child and offered a prayer of thanks right on the platform for their safe journey before helping with their baggage. The children could barely sit still in the wagon as they clip-clopped through dizzying activity to the house of a friend on Pacific Avenue near Polk Street on the city's South Side. They kept snapping around to marvel at buildings as high as ten stories and to stare at steam shovels digging foundations for even taller structures. Given the length of the family's separation and the drama of their journey, one would hope that Moses recalled more of the emotion of the reunion. But he did not, so there is a certain sense of anticlimax about his account of the final stage of their epic journey. What was clear was that the Annenbergs, crammed into two rooms of the friend's small house, were exhausted, bedraggled, flushed with excitement and anxious to find their own place.

Four days later, Tobias borrowed the wagon again and moved everyone to permanent quarters, an apartment on Fifth Avenue between Polk and Harrison streets near the old Allen B. Wrisley Soap Works. "From this point on," Moses wrote later, "the real problems for the future began."

2

CHICAGO

———

UNTIL THE 1830s, Chicago was little more than a desolate trading outpost, thirty people living in a handful of fur traders' shacks clustered outside the walls of Fort Dearborn on the marshy prairie mudflat at the mouth of the Chicago River. In 1837, the year Chicago incorporated as a city, its population was only 4,200, but the surge was about to begin. "I wish I could go to America if only to see that Chicago," Chancellor Bismarck told Philip Sheridan in 1870 when the Civil War general visited Germany.[1] By 1893, the year it beat out New York for the World's Columbian Exposition, marking — a year late — the four hundredth anniversary of Columbus's discovery of the New World, Chicago was home to a million people and the world's most dynamic city.

The first burst in Chicago's volcanic growth was ignited by the completion in 1825 of the Erie Canal. The 350-mile waterway stretched from Albany to Buffalo and joined the Hudson River with Lake Erie. More significantly, it connected the East Coast and Atlantic states to the Great Lakes. Because the canal was easier to navigate than the flood-prone Ohio River, the major highway for commerce and westward migration shifted north. The rapid expansion of the nation's railroad system did the rest, making Chicago first a rail hub and then quickly the great midcontinental transportation center.

When the Illinois and Michigan canal was completed in 1848, linking the Mississippi system to the Great Lakes, Chicago's status as a national water gateway was secured. Its fourteen miles of river docks made it the nation's greatest inland port. In 1852, the first through train arrived in Chicago from the East. That same year, the Chicago Rock

Island line began service to Joliet, Illinois, giving Chicago its first rail link to the Mississippi River, the nation's most important waterway. Soon the Rock Island line extended north to Minneapolis–St. Paul, south to Galveston, west to Denver and east to Memphis along nearly eight thousand miles of track, all of which funneled into the boss city.[2]

So fast did trade begin moving then that by 1860, Chicago was shipping more wheat and corn, more beef and pork, more lumber and steel, than any other city on the planet. The new train and waterway networks brought corn from Iowa, wheat from Kansas, beef from Texas, steel from Pennsylvania and workers from all over the nation and world.[3]

A setback which would have undone most cities only inspired Chicago. The summer of 1871 broke every record for dryness. On the October 8 front page of the *Tribune*, a local fire insurance company advertisement warned, "Fire, fire. Prepare for fall and winter fires."[4]

That very Sunday evening, a fire started on the property of Mrs. Patrick O'Leary on the city's West Side. Fed by the cheap tar-paper-and-green-pine wooden buildings thrown up in the city's race to greatness and pushed by southwest winds off the prairie, the blaze spread eastward for two days, leaping the Chicago River and finally stopping only when the flames reached Lake Michigan. The worst natural disaster in American history until then, the blaze consumed four square miles of city center, destroyed seventeen thousand buildings, killed three hundred people and left nearly a hundred thousand homeless.

The Chicago Historical Society, which held the original copy of Lincoln's Emancipation Proclamation, burned to the ground. So did Ramrod Hall, the city's biggest bordello, forcing Madam Kate Hawkins to take her trademark horsewhip and fifty girls and flee to Lincoln Park, where they huddled with thirty thousand other terrified refugees under a flame-red sky filled with flying embers.[5]

"How the city is to recover from this blow no one can yet see," said Frederick Law Olmsted, the landscape architect who designed New York's Central Park and the grounds for the 1893 Chicago exhibition. "But that it will presently advance and even with greater rapidity, those most staggered and cast down by it have not a shadow of a doubt." Olmsted's words were more prophecy than prediction. Chicago's recovery turned out to be more astonishing than the calamity itself.

"Chicago Shall Rise Again," blared the *Tribune* on October 11. And within a week of the last flames' being extinguished, the city had already put up more than five thousand temporary structures and started construction on two hundred permanent buildings. Convinced that they had survived a test of biblical proportions, Chicagoans believed they could rebuild a safer, more modern and more beautiful city that would be the epitome of the very best any city could offer.[6] When English aristocrat Lady Duffus Hardy visited in 1880, she expected to find "traces of ugliness and deformity everywhere," she admitted, "but Phoenix-like, the city had risen up out of its own ashes, grander and statelier than ever."[7]

New technology, including the Otis elevator, which made skyscrapers possible, and the refrigerated freight car, which fostered a centralized national meatpacking industry, plus a nearly infinite supply of cheap immigrant labor would help Chicago create a metropolitan colossus between the prairie and lake.[8] "The first of the great cities of the world to rise under purely modern conditions," wrote Henry B. Fuller, one of the city's early novelists. This drive to modernity was not hurt, Fuller noted, by Chicago's being "the only great city in the world to which all its citizens have come for the one common, avowed object of making money."[9]

The Annenbergs were no different from others drawn to the city. They were looking for a chance to improve themselves. Tobias had to make a better living than he ever had before to support such a large family, and he had so far earned little. Most of what he had saved had gone to pay for the family's crossing. If it had not been for his own discipline and abstemiousness, he would have had little to show for his three years. He had never shied away from hard work, but the competition for jobs and for decent wages was brutal.

Tobias had no qualifications to be a skilled laborer. The skilled workers — the machinists and carpenters, cabinetmakers and upholsterers — were the aristocrats of Chicago's working class. They were paid relatively well and worked reasonable hours. Architectural ironworkers, for example, had a union contract guaranteeing an eight-hour day, with a half day on Saturday, and a minimum salary of thirty-eight cents an hour plus overtime.

The vast majority of Chicago's workers, however, were unskilled. As the American economy was transformed in the late nineteenth century by mass production, employers used more machines, and hired laborers with fewer skills who worked ten or more hours a day, six full days a week. These workers often faced seasonal layoffs and had no guarantees they would be rehired because they were so easily replaced. To find work, men had to report early, often before dawn, yet might not be employed for hours, if at all. They might then work a few hours or until 10 P.M. In either case, they were only paid for the hours they worked, often at salaries of twelve to fifteen cents an hour. A $9-a-week wage was common.

Yet they kept coming, from dirt farms and small towns around the United States as well as from overseas. Theodore Dreiser, who appreciated Chicago's depth, color and complexity the way Charles Dickens understood London, wrote in his 1900 novel *Sister Carrie* that the city was "a giant magnet, drawing to itself, from all quarters, the hopeful and the hopeless." Some worked in appalling conditions, as Upton Sinclair detailed in *The Jungle*, a horrifying 1906 account of life in the blood- and gore-drenched meatpacking industry. Jobs bashing cows to death with sledgehammers or slicing the necks of pigs squealing as they came dangling on a chain down an assembly line could be learned in a few hours or days by men who spoke no English or had only farm experience.[10]

Most small factories were crowded, noisy and filthy, with little light and littered floors. Machines rattled and chemicals stank. Some workers stood in fluids that ate through their shoes and left festering sores on skin that never healed. Yet any job for almost any wage was better than being unemployed. Still, conditions were so bad, so polluted, so corrupt, that unrest grew.

The conditions that Dreiser and Sinclair and later Sherwood Anderson and Carl Sandburg wrote about were all evident in 1885 when the Annenbergs were reunited. The following year labor agitation became so severe that there was a riot in Haymarket Square, where fifteen hundred people gathered to demand an eight-hour workday. When police tried to disperse the crowd, a bomb exploded. Seven policemen and four others were killed and more than one hundred were injured. In New York, streetcar workers struck, tying up most of the city until the motormen agreed to accept $2 for a twelve-hour day. In 1886, Samuel Gompers, a thirty-five-year-old immigrant cigar maker, founded the American Federation of Labor (AFL), which became the primary organizing force for unions. That year 610,000 workers walked picket lines, the worst year for strikes in nineteenth-century America.

Despite the furious growth and industrialization, there was little guarantee a family as large and unskilled as the Annenbergs could survive, let alone thrive. Tobias had arrived with no money and spoke no English. If he had not been able to turn first to several relatives who had preceded him to the United States, there's no telling what would have become of him. They included the Cusworms of Cincinnati, who earned a comfortable living manufacturing cigars, the Harrises of Denver, who did well in the Leadville and Durango silver boom, and the Stones of Chicago, who put up Jacob. Mrs. Cusworm was Tobias's sister; Mr. Stone, his nephew. Mrs. Harris was Sheva's sister. Their stories, how they arrived in the United States, raised families and became successful were lost from family lore. But according to Moses's later account, it was hand-me-downs and a $5 donation from them that allowed Tobias to fill a handcart with scarves, mirrors, combs and thimbles and begin peddling house to house.

He made little progress that first winter of 1882 until he made a breakthrough when canvassing a neighborhood of Swedish immigrants. "One day he passed a little hotel on Hubbard Court where several people were sitting in the lobby," Moses recalled, from one of his father's earliest stories. "The weather was below zero and my father made motions through the window, blowing on his fingers to warm them.

"He was finally called in by the proprietor whose name happened to be Johnson and who discovered my father spoke his native language. The Johnsons took father in, treated him very kindly and bought his entire stock of notions. And that was father's real start. His friendship with the Johnsons continued for many years and they remained social friends and customers as long as they lived."[11]

The Johnsons were part of a contingent of fifty thousand Scandinavians in Chicago in the mid-1880s, more than in any other city in America. They were the paragon immigrants in the press and literature of the day: virtuous hard workers who raised good families and maintained spotless homes and businesses. In that regard, the Scandinavians were considered polar opposites of the Irish who had come to Chicago in the 1830s to dig the Illinois and Michigan canal. Their ranks swelled after the potato famine of 1845–48 killed nearly a million people and forced another million impoverished Irish to leave their homes. Streaming into Chicago, they spoke English and found work quicker than other immigrants. But many also lived in rat-infested hovels near the junction of the canal and the Chicago River, where cholera, tuberculosis, scarlet fever and alcoholism incubated. Others spread through the city, clustering around churches and eventually dominating the police and fire departments and, before long, the city's Democratic party politics.

Unlike the Irish, the more numerous Germans tended to cluster in neighborhoods, as did the Jews and later the Italians and Poles. The Jews who arrived before 1881 were more prosperous and included the Sears, Roebuck partner Julius Rosenwald and the shoe and clothing manufacturers who built Florsheim and Hart, Shaffner and Marx. As part of the post-1881 wave of "new" Jews, Tobias had initially lived in the Jewish ghetto around Maxwell Street. Nearby, in 1889, social reformers Jane Addams and Ellen Gates Starr established Hull House to provide community and social services for poor immigrants. Each morning, scores of long-bearded Jewish peddlers in black coats and hats bade good-bye to wives wearing shawls and wigs, poured out of crowded tenements and pushed their carts across the city.[12]

Tobias was no different from the other peddlers. And like most of his fellow immigrants, he was driven to succeed. With his ear for languages, his English improved quickly along with his peddling. While figuring out which streets and corners, sometimes a mile or more from the Jewish ghetto, were the most lucrative, he was always on the lookout for a store. He did not want to remain outside. The streets were either roasting or freezing, dirty and down-market, filled with pickpockets and con men, hustlers and streetwalkers. Youths chased peddlers, called them "dirty Jew" and tried to pull their beards or knock off their broad-brimmed hats. By any measure, physical, economic, mental or moral, working outside on the unpaved streets and wooden sidewalks was uncomfortable. Tobias had had a store in Kalvishken and it was a store that he wanted again.

It is not clear how long it took him to put together the money, but after the family arrived, he gathered $150 of savings that he and Jacob had hidden under their floorboards as down payment on a storefront at 1255 South State Street. It was not far from Maxwell Street and its morning market, but, significantly, it was a mixed neighborhood and not the heart of the Jewish ghetto. Sheva and the older girls waited on customers. Sister Eva started work at the Boston Store, which became a popular chain in the twentieth century. Max, Moses and the younger girls started school in the neighborhood. As in Kalvishken, the family moved into rooms in the back of the shop.

Next door lived another immigrant family, the Domkas, and their seven children. Christian and likely Catholic, the mother was Polish and the father a well-educated German. Using a mixture of High German, Plattdeutsch and the English the youngsters were learning as fast as they could, eight-year-old Moses managed to make friends with Jacob Domka. Moses recalled how one winter day he looked over the fence and saw the boy sitting on a new red sled.

" 'Where did you get the sled, Jake?' "

"Santa Claus," he replied.

In his memoir notes, Moses related how that was the first he had ever heard of Santa and how he quickly wanted to know more about strangers bringing presents. Jake, he said, explained how anyone could get anything one wanted on Christmas by making a list and sending it to Santa Claus. Moses ran inside and asked Jacob and his sister Eva to help him write a list, but their own knowledge of Santa Claus was limited. "I finally was told exactly how it was done, which of course, left me out completely because we could not afford such luxuries."

Then there was the pants problem. Neighborhood boys Moses's age and a few years older all wore short pants, but Moses owned only two pairs of long pants. "I felt the embarrassment keenly whenever I went out to play. I continued to ask my father for a suit of clothes in keeping with the American style, but he always told me we could not afford it because a short pants suit cost at least $2.50."

Sheva was more sensitive to the awkwardness her youngest son felt. She managed to buy shorts at cost from a distant relative named B. Wartelsky, who had a department store at Thirty-sixth and Halstead Streets. The shorts made a big difference. From that moment on, Moe, as his friends called him, began to feel he really belonged in Chicago.

The importance of belonging varied among immigrants. Some, usually the older ones, stayed close to their neighborhoods, their churches and temples, saloons and markets and spoke and read newspapers in their native language. Younger arrivals more commonly could not assimilate fast enough. Whether the Santa Claus and pants stories were accurate or apocryphal, what was certain was that Moses and Max were shedding their old-world identities the way snakes crawl from their skin.

This was particularly true of school. Moe had had only one year of formal education before leaving East Prussia. At the age of eight, he entered second grade at the predominantly Irish Haven School at Fifteenth Street and Wabash Avenue, part of the South Side Irish "patch." His first teacher was Josephine O'Sullivan and Moe loved her, especially when she showed off to Principal Bannon his compositions and the precise penmanship he would retain all his life. "Principal Bannon was a real fine American character," Moses maintained. "His discipline and management of the children were wonderful. Everyone had the highest respect for him."

From Miss O'Sullivan's, he went to Miss O'Rourke's third-grade class. "The impression of her teaching remains with me to this day," he wrote a half century later. "She was most able, not only in reading, writing and arithmetic, but in every respect that would interest young children between the ages of nine and twelve." Miss O'Rourke read regularly to her class about everything — from adventure stories and history to geography, the horrors of cruelty to animals and the benefits and punishments to be derived from right and wrong behavior — which marked the start of a lifelong obsession with reading. "I was so interested, and my lessons became so perfect, that she advanced me, without examinations, to the fourth grade, into a room taught by Miss Wolfe."

An unfortunate mistake, as it turned out, for the eleven-year-old and Miss Wolfe clashed immediately. "I was called upon to spell a very simple word, 'lightly,' which I knew very well. But because she said 'lit-tel-ly,' I did not know what she meant, so I tried it several ways and failed. Then she called on Sonny Weinberg, who had been in her room for quite a while. When I heard him spell it, I was chagrined and embarrassed and could not restrain my anger, so I stood up.

"Had you pronounced that word correctly, I could easily have spelled it."

The astonished Miss Wolfe turned red and reached for her ruler. "Young man, I will send you back where you came from!"

"You will not send me anywhere," the defiant Moe replied, packing up his books. "Since I can learn nothing in your room, I am leaving."

The story is amazing in itself and for its implications. Here was a gifted student who, after his first unpleasant brush with education in East Prussia, had grown to enjoy school. Yet he became enraged over an inconsequential incident, walked away from school and never returned. Moses told the story on himself in his unpublished notes and repeated the story without regret years later to his own children. There is no indication that they were curious about why he would have acted that way or whether they wondered if there was more to the story. That may be because they knew the cause, which he touched on when he confessed that he could not restrain his anger.

Moe had a colossal temper, a blast that could appear from nowhere and leave his children quivering and associates with their mouths agape. "He could be really attractive, and amusing and a likable fellow," attorney Richardson Dilworth said decades later of his client and friend, the adult Moses, "but he could also be crude and rough and he had an absolutely vicious temper."[13]

The fourth-grade outburst was the first recorded example of the impulsive and self-destructive behavior that would alter Moe's life repeatedly. This impulsiveness would sometimes prompt risk-taking that yielded brilliant results but eventually led to his ruin. This acute sensitivity to criticism would metamorphose into feelings of persecution that repeatedly provoked bad decisions. The source of this rage is harder to pin down without moving into psychobiography. But those years when he was six and seven, standing all alone day after day by the Kalvishken lake to feed his family, must have been seminal. His father and eldest brother, Jacob, had left home. He was jealous of his favored older brother Max, who received presents but got away with refusing to fish. The respect he had for his parents for moving to America was diminished by their reaction to his decision to quit school. They did not chastise him, make him return, or even force him, as many immigrant parents did, to find a job to support the family. All that suprised him.

Instead, for the next six months, Moe took to the streets. Hanging out with neighborhood boys, most of them Irish, who had also dropped out of school because there were no laws making attendance compulsory, he played stickball, rolled dice and worked to become expert at marbles.

The boys organized the Shamrock Athletic Club in a dim, dusty and abandoned coal shed. Dues were fifteen cents a week and brother Max, also a truant, became treasurer. They set up a used punching bag, and Barney Kapples, a journeyman boxer, gave them some old, worn gloves and showed up occasionally to teach the rudiments of boxing.

Moe, Max and Shorty Gelder were the only Jewish members. The fact that the team was mixed at all reflected the easier mingling of ethnic groups in Chicago than, say, on the Lower East Side of New York, where neighborhood boundaries were more distinct and inviolate. It helped that Shorty was a good pitcher and the brothers good athletes, by Moe's account, the stars of the Shamrock baseball team, which had been winning most of its games. When challenged by the Bright Diamonds, an all-Irish team from Thirty-fifth and Halstead, deeper into the South Side on almost pure Hibernian turf, Moe had his first brush with anti-Semitism in Chicago.

"Just as we were reaching their neighborhood, a small, freckled-faced Irish boy sitting on a fence spied us and yelled, 'Oh, look at the Sheeny Shamrocks.'" Moe did not lose his temper, but neither did he forget the incident. "That remark so affected our morale that we lost the game by a very large margin." The Irish kids on the Shamrocks were more upset at the slur on their name. Max, three years older at fourteen, came up with a solution. They dropped the Shamrock name and began calling themselves the Glen Athletic Club so the Jewish kids could stay as members without angering Irish outsiders. The games went on.

A few weeks later, Moe reacted differently when an Irish teenager stood outside the Annenberg store shouting, "Sheeny, sheeny, get me a sausage." When Tobias did nothing, Moe grabbed a baseball bat and slipped out the rear of the store. He crept up behind their tormentor, smashed him across the back and yelled, "Here's your sausage."[14] That was the last instance of taunting outside the Annenberg shop.

In their teens, the brothers were fast slipping beyond parental control. They drank in the Glen clubhouse, where Max passed out after a New Year's Eve meal of whiskey and pigs' feet, a local saloon delicacy. Had Tobias heard about the pigs' feet, he would have been furious, but he never found out. Increasingly, parents and boys were living different lives. Tobias and Sheva became more involved in Jewish affairs. The very devout Tobias became president of his local synagogue. Sheva, who owned no wig in Kalvishken, bought one in Chicago and shaved her head in keeping with orthodox practice, delighting her husband.

The further their parents moved into the Jewish community and spent more time with other immigrants with similar backgrounds, the faster and deeper Max and Moe moved away from the synagogue into their own new world, on the street and on the make. Despite being raised in a very orthodox home, neither was religious, although Max, who made a greater effort to please his father, often joined Tobias for morning prayers. Not Moe. By the age of thirteen, Moe had been out of school and on the streets for two years. He was strong-willed, had no interest in religion and no intention of pretending otherwise. Tobias tried literally to tug his son into line. He pulled Moe's ears to force him to pray and banished him to his room when he refused.

The punishment meant little because Moe argued successfully that he had to leave the apartment to work. Tobias and Sheva were upset by his rebellion because they had experienced less of it with Jacob and Max. But they also realized that Moe's world in Chicago was profoundly different from what they had known in East Prussia. Moe was committed to the family and was neither rude nor rebelling against them. But his increasing passion to make money and a name was not one they shared.

Moe had little spending money, but he could see that many men on the street were flush with cash, whether they were businessmen in private carriages or gamblers in Stetsons from Mississippi river boats. Tobias had no money to hand out, so Moe's first job was helping a vegetable seller for fifty cents a day. When Max was hired as a messenger for American District Telegraph, he persuaded the company to take on Moe as well. In the early 1890s, an army of messenger boys raced around Chicago because few phones existed and almost all urgent communication was conducted by telegraph. The telegraph had been in use in the United States since 1844 when Samuel F. B. Morse first demonstrated its use for Congress, but it was 1875 before Alexander Graham Bell invented the telephone. When the Annenberg boys started at ADT in 1891, only the wealthiest families — the Armours, Pullmans and McCormicks — had telephones at home. The few public telephones were in first-class hotels, and saloons and pharmacies. The most efficient means of staying in touch for everyone else proved to be quick young men who knew their way around the city.

One man living in the Palmer House Hotel, for example, hired Moe by the hour to run back and forth to the Chicago Stock Exchange keeping him supplied with the latest quotations. When the job was done, Moe often received two tips. "Traction, my boy," the man would say, referring to the expanding streetcar or trolley companies and handing Moe a nickel. "There's money to be made in traction." It was not advice Moe followed then, but he remembered it.

When Moe turned fifteen, he switched from day to night messenger duty which often involved, as he described it, "assignments to carry messages into the highest and lowest classes of assignation houses," or brothels, which were then legal. They ranged from the squalid twenty-five-cent cribs to dollar houses and to the rococo five-dollar bordellos on South Clark Street, where string and brass musicians played and women in silk gowns passed champagne in silver goblets around rooms hung with Victorian still lifes and Belgian tapestries. He loved the work, he explained without the slightest embarrassment. It was exciting, exotic and, most important, "usually tips on those assignments were far more generous than on others." For men who had not bought the *Sporting and Club House Directory* from the newsstand and did not know where to find the working girls, Moe would make the introductions himself.

After two years with the telegraph company, Moe's temper got the better of him again. A quarrel with another messenger, about what he did not specify, began in the dispatch office. The young men went into the alley outside to settle it. Moe, used to boxing at the Glens' clubhouse and wrestling with his brother Max, had the other boy down when the night manager intervened, pulled Moe off, put his opponent on top and strode back inside. Moe exploded at the display of favoritism. His adversary "could not hold me down, so I rose quickly and forgot about my fight with him and thought only of the unfair tactics of the night manager. I was so enraged I picked up a large stone and threw it through the window at him."

That was the end of that job. Getting a reputation as a hothead and unable to find other work for weeks, Moe took to fishing for pike in Lake Michigan and the Chicago River. The hours away from the hubbub of the city center allowed him to indulge his passion for fishing and calmed him down, but only temporarily. As he grew older and faced other demands, Moe developed a more complex and responsible character. But a major theme of his youth, and one that remained an undercurrent throughout his life, was unbridled aggression.

Native intelligence, raw temper, quick fists and an independent spirit were Darwinian traits for surviving on Chicago's mean streets and would account for much of Moe's early success. Jewish boys weren't the only street kids with such talents. Plenty of Irish, Italian and Polish boys and others used them as well. The others, however, had not been hounded out of Europe the way the Jews had been. Bullied young Jews could not fight back there, but in the United States they could and often had to. Like Moe, they went straight from the boat to the street. Their fathers were peddlers, tailors or merchants. Rarely were there established family businesses to join. Those who bypassed the synagogue were not going to become Yeshiva boys, one option for bright young Jews. Those eager to fight had other options and became tough businessmen or gangsters like Benjamin "Bugsy" Siegel, Arnold Rothstein and Meyer Lansky. Later, there would be questions for years as to whether Moe was one, the other or both.[15]

Eventually Moe was hired as a switchboard operator in Wright's Livery Office on Plymouth Court next door to what in the 1920s would become the Chicago office of the *Daily Racing Form*, which Moe would own. In 1893, the livery business paid him a base salary of $20 a month, a fraction of what he would be making on that street in three decades, but enough to keep him happy then.

Moe had been comfortable around horses since growing up near the stud farms between Kalvishken and Insterburg. And it helped that the managers, Messrs. Dwelle and Bay, liked him. When he wasn't handling phone orders for taxis or wagons, they taught him about the animals, stabling and how to drive all sorts of carriages, including landaus, stanhopes and tandems. The extra training allowed him to supplement his income delivering private horse rigs to owners and helping out at weekend tally ho hunting and riding parties, his first close contact with genteel society.

Moe took a major step upward at sixteen when he was named day manager of the livery office at the Grand Pacific Hotel, meaning he ran the cab stand. The job was good, but what really mattered was his new environment. Out of the neighborhood and away from the peddlers, Moses's horizons were expanding. The Grand Pacific stood on LaSalle street, next to the Board of Trade Building, in the heart of Chicago's business and investment center. Run by John Drake, whose family would later build the Drake Hotel at the north end of Michigan Avenue, the Grand Pacific had an opulent lobby and an elegant dining room and was the gathering place for Chicago's Republicans and the city's top speculators.

"It represented, better than any other hotel in the city, the intimate Chicago connection between luxury trains, big passenger terminals and grand hotels," wrote Chicago historian Donald Miller. "Built a few hundred yards from the Van Buren Street station with money from the railroads using the terminal, it had doormen who sent drivers around to pick up arriving guests and drop them off at its glass-domed carriage rotunda."[16] Moe was intrigued by the environment. Obviously not everyone lived the way the Annenbergs did on South State Street. Increasingly, he began to appreciate the links between money, milieu, influence and a better life.

Most days, John Drake dropped by Moe's small office, often accompanied by Franklin Parmelee, the wealthy owner of the Parmelee Transfer Company, a freight haulage firm. Parmelee was as eccentric as he was successful. Just before 11 A.M. each day, he appeared at Moe's desk to order a shebang, a one-horse carriage, for the few blocks' ride to the old *Tribune* building at the corner of Madison and Dearborn. On the ground floor there was an optometrist's office with a clock in the window. Parmelee would adjust his watch, return to the hotel and tip Moe twenty-five cents. The young man decided then that his benefactor was as odd as he was generous, but later, he drew a more thoughtful conclusion. "My experience as a messenger and in the livery office, handling the public with their idiosyncrasies and different characteristics," he decided, "helped considerable [sic] in sharpening me up for the future." What he meant was that he liked being around the toffs and was learning how to deal with them. They were different from the almost clichéd, one-dimensional figures he was used to. They were not only wealthier and more successful, but more complex. To emulate them, he needed to learn more because he realized, as in the case of Mr. Parmelee, that his first impressions were not always accurate.

Brother Max was by then twenty, working as a bartender in Russick and Levin's and regaling the family nightly with tales of his adventures in the busy saloon. Moe's brother-in-law Samuel Epstein, who had married sister Eva, was also in the saloon business, which in the rankings of neighborhood institutions came immediately behind the family dinner table and local church. Epstein had become ill with whooping cough — endemic in some ethnic ghettos — and Tobias and Max suggested that Moe help the family out by stepping in for Samuel. Surprisingly, because he had so enjoyed the classy circumstances of the Grand Pacific and liked John Drake, Moe nonetheless agreed to make the change.

Several factors were involved. Most important was that for all his differences with Max and his parents, Moe cared deeply for his family. He also explained later in his memoir notes that he saw little opportunity for advancement in either the livery or the hotel business. However grand the location, Moe was too ambitious to be content with running a cab stand the rest of his life. At seventeen, he knew a bar would be more fun. Alcohol was not the lure. Moe drank, but not much. The real attraction was that the saloon was the switching yard for information in a neighborhood. News was passed on, job openings discussed. Union bosses met with members. Politicians gathered and birthdays and weddings were celebrated.[17] "Having heard so many stories from Max about how interesting saloon work was, I did not require much family influence. I too wanted to be a 'big shot' with a white jacket and apron."

For the next two years, Moe, Max and brother Jake worked in a variety of saloons near the Chicago River and on the tough South Side, where it was not unusual for the white jackets to be stained with blood from brawls. At one point, Max and Jake ran their own bar at LaSalle and Thirtieth, a neighborhood Moe himself described as "infested by some of the worst criminals in Chicago." The Ward brothers, regular customers, specialized in bogus checks. Dan Cronin was a cat burglar. One Eyed Beck Moriarty lost his eye in a botched attempt to rob a craps game. When J. J. Gallagher shot up the Annenbergs' saloon one evening, Jake had him arrested. He was fined $25 and costs and held in jail for fifty-three days. The day he was released, Gallagher returned to the bar and bought several rounds, all the while taunting, "You owe me twenty-six fifty, Jake, and I'm going to collect it one day."

Jacob and Max, armed with a gun and an ax handle, usually took turns sleeping in the bar, but that night Max had a late date and Jacob took the evening's receipts of $80 to his apartment across the street. Moe was deputized to sleep guard. At 3 A.M., pistol shots woke him. Jake was shooting out his window and shouting for the police. While he slept, burglars had climbed through his window, pulled his trousers from under his pillow and escaped with his wallet and watch, waking Jake at the last instant. That morning, Gallagher arrived at the saloon, bought a round for all, looked up at the bartender and said, "We're even, Jake. You don't owe me anything anymore."

Jake could not pin the robbery on Gallagher for the same reason he and Max were unable to keep the saloon business afloat. They were surrounded by lowlifes and neither was a very good businessman. At Tobias's urging, Max abandoned saloons and, like his father, who had always been a shopkeeper, decided to try the grocery business.

During this period, Moe and Max got along better than they did throughout most of their lives. They dressed alike, were often taken for twins, and were spending so much time together that when Max began courting Etta Lando, Moe dated her sister Susie. That relationship broke up the day Max and Etta married. Because marriage meant that Etta would stay at home and no longer bring home the $16 a week she earned working at the Boston Store, in the midst of the wedding party Etta's father lamented to Sheva and Tobias: "What have I got out of it? And now Moses wants to get married too. Susan will quit her job at Seigel's and I'm going to lose again."

It was not the first time there had been difficulties at an Annenberg wedding. Tobias had been determined from the moment the family had arrived in Chicago, as Moses put it, "to get rid of some of the daughters" to ease the burden of feeding and clothing so many children. Romance was not a factor, although Anna, the second Annen-berg daughter, was a head-turning girl with long dark hair, rosy cheeks and a voluptuous figure. The marriage brokers had no problem finding a husband for her, which was unfortunate for Anna. She would have been better served had the family been less eager to push her out the door.

The lucky groom was a peddler from Texas named Samuel Bal-chowsky and the union was a disaster from the outset. "He was a plain character, uneducated, rough and tough in his behavior," Moses recounted. If those traits weren't a red flag, his wedding-night behavior should have been enough to call the match off. He pulled out a pistol and began shooting at several boys trying to disturb the ceremony.

Besides creating hysteria among the family and wedding guests, who dived under tables and behind chairs, the shooting was as dreadful an omen as Balchowsky would be a husband. Three children were born, but Sam's temper was uncontrollable and his brutality toward his children beyond all bounds. Two died young, while "my sister Anna," wrote Moses, "died of grief, aggravation and cancer at the age of forty-two."

Moe had no intention of getting married yet, but his parents were pressuring him. "It was my parents' wish that all the children should marry early and I was next on the list," he explained, "but it was also their idea that we should be in business for ourselves when we mar-ried." Establishing a business was much more difficult than finding a spouse. Many immigrant families were large, and as Moe put it, "there were plenty of women to be had as a wife, so a wife was a secondary consideration." Those priorities would never change for Moe. To his dying day, business would always come first.

Because a storefront shop was what the family understood, Moe had been saving money through much of his teens and had built up a nest egg of $500. Brother Jacob, who was then a street-car conductor, had helped Moe scout locations. When they found one that looked suitable, Moe went to his parents, who according to family tradition acted as bankers for all the unmarried children. But when Moe told them that he found a spot and asked for his money, they blanched. Tobias began to stammer. There was a problem, he explained in embarrassment. They had loaned Moe's money to Max. Moe was furi-ous. "Chagrined and disappointed," was how he described his reac-tion. He managed to hold his temper in check, but that would never have been the case had anyone other than his parents been responsible.

He was particularly annoyed, though not much surprised, that Max was the beneficiary. "It must be remembered again," he wrote, "that Max was always Father's favorite son."

Moe had long been conflicted about Max, both resenting and loving his brother. But this turn of events, no less than a betrayal by his parents, intensified a growing sense in Moe that he had to become self-reliant. Right then, though, he had no choice. The best chance he had of getting his money back was to do what Sheva and Tobias recommended: become a partner in Max's grocery store.

Moe was not thrilled with the idea because his brother's shop had just burned down. While Max and Etta were walking upstairs to bed, she had slipped and dropped the kerosene lantern, setting a fire which destroyed the premises. Still, Moe saw no alternative. At least the property had been insured. He and Max used the payout to rent another building and restock.

Once he was in business, Sheva and Tobias turned up the pressure again for him to marry. When he did, the marriage was most likely arranged, like sister Anna's. Most marriages in the Jewish immigrant community at the time were brokered. Moe, though, did not say what happened. Other than noting that he was working at the store with Max when he married, there was no mention in his memoir or in other family records of his first contact with Sadie Cecelia Friedman nor anything about their wedding. Perhaps if there had been shooting, the record would have been more complete.

Two years younger than the twenty-two-year-old Moe, Sadie was born in New York City on June 3, 1879, the daughter of Morris Friedman, a German Jew who had emigrated from Berlin in 1862, twenty years before Tobias Annenberg left Kalvishken. A shoe and boot merchant who would live to the age of ninety-seven, Friedman moved his family to Chicago when Sadie was a child. She grew up there and had had at least two years of high school when she married Moses in 1899.

Her family was more acclimatized to the United States than the Annenbergs. Sadie was not an immigrant, as Moses was. She had not experienced the harshness of life in Eastern Europe and had not been forced to flee the pogroms or worry about surviving an Atlantic crossing, perhaps to be rejected at the immigration desk and sent back. Her roots were in America. She did not have to claw her way up as Moses did. Her mother died when she was ten, but Sadie grew up with a loving father and three brothers. They doted on her, the only Friedman girl, creating a profoundly different environment for her than Moses, the eighth of eleven children and the third of three boys, had known. Sadie also had years more formal education than her husband. Unlike Moses, who was volatile, with a quick temper and little time to waste, she was calm and had time for everyone. She was a nurturer and a pleaser. Moses described himself as a hunter and hungry wolf. No one who knew them disputed either characterization.

In looks, Sadie was a Rubens, Moses, an ascetic El Greco. She had a creamy complexion, was five feet three inches tall, slightly round and full of soft curves. Moses was dark, almost Moorish, a half inch shy of six feet, all sharp angles, wiry and so lean as to be bony.

Sadie had long red hair which she wore up in a twist and large, liquid, doe-like eyes that suggested all would be right with the world if only you were swept up in her comforting, full-bosomed embrace. Moses had close-cropped dark brown hair, was thin lipped, with a high forehead, strong square jaw and brown piercing eyes that could flash into a glare. Few women looked more motherly than Sadie, few men more intimidating than Moses.

Soon after marrying Sadie on August 20, 1899, Moe's relationship with Max at their store began to sour. The trouble was reminiscent of Max and Jake's money-losing saloon venture, and Moe was quick to blame his brother. "Max was the boss," Moe said, "and he overbought and overborrowed in every direction, doing everything he could to get credit."

There was so much competition from other stores and vendors that Max started selling their entire stock below cost. "We must have leaders," Max insisted. Soon every bit of merchandise was a loss leader. After only seven months in business, the two brothers owed $518 to provisioners Read Murdock, $300 to the chicken dealers Viles and Robbins, $300 to their Uncle Cusworm, the cigar manufacturer from Cincinnati, whose loan Tobias had personally guaranteed. They were so mired in debt that the creditors took over the store.

By then, the century had just turned. Moe Annenberg was twenty-three and did not have a nickel to buy the Duke's Mixture tobacco that he liked to smoke. He owed two months' back rent on their apartment. The gas man had just left a final notice, a serious matter in Chicago in February and especially worrying because Sadie was six months pregnant. Moe had no idea what he would have done if William Randolph Hearst had not chosen that moment to move into Chicago.

3

HEARST

———

NINE DAILY NEWSPAPERS were operating in Chicago in 1900 when William Randolph Hearst decided to launch the *American*. The leading paper, then as now, was the *Tribune*, although Joseph Medill had nearly run it into the ground in the 1850s in his costly effort to elect downstate legislator Abraham Lincoln president. In the 1930s Robert McCormick would transform it into the most widely read broadsheet in America with its muscular conservatism, vigorous support of isolationism and venomous opposition to Franklin D. Roosevelt's New Deal.[1]

At the turn of the century, the *Tribune* was a genteel paper of record, a bulwark of taste in a bawdy frontier city that Dreiser portrayed as "singing of high deeds and high hopes, its heavy brogans buried deep in the mire of circumstance." That *Tribune* was the conscience of Chicago, condemning shoddy public construction and railing against vice and official corruption. Sixty Chicagoans then owned cars, enough for the paper to seek imposition of a twelve-mile-per-hour speed limit.

"News and Views of the London Times" ran on the paper's front page as did dispatches on the Boer War from the English war correspondent Winston Churchill. Gossip about European royals and nobility graced the editorial page in a column titled "Letter of Marquise de Fontenoy." The paper was thrilled when the Chicago Horse Show that year ruled that female competitors must ride sidesaddle and not wear the split skirts that made young ladies look like cowgirls. More editorial praise was directed at the Swift Packing Company for its decision not to hire cigarette smokers.

Tribune executives were uncomfortable with the unfortunate commercial aspects of publishing. Calling subscribers or seeking advertisements was something other papers did, but the *Tribune* was flush with money. Its owners, the McCormicks, had made their first fortune inventing the reaper and founding International Harvester Company. There was little need for them to focus on the bottom line.

At the *Tribune*, ads came "as the wind comes, on [their] own and unsolicited." Editorial copy ran separately from advertisements. When there was a rare promotion, such as free plates as an incentive to subscribe, editor Robert Patterson selected the best of the choices his circulation staff offered. "By God," he said, "if we're going to be a whore, we're going to be a good one."[2]

The *Tribune*'s approach made it the classiest daily in town, but not the biggest. Circulation lagged far behind that of the *Daily News* and *Morning Record*, owned by Victor Lawson, who chased the larger mass market of immigrants and laborers by running sensational stories, frequently about crime. Hearst, however, was about to make Lawson a historical footnote.

Hearst was only thirty-seven, but already the best-known publisher in America when he arrived in Chicago. He was born in San Francisco in 1863, the son of George Hearst, a prospector and geologist who made a fortune in Nevada's Comstock silver lode and Montana's Anaconda copper mines and then went on to buy the *San Francisco Examiner* and later serve as a U.S. senator from California. Young Hearst was twenty-four when he persuaded his father to let him edit the *Examiner*, employing what would become his trademark blend of oversized banner headlines, aggressive, sensational stories, lavish, exclusive pictures, plenty of cartoons and down-to-earth commentary.

According to his biographer W. A. Swanberg, Hearst would cover the floor of his office with newspapers, turn the pages with his feet and tap with his toes the few stories he found acceptable, or more commonly, those he thought read like a telephone book. The publisher's ideal newspaper, said Swanberg, would have been one in which "the Prince of Wales had gone into vaudeville, Queen Victoria had married her cook, the Pope had issued an encyclical favoring free love . . . France had declared war on Germany . . . and the Sultan of Turkey had converted to Christianity — all these being 'scoops.'"[3]

In 1895, Hearst charged into New York, paid $180,000 for the *Journal*, which sold a measly 77,000 copies a day, and began competing with Joseph Pulitzer's *World*, the globe's biggest daily, with a circulation of 800,000. The odds of the *Journal*'s overpowering the *World* would have been about the same as Iceland's chances of successfully invading the United States. As Swanberg put it, Pulitzer was at first "not even aware of the gnat buzzing around his head." He was not unaware for long.

Hearst dropped the *Journal*'s price to a penny and doubled its size to sixteen pages. Within two years, Hearst had boosted the circulation of the *Journal* to 960,000 by campaigning to make William Jennings Bryan president, calling for war with Spain, detailing endless corruption scandals, advancing spurious scientific "breakthroughs" about vampires and the like, and printing a comic strip featuring a street urchin in a yellow robe who became known as the "yellow kid," from which the whole genre of sensational journalism took its name.[4]

One of the high, or, more precisely, low points of the "yellow journalism" era involved Hearst's virtual sponsorship of the 1898 Spanish-American war. He sent thirty-five writers and editors to Cuba to chronicle the island's struggle for independence from Spain, including lurid tales of Spaniards raping Cuban women and killing their children. The stories often bore little relationship to the truth, but they were great circulation builders. In Chicago, publishers and editors of second-tier tabloids who had watched Hearst trounce Pulitzer on his own turf in New York quaked at the prospect of Hearst's arrival in their city.

Hearst came not just to extend his newspaper empire — which grew to twenty-two dailies and fifteen Sunday papers, a host of supplements and a claimed readership of one in four families in the United States — but as part of his plan to enter politics. In Hearst's case that meant to be president of the United States.

His political opening came in Washington on May 19, 1900, when Senator James K. Jones nominated him to be president of the National Association of Democratic Clubs. To oust Republican president William McKinley and elect Democrat William Jennings Bryan, Jones told him, the party needed a powerful newspaper in Chicago. In return for the presidency of the Democratic Clubs, which Hearst expected would put him on the ladder to the presidency of the United States, the publisher agreed to have a paper in operation before the summer's political conventions.

In New York, Hearst summoned Solomon Carvalho. "I wish you would go out to Chicago and start a paper," he told the wily business manager he had hired away from Pulitzer. "Let's call it the *American* and have the first issue on the streets before the Fourth of July. Can you get away?"

Carvalho understood that Hearst was not asking, but telling. He also knew that to get a paper going from scratch took months. To do it in six weeks was impossible at worst, prohibitively expensive at best, even for Hearst, who had inherited $17 million from his father. Carvalho did not say that. Instead, giving himself a moment to think, he picked up a pair of editorial scissors from Hearst's desk and began trimming his goatee and letting the hair drift down onto the publisher's thick Belgian carpet.

"It's a tough town," he finally replied. "We'll have to shoot our way in."

That was fine with Hearst. "Take all the ammunition you need," he instructed, his high-pitched voice uncommonly mellow.[5]

To meet the deadline, which was both Independence Day and the first day of the Democratic national political convention in Kansas City, Carvalho left for Chicago on May 20 and began putting in twenty-hour days. He rented an old building at 216 West Madison Street near Franklin. The pace of activity there over the following weeks and beyond caused journalists to call the *American* "The Madhouse on Madison Street," an epithet that stuck for the fifty-six years the paper survived. "Noise and confusion reigned," wrote reporter William Salisbury. "Telegraph keys and typewriters clacking, feet running, voices shouting, often cursing."[6]

When Hearst could not lease freight cars to transport new presses to Chicago in time, he hired Pullman cars and ripped out the interiors. Carvalho contracted for ink, paper and furniture and still found time to buy away from the *Daily News* their rights to advertise on the city's street-corner trash cans.

Hearst's formula always included hiring the best writers and editors for the best pay. Reporters earning $20 a week found calling cards stuck in their typewriters saying, "Mr. Hearst would be pleased to receive you." If they took up the invitation, as nearly all did, they found he offered up to $50 a week. The *Tribune* and *Daily News* each sold for three cents a copy. Hearst's *American* cost a penny. He planned to lose money initially and did. He also expected soaring circulation which would lead to increased advertising revenues and a quick reversal of the start-up losses.

The first edition of the *American* rolled off the presses the evening of July 2 with a touch of typical Hearst showmanship. William Jennings Bryan, who was in Indianapolis, pressed a key that sent the message "Start the presses." The *American* was in business to be the voice of Democrats and of the working class. It supported Bryan, his proposal for the free and unlimited coinage of silver, the eight-hour workday, a full lunch bucket for every worker and the establishment of controls on the trusts, monopolies like Standard Oil, whose interlocking directorates stifled competition.

Fresh editions — nine a day — flew off the *American*'s presses. The front page of the newspaper, which was the model for Ben Hecht's hit play *The Front Page*, was laced with stories celebrating scandal, crime and orgy under such five-inch headlines as: "Woman Shoots Her Prosecutor," "Gangs of Ruffians Hired to Insult Bryan," and "Beautiful Young Woman Victim of Poison Plot." Editors loved working the words "poison" and "young woman" into as many headlines as they could.

When news was slow, the paper manufactured it. The *American* brought Carrie Nation, the temperance agitator, from Kansas to Chicago to smash up saloons. In New York, Pulitzer's *World* sent Nellie Bly around the world to prove it could be done in less than eighty days. For Chicago, Hearst editors picked three high school students, from New York, San Francisco and Chicago, to race around the world by different routes. The editors decided that the Chicago boy — who was Irish and selected because Irish immigrants were arriving in large numbers — would win because the *American* needed a bigger circulation boost than the *Journal* or *World*.[7]

To fill so much space so quickly, writers had to be as creative as the editors. Those who were not were sometimes fired within a day or two of being hired. William Salisbury was let go when his editor preferred a rival paper's version of a house fire. "The rescue of several persons from a tall building by a human ladder formed by firemen was described, but no such rescue had taken place. It was a one-story building and no ladder was used at all," Salisbury lamented. Facts were secondary. "I was told never to let a paper outdo the *American*."[8]

Editors were no less vulnerable than reporters. Hearst tore through twenty-seven city editors in the *American*'s first thirty-seven months.[9] The key to success, he believed, was to grab a reader's attention fast. As columnist Arthur Brisbane told rewrite men, "If you don't hit the reader in the eye with the first sentence, don't bother to write the second."[10]

If producing the paper required a madhouse effort, getting it delivered involved just as much bedlam. On June 22, ten days before the *American* started rolling off the presses, Solomon Carvalho hired Max Annenberg. Max was working for the *Tribune* at the time, but when Carvalho told him the *American* would pay twenty-five cents for each subscription he sold, he quit on the spot to join Hearst. As Moe wrote in his notes, with a mixture of admiration and resentment, "Max could always get a job in a hurry and could always get himself into a most favorable position with the boss."

Max had an early start as a newsboy. Within weeks of the family's arrival in Chicago when he was eleven, Max had begun selling papers at the corner of Twelfth and Wabash Avenue, making a penny for each five papers he sold. He parlayed that street experience into a job in the publicity office of the 1893 Columbian Exposition, where, as he put it, at eighteen, "I was practically the circulation manager of the *Illustrated World's Fair.*"[11] That newspaper was published daily during the seven-month fair, which brought twenty-seven million visitors to see exhibits from seventy-two countries on the site near the University of Chicago.[12]

Max did not work again at a newspaper until 1899, when, at the age of twenty-five and after his last job in the grocery business with Moe, the *Tribune* gave him a tryout as a subcription salesman, or canvasser, as the job was called then. He had been there for several months and was making a name for himself when Carvalho hired him. As soon as Max began on Madison Street, he brought over Moe, who ever since their grocery store partnership collapsed had been trying to survive financially by selling scrap iron and bartending.

The circulation business baffled Moe at first. He knew nothing about newspapers beyond reading them as he read everything he could get his hands on, including novels and history books. At a time when most newspapers sold on newsstands, he did not understand the significance of home delivery. Customers were fickle. They bought one paper one day, another the next, depending on the appeal of headlines or features. Subscriptions and home delivery locked in reader loyalty and would become tremendously important. Moe had never approached a customer directly to sell a particular product and admitted, "Never having solicited before, I found the task very difficult to begin with."

He started by listening to the other salesmen, who emphasized that the *American* was the best-edited paper in the city. At the outset, armed with that simple claim as his entire sales pitch, Moe took to the streets he knew so well and began putting in brutally long hours to see more potential subscribers than any other salesman. "I was so hungry for success after the hardships endured and failures suffered," he wrote for his never-published memoir, "that my one wish, for which I prayed night and day, was for an opportunity to demonstrate how earnestly and hard I could work if only I had a chance."

Once Moe began, holding him back was difficult. After selling to everyone he could find in his territory, he thought nothing of moving over and working in someone else's, which infuriated them. "My plan of soliciting was very simple," Moe explained. "Upon being given audience and learning that the prospect had not yet seen or read the *Chicago American*, I would begin by telling her how ably the paper was edited, and would point to the various contributors page by page. I would then finish by asking her to please try it for a month for only 25 cents and if she was not satisfied, she could stop. After securing the signature of the prospect, who was usually a housewife, I would thank her and tell her that someone would come from the office in a day or two to verify the order, so please tell your husband about it so it will go through. Otherwise, if the order comes back no good, I might lose my position.

"That simple little 'goodbye statement,'" Moe believed, "was the reason why my orders held up to such a high percentage over all the other solicitors." Salesmen were fired right and left, but as one of the more dependable and successful ones, Moe was always kept on. Each day, he grew to love the job more. When Max was promoted to oversee circulation in Englewood, a tough, working-class neighborhood southwest of the University of Chicago, Moe went along. After three months, Max returned to Madison Street headquarters and Moe took charge of Englewood. That, he wrote, "was when the real fun began."

Circulation men were responsible for more than selling subscriptions to ever larger territories. They also had to ensure that the papers were delivered. In a turbulent, unruly city like Chicago, no Marquis of Queensbury rules governed the furious competition for readers among ten papers. Dealers had no compunction about stealing bundles of papers belonging to a rival and throwing them into Lake Michigan or the Chicago River or setting them afire. Dealers who handled one paper were discouraged from selling another. If they disregarded the warnings, they were often beaten up or their kiosks were turned over or destroyed. And because the *American* was the new paper, it had to force itself in, just as Solomon Carvalho had predicted to Hearst.

Moe was ready to do whatever it took. He was used to bar fights. When he worked at the saloon on the corner of Archer and State Streets, a crowded hangout for construction workers and prostitutes, Moe had constantly been breaking up brawls. Invariably he took the side of the hookers. He had been comfortable around them since his days as a telegraph boy, when they often tipped him better than the johns for whom he was running messages.

Bartending was for choirboys compared with circulation work. To supply the corner kiosks and have the carriers on their way with the first morning editions, Moe had to arrive in Englewood by 5 A.M. He rose at 3:30 A.M. to a hot cup of coffee and full breakfast prepared by the always cheery Sadie. At the corner of Clark and Archer, he boarded the 4:15 A.M. Wentworth Avenue streetcar and rattled and swayed his way due south in the pitch black of predawn.

"The other papers, especially the *Daily News* and the *Tribune*, which were powerful and had entrenched circulations, were very fearful of the Hearst invasion," Moe wrote. "The *Daily News* resorted to every available means to stop the Hearst circulation and strengthened themselves further by engaging a strong-arm squad to enforce their policy." The *American* retaliated in kind. "We were compelled," Moe explained, "to do the best we could by establishing our own avenues."

The avenues were bloody and whether Max and Moe were the instigators or the retaliators, there is no question that they were full participants in the *American*'s battle to establish itself in the opening years of the century. The strain of the Hearst offensive increased by the day. As competition rose, so did intimidation. "The more I tried to force the sales of the Hearst papers, the more I was antagonized by the *Daily News* organization," Moe recorded decades later. "I was threatened every day with extermination for my efforts and I would leave my home, as a result, with a revolver in each of my coat pockets, ready for action."

He organized his own gang of neighborhood toughs and learned on the street about organization, leadership and loyalty. He handed out baseball bats and spoke with his team constantly about strategy and tactics, when to attack boldly, when to regroup and use subterfuge. And because such fellows followed doers, not talkers, Moe led the way with his own fists and swinging his own bat. One 5:30 A.M. Englewood fistfight between Moe and a *Tribune* seller ended after young Annenberg had beaten his opponent so bloody that both were arrested and tried later that morning at police court on Wentworth Avenue. "My boys were all witnesses testifying that the *Tribune* man assaulted me first," wrote Moe, "when old Judge Dugan peered over his glasses at my unmarked face and stated sarcastically that 'He must have hit you with a quill feather.'"

Taking the lead in fights endeared Moe to his troops. "Gradually I won their confidence to a degree that they would do more for me without pay than the *Daily News* could have done for pay. And," he added proudly, "my boys were no cream puffs."

His boys were young mobsters. Several became killers. Among them were Mossy Enright, who was shot to death in a 1920s gangland fight; Tim Murphy, slain in a mob feud; Diamond Dick Torpy, gunned down in a private dispute; James Ragen and Mickey McBride, who in the 1930s ran the racetrack newswire Nationwide News Service for Moe; "Schemer" May, an Irish brawler who worked for Ragen, and Eddie "Bricktop" White, whose face would turn as red as his hair as he sprinted down Sixty-third Street, a bat in each hand, in pursuit of a *Daily News* intimidator. "This was the nucleus of my little army," wrote Moe. "And they had friends on whom they could call. As a result of my efforts and the help of those boys, we were able to break through the resistance of the *Daily News*."

With the help of the boys, a penny sale price and papers packed with sensational news, often from the neighborhood, sales of Hearst's paper soared in Englewood. From the corner of Sixty-third and Wentworth, Moe was selling up to a thousand copies a day of the *American*, while the *Tribune*, whose primary audience lived far from Englewood in the more exclusive lakefront neighborhood, sold seventy-five copies a day. To mark his success, Moe was asked to take over Woodlawn, an area about a mile and a half east of Englewood near the Washington Park racetrack.

One day during race season, Moe was on the corner of Cottage Grove and Sixty-third Streets selling the *American* when "one of the ugliest looking human specimens that I have ever seen" approached and without warning hit him in the face as hard as he could. The blow did not land squarely and Moe responded by punching his assailant's head as fast as he could. His much bigger attacker was surprised by Moe's resilience. The two grappled and fell to the ground. As they rolled around, a second attacker raced up to kick Moe, but was knocked back by a gathering crowd.

The two attackers fled, but Moe learned their identities. The next morning, with what he called his little army in tow, Moe marched into the *Daily News* and demanded to see the circulation manager. When he emerged, "I told him in no uncertain terms that I knew the attack upon me was inspired by him and that if there were any recurrence, I would retaliate on him personally in the same manner. That," Moe explained, "put a quietus on the slugging tactics for the time being."

With the message delivered, Moe and his crew took off after his two attackers. It was fortunate he didn't catch them because if he had, Moses Annenberg would have been jailed in his twenties. He admitted later that he intended to kill the man who had first hit him, a *Daily News* tough named Touse. "Had we found him, I am sure that would have been the end of Mr. Touse," he wrote. "However, we learned later that he had left the city on a freight train, fell off near St. Joe, Michigan, and was cut to pieces under the car wheels. That saved us the trouble of exterminating him." And of being prosecuted himself, a possibility which never dawned on him in moments of fury.

Soon after the Touse incident, Moe was promoted to circulation manager for the entire South Side of Chicago, which meant a $5-a-week raise to $19 and more responsibility. Although the *American* was an afternoon paper, Hearst produced earlier editions to compete directly with the morning dailies. As deadlines advanced, Moe had to arrive at 1:30 A.M. to make certain the morning editions arrived and were distributed. Leaving a bundle of papers unprotected on the street guaranteed they would disappear within minutes.

If a driver failed to show up, Moe took his place. The worst route was around the Union Stock Yard, the mile-square city of commerce and death which was built in 1879. By the turn of the century it was home to a workforce of twenty-five thousand men, women and children who bought, sold, killed and processed fifteen million animals a year. On the southwest side of the city, the stockyards were surrounded by a desolate warren of narrow, muddy streets, ugly shanties and small, dirty shops where it was difficult to deliver papers and harder to collect subscription fees. A sickening stench of animal fear, decaying meat, blood, dung and urine permeated the neighborhood year-round.[13]

When the regular stockyard driver became ill, Moe drove the route for six winter weeks, the temperature below zero much of the time.

Every day, he woke up at midnight, walked to a stable, hitched a horse to a wagon, picked up his load of papers and started delivering at 2:30 A.M. Finishing at 7 A.M., he went home, ate breakfast, slept until noon, got up again and repeated the earlier schedule for the afternoon papers. He was relieved when the regular driver returned, but Moe had gained valuable experience. No circulation man in Chicago combined his intelligence, drive, toughness and grasp of the job's details.

Any neighborhood where Hearst's *American* did not dominate, he considered a personal challenge. One *Daily News* stronghold was the largely black district near Thirty-ninth and Cottage Grove on the South Side, which Moe was determined to take over. The situation was complicated by the fact that the *Daily News* operation was organized around a newsstand whose owner was crippled. "I met many difficulties on account of the natural sympathies of the neighboring hoodlums for the crippled corner man," noted Moe. Every time Moe tried to persuade the man to handle the *American*, the *Daily News* men would throw the Hearst paper into the street.

Moe explained to the *American*'s circulation manager, John Eastman, that he had a special problem. Eastman told him to hire whomever he needed "for the purpose of securing fair representation." Moe hired eight toughs from the stockyards at $3 a day and brought in a prizefighter on the Hearst payroll named Jack Daley. For three weeks, copies of the *American* were sold, until Eastman complained about the cost of the muscle. Moe moved quickly to force a resolution.

One of his men called the *Daily News* circulation chief, pretended to be a son of the crippled newsstand operator and claimed that sluggers for the *American* were destroying his papers, then settled back to wait. The *Daily News* promptly dispatched a wagon full of its own black toughs for the showdown and walked into Moe's ambush. The leader, a man named Clark, leapt from the wagon, muttered, "There's going to be some real doing today," and as he approached Moe's *American* gang, appeared to make a motion toward his pocket. "Quick as a flash, one of our members struck him in the face," Moe later wrote, "and another fired a bullet into his head." Clark's revolver dropped from his pocket onto the wooden sidewalk.

Lawrence Finn, who managed the Thirty-ninth and State Street neighborhood for Moe, was indicted for murder. Defended by Hearst attorney Clarence Darrow, already on his way to building a reputation as a defender of hopeless causes, Finn was acquitted. More significantly, Clark's death meant the *American* took over the black neighborhood, or as Moe put it, "the episode went a long way toward clearing up a most difficult situation."

Moe had nothing against the black newsboys working for the *Daily News*. There is no indication that he had any innate biases or racial prejudices, probably because he had grown up in a mixed neighborhood and had hung out with kids from different ethnic groups. From the Grand Pacific Hotel to the Archer Street saloon, he had dealt with a hefty cross-section of society. He was making judgments based on people's abilities to get a job done, not on their origins or how much schooling they had. The fact was that the black newsboys knew the territory well. If he could get them working for him, he knew he would have an easier time controlling his new neighborhood.

To switch their loyalties, he became friendly with several blacks in the area and discovered that the newsboys lived together in a group house. The *Daily News* neither owned nor rented the property, but paid a local circulation manager, who rented it month-to-month in his own name. Moe immediately went to the owner and arranged a two-year lease. Assuming control of the Daily News Boys Home, he installed his black friend Mose Walker as manager, improved the boys' meals, beds and salaries, and in one brilliant, nonviolent move, knocked the *Daily News* out of circulation in black neighborhoods on the South Side.

Hearst did not know the Annenbergs in the first years of the new century. He delegated, rarely dealt with junior underlings and kept his distance from the seamier aspects of what he knew was involved when a Hearst paper shot itself into a new territory. His Chicago executives, however, had nothing but praise for Moe. His tactics concerned them less than his results. When the motto of Chicago's circulation men was "Sell 'em or eat 'em," few *American*s remained unsold in Moe's territories.

Promotions kept coming. To subscription manager, which he disliked because it cooped him up at headquarters. He asked for outside duties and was named the *American*'s top road man, responsible for the circulation of the *American* in other cities. The *Sunday American*, for example, was packed with features, comics and advertising and sold as many as twenty-five thousand copies in cities as far away as Cleveland and Columbus.

When William Randolph Hearst ran for president in 1904, Moe was assigned to help boost his campaign in Indiana. Hearst was a U.S. congressman from New York at the time, but as his father, George, had been U.S. senator from California when he died in 1891, the publisher's ambition was targeted for the top. Based in the Claypool Hotel in Indianapolis, Moe was assigned to blanket the state with Hearst newspapers, whose editorial pages were devoted to pushing the candidacy of the man his Chicago editors called "the Great White Chief."[14]

Cracking Indiana, never mind defeating President Theodore Roosevelt, proved more problematic than knocking off Joseph Pulitzer in New York or Victor Lawson in Chicago. Hearst won the Iowa convention, but in Indiana, Democratic party boss Tom Taggart opposed Hearst, who was accused of trying to buy the nomination and overrun the state with "a gang of paid agents and retainers."[15]

Moe was among them. He spent six months in Indiana as part of a Hearst campaign team that, as he described it, "worked and schemed night and day," spent $300,000 and managed to capture only two delegates. From there, Moe went to the Democratic national convention in St. Louis, "where again I did everything possible to spread Hearst propaganda," but met with the same result. Hearst expected to be nominated by William Jennings Bryan, whom he had championed twice previously. The publisher was crushed when Bryan instead nominated a Missouri senator who had no chance. Eventually, the Democrats nominated Alton Parker, the stolid, dull chief judge of the New York State Court of Appeals, who himself was annihilated by Roosevelt in November.

Moe worked in Indiana directly for Andrew Lawrence, an editor on the *American* who had been assigned purely political duties during the campaign. Once Hearst was out of the presidential race, Lawrence persuaded the publisher to create a separate morning edition of the *Chicago American* and put him in charge. When Hearst agreed, Lawrence hired Moe as his circulation manager. Max stayed on as the assistant to Berthold Yokel, circulation manager for the *Evening American*.

Although they were working for the same paper, Moe's new post on the morning edition actually put him into direct competition with Max. Because different staffs put out the papers, some competitiveness was inevitable. What made this situation worse was a business plan for the morning paper that guaranteed the brothers' rivalry would intensify.

Hearst had been willing to launch the morning edition, but he refused to incur additional operating costs. Lawrence was so eager to run his own paper that he agreed, only to tell Moe to operate as best he could with the *American*'s overall circulation department controlled by Yokel and Max. Those two had no stake in helping Moe succeed at their expense. Instead, they ordered their circulation men not to work for the morning paper, but allowed them to work for the rival *Morning Record*, owned by Victor Lawson, who also owned the *Daily News*. Outraged at this treachery, Moe appealed to William Leach, publisher of the *American*. Leach agreed with Moe that the arrangement was senseless and fired Yokel but retained Max. Moe was not appeased.

The rivalry became so intense that one day when Max's tactics infuriated him, Moe exploded, grabbed a baseball bat and charged into the *American*'s circulation office in search of his brother. He had to be physically restrained. Lawrence asked Hearst for advice, then summoned Moe and told him that while he admired his spirit, he could not condone his behavior. Moe said he could not run a circulation operation when his older brother controlled the resources and was determined to prevent him from succeeding. Impulsive as ever, he quit on the spot.

It was time for him to do something else. Moe had briefly tried operating a newspaper distribution business in Aurora, Illinois, where his brother Jacob ran a scrap iron business. He never spent enough time or effort in Aurora to make the business work, but he did notice that "wholesale distributors with far less talent than I" were making far more comfortable livings with much less effort and tension, sometimes six or seven times the $3,000 a year he was then earning at the *American*.[16]

If emigrating from East Prussia had been the first turning point in his life, he was now facing the second. Several factors would determine his direction. One was the level of violence in the circulation business in Chicago. He had already had several close calls and foresaw that the situation would get worse — as it did after 1910 — and that he would inevitably be targeted. That prospect terrified Sadie, who pleaded with Moses to be careful.

A second factor involved his growing family responsibilities. He and Sadie had been married a year when their first child, Diana, was born in 1900. Esther, or Aye as she was known, arrived a year later. Pearl, who became Polly, was born in 1903 and Janet, known as Jan, the following year. Then, in 1905, Diana died of tubercular meningitis. Sadie and Moses were devastated and a pall fell over them both. Sadie was inconsolable and for years could scarcely tolerate having any of her three surviving children out of her sight. Terrified that she might lose another, she was exhausted from waking up repeatedly throughout the night to check their cribs, making certain none had a fever.

Diana's death had a lasting effect on the family. One result was that Sadie and Moe would raise their children with an indulgent love in which much was given and little demanded beyond obedience and decent, polite behavior. Another was Diana's role as catalyst in later years for Sadie's and the Annenberg children's generous philanthropy in the medical field. Less than a year after Diana's death, Sadie gave birth to another daughter, Enid, the final member of what would be considered the elder group of Annenberg children. Her birth worried Sadie as much as it delighted her. Ever since its founding on the mud-flats, Chicago had been plagued by health epidemics, from cholera and typhoid fever to dysentery and diphtheria. Sadie had lost confidence in the city as a place to raise their children. She did not insist that Moe move. That was a decision for him to make, but she voiced her concerns. And Moe, who appreciated her intelligence and shared her feelings about the health of the children, paid attention.

Finally, there was the problem of work. Reporting to Max at the *American* had been untenable. And trying to support a family of six on a $60-a-week salary was no better. Moe wanted more money, more security and a healthier environment for his family. He was maturing.

Moe had his eye on Milwaukee, ninety miles north, where he knew that the newspaper distribution system was haphazard and poorly run. With some research, he found that each of Chicago's ten dailies maintained its own circulation office in Milwaukee and each was losing money. He proposed merging all of them into a single office that he would manage, and the publishers agreed to give him a chance.

He needed $2,500 to establish himself in Milwaukee. He had $1,000 saved and approached Jacob to borrow the additional $1,500. Jacob agreed, but, unsentimental as always and every bit as tough as his two younger brothers, insisted on rigid terms. He demanded 7 percent interest, a promissory note, and, as security, $700 worth of Sadie's jewelry, which he later lost, causing another fraternal rift which lasted for years. As Jake listed them, Moe agreed to all the conditions. He made quick decisions and acted on them even faster. The day Jake handed over the money, Moe hurried to the Milwaukee train station and bought six tickets.

It was October 1906. Six months earlier the worst earthquake in U.S. history had devastated San Francisco. While the city by the bay was still digging out, the city on the lake was celebrating an all-Chicago

World Series. Moe was not much of a baseball fan, but he wanted to see his South Side White Sox knock off the mighty Cubs, whose 116 victories that year were the most any major league team had won in a regular season in the twentieth century. Two days after the "hitless wonders" White Sox upset the Cubs and their infield stars Tinker, Evers and Chance in six games, the Annenbergs were on their way to Milwaukee.

4

MILWAUKEE

W HEN SADIE, MOE and their four daughters clambered down from the train in Milwaukee in 1906, he was twenty-nine years old, had quit a $60-a-week job and was $1,500 in debt. When he left Wisconsin in 1920, Moe had eight children, was making $300,000 a year and had a net worth of $2 million. By every measure, the family's fourteen years in Wisconsin were fruitful. Moe, a loner unable to count on anyone else and determined to succeed on his own, had a simple explanation for how he did it.

"It's the difference between the well-fed house dog and the hungry wolf," he said. "You never hear of a well-fed house dog going out to hunt for food. But the hungry wolf must hunt, or starve. I was a hungry wolf. I had a large family. I had to hunt or starve. I learned how to hunt. And I kept it up."[1]

The family moved into a house at 715 Van Buren Street. A mile away at 450 Broadway, Moe set up the Chicago News Company, which later became the Milwaukee News Company, and began receiving daily by train the ten Chicago morning and evening papers plus a broad selection of magazines, including the popular *Ladies' Home Journal* and *Saturday Evening Post*. Cyrus Curtis, president of Curtis Publishing which owned the *Saturday Evening Post*, was so pleased with his increased circulation in Milwaukee that he gave Moe a gold watch inscribed with thanks "for unusual services."

Those services included making clear to retail outlets that taking the *Saturday Evening Post* was required if they wanted any of Moe's other newspapers and magazines. There was nothing illegal or even unseemly about the arrangement. It was tough, Chicago-style business.

Moe was leveraging his advantage, a strategy he followed as long as he stayed hungry.

Within months of his arrival, Moe was earning $150 a week, but he had just begun to hunt. With only four years of primary school, he had no formal business training, no financial or accounting expertise. But his half-dozen years with Hearst had given him sufficient education to organize a lean and tough circulation system and to begin dominating competitors. In 1908, the first year the Chicago News Agency was included in *Wright's Directory of Milwaukee*, it was one of fifteen city news dealers listed. When the 1916 edition of *Wright's* was published, only Moe's agency was still in business.

He added product lines which Milwaukee's news dealers had not carried: tobacco, cigarettes and cigars, candy and souvenir postcards. As his city-wide business grew, he took over other newsdealerships far beyond Milwaukee, mostly organizations which had been unable to compete with him. "Whenever an agency was not operating successfully, the publisher would call me in," Moe said. "I would pay the deficit owed by the agent and the business would be turned over to me."[2]

Distributing both the Chicago papers and later local dailies and weeklies, he bought or established distribution agencies in Oshkosh, Racine and Kenosha in Wisconsin, then expanded to Peoria and Aurora in Illinois, Louisville, Kentucky, Akron and Youngstown, Ohio, Elizabeth and Trenton, New Jersey, San Francisco and Los Angeles. After a decade in Milwaukee, he owned thirty distribution agencies nationwide.

Moe worked closely with the newsboys who delivered his papers and magazines. He not only knew their kind from Chicago, the scrappy kids and young men who headed out on their rounds before dawn, he had been one himself. He told the newsboys about fishing for the family supper in Kalvishken, dealing with hookers on the make and cops on the take during his messenger and bartending days, and about battling *Daily News* sluggers on Chicago's South Side. Moe was a good boss and they enjoyed working with him because he knew what he was talking about. He did not ask them to do anything that he had not already done himself or was not willing to do again. He was demanding, but he did not stand on formality or seniority and he pushed no one harder than himself. The industrious ones were treated well, stayed with him for years and went on to become successful wholesalers themselves.

Distribution was the core of Moe's business, but his best idea, the one that gave the family its single biggest cash infusion and the one that eight decades later his descendants continued to speak of in awe as his most brilliant move, came from Sadie. He was sitting at home one evening in 1913, trying to come up with a plan to make his fortune. Something simple, something women needed or wanted was what he was looking for because, as he knew from his first days of selling subscriptions to the *American* in 1900, it was women at home who signed up when salesmen came by.

"Selling things through newspaper coupons was not new then. College pennants had been popular: cut out the coupon, send ten or twenty cents and get the pennant. Everybody had a den and they went well, but the business was played out. I was looking for something new, something housewives might want . . . something that would have a serial quality, which women would buy and repeat."

Because Sadie ran the house, he asked her which of the more durable household items she bought most often. "Teaspoons," she replied.

Instantly, Moe sensed she was right. "That's it," he said, turning to his children. "Mother has just made us a fortune." The children giggled and clapped their hands although they had no idea what their father was talking about. His enthusiasm was bewitching.

Instead of college pennants or plates, Moe would use silver teaspoons as a promotional incentive to increase newspaper sales.

"I conceived the idea of having teaspoons with the state seal on the handle. I ordered 30,000 spoons in six lots of 5,000 each with the seals of Wisconsin and the five neighboring states."

As he always would when starting a new business, Moe set up a separate organization, the International Souvenir Spoon Company, and contacted W. M. Rogers and Sons to produce samples that he showed to circulation directors of the papers he handled.[3] Soon after they agreed that the idea was a likely winner, newspapers across the country were participating in the promotion. Each paper carried the subscription advertisement and sign-up coupon. The subscriber cut out the coupon, presented it to certain newsstands and for fifteen cents extra was given the silver spoon. Each week a new spoon was available. And while Moe knew he was on to something, he was stunned by the demand.

"My wife was right," said Moe. "Every woman in creation seemed to want those spoons."[4]

The *New York Sunday World* sold 150,000 spoons a week. The *Chicago Examiner,* 100,000 a week. Moe signed up papers in nearly every state and Canada by including the seals of each of the forty-eight states and Canadian provinces. He was preparing to take the campaign into Europe when World War I broke out and ended that plan. The promotion lasted more than a year. Early on, William Randolph Hearst tried to steal the idea and persuade the chairman of the International Silver Company, a man named Wilcox, to sell the silver to him. "Those spoons were contracted for with Mr. Annenberg," Wilcox replied. "He made the deal. This was his idea." Moe thought no less of Hearst when he heard of the publisher's attempt. He was not even surprised. Hearst sought advantage the way a shark sought lunch. It was part of his nature. But Moe did resolve to take extra care if he ever had any future dealings with the publisher.

When the totals were in, Moe had sold one hundred million spoons and had collected a percentage on each sale. At the age of thirty-six, he had made his first million dollars and was rich enough to begin branching out into investments other than distribution.

He did not know much about any other businesses, but just as he was happy to teach the tricks of the news agency trade to his distribution team, he wanted to keep learning. He researched his next step with the help of Frank Mulkern, a Milwaukee celebrity known as the "millionaire newsboy" because he too had started out peddling newspapers. Mulkern taught Moe how easy it was to borrow money from banks, putting other people's money to work to leverage income. Moe went into the taxicab business with Mulkern, and founded one of the first electric car dealerships, the Chicago Electric, though he owned a six-cylinder Winton himself.

One of his best investments was building Milwaukee's largest parking garage. Henry Ford had introduced his Model T in 1907, the same year General Motors was created, and eight years later Moe saw the $850 "flivvers" turning up and parking haphazardly all over downtown. Anticipating that the congestion in the city would worsen, he built the garage and to promote it bought an advertising supplement in the *Milwaukee Journal* featuring pictures of the building and ads from contractors who had worked on the structure. Proud of what he had done, he sent his brother Max a copy of the paper.

Several days later, back in the mail came the ad. On it Max had scrawled: "Stop building garages with *Chicago Tribune* money." He had not, though, spent any *Tribune* money on the garage. The *Tribune* was not paying him that much anyway. Of the twelve thousand papers he was distributing daily and fifty thousand on Sunday, the *Tribune*s were not even the biggest part. Except for a First Wisconsin bank mortgage, every penny in the garage had been his own. Uncharacteristically, Moe cried when he received the letter. He was upset and angry with himself for asking Max for recognition that he should have known would not have been forthcoming. And he was upset with the realization that their relationship was beyond redemption. With the exception of the funerals of Tobias in 1910 and of Sheva five years later, the brothers rarely saw each other during the fourteen years Moe lived in Milwaukee. After this letter, the brothers did not speak for three years and even after they resumed it, their contact was perfunctory. Asked years later to confirm that he and his brother were again cooperating, Max replied, "I did not say we cooperated. I said we were on speaking terms."[5]

In addition to the garage, Moe built and bought two theaters, bowling alleys, billiard parlors, stores and apartments. Five properties, including the theaters, provided revenues until 1948, when they were sold for $1.75 million. Milwaukee's beer barons were richer, but Moses Annenberg was the city's Croesus. He had been a silver man from William Jennings Bryan to teaspoons, but now everything he touched turned to gold.

The family was expanding as fast as his business. Moses, as he went back to being called in Milwaukee, came from a large family and wanted a large one of his own. That was fine with Sadie, who after giving birth five times in Chicago, had four more children in Milwaukee. Three were girls: Lita in 1909, Evelyn in 1911, and Harriet in 1914, an inseparable trio known as the three little bears. There was never any question that Moses and Sadie wanted a boy. Sadie was close to her own brothers and father and each time she was pregnant prayed for a boy if, as she said, it was God's will. Moses, surrounded by females, loved his daughters, but he had an old-world attitude about women. To extend the family name and inherit his business, he needed a son.

They would have only one. Walter Hubert was born on Friday the thirteenth of March, 1908, at 1:30 P.M. at home at 742 Jackson street. He was named, the son explained later, for Walter Hubert Inman, a newsman in Cleveland whom Moses admired. The birth was difficult. The baby was in breech position and might well not have survived had Sadie not been so strong and if Dr. A. W. Myers had not been on hand to assist. The combination of near tragedy and sole son ensured from that moment that the attention paid to young Walter would be extraordinary.

Some supersitious families considered it bad luck to have a child on Friday the thirteenth. Not the Annenbergs. Walter was their third consecutive child born on a thirteenth, albeit the only one on a Friday, and forever after, the family considered thirteen its lucky number.

There were no vital statistics on the birth certificate regarding the newborn's weight or length. There were two boxes on the form which asked the doctor to state yes or no as to whether the child had any physical defect and if yes to state its nature. Neither box was filled in, but Walter was born with a minor defect. His right ear was withered to a small stump of cartilage and he was deaf on that side. Moses was overjoyed that he had a son, but concerned about his ear, and, according to Walter's sister Evelyn, disappointed that his heir was not perfect. Moe's older brother Jacob had had a hearing problem too and he understood the frustrations such a disability could cause. Still, he was also grateful that his son otherwise appeared to be healthy.

Being the sole brother in a sea of seven surviving sisters guaranteed a special role for Walter. From the outset, he was his parents' undisputed favorite. The children were all "like the fingers of my hands," Moses often said, extending his palms forward. Walter, though, was more than a finger. "My right arm," Moses called him.

His mother and sisters did not call him Walter. To them he was always "Boy," the nickname Sadie was still using when Walter was in his fifties. When she did use his proper name, it was a sure sign he was in trouble. "She had a phrase whenever I did something that she didn't like," he said. "'Now, Walter, think about that more carefully. Now Walter.'" His father never used the nickname. To Moses, he was always Walter.[6]

With one exception, life was quite idyllic and mostly fun in Milwaukee. When Moses was not at home, which was frequently because he worked long hours and traveled by train to distant distributorships, the house was a rambunctious madhouse of siblings cavorting, friends racing through, playing games, throwing balls, staging puppet shows, making snowmen in the yard. Sadie was constantly fussing about like a mother hen. Whenever the girls or Boy left the house, she wanted them looking perfect. Even before the money began to roll in, there were no torn or patched dresses or suits on her children. Each morning she made certain the girls brushed their hair so she could pin on big, freshly ironed hair bows. Boy had his collar inspected and his finger-nails checked. Before leaving, each child was hugged and kissed.

When Moses was home, the atmosphere changed. For all the joy in a house full of kids and parents who loved them, there was a constant undercurrent of tension and anxiety because Moses was so intense and still prone to violent outbursts. He set aside Sundays to spend with the family and the mood was light, but the tone was different than when he was away. An edginess set in. Sunday mornings he gathered the children around and flipped through the *Milwaukee Journal* until he found something he thought they would enjoy, like a photograph of a dirigible, and he would take them on a fantasy journey to Japan for the coronation of the new Taisho emperor, where all the women were in long gowns that he would describe in exquisite detail. He had never been in Japan, but he rarely slept, was an omnivorous reader and forgot nothing. When the superliner *Titanic* sank in 1912, he told them all about icebergs.[7]

Almost any story about Theodore Roosevelt, who was president when Walter was born, led to the retelling of how Teddy was almost assassinated just a few blocks from their house while he was running for president in 1912 as a Bull Moose. Moses described how the assassin's bullet was slowed when it smashed into Roosevelt's fifty-page speech text and how, with blood seeping through his shirt, the former president insisted on delivering his entire eighty-minute address, the audience leaning forward and expecting him to collapse at any instant.

On other Sunday mornings, Moses described his companies and explained how he was building stores with apartment buildings above them equipped with the new Murphy beds that folded up into the wall. He detailed how newspapers and magazines were printed and distributed and how his holdings were growing. Periodically, he had them write down lists of his companies. Each time the lists grew longer. The variety of the stories and the realistic detail enthralled the kids. There did not seem to be anything Father did not know or could not do.[8]

He even taught himself to play the violin. Moses had no musical training, but he owned a massive collection of opera and classical records which he listened to on a phonograph. From listening, he learned enough to play in unique style. He braced the violin between his knees like a cello while the hushed children sprawled around his feet.

When he came home from work during the week, he was often tired and more prone to be irritable. Like Sadie, he wanted the children well dressed and well behaved; unlike her, he also wanted them quiet and, on occasion, silent. If he were upset or mulling a problem, he sometimes ordered that there be no talking at the dinner table, a difficult command to obey in most houses with children, let alone eight.

Yet when Moses wanted silence, he got it. "He was very strong-willed, very," said Evelyn Annenberg, his sixth surviving daughter. "When he said no talking, no one would talk."[9] "His word was law," said Ronald Krancer, son of second daughter Polly.[10] Except for a slurp of soup or the clank of a utensil on a plate, the table, including Sadie, ate in complete silence. If anyone slipped and did speak up, Moses's rage set the children quivering. "My mother was very afraid of her father," said Cynthia Polsky, daughter of Lita Annenberg, the fifth daughter. "She admired his energy and his brilliance, but she was afraid of his temper and fearful of incurring his displeasure."[11]

Moses did the damage with his voice and mood. Neither he nor Sadie believed in physically striking their children. The girls were never hit. When Boy was seven, he was given a tool kit which he used to chisel holes in the windowsills of their rented house. The landlord heard about the damage and threatened to sue, and Moses gave his son a severe tongue lashing. The next time Walter was not so lucky. When teasing Lita, he sicced the family's pet bulldog, Wrinkles, on his sister. As Wrinkles lunged, Lita raced backward up the stairs, tripped, fell and broke her arm. "I caught hell," said Walter. "That was the only time I got a beating."

As the children grew, they increasingly came to consider their father a man of Wagnerian complexity. He was knowledgeable, confident, generous, supportive, and loving. Yet he was also prone to violent mood swings in which he turned furious and profane or icy cold and vindictive. Years later, when Enid said she wanted to adopt a daughter and name her Diana "so we would have another Diana in the family," Moses immediately became enraged.

Sadie had talked with her children about Diana, but Moses had completely internalized her death. Enid, who had no idea how he felt, believed she was memorializing Diana. Her father quickly set Enid straight. He did not want the name used and no other Annenberg descendent was ever called Diana.

What upset him more, family members recalled, was that Enid wanted to give the name to an adopted child, not a blood relative. "You would call somebody else's mistake after my beloved child?" Moses bellowed at her. "I would never speak to you again as long as you lived if you did such a thing." Enid immediately backed off on the Diana, but when she adopted a daughter anyway and named her Pamela, Moses refused to speak to her for three years despite every effort by Sadie and the children to bridge the rift.[12] He abhorred the thought of the Annenberg bloodline being corrupted by any outsider.

When Rabbi Hirschberg of Milwaukee's Temple Emmanuel announced a fund drive, Moses sent a check for $2,000. He was a member of the synagogue but did not attend services, having little regard for any organized religion in general or this rabbi in particular. Sadie, however, attended services regularly and the children went to Hebrew school. After receiving the check, Hirschberg called and asked to see Moses at his distributing company office. Expecting a thank you, Moses invited him over and greeted him with respect. Hirschberg sat and the next words out of his mouth were, "Mr. Annenberg, you who drive around in a big Winton six and I, who do you the honor of coming to your office to protest the size of your contribution . . ."[13]

Moses stood up. "Out. Get out of my office," he said, his voice a menacing whisper. "Immediately." The rabbi was uncertain he had heard correctly and hesitated. "Out, or I'll throw you out," Moses repeated, his voice rising and face turning red. As Hirschberg scuttled through the door, Moses shouted after him, "I resign from Temple Emmanuel."

When he came home and informed Sadie what happened and that he was withdrawing the children from Hebrew school, she was stunned, although she agreed that the rabbi's behavior had been shocking and arrogant. The children were ecstatic. "That was the end of our religious training," Walter chuckled later. "Mother was a bit embarrassed, but we couldn't believe our good luck, that we didn't have to light candles or learn Hebrew. We stopped going immediately."

While Moses did not put much stock in religion, he put a high priority on readying Walter for a life that would be more challenging than what he was experiencing inside the overly protective Annenberg cocoon. Walter needed help because his problems were mounting.

His sisters never spoke with him about his deformed ear, but other children repeatedly teased him. "I was a bit sensitive to it," he admitted. Aye, his eldest sister, came to his defense several times. Walter got into a fistfight after one boy called him "tin ear." "I struck the fellow and that was the end of it," he said. If anything, it was just the beginning.

Nothing could be done to help him hear on the right side. The only sound he could pick up was the ring of a specialist's tuning fork placed directly on his ear bone. Plastic surgery was considered. A Milwaukee doctor had experimented with ear and nose replacements and told Moses he could fix up his son with a plastic ear, but would first have to cut away the cartilage. Walter balked. Moses took him to St. Louis to see another ear specialist, but plastic surgery was in its infancy and the results looked artificial to Walter. "My father said, 'Walter, I leave it up to you,' and I said, 'No, Dad, I don't want to live through that.'" So the ear was left alone. Walter already favored his left side. He wrote left-handed and later played golf left-handed. When he became a newspaper executive, all pictures of him were taken almost exclusively from the left side. If there was no way to avoid a right-profile shot, the photos were often retouched.

In addition to the ear problem, Walter had a pronounced stutter that he worked diligently to overcome throughout his life. He could speak, unlike some stutterers who can barely get a word out, but the disability was serious and had a profound effect on Walter's psyche and behavior.

When he was a child in the early years of the twentieth century, there was no clear understanding of what caused stuttering, although it is a malady which has been chronicled and analyzed for twenty-five hundred years.

"At one time or another, stuttering has been popularly traced to childhood trauma, sibling rivalry, suppressed anger, infantile sexual fixations, deformations of the tongue, lips, palate, jaw or larynx, chemical or humoral imbalance, strict upbringing," Benson Bobrick wrote in *Knotted Tongues*, his insightful 1995 study of its history and causes. "Mounting clinical evidence today, however, indicates that stuttering is, after all, an inheritable, physically based problem involving some neurological defect in brain function, perhaps pertaining to the auditory feedback loop and anomalies of sound transmission through the skull."[14]

Walter's stuttering was most likely related to his hearing problem. Not all deaf or partially deaf persons are stutterers, and none of Walter's siblings stuttered. But because he could not hear properly, there may have been a disruption of the precise coordination of the hundred or more muscles used to produce speech. It was impossible to know that for certain when Walter was a child, because there was no way of determining the extent of the defect that affected his ear and hearing.

What was clear was that the stutter made Walter extremely shy and sensitive. And it would be a key to his being an intensely private adult. That he should be shy was understandable. "Stammering in a child rises as a barrier by which the sufferer feels that the world without is separated from the world within," Charles Dickens, a discerning observer, but not himself a stutterer, wrote in 1856.[15]

And how could it be otherwise? "Stuttering is an affliction that renders defective the uniquely human capacity for speech," Bobrick explained. "The dignity of the person, his distinctive humanity and even his soul, as made manifest in rational discourse, was (and is) by tradition associated with speech. Together with the capacity for thought that it expresses through language, speech defines us as human more adequately than any other faculty we have. Its deprivation — in stuttering, its audible and visible disintegration — cannot but be felt as a catastrophe."[16]

It was a catastrophe. "The stuttering wasn't just hard for Walter," said his sister Evelyn, "it was awful."[17] He did endless exercises reading aloud: "My aunt won't untie a knot. . . . Mama and Papa went away at noon. . . . Pin a pad upon a pony. . . . May I eat a muffin, Mama? . . . Fifty fought fifteen." Page after page of lists of words, phrases and sentences. Over and over again for what would ultimately be the better part of a century. In his eighties and nineties, Walter continued to do his speech exercises daily, a sign that he was never "cured" and of his determination and discipline. Every day he would have to prove again that he could speak.

Moses took Walter to the best speech disorder specialists and therapists. He was not insensitive to his son's shyness. But he worried that the combination of Walter's withdrawn, insecure nature and the fact that he was surrounded by women could result in his only son turning out too soft and ill-equipped to compete against life's challenges. When he came home one evening and found that the girls had dressed up Boy with a hair ribbon, Moses flew into a fury. He assembled the girls and Sadie and laid down the law: "Never, ever again will you do anything like that."

Moses had reason to be concerned, because as a child and young man Walter was anything but tough. Like his sisters, Walter was well dressed and well behaved, but he lacked any of the combativeness Moses had shown at his age. With his friend Kirby Robb, Walter carried pet hamsters around in his shirt. He nursed a fawn with a baby bottle. He swore off hunting in his twenties after he wounded a deer on a hunt, and followed it for hours, hearing its anguished cries. "The poor thing sounded human," he said. "I could never shoot anything again."[18]

An insightful boy, he understood his father's intentions. "He was rather fearful," said Walter later, "that I would not have the sense of urgency that he thought I should have." Which was a reasonable fear because Walter had everything he wanted and no reason to show exceptional drive. Moses was not without guilt when it came to indulging Walter. When Walter was four and five, Moses loved to take his son to the news agency, open the cash drawer and have him grab as many coins as he could in one swoop with his two pudgy fists. Being spoiled was fun, but it came with a price. "I was spoiled, but I was a curiosity, the only boy with seven girls. Looking back, though, that may have been a mistake," said Walter. "I probably should not have had everything that I wanted."

But he did have everything, so Moses decided to toughen him up. He brought home a boxing bag and, just as he had learned with the Shamrocks in Chicago, taught Walter how to punch. When the family moved to the tonier East Side of Milwaukee near Juneau Park and into a brick Edwardian house at 485 Marshall Street, Moses installed a billiard table and spent so many hours late into the night teaching Walter how to play that Sadie pleaded with him to let Boy go to bed and get some sleep so he would not fall asleep at school.

Unlike his father, Walter was not a natural athlete, which was evident on family vacations as well as around the house. "An average hack," was how Walter later described his skills. In summer, the family often rented a house on Paw Paw Lake in southwest Michigan near Kalamazoo, where they swam and canoed and Moses could fish. When he turned twelve, Walter began spending two months each summer at Camp Yukon, a boys' camp near Augusta, Maine. "On Lake Cobbosseecontee," he specified seventy-five years later without missing a beat or, significantly, a syllable.

At Camp Yukon, he hiked, swam and played baseball and tennis, but no sport consumed him. One summer he was awarded a small hatchet as "neatest camper." Another year he won a small silver cup inscribed "most improved" camper. Eight decades later, he laughed heartily as he plucked the polished cup from a shelf in the "Room of Memories" at his Rancho Mirage, California, estate, where it sat between an autographed picture of President Ronald Reagan and the certificate of knighthood presented to him by Queen Elizabeth II. "I must have been pretty bad if 'most improved' was the best they could come up with for me."

Having had so little education himself and more aware by the day of what he had missed, Moses sent all the children to private school. Not all were good students. Aye was the best, innately bright and scholarly. She later graduated from the University of Wisconsin, the only Annenberg child to finish college. Polly and Jan, the second and third sisters, were mischievous and uninterested in school. They repeatedly played hooky and went to the Milwaukee Athletic Club, where they had manicures and had their hair done. "They were incorrigible," said Walter. Once when Sadie and Moses went to New York for a week, Polly ordered a ton of sand delivered, brought in umbrellas and hosted a beach party in the living room. By the time her parents returned the sand was gone, but enough evidence remained so that Polly had to confess and was grounded.

Walter was sent to the German-English Academy, Milwaukee's answer to Groton or Exeter. It had been turning out Ivy League–caliber students since 1851, when natives of Germany made up more than one-third of the city's population. It featured a Teutonic regimen designed to build a strong mind in a strong body — mornings were devoted to developing the mind, afternoons, the body. Moses dropped Walter off for classes, which began at 8:45 A.M. and continued until 4 P.M., with ninety minutes for the boys to go home for lunch. German language and cultural study was required, each of which had a lasting effect. In his eighties, Walter could still say at lunchtime, "Wir mussen sandwiches machen," when it was time to make sandwiches. His favorite was mortadella bologna, which he shipped in several times a year from Usinger's, Milwaukee's great sausage maker.

Walter loved the school, which he attended from age six to twelve. Finally he had boys to play with, a decided change from home. Frank Spigener headed the school from 1927 to 1954, well after Walter left, but his philosophy was no different from the credo inculcated during Walter's years: "When money is lost, nothing is lost. When health is lost, something is lost. When character is lost, all is lost."[19] As years and decades rolled by, Walter became more convinced that the key to everything was character.

The outbreak of the First World War meant that the years he attended, from 1914 to 1920, were the most traumatic in the history of both the school and Milwaukee. When Germany invaded Belgium and

France after the June 1914 assassination in Sarajevo of Austrian arch-duke Franz Ferdinand, Milwaukee was the most Germanic city in the United States. The great surge of immigration in the latter half of the nineteenth century which had made it an almost European city had slowed, but at the onset of the war, three-quarters of Milwaukee's citizens were either immigrants or had a foreign-born parent. In one ten-block central area of the city, 54 percent of residents described themselves as being of "Teutonic background." Nearly one-quarter of the residents spoke German exclusively, while an equal number were more comfortable speaking German than English. The German-American Alliance, organized in 1901 to promote ties between the countries, boasted thirty-seven thousand members in Wisconsin, most of them Milwaukeeans.[20]

Nowhere in the United States was the reservoir of goodwill for Wilhelm II deeper than it was in the city whose first citizens bore such names as Pabst, Blatz, Schlitz and Uihlein, the brewers who made Milwaukee famous. Joseph Uihlein Jr., whose family founded and owned the Schlitz brewery, was Walter's best friend at the German-English Academy and decades later remained close.

Until the kaiser's armies began moving, many Americans considered Germany to be the land of Goethe, Wagner, bratwurst and beery camaraderie. When it suddenly became the land of the Hun and virtually anyone who spoke German came under suspicion, Milwaukee, the Munich of the Midwest, was divided.[21]

Milwaukee's newspapers spoke for different factions. When the Cunard liner *Lusitania* was sunk by a U-boat torpedo in 1915, killing 1,198 passengers and crew, including 128 U.S. citizens, the *Free Press* blamed the tragedy on an internal explosion. The *Journal*, however, won the 1919 Pulitzer Prize for its coverage of the war, in part for its readiness to pursue local citizens who, said the prize citation, "put Germany above America."

A week-long flea market to raise funds for German, Austrian and Hungarian war victims drew 175,000 people from Milwaukee and brought in $150,000. But when the Chicago Symphony visited the Pabst Theater, it refused to play Brahms, Wagner and Beethoven. At the same time, spectators at German-English Academy athletic events hollered anti-German epithets. When the United States joined the war in 1917, paving stones were hurled through the windows of the academy while Walter was attending class. The school got the message, dropped German from the curriculum and changed its name to the

Milwaukee University School. In short order, the Germania National Bank became the Commercial National Bank, the Deutscher Club became the Wisconsin Club and sauerkraut, a staple in nearly every bar and restaurant, was renamed "liberty cabbage."[22]

With the exception of the hostility aimed at the school and the fact that the silver spoon campaign never made it to Europe, the war had little immediate impact on the Annenbergs. Moses was busier than ever, but not too busy in late 1917 to take a call from the *Examiner* in Chicago asking him to come down and see Arthur Brisbane, Hearst's chief editor and columnist, who was then probably the most widely read journalist in America. Brisbane's opinions, said the *New York Times*, "were like those of a prophet to his disciples."[23] Moses was a huge fan of Brisbane's columns, which he regularly read aloud to Sadie and the children. He had met the editor only briefly while running the *Examiner*'s circulation department, but in the intervening years, Brisbane had become an almost mythic figure to Moses. He was delighted with the prospect of seeing him in Chicago.

"He told me, 'Annenberg, I am coming to Milwaukee to acquire some newspapers, but I want you to help me with the circulation. How do you think Milwaukee will receive me?'

"I said, 'I think they will receive you very well. And I will be very happy to help you, but I have a business of my own which requires all my attention, so I could not work for you exclusively.'"

They agreed to meet the next afternoon at the Hotel Pfister, Milwaukee's finest. The next morning, when Moses stopped at the Wisconsin National Bank to make a deposit, he mentioned that Brisbane was coming. The bank president said he would like to meet the great editor, and Moses promised to try to bring him over after their meeting.

Brisbane arrived in Milwaukee with a dozen executives to head various departments of the three papers he planned to buy — the *Daily News*, the *Free Press* and the *Evening Wisconsin* — and merge into a new paper, the *Wisconsin News*. He immediately resumed his pitch to Moses to run circulation. Moses resisted and the conversation seemed to be going nowhere until he mentioned to Brisbane that the local bank president wanted to meet him.

Brisbane was always happy to meet bankers, ideally to borrow their money, and he was delighted at this opportunity. He had a private forty-minute meeting with the man, emerged, grabbed Moses by the arm and said, "Annenberg, I've changed my mind completely. You're going to be publisher of the paper."

Moses was startled and put him off. "I don't know enough about the paper business to take on that responsibility."

"You're foolish," Brisbane retorted. "You have a large family. There is no limit to where you can go as publisher. You can go to Congress. I will write your speeches."

Moses was overwhelmed. His star was rising in Milwaukee, but at most he was then a successful local entrepreneur. Brisbane — charming, urbane, a man of the world — was a household name. Moses knew the circulation side of newspapers as well as any man in the country. Being a publisher, however, implied a certain stature in a community. Publishers discussed commercial ventures over lunches in exclusive clubs. At a time when the "church-state" divide between a newspaper's news and business sides was ill-defined or nonexistent, publishers opined from editorial pulpits. He had no such experience, but the offer held great appeal.

"I was quite dazzled," Moses admitted. "I was so fond of him and because I had followed his editorials, particularly his Sunday sermons for so many years, I wasn't in a position to refuse almost anything within reason. So I went to work for him for practically nothing, no salary, and $100 a week for expenses."[24]

Only after Brisbane left did the flattered Moses figure out why the editor had changed his mind and asked him to be publisher. The bank president had told Brisbane how wealthy Moses was. "Until Mr. Brisbane learned that," Moses wrote in his memoir notes, "I was just a news dealer."

Owned until then by pro-German interests, the papers by 1917 were hemorrhaging money and readership and eager for a buyer. Neither Moses nor Brisbane put up any money. The bank loaned $100,000 for the purchase. Moses started work and discovered right away that there was more reason than a pro-German tilt for the papers' loss of readers: the reporters were not working.

The first evening he walked into the newsroom, a crowd of reporters clustered around the copy desk shooting craps.

"Hey, you guys," said Moses. "That's not allowed."

They ignored him until Moses finally reached in, grabbed the dice and threw the pair out the window. He turned around and told the grumpy reporters that that was it; no more gambling.

The next evening, he walked in again and found the game back in progress. Because he had just taken over and preferred to cajole rather than antagonize his new staff, he tried another tactic. He pushed into the crowd and placed a $20 bill on the desk. "Fade that," he said as he lit up one of the twenty-five Pall Mall cork tips a day he was then smoking. The men looked at each other in consternation. They had been playing for pocket change. The police reporter dug into his pocket and produced $1.82 in coins. A rewrite man had $2. Everyone chipped in until they could cover Moses's twenty. The dice rolled, and Moses lost. Twice more he lost. "The hell with it," he said finally. He laughed with the players, threw the dice out the window once more and stalked out of the newsroom on the heels of a copyboy who was already in pursuit of the dice.[25]

He had more impact on the papers than he did on the dice. Over the next two years, Moses killed the *Free Press*, merged the *Daily News* and *Evening Wisconsin*, opened the *Wisconsin News* in a new building, doubled the paper's price from one to two cents a copy, trebled advertising revenues and raised circulation from twenty-five thousand to eighty thousand. The staff, including the craps shooters, grew to love him. He doubled their payroll and treated them in a friendly fashion. He called everyone by his or her first name. If a reporter or ad salesman did a particularly good job, Moses took him fishing and passed on a bonus. In summer, he hosted picnics for the entire staff. One year, the advertising staff was so large that the photographer needed two shots to fit everyone in the panoramic group photo. Moses stood on one end of the group for the first frame, then ran to the other end to pose with the others. When the photographer spliced the negatives together, there was Moses in both places. It was a fair metaphor for a man moving as fast as Moses was in Milwaukee.[26]

When Moses asked Brisbane for $10,000 to make additional improvements in 1919, Brisbane refused to give him a nickel. Instead the columnist sold his interest in the paper — which had cost him nothing — to Hearst for $150,000. His audacity stunned Moses, an audacious man himself, and his admiration for Brisbane grew.

Moses continued to run the paper for Hearst. Brisbane had noted in his November 18 announcement of the sale, "The businessmen of Milwaukee know how greatly Mr. Annenberg's energy and ability have contributed to the rapid growth of the *Wisconsin News*."[27] As circulation and profits continued to climb, Hearst took closer notice. In 1920, Joseph Willicombe, the publisher's personal assistant, cabled Moses. Hearst was on his way to the West Coast and would like to meet Moses in Chicago.

"I met Mr. Hearst. He complimented me for what I had been able to do with the *Wisconsin News*. And he said that Milwaukee was entirely too small for someone of my ability. He asked me to come to New York to take charge of the circulation of all his newspapers and magazines."[28]

Hearst had read him well. Moses was forty-three, his family was complete and he had outgrown Milwaukee. He had used his time there the way an athlete hones skills in the minor leagues before moving up to the majors or an executive builds credentials in the provinces and is then summoned to corporate headquarters. Ambitious and determined, Moses had developed into an entrepreneur, a man who had built his businesses on his own, yet had also shown an innate ability to manage others. He had learned about banks, finance and credit, knowledge he had never had in Chicago. He had developed a patina of social and civic skills that were reinforced by a soaring level of confidence from his financial success and the influence he had in the city. All in all, Milwaukee gave Moses the equivalent of the formal schooling he had never had. There were gaps in that education though. One important deficiency was that he was unaware of how much he still did not know. He had demonstrated what a hungry wolf could do, but he had operated as a lone wolf, still intensely competitive and self-reliant. Still, he had come a very long way in fourteen years, from a callow debtor trying to carve out a better life to a millionaire with elevated sights. And he had found invaluable patrons in Hearst and Brisbane, men who would influence him the rest of his life.

Not that Moses intended to rely on either of them. He had no intention of giving up his distribution agencies or any of his real estate holdings. He accepted Hearst's offer on the condition that he could continue to operate all his own businesses. The publisher had no objection.

As soon as Hearst agreed, Moses's impulsiveness kicked in. Within forty-eight hours, he had pulled the children from school, closed the Milwaukee house, put his assistant Aaron Trosch in charge of Midwest operations, leased an apartment in Manhattan and an estate on Long Island and hired a private railroad car for the journey east. The ten Annenbergs were moving to New York in a style that marked the next phase of their lives.

5

NEW YORK

———

IN THE 1800s, Great Neck was to New York City what Kalvishken
was, more modestly, to Insterburg, a rural breadbasket. Farmers
packed horse-drawn wagons high with meat, vegetables and hay
from the pastures, orchards and farms around the town on Long
Island's north shore and brought the produce across the Sound and into
the city on ferries that began service in 1785. By the end of the nineteenth century, more traffic was coming from the other direction. Great
Neck's sheltered waters, sandy beaches, and soft, fair breezes had
begun to attract the wealthy seeking relief from Manhattan's summer
heat and drawn by the velvet lawns, gardens and verandahs on which
they could stretch out and relax.

Along with their architects and money, butlers and governesses,
polished Pierce-Arrows and sleek yachts, the new arrivals brought a
new social order. "There was a steady absorption of land on the North
Shore by great estates, creating an aristocracy of Long Island," noted a
local realtor in 1900. "Great Neck with its miles of bridle paths, acres of
golf courses and ideal bathing, boating and other sources of amusement is placed among the foremost ranks of America's most desirable
communities." By 1919, when the Volstead Act initiated prohibition
and the twenties loomed ready to roar, Great Neck had become the
Riviera of Long Island.[1]

Yachtsman William Vanderbilt, a younger brother of Cornelius's,
lived in Great Neck. So did Henry Phipps, who started as an office boy
and created his own $100 million fortune as a partner of steel magnate
and philanthropist Andrew Carnegie. Alfred P. Sloan, the president of
General Motors and Ellsworth Statler of the Statler Hotels, were Kings

Point neighbors. Harry Sinclair of Sinclair Oil was driven daily to prison by chauffeured limousine from his Kings Point home after his conviction for contempt of the Senate in the 1923 Teapot Dome scandal. Ring Lardner, the humorist and short-story writer, and Herbert Bayard Swope, the executive editor of the *New York World*, whose war reporting in Germany won him in 1917 the first Pulitzer Prize and made him one of America's best-known journalists, were also Great Neck residents.

The H. P. Booth property on East Shore Road — the family's money came from the Ward Shipping Line — was the model for Jay Gatsby's mansion. The Booth waterfront was where one stood to spot the green light on Daisy's dock across Manhasset Bay in Port Washington, or East Egg as F. Scott Fitzgerald called it in his 1925 masterwork, *The Great Gatsby*.[2] Walter Chrysler moved to Stepping Stone Lane in Kings Point when he purchased Henri Bendel's estate after the milliner's daughter drowned. The auto magnate's next-door neighbor was Moses Annenberg.

Moses bought his property from George M. Cohan, the prodigiously talented musician and showman responsible for twenty Broadway musicals. His songs — "Give My Regards to Broadway," "You're a Grand Old Flag" and "Over There," which he wrote in 1917 for the troops leaving to fight in Europe — were national favorites.

Like the man, Cohan's Kings Point property was extraordinary. Larger than Walter Chrysler's land, the new Annenberg estate spilled over thirty-six acres of lawns and forests on both sides of Stepping Stone Lane and Kings Point Road. When Sadie Annenberg's father, Morris Friedman, visited the first time from Chicago, where he lived in a duplex, he was astonished by the property's vastness. "Why on earth did you buy a house in a park?" he asked his daughter. Because it had enough bedrooms for eight children, she replied.[3]

And a few to spare. The white house had thirty-two rooms, including a bowling alley, a billiard room, a music room with a grand piano and ten bedrooms. The grounds featured a sixteen-stall stable for ponies and horses, bridle paths, a small racetrack, handball and tennis courts, and two swimming pools, one for adults, the other for children.

Arthur Brisbane had found the property and shown it to Moses because he knew it was big enough for the ten Annenbergs, plus visiting relatives and friends. There were other houses available that had enough space for the family. The reason Moses bought this one was that Brisbane urged him to. To Moses, the editor and columnist was a great man — charming but tough, well read and cultured, fascinating to be with and hugely successful. Moses wanted to be more like him.

Until then, Moses had not had a role model. He had moved well past his father, Tobias. He had little respect for his brothers. Max, who also moved to New York from Chicago to work for Joseph Medill Patterson's new tabloid, the *Daily News*, would be a circulation man until the day he died. There were a few businessmen in Milwaukee from whom Moses had learned, but he had never connected personally with anyone as famous, stimulating, and with such over-the-horizon ambitions as Brisbane. The newsman's natural ability to connect with average Americans through his column had given him great influence, considerable affluence and overwhelming confidence. In Brisbane, Moses finally had someone he respected from whom he could learn. So if Brisbane thought the Cohan estate was the place to live, that was good enough for Moses.

The property was the first and most visible manifestation of a remarkable change in lifestyle that the Annenbergs were undergoing. In Milwaukee, they had lived in a comfortable but modest home near the lake on a half acre of land with a backyard and had a cleaning lady, a driver and neighbors. The children attended good schools. They lived at home and played mah-jongg and canasta and listened to records on the Victrola. On Long Island, almost overnight, the Annenbergs moved into a different world of great extravagance.

The children were or would be sent off to boarding and finishing schools. Home was an estate, with the staff of a small corporation. There were stable boys and gardeners, upstairs and downstairs maids, butlers, drivers, a cook, a kitchen helper and a laundress. Tennis coaches, riding instructors and piano teachers came regularly to tutor. The children had grown up eating solid, basic German food: roasts and schnitzels, sausages and potatoes. The cook now prepared game birds and soufflés, fish baked in parchment, and oysters and clams, which Moe loved, but which Sadie, a practicing Jew who would not eat shellfish, disliked having in the house.

Moses had become rich in Milwaukee, but only since hiring the private rail car to bring the family east had he begun to live rich. Because all that mattered to him was business and his family, he wanted them to enjoy the benefits of his success. He was a classic parvenu but had worked hard to become one. He had started with nothing but a hand-me-down fishing pole to feed his brothers and sisters, four years of school and a tenacious determination to defend his street corner and later his growing interests and family livelihood.

Now that he was financially successful, he was not content to sit back and say, "Enough," the way many executives did. A hunger to do more and to rise higher had pushed him from the muddy streets on Chicago's South Side to a palatial mansion overlooking the yachts on Long Island Sound. The Annenbergs were living out one of those exotic fables Moses used to create for the children when they gathered around his feet on Sunday mornings in Milwaukee.[4]

Moses had not uprooted the family and moved from Wisconsin to New York merely for the money or a fancier house. The $50,000 salary he earned from Hearst was one-sixth what he was earning from his own enterprises. The prospect of greater riches was a draw, but the lure of New York involved other factors as well.

The big attraction was the chance to work with Hearst and Brisbane. Both were rich, Hearst fabulously so, but, like Moses, neither eased off working. They were far from working class, but Moses liked the fact that they championed in print the working man and his family.[5]

Next, to a self-starter like Moses who constantly sought to improve himself, New York offered the ultimate challenge, the chance to be the nation's circulation king, the biggest and best in his business.

Finally, New York offered the family an opportunity to assimilate into American culture and society at the highest attainable level, an opening few immigrants would reject.

That Moses could build a bigger fortune was, after his success in Milwaukee, never in doubt. Assimilation and social acceptance were another issue and far from guaranteed. Moses may not have practiced his religion, but he remained an Eastern European Jew who had crossed to America in the third and least socially acceptable wave of immigrants, the "new Jews."

The earliest settlers were Sephardic Jews whose ancestors had been expelled from Spain and Portugal in the fifteenth century. Twenty-three of their descendants arrived in the colonies by accident in 1654 when their ship was seized by a French privateer on its way to New Amsterdam, the Dutch colony that became New York.[6]

More than a century later, when the first U.S. census was conducted in 1790, about two thousand Jews were determined to be living in the new United States. Because they numbered so few in a population of 3.9 million, and were scattered throughout the former thirteen colonies, had fought in the revolution and were for the most part successful merchants, they mixed primarily with non-Jews, who accepted them with relative ease. The scarcity of rabbis and Jewish women meant that the mixing extended to widespread intermarriage. This group was the elite, whose numbers included the founders of such Establishment institutions as Columbia University, the New York Stock Exchange, the Boston Athenaeum and the American Medical Association.[7] "This then was the classic period of aristocratic assimilation," wrote sociologist Digby Baltzell in *The Protestant Establishment*, "and even today there are leading families within the old-stock and Protestant upper class, some of whose ancestors were prominent Jews during the colonial period."[8]

The second group came in 1848, the year in which the failure of the revolutionary liberal movement in the German states forced dissidents to flee for their lives. By the 1870s, some of these families, including the Seligmans, Guggenheims and Lehmans, were already established and very wealthy. "Proportionally speaking," wrote historian John Higham, "in no other immigrant group have so many men ever risen so rapidly from rags to riches."[9]

These Jewish immigrants were also accepted into the highest reaches of society and even, in some cases, founded the clubs that would help define that culture. Investment banker Joseph Seligman in 1863 helped found the Union League in New York. In 1871 sugar merchant Moses Lazarus was one of the founders of that city's Knickerbocker Club. "Even as late as the 1870s, when young Louis D. Brandeis was welcomed into the best Boston society," wrote Baltzell, "Jews still belonged to the best clubs in many cities."[10] Most immigrants did not want to remain outsiders; they wanted to assimilate as quickly and as fully as they could into American culture, society and corporate life.

By the time the Annenbergs arrived in the mid-1880s, however, the assimiliation process had become more difficult because the third wave of immigrants — "the largest exodus since the one from Egypt," wrote Stephen Birmingham[11] — was different in every respect save religion from those Jews who had arrived earlier. Many more immigrants came in this third segment, most of them Russians and East Europeans who were not merchants but poor, ragged, tough and idealistic laborers of lower class. "In practice, tone and theology," wrote Nathan Glazer and Daniel Patrick Moynihan in *The Melting Pot*, "the Reform Judaism of the (earlier) German Jews diverged from the Orthodoxy of the (later) immigrants as much as the beliefs and practices of the Southern Baptists differ from those of the New England Unitarians."[12]

The absorption of the Annenbergs would not be easy, but it began in earnest on the lawns, pony paths and drawing rooms of the Long Island estate, which they continued to call the Cohan house. The education and assimilation continued in Manhattan, where the family maintained an apartment and where Sadie stayed with the girls when they were at school. In the 1920s, their first apartment at 246 West End Avenue, not far from William Randolph Hearst's triplex on Riverside Drive, was a spacious and light-filled flat with a view of the Hudson River.

The next was a sprawling penthouse at 1175 Park Avenue, although it was not so big as to offer a bedroom for each child. Aye, the eldest, was away at the University of Wisconsin. In the city, the three youngest girls went back to sharing a room. The girls spent more time with Sadie because their father's schedule had become so hectic that he rarely slept more than four hours a night. At Kings Point, he would walk the dogs, but any other free time he had was devoted to reading, increasingly biography, history and philosophy. Anyone who had known Moses twenty-five years earlier when he was brawling on the South Side of Chicago would have found it unbelievable, but he became a devotee of Spinoza once Brisbane suggested he read the works of the Dutch philosopher and pantheist.

Moses worked very closely with Brisbane, or "A. B." as he called the editorial chief for Hearst, who was known as "W. R." Moses adopted the style, popular with corporate titans of the era, and became "M. L.," for Moses Louis, his middle name, which is how nonfamily members addressed him from then on. At home, he remained Father, or Dad, except to sons-in-law, who he decided should call him "Governor," not in the honorific sense, but more as "guv'nor," period slang for one in charge.

Initially, Moses's work with Brisbane was all related to the huge Hearst empire which had expanded to thirty-seven daily and Sunday newspapers from Boston to San Francisco and nine magazines, including the high-selling *Harper's Bazaar, Cosmopolitan* and *Good Housekeeping*. Brisbane shared Moses's delight in their working together on the Hearst executive council, the publisher's in-house privy board. He was convinced no one in America had a better grasp of circulation matters than the man who had made him a $150,000 bundle on the *Wisconsin News*.

On the wall outside his office, Moses framed a letter from Brisbane: "When I persuaded you to come to New York and presented you to Mr. Hearst, I told him I was doing him a much greater favor than if I had given him one million dollars in cash."[13]

If the compliment had come from Hearst himself, Moses would not have been any more pleased. Brisbane was a dozen years older than Moses, but they shared a number of similarities: each was a self-taught, highly intelligent, ambitious workaholic. "He couldn't stop himself working," Moses said. "It was work every moment of his life, on trains, in automobiles and everyplace. Just work, work, work. That's all he ever thought of."[14]

The best-known columnist in the country from 1910 into the 1930s, Brisbane was as facile as he was diligent. He dictated his twelve-hundred- to fifteen-hundred-word daily column in thirty minutes, talking constantly as he bustled about, his arms loaded with newspapers, producing part of the five hundred thousand words he wrote yearly. He took pride in his output and the fact that he was the highest-paid journalist in America. Other journalists cringed when he frequently introduced himself by saying, "I'm delighted to meet you, sir. Do you know that Mr. Hearst pays me a salary of two hundred sixty thousand dollars a year?"[15]

Brisbane started in journalism as a $15-a-week reporter on the *New York Sun*, where he became so passionate about his work that his father and stepmother, fearing for his health, took him to recuperate in France and Germany, where he studied languages, literature and history. He returned to New York to spend most of the 1890s writing and editing at Joseph Pulitzer's *World* before joining Hearst's *New York Journal* in 1906.

His contract called for a base pay of $150 plus a dollar for each one thousand readers he added to the paper's circulation. Starting work at 4:30 A.M., he sensationalized the *Journal* and had it on the streets of New York hours before the other evening papers. He was forced to operate under certain restrictions: the *Journal* was noted for Hearst's twin lists: Goody and Shit. Those on the Goody List could be mentioned only in flattering terms; those on the Shit List, which at one point had two thousand names, invariably headed by Hearst's nemesis, New York's Democratic governor Al Smith, were either to be unmentioned or written of with disparagement. One reporter's full-time assignment was to read the paper in makeup each day to insure that the sanctity of the lists was preserved. Neither the lists nor much else proved any obstacle for Brisbane. Within seven weeks of taking the job, he boosted the *Journal*'s circulation past the *World*'s and made himself the talk of the industry.[16]

His columns were the editorial equivalent of cartoons, set in large type with wide columns, short paragraphs and even shorter sentences, often only three or four words. Few subjects escaped his eye and pen. His speciality was simplifying a complicated subject or, as his critics charged, grossly oversimplifying it. He was a columnist/philosopher who looked like a sage, with an immense head and towering brow that earned him the nickname Double-Dome. In his column titled "Today" which appeared on the front page of most Hearst papers, he wrote homilies on justice, gambling, prizefighting, religion, debt, drink, crime and self-control. He might discuss Nero, the infamous Roman emperor, whom he considered the greatest man who ever lived, or the likelihood of a man's winning a boxing match with a gorilla, or the superiority of people with blue eyes. "It annoys many when I write about blue eyes, but any man who ever amounted to a damn in history had them, even men like Napoleon from Corsica and Caesar from Rome."[17]

If Hearst did not like what Brisbane wrote, it did not run, but that happened rarely. "I write what I please and he publishes it if he pleases," Brisbane explained. There was no question in Brisbane's mind that the ultimate arbiter of everything that went into his paper was Hearst. "He rules his papers absolutely. Occasionally, if he sees something in the paper that he does not like, he throws it out, naturally. The papers are his property." Moses agreed with such reasoning and adopted a similar policy when he again became a newspaper publisher.

The reason Brisbane had almost infinite latitude was that he and Hearst — who were so close that for a while they lived in the same house — shared almost identical ideas about editorial policy. A. B. denounced politicians, supported women's suffrage and predicted developments in the air travel and automobile industries. Consistency was never a virtue of his. He so savaged Woodrow Wilson during the First World War that he was criticized for being pro-German and a traitor. When called to appear before the Senate three weeks after the end of the war, Brisbane claimed that he had strongly supported the war effort. Although he flip-flopped constantly on other subjects, his readers never seemed to care.

However contradictory, his views were upbeat and always popular. "When he did not deal with national affairs or other actualities, he philosophized in his own typical way in what he called 'sociological discussions,'" wrote the *New York Times*. "He would devote a column to a dissertation about the size of George Washington's feet or to speculations about a flea's ability to jump. All such minor problems he set forth in his characteristic short and entertaining way. He seemed to understand the man in the street, but he did not bother to write up to the public. His enemies accused him of scattering obvious platitudes, but the newspapers thrived."[18]

In personality, Brisbane was as complex and mercurial as Moses. Brisbane, wrote biographer Irving Dilliard, "depending on circumstances or the company he was in, was companionable or abrupt, affable or cold, generous or niggardly, idealistic or cynical."[19] Like Moses, he was an exceptional businessman whose income allowed him to invest heavily in outside interests, primarily high-end New York real estate.

Brisbane had a skilled eye for property, and often wrote about real estate in his column. Either foresight or insider information allowed him to buy land in New Jersey near the entrance to the Holland Tunnel before its construction plans were announced. He bought several Manhattan hotels with Hearst. His personal property included his primary residence at Allaire, a three-thousand-acre estate in New Jersey, and an apartment at Fifty-third and Madison in Manhattan, as well as homes in Hempstead, Long Island, the Catskills and Miami.

Each locale had an influence on Moses's life: the New Jersey estate determined where Walter went to school; Hempstead was an easy drive to the Cohan estate, which Brisbane found for the Annenbergs, as he did their first apartment in the city; Moses would later buy a fishing camp in the Poconos similar to Brisbane's in the Catskills and would also move to Miami. They spoke to each other on the phone several times a day and met for lunch three or four times a week. No one outside his family was closer to Moses during the 1920–1935 period than Brisbane.[20]

Despite their friendship and the admiration Moses had for Brisbane, their business partnerships were never easy. Moses was invariably required to provide the financial heavy lifing, just as he had in Milwaukee at the *Wisconsin News*. In New York, the A. B. and M. L. A. Investment Company bought a building at 515 Madison Avenue, then one at 810–812 Fifty-seventh Street, followed by the Ritz Tower land on Park Avenue and another building at Fifty-ninth Street and Park. Each deal was a struggle.

"In each instance, I put up several hundred thousand dollars," said Moses. "Brisbane put up nothing." As soon as the investment looked profitable, Brisbane "would start a quarrel and take control of the property."

On the Fifty-seventh and Park Avenue property, site of the Ritz Tower, they planned to build a fourteen-story building.

"A few days later, Brisbane would say, 'Annenberg, fourteen stories is not enough. We should have at least twenty-four stories.'

"And I'd say, 'A. B., that's too much of a gamble. I don't know if that location requires that high a building.'

"'Doesn't cost anything to go up in the air. The air is free.'

"I'd say, 'Maybe . . .' A couple of days later he'd come back at me.

"'I don't think twenty-four stories is enough. I think we should have thirty-six.'

"And I'd say, 'A. B., that is way over my head. I don't see how we can successfully finance such a thing. I don't think there's enough demand for that kind of building.'

"'Well, it's easy to see, Annenberg, that we can't agree on anything.'

"On that one, I was glad to get my money back without interest."[21]

Three times Brisbane undercut Moses. On the Fifty-seventh Street property, the editor demanded a perpetual lease on the building's penthouse. Moses refused. "I told him if I ever wanted to sell the property, his lease on the penthouse would materially depreciate the property." They built anyway.

On the Fifty-ninth and Park property, Brisbane insisted that Moses put up all the money, but that they nonetheless be co-owners. When property values shot up soon afterward, Brisbane again insisted on buying a controlling interest at the original price from Moses, who once more went along.

Moses had not been so betrayed since his parents turned over his childhood savings to his brother Max. And no one had ever taken advantage of him twice. It never would have happened had Moses not been so determined to maintain his friendship, and if Brisbane had not constantly reminded Moses of how much he had done for him. Yet there were limits. Moses became fed up with Brisbane's antics on a property on Fifty-ninth Street. "All of a sudden, out of a clear sky, he started the same thing all over again. If I didn't turn over the property to him at what it cost originally, he was going to the two adjacent plots, buy those, put up a tall building to deny me light and muscle me out."

Moses was infuriated, but instead of a temper tantrum, turned calculating. He insisted to Brisbane that he would not be muscled and
went to work. The very next day, Moses bought the two properties that
Brisbane had mentioned and went back to see his partner.

"A. B., you gave me a fine idea yesterday about acquiring that
property next door to ours. I bought those buildings and am going to do
exactly what you threatened to do to me, use that corner for a light
shaft."

Brisbane was thunderstruck. His eyes widened. "You shouldn't do
that to me, Annenberg. We have been friends for so many years. I
brought you to New York. I introduced you to Mr. Hearst."

Moses was tough, but he did feel obligated to Brisbane for the
Hearst connection and he could not sever a relationship that involved
so much more than business. Moses had met many people in New
York, but at heart, he was a loner and Brisbane was one of his few real
friends. They went to the fights together and the racetrack. Brisbane
often came home with him and mixed with the family. For Moses, Brisbane was the older brother he would have preferred to Jacob. So Moses
did not follow through on the threat. Brisbane paid him $60,000, which
was $60,000 more than he had ever paid before, and Moses made him a
partner in the two properties. A year and a half later, Moses bought him
out for one million dollars in cash.

Their most troubled venture was owning the *Elizabeth Times* in
New Jersey. Brisbane bought it in 1924 with the expectation of
reselling it to Hearst, just as he had done a few years before with the
Wisconsin News and the *Washington Times*. But Hearst decided not to buy
the *Elizabeth Times* and Brisbane panicked.

He was losing $1,800 a week and begged Moses to help him out.
Moses had no interest in assuming such a loss, but took over the paper
with two partners when Brisbane promised to turn over his stock, to
write the paper's editorials, solicit ads, provide his daily column and
give Moe enough copies daily of his flagship paper, the *New York Journal,* to wrap around the *Elizabeth Times*. Five months later, Brisbane
had not made good on a single pledge. Moses and his partners finally
sued the columnist for $90,000 and settled for $25,000. Moses realized
that his partner shared many traits with con men, but he could not help
himself.

"It was all blackjack stuff," Moses told an interviewer a few years
later, referring to how he was psychologically clubbed into following
the Hearst editor. "But I liked Brisbane immensely and I felt I would

go the limit in trying to help him out, even at financial loss to myself. In spite of all his shortcomings, I just couldn't help but love the man."

Did he understand that he was being used? "No question about it," Moses acknowledged. "You paid a price for his friendship. He was in a hole and whenever he was in a hole, he didn't care whose friendship he worked on. He was the type of person who just wouldn't take a loss." That included cards. Playing poker once on a train, Brisbane turned desperate after losing several hands, began to bluff, and lost more. There was $400 in the pot and Moe had a pair of kings.

"He raised several times and bet as if he either had two pair or made his flush. I called him, and he said two pair, turned the cards upside down and threw them into the deck. I picked up the cards, turned them over and said 'A. B., you haven't got two pair; you've only got a pair of fours.' He said, 'Oh, I must have been mistaken, Annenberg,' but he became so angry because he felt humiliated."[22]

The better Moses got to know his hero, the less he believed him. And there was always a part of Brisbane that worried Moses, the fact that the columnist was much closer to Hearst than he was and could hold that over him. In the middle of the *Elizabeth Times* fight, Moses told Brisbane that because he had not fulfilled any of his promises, he, Annenberg, intended to pull out and quit the paper.

"If you quit the *Elizabeth Times*," A. B. responded, "you will have to quit all the other businesses you have."

"In the future," Moe replied, "I will do business with you only in legal form."

"I may see to it," said Brisbane, "that you have no business in the future to look after."[23]

When the suit was resolved, the men patched up their differences and resumed a friendship that endured until Brisbane's death on Christmas Day, 1936, just hours after dictating his final column. But Moses never forgot the threat. For all the financial and personal turmoil involved, the property ventures with Brisbane did turn out to be lucrative. Yet Moses had also learned an important lesson about the perils of depending on a partner whose behavior he could not control.

At the time of the *Elizabeth* dispute in 1925, Moses was forty-eight and missed the feeling of total self-reliance that he had first experienced fishing alone as a six-year-old in Kalvishken and relished when running his business in Milwaukee. He enjoyed supervising Hearst's interests, but he preferred to regain his independence. By the mid-

1920s, it seemed that a purchase he had made a few years before would make it possible.

IN 1922, Moses had received a phone call from Frank Brunell, a one-time copy boy with the *Cleveland Plain Dealer* who moved to Chicago and a job with the *Tribune,* where he worked his way up to become sports editor. He was an excellent editor and launched a major expansion of sports coverage, including horse racing. The sport had become so popular in the late nineteenth century that major stakes races were inaugurated, including the Belmont in 1867, the Preakness in 1873 and, two years later, the Kentucky Derby. Chicago was caught up in the boom and became a racing center in 1884 when Washington Park opened with a superb mile-and-an-eighth track that was the equal of any in the nation. Its major race, the American Derby, offered the world's biggest purse, twice that of the Derby at Churchill Downs .[24]

Washington Park was only one of five tracks operating in or near Chicago. There was so much action that Brunell considered starting a newspaper devoted entirely to racing. Others had tried and failed, but what made Brunell's idea different was his focus on statistics. His plan was to pinpoint a horse's position as he rounded the track through fixed points of call. Brunell resigned from the *Tribune,* polished up a business plan with his wife, who had a sharp financial mind, and published the first edition of the *Daily Racing Form* in 1894. Twenty-eight years later, Brunell was sixty-nine years old, exhausted, and his wife was ill. They had $6 million invested in bonds and no children. He wanted to sell his paper, retire and enjoy life while they were still able.[25]

He called only a few people. He had met Moses on business trips to Milwaukee, knew that he loved newspapers, that he had a big job with Hearst and was in good financial shape. The selling price of $400,000 covered the *Form's* headquarters in Chicago, another office in New York, and an outpost in Buffalo, New York, which serviced patrons across the border in Canada. Moses liked Brunell and he knew Washington Park well from selling newspapers in its shadow at the turn of the century. He could see that racing was a growth industry and that there was plenty of room to expand the *Daily Racing Form.* Brunell opened his books and showed Moses that he had been clearing between $175,000 and $200,000 a year.[26]

"How do you want the money?" Moses asked. "Cashier's check?"

"No," Brunell replied, "I want cash."

Moses agreed and immediately called Peter Brady, president of the Federation Bank and Trust Company at Thirty-fourth and Eighth Avenue, which maintained both his substantial personal account and several corporate accounts for Hearst. During the day, Brady was a respected banker. After hours, he was better known as the handsome bachelor escort of Louella Parsons, queen of the gossip columnists, a star of Hearst's *New York American* and a confidante of Marion Davies, Hearst's mistress.

Moses explained that while he was still working for Hearst, he was buying the *Daily Racing Form* for himself and needed $400,000 right away. "Wrap it up in newspaper and my son and I will be over to pick it up."

Brady was very friendly with the top Hearst executives and had known Moses since he arrived in New York. "You're going to carry four hundred thousand dollars over to Frank Brunell's like a fish under your arm?" he asked, roaring with laughter. Moses laughed along and said that was exactly what he had in mind except he was going to let fourteen-year-old Walter carry it.[27]

An hour later, Moses picked up the foot-square package and handed it to his son. Together they walked the four blocks to Brunell's apartment, where Moses signed the papers, and assumed ownership of the *Daily Racing Form*. In the first year Moses owned it, the paper would bring in $1 million of revenue and clear the purchase price in profit.

6

SPORT OF KINGS

ORSE RACING never interested Moses Annenberg. He never owned a racehorse or a piece of a racetrack, although he had offers to buy each many times. He went to the track infrequently. The box seats he held at Hialeah were usually passed on to business associates or friends and, later, to his lawyers. He rarely bet on horses.

Not that he had anything against them. He liked to ride and was a respectable horseman. He kept a half-dozen mares and geldings stabled at Kings Point, where instructors came to teach the girls and Walter, as he put it, "for their amusement and their health." He had a favorite horse of his own, a chestnut colt named Dusty. Moses kept him at Sunnylands, the family vacation retreat he later purchased in the Poconos where he went to relax and fish for black bass.

Nor was Moses opposed to gambling. On the contrary, he enjoyed a good wager. He was a decent poker player, comfortable with pots worth $500 or more a hand and a regular game where the night's winnings might total $5,000. He loved pinochle, carried two decks of the cards in his briefcase, and on occasion sent frantic cables to Chicago to summon an employee who played well to hop on a train to New York and join him for games. Roulette was another favorite. He knew the odds were against him, understood that he would lose, always did lose, and justified the losses as the price of the pleasure. Asked once if he had much gambling income, he replied, with a grin, "None, but I had a lot of outgo."[1]

Racing had less appeal because he considered the sport a mug's game where the bettor had no control over the outcome and was invariably at the mercy of others who did have control. He understood that bettors and fans either disagreed with him or did not care. He counted on them to react that way. Whatever he felt personally about racing meant less than the fact there were plenty of people who loved to watch horses careen around a turn or thunder down the stretch, were thrilled by a close finish and were certain that on the other side of that betting window were riches to reward their shrewd prognostication. All that separated them from success was the right information.

Like the distiller who does not drink, the athletic coach who could not play the sport he teaches, or the prospector who discovered the path to real wealth was putting aside his metal sluice pan and selling equipment to gold bugs, Moe was only interested in delivering the information which allowed others to play the game. He had delivered information in various forms in Chicago, Milwaukee and New York. No one, it could be argued, did that better. Now there was a booming demand for race information. Before and during the First World War, interest in racing dipped, but in the roaring twenties, just when the aging Frank Brunell lost the energy to publish the *Daily Racing Form*, there was a sharp rebound of interest in the turf, a wave Moses caught perfectly.

His genius had nothing to do with either horses or the tracks. Instead, he recognized that millions of racing fans wanted to be part of the sport and bet, but had little information about the horses. In the *Daily Racing Form*, Frank Brunell had already created a matrix, or form, for presenting the data. Brunell's brilliance had been in concluding that a horse's past performance was the best indicator of how he would run the next time out. Moses would take those performances to the masses.

Daily Racing Form charts included meticulous records of the breeding, morning workout times, personal idiosyncrasies and past performances of every horse entered. This last item included not just where the horse finished in the field, but the class of the competition and each horse's position at every stage of each of its races against all its opponents. Crews of race callers, clockers and clerks from the newspaper sat in booths in the press box and on the grandstand roof at each racetrack to call out the facts in a mad gibberish that sounded like a tobacco auctioneer's spiel, then record and transmit by telegraph to headquarters the information at each furlong and fractional milepost along the course. The data was as staggering in its detail as it was astonishing in its accuracy. The *Daily Racing Form* was "indispensable," according to *Ainslie's Complete Guide to Thoroughbred Racing*, the sport bible, which added, "It is impossible to handicap a field of horses without this newspaper."[2]

As Richard Sasuly, author of *Bookies and Bettors, 200 Years of Gambling*, explained: "Unique among serious gamblers, the horseplayer depends heavily on his analysis of information encoded in the *Racing Form*'s dense columns of numbers in the past performances. A poker player who brought a book with him to the card table would expect laughter. A blackjack player who laid a counting device beside his cards in a Nevada casino would be astonished if he were not summarily thrown out. At roulette wheels in Europe, aged devotees sometimes fumble with endlessly long rolls of numbers, hopelessly seeking to find an imperfection in the wheel. With horseplayers too, the search often fails. But the player has no hope at all unless he buries himself in the published information."[3]

When he purchased the *Daily Racing Form* from Frank Brunell, Moses brought in four associates from the Hearst executive council: Joe Bannon, circulation director of the *New York Journal*, Hugh Murray, a nephew of Randolph Hearst's, Joseph Moore and William McMurray. Unlike Moses's arrangement, their contracts with Hearst did not allow them to operate their own businesses, but they agreed to be partners as long as Moses ran the operation. Why Moses brought them in, especially as equal partners, is not clear. Moses did not say and years later his son Walter could not explain, either. Each of them had an equal interest, but Moses financed Moore and McMurray, Murray contributed an undisclosed amount and Bannon put in about $4,000.[4]

At the time they took over the newspaper in 1922, there were twenty-nine tracks operating in the country, although not simultaneously. Like golf and tennis pros in later years, the horses followed the weather. Chicago, Toronto, New York and New England tracks operated in summer, when the northern sun set late and temperatures were too high to race in Florida. When the seasons changed, the horses and their entourages of trainers, jockeys, clockers and touts shifted south and west.

The first operational move Moses made was to go national with the paper, which cost twenty-five cents rather than the three-cent price of most regular dailies. He set up newspaper offices and printing facilities in Toronto, Chicago, Cincinnati, Miami, Houston, Seattle and Los Angeles and circulated the six-day-a-week paper through the national distribution agency he had organized in Milwaukee and maintained from New York. He was as determined to control the distribution of essential racing news as he had been circulating his other papers in Milwaukee and Chicago.

He played hard and seized every available advantage, but there was no evidence he operated any more roughly than his competitors. Rumors that he forced Brunell to sell to him have no basis in fact, according to Joe Hirsch, dean of American turf writers, whose 1994 book *The First Century* chronicled the *Daily Racing Form*'s first hundred years. When Sol King, publisher of New York's *Daily Payoff*, sued Moses and the *Daily Racing Form* for having a racing news monopoly, slashing the tires of King's trucks and sabotaging his printing plant, the case was thrown out for lack of evidence.

It was true that independent distributors were forced to take the *Daily Racing Form* if they wanted to sell any of Hearst's newspapers and magazine titles, whose national circulation Moses completely controlled. That was a common hardball circulation practice and one that Moses used in Milwaukee. To minimize competition to the *Form*, he bought small local racing sheets. In New Orleans he paid $50,000 for the Bulletin Printing Company and in San Francisco $4,000 for the *Peerless Overnight Handicap and Run Down Sheets*.[5] To keep costs low, he monitored circulation so that his distributors would sell out or come up a few copies short, which increased reader appetite and meant he did not have to accept returned copies.[6]

By 1926, his own businesses — the *Daily Racing Form*, the distribution agencies and major real estate holdings in New York and Wisconsin — were taking so much of his time and energy that Moses gave up working for Hearst. He was forty-nine, far more confident than he had been when he arrived in New York six years earlier, and had lost interest in working for someone else. There were no hard feelings. For all his outside distractions, he had delivered for Hearst, increasing circulation revenues $5 million each year he had held the distribution job. Besides having more titles to sell, he attributed his success to "moving about the country, jacking up rates wherever possible, putting in more efficient distributing methods and keener men."[7]

He kept in contact with Hearst after he quit, because he had more admiration for him than when he started and he wanted to keep the mercurial publisher on his side as a business ally. Hearst was happy with the arrangement. Annenberg had served him well, and in the 1930s he invited Moses to visit him at San Simeon, his spectacular 165-room castle on a 275,000-acre ranch with fifty miles of shoreline halfway between San Francisco and Los Angeles. As part of his never-ending campaign to educate Walter by introducing him to the nation's movers and shakers, Moses brought his son along. They dined with Hearst and the actress Marion Davies, his mistress, and swam in the castle's elegant Neptune pool.

Moses had long understood how to compete locally, but working for Hearst had taught him to think bigger. After six years of owning the *Daily Racing Form* and mastering the basics, Moses realized that if he continued to buy racing publications, there was a good chance he could end up controlling the entire track news industry. In 1928, his partner Joe Moore took over the *Morning Telegraph*, more of a general entertainment guide with featured news about the theater and motion pictures, but it also ran racing news and so competed with the *Form*. Founded in 1833, the Telegraph hired a columnist early in the twentieth century named William Barclay Masterson, who had a broad background on which to base his views. Better known as Bat Masterson, once a Kansas sheriff and later a peace officer in Dodge City with Wyatt Earp, the quiet, stocky columnist regularly interrupted his writing to welcome to the *Telegraph* offices a string of admirers, such as boxers Jim Jeffries, Jack Johnson and Jack Dempsey. When he wasn't writing or greeting, he acted as a bodyguard for the paper's editor until one day on deadline when the old marshal keeled over at his desk, victim of a heart attack.[8]

By the mid-1920s, the paper was nearly insolvent and was sold to a Georgia printer named Roi Tolleson, who preferred handicapping to printing. Tolleson's knack for picking winners collapsed along with his ability to make a profit on the *Morning Telegraph*. Unable to keep pace with the competition posed by the *Daily Racing Form*, he sold the *Telegraph* to Moore, who could not run it either. Moore hired mediocre reporters at ridiculous salaries of up to $300 a week, increasing the weekly overhead by $25,000. When the stock market crashed, Moore went down too and Moses bought him out. "The honeymoon is over," said the new proprietor, who fired the overpaid unknowns and revamped the paper in Hearstian style. Moses hired top reporters, a fashion editor and sports writers and brought in Ring Lardner to write three columns a week. He made the *Morning Telegraph* newsier, sportier, punchier and horsier, and raised the price from a nickel to twenty-five cents.

He then used the *Telegraph* to oust his partners on the *Daily Racing Form*. Just as he had grown tired of being a Hearst employee, he was fed up with partners and sharing profits when he had produced most of the revenues. There was no question that he was the brains of the group, and while partners had helped get the project off the ground, he was ready to revert to lone wolf status. There was no evidence he harbored any doubts about cutting his partners loose, but if he did, they disappeared when they were all indicted, leaving Moses feeling betrayed.

THE INDICTMENT in Baltimore involved a weekly scandal tabloid called *Baltimore Brevities*, which was printed on the presses of *Running Horse*, another track paper owned by Moses, Murray and Bannon. The key charge was sending "lewd and obscene material" through the mail, although what was lewd or obscene about *Brevities*, a Hearst-style exposé sheet that targeted lurid sex crimes and police and political corruption, was left unspecified.

What drew the authorities' attention was an item in the September 1932 issue which was critical of the Federal Bureau of Investigation. FBI agent J. S. Egan wrote a memorandum about it to J. Edgar Hoover, who was notoriously thin-skinned about criticism of the agency he was building, to alert the director. "If it was criticism of the Bureau, it must have been by some disgruntled ex-employee," he wrote Hoover, who launched an investigation. The *Brevities* case marked the beginning of an FBI dossier on Moses that eventually totaled more than four thousand pages of agent reports.[9]

Baltimore Brevities was the target, but as part of his strategy of transforming all his local ideas into national sellers, Moses was also publishing *Philadelphia Brevities*, *Washington Brevities* and two other gossip tabloids, *Chicago Hush* and *New York Hush*. They had circulations of about forty thousand and were popular in the way in which *Hollywood Confidential* would be popular in the 1950s, risqué enough not to be left out on a living room coffee table but tame by modern standards. As far as Moses was concerned, they were money spinners that were popular and filled the down time between press runs of racing news.

Terrified by the indictments, Moses immediately altered the *Brevities'* editorial content. The November 1932 issue of the magazine included a statement titled "Our New Policy," which stated, "We believe the paper has, in a large way, served the community by dragging to the glare of the pitiless sun of publicity certain conditions which have been much corrected. Our work in this direction is nearly over and, understanding that, *Brevities* prepares to abandon a great portion of its exposé policies and instead concentrate on giving odd and

unusual bits of news about Baltimore and the vicinity, political side-
lights, sport items and society notes and other departments which we
believe will make interesting reading. Practically all stories relating to
sex will hereafter be omitted. We hope this new policy will find favor in
the eyes of our friends — as well as those who have declared themselves our enemies."[10]

Although Moses was indicted, he was not prosecuted. Neither was
Murray or Bannon. But Moses was furious that his two partners
claimed that they knew nothing about *Baltimore Brevities*. They had
never even seen a copy of it, they maintained, which was hardly true.
FBI agent reports specified how the magazine circulated to their
offices. Joe Ottenstein, a former Milwaukee newsboy and faithful
retainer who ran Moses's distribution agency in Washington, took the
fall, was fined $5,000 and sentenced to eighteen months in federal
prison, which was suspended.

After the Murray and Bannon denials, Moses was determined to
oust the men from the *Daily Racing Form*. When they refused his buyout offer, he used the *Morning Telegraph*, which he owned outright, as a
club to beat down the *Daily Racing Form*, which they partly owned. He
boosted racing coverage in the *Morning Telegraph* and cut its price from
a quarter to a dime. At the same time, he maintained the price of the
Daily Racing Form at twenty-five cents, reduced its coverage, and
ensured that his distribution agents gave it secondary consideration.
The message to Bannon and Murray was clear. Moses was ready to put
out of business the paper he owned with them to keep alive the one he
owned by himself.

They protested and sued him for mismanagement, but while the
case languished with lawyers, Bannon and Murray saw their equity
vanishing. When Moses offered them $1 million apiece for their shares,
each accepted. He speeded up the process and guaranteed that he
would break their resolve by dangling a $250,000 bonus to the man
who sold first. That was Bannon. Each later complained, but Moses figured that a return in a decade of more than ten times their initial
investment was a reasonable profit. He could afford to be magnani-
mous. Viewed another way, the settlement was an extraordinary bargain. Within two years of owning the *Daily Racing Form* outright, the
Annenbergs were netting $2.5 million profit from it annually. They
would own the *Form* for more than sixty years and the *Morning Telegraph* for nearly a half century, cash cows which poured hundreds of
millions of dollars into the family coffers.

Moses also created a monopoly, although he and the *Daily Racing Form*'s managers avoided use of the word and took steps to make sure that they would not be prosecuted for controlling one. "Competition was absolutely minimal," a senior editor conceded years later, "but whenever that ugly word 'monopoly' was mentioned, we'd say that we sold the charts to the newspapers, which we did for ten to twenty-five dollars a day, so how could we have a monopoly? We always got around it that way because we never wanted to be perceived as having no competition."[11]

Once Moses cornered the market on information for the amateur horseplayer, he went after the professionals. Bookmakers, who were illegal but by no means out of business, needed race data quicker and in greater detail than average bettors. "Handbooks" barely eked out a retail living. These were bookies working a beat alone like a milkman, visiting homes and stores every day to take bets from regular customers.[12]

The big, wholesale money was in horse parlors, or offtrack betting when it later came to be legalized, where the action increased many times over for bookies who knew the score.[13] These parlors, which handled three out of every four dollars bet daily, had everything a track had except horses. Wall sheets provided all the race information. There were easy chairs to encourage customers to stay and bet a few more races. In some deluxe establishments with higher minimum bets, admission was by membership card and complimentary platters of roast beef and pitchers of beer were laid out on buffet tables. In other neighborhoods, where fifty-cent and dollar wagers were accepted, cash bars and sandwiches were an important source of revenue.

There were betting and payoff windows, and boosters and shills who circulated through the crowd encouraging bets. Loudspeakers for the race callers kept patrons informed with an unending stream of information as horses headed from paddock to starting gate at tracks all over the country. These bookie parlors were illegal too, but they existed everywhere, from one or two in small towns to an estimated nine hundred in Chicago. And because they were illegal, other elements were drawn to the mix, including police protection, gangsters and racketeering, and political corruption.[14]

The daily papers, even the twenty-eight- to forty-page *Daily Racing Form* published in seven editions from seven cities, were not enough for these professionals, who needed up-to-the-minute information about everything that had happened since the paper was printed. Horses were scratched. Jockeys switched mounts. Weather and track conditions changed. Each affected horses in different ways: some were "mudders," while others ran poorly on wet, sloppy tracks. Changing weather meant changing odds. This late-breaking information was conveyed to a certain degree by various betting tools, including scratch and run-down sheets, the up-to-date lists of horses and jockeys which were published twice a day locally, and wall sheets, big posters with the latest listing of odds and results. Moses cornered the market in all of them. The kind of bettors who play slot machines bought local tip sheets, predictions of likely winners which any tout could turn out. Those local sheets were not worth Moses's time, but he did gain control of the national tip sheets.[15]

From tip sheets to national dailies, all the published material was lucrative. The biggest money of all, the racing equivalent for Moses of the silver spoon newspaper promotion, was not the printed word at all, but the telegraph wire which delivered all this up-to-the-minute information. The leased telegraph wire went to every organization that wanted it, including legitimate news agencies such as the Associated Press and United Press, regular newspapers and any subscriber interested in racing news. There was no question, however, who the primary recipients were — the more than fifteen thousand bookmaking establishments that the Department of Justice estimated were operating in the late 1920s and 1930s. One of Moe's closest associates, a *Philadelphia Inquirer* editor named E. Z. Dimitman, conceded in an unpublished monograph about his boss, "There is no doubt that many of the subscribers were bookmakers, who found it convenient to receive this statistical and result information from established and authoritative sources."[16]

Moses did not create the leased horse wire. The racing wire had been in operation since the late nineteenth century, but the first person to make money with it was a clever telegraph operator named John Payne, who in 1907 established the small Payne Telegraph Service to distribute racing news from tracks around Cincinnati. He was so successful that he branched out to other cities, including Chicago, where later that year he went into business with gambling boss Monte Tennes.

One of the smartest, most resourceful and ruthless racketeers in Chicago, Tennes ran gambling on the North Side. His war to oust his South Side rival James O'Leary and West Side boss John Rogers and become Chicago's undisputed gambling overlord involved machine guns, bombs, arson, police investigations, corruption scandals, prosecutions and a general reign of terror for the city's horse parlors. The violence failed. Tennes won the war after agreeing to pay Payne $300 a day for exclusive race results, the edge he needed over O'Leary and Rogers. Tennes relayed the results to the horse parlors and bookmakers, who paid him $50 to $100 a day plus one-half of their total receipts, from which he paid one-half of their losses.[17] To connect with Payne's service, Tennes organized the General News Bureau, his own wire service, in 1907. Then he shoved Payne out of business and became the city's undisputed gambling kingpin, making several million dollars a year, and a significant power in local politics.

Protected by friends in high places, Tennes acted in the early 1920s like the well-to-do citizen he had become. "Why, I haven't been in the gambling game for years," he told a reporter. "I'm not a handbook maker. I'm a newspaper man." When the Interstate Commerce Commission investigated his wire business and he was indicted in 1920, his lawyer was Clarence Darrow.[18]

By 1927, Tennes was old and scarred, and his General News Bureau was under siege by a new generation of Chicago mobsters. Tennes got along with John Torrio, the mobster who ran much of Chicago's liquor and speakeasy rackets. He did not have the same working relationship with Torrio's top lieutenant, a thug named Al Capone. When Capone took over after a mob battle forced Torrio to flee the city, Tennes decided to sell half his interest in the General News Bureau. Knowing Moses had full staffs at every racetrack to service the *Daily Racing Form*, Tennes came to New York and told him the business would earn no less than $400,000 a year, but that he was no longer capable of protecting himself or his investment.

Moses liked the number but understood the pitfalls of the racing wire. The first thing he asked Tennes was who were his clients.

"He said he supplied anybody," Moses recalled. "I said, do you supply bookmakers? He said yes. I said, is it legal? He said by all means." He asked Tennes the name of his law firm, which was Winstead, Strong and Shaw, one of the best in Chicago. "Whereupon we went to the offices of Winstead, Strong and Shaw and they too told me that the business was legal in every respect and went so far as to apprise me that the business had been under scrutiny and that Mr. Tennes had been hailed [into court] and had been acquitted of any improprieties."[19]

Their explanation was reassuring. Still, Moses knew that if he took on the wire, there was a thin line separating the legal and crooked sides of the business. He talked it over with his Chicago attorneys, Weymouth Kirkland and General Roy Keehn, once head of the Illinois National Guard.

"They told him racing results were news and that he would be collecting and disseminating news," Walter said later. "Providing news was no different, in their opinion, than manufacturing playing cards. If people use the cards to gamble or the wire to gamble, that's not your business, that's their problem. He wasn't gambling. Race results are news. After all, the Associated Press and others were getting the results, too."[20]

Moses wanted to believe. The national potential of the wire intrigued him. Given the interest in the *Daily Racing Form* in Canada, there were north-of-the-border possibilities as well. He was further reassured by the fact that the Payne and Tennes operations were not the only wires. Other apparently legal services delivered similar information. The potential was there to incorporate them and operate an international racing wire service. Combined with his publications, Moses would have total control over the industry's news. Not only was that the kind of challenge he loved, the prospect for reward from such a monopoly was almost limitless.

Walter Annenberg was only nineteen at the time, but he knew about the racing wire from schoolmates and friends who placed bets through race parlors. There was no one Walter respected or loved more than his father. The number of times he questioned his judgment could be counted on his thumbs. But in this instance, he was certain that his father was making a mistake. The family's businesses were hugely profitable. In May 1923, Moses had set up the Cecelia company, from Sadie Annenberg's middle name, as an umbrella organization for all the increasingly varied enterprises he owned: racing publications, motion picture magazines, real estate, the network of distribution agencies and a stock brokerage house. By 1927, Cecelia included more than forty ventures. The *Daily Racing Form* was making the family wealthier than ever.

Walter begged his father not to get involved with the wire. "I knew there was a vulnerability because many of the clients were bookmakers," Walter said later. "I told him that I wished that he wouldn't do this." But when he voiced the warnings, his father paid him little heed.

After listening for just seconds, Moses interrupted and said he had made up his mind. He saw nothing illegitimate or illegal about providing racing information. "This is news," he declared, "not gambling."[21] A few decades later, offtrack betting was legalized and modern casinos earned billions in legal profits, in part from the instantaneous electronic transmission of sports data, including that from tracks.

The situation was different, however, when Moses made his decision, which turned out to be a crucial turning point for the family. By then, he had spent twenty successful years working in Milwaukee and New York and putting his Chicago past behind him. From time to time, his brother Max's misdeeds in the full-scale circulation warfare that plagued Chicago from 1912 to 1914 and led to the gang wars of the 1920s would be attributed to him, but for the most part, Moses had shed the tainted associations of his rough Chicago youth. He was never a softie as he built his reputation, but few very successful businessmen in those years were.

John D. Rockefeller, for example, was a masterful executive, but also used notorious tactics to create Standard Oil, a monopoly which refined and sold 90 percent of America's oil. The nation's first billionaire colluded with railroads to secure preferential rail tanker rates, used predatory pricing and industrial espionage and bribed politicians on the way to becoming the world's richest man. In later years, the Pew brothers of Pennsylvania's Sun Oil told Walter how Standard Oil thugs burned down their oil derricks. The titan's great-grandson, Senator John D. "Jay" Rockefeller, conceded, "The business practices then were completely different from those of the modern era."[22]

Even by the standards of the time, however, the racing wire was notorious. Purchasing it was the biggest mistake of Moses's mature business life. Everything that later happened to him, and ultimately to Walter, stemmed from this decision. Moses would forever insist that he did nothing wrong with it, but regardless of his rationalizations and denials, the wire was a criminal tool. Owning it would tar him again with dark, unsavory associations and give his enemies, who began to multiply in number and influence, powerful ammunition to use against him.

7

THE WIRE

———

T HE CHICAGO GAMBLING WORLD was no place for the meek in 1927 when Moses paid Monte Tennes $650,000 for a 50 percent share of the General News Bureau. That year Al Capone made $105 million, according to the Treasury Department, which was not only the highest gross personal income any U.S. private citizen had earned until then but was also $35 million more than Henry Ford made in his best year.[1]

Most of the twenty-eight-year-old gangster's money came from the massive quantities of illegal whiskey that the underworld had been shipping into the United States from Canada and the Caribbean since Prohibition began in 1919. But he also controlled Chicago's prostitution, dance halls, speakeasies, roadhouses and nonracetrack gambling.

A hood imported from Brooklyn, Capone took over as boss of the Chicago bootlegging operation in 1925, a year after he arranged the killing of rival mob boss Dion O'Banion, a slugger in the circulation wars who once tried to kill Max Annenberg. The following year, gunmen firing machine guns from eight black sedans parading single file down the main street of Cicero, Illinois, in broad daylight peppered Capone's headquarters in the Hawthorne Hotel. No one was killed, but the attack underscored the lawlessness of the day, which peaked in the 1929 St. Valentine's Day massacre in which seven members of the Bugs Moran gang were shot to death in a North Side garage by killers sent by Capone.

The homes of the city comptroller, a senior judge and assistant state's attorney were all bombed in 1927, the same year Capone decided to move in on the bookie joints. The situtation was too unnerving for Monte Tennes, who'd had a long run and wanted out, but not for Moses, who saw an unprecedented business opportunity. He had no control over the bookie parlors and wanted none. Nor did he have any intention of getting tied up with Capone. There was no evidence that Moses ever met the mob boss or had anything to do with him. On the contrary, Capone's men would try to kill Moses because he would not share his racing news monopoly. Still, many of Moses's friends and Hearst associates frequently met mobsters who were some of the top celebrities of the era. Arthur Brisbane knew Capone well enough to get the only interview with him (in prison) after the Lindbergh baby was kidnapped in 1932. The columnist wanted to know if his underworld contacts could rescue the child.

Moses did not care who ran the horse parlors or handbooks as long as he could move racing information along wires leased from AT&T. The phone company didn't care either. As long as nothing patently illegal was involved, it leased its wires to whoever would pay for delivery. If someone wanted to place a bet at the other end, it was out of Moses's hands. He understood that bookies were illegal, but he did not believe they should be. He believed that all business involved risk-taking and thus was not very different from gambling. Indeed, life was a gamble. People could buy stocks or bonds, grain or hog bellies, or real estate. It was all speculation, he said, and no one thought those pursuits were illegal.

You could gamble at a track, so why was offtrack gambling illegal? To Moses's thinking, there was a class factor involved, and something was inherently unfair about the entire system. Not everyone could visit a track. Millions of factory workers and day laborers could not get away from their jobs during the week or leave their families on a weekend. Thinking along the same lines that would lead to the legalization of offtrack betting four decades later, Moses wondered why they should be denied the opportunity of placing a wager. "It isn't right to deprive the little people of a chance to be lucky," he told Walter. "How many people can take the time off to go to a racetrack?"[2]

Although he promised Moses he would remain his partner for a minimum of five years, two years after he sold him fifty of his one hundred shares of the General News Bureau Tennes took himself completely out of the business. He sold forty of his remaining shares to Jack Lynch, a local gambler, and the final ten shares to his nephews Lionel and Edward Lenz. The Lenzes were irrelevant, but Lynch was the liaison to the handbooks and horse parlors and a man with numerous links to the Capone gang. A well-known character in local gambling, Lynch owned a combination bar, poolhall and bookie joint named the Den of Immunity, which the police conveniently did not bother. Another of his establishments, the Sportsmen's Club, was cited in a 1916 Chicago Crime Survey report as a place where regular police payoffs were made. Lynch was at home with any handbook or in any horse parlor. "I wanted Tennes to stay," Moses said, "but when he sold to Jack Lynch, who hád been in the bookmaking business for years, I had a partner I didn't relish."[3] The comment was disingenuous. Moses took no steps to separate himself from his new partner. He did not consider selling his shares and withdrawing, buying out Lynch or building an in-house firewall. Instead, to supervise the General News Bureau and expand it nationally, he hired a deputy straight from the Lynch school.

He was James Ragen Sr., an old friend from his early newsboy days who had risen to become circulation manager of Hearst's *Chicago Examiner*. Ragen was well qualified to run the General News Bureau. He knew the distribution game, was very street smart, had outstanding leadership capabilities and was as tough, irascible and loyal as they came. Ragen had been a member of a gang of Irish bruisers organized by his brother Frank and called Ragen's Colts, which had done its share of slugging for Hearst. Twenty-five years earlier, when *Chicago Daily News* publisher Victor Lawson unleashed on Hearst drivers and newsboys a boardinghouse full of thugs, Moses had called on the Colts for help and the Ragens delivered. Just when Moses was leaving for Milwaukee in 1906, Ragen was arrested for killing a man in a fight, but he pleaded that he had acted in self-defense and was acquitted.[4]

Moses liked and trusted Ragen and gave him a free hand to run the General News Bureau from the Cecelia headquarters in Chicago. The offices were located at 431 South Dearborn Street, a few blocks south of the Loop, and along Plymouth Court, a street behind the Dearborn building which was home to so many of Moses's enterprises that it became known as Annenberg Alley. The intention of Moses, who in late 1929 was fifty-two and a multimillionaire who had avoided ruin in the crash, was to duplicate his success with the *Daily Racing Form* and make the General News Bureau the nation's dominant, and ideally sole, racing wire. Moses was the strategic mastermind; Ragen, the tactical implementer.

When they began, there were nineteen racing wire services in operation nationally. The majority were local, but four were large, multistate services: the General News, run by Moses; the National; the Empire News; and the Greater New York. By 1936, there was only Nationwide, owned by Moses.[5] Using persuasion and muscle, he swallowed up the others just as thoroughly as he had taken over all of Milwaukee's distribution agencies. Next, he put into place the same strategy and tactics that had made the *Daily Racing Form* dominant in print.

His first move was to run General's wire into the newspaper and magazine distributorships he had in operation from coast to coast. Those distributors supervised sales and service to local customers, a highly lucrative add-on to the publication business they were handling. Other small services were purchased outright and rolled into General. Ragen and his men dealt roughly with those who did not want to sell.

Alfred Kelly was one. He was an independent who ran a small local wire in Philadelphia. Kelly took the National service, for which he paid $40 a week. In turn, he serviced thirty-four customers at an average fee of $25 a week, clearing slightly more than $700 for himself. General News asked Kelly to buy from them. He declined, saying he was content with National. General then bought out National and went back at Kelly. He declined again and switched to Empire, where he paid $60 a week. General then bought Empire and sent its Pennsylvania manager, Patrick Burns, to Kelly with a third offer. General wanted to supply his customers directly. If Kelly agreed, he would be put on the General payroll for $100 a week. For the third time, Kelly said no thanks.

Ragen called him; Kelly would not budge. Finally, a frustrated Patrick Burns called Kelly's wife, Margaret, at 3:30 A.M. "Tell that long-legged, son-of-a-bitch husband of yours to be at the Jefferson Building at 2 P.M. today. Mickey Duffy's taking over this case and if your old man doesn't show, he can expect a pineapple [bomb] delivery at the office."[6]

Kelly showed up. He knew and liked Duffy, a top Pennsylvania gangster, who was later shot to death in Atlantic City. He doubted that the mobster would line up with Ragen against him. Yet, when Kelly arrived at the General News office, there was Duffy to close the deal or else. He urged Kelly to come on board for $150 a week and a share of the profits from his old customers. With a curse and a sigh, Kelly recognized the inevitable and signed on, the last of the independents to come aboard.[7]

The General News bought out the Greater New York service for $110,000. The National was absorbed when General agreed to pay its owner, Joseph McFadden, $10,000 a year for fifteen years. Buying Empire News, the last other major service, called for ingenuity. Ragen discovered that a telephone company employee bribed by Empire was diverting to Empire the General News wire feed from Chicago to the East Coast.

Ragen's boys dealt with the problem brilliantly. When General received the latest results, it temporarily shut down its wire, denying the information to its own customers and the thieves at Empire. Clerks from the General News phoned the results to their own bookies to keep them informed, while simultaneously dispatching runners to Empire bookie parlors to bet large sums on horses that General already knew had won. The General News agents later explained to the victimized bookies what they had done and how it might just keep happening if they kept their business with such a disreputable lot as the Empire service. In a wise public relations move, General reimbursed the bookies for their losses.

The parlors which had been stung were grateful, found the argument compelling, and shifted their accounts. Soon after, Empire accepted General's $300,000 offer and joined the Annenberg stable. By the end of 1930, through a mix of legal maneuvering and high-pressure threats, Moses had the racing wire business sewn up and thriving.

From each of the nation's twenty-nine tracks, the wire connected across the U.S. and into Canada, Mexico and Cuba. Moses was AT&T's fifth largest customer nationally, paying $43,000 a month to lease private long-distance lines and Morse telegraph terminals. He had outlets in 223 cities in thirty-nine states, links to every legitimate news organization that needed racing news and most of the nation's fifteen thousand bookie joints.[8]

There was only one problem. Moses still had Jack Lynch as a partner. Because Moses had done all the thinking and Jim Ragen the operating, Moses saw no reason to keep Lynch in the business and sharing profits exceeding $1 million a year from the wire alone. Just as he had eased Joe Bannon and Hugh Murray out of the *Daily Racing Form*, he decided it was time to assume full control. He did it by adopting almost precisely the same strategy he had used before.

In the *Daily Racing Form* case, Moses used the *Morning Telegraph* as a stalking horse. This time, when Lynch turned down his buyout offer, Moses came after his partner with a pincer movement. It was designed to undercut Lynch in two areas, the telegraph wire and the run-down sheets which listed the latest information on horses, jockeys, weights and track conditions and were an integral part of the electronic service.

The General News had had a subsidiary which printed these sheets, but without telling Lynch or the nephews Lenz, Moses established another firm, Universal Publishing, to publish the same information. In five years, company secretary Edward J. R. Kelly paid $900,000 in cash to Ragen as General's share of the sheet printing revenues alone.[9] Beyond Chicago, Moses bought the Bulletin Printing company in New Orleans for $50,000, the Overnight handicap and Run-Down sheets in San Francisco for $4,000, Abe Markewitz's operation in Los Angeles for $1,100, and the Wallwin Press in New York and again went into competition with himself, but with a twist.

Ragen sold the run-down sheets at cut-rate prices, won a customer following, then, based on a strategic decision made with Moses, had the wire broadcast odds and results using numbers instead of horse names. For example, horse number 612 would go off at 5–2 in the third at Saratoga, not Sunny Boy.

To know the identity of horse 612, a bookie had to buy Universal's run-down sheet, which included the horse's name and number. If a bookie took only the wire service, he had no access to the code, which changed daily. There was a simple and legitimate explanation for anyone who complained: the code offered security, protecting both the wire and the bookie from theft or manipulation of the odds and results.[10]

The fee structure then changed. Run-down sheets that had covered all the tracks in operation on a given day now covered only one track. If seven tracks were operating, a bookie needed seven sheets. Sheets had cost a dime; a whole set now cost seventy cents. Each horse parlor needed from a half dozen to two dozen sets. If each of Chicago's five hundred to nine hundred fully equipped parlors spent $7 a day buying ten sets, the income for run-down sheets alone would be a minimum of $3,500 a day.

After taking over the publishing side of the wire, Moses went after Lynch and full control of the wire itself. He did it in 1934 by establishing a second wire, called Nationwide News Service, which he owned completely, and setting it into competition with the General News, of which he owned 50 percent, but controlled because his man Ragen was the general manager. Moses and Ragen shifted the customers who subscribed to General over to Nationwide, taking a short-term loss at General, but making it back at Nationwide. In 1934, General showed a profit of $1.435 million and Nationwide a loss of $3,788. At the end of 1935, General had lost $45,634 while Nationwide registered a $1.1 million profit.[11]

A furious Jack Lynch, discovering, as had Bannon and Murray, that he had been made a fool of and that his assets were slipping away, first demanded an accounting and then tried to have Moses killed. "Annenberg was marked for a 'ride,'" according to FBI agent Louis Loebl. "He missed this in the fall of 1934 by just one minute, having boarded a train not more than sixty seconds before a gang rode up to rub him out."[12]

When the planned shooting failed, Lynch went to court and filed suit against Moses for mismanagement of the General News. Moses was straightforward in his defense, explaining precisely what he had done and why. When Lynch's lawyers detailed the methods employed — the rate cutting, the wire deadening, the codes installed — Moses offered no denials. He had been applying established business practices. As for owing Lynch money, Moses's defense was breathtaking in its audacity.

"It appears on the face of the bill of complaint," his lawyer Weymouth Kirkland told the court, "that the subject matter of the lawsuit is a division of profits made by supplying operators with certain essentials which are necessary in the conduct of said gambling or handbook business. Equity will not take jurisdiction of an accounting between participants in an illegal business."[13] As precedent, Kirkland's associate Robert Golding cited a 1725 English court decision in which the judge threw out a case in which a thief sued to have another robber pay his portion of the spoils. "There they wanted a division of spoils by robbers," said Golding, "here they want a division of spoils by gamblers."[14]

Lynch could not believe what he was hearing. But Charles Bidwell, a Chicago run-down sheet printer and an owner of the Hawthorne racetrack whom Lynch had also sued for cheating him, used even blunter language in his defense. "It appears that the subject matter of that suit is the division of loot, alleged to have been procured by supplying the instrumentalities indispensable to the operation of poolrooms and handbooks," Bidwell's lawyer maintained. "A court of equity will not entertain an application for accounting between alleged co-adventurers in an alleged criminal enterprise, nor aid the participant therein to recover his alleged share of the loot."

In addition to its brazenness, there were two other stunning aspects to Kirkland's defense: one was his concession that the profits came from an illegal enterprise; the second was the judge's willingness to accept the arguments that the court should not be involved in the lawsuit.

As the case dragged on, Lynch realized the court would throw his suit out. He turned to the mob for satisfaction. "Chicago's biggest gambling war — a colossal struggle for millions of dollars — will be fought with guns unless a compromise is quickly made," blared out the *Chicago American* on December 21, 1934. "Gangsters, gang weapons and gang methods will decide the struggle between Jack Lynch, veteran Chicago gambling boss, and Moe Annenberg, national racing paper owner, for control of the vast system that disseminates racing news to the thousands of Chicago handbooks."

The *American*, where Moses worked before moving to Milwaukee, declared that the Capone mob was backing Lynch. That was no surprise. When Lynch was kidnapped by a rival gang in 1931, Capone himself, cooperating with the Chicago police, conducted the negotiations with the kidnappers and personally handed over the $50,000 ransom that secured his release. But Capone was not around for Lynch's feud with Moses. He had been indicted for tax evasion in 1931, sentenced to eleven years in prison and was sitting behind steel bars at Alcatraz, tertiary syphilis eating away his brain. The remnants of the Capone gang were ready, though, including Frank "the Enforcer" Nitti, who won his nickname for providing such services for Capone, Dan Serritella, a crooked state senator with long ties to the gangster, and Marty Guilefoyle, a northwest side mob boss.

Backing Annenberg was Ralph O'Hara, the brutal organizer of the Chicago Motion Picture Operators Union. Twice in the previous three years O'Hara had shot and killed men. Each time he was acquitted. "O'Hara's forces are being recruited from the unattached members of Chicago's underworld," wrote the *American*, adding, "but it is known that gunmen have been recruited from New York. Many eastern bad men are already on the ground, ready for bombings, battles and gangland 'rides.'

"The higherups in Chicago's organized gambling — the politicians, police and syndicate chieftains who split the lion's share of the millions and millions of 'sucker' dollars which bettors drop in Chicago's poolrooms — are panicky in face of the impending conflict, and are powerless to prevent it. The reason they are powerless is that they have collected graft from both sides."[15]

For all its breathless, frenzied prose, and probably plenty of hyperbole, the newspaper was right about the graft. By his own admission, Jim Ragen had been paying off every politician in sight and beyond to keep Moe's wire operating at peak efficiency. "From 1933 to 1936, while I was managing General News and then Nationwide," Ragen said, "I paid $600,000 to politicians throughout the United States for political campaigns. We would set it up in our records as non-deductible items and pay the tax on it."[16]

The politicians dealt with the Lynch-Annenberg battle by going nowhere near it. Frank Nitti had his own solution, which would have also resolved a pressing problem the Capone gang faced in 1934. Prohibition had been repealed in 1933, knocking the bottom out of the bootleg liquor industry. The gang was attempting to make up its shortfall by investing elsewhere, but nightclubs and prostitution were much less profitable than whiskey. Many nightclubs and roadhouses offered gambling, but the games only drew customers at night. Nitti and Guilefoyle wanted more hours with clients and decided that bookmaking would bring in customers during the day with the profit potential of smuggled liquor. The only obstacle to controlling bookmaking, Nitti decided, was Moses Annenberg. Since Moses was unwilling to go along, Nitti concluded that the only solution was to kill him.

Nitti approached Ragen and suggested that he switch sides. The mob did not want to kill him, because they needed Ragen to run the wire. A dozen years later, there would be no mitigating factors, and the second shotgun attack on him in a fortnight would kill James Ragen. In an affidavit released after his death in 1946, Ragen recalled Nitti's proposal, that he "go along with the syndicate and put Annenberg out of business."

"The syndicate is trailing Annenberg twenty-four hours a day," Ragen later quoted Nitti as saying in 1934, "and if you will come along with us, we will kill him within twenty-four hours."[17]

Ragen, who was as stubborn as he was incapable of being muscled by anyone, turned Nitti down and told Moses of the approach. Moses knew that he was in danger. The two discussed options to avoid bloodshed. The Cecelia headquarters were well protected and Moses traveled with bodyguards. He was not foolhardy. With eight children, the last thing he wanted was a war. He had no intention of giving up what he had worked so hard to win, but he preferred winning with brains rather than brawn.

When Judge John Prystalski dismissed Lynch's suit, Moses made two overtures. The first was to his former partner. He did not want to sit through another trial or in the sights of a contract killer. He approached Lynch and offered $750,000 for his share of the General News, the equivalent of one-half of one year's profit. Lynch, who was contemplating an appeal to the Illinois Supreme Court, recognized that by the time that court heard the suit, there would be no money left in the General News Bureau. Still furious at having been out-smarted, he grudgingly accepted Moses's offer.

Ragen made the second approach. The day Lynch accepted the buyout, Ragen delivered $100,000 in one-hundred-dollar bills to Frank Nitti for what he later testified were "services rendered." He never said what the services were, but the implication was obvious: Nitti and the Capone remnants were paid off to lay off. And they did.

Moses promptly closed the General News and folded what was left of it into Nationwide. "This was a fight between two companies just like Joe Louis against Max Schmeling and Schmeling lost," was Ra-gen's summation. The outcome left Moses like Louis, the undisputed champion, controlling all published and electronic racing information nationwide, an extraordinary monopoly which was never duplicated. He had vanquished all his rivals in racing news. He had survived grudges and mob vendettas. His wealth was enormous. The FBI esti-mated in 1936 that he was earning $6 million a year from Nationwide, the *Daily Racing Form*, their subsidiaries, and from his distribution agencies, real estate holdings and investments, including those in an insurance company.[18] He was so successful that he could be magnani-mous when Stanley Kahn, who married his third daughter, Jan, and worked for Moses, suggested that he go after a few of the last scratch sheets he did not own.

"After carefully thinking it over," Moses wrote his son-in-law, "I come back to the conclusion that I have related to you many times, that I am reluctant to risk my present position for all the possibilities that were offered in the way of additional earnings.

"You complain that the scratch sheet has injured the sale of our rac-ing papers, and then in the next breath you say that we are ahead of last year in circulation in spite of a raise in price. So, the two statements do not reconcile.

"Besides, we simply cannot have everything, and like Mussolini when he started out to grab Ethiopia, he had to very carefully consider what he might be plunging into; but Mussolini had nothing to risk because Italy was on the bum and those who might have opposed his ambitions had by far and away much more to risk than Mussolini.

"Our position is similar to that of the English nation. We in the racing field own three-quarters of the globe and manage the balance. In other words, the few little nations that are left have to pay us tribute to continue. Now why isn't that the most beautiful and most satisfactory position to be in which ought to satisfy even me?

"Have you ever stopped to figure our earnings and how they might be upset by a little mistake such as we are discussing? For example, we have a number of enemies with unusual ability that are eager for a chance to get even with us and upset the monopoly, who would be willing to work for almost nothing just for revenge, and who would contribute their talent more enthusiastically than our own people just for a chance to upset our applecart." If he kept pushing, he concluded, "we might find ourselves with many regrets."[19]

Written in May 1936 when he was approaching the height of his power, the letter was revealing of Moses. He had a precise awareness of his dominance. He knew that he had real enemies. He was wary about overreaching, the first hint of concern about greed and arrogance. There was nothing modest in comparing the Annenbergs and Cecelia Corporation with the mighty British empire, but neither was he bragging. In the narrow world of racing news, he was the empire.

There was no coyness in his recognition that he was in a "beautiful and satisfactory position," but there was a wistful quality to his question, directed more to himself than to Kahn, as to why that position was not satisfactory. It seems clear that Moses wanted it all. He had been remarkably successful, so far never beaten: as a street slugger, a circulation executive, distribution agency tycoon, or racing information monopolist. He was smarter and tougher than any of his competitors, all of whom he had vanquished. His confidence was not only overpowering, it had spilled over into arrogance.

Not enough to blind him. Moses was fully aware that he was in a shady business. He understood exactly with whom he was dealing. He was proud of what he had accomplished, but he was not proud of this business, nor was his family. He did not want his obituary to read that he was the master of the racing wire and, indeed, when he did die, the full-page obituary in his own newspaper devoted less than a sentence to his involvement with Nationwide.[20]

He had Walter working for him at Cecelia, signing checks so he could learn the basics of his other business. But Moses deliberately isolated his son from the racing wire. "He did not want me to have anything to do with it," Walter acknowledged. "He was not completely comfortable with the people he worked with."[21] Walter was not at all comfortable with them.

The wire had been a means to an end for Moses. It made him wealthy and gave him status, although not the permanent status he sought. He was the biggest fish in the racing pond, but he knew enough about fish and ponds to understand that he wanted to move into a bigger pond with cleaner water, fewer weeds and a better class of fish. He wanted his family associated with something that would endure, an institution with character that would be the core of a community and which he would be proud to have his only son inherit. When he thought about it, there was one obvious route to take. What he enjoyed and understood best was daily newspapers, the kind William Randolph Hearst and Colonel McCormick published. Ragen could keep running the Nationwide wire. He had solid editors at the *Daily Racing Form* who needed only minor supervision. He would buy a newspaper. That would be his legacy, not the racing wire.

8

SCHOOL DAYS

———

THE WHOLE NOTION of his legacy intrigued and confounded Moses. He had made a great deal of money in a disreputable field and up until then, money was a sufficient measure of success for a man who had been trying to better himself almost entirely on his own. He ran his own businesses, devoted hours a day to self-education, reading and listening to classical music, and when he had spare time, escaped to a lake with his tackle to fish alone. Soon he would become fascinated by politics and influence and his goals would change. There would be a breakdown in the compartmentalization of his life in which the left hand made money, indulged his children and turned up the volume on Prokofiev, while the right hired sluggers and extortionists and cut associates out of partnerships.

Throughout this period, there is no evidence that he spent much time thinking about his own reputation. Criticism did not seem to bother him. Most he attributed to jealousy of his financial success. He was not driven to social climbing. Although he lived alongside society's panjandrums in Kings Point, he was not drawn to fraternizing with them, either over gin and tonics on their sweeping lawns or on the decks of their yachts or in the stalls at the opera. He preferred to play pinochle or buy another business.

His children were another matter. Like many of the newly wealthy, he wanted them to have everything his parents had been unable to give him, from clothes and cars to luxurious homes and a ready flow of money. He made few demands of the girls. The seven daughters were raised almost exclusively by Sadie. Walter was another story. His only boy, the child who would inherit all the companies Moses had built, was marked for special treatment from the outset. Moses's plan was to give him the best education he could in life and business. That called for both keeping Walter by his side and separating him from the indulgent harem of women at home.

Walter had been fourteen in 1922 when Moses brought him along when he bought the *Daily Racing Form* from Frank Brunell. Walking through Manhattan with $400,000 in cash under his arm was a thrill, but by no means the most significant experience he had that year. Buying his first pair of long pants from Brooks Brothers was a bigger deal. So was enrolling at the Peddie School as a Baptist.

Arthur Brisbane suggested Peddie when Moses asked him to recommend a prep school. Moses knew nothing about such schools and his only stipulation was that he wanted a good, not too snobby boarding school within an hour's drive of New York. Brisbane knew Peddie because it was in Hightstown, New Jersey, near Princeton, close to his farm. Walter was more than ready. He had had a difficult experience with school since arriving in New York.

Despite regular speech lessons in Milwaukee, by the time he left there after the sixth grade his stutter had not improved. If anything, as he moved into adolescence, it seemed more pronounced. To reverse that, Walter spent his first year in New York attending seventh grade at a small private school in Manhattan. That school left no impression because he spent almost the entire year taking intensive speech therapy lessons with a German woman who lived at Broadway and 103rd Street.

Sadie and Moses realized the impediment could cause him serious academic and social problems, and they were determined to try to ease his transition to his next school. There were no shortcuts to improvement, just hours and hours of daily oral exercises: practicing the correct way to swallow and breathe, the proper tongue placement against the teeth and roof of the mouth, and endless repetition of hard-to-pronounce words and phrases: *Emma, do you know my mama? I owned a wooden pump. My auto waited a time at a depot uptown today. My food fed fifty. I viewed a fat dove at a fountain. I found a definite divide on a mountain.*[1]

Page after page of words, phrases and sentences. Over and over again. *M*s, *P*s, *T*s, *V*s and *W*s were all exceptionally difficult for him. A simple question such as "What is your name?" could cause agony as he struggled to get out, "My name is Walter." Sometimes he pounded his desk in frustration; other times, he sobbed in humiliation. But Beezie Binks, as his sisters then affectionately called the teenager, never quit.

Peddie was a solid but not very well known school in the 1920s, certainly not as famous as its neighbor Lawrenceville, which was larger and a half century older. Peddie, though, was a more egalitarian place than Lawrenceville or Groton or Choate or any of the other WASP prep schools which were also within an hour of New York — schools less likely to welcome a Jewish boy who was perfectly polite but neither academic nor athletic, with no distinguished pedigree or social graces and whose most pronounced attributes were a stunted ear and an awkward stammer.

Peddie was founded as a Baptist school in 1864, a time when independent educators in the United States not only welcomed the union of education and religion, but considered positively dangerous the idea of dispensing knowledge which did not incorporate moral training. Peddie's original charter specified that the school was not founded "for commercial ends, [or for] creating physical prowess or mental acuteness, but for the development of students in whom ideas should be dominant. It was the dream and the plan of those laying the foundation that in the curriculum and in the teachers should be God, morality, high ideals, and the finest manhood."[2]

Had there been greater sensibility about "commercial ends," the school might not have faced extinction after its first half-dozen years. It was known then as the New Jersey Classical and Scientific Institute and the board of trustees offered to rename the school for anyone who would donate $25,000. Thomas B. Peddie, a Scottish immigrant who had come to America in 1833 at the age of twenty-five, made a fortune manufacturing leather trunks and luggage, and served as a New Jersey state legislator, as mayor of Newark and as U.S. congressman, stepped up with the money in 1872. Although he never knew Walter Annenberg, Thomas Peddie had a surprising amount in common with the young student whose generosity to ensure the school's future would one day far exceed the Scot's. Just like Walter, the original savior was one of eight children and, according to the official history of the school, "unsophisticated, almost shy, he was hesitant and slow in speech, probably a bit sensitive about the Scottish burr."[3]

When Walter applied to Peddie, the headmaster was Roger Swetland, a man who, in appearance at least, bore an astonishing resemblance to Arthur Brisbane. Swetland had been running the school for a quarter century and would continue in the top job for another dozen years. Like other long-term school builders such as Endicott Peabody, who directed Groton for fifty-six years, Frank Boyden, the head of Deerfield for more than sixty years, and Alfred Sterns, Andover's head for thirty years, Swetland was a man of unquestioned authority. He had a powerful voice and physique, indefatigable energy, decisive judgment and the inclinations of a rigid disciplinarian. Flogging was a regular part of his training regimen. According to Peddie historian Carl Geiger, "the rod was not spared nor the youngster spoiled."[4]

Moses thought Swetland was pompous and a bit of a "windbag," but he recognized that the no-nonsense headmaster might toughen up Walter, which he felt his son needed. He also liked Swetland's policy of limiting each student's allowance to two dollars a week so the wealthier students would not feel advantaged. Moses knew that was the better way to raise a child, but he also recognized that he was unable to follow the advice himself. He was forever giving money to his own children, and especially to Walter. Having encouraged Walter to forage for change in the till at his Milwaukee news agency, Moses had moved up to shoveling dollars at his son, often in the hundreds, or if he won big at poker, occasionally in the thousands.

Walter maintained later that his father was so generous because Moses had had so little money himself as a child. There was a certain logic to the explanation. For every Rockefeller who wanted to isolate his children from extravagance and impress upon them the values of abstemiousness, there were a dozen first-generation millionaires, including Moses, ready to spoil their children. One wonders, though, if there were another reason. Walter always played down the significance of Moses's bouts of rage because he believed that to discuss them with anyone, including family members, was tantamount to criticizing his father. His sisters were not so reluctant. Although there is no documentation of cause and effect, the extent of their fear when he erupted suggested guilt on his part. The payoffs may have been to help counter the terror of the rages.

Sadie did not like the idea of her only son leaving home so early, but she was grateful he was not going far and she had high regard for Peddie. She was never the disciplinarian that Moses was, but she knew Walter was at an age when he needed a more masculine environment. And she was very impressed by the preppy dress code. One of the first things she mentioned on her initial visit was how well dressed the Peddie boys were, so proper in their required slacks, jackets and ties.

The mother who inspected her daughters to ensure that they wore clean gloves when they left the house would be thrilled when Walter went to college and was voted "best dressed." Moses, though, was disgusted. He felt that Walter was too concerned with appearances, and not enough about more serious matters. Walter was the son of a rich man, but Moses hated the idea of his ending up as another rich man's son. He wanted his son to be confident about money, including being able to deal with large sums, but he did not want him to take affluence for granted or assume that he did not have to work to succeed.

Walter was readily accepted at Peddie, but Arthur Brisbane had not been certain that he would be. Brisbane filled out the application for him and on the line set aside for "religious affiliation" wrote in "Baptist." "Brisbane did it," Walter explained. "Years later I asked to see the application. There it was: religion, Baptist. I said, 'Well, this is ridiculous.' But Brisbane knew all the headmasters were Baptist ministers, so he figured I ought to enter as one. He thought it was a prudent thing to do if I were going to get in with the headmaster in a friendly fashion."

Prudent meant play it safe, but it also suggested Brisbane's economical approach to truth. Moses's failure to complete the application himself, or to correct Brisbane's misstatement, hinted that for all his confidence in business, Annenberg had no intention of taking chances with his son's education or on such alien territory as a prep school.

As an adult, Walter laughed at the petty deception which, as he acknowledged, was ridiculous because it was clear to Swetland or anyone else that the Annenbergs were not Baptists. The headmaster ignored the fabrication. Because he was agnostic, it meant nothing to Moses, but the lie bothered Sadie. She could accept the fact that her husband was not religious but found it more difficult to deal with the gaps in her children's religious upbringing. She was very troubled when Walter did not make his bar mitzvah when he was thirteen, but she could not convince her husband or her son of its importance. Walter shared his father's lack of interest, but Sadie regretted that her son was so removed from his religion.

EXCEPT FOR THIS INCIDENT, in which he played no active role, Walter never denied his Jewishness. He never called attention to his religion, but neither did he hide it. Throughout his life he would have Jewish and non-Jewish friends, would date and marry Jewish women, and would be very generous to Jewish causes and philanthropies. He denied that the "Baptist" incident troubled him, but even some of his closest friends wonder. "He laughs now," said one, "but he knew it then and can you imagine how awful that was, forced to conceal your identity?"[5]

If it were awful at all, the incident was not enough to diminish in any way Walter's five-year experience at Peddie, perhaps the happiest period of his life. When he entered in eighth grade, he was lonely and homesick during his first months. But as a genial boy eager to make friends, he became quickly acclimated. It helped that he liked his first-year roommate, Williston Case, brother of Clifford Case, later the U.S. senator from New Jersey. And while he was no athlete, Walter enthusiastically threw himself into the sports that were required of all students.

Five feet eight and slender, "Annie," as he was known, played league or intramural basketball and baseball in eighth and ninth grades, or the second and third form according to the English prep grade designations which Peddie adopted. He never earned a varsity letter, but not for lack of effort. For three years he was a shot-putter on the track squad. "I never put it very far," he conceded, "about thirty-eight or forty feet, but it was fun." He played third-team football as a sophomore and junior and, understanding his limits, wisely coached intramural football as a senior.[6]

In his upper-form years, he lived in Trask Hall, an ivy-covered brick dormitory, where his roommate was Roy Thompson, whose father owned coal mines in western Pennsylvania. With some extra money slipped him by his father, Roy bought a beat-up Ford roadster and hid it in the woods on the far side of Peddie Pond because the school did not allow students to have cars. On weekends, Roy, Walter and other boys would sneak into the forest, push the car onto a dirt road, drive the six miles to Princeton junction and take a train into New York, which was also forbidden. "Fortunately," Walter said when later recounting those years, "we had an understanding proctor."

He became a popular enough student that whether he was along or not, it became a practice that whenever anyone from Trask House went to Manhattan, that student had to go to the Waldorf Astoria Hotel, then at Thirty-fourth and Fifth Avenue, and purloin anything he could find with the monogram "WA." Towels, ashtrays, shower curtains, sheets, glasses, ashtrays, plates, silverware, anything that was not nailed down ended up in Walter's room. "Of course it was a prank," he said, "but I had a pretty full collection. We did it over a two-year period and I had more than a hundred objects all initialed 'WA.'"

Such a full collection that a shocked Sadie Annenberg thought she had stepped into a Waldorf stockroom when she visited Walter's dorm room one day. She immediately made him call Oscar Tschirky, the manager of the Waldorf, confess to what he had done, apologize and make arrangements to return all the stolen pieces. It took two bellboys to unload them from his mother's limousine. "I said, 'Mr. Oscar, I didn't want to, but my mother insisted I bring these back.' He laughed all about it, took me down to the dining room, ordered me a porterhouse steak and sat with me while I ate it. Oscar of the Waldorf, God, he was really something."[7]

On another occasion, it was Moses who was dismayed. Roy and Walter drove to Princeton, pooled $5 and bought an open-cockpit plane ride with a barnstormer. They had a ball, but when Walter told his father about the experience, Moses was furious. "My father was really annoyed about that. He was very protective. He didn't want me to fly, he didn't want anything to happen." Moses was terrified of flying himself and took the train everywhere; even if Walter was not nervous, he worried about losing his only son and heir.

A more traditional German father than his own upbringing might suggest, Moses never considered entrusting his affairs to his daughters regardless of how intelligent or capable one or more might be, a philosophy that would later lead to problems in both his and Walter's families. Walter would be in charge no matter what happened, so he had to be healthy and prepared.

School was only one element in Moses's preparation plans. In the summer of 1923, he and Sadie took the four eldest girls and Walter on a European tour. Moses was determined to do his first real vacation in proper fashion: first class on the Cunard Line to Southampton, with stays in fine hotels in London, Paris and Berlin, where the family rode in a horse-drawn carriage around the Tiergarten — Walter and his father wearing straw boaters — and to the train station through which Moses had passed thirty-eight years earlier on his way to America. Moses asked Walter to keep a diary to recall his experiences. When he looked at it years later, Walter burst out laughing. Nearly every day, he had written the same entry: "Ate and fooled around."

From Berlin, Moses escorted everyone to Kalvishken so Sadie and the children could understand the family's roots. Although often hidden, there was a sentimental side to Moses, who wanted to see what the place looked like. The bullying blacksmith was dead, but several neighbors remembered Moses, which delighted him. Like a lord of the manor rewarding his tenants, he handed out gifts of money, shoes and candy. Excited and animated, he pointed out to the children and Sadie the lake where he had fished and showed them where he had placed his fish traps. The kids did all they could to keep from yawning.

"It was just a burg with a few simple houses," Walter recalled. "It was important to my father that we saw it, but it was not the sort of place you would want to visit again."[8] Moses was annoyed that his children were not more excited. One of the purposes of the trip had been to show them just how far he had come up in the world so they wouldn't take their new status for granted, but he doubted that the lesson had taken hold.

After Kalvishken, the family traveled by train to Salzburg for the music festival which Moses was especially eager to hear. They stayed at the Imperial Hotel, where they waltzed in evening gowns and dinner jackets. A dance instructor had come to the Kings Point house, but Walter had never danced in public, nor had he ever been in a ballroom.

He took to dancing the way a bird takes to wing. He was not a good athlete. Evelyn was the only family member who was talented at sports, but on the dance floor, Walter had an inherent, natural grace. Aye, Polly, Jan and Enid all discovered that they too loved to dance, swirling around the ballroom to the strains of Johann Strauss, their long evening dresses rustling as they spun. The experience was so romantic, so much fun, that forever after, dancing became the family passion. Weddings, anniversaries and birthdays were never organized without a dance band or mini-orchestra on hand. No sooner was the group warmed up and a few bars into its first number than the Annenbergs tumbled out of their chairs and headed onto the dance floor.

A few days after Walter returned to Peddie in September 1923, Arthur Brisbane came by to pick him up and take him to the New Jersey training camp of Luis Angel Firpo, the "Wild Bull of the Pampas," who was preparing to fight heavyweight champion Jack Dempsey. Firpo had arrived in the United States with a woman not his wife, and some newspapers were speculating that unless boxing promoter Tex Rickard did something, his challenger might be deported before the bout for violating the Mann act, which prohibited transporting women across borders for immoral purposes.

With Walter in tow, Brisbane walked straight up to the giant and asked, "Are you going to be deported?"

"No deporto. Fighto," Firpo bellowed. "Ricardo, he fixo."

Walter was fascinated by the exchange and amazed by Brisbane's access. Stories about Firpo and Dempsey had filled the sports pages for weeks, and here was Mr. Brisbane just walking up and speaking with the fighter.

The following week, on September 14, Brisbane took Walter and Moses to the fight at New York's Polo Grounds, where he put the fifteen-year-old next to him in a front-row press seat. On the other side of Walter sat the journalist Damon Runyon, who later befriended him. In the first round, Firpo knocked Dempsey through the ropes and right into the laps of Walter and Runyon. The two of them helped push the champ back into the ring, where Dempsey proceeded to knock the Argentinian down nine times, the last one for a second-round knockout to retain his title. Walter, sweaty and rumpled from his encounter with Dempsey and with the shouts of the crowd ringing in his ear, was thrilled.[9]

Following his junior year, three years after his first trip to Europe, Walter went back. Young Americans frequently made such trips in the years after World War I and during the 1920s. French was the international language of the day and of culture. Paris, the capital of elegance and art, was the most popular destination. Less than a year later, in May 1927, Charles Lindbergh would fly his single-engined *Spirit of St. Louis* from Long Island to Paris in the first solo transatlantic flight.

Most of the travelers, even the young ones, were well off. Young men went for adventure, exploration and "experiences"; young women traveled with chaperones for a dusting of culture and to learn how to distinguish a Manet from a Monet. Walter and his cousin Stanley Rose sailed first class on the *Mauretania*, with a full complement of suits and evening wear, stayed at the Savoy in London and the Crillon in Paris, drank champagne, learned to tango and had a wonderful time.

Paris was hopping in 1926. Josephine Baker, the United States–born star of the Folies Bergères and darling of café society, opened her own nightclub while Walter and Stanley were there. Gertrude Ederle, the nineteen-year-old Olympic swimming champion from New York, arrived and in August became the first woman to conquer the English Channel by swimming from Calais to Dover in a record fourteen-and-a-half hours.[10]

Walter and Stanley cruised the jazz joints of Montmartre and Pigalle, the nightclubs of the Left Bank and drank wine at 32 rue Blondel, which was renowned for its attractive waitresses in high heels and nothing else. They toured the House of All Nations, once a legendary bordello for European royalty, but only a museum by the time of their visit. "They took you around the bedrooms like Tussaud's wax works and told you about the clients," said Walter. One room boasted a hoist built for King Edward VII, who in 1901 succeeded his mother, Queen Victoria, on the British throne. Because he was a portly monarch with a large belly and a prodigious sexual appetite, an apparatus had been constructed with stirrups and special supports for the object of his desires. "He stepped in there as if he were going into a stall," Walter said, chuckling.[11]

Although he loved a good time and had a eye for attractive women, whom he had no qualms about asking to dance, Walter kept his eighteen-year-old libido in check. A consummate pragmatist, Moses had given his son the full sex talk before Walter left New York and scared the daylights out of him. "I was very circumspect because my father talked so much about venereal disease and how careful you had to be. I was really terrified of that, so it cooled my ardor quite a bit."[12]

When he returned from Europe for his senior year at Peddie, he had gained considerable confidence, which offset the loss of what little interest he had in studying. He had never been much of a student. "He never worked his hardest while he was here," said Carl Geiger, an English teacher Walter much admired. "He enjoyed life too much for that."[13]

One of the few academic pursuits that interested him in his senior year was the work of F. Scott Fitzgerald, which in addition to the just-published *The Great Gatsby* included a series of short stories and two other books, *This Side of Paradise*, about his years at Princeton, and *The Beautiful and the Damned*. When two books about Fitzgerald were reviewed by Lord Snow in the *Financial Times* in 1973, Walter, then the U.S. ambassador to Britain, dashed off a note of appreciation to him in which he told how nearly a half century before, he had "devoured" the author and "would dream of my participation as a central character in his writings."[14]

The remark revealed a romantic and contemplative streak in Walter that he did not often express but which would become more apparent as he grew older. It's easy to understand Fitzgerald's appeal in the 1920s for a young preppy like Walter. In his 1925 masterpiece *Gatsby*, he created glamorous characters whom Walter wanted to emulate on Long Island, where the Annenbergs lived. Moses had not yet purchased the racing wire, so the fact that Jay Gatsby was a rich racketeer with shady connections had no threatening resonance. On the contrary, Gatsby's transformation from rogue to admirable character as his love for Daisy Buchanan develops would have been as irresistible for Walter as it was for millions of other readers.

Burying himself in Fitzgerald, however, was not the main reason he fell into a senior slump which left him with these final grades: algebra review, 75; biology, 75; English V, 76; English history, 75; German III, 85; plane geometry, 85 and public speaking, 75. The stock market was the culprit. He became completely wrapped up in it.

Moses had launched a stock brokerage house — Annenberg, Stein and Company — at 60 Broad Street and Walter became friendly with the chief cashier. Moses invested and taught his son the basics but was not a speculator nor an active trader himself. He liked blue chips — General Electric, American Telephone and Telegraph — and shares in companies whose products or management he knew well. He also favored Pullman and General Motors, whose chairman, Alfred P. Sloan, he had met and to whom he introduced Walter. The public company he knew best was First Wisconsin National Bank, which had backed his distribution business in Milwaukee and financed the *Wisconsin News*. In the thirties, Moses became that bank's largest individual shareholder.

Walter took to stock trading the same way he had to dancing. He loved it and was good at it, a natural from the start. He could scarcely wait to get to the public telephone between classes and call the chief cashier, who would place his orders. Since hearing his father explain the primary requisite of quality management for the success of any company, then meeting Sloan and deciding the auto magnate was a genius, Walter's favorite stock was General Motors. He would be so loyal to "Motors," as he called it, that in the 1990s he owned ten million shares and for a while was the largest individual stockholder in the nation's biggest company.

Walter started trading with several thousand dollars Moses had won at poker. With the advice of the cashier, but not of his father, who had little knowledge of what he had instigated, Walter quickly became an active day trader. "If you bought in the morning and sold before the close, you didn't have to put up any margin if you had credit," he said. "My father owned fifty percent of the brokerage, so my credit was fine."[15]

So were his picks. He was speculating, but not in unknown start-ups or penny stocks. He foresaw, as his father had when he built the parking garage in Milwaukee, that the car industry would only grow. In addition to Motors, he bought Willys Overland and Packard, and Chrysler stock because he admired Walter Chrysler, their neighbor in Kings Point. Another company he liked was Radio Corporation which took over Marconi Wireless in 1921 and would become RCA, the Radio Corporation of America. Walter was certain that radio would become huge. He was only reinforced in that belief in the 1930s after his father introduced him to chairman David Sarnoff, the kind of deliberate, serious, solitary and yet visionary executive that he would one day become himself.

His classmates knew what he was up to, but Walter was reluctant to give them advice because he did not want to feel responsible for any losses they might suffer. The teachers were another matter. He may not have excelled in math, but Hyster Harnberger, who taught him mathematics and Latin, and Fred Farris, his history and English teacher, discovered that they had a financial wizard on their hands. They often asked what he favored, and Walter was happy to pass on his analysis. He especially liked Harnberger, a Pennsylvania Dutchman, with whom he shared liverwurst sandwiches late at night while talking about school and the market. Seventy years later, Walter relished recalling those evenings and telling how Hyster's son, a throat surgeon, had served in Korea and wrote a film proposal that eventually became the hit movie and television series *M.A.S.H.*

Elected to the senior prom committee, he tried something no one had ever thought of before: soliciting the merchants of Hightstown for $25, $50 and $100 advertisements in the prom program. "I don't know why it had never been done," he said. "I had seen ads in college magazines, so it seemed a natural to me." The local stores responded so well that 1927 marked the first time a Peddie prom cleared a profit.

Walter profited so much from trading all year that during his final year he donated $17,000 to Peddie for the construction of a cinder running track. He thought hard about the donation, his first charitable gift. He did not want merely to leave something for the track and field team, no matter how much he enjoyed competing. He wanted to leave something enduring that Peddie could leverage, the foundation on which he would also base his future philanthropy. Walter figured that because no other schools in the neighborhood were equipped with a cinder track, Peddie could rent out its facility and thereby pay for its maintenance. "I wanted to give something," he explained, "that could be a revenue producer."

When he graduated in June 1927, Walter was as well known on campus for his financial acumen as football captain Richard Walsh was for sport. Walsh was voted "best athlete," but "Annie" walked away with "best businessman" and "most likely to succeed," quite an improvement from junior year, when his sole class superlative was "noisiest."

Sadie and Moses were pleased with the Peddie results. Walter had made good friends, had fit in well with both boys and teachers, had lost some of his shyness, learned a great deal about the world and met a few decision makers who helped run it.

He had reached another plateau, but before he left for university, Moses gave him a different sex talk. "You're old enough now to have a woman," he told his nineteen-year-old heir. He would find him one if Walter wished. Walter considered the offer but turned it down. "No, I'm not ready," he said slowly after some thought. Then, just as carefully, he added, "I should be in about six months."[16]

Walter fulfilled the forecast almost to the day. He did it on his own, with no help from his father, although Loretta Paganini did work in his father's Chicago office. She was his age, very attractive and fun, and Walter never lost track of her. Seventy years after their first intimate romance, and decades after he had last seen her, Walter still wrote her an occasional friendly note, from time to time enclosing a $1,000 check or another remembrance for old time's sake.[17]

His parents let him choose where he wanted to go to college, but Walter did not want to attend college at all. He wanted to trade stocks full-time and argued that six of his sisters had not gone, but Sadie and Moses would not hear of his dropping out. So at Moses's urging, he opted for business, which was all he knew and what interested him most. He had no ambition to be a doctor, lawyer, architect or writer or anything else. And since there was never any question that he would ultimately follow his father and take over Cecelia, the family business, he went along with Moses's wishes. "His father was a bit of a tyrant and very tough with him," said Morton Wilner, a college classmate who became Walter's brother-in-law. "Walter was M.L.'s heir and that was all there was to it. M.L. was going to forge him in fire."[18]

Moses pushed Walter to attend the Wharton School of Finance and Commerce, the first U.S. business school, at the University of Pennsylvania in Philadelphia. His grades were not good enough to get him into

Yale, Harvard or Princeton and even if they had been, he would have had difficulty being admitted because those universities had "Hebrew quotas" at the time. Neither Penn nor Columbia had such restrictions, but Columbia was too close to home and its business school was not as distinguished as Wharton. Another, equally important, factor behind the choice of Wharton was the presence at Penn of a renowned speech disorder clinic headed by Edwin Twitmyer, a nationally known speech pathologist, who saw young Annenberg regularly and redesigned his elocution exercises.

Walter moved to Philadelphia in September 1927, with a Cadillac convertible roadster and a raccoon coat. "Mort, why are you walking around in that thin cloth coat on this cold day when I've got this fur on?" he asked classmate Wilner jokingly. Wilner and Walter met through Phi Sigma Delta, the Jewish fraternity they both joined because Jews were not allowed to pledge gentile houses.

"I never thought of myself as a boy from a Hebrew background," Walter said, "but I had to recognize it as other people saw it." He and his fellow fraternity members took pains to be well dressed, to behave well and give no cause for criticism. He would take chances in business, but he never wanted to rock the boat socially. "I had to regard myself as a missionary in terms of the way I conducted myself." Wilner felt much the same, even as he went on to be first in his class, captain of the baseball team for two years, and the football quarterback who beat Navy 7–2 on a 55-yard touchdown run in 1929.

In the fraternity house, Walter was as popular as he had been at Peddie. "The other fellows all looked up to him," said Wilner. They did not admire him for his academic, athletic or social prowess, because those were not his strengths. They did, however, have a high degree of respect for the diligence he put into the elocution regimen given him by Twitmyer. Every day Walter locked himself into Phi Sigma Delta's communal bathroom so he could recite his lessons out loud without disturbing the other forty boys in the house. "He's going *a, e, i, o, u,* all the vowel sounds, out loud over and over," said Morton Wilner. "He'd be assigned to read parts of the dictionary, to pronounce every syllable and the meaning of every word. That's how he's got this big vocabulary."[19]

As his vocabulary grew, so did Walter's portfolio. He had been at Wharton only a few months when he recognized that its classes held no more appeal for him than Peddie's had. Business and management theory, the geometry of marketing and calculus of budgeting, were too hypothetical, too unreal. He hated writing term papers or anything longer than a page. "I was bored stiff," Walter said. He began cutting classes and hanging out at a brokerage office on the corner of Walnut and Broad streets. DeBenneville Bell was the office manager. Known as Bert, he was the son of an old Main Line family: his father was Pennsylvania's attorney general; his brother, governor. Bell was well known in Philadelphia for having quarterbacked Penn to an upset over mighty Michigan in 1915 before losing to Oregon in the Rose Bowl. He became much better known after 1946, when he was named commissioner of professional football.

Until 1928 Bell was an assistant coach of Penn's team. In 1933, he and three Penn friends borrowed $2,500, bought the Frankford Yellow Jackets National Football League franchise, moved the club from Delaware to Philadelphia and renamed the team the Eagles. Bell was thirty-three and Walter nineteen when they met in the brokerage, but the older man shared some traits with the student he befriended. Biding his time between football jobs, Bell was a rich kid whose beak nose was as conspicuous as Walter's ear, and school had also offered him the same means to his passion. He bounced through three prep schools studying football and little else before he made it to Penn, where he failed to graduate. At the brokerage, he and Walter talked of those things as well as the stock market, which they both played with abandon.

The market was in as ebullient a mood as the nation. Wall Street had been the center of the global financial universe for a decade, succeeding London, which had been the world's banker for a century until the First World War. By the latter half of 1927, when Walter started at Wharton, the national mood was buoyant. Lindbergh crossed the Atlantic, sending airline stocks soaring, Babe Ruth had hit sixty home runs, a mark that would stand for three decades, and flappers' skirts were as high as the market, which had been setting records each year since 1924.

Calvin Coolidge was in the White House with a light hand on the economic tiller. When he said, "The chief business of the American people is business," Silent Cal was not just talking. Unemployment and inflation were low. He had cut taxes three times and dropped the national debt $2 billion. His Treasury secretary, Andrew Mellon, was one of the most staunchly probusiness cabinet members in history. According to Wall Street chronicler John Brooks, Mellon "subscribed fully to the view that unrestrained stock speculation was a virtually unmixed blessing to the economy."[20]

Walter did not disagree. "Never had there been a better time to get rich, and people knew it," wrote economist John Kenneth Galbraith.[21]

Before the end of his first year and before his finals in May 1928 which he had little chance of passing, Walter told his father he wanted to drop out of Wharton and play the market full-time. He knew his father would be upset and he was not disappointed. Having had so little education himself, Moses had come to appreciate what he had missed and said Walter was a fool to walk away. He did not like what the decision suggested about Walter, that when challenged he was more likely to fold than persevere. Walter disagreed. He respected his father's opinion and understood his disappointment, but he was not plagued by self-doubt. He was confident about his decision. He wanted to spend more time at the brokerage office and make his fortune as his father had done. Once Moses saw Walter's mind was made up, he decided against trying to change it. "You're making a mistake," he told his son. "You will regret this later in life, but it's your decision."

Walter spent the remainder of 1928 and 1929 trading stock full-time. The Dow Jones index was up 255 percent for the decade. "By the summer of 1929, the market not only dominated the news," Galbraith wrote, "it dominated the culture."[22] Brokerage offices operated in resort hotels in Palm Beach, Newport and the Catskills and on such transatlantic liners as the *Ile de France* and *Berengaria*. No one in the market could stand being out of touch.[23]

Walter scoured the financial press, followed company and brokerage reports, listened to tips from brokers and his cashier friend at Annenberg, Stein and Company. In eighteen months, beginning in midyear at Wharton, the twenty-one-year-old had rolled up a portfolio worth $3 million, some $28.3 million in current dollars.

Moses warned him to be careful. Manipulators were busy targeting stocks. Radio Corporation rose from 85 in 1928 to 549 in 1929. The market had tumbled in June 1928 when Coolidge announced he would not run again, but Walter paid no heed. He was very thinly margined, buying stocks for no money down or five to ten cents on the dollar and borrowing the rest. But he felt invincible.

On Friday, October 25, Moses sold all his stock. The market had fallen badly on Thursday, and although it recovered, the elder Annenberg believed the orgy of speculation was over. The Dow Jones Industrial Average had more than quadrupled since 1924, climbing from 88 to 381. His father told Walter that he had pulled back, but on Monday, October 28, Walter was still busy trading. "I couldn't believe it was going to crash. I thought it would go on forever," he said. "But I was just a pigeon."[24]

On Tuesday, a record sixteen million shares were sold and the Dow fell 30.57 points. More than $30 billion disappeared from speculators' accounts. Margin calls forced the Annenberg, Stein cashier to sell Walter's shares. By the close of business, Walter's $3 million portfolio was gone and he was $350,000 in debt.

9

BOY ABOUT TOWN

———

WALTER'S SELF-ESTEEM CRASHED along with the stock market. A multimillionaire on paper midway through October 1929, he was panic-stricken and bankrupt seven months past his twenty-first birthday. He was also a shortsighted college dropout. "The biggest mistake I ever made," he acknowledged later. "Leaving Wharton was ridiculous."

It began to dawn on him that he was nowhere near as smart as he thought he had been only days before the crash. When Moses asked to see him after the market plunged, Walter went with a mixture of stomach-churning dread, confusion and desperate hope that his father would have some answers for him. Walter had no idea how to pay off his debt, but he was less worried about that than he was about the reaction of his father. Moses had given him full warning about speculating, but by ignoring his cautions, by not even hedging, he had been monumentally stupid.

Moses already knew from the Annenberg, Stein office about Walter's losses, but he wanted to hear the explanation directly from his son. As soon as Walter finishing laying out the details, Moses reacted. "I'm not going to let you go through bankruptcy," he said without hesitation. "I don't want you to have that on your record." At that moment Moses had a net worth of $8 million dollars, an annual income of nearly $600,000 and could absorb what he was about to offer. "If you will swear to me that you will never again trade on margin, I will pay your losses." Walter leaped from his chair, grabbed his father's hand and shook it hard and long. "Dad, you've got a deal."

From that day on, he later said, his father's admonition to "let this be a lesson to you" rang in his ears and "never again did I trade on margin." In case temptation arose, he would never have the opportunity to do it again at Annenberg, Stein. Immediately after the crash, Moses closed the brokerage.

Something, though, needed to be done for Walter, who was adrift and whose demonstrable talents stopped at dressing well. He had shown little ambition beyond ordering wisely at good restaurants and enjoying himself. Moses saw that his worst fears were coming true. Walter was overindulged and undermotivated. He was living at home, pampered and adored by his mother, deferred to by his sisters, with too much pocket money and too few responsibilities. He was not a mean-spirited young man, not a heavy-drinking, skirt-chasing playboy, but Moses would almost have preferred that to what Walter was becoming. It was time to bring Walter into the business, give him some purpose and begin training him for the day when he would take over, because there was never any doubt, or even discussion, about it. That he would take over was a given.

Moses had incorporated his businesses in 1923 as the Sheva Leah Pismon company, named for his mother and grandmother. Five hundred shares of stock were issued initially: 449 for Moses, 50 for Sadie, and one share for Arnold Kruse, the chief financial officer. Two years later, the name was changed to Cecelia Investment Company, for Sadie's middle name.

Cecelia, as Moses explained to his lawyer Thomas McEntegart in 1926, "is supposed to operate as my holding company which was organized for the purpose of holding everything that I own." Initially, it held the newspaper and periodical distribution agencies, the *Wisconsin News*, the A. B. and M. L. A. Investment Company that he ran with Arthur Brisbane, and the *Daily Racing Form*. By the late 1930s, Cecelia comprised more than seventy-five corporations, with gross revenues of $20 million.

From the outset, Moses arranged that Walter would inherit the company. In a letter to McEntegart, written on the eve of his departure on another trip to Europe, Moses asked the lawyer to prepare a will which would give Sadie a minimum of $1,000 a week for life; equal shares of his estate to his married and unmarried daughters; and to the then eighteen-year-old Walter, "at least four times the consideration of any of the other children."[1] Moses's dominance of the family was so all-powerful that his daughters, at the time they became aware of what he had done, neither questioned nor disputed the primacy Moses assigned his sixth-born, which was nothing less than slightly enlightened primogeniture. In classic primogeniture, under the feudal system of medieval Europe, the women would have received nothing.

Cecelia was headquartered in Chicago and Walter lived at home in New York, so his job responsibilities in the early 1930s were minimal. He occasionally traveled by train to Chicago, where he stayed at the Drake Hotel at the northern end of Michigan Avenue. On one 1931 trip with his father, Moses marched him into the First National Bank of Chicago office of Edward Eagle Brown. As Moses's business fortunes soared in the 1930s, the bank was his biggest lender, and Brown, the former chief counsel who would become its long-serving chairman, was the brains of the bank. "Sit down, Walter," the then vice president said to the twenty-three-year-old. "I want to give you a lesson in investing."

"Let's take real estate," Brown began. "Your father has done well in real estate and you may be interested as you get older. Always look for a corner property in a successful new suburban community. If you can't get the corner, get the property next door because if anyone wants to expand the corner they will need your property. If you need money sometime, get a loan, but don't sell the property. Sit, sit, sit. The big money in real estate is in sitting.

"Now, let's take equities," the banker continued. "There are two things to remember. Number one by far is quality of management; you must observe their character. Number two is, are the products wanted by the public? That's all you have to know. Then it's the same story. Sit, sit, sit. If you are confident that you have a solid company run by people of good character, never be in a hurry to sell. It takes endless patience and very few people have endless patience, but you will learn that you will do better with your backside than you ever will with your head."[2]

After his tumble on Wall Street, Walter knew more about downside than backside, which is why Moses had brought him to the banker's office. He would not give Walter much responsibility at Cecelia, but as a powerful manager, he made a point of introducing him to business titans whom he admired. Brown was one, as were William Randolph Hearst and Colonel Robert McCormick. Another was General Motors president Alfred P. Sloan.

Sloan spent two weeks a month in Detroit, but he was based in New York and had a twenty-five-acre summer estate in Great Neck, where the teen-aged Walter met him in the 1920s. A management genius, Sloan became president of General Motors in 1923 and transformed the company from a cluster of loosely related units into the model of a modern business structure and ultimately, after it blew past Ford in the late 1920s, the world's largest corporation. Like Walter in his twenties, Sloan was a bit of a dandy. He often wore a pearl stickpin in his tie; his breast pocket always featued a cascading silk handkerchief. Slightly deaf, which made him an intent listener, Sloan was more scholarly than Walter and had graduated from MIT in three years, but he had had a similar upbringing in a house full of servants, thanks to his father's prosperous tea-and-coffee importing business.

Sloan's greatest talent was organization. GM was a behemoth, but he kept it mobile by centralizing administration and decentralizing production, the model Moses used at the *Daily Racing Form*. Sloan acted as the chief of staff, planning and guiding strategy, while trusted division head lieutenants implemented tactics. "The whole objective of industry should be to reduce prices," was a Sloan saying. "That's what produces employment and expands business."[3]

Walter was tremendously impressed by the man whom he knew only slightly but understood to be the world's leading business executive and a man of sterling character. The Sloan Foundation that Sloan established in 1934 financed social and medical research, primarily in cancer through the Sloan-Kettering Institute in New York City, named also for his GM research chief Charles Kettering, the inventor of the electric self-starter.

Walter had begun speculating in "Motors" stock immediately after meeting Sloan. He read all he could about him in business journals and while a senior at Peddie in autumn 1926, he noted that GM production was up nearly 40 percent over the previous year's quarter. He was further impressed by the quarter-billion dollars the company paid that year in dividends, including a four-dollar-a-share bonus to show confidence in the future. To Walter, Sloan epitomized quality management and there was no question GM made products the public wanted.

AT CECELIA, Walter's primary duty in his early twenties was signing checks, a task he performed for years. Between 1932 and 1936, he estimated that he signed from five to fifteen thousand checks. Moses wanted him to understand where the money was coming from and where it was going, but Walter had no authority to do anything but sign what he was told by his father or Arnold Kruse, the CFO who had worked with Moses since 1922, or Joseph Hafner, who starting in 1933 was Cecelia's chief bookkeeper. Moses knew how to make money, but none of the three was a financial professional. Neither Kruse nor Hafner was a certified public accountant. As for Walter's knowledge of bookkeeping and accounting, said Kruse, "I believe he knows less about it than any man I ever met."[4]

A bookkeeper could have signed most of the checks. If one had, or if Moses had employed a top accounting firm to monitor his books, he might well have avoided the morass of investigations that later nearly destroyed the Annenbergs. But Moses saw no operational job for Walter other than to have him by his side. He did not trust his son to lead a division of Cecelia or even an individual company, no matter how small. He loved Walter, but he did not respect him. When Walter spoke up, invariably plagued by his stutter, Moses often lost patience and cut him off. "What do you know?" he asked. "You have no idea what the hell you're talking about." Walter, humiliated, would cringe and go silent.

Moses also isolated Walter to protect him. He did not mind Walter's involvement with the distribution agencies or real estate investments. He had few qualms about the *Daily Racing Form*, which was clearly legitimate, but he did not want Walter to work there and certainly not at the racing wire or run-down sheet operations.

"Since Walter had just come of age, his family and he were then, and continued to be, anxious for him to get into a line of endeavor divorced from racing publications and racing news service," explained Weymouth Kirkland, who was Moses's lawyer in the 1930s. "It was this same motive that led in 1932 to the investment in the *Miami Tribune* and Walter's apprenticeship there and later . . . to the purchase of the *Philadelphia Inquirer.*"[5]

For all Moses's public testimony about the probity and propriety of his racing endeavors, the fact that he refused to let Walter work there undercut his protests and was the best evidence that he was aware that his racing operations were less than reputable. He had no such compunctions about hiring other relatives. Five sons-in-law — Kenneth Friede, Robert Friedlob, Stanley Kahn, Stewart Hooker, and Herbert Krancer — worked for Cecelia on racing business; he offered a job to Ivan Annenberg, his brother Max's son, but Ivan turned him down.

Signing checks and sitting at his father's side did not cramp Walter's social style. There were sixteen million Americans out of work during the Great Depression — one-third of the national work force —

and the country's gross national product dropped from $104 billion in 1929 to $56 billion in 1933, but the Annenbergs sailed through unaffected.

"I didn't feel the Depression at all," said Walter. "I always had a pocketful of money." Later, he realized "that isn't really good for a young person." Instead of being given what he needed, he should have worked harder for it himself. It was a lesson he would apply later to his own children, but it was not a concept he appreciated at the time.[6]

Never close to cousin Ivan, who was three years older, Walter went back to Europe twice with cousin Stanley Rose, wining, dining, dancing and cavorting. Walter was a handsome young man with thick dark hair, the build and gait of a middleweight boxer, penetrating eyes, a shy smile, heartier laugh and a quick retort to all but Moses. Impeccably dressed, he bought his clothes off-the-rack at Brooks Brothers and J. Press, and the slacks, sport coats and suits were always freshly tailored and pressed. For a while, he drove around in one of the family Cadillacs, but soon bought a coffee-colored Lincoln convertible with wire wheels and a windshield between the front and back seats.[7]

He thought nothing of taking a boat to Havana, checking into the elegant National Hotel and ordering a tin of caviar in the grill room. The manager, uncertain that the twenty-six-year-old could afford the luxury, stationed an armed policeman by Walter's table until he pulled out a wad of cash and the cop was withdrawn. On one trip, Walter saw gamblers waiting hours for the airlifted arrival from Miami of the *Daily Racing Form*, paying $5 for copies regularly priced at twenty-five cents. It dawned on him that his father's monopoly accounted for the price. "The lesson of essentiality that I saw in Cuba never left me," he said later.[8]

His father begrudged him none of the trappings of wealth. Like other immigrants who arrived in the United States with nothing and made a fortune, Moses did not mind spending whatever it cost to keep his family looking successful and well maintained. He owned sixty suits at a time himself, but never a dandy like Walter, wore only one or two of his favorites regularly. Walter loved elegant shoes of buttery leather in a variety of styles: loafers, wing-tips and brown-and-white saddles. Moses wore only black shoes, which he hated to change. He usually wore the same pair for as long as two years or until they were beyond repair.

During the early and middle 1930s Walter played his way through the drawing rooms and nightclubs of New York, Chicago and Miami café society. Ginger Rogers fascinated him when she appeared in George and Ira Gershwin's hit musical *Girl Crazy* on Broadway in 1930. He took her to lunch several times, advanced to dinners and danced with her at the Waldorf-Astoria. That was three years before Fred Astaire teamed up with her for the first time in the Hollywood musical *Flying Down to Rio*. Ginger's mother, Lela McMath, put a stop to the romance with the then twenty-two-year-old Walter on the grounds that he was too old and sophisticated for her nineteen-year-old little girl, who had already been divorced once and would be again four more times.

Walter moved on and next fell for Ethel Merman, who, like Rogers, made her Broadway debut in *Girl Crazy* and stopped the show when she swung into "I Got Rhythm." Merman had been born Ethel Zimmerman across the East River in Queens. She had a solid family, was the daughter of an accountant in a Wall Street brokerage and was only ten months younger than Walter. She had been a stenographer at the B. K. Vacuum Booster Brake Company on Long Island, but young Annenberg had first seen her at Les Ambassadeurs, the New York nightclub where she sang with Jimmy Durante. Soon after she hit Broadway, they were having Friday night dinners with her parents at their apartment on Central Park West and spending occasional weekends together in Philadelphia. She was great company and it was a serious romance that lasted until 1934, when she starred with Eddie Cantor in Sam Goldwyn's *Kid Millions,* a movie that could have been named for Walter.

Walter was no less taken with showgirls. In New York he was captivated by Peggy Hopkins Joyce, the Elizabeth Taylor of her era. A gorgeous Ziegfeld Follies girl, she had the smile of a toothpaste model, a lively sense of humor and a first-rate brain which entranced five wealthy husbands and a skein of lovers, including the Annenbergs' Kings Point neighbor Walter Chrysler. In the midst of the Depression, newspaper readers lapped up stories of her multimillion-dollar divorce settlements and the jewelry and Rolls-Royces her gentlemen friends lavished on her. Walter visited her in the Dorset apartment where she was kept by Chrysler. As she laughed and joked about her elderly benefactor, Walter and his friends smoked Chrysler's cigars and fanned themselves with the $10,000 checks he had left her.[9] She was smart, fun and irreverent and Walter loved talking with her, but he was too young for her and she too experienced for him for their acquaintanceship to develop into anything more. He became more involved with another less well known but equally stunning Ziegfeld girl, Lillian Vernon. "She was a great beauty and great company," Walter confirmed years later. "I had a wonderful time with her in Florida."[10]

None was marriage material. They were not interested and neither was Walter. Throughout his twenties, marriage scarcely entered his mind. And for all his socializing, bedding women was less important than being with them. Always comfortable with women, he had more women than men friends. Much of that was the result of living with seven sisters and a mother whom he adored. More familiar with them, he was less tense and self-conscious around women, less anxious than when he was with his father or other men, where he felt more competitive. He stuttered noticeably less in the company of women.

ONE OF MOSES'S newest publications, a fan magazine called *Screen Guide*, was written and published in Los Angeles. Filled with photos of starlets and leading men and glowing profiles that read like rewrites of studio public relations handouts, which in many cases they were, *Screen Guide* was launched in 1932, easing Walter's entree into Hollywood just as the movie capital was taking off.

Al Jolson's *The Jazz Singer*, the first full-length successful talking picture, debuted in 1927, the year the Academy of Motion Picture Arts and Sciences was founded by MGM's Louis B. Mayer and the "Oscar" award made its first appearance. In *Screen Guide*'s first year, Katharine Hepburn won her first Academy Award for *Morning Glory* and Charles Laughton won the Best Actor award for the *Private Life of Henry VIII*. A year later, in the depths of the Depression, the nation was cheered up by Frank Capra's comedy *It Happened One Night*, which swept all the top prizes, including Best Picture and Oscars for Claudette Colbert and Clark Gable.

Walter did not think much of the magazine, but he loved the fact that it gave him a regular excuse to take the train to California — Moses still did not want him flying — where as the owner's son he was treated like visiting royalty. Walter kept in touch with William Randolph Hearst and Marion Davies, whose latest movie was *Going Hollywood* and who invited him one evening to a costume party at her beach home in Santa Monica, where Walter met her costar Bing Crosby. "All the guests were told to get outfitted at the Western Costume Company, and Hearst picked up the tab for everybody," Walter recalled. "I went in a Mexican outfit with a big sombrero. What a party!" Everyone was there, from Norma Shearer, Helen Hayes, and Lionel Barrymore, each of whom had already won Academy Awards, to a rising twenty-nine-year-old actor named Cary Grant, who was winning raves for his performances in *Blonde Venus* with Marlene Dietrich and *I'm No Angel* with Mae West.

He met Jack Warner, the head of Warner Brothers studios and one of Hollywood's great storytellers, who told Walter how his own father, Ben, had fled pogroms in Poland and immigrated to the United States the year after Walter's grandfather Tobias left Kalvishken. The Warner connection would lead to two other friendships. One, fleeting, was with June Travis, a young actress as charming as she was beautiful, the daughter of a vice president of the Chicago White Sox. The gossip sheets linked Walter romantically with her, but she was more entangled with a fellow Illini named Ronald Reagan, who was making his film debut in 1937 in *Love Is On the Air*. Reagan, three years younger than Walter, became a lifelong friend, and Walter became one of the staunchest supporters of the future California governor and president.

On one of his trips west, Walter stopped in San Francisco to meet another businessman whose exploits intrigued him: Amadeo Peter Giannini, founder of the Bank of America. Walter had read about him, recognized in him a corporate visionary along the lines of Alfred Sloan and had written to ask if the banker would meet him.

Giannini, a Genoese peasant by ancestry and a Roman patrician by nature, had been born in a cheap hotel room in San Jose, California. A natural trader, he had left his stepfather's produce business in 1904 to establish the Bank of Italy in San Francisco in a remodeled saloon. He catered to small merchants and laborers, many of them Italian, and tramped the streets soliciting business, to the horror of the city's staid, traditional bankers. Two years later, during the San Francisco earthquake, he salvaged $2 million of his depositors' funds, dashing through fire and destruction in a wagon to his bank and carting away the cash, gold and securities under a layer of vegetables. As soon as the flames died down, the Bank of Italy reopened for business, the only bank that did. Giannini's name became synonymous with integrity and daring, a reputation enhanced a year later in the national panic of 1907, when he paid depositors in carefully hoarded gold while other banks issued certificates for cash.

The founder of regional branch banking, Giannini bought and built scores of banks through the 1920s, convincing communities — if not always independent bankers — that a big bank's branch could put more resources into a town and reduce fear of bank failure. In those years, when many bankers considered Hollywood a financial risk, he loaned large sums to Charlie Chaplin, Darryl Zanuck and producers as far afield as Broadway, where he served Florenz Ziegfeld. His bad-loan rate was infinitesimal and in the 1930s, he consolidated his banks into the Bank of America. His story and success fascinated Walter. A big, thick-armed man with a white mustache and an ample middle, Giannini took the twenty-eight-year-old to an Italian restaurant where they ordered heaping bowls of spaghetti. He talked to Walter about his customers. Working people, the masses, had made him, he told him. Bankers who loaned to the favored few had tried to shut him down, but he had triumphed by giving the public what they wanted — convenient, trustworthy service. Big banks were not bad as the federal government would have you believe, he told Walter. He had a vision in which his bank would blanket the nation, not just California. He even talked to Walter about philanthropy. "Hell, why should a man pile up a lot of goddamned money for somebody else to spend after he's gone?" Giannini asked, presaging his later gifts to education and medical research.

Every aspect of the meeting made an impression on Walter: from the pasta, which became his favorite dish, to the idea of mass marketing, even targeting one's own philanthropy, and to a Bank of America where Giannini's successors would operate in every state. Walter was so taken with the banker's vitality and vision that he began buying Bank of America stock at every opportunity.

Such experiences created enduring impressions on Walter. He had lasted only a year at Wharton and to those who did not know him — as well as to some who did — he looked like a mama's boy and a loser as he trailed on the edges of his father's shadow. But there were other lessons he was absorbing. Analyzing the thinking and styles of top managers was among the most important. He was also trying to turn his stuttering and hearing loss to an advantage by concentrating on listening closely. Less eager to hear himself speak, Walter was developing a technique of sitting quietly and evaluating as others spoke. In later years, executives would describe him as perhaps the best listener they knew.

Although Moses had made few demands, he was serious about training his son. When he began publishing the *Miami Tribune* (see Chapter 10) in 1934, Moses gave Walter, then twenty-six, the title of business manager, which meant he watched his father manage the business, and encouraged him to write. Walter did some reporting and

wrote an occasional column called "Boy About Town," which mimicked Walter Winchell's "Man About Town" column for Hearst, played
off his family name, "Boy," and revealed that he really was more boy
than adult as he collected gossip and news items.

Using a style that tracked Winchell down to his tri-dot ellipses
between items and presaged such great later city columnists as San
Francisco's Herb Caen and Chicago's Irv Kupcinet, Walter offered a
mix of musings and goings-on about town:

> "Did You Know That: Miami Beach has about three
> women visitors to each male visitor, a very nice situation
> for the men ... John Law, popular polo star, is absent
> this year, an operation being the barrier ... the bulk of
> [Hialeah track owner] Joe Widener's fortune is reputed to
> be his holdings in Pennsylvania Railroad, Baltimore and
> Ohio Railroad, American Tobacco Company and Phil-
> adelphia real estate ... President Roosevelt's favorite
> cigarette is Camel and he smokes about a package a day,
> in addition to several cigars and a pipe ... Arthur Bris-
> bane, besides being an authority on economic, political
> and social conditions is a connoisseur of wines and an
> expert judge of horses and cattle ...
>
> [There were also,] "Those seen at the Thursday
> Night Waltz: ex-Governor Cox impatiently smoking cig-
> ars all evening ... Gene Sarazen displaying what the well-
> dressed golfer should wear ... Bernard Gimbel figuring
> the window dressing possibilities of the champion ...
> Barney Baruch Jr., attempting to sell the evening short
> but not finding any takers ... [or his candidate for] Nom-
> inated to sleep on a cactus plant: The man responsible
> for those handbills which are printed after the races in
> the nearby woods and are annoyingly thrown in your car
> [with nary a mention that such information was available
> from the next Daily Racing Form] ...
>
> [And] "Dear Diary: Just managed to pull myself out
> of my warm blankets. Looking at the clock I discover
> much to my surprise that it is noon. After thawing out in a
> hot tub, I managed to find some clothing which would do
> Admiral Byrd nobly on his present expedition. Brunch-
> ing on orange juice, oatmeal, chicken livers, scrambled

eggs, wheat cakes, toast and coffee, I was considerably
fortified to face the icy blasts of the great outdoors."
[This last on a chill March 18, 1934.]

Walter knew Winchell, but his real journalistic mentor in the thirties was Damon Runyon, who succeeded Arthur Brisbane as Hearst's
top columnist and whom Brisbane called, "the best reporter in the
world." "I used to meet him late, around midnight, at the Beach and
Tennis Club in Miami Beach," said Walter. Runyon, nearly a quarter
century older, let him tag along until dawn, a normal work shift. "He
was a damn good friend, advising me, tipping me off about what
was newsworthy, telling me where to be careful. He just happened to
like me."[11]

Runyon got his start in sports, which attracted Walter as well. The
writer once owned a semipro baseball team, promoted boxing matches
and won a huge audience by writing colorful human-interest stories
which mostly ignored the game's technical details. He covered everything from political conventions, heavyweight boxing matches and
murder trials to General John "Black Jack" Pershing's 1916 expedition
into Mexico for Hearst's *New York American*, before writing *Guys and
Dolls*, his first collection of short stories, in 1931.

Working Broadway between Forty-ninth and Fiftieth Streets, Runyon chronicled in his own "slanguage" the gamblers, gigolos and gangsters, the chorus girls, hookers with hearts of gold, broken-down
athletes, and Wall Street sugar daddies with "plenty of ticker." They
were an assortment of seedy but likeable rogues with names like Sam
the Gonoph, Harry the Horse and Dream Street Rose, and Depression-
era readers, not to mention Walter, could not get enough of them.[12]
When Walter wired Runyon once to comment on several of his characters, the writer, a kind man who went out of his way to encourage him,
cabled back his thanks, adding generously, "I only hope you never start
writing stories like that yourself in that style or you will make me look
like a sucker."[13]

Runyon obviously did not need to worry. Walter never tried to write
about some of his best experiences. One involved Huey Long, the
clever demagogue who ruled Louisiana more as dictator than governor
and maintained his control when he moved to Washington, D.C., in 1931
as a U.S. senator. Because the "Kingfish" was such a character, Walter
wanted to meet him, and in late 1934, when Long was thinking of running for the presidency, the *Miami Tribune* columnist asked to see him.

"Son, I'd be delighted to visit with you," Long replied.

Walter drove to New Orleans, met Long in his office, talked for ninety minutes about Long's possible presidential run and heard some tales.

"He told me about when he was first running for governor, he was up in this small community on a river where there was a pulley arrangement to pull people from one side to the other. The elders said to Long, 'Will you build us a bridge if you're elected?' and he replied, 'Oh, I'll certainly think about that.' So he was elected and they never heard from him again, so they sent the delegation that had met him when he was campaigning to Baton Rouge to ask what happened to their bridge.

"He said, 'There are just so many communities that need bridges.'

"'But Governor, what are we going to tell our constituents when we go back and say there's no bridge?'

"Long said, 'Just tell them Old Huey lied,'" said Walter, howling with laughter at the story. "Can you imagine that nerve?"

After their talk, Long, who had taken a liking to his young visitor, asked Walter to join him for dinner at a roadhouse on the edge of town. "Why don't you come with me." Walter accepted.

"After dinner, he said, 'You know, in the back of this roadhouse, there's some gambling going on. Would you like to have a look?'"

Walter would. "So he introduced me to the manager, and then I heard him say, 'I'd hate to have my young friend here lose any money.' So I started playing roulette.

"I used to play 9, 19, 21, 25 and 29. And number 9 came up three times in a row. So I figured someone upstairs was controlling where that ball dropped. I won about three thousand dollars in fifteen minutes and said to the senator, 'I'd better stop. This is too rich for me.'"

Long put his arm around Walter's shoulder and grinned, "Y'all come back now." Walter said he would. He was alternately intrigued and embarrassed about his gambling success, which is why he filed this story away in his mind, though he did want to write about Long's campaign. But a year later, Long was dead, assassinated ten days past his forty-second birthday at the new state capitol he had built at Baton Rouge.

At about the same time, Moses asked Walter to stop writing "Boy About Town." "My father thought I was developing a character like Walter Winchell's and he didn't like that," said Walter, who did not try to change his father's mind. "He thought Winchell was scoring on everyone, too many cheap shots and he did not want me doing that. I hated giving it up, but he was right to make me stop. He was afraid it would affect my character later in life."[14]

Relinquishing the column allowed Walter more time away from the paper, some of which he spent with his father on a luxurious ranch Moses had bought in eastern Wyoming while on a trip to Yellowstone Park. Driving through Beulah, Moses stopped for dinner, liked the trout he was served and asked where they had been caught. Sand Creek, he was told, a nearby stream. An easy mark on trout if little else, Moses changed plans and stayed overnight in Beulah. In the morning, he drove to Frank LaPlante's trout farm, looked at the beautiful salmon-colored cliffs and the clear, fast-flowing stream and asked how much he wanted for the place.

LaPlante did not want to sell. Moses pressed. After some banter, LaPlante decided the best way to drive off his pushy visitor was to name an outrageous price for an unimproved 650-acre property in the middle of nowhere with no buildings, electricity, running water or paved access road.

"Twenty-seven thousand dollars," he said.

"Sold," Moses replied.

Over the next two years, Moses spent an additional $270,000 buying a total of two thousand acres. He put a sixty-five-man crew to work on a mound of huge building logs. The main lodge, with its eight bedrooms, six baths, large dining room and poolroom, was built from the logs and filled with fine hand-carved Western furniture. Each room had its own motif: moose, elk, cattle, sheep, bear and mountain goat. The beaded horsehide bedspreads and draperies in each room were embroidered with the animals. Beds, two to a room, had matching animals carved into the head- and footboards. Hat and clothing racks were made from elk horns. A stuffed coyote held a lamp in its teeth. Animals were carved into the armrests of the living room chairs, while a bear chugging a bottle of beer was the bar centerpiece.[15]

There were no cattle on the ranch, but there were forty elk, twenty deer, antelope that Walter fed by hand, and flocks of wild turkey, ruffed grouse and duck, which Moses enjoyed both swimming in his man-made lakes and roasted on his table. Carpets of sod were imported and rolled down on the dry terrace in front of the ranch and six guest houses. He constructed a hatchery, brick-lined trout breeding ponds, a nine-car garage and a barn with an automatic drinking fountain in each stall for the ranch's thirty-three horses. Stone arches built over the new entrance road bore the simple name in foot-high letters: Ranch A, for Annenberg.[16]

Moses and Walter loved Ranch A. Sadie and the daughters hated it. They did not like to fish, which was the property's primary function. With the exception of Evelyn, who played any sport, out-of-doors for the Annenberg sisters meant the seven-block walk between Bergdorf Goodman and Saks Fifth Avenue. They were Park Avenue women for whom the natural beauty of Wyoming and the urban delights of Beulah held little attraction. They visited Ranch A after it was completed in 1933 and never returned, thereafter staying close to Kings Point, Miami Beach and midtown Manhattan.

Moses, though, liked to spend a full two months on the ranch in the summer. He brought along his cook, Rose Babos, a plump matron who had been both a registered nurse and a school principal in her native Hungary. She immigrated at the turn of the century and had cooked for Albert Lasker and Julius Rosenwald, the president and chairman of Sears, Roebuck who was one of the nation's great philanthropists. Rose specialized, not surprisingly, in Hungarian and Eastern European dishes: boiled chicken in casserole, noodle puddings, strudels, and fish in every variety from steamed and baked to sweet and sour. When Moses traveled she packed his favorites in aluminum tins and dry ice and shipped them to him air freight, spending as much as $30 in mid-Depression to send a double serving of chicken paprikash to the West Coast.

Walter never stayed the whole time with his father. Two months was too much isolation for him. And after several years, Moses too lost interest in Wyoming. It was gorgeous and he loved the quiet and the time it gave him to sit and read and think, but it was so far away and most of the family would not use it.

Ranch A illustrated also how easily Moses became bored with projects. A true entrepreneur, he relished new undertakings, designing them, getting them up and running, then turning them over to others to manage. Ranch A fit the pattern. Creating the property was more interesting than maintaining it. The same was true of his real estate and distribution agencies. By the mid-thirties, he spent little time on them.

Walter recognized how his father operated, and as he grew older, more confident and serious about assuming responsibilities, he spoke up more. He was particularly disturbed about Moses's plans to build a high-rise hotel in Miami at a cost of at least $1 million.

"Within the last year I have secured your promise on more than one occasion that we would not become involved in any new business ventures but that we should endeavor to solidify and consolidate our present enterprises," Walter wrote him in 1939 when Moses's legal problems were escalating. "To consider a development of this magnitude and approach it as a sporting proposition leaves me exceedingly unenthusiastic, especially since we have so many interests that need nursing if they are to eventually succeed." Then Walter went to the heart of the matter. "I fully appreciate your restless and roving nature and further recognize how you thrill and derive pleasure out of new things," he went on. "I likewise have observed how you cool off and lose interest after new things get under way. Someone then has to be found to wrestle with the baby."[17]

Walter wound up wrestling with the Ranch A baby, unloading it after Moses lost interest and went looking for a retreat closer to home, one that might draw more of the family and would be accessible for his senior staff. Moses was always generous in that regard, lending out his vacation places to friends. After moving to Philadelphia in 1936, he found what he was looking for, a five-thousand-acre mountain estate in the Poconos, near Milford, Pennsylvania, and halfway to New York. The property included a comfortable main house and farm, several hundred acres of forest and the Big Log Tavern Lake, site of the drowning of the estate's previous owner, Thomas Mitten, chairman of the Philadelphia Rapid Transit Company, the city's trolley and subway lines.

"Most Philadelphians who move and live in the upper reaches of politics, journalism and big business would shudder at the memory haunting the private lake where Mitten was drowned while his street car empire collapsed," said one report announcing the sale. That did not bother Moses at all. To him, an estate sale, in both senses of the word, was an opportunity. The property had been appraised in 1935 for $185,000, but Moses suspected he could get a good deal. He offered $100,000 to Albert Greenfield, a Philadelphia real estate mogul who was Mitten's executor. "In all probability, the property may be worth more than the amount I am offering," he wrote Greenfield, who for other reasons became Moses's sworn enemy. "But that is positively all it would be worth to me."

The offer was good for a week only, but there were no other bidders, so Moses's brinkmanship worked. He named the estate Sunnylands and made the three-hour drive up to fish and ride as often as he could from Philadelphia, frequently inviting up his senior editors and business friends for cookouts and fishing weekends.

Walter went often because he enjoyed being with his father. While Sunnylands was by no means on any direct route to New York City, it was not that far out of his way. New York was exerting an ever stronger pull on him in 1937 because his mother and sisters had elected to live in Manhattan. They refused to be around Moses while he was carrying on with a bosomy blonde younger than most of his daughters.

10

MIAMI

———

W HEN MOSES WENT LOOKING for a newspaper in the 1930s to put distance between himself and the Nationwide wire and to give Walter a more reputable place to work, logic, sun and demographics drew him to Florida. The state had been through a boom-bust cycle in the 1920s. The boom was sparked by a real estate frenzy, Prohibition, rampant rum-running from the Caribbean and an all-out effort to attract well-to-do tourists to a relaxed pleasure dome where gambling, horse parlors and racetracks flourished. The bust began when the bottom dropped out of the overhyped land boom, two deadly hurricanes slammed into Miami and Palm Beach, the stock market crashed and the Depression began.

The bloom wasn't off the boom for long. When the economy was flying high in the 1920s, Miami, and particularly its upper-crust neighbor Miami Beach, were snobby, restrictive resorts with a strong anti-Semitic flavor. Jews had been unwelcome in Miami Beach since the first causeway linking the sandspit to the mainland opened on New Year's Day in 1920. New luxury hotels under construction included warnings in their brochures that accommodations were reserved for gentiles. Those who missed the red flag arrived at registration desks with signs which boldly announced No Jews. Battered economically by the end of the first cycle and the Depression, Miami found out it could not afford to be so restrictive.

In 1930, the Surf Club was founded when former Ohio governor James Cox resigned from the Bath Club because it refused to admit his guest Adolph Ochs, who owned the *New York Times*. Jews began to discover Miami Beach and new hotels were built to serve them, in some cases by Jewish contractors and investors. These northern Jews, many from New York, the new construction, and a party atmosphere stoked by gambling sparked much of the 1930s growth spurt. It was with this surge of new arrivals that the Annenbergs came to Miami Beach. Moses had often traveled to Miami, where the *Daily Racing Form* was published in a dilapidated building at Northwest First Avenue and Twenty-first Street. The family began coming south in the winter of 1931, staying at the comfortable Hotel Alamac. That was the year the state legislature approved jai alai and pari-mutuel betting for horse and dog tracks, giving Dade County a boost. Joseph Widener rebuilt Hialeah Park, transforming what had been a serviceable but drab course into a showplace that drew up to forty thousand patrons daily. He did not like horse parlors because he was convinced bookies took business away from his track, and for a while, he prohibited the Nationwide wire service from setting up at Hialeah. Moses responded by positioning an observation balloon over the infield to record results.[1]

Two years later, Moses bought an elaborate Italian Renaissance oceanfront villa for $135,000 from Albert Erskine, the president of Studebaker Corporation and Pierce-Arrow Motors. The two-story residence at 4815 Collins Avenue, the *Chicago Tribune* rhapsodized, was "a veritable dream palace, constructed about a patio and overlooking a superb vista of sea and formal landscaping."[2]

There were two things about the house that Moses liked: it was big enough so that all the family could stay there at once, and it was grandiose and well located to serve his purposes. The family was growing fast. Daughters were marrying, in several cases young men whom Moses hired and paid well enough to support their wives in the manner to which they had become accustomed. He dressed Sadie and the girls in the best fashions, in flattering gowns with stunning jewelry. There was more to spoiling them and showing them off than guilt payback for outbursts of rage or for being tied up in an unseemly business. Having his family look good made him look better. Moses may have been the king of racing information, but he was not to be confused with the general manager of the Associated Press or the chairman of Dow Jones. A well-housed and beautifully turned out family elevated the image of the Annenbergs and in certain quarters gave Moses heightened respectability.

The house was significant in that regard. Named Casa d'Oro, or House of Gold, it was smack in the middle of Millionaires' Row on the ocean side of Miami Beach. For a man looking for respect as a businessman and patriarch, the location, like that of the Kings Point house, mattered more than the glorious ocean view, swimming pool and formal grounds. His immediate neighbors included J. D. Hertz of rental cars; Albert Lasker, an advertising kingpin; W. O. Briggs, of Detroit autobodies; Gar Wood, the speedboat king; Frank Gannett, whose newspaper chain was based in Rochester; and Harvey Firestone, the Akron tire manufacturer. Writer Damon Runyon lived a short chauffeured drive away just off the causeway, while Arthur Brisbane wintered on the ocean side of Brickell Avenue in Coral Gables. Both met Moses for lunch at the Beach and Tennis Club, where talk often turned to the local newspapers.

Four papers operated in Miami during the boom, but after the collapse and market crash, only two survived. The morning daily was the *Miami Herald*, which was published by Frank Shutts, an Indiana lawyer who had come to Miami as a federal receiver to handle the bankruptcy of a local bank. The bank's largest depositor was the Florida East Coast Railroad, built by Henry Morrison Flagler, cofounder with John D. Rockefeller of Standard Oil and a financial backer of the *Herald*. Shutts liked the climate, decided to stay and opened what became a respected law firm. He became prominent in city politics and took over the paper, transforming it into the mouthpiece of the Shutts political machine, which dominated Miami and Dade County.

The other paper to survive was the *Miami Daily News*, owned by James Cox, who was the former governor of Ohio and the 1920 Democratic party candidate for president. The colorless, flat-faced Cox and his running mate, Franklin D. Roosevelt, were swamped that year by another Ohioan, Republican Warren G. Harding, and his number two, Calvin Coolidge. Now, Roosevelt was in the White House. Cox's paper, which was actually run by his son-in-law Dan Mahoney, held sway in Miami Beach, where Cox used its political muscle to counter the Shutts machine.

In the winter of 1933–34, his first full season at Casa d'Oro, Moses agreed, "purely as a sporting gesture," in his words, to join a small group of investors backing a seasonal daily called the *Miami Beach Tribune*. The paper operated for three months and lost money. When it suspended operations at the end of the season, the other investors dropped out leaving Moses's printing company with the debt. At about the same time, a newspaper broker asked Moses if he was interested in buying the *Miami Herald* for $1.5 million because Shutts was ill and going blind. Moses was interested, but when the price was raised to

$1.8 million and neither earnings nor circulation figures were available, Moses declined to make an offer. Nor was he interested several months later when Shutts offered incomplete financial figures and raised his price to $2.8 million.

Moses claimed that he was being trifled with and his time was being wasted by an unprofessional publisher. After he turned the second offer down, Moses maintained that Shutts turned on him. "Immediately thereafter," Moses said, "Mr. Shutts began to express himself publicly and otherwise in a derogatory manner about me personally, deliberately misinterpreting my aims, my connection with the *Tribune* and my various other business interests," meaning Nationwide and its bookie connections. "I became the subject of Mr. Shutts's wrath all because I refused to become interested in paying $2.8 million for a cat in a bag."[3]

His competitive juices flowing, Moses decided to restart the *Miami Beach Tribune*. He had little respect for either the *Herald* or the *Daily News* and understood that Miami was a wide-open town where the hot issues were gambling and political corruption — a perfect environment for a muckraking tabloid he could also use to keep an eye on his own interests. During the summer of 1934 he discussed his idea with Paul Jeans, an energetic editor in the Chicago office of the *Daily Racing Form*. Moses liked promoting insiders, whether they were newsboys, distributors or editors. He liked the boyish-looking Jeans, who had worked for him for fourteen years, had a million ideas and was eager to put them to work.

When the *Miami Beach Tribune* went through bankruptcy proceedings that summer, Moses was the sole bidder for its remaining assets, which were not much more than its name and a contract with United Press. He renamed the paper the *Miami Tribune* and gave Jeans nominal control of the business and editorial sides. There was never any question that Moses, who loved every detail of the news business and was at his desk in the *Tribune* office every day, maintained overall control and had his fingerprints on every important issue.

"'Print the news,' he told me," Jeans later wrote. "A newspaper to be successful must serve the public. You can't serve the public by keeping a story out of the paper because it might hurt some advertiser or politician. When you take an editorial stand on anything, consider whether it is in the editorial interests of most of the people of the community, not whether it will damage the interests of the paper. I'd rather operate the *Tribune* at a loss as long as I can afford to do it, than to have it financially successful but unable to command the confidence and respect of its readers."[4]

Jeans wrote that he could not ask for any more from his proprietor, and that Moses stuck to his resolve "when the *Tribune* locked horns with the political oligarchy that ruled Miami and Dade County, when the state government joined in the attempt to crush the young upstart, when death threats became a daily occurrence. . . . Incensed politicos hurled one criminal libel case after another at us; a gunman lawyer invaded our office and shot down one of our reporters, politicians in Tallahassee sent a hired thug to 'get' me, the *Miami Herald* launched vicious personal attacks on Mr. Annenberg; blackmail sheets, financed by the city hall gang, made vicious, false and ridiculous accusations."

Finally, noted Jeans, "even Mr. Annenberg's good friend Arthur Brisbane advised him to lay off because he feared that the men we were attacking would have him killed or harm his family." Brisbane would know. Shutts was one of the columnist's vast number of good friends.

Jeans bought the syndicated columns of Walter Winchell, Westbrook Pegler and Eleanor Roosevelt, priced the paper at two cents and in Don Quixote fashion charged into the swamp of Florida's political corruption. The model was Hearstian: rowdy and combative. There were circulation contests, centerfolds of bathing beauties, huge photos of train wrecks and banner headlines and gory details of crimes. There was also responsible and penetrating reporting of life in the black communities, including stories on joblessness and problems with health and the lack of basic utilities, the kind of reporting that most papers did not do, certainly not the *Herald* or *Daily News*.[5]

The *Tribune*'s first big opening came with a break in the mob policy that had designated Miami off limits for settling feuds so that all could enjoy its winter comforts. Soon after Christmas 1934, the bullet-riddled body of Miami gambler and bookmaker George "Skeets" Downs was found on the edge of the Everglades. His was the second killing in two months. Miami bookmaker Leo Bornstein had been slain in a hail of machine-gun-fire when he answered a telephone in an apartment lobby. The Bornstein killing took place before the *Tribune* resumed publishing, but the Downs shooting gave fresh life to the earlier story. The *Tribune* played both to the hilt, with huge black headlines and pictures of the bloody corpses.

Three weeks later, on January 16, 1935, federal agents killed bank robbers "Ma" Barker and her son Fred after a five-hour gun battle at their hideout near Oklawaha, Florida. The *Herald* played down the story, which was a mistake, as the Barkers were as well known as John Dillinger, Baby Face Nelson and Bonnie Parker and Clyde Barrow. The *Tribune* printed extras on the shootout and sold out as fast as they could print them.

Then Joe Adams, the respected manager of El Comodoro Hotel, was arrested for helping to hide Alvin Karpis, the notorious partner of Fred Barker in the kidnapping of a Minnesota banker freed after his family paid a $200,000 ransom. That same week, two gunmen followed Mrs. Margaret Bell of New York to her suite at the Miami Biltmore and robbed her of jewelry insured by Lloyd's of London for $185,000. An investigation revealed that thousands of dollars were to be paid to police and prosecutors as part of an insurance fraud scheme. Lloyd's detective Noel Scaffa, convicted himself, testified, "You talk about fixing prosecutors in Florida just as you talk about taking a drink."[6] With such rich material, the *Tribune* could hardly keep up with the news.

A grand jury sitting to consider the Downs and Bornstein killings failed to indict anyone for those deaths, but did bring charges against criminal court Judge E. C. Collins for accepting a bribe. Collins was a prude, the head of the men's Bible class at First Baptist Church and an upright member of Miami's resident citizenry. Out of sympathy, the *Herald* went with a one-column headline; the *Tribune* splashed the judge's story all over its front page. "City Hall is filled with crooks," Jeans shouted after closing the story. "We're going to clean up this town and fire all our big guns."[7]

The paper trained its guns on Miami's public officials, and charged that city hall, the police and the county prosecutor's office were all involved with the underworld. The barrage was so intense that the cautious Walter Annenberg wrote *Tribune* attorney Victor Miller to ask why Jeans was "slandering" one official rather than praising his opponent. "But then, knowing Jeans' nature," Walter continued, "I realize he is only at his best when he has the clubs out browbeating somebody or something."[8]

Mayor Everest Sewell, who had been untouchable in Miami for a quarter century, ever since he raised the early money to publicize Miami and draw the northern tourists south, was apoplectic over the *Tribune*'s attacks. He sued Moses and Jeans for libel and published a circular about Annenberg's experiences with the racing wire and in the Chicago circulation battles. On some points he confused Max Annenberg with Moses, who countersued Sewell for $100,000.

The *Tribune* increased the pressure. As soon as the Miami Beach council voted to outlaw gambling, the *Tribune* revealed that council member Art Childers had voted for the ban because his gambling club, the Royal Palm, was not on the beach and would benefit from the ban.

The tabloid was making a major impression on Miami. In its first year, it repeatedly embarrassed the *Herald* and *Daily News*. They were get-along Establishment sheets which rarely probed deeply into the city's underbelly. Miamians were startled and fascinated by the *Tribune*'s revelations, and when Jeans cut the price to a penny, the tabloid's circulation soared to fifty thousand daily.

Jeans was as inspired on regular breaking stories as he was on political muckraking. When high winds and huge surf pummeled Miami on September 2, 1935, the weather bureau said that a hurricane was coming but mistakenly advised that it would pass south of the Florida Keys. The Florida East Coast Railway sent a train south to evacuate residents as a precaution, but when it failed to return, Jeans realized something was wrong. He sent out two reporters and a photographer, who discovered that the train and the highway had been washed away and that more than four hundred people had died when winds of 150 miles per hour and waves eighteen feet high hit the Keys. The *Tribune* produced an extra with dramatic photos of the destruction, which was the first the *Herald* or *Daily News* knew of the storm. For days, the *Tribune* dominated the story, bannering everything from the shoddy reporting from the weather bureau to exploitive undertakers and the death of a madam on whose body was found $1,000 in cash. Circulation climbed another ten thousand.[9]

Moses loved the competition as much if not more than his editor. In late March 1936, he ordered three different copies of the *Tribune* printed in advance of the execution of Bruno Hauptmann, the convicted kidnapper and killer of Charles and Anne Morrow Lindbergh's baby. Headlined "Hauptmann Executed," "Hauptmann Reprieved," and "Hauptmann Pardoned," the papers were bundled and stored in a Miami warehouse. As the execution approached, Moses hovered by the United Press wire, chain-smoking Pall Malls. When the bulletin chattered across the wire, he shouted into an open phone, "He's executed. Go with the execution." The first *Tribune* extras were on sale in less than ten minutes, swamping the *Herald* and *Daily News*.[10]

Next, the state legislature tried to cripple the *Tribune* by permitting publication of racing news only by papers which had been publishing continuously for two years or more, meaning that only the

Herald and *Daily News* qualified. The legislation failed, but it reminded Moses that big companies required powerful friends in political places. Milwaukee had been clean, but he had seen in Chicago and New York that businessmen needed understanding politicians to survive, let alone thrive.

To that end, the *Tribune* put up three candidates in 1935 for the Miami City Commission. Scrawny, elderly businessmen, they were dubbed the "Three Musketeers" by the *Herald*. The *Tribune* adopted the label and used it to promote the three unknowns so skillfully that they made a good showing, though none was elected. Moses tried again in January 1936, when he told Jeans and Howard Hartley, the *Tribune* correspondent in Tallahassee, that he wanted a candidate he could support for governor.

Peter Tomasello, an Orlando lawyer and member of the state legislature who had announced his candidacy in the Democratic primary, looked promising. Hartley later testified to a Pennsylvania legislative committee investigating the racing wire that Moses sent him to call on Tomasello with a $2,500 campaign contribution. The young legislator then came to Miami and met Moses at the Alcazar Hotel, where he started to describe his platform.

"'I don't give a damn about any platform,'" the publisher interrupted. "'I just want you to obey orders.'"

"'Okay,'" Hartley quoted Tomasello as saying. "'I can obey orders.'"

Instantly, Moses's tone changed. "'Young man, you can go far in politics,'" he said. "'I like you and you have a nice personality. First, we are going to make you governor and then we are going to send you to the United States Senate.'"[11]

What Moses wanted was approval of two bills by the legislature in Tallahassee. Prepared by *Tribune* attorney Victor Miller, one bill was to legalize offtrack betting; the other to legalize casino gambling. His critics accused him of being greedy and crooked, but to Moses, his reasoning was straightforward. Years later advocates of legalized gambling succeeded after making the same argument.

A total pragmatist, Moses believed that since gambling was already taking place everywhere and was an enjoyable pastime, there was little reason not to legalize it. He was benefiting through sales of the wire to the horse parlors and handbooks, but so were gangsters. If gambling were legal, he argued, his information business would profit, but the crime element would be reduced, payoffs could be eliminated, the state and cities would benefit from taxes, and everybody would be better off.

Whether Tomasello accepted the argument or, more likely, was looking for more "campaign contributions" is not clear, but he did agree to support Moses's bills if he were elected and to use his influence with the legislature to get them through. That was good enough for Moses, who promptly handed over $10,000 in four installments of $2,500. The *Tribune* backed him for the nomination, but Tomasello proved to be so inept a candidate that Moses gave up on him and the lawyer was badly defeated.

Putting the governorship behind, Moses turned his attention back to Miami, where he and Mayor Sewell were at each other's throats. Sewell said he wanted to shut down the horse parlors and put Nationwide out of business in Dade County. Moses charged that Sewell and Miami's police chief, Sam McCreary, were corrupt and stepped up his attack. Accusations that Annenberg was acting out of resentment that Sewell and McCreary had closed one hundred handbooks "were so ridiculous that everybody laughed," wrote *Tribune* editor Jeans. "Miamians knew that the police had not closed any handbooks." He ran lists and photos of those operating, including two adjacent to Sewell's office.[12]

The *Tribune* exposed how Parker Henderson Jr., son of a former mayor, controlled the city's bailbondsmen and had helped Al Capone buy a home on Palm Island and how McCreary was involved in a cover-up of the bolita numbers racket and in a complex web of bribery, kickbacks and a police brutality cover-up. The grand jury then validated much of what Moses and Jeans had been trumpeting in the *Tribune*, stating:

> We have obtained increasing and conclusive evidence that organized crime has almost reached the point of a monopoly, for which two primary factors are, in our opinion, responsible. One of these factors has to do with the conduct, officially and otherwise, of men who constitute part of our governmental machinery entrusted with the duties of fostering and maintaining orderly government and protecting communities against crime and vice, and vested with the powers of enforcement.

McCreary was forced to resign as police chief. Sewell was ousted as mayor and a multitude of city officials were indicted for conspiracy to defraud the city. McCreary was succeeded by Andrew Kavanaugh, former chief of police in Rochester, New York, who came "ostensibly to clean up the city's graft-ridden police department and enforce the law," Jeans wrote. "Actually, the purpose for which he had been employed was to put the *Tribune* out of business."[13]

Kavanaugh, backed by *Herald* publisher Frank Shutts, launched a crackdown on the horse parlors, a strategy Jeans wrote was "stupidly" based on the theory "that M. L. Annenberg and the *Tribune* could be stopped if all the handbooks were closed." But, the editor continued with a blast of righteousness, "whether the handbooks operated or not, made not a whit of difference to M. L. Annenberg and the *Tribune* so long as their operation did not involve the corruption of city officials and the police department as it always had under the rule of Shutts and the city hall gang."

In fact, the handbooks reopened as soon as they were closed and Moses suffered very little damage. If anything, he was on a roll in Miami. The politicians he had opposed were out of office. The *Tribune* was moving into the black financially, allowing Moses in 1936 to spend $300,000 on a new printing plant and offices for the paper.

Clouds that Moses could not see, however, were gathering. In Washington, Congress had asked the Federal Communications Commission to probe the American Telephone and Telegraph Company, which controlled all the nation's long-distance lines and nearly 85 percent of its 17 million telephones. In the course of the investigation, the FCC took up the question of AT&T's supplying leased lines to the racing wire and specifically Nationwide. Kavanaugh, who was then also serving as head of the International Association of Chiefs of Police, was called as a witness in March 1936 and testified that two hundred bookies subscribed to Nationwide in Miami, part of an empire that earned Moses $6 million a year. He did not give a source for the income figure, but it was repeated, including in FBI reports, cited as fact and would later be used as evidence that Moses had one of the highest annual incomes in America.

The *Herald* and *Daily News* printed Kavanaugh's testimony on their front pages. Moses countered by publishing a lengthy statement in which he portrayed himself as a former businessman with many investment interests whose character the locals were impugning because he had exposed widespread corruption in Miami. Some of his rejoinder was laughable, expecially his innocents abroad defense that much of his business had been conducted in Milwaukee, "which is known all over the world as 'the crimeless city.' That is the chief reason why I find it a little difficult to acclimate myself to the goings-on in Miami." This from the partner of Monte Tennes and Jim Ragen. He had launched the *Tribune*, he explained, to "hasten the manifest destiny of Miami," but his success had "earned the enmity of our competitor, which has from time to time resorted to unscrupulous efforts to besmirch my character."

He gave a vigorous defense of legalized gambling, pointing out that thirty-four states, including Florida, allowed betting on horse and dog races, and that in Britain racing was an honorable sport, "fit only for kings." He dismissed, without denying, Kavanaugh's estimate of his income at $6 million and declared that he had never had an interest in any gambling business or owned a racehorse or shares in a racetrack.

MOSES'S SELF-RIGHTEOUSNESS would have been more impressive had he not offered an explanation of how Cecelia operated that a modern-era spin doctor would have admired. "A corporation *in which I am interested* owns stock in approximately sixty other corporations which are listed on the New York Stock Exchange. *One of the unlisted stocks* is that of a corporation engaged in the business of gathering sporting and racing news. This organization, *as I understand*, serves hundreds of subscribers and newspapers with racing news and racing results. The business of this organization has thus far been legal in every respect. It is said, however, that some of its subscribers have misused the racing news for gambling purposes. The same might be said of every newspaper in the country which devotes generous space daily to racing charts, selections, entries, results and tips of every kind and character, and of radio stations that broadcast racing results."[14]

The circumlocutions in italics are the words of a man with something to hide. He did not say, "I own a conglomerate, one part of which is the Nationwide wire service which provides racing information to newspapers and bookies." If he had, Moses would have been more credible. Instead, his sanctimony was disingenuous. The attacks and his response raised core questions about Moses. How much was he sinning and how much sinned against? He denounced crime and corruption but was clearly involved in plenty of shady dealing. Was he a hypocrite or did he believe what he was saying? Or was Moses so able to compartmentalize aspects of his life that he was unable himself to distinguish right from wrong?

Understanding his culpability or innocence is essential not only to understand his character but to comprehend all that happened to

Moses from Miami onward. The self-righteous and disingenuous aspects are the easiest to understand. Those are characteristic traits in many business barons, from Rockefeller to Microsoft chairman William Gates. They are delivering a unique and necessary product for consumers, is how their argument usually goes. Their companies perform better than disgruntled, less capable competitors who question their practices and resort to slander and lawsuits to curb their higher-flying talents and efficiencies. Moses repeatedly made the same case.

He was sinned against. He was criticized and undermined for his efforts to root out corruption. He was not a hypocrite about gambling. He was consistent in his belief that it should be legalized, and he lobbied openly for its acceptance. He seemed honestly to believe what he was saying when he adopted the Chamber of Commerce defense about his publishing tactics, that he was helping Miami become an all-purpose entertainment center and why not on his terms. At best the strategy was genuine; at worst, phony and calculated to keep the horse parlors open. Most likely, it was a combination of both, and aggressive good business.

That last may have been a gray area, but he also sinned. The Nationwide wire was corrupt and Moses knew it. From his days on Chicago's South Side to seizing control of all Milwaukee's distribution agencies to expanding the *Daily Racing Form* nationally and crushing all competition to Nationwide, Moses's goal was a national monopoly on racing information. He wanted control and maximum profits. He knew every detail of the business, and there is no evidence that he ever balked when faced with a questionable means to his desired end. His denials of criminal links notwithstanding, it was his determination to maintain Walter's purity that refuted his contention.

It would be easy to label Moses a hypocrite, but hypocrisy is a shallow failing. Moses was more complex, a man with a paradoxical, almost schizophrenic duality, traces of which would surface later in Walter's own contradictory nature. Moses denounced crime and corruption — and meant it — yet ordered an underling to have a competitor desist or see his business demolished. He made idealistic pronouncements about journalism, which he believed, yet ruthlessly suborned journalistic ideals for personal expediency. He sheltered his family and tried to lead a respectable family life, yet kept a longtime mistress and constantly consorted with shady characters in questionable enterprises. He belittled his son and gave him money. He kissed his daughters, then erupted in rage and instructed them not to speak. The contradictory characteristics would appear again and again.

CHARGES AND COUNTERCHARGES traded, Moses and Jeans resumed their "throw the rascals out" campaign. "Throughout the winter of 1935–36, gambling was wide open in Miami and Miami Beach," wrote Jeans. "Virtually every known public enemy in the country who was still at large was known to be in Miami or Miami Beach. . . . The result was one of the worst crime waves that south Florida has ever seen. Robberies, stick-ups and other crimes of violence raged unchecked as the police departments failed to take any decisive action. Kavanaugh's raids stopped."[15]

When former mayor Sewell maintained at a civic meeting after the Kavanaugh and Moses counterclaims, "We never had any trouble here until they came in and started messing around," the *Tribune* proudly agreed in a full-page editorial, "Mr. Sewell is right: the city hall gang never did have any trouble until the *Tribune* started."

Sewell retaliated by taking his complaint to the FCC. On April 21 he wrote FCC chairman Anning Prall and offered to come to Washington and testify how Moses Annenberg was "a menace to a community." Sewell complained that he had been libeled repeatedly by the *Tribune*, but that Annenberg had "very able" lawyers who had prevented a trial. He was not opposed to horse racing, "which is a very fine sport for those who can afford to attend the races," Sewell explained. "It was the bookmaking joints, these schools for creating gamblers of our youth and clerks and making a great many of them thieves."[16]

Three days after Sewell wrote the FCC, Governor Dave Sholtz wrote FBI director J. Edgar Hoover about "helping us rid the state of Florida of Annenberg and his Nationwide news service." "The only way I can see that this sort of thing can be broken up is through the cooperation of your department. . . . Break up Annenberg and his connections and you will break up the major sore spot in this country."[17]

Kavanaugh followed Sholtz's letter four days later with his own from "Andy" to "my dear Edgar." "I am waiting patiently, and in fact, I am praying for the Attorney General to find some law or some way of assigning you the job of investigating the activities of the wire service controlled by Moe Annenberg because I know if you do investigate, oh boy, about a year from now what you will have learned of the activities of the underworld will lead you to believe what you knew up until that time was just a little sketch of what is actually happening."[18]

None of the three realized any immediate gratification. On the contrary, in the 1937 campaign for Miami's civic commission, the *Tribune* endorsed and heavily promoted three outside candidates over three incumbents supported by Sewell and Shutts and reveled in their upset victory. Moses hailed the triumph of honest government and his new board expressed their gratitude for his support by firing Kavanaugh, who was hired by Wilmington, Delaware, to be its police chief. That was not, however, the last of Kavanaugh, who lost the Miami battle but would surface again through the offices of his friend "Edgar" to ensure that Moses ultimately lost the war.

Then, however, the fifty-nine-year-old Moses was a happy man. "My work keeps me interested to a point where I forget age," he wrote to Bessie Bernstein, an old girlfriend whose husband had lost his job and whom Moses agreed to help. "I hate to hear you talk about our not being here much longer. You talk like an old grandmother. Personally I do not feel much different than when I was twenty-five."[19] He was eager to keep the *Tribune* operating and extolling the new Miami government he had worked so hard to put in place.

His attitude changed overnight in April 1937. Paul Jeans and Victor Miller were driving back to Miami from Tallahassee, where they had been seeing state legislators, when the speeding Miller swerved to avoid several cows on the road. Careening across the median, the *Tribune*'s editor and lawyer smashed head-on into a car driven by a tourist from Cincinnati. All three were killed instantly.

The death of his feisty editor shattered Annenberg and killed the *Tribune*. Six months after the death of Jeans, an exhausted Frank Shutts sold his *Miami Herald* for $2.5 million to John Knight, a newspaper publisher from Akron who was in the early stages of building a substantial newspaper empire. Two weeks later, at the suggestion of Cleveland newspaper broker Smith Davis, who believed Knight could establish a monopoly in Miami, Knight went to see Moses.

"Mr. Annenberg," said Knight, "I know you are an extremely busy person, so I'd like to ask you three questions. Number one, do you think there's room in Miami for three papers?"

"No," Moses replied.

"My second question is, would you sell the *Tribune*?"

"Yes, I would sell."

"My third question is, how much do you want for it?"

"A million dollars," Moses replied.

"I don't have a million dollars," Knight replied.

"Then what do you have?"

"I have a little paper in Massillon, Ohio."

"And where the hell is that?"

Knight explained that it was twenty miles from Akron, that circulation was about ten thousand but the paper netted $50,000 a year. "I believe you are losing two hundred fifty thousand dollars a year in Miami. Maybe we could work a swap?"

Moses nodded. "What's your proposal?"

The haggling went on for some weeks, but eventually Moses sold the *Tribune* to Knight for $600,000 and the *Massillon Independent*.

On December 1, 1937, Moses's last day as *Tribune* owner, he published a front-page final editorial, announcing the paper had been sold to Knight and congratulating himself for cleaning up Miami.

"The job wasn't easy, but once I was in it, there was no turning back. There was nothing to do but go straight ahead, fearlessly opposing the desperate efforts of the 'City Hall Gang' to save itself."

He was proud, he wrote, that "city government was returned to the people. In the election of the new city commission, good government won its major victory in Miami. I am proud that the *Tribune* helped to put the new commission into office. I have accomplished all I set out to do. . . ." The city, he concluded, "is in good hands. The *Tribune* is in good hands. Nothing remains but to go ahead."[20]

Knight locked the building and closed the paper later that day. A month later, several of the new city commissioners were charged with trying to extort $250,000 from the Florida Power and Light Company. James Cox's *Daily News* launched a recall campaign of two commissioners Moses helped elect and of the new mayor they had selected. The recall failed, but in the 1938 election, with no *Tribune* behind them, Moses's slate was swept from office, replaced by Everest Sewell and the "City Hall Gang," which returned Sewell to the mayor's office. Cox's paper chronicled the recall effort and turnaround, for which it won the 1939 Pulitzer Prize for public service. By then, Moses was operating in Pennsylvania, where he was up to his eyeballs in another political fight that made his Miami experience feel like a day at the beach.

II

PHILADELPHIA

I
F Moses Annenberg had moved anywhere other than Philadelphia after Miami, he would have avoided a unique set of political and journalistic circumstances which preordained trouble.

He nearly settled elsewhere. While living in Miami, he tried to
buy the *Milwaukee Journal,* which would have meant a return to a city
that he and his family knew and loved and where he was respected. He
had maintained business ties to Milwaukee, which remained the hub
for his distribution agencies even after they were officially headquartered at the Cecelia offices in Chicago. By the mid-1930s, he was also
the largest individual holder of the Wisconsin Bankshares Company
stock that he had been accumulating for two decades. But the *Milwaukee Journal* spurned his $7 million bid, so he remained on the lookout
for another high-quality paper where he could have a voice, train Walter and ultimately turn the publication over to his son.

Moses had known before Paul Jeans died that the *Miami Tribune*
was not the proper monument or legacy. After living in Miami for two
and a half years, Moses believed the city was second-rate, not good
enough for a man who wanted to dominate every field he entered,
whether it be racing news, indulging his family, or building estates,
ranches or a big-city newspaper. Like Hearst or McCormick, combative conservatives and ruthless competitors for whom he had the highest respect, Moses had developed strong opinions about the rights of
individuals, especially businessmen, and the role of government in
their ventures, and he wanted to state them in an established and
respectable forum.

There were few papers in America in the 1930s that were more established or respectable than the *Philadelphia Inquirer.* In 1936 the *Inquirer* was already 107 years old. Taking into account various mergers and consolidations, the paper's lineage extended back to the *Pennsylvania Packet*, which first published on October 28, 1771. With its roots in the revolutionary origins of the Republic, the *Inquirer* called itself the oldest daily in America. The newspaper backed Democrat Andrew Jackson until the president withdrew government deposits from the Bank of the United States, fearing that its financial power was a threat to democracy. It dabbled with the Whigs until that party disintegrated, and the *Inquirer* threw its weight behind Republicanism during the Civil War, when even Confederate commander Robert E. Lee held the reliability of the paper in high esteem. In Philadelphia, the *Inquirer* both shaped and reflected Republican control of the city from about 1860 until 1950.

When Moses heard about its availability, the *Inquirer* was well known as the bible of the Republican party in Pennsylvania, but for all its respectability, the *Inquirer* had in recent years fallen on hard times. The change came in 1929, not because of the Crash, but as a result of the death of publisher Colonel James Elverson Jr. The colonel, whose honorary rank was awarded by two Pennsylvania governors, was a fun-loving rogue with a high appreciation of beautiful women and fine sipping whiskey. A fervent boatman and sailor, he maintained two yachts for himself and a third for his wife on the Delaware River.

The Colonel built the *Inquirer*'s $10 million home, a luminescent white building topped with a soaring tower that straddled the Reading Railroad tracks on North Broad street and overlooked City Hall. Completed in 1925 and named for his father, from whom he had inherited the paper, the Elverson Building contained a state-of-the-art newspaper plant and on the twelth and thirteenth floors an elegant duplex apartment for the publisher and his wife. The walls of the suite were covered with what one *Inquirer* editor called a "not overly selective" collection of art, a hodgepodge which did include five Corots, for one of which, *Les Baigneuses des Iles Borromes*, Elverson had paid $50,000. In the few areas not covered by paintings or sculpture, he displayed his collection of scores of antique and modern clocks, each of which chimed so loudly on the quarter hour that when he suffered his fatal heart attack climbing from bed at 7:30 A.M. on January 21, 1929, his wife was able to fix precisely the moment of his death.[1]

Because the colonel had no children, ownership of the *Inquirer* passed to his sister Eleanor, who in 1894 had married Jules Patenotre, the French ambassador to the United States. A few years later, during the Spanish-American War, Patenotre was transferred to Spain, where the beautiful Eleanor was known as the "Pearl of Madrid." By the time her brother died and left her the *Inquirer,* Eleanor was a sixty-six-year-old widow living in Paris with her journalist son, Raymond. Mother and son hurried to the United States to examine their inheritance, which was then the leading morning paper in Philadelphia, with a circulation of 288,494 daily and 498,281 on Sundays. The task of managing the paper was beyond her, nor did Raymond care to try. He was busy developing his own string of small, inconsequential newspapers in France, including the aptly named *Le Petit Journal,* and building a political career that led him to serve as economics minister in four prewar French governments.

Complaining that Philadelphia was provincial and filthy, "not like Paris at all," Madame Patenotre ordered spending cuts in all departments, instructed the business office to mail her a weekly check for $25,000 from the paper's profits and promptly sailed for home aboard the *Mauretania.* With no leadership to replace the colonel, the decline of the *Inquirer* commenced. Madame had been quite correct in one assessment. Philadelphia was indeed more provincial than Paris, but a more severe problem for her newspaper was the deep provincialism of the *Inquirer* editors. Putting out a newspaper in the 1920s had been relatively easy. There was fascinating news everywhere an editor turned: Prohibition and Al Capone, the Scopes trial pitting Bryan against Darrow, the Lindbergh transatlantic flight, the Leopold-Loeb murder case, the rise of Hollywood as well as the seamy side of filmmaking illustrated by the Fatty Arbuckle scandal, the great sports heroes Babe Ruth, Bill Tilden and Red Grange. The list was endless.

When the balloon burst in 1929 and the nation lost interest in the flamboyance of the twenties and needed to understand the impact of the slump in business and precipitous rise in unemployment, the *Inquirer's* editors were out to lunch. Literally. They lunched daily on three-course meals of roasts served from wheeled serving carts at the Union League club, a cathedral of Philadelphia conservatism, where it was considered poor taste to discuss the plight of millions of unemployed. With their man Republican Herbert Hoover in the White House, the editors banned use of the word "Depression" in news columns. No mention of local or national unemployment was made.

No statistics on the subject were printed, even when released by the Department of Labor. If a local factory closed and dozens or hundreds of workers lost their jobs, the paper did not report it. If readers wanted vital news of the economy, they had to look beyond the *Inquirer*. Only when banks began to fail in Philadelphia, as they collapsed across the country, was a small announcement buried back on the financial pages near the stock tables, never on page one.

A year after the Patenotres returned to France, they sold the *Inquirer* for $10.5 million to the Curtis-Martin corporation, which owned two other Philadelphia papers, the *Public Ledger* and the *Evening Ledger*. The company was named for its two owners, Cyrus Curtis, owner of the *Saturday Evening Post* and *Ladies' Home Journal*, which Moses continued to distribute, and his son-in-law John Martin, a former ink salesman who managed the Curtis newspaper properties. The change of management only accelerated the *Inquirer*'s decline. Merging the *Inquirer* with the *Ledgers* failed to turn around the deteriorating situation. Curtis, eighty-two when he took over the *Inquirer* in 1931, was dead within eighteen months. Martin suffered heavy losses in the stock market and could not keep up payments on the paper. Three years after they had sold it, ownership of the *Inquirer* reverted to the Patenotres, who remained absentee proprietors in Paris as the paper continued its slide.

By mid-1936, when the Patenotres looked again to sell, both the United States and the Philadelphia newspaper scene had undergone dramatic changes in the seven years following Colonel Elverson's death. Hoover had been defeated by Franklin Roosevelt. The Depression was not over. There were 12.8 million unemployed in 1933 and 9 million remained out of work in 1936.[2] The economy would not truly recover until the 1940s, when heavy military and defense spending programs began. Still, the economic, agricultural and relief policies of the New Deal launched in Roosevelt's first term had gone a long way toward restoring national confidence and mitigating the worst effects of the downturn.

In June of that year, more than one hundred thousand of the Democratic faithful massed in Philadelphia's Franklin Field stadium, where they sat in humid, steamy weather through no fewer than fifty-six seconding speeches before Roosevelt made his slow, stiff-legged walk onto the stage to accept nomination for a second term. The next morning, the *Inquirer* ran a story on his appearance, but every detail of the convention and presidential remarks were splashed across the front page and inside Philadelphia's other morning paper, the more aggressive and dynamic *Daily Record*, which had already published a half million copies of a special issue devoted to the Democratic gathering.

Just as the *Inquirer* had turned moribund beginning in 1929, the *Record* was nearly defunct in 1928 when it was purchased from the Rodman Wanamaker estate by J. David Stern, the scrappy owner of the *Camden* (New Jersey) *Morning Post* and the *Camden Evening Courier*. The Wanamakers had long been involved in Philadelphia newspapers, owning the *Morning Telegraph*, the *Philadelphia Press*, the *North American* and the *Record*, but each paper died or was sold. The family was as unsuccessful in the news business as it was successful as merchants and store owners.

Born into Philadelphia's upper-class Jewish gentry, Stern started his news career as a cub reporter on the *Public Ledger* in 1908 and knew every phase of the business from working in the news, business and advertising departments of a variety of papers from the mid-Atlantic to Rhode Island and Illinois. In 1911, when he was twenty-five, he bought the *New Brunswick* (New Jersey) *Times* for $1,500, launched a campaign to clean up municipal government, then sold the paper for $25,000.

He had owned the *Philadelphia Record* for eight months when Colonel Elverson died and threw the future of the *Philadelphia Inquirer* into question. As the *Inquirer* waned in news coverage, community influence and advertising linage, Stern's *Record* waxed, with new promotion and circulation schemes, aggressive ad sales, improved coverage and gains in circulation. While he labored to improve the *Record* and *Camden Post*, Stern also bought the *New York Post*, that city's biggest evening daily, for three million dollars in 1933 when it was losing $25,000 a week, all with a mind toward building his own publishing empire at the opposite end of the political spectrum from Hearst and McCormick.

His finances were tight, but when Franklin Roosevelt addressed the throngs in Franklin Field, the chunky and ebullient Stern was riding high. His *Record* had stormed past the *Inquirer* to record the highest circulation of any paper in Pennsylvania. From an anemic 123,000 readers in 1928 when he bought it, the paper had nearly tripled in circulation to 315,000. By contrast, the *Inquirer* was still under 290,000, almost exactly where it had been eight years before when Colonel Elverson died.

More important than numbers was the matter of power. For decades, Pennsylvania had been a Republican state and Philadelphia a GOP stronghold. Stern, however, was a crusading liberal Democrat, and with Roosevelt in the White House the political landscape was shifting his way. A dyed-in-the-wool, full-throated New Dealer, Stern was a "B. C." Roosevelt man, meaning a supporter Before Chicago, where FDR was first nominated for president in 1932. The backing of the *Record* was instrumental in putting George Earle in the Pennsylvania governor's mansion in 1934, the first Democrat to run the state since 1890. That same year party boss Joseph Guffey became the first Democratic senator from Pennsylvania since 1875. Pennsylvania's Democrats, after a long, lonely wandering in the Keystone State's political wilderness, were on the move.

Philadelphia was changing too. The Great Depression and the New Deal had turned the machine-run city into a union town. The *Record* was the first paper in the country to sign a contract with the newly organized Newspaper Guild. Stern resigned his membership in the American Newspaper Publishers' Association in protest against what he called the group's "unfair attitude" against the union. Later, he was horrified when the guild, in a moment of foolhardy shortsightedness, turned on him, its most enthusiastic patron, and struck the *Record* for a crushing three months.

The very June day that Stern was welcoming his hero President Roosevelt to Philadelphia for the Democratic party convention, Moses Annenberg climbed from his trout stream at Ranch A in Wyoming to take a phone call from George Schroder, a Pittsburgh newspaper broker, who told him that the *Inquirer* was again for sale. Moses immediately dispatched — not Walter, who he felt was not up to the job — but his son-in-law Stanley Kahn, who was married to daughter Jan, to Paris to negotiate with Eleanor and Raymond Patenotre. Kahn was successful, returning with a purchase option, and on July 31, 1936, Moses announced that he had bought the *Philadelphia Inquirer.*

If he had set off a bomb at high noon in City Hall, Moses would not have made a bigger impact on Philadelphia. The Establishment of the fustiest, most conservative big city in America, where Benjamin Franklin had been a member of the local press corps, was stunned by news that the nation's leading purveyor of racing information was assuming control of their hallowed institution. Philadelphians knew next to nothing about Moses and he as little about their city and state. Pennsylvania was what he saw out the window of his Pullman car racing on business trips from Milwaukee and Chicago to New York. What little Philadelphians knew about Moses was not good and would turn worse when Stern told them more.

The first shots fired came from Stern's *Record* with a story noting the sale to Moses. The article began on page one and continued for almost four columns, characterizing Moses as an undesirable character, an associate of underworld figures and a major player in the Chicago circulation wars. Stern had heard a few days earlier from department store magnate Bernard Gimbel, one of his biggest New York advertisers, that Moses was buying the *Inquirer.*

"He's tough competitition," Stern said.

"The toughest," Gimbel replied. "In Miami Beach I saw the way he works at close range. Jim Cox, the publisher of the *Miami Daily News,* can tell you. If you think you've had competition from Jack Martin, you're due for a big surprise."

"The bigger they are, the harder they fall," said Stern with a forced cockiness. The publisher admitted in his memoirs, "I tried to appear nonchalant, but I had a sinking feeling. The Curtis-Martin organization was soft competition. Now the opposing team was putting a Red Grange in the line-up."[3]

In a panic, Stern contacted Mayor S. Davis Wilson with an absurd story about Moses coming to town at the head of a mob of gun-toting gangsters. The mayor fell for Stern's fantasy, but when Wilson asked for protection from the Philadelphia FBI office, the agent in charge saw the story for the nonsense it was and ignored it.[4]

Other publications dipped selectively into Moses's background. *Newsweek* wrote that Annenberg's name "once struck terror in the hearts of strong men." The magazine explained that he and his brother, "former butchers," had worked for Hearst and that "as circulation hustlers, they pounded their way to fame." The brothers' helpers, it added, "are generally given credit for sowing the seeds that made Chicago and gangland synonymous."[5]

Time gave a fuller and more accurate account of Moses's history and business interests. While noting Moses's experience for Hearst in Chicago, it wrote that "the tough tactics of that era gave to Mr. Annenberg and his older brother Max a sinister aura which dogged them throughout their careers." Yet *Time* also described Moses as soft-spoken, his seven daughters as "so attractive that all have been married," and the Kings Point house as "teeming with in-laws and grandchildren like an old-fashioned Milwaukee home." His Nationwide news service furnished sporting and racing news "to all comers, including Associated Press, United Press, hundreds of U.S. dailies and, inevitably, countless bookies and handbook operators," but it went on to note that Annenberg himself was "no gamester, places no wagers" and that "he is wroth when publisher-rivals refer to him as 'Moe Annenberg, the gambler.'"[6]

While those and other publications focused comment on Moses's past, there was also curiosity about whether Moses was fronting for Hearst. "Of prime interest to the trade was one question," said *Business Week*. "Did Mr. Annenberg represent William Randolph Hearst who was his boss for 26 years?"[7] There were several reasons for the fascination with Hearst. First, in the mid-1930s Hearst's newspaper ownership was up to thirty-three U.S. papers with a combined circulation of eleven million daily. Second, Hearst had long been interested in cracking the Philadelphia market, but he had never actually launched an effort to do so, which had locals believing that at any moment he might. Third, only nine months before Moses bought the *Inquirer*, Stern had publicly dared Hearst to establish a newspaper in Philadelphia.

The challenge had come about in November 1935 when Hearst placed an anti–New Deal advertisement in each of his newspapers plus sixty others, including the then Patenotres' *Inquirer*. Entitled "The Rake's Progress, or The United States is wasting its substance in riotous extravagance," the ad said, "Before the times of Woodrow Wilson and Franklin Roosevelt, the United States had practically no national debt. Now we have a formidable national debt of some thirty thousand million dollars, which is continually increasing. . . . The most important thing before this nation at this moment is to reduce expenditures, to reduce the national debt, to reduce taxation, to reduce the burdens upon business and upon labor. This is the ABC of economics, but unhappily there are a lot of people in Washington who do not know their ABCs."

When Stern saw the ad in the *Inquirer*, he reprinted it free in his *Record*, adding in a front-page editorial: "Let Hearst, arch reactionary, battle the liberal *Record* at close range and let Philadelphia citizens be the jury. . . . Philadelphia is one of the few cities in the country where Mr. Hearst has to pay for space to place his views before the public. . . . We suggest that Hearst immediately remedy this situation by purchasing a Philadelphia newspaper. . . ."[8]

Hearst did not. The only Hearst contribution to the *Inquirer* was that Moses was a self-taught Hearst protégé. He denied emphatically and truthfully that Hearst or any secret backers were involved. He had bought the *Inquirer* for himself and intended to run it himself. "I am primarily interested in the publishing business," Moses declared, "and with the acquisition of the *Philadelphia Inquirer,* I feel that my ambitions have been fully realized." This also was true. After his death, in a memorial book published privately by the family, Walter called his father's purchase "the realization of a lifelong ambition. It marked the first untrammeled opportunity . . . in which he could give free rein to his ideas."

Because his ideas largely mirrored those of his mentor Hearst, the *Nation* weekly was on target when it said that Moses's purchase was "a matter of first-class journalistic interest." Stern, the *Nation* pointed out, "alone among newspaper proprietors has dared to criticize him [Hearst] openly. New Deal Senator Guffey and Governor Earle of Pennsylvania are reported to have an interest in Stern's papers and Stern and his associates stand high in the councils of the New Deal, while Hearst and his friends are running the Republican party." Pennsylvania, it continued, would be crucial in the 1936 presidential campaign, and in 1940 Earle might well run for president himself. "The ownership of a leading paper of Philadelphia becomes, therefore," the *Nation* concluded, "a matter of national concern."[9] From every vantage point, it was clear that a donnybrook was brewing in the City of Brotherly Love.

Lost in that later furor was the fact that when he bought the paper, Moses was actually a Democrat. He had never registered as such because he had never been much of a party person and had taken few national political stands. He supported Hoover in 1928 after admiring the Republican's handling of war relief in Europe. Four years later, Hoover's inability to cope with the aftermath of the crash, Depression and a sharp increase in crime engendered by Prohibition sent Moses and millions of Americans across the aisle to the Democrats and Roosevelt.

Roosevelt had been in the White House barely four months when Moses sent him a breathless gush of a telegram. "The success which is crowning your efforts in the most difficult task since the reign of Washington and Lincoln is deserving of the highest appreciation that can be shown you by the American people. I was highly enthusiastic about your candidacy before your election, but what you have performed since your election is beyond my most sanguine expectation. Please count on us in all our printing plants for cooperation in raising the wages of our employees. We pray for your continued success and long life."[10]

Such effusiveness was out of character for Moses, yet his reaction to Roosevelt was not atypical. It reflected a broad sense of national relief with and gratitude for the president's quick action to get the country moving, shoring up banks, granting loans to avert foreclosures, passing relief and recovery legislation and establishing civil works programs to provide emergency jobs. From 1934 to 1936 in Miami, Moses remained an ardent Democrat who not only backed FDR but also published Eleanor Roosevelt's syndicated column in the *Tribune*.

When he announced in Philadelphia that the *Inquirer* would "continue to uphold the principles and policies of the Republican party," Moses the Democrat was not absolutely certain that it would. "However honorable or revered, he could not permit dead men's ideas to dominate the property," was how a 1939 authorized history of his *Inquirer* purchase described his attitude. For all his thrashing around in Miami, he was a political neophyte operating for the first time on a national political field and seeking his footing. For the time being, he was willing to give Roosevelt a chance to modify his first-term emergency measures and move to the right in a second term.

In November 1936 the *Inquirer* supported Republican challenger Alf Landon of Kansas. Moses, though, voted a second time for Roosevelt. So did Walter Annenberg and most of the rest of the country. "As Maine goes, so goes the nation," was the old political saw. In November, Roosevelt campaign chairman James Farley reworked the axiom to "As Maine goes, so goes Vermont," the only two states Landon carried. Roosevelt brought home the other forty-six states, 523 electoral votes and the most impregnable political mandate of any president. With more pressing priorities than politics, Moses settled into his third-floor office at the *Inquirer* to begin resuscitating his paper and establishing his own reputation as a great publisher.

He was thrilled with his new property. Arthur Brisbane was among the first to contact him after the purchase. The columnist was worried that his old business partner had erred badly by going into Philadelphia. The paper was at death's door and the competition with Stern was fraught. Moses would hear none of it.

"From your remarks about the *Philadelphia Inquirer* I am of the opinion that you are not sufficiently familiar with the situation. The *Inquirer* is a very fine property in its entirety with a wonderful record as to its past. Its equipment is second to none in the world, and in spite of what it had to suffer from the many changes and foreign ownership, it has coasted along practically without any captaincy for several years and yet under these conditions retained a circulation of 300,000 daily and in excess of 700,000 Sunday," he wrote Brisbane on August 13, 1936.

"From now on it can only get better. I do not fear any competition from anyone. We have first of all excellent merchandise to sell, and I also feel that I know quite a little about the paper business thanks to you and the Hearst organization where I received a most excellent college education that will serve me well should I encounter difficulties. I do not underestimate anyone including Stern and I earnestly hope he underestimates me."[11]

To keep Stern guessing, Moses never denied published reports that he had paid $15 million for the *Inquirer*. He took more delight in the repetition of rumors that he had paid the entire amount in cash carried to the hand-over in suitcases. In fact, he paid $1 million in cash — to ensure the Patenotres did not renege — borrowed another $3 million, mostly from the First National Bank of Chicago, and assumed $6.8 million in debt. But the more money he appeared to have, the more the cash-strapped Stern could worry. Stern fretted so much that he sued Annenberg as soon as he arrived in Philadelphia.

Stern charged that one of Moses's men told a newspaper distributor in Wilmington, Delaware, that because he was favoring the *Record* he should sell out or he would no longer be allowed to sell the *Inquirer*. The distributors in fact were favoring the *Record* because the *Inquirer*, incompetently run by the Patenotres, had allowed their distribution system to collapse. Moses, who understood circulation better than anyone, would not tolerate the *Record* being stacked on top of newsstands with the *Inquirer* always buried below, so he moved to establish his own system.

Stern reasoned rightly that if Moses controlled the distributors, he could destroy the *Record*'s circulation or force the *Record* to establish its own expensive distribution system. When Stern filed suit, his lawyer had a well-dressed process server infiltrate a reception Moses was hosting for local VIPs and serve the subpoena. "A fine welcome to Philadelphia," Moses snorted. "When I get off the train Dave Stern has me arrested."[12]

At the heated hearing, a handsome young lawyer named Richardson Dilworth represented Moses. An ex-marine with a distinguished record in the First World War which he would match in the Second,

Dilworth was all combat infantryman in the courtroom. He put up such a fight on Moses's behalf, interrupting the proceedings and the opposing counsel, that the judge repeatedly held him in contempt, time after time fining him one hundred dollars. At each outburst, Moses pulled out his billfold, which was stuffed with thousand- and hundred-dollar bills, calmly peeled one off and handed it to Dilworth to give the clerk.

"Stern didn't have a case, but the judge was a friend of his and terribly prejudiced against Annenberg," Dilworth later told Philadelphia journalist Peter Binzen, adding with a booming laugh, "Stern had given him this cartoon of Annenberg beating a crippled newsboy over the head with his own crutch. That judge believed everything Stern told him. He just hated old man Annenberg."[13]

Although he hated Moses — "he thought it was a tragedy old man Annenberg had come to Philadelphia and he wanted to drive him back to Chicago or Milwaukee," Dilworth said — the judge was fair and ruled that Moses had the right to establish his own distribution system. Moses was so pleased with the victory and Dilworth's truculence that he hired him as general counsel for the *Inquirer* at an annual retainer of $50,000. Years later, backed by the *Inquirer*, Dilworth became Philadelphia's combative district attorney and then its excellent mayor.

Stern next figured that Moses would try other strong-arm tactics. He hired a Chicago detective agency whose operatives, Stern said, could identify Moses's men who came to Philadelphia. He sent a reporting team to Chicago to write a series on the circulation wars. He phoned the White House and asked that FBI agents be sent to Philadelphia to guard against an onslaught of what he called "Chicago thugs." Governor Earle and Mayor Wilson assigned state and city police to protect the newsstands. Nothing happened. Moses had no intention of using muscle in Philadelphia. He was determined to have his paper circulated, but he approached the task as a serious publisher who knew that any such tactics would subvert his effort.

Moses spent millions on circulation promotion. Recalling methods he had used thirty years earlier, he ordered an army of subscription sellers into the streets and spent $25,000 a week on lavish premiums and such give-aways as watches and crystal bowls. A $4 subscription earned a $12 wall clock. He added a South Jersey edition to compete directly with Stern's *Courier-Post* and staffed an office in Camden with more reporters and photographers than Stern had. Soon he was cutting deeply into his rival's bottom line. "The steady earnings of the *Courier-Post* were cut in half. The *Record*'s net was reduced a third," Stern acknowledged. "I had counted on those earnings to offset the [*New York*] *Post*'s losses."[14]

In the *Inquirer* newsroom, there had been nothing but gloom before Moses arrived. The paper was dying, and if management dining on starched linen at the Union League did not understand that, the reporters and copyeditors eating sandwiches around the rim of the news desk did. The best writers had been drifting off since Elverson died. Less space was devoted to news as the Patenotres squeezed spending to bolster their weekly check to Paris. On Moses's second day as owner, he ordered that the paper go up four editorial pages, two each for news and features.

City editor Eli Zachary ("E. Z.") Dimitman was summoned to the publisher's office. There was no small talk. "Sit down," Moses ordered brusquely. "How many reporters and editors do you have?"

"About fifty," Dimitman replied.

"You need more?" Moses asked.

Dimitman paused. The edit staff was at its lowest level in a decade. Figuring he would be lucky to hire half of what he asked for, he said he could use six or eight more.

"Hire twenty," Moses snapped.

Back at his desk, Dimitman remembered what happened the last time he was given an order to increase staff, by Curtis-Martin. He had hired ten men and after six months was ordered to fire five as a cost-cutting measure. He fully expected the same to happen this time.

Moses left on a business trip to Chicago. When he returned in two weeks he immediately summoned Dimitman. "Did you get all twenty?"

The editor was nonplussed. "I got five, all topnotch men. They're either here or on their way," he reported.

Moses's eyes flashed, his face turned crimson and he began shouting. "Goddammit, I told you twenty. When I give you an order, you son of a bitch, I want it obeyed. I'm not paying you to second-guess me. It's time you people realize I mean exactly what I say. Now do as you were told."[15]

Instead of feeling chastised, Dimitman was elated. This proprietor said what he meant and meant what he said. E. Z. began hiring in earnest.

Next, Moses called a staff meeting. He was a businessman with plenty of money, but he wanted his editorial and business executives to understand that he had not bought the *Inquirer* merely as a financial proposition. Obviously, to be successful, any institution had to pay its own way. If it deserved support, it would succeed, he believed; otherwise, there should be no surprise when it failed. He was determined that the *Inquirer* succeed, but financial success was only one factor. He was a crusader at heart, as he had demonstrated in Miami, and more important to him than money at this stage was that the paper stand for something.

"A newspaper is not living up to its real power in a community unless it *does* something," he told the assembled editors. "A paper that isn't willing to stand up and fight for the rights and the happiness and health, the general welfare of the community which supports it, isn't worth printing, and it certainly isn't worth owning. I want the *Inquirer* to be the eyes and the voice and, if need be, the good hard fists of the citizens of Philadelphia and Pennsylvania."[16]

In that same meeting, Moses proposed that the paper drop its party label, go independent and support Roosevelt. The editors were horrified by the prospect, with only three months remaining in the presidential campaign, and they raised such a fuss that the publisher relented. Immediately after FDR's November landslide, however, Moses announced on the editorial page that the *Inquirer* would thereafter be politically independent. Having introduced the slogan "All the news without fear or favor" to the masthead of the *Miami Tribune*, he added a new motto below the *Inquirer* logo: "An independent newspaper for all the people." In a signed editorial he explained the change and his vision of the *Inquirer* as a vehicle for public service:

THE INQUIRER'S PLATFORM

To print the news accurately and fearlessly but never to be content with merely printing the news; to strive always to uphold the principles of our American democracy, to war relentlessly against alien 'isms,' to fight intolerance, to be the friend and defender of those who are persecuted and oppressed; to demand equal justice for employer and employed; to work for the advancement of industry in Delaware Valley and Pennsylvania; to oppose political hypocrisy and corruption; to fight and never cease fighting to maintain the sanctity of personal liberty and the inviolability of human rights.

They were not postcard maxims for Moses. This was his philosophy and just as he meant what he said when he gave Dimitman orders, he believed what he said when he articulated essential principles. The only problem was that he believed just as strongly in his right to do whatever he wanted, another indication of his capacity to compartmentalize his life. When his actual behavior veered from those ideals, a considerable distance on several occasions, Moses saw no ambiguity. Instead, like an avenging prophet, he would insist that his actions were entirely consistent with his philosophy. His tyrannizing of some politician or news or business competitor, he actually believed, was part of the good fight, in pursuit of a noble goal, certainly not intolerance on his part. He was far from the only newspaper proprietor who operated that way. William Randolph Hearst and Colonel Robert McCormick acted similarly on a larger scale. Each was a model for Moses, as Rupert Murdoch would have been had he been a contemporary.

There was also a jingoistic streak in Moses, who like so many first-generation immigrants considered America the land of opportunity for people willing to work hard. Having struggled and succeeded without outside help, he was a flag-waver in terms of U.S. core principles — as he interpreted them. As he became more involved with the *Inquirer* and politics, he no longer visited abroad, traveled infrequently to Chicago and even more rarely beyond. In replying to Brisbane, who was vacationing in France when he forwarded his concerns about the *Inquirer*, Moses urged the columnist to return soon to America, "the only land that is at all worthwhile."

In late 1936 and early 1937, Moses devoted himself to improving the *Inquirer*. He did not just monitor editorial policy, but plunged with enthusiasm into every area of the newspaper business. He rose before dawn to ride delivery trucks, timing traffic lights and making certain drivers were taking the shortest routes. Other days, *Inquirer* drivers would find him at 5 A.M. chatting with newsboys on a street corner and waiting to see if the paper arrived on time. He visited news kiosks around the city and suburbs and, without specifying, simply asked for a paper. If the seller handed him a *Record*, Moses paid the three cents and walked away. If he were given an *Inquirer*, Moses paid five dollars and told the seller to keep the change. Soon, all over the city, if a customer failed to specify, he or she was given an *Inquirer*.[17]

To boost Sunday circulation, then at about seven hundred thousand, Moses instructed Dimitman to produce a pre-date, an issue rarely produced now, but a popular Hearst novelty in the 1930s. Pre-dates were usually printed a week in advance and consisted of all the comics and features, plus a thin news section which included little news beyond recapitulations of old stories and analyses, or in the Hearst papers, a heavy infusion of stories with lots of sex and violence. Sent by train and truck across the country three to five days in advance of their street sale date, pre-dates were cheap to produce, good advertising revenue producers and circulation builders in that they were distributed far afield almost magically on the date they were officially published.

When Moses asked Dimitman on a Wednesday to produce a pre-date, the city editor had no idea where to start. He'd heard of them, but had never seen one. He scrambled to find Hearst samples in Boston and New York, collected them by Friday and discussed with several editors how to adapt the Hearst crime-and-sex formula to Philadelphia. Dimitman thought he would have a month to plan and produce the first issue until Moses came by his desk that afternoon.

"Do you have my proofs?" he asked.

"What proofs?" Dimitman responded.

"The pre-date," said Moses. "We go to press Monday."

Stalling, the city editor said he would set the pages Sunday when news was slow and the composing room available. He would give him the proofs on Monday. Moses said okay and left. Dimitman moved a desk into a corner, grabbed three of his best reporters and spent the weekend laying out and writing the first pre-date. On Monday the proofs were on Moses's desk. "Never a dull moment with Annenberg, eh?" the owner said, grinning at his editor.

The "jack rabbit" edition, as Moses named it, ran until newsprint shortages during World War Two forced its elimination. At its peak, some three hundred thousand copies of the edition were sold weekly in nearly every state, Canada and Alaska. That pushed total Sunday circulation to more than one million and along with it the newspaper's rate base, which sharply increased advertising revenues.[18]

Popping into story conferences and generating ideas was another favorite Moses tactic.

"Do you know how much pawnbrokers charge those poor unfortunates who have to patronize them around this town?" he asked Dimitman one day.

"No idea," the city editor replied.

"Well, I do know and it's at least sixty percent a year," said the publisher. He began describing how Philadelphia's poorest and neediest families were pawning whatever they owned, even their clothes, to pay rent or buy food and were then forced to pay usurious rates to redeem their collateral. "He was a master at painting a verbal picture and all but had his editors in tears," said Dimitman.

Illinois, where Cecelia was based, had laws limiting the amount of interest a pawnbroker could charge. Moses believed it could serve as a model for Pennsylvania, where pawnshops charged up to 276 percent annual interest, sold unclaimed pledges without notification and returned nothing to their customers. "Pawnbrokers are mean, cold-hearted bastards. They'll take advantage of any poor son of a bitch who doesn't know any better. I want you to do something about it. Get the word out and change the legislation."

He suggested an illustration for the first crusading story. He wanted a photo of a tired, elderly woman, hands scarred from over-work, dressed in black with a skirt down to her shoes, wrapped in a black shawl. The picture had to be taken in front of a pawnshop with three gold balls over the woman's head and the word "pawnbroker" visible in the window behind her in case some readers failed to com-prehend that the balls symbolized the pawn trade. The next day the photographer returned with precisely the image Moses requested, the campaign was launched, the evils were exposed, reform plans were proposed and blame was laid at the feet of Governor Earle.

Earle actually endorsed the *Inquirer*'s suggested bill and after a fight with the pawnbrokers' lobby, the legislation passed unanimously and limited rates to betweeen 12 and 24 percent. While the campaign was a populist victory for the *Inquirer*, it was also Moses's first statewide crusade. Significantly, he had been unable to resist bashing the state's ranking Democrat even though Earle had been on his side, a poor augury for more serious future battles and a reminder that Moses had an uncanny instinct for alienating his friends.

Soon he was pushing for all sorts of populist legislative adjust-ments. The first autumn he lived in Philadelphia he discovered that the state's restrictive blue laws, which forbade shopping or frequenting bars on Sundays, also prohibited residents from fishing. He had no dis-pute with what he called the Sabbatarians, but, a fishing addict him-self, he was indignant that a man who worked what was then a regular five-and-a-half-day week, could not relax with a rod and reel on his one full day off. His attitude echoed his feelings about offtrack betting. Not everyone who liked to wager on a horse could get to a track; not everyone who liked to fish could get to a lake Monday through Saturday. He was looking out for the little person. A series with photos of unhappy men with tackle and unfished-in lakes ran and the legislature amended the law to allow deprived anglers to enjoy their Sundays.

When on his first Fourth of July in Philadelphia he read the *Inquirer* story about the worst casualties in a decade from fireworks — three children killed, several blinded and others mutilated or injured — he smashed the desk with his fist. "I'm going to stop that." The *Inquirer* launched a successful campaign to ban the indiscriminate sale of fireworks. A year later the perennial story reported one minor injury statewide. "That's more like it," he said, wagging the copy under Dimitman's nose.

At the *Miami Tribune*, he had initiated a program in which the paper awarded $50 to the policeman of the week, and $100 to the one selected officer of the month. Critics claimed that the program was thinly disguised bribery, but Moses scoffed at the charge, and after watching Philadelphia policemen directing traffic in a snowstorm instituted the *Inquirer* hero awards. Each month at a public ceremony, the *Inquirer* gave a medal and $200 to the police officer, fireman or park guard whom a nonpartisan committee determined had performed the most meritorious service during the previous month. Dependents of any city guardian who died on the job were given $1,000. In the program's first five years, $19,200 was passed out to award winners and an additional $22,000 to dependents.

Moses's employees had been terrified of him when he arrived. He was tough, brusque, crude around men and his occasional flashes of vicious temper were monumental. Yet over time, they became devoted to him because Moses also had tremendous talent, an earthy charm, a readiness to mix with staff and call everyone by name and because he had such love for the paper. "He was hearty, with a good sense of humor," said Shirley Katzander, who was hired as a reporter at nineteen. "He came in, never without a coat and tie, and when he walked through the newsroom, he showed a true interest in people. There was a great kindness to him. To me he was no demon, but absolutely adorable."[19] There was also a palpable sense of an electric current coursing through the building when he was around, an energy easily felt by anyone who came upon him.

"Annenberg hurried in, his head extended forward from his shoulders, walking as a man pursuing a purpose always slightly ahead of him," was how Sunday magazine editor Emile Gavreau described their first meeting. "He was eating oranges and flung the skins over his shoulder as though they were discarded projects whose substance he had devoured. He had a lantern-jawed face whose lines somehow reminded me of the smart horses which had made him a millionaire, but here the resemblance stopped. His features had a mixture of jovial brutality and rapid perception. He was tall, rangy, with the nervousness of a gray wolf and during business hours wore the alpaca coat which drapes the individual behind the counter of a pawnshop. . . . [He] held me with a cold and fascinating glance. There was a sinister suggestion of strength and rapaciousness in his thin frame. His humid eyes, rather close together, seemed to darken from a grayish color and mingled cunning and suspicion behind their penetration."[20]

Moses came to the newsroom every midafternoon to discuss the next day's paper. But he also often restlessly walked the halls with a long, loping stride. "Keep your eye on the ball," he would holler, passing some editors. At lunch, he rarely ate out or in his office, but sat alongside his editors at the round central table in the cafeteria. "Eating with the common people," he called it without a hint of condescension. He'd tell stories about Brisbane, how he had read his column aloud for years to his children and how Brisbane had introduced him to Spinoza. "He's got something on the ball," Moses observed of the seventeenth-century Dutch philosopher and pantheist who held that God is nature, a concept which the supremely pragmatic Moses spent little time exploring. "But he spends too much time watching the bases instead of throwing to home plate."

Subeditors were in the habit during the Patenotre period of hanging red tags on desk lamps saying, "Please turn off when not in use." Moses took the opposite tack. When an underling suggested that an idea was expensive, the publisher generally snapped, "It's my money, isn't it?"

A paternalist in every sense of the word, he gave management advice to young editors. He told one editor to watch out for his assistant. When the editor asked why, Moses explained that when he called, the assistant told him the editor was not there.

"But I wasn't," the editor exclaimed.

"Yeah, but he shouldn't have told *me* that," said Moses.[21]

The publisher handed out cash for food to reporters and editors working late hours. He approached staffers with new babies and described the joys of family life, handing over one or two hundred-dollar bills before moving on. He took flowers to the hospital on a Sunday for one ailing secretary, discovered she had no radio to occupy her, found a shopkeeper who would open his store and returned with the radio. Editors were invited to Sunnylands in the Poconos to fish and ride.[22]

After work, instead of returning to his suite at the Warwick Hotel, he and Dimitman frequently rounded up as many as a dozen pretty stenographers or women from the advertising department to join them at one of his favorite hangouts, "Benny the Bum's," where he slipped the orchestra leader ten dollars to play "A Bird in a Gilded Cage," a popular hit in 1900. In the midst of the raucous bonhomie, he listened quietly, his eyes often tearing up until he caught himself, laughed and ordered the song played again.[23] When Benny's closed, Moses often hung around, flirted with the girls and played the piano.

Walter, who was vice president of the *Inquirer* and sat at the desk next to his father, came along on occasion but never felt comfortable at Benny's or any of his father's watering holes. Walter was twenty-eight when he and his father moved to Philadelphia, but he seemed much younger and was completely overshadowed. Moses was rough-hewn, outspoken, confident and exuded power. Walter was shy, hesitant and prudish.

"There was a sense of weakness to Walter," said Shirley Katzander. "He never seemed to assert himself."[24] Marion Hoeflich, Moses's secretary who married editor E. Z. Dimitman, said that "Walter was the apple of M. L.'s eye, but he didn't look very promising. If he asked Walter a question and Walter didn't know the answer, M. L. would just lay him out, right then and there. He'd yell at him and say, 'If you don't know what you're talking about, don't say anything.' It was sad to watch, but he was trying to get Walter to straighten up and fly straight."[25]

"Walter adored his father," Richardson Dilworth confirmed. "He really adored him and yet the old man treated him just like dirt. But he always wanted him around. If Walter spoke up, the old man said, 'You don't know your ass from third base, shut up,' that kind of stuff."[26]

In later life, Walter insisted that his father was wonderful to him, conceding only that "my father could be firm" because he, Walter, needed it. Moses was not wonderful, but Walter preferred to blame himself rather than his father because he was all too mindful of his own deficiencies: he could not speak properly, he had an imperfect ear and he seemed to know so little. Neither physical problem was his fault, but each understandably upset him. There is no evidence, even in the most impulsive fit of pique, that Moses ever criticized his son about his physical disabilities.

Walter also blamed himself for dropping out of Penn. He felt guilty about his father rescuing him from the stock market and about not having a real job where he could learn the business ropes. He had also been indulged and cosseted by his mother and elder sisters, who asked nothing of him. And it was not as if his father beat him or sent him away. He belittled him. Enid, the fourth daughter and Walter's immediate elder sibling, tried to explain to her brother what she saw happening. "We must remember that our dear Papa is not one to hand out roses," she wrote. "Being of the German school he could not let praise pass his lips too often."[27] Walter concluded that he was only getting what he deserved. "I wasn't worth a damn in those years," he explained later. "I was pretty much a playboy and didn't amount to much until I was about thirty."[28]

Although there was tension in the father-son relationship, Moses was at least devoting a lot of time to Walter. The women in the family he ignored. They were Sadie's responsibility. He did not care whom they married nor did he show any concern when their marriages broke up. When Evelyn eloped as a teenager, she expected her father to be upset, angry or both, but Moses did not seem to care at all. He merely instructed Sadie to accompany the girl on her honeymoon, which she dutifully did.

As modeling clay, the girls did not interest him. Aye, the eldest, was considered the smartest child even before she finished university. She wrote her father business suggestions, giving him advice on expanding franchises, and evaluated his employees. Aye wanted to be molded, yet Moses never gave a hint that he took her seriously. The only child he wanted to develop was Walter. He wanted to make him into a better Moses.

He gave Walter what he, Moses, lacked: style, polish, formal education, social acceptance, and a newspaper with a pedigree. Walter did not comprehend at first what was happening because he was adrift. On the one side he had the unconditional love of a mother whose support could not be driven away; on the other, a father whose yelling compensated for his overindulgence, but whom Walter could never please because he could never be a complete extension of Moses. The love and warmth he had inherited from Sadie ensured that distinct and dueling personality traits would eventually be manifest in Walter: qual-

ities of fierce independence, business toughness, and his own erup-
tions of temper — based on stuttering frustrations, paternal genetics
and spoiled-child syndrome — combined with extraordinary kindness
and generosity.

In their early days together at the *Inquirer,* Walter was wrestling
with another problem that caused him much more anguish than his
father's "firmness." Soon after moving to Philadelphia, Moses installed
a live-in girlfriend named Gertrude Boze in his suite at the Warwick
Hotel. A beautiful young woman with softly curled blonde hair, Trudy
Boze first surfaced in 1935 on the payroll of the *Daily Racing Form.* She
was listed as Moses's secretary and paid $150 a week, about four times
the going rate.

When government prosecutors later investigated Moses, they
alleged that she did no work. That was untrue. Trudy was his mistress,
but she was also his personal secretary. She traveled everywhere with
Moses after 1936, including the sleeper next to his on the overnight
train to Cecelia headquarters in Chicago. She was on constant call, she
said with a straight face to one investigator, in case anything came up.
When she approved accounts from the Warwick Hotel, bills from merchants or paperwork from the Cecelia office, she signed "Mr. G. Boze,"
so as not to reveal her gender.

Sadie Annenberg and the girls were distraught about the affair. It is
unclear whether it started before Moses left Miami, but as a result,
Sadie neither moved to nor visited Philadelphia, choosing instead to
live in New York. "It distressed my mother because she was very
devoted to my father," said Walter. Sadie did not discuss the situation
with anyone. "Mother was just stoic about it," he added.[29] There was
never any question of divorce or of Moses cutting down his hugely
generous support of the family, nor even evidence of sharp friction
between Sadie and Moses. On the contrary, they regularly exchanged
loving letters.

"First, I want to acknowledge your sweet note received today," he
wrote to "My dear Wife" in December 1936, "and to tell you how
much I miss you and how much I regret not having been able to be
with you and the family as much as I should have liked to have been.
However, you should know that you and the children are constantly on
my mind and in my thoughts and that I feel that the only thing I have
to live for is the happiness of my family."[30]

Such letters, typed by his secretary, offered little comfort to the
daughters, who felt crushed by their father's betrayal. "My mother was

so good and kind and understanding that she probably realized that if you have nine children, you're not as attractive sexually," said Evelyn Annenberg Hall. "I loved my father, but when we were aware of that girl, I didn't like him anymore. I was not so much angry as I was disappointed in him as a person."[31] A half century later, Evelyn blamed "that woman," meaning Trudy, for her father's problems with the government.

Walter was more conflicted than his sisters because he worked with his father every day, saw Trudy at the Warwick and also agonized over his mother's pain. Unlike his father, who only went to New York every few months, Walter shuttled almost constantly between Philadelphia and New York to spend as much time as possible with Sadie, whom he respected as much as he cherished. They did not talk about Trudy or Moses's other infidelities. "Even with Trudy living in, the old son of a gun had a wandering eye," said Marion Dimitman, his secretary at the *Inquirer*. "And he was good at it; M. L. could charm you right out of the trees."[32]

Although he lived in a separate suite, Walter grew uncomfortable staying in the same hotel with his father because it made him feel like a traitor to his mother. "It was very hard for Walter, who adored both his parents, living down the hall from his old man with the babes around," said Richardson Dilworth.[33]

Walter finally moved out and into an elegant apartment in the Rittenhouse Plaza on Rittenhouse Square, the most glamorous of the five original city parks laid out by William Penn and Philadelphia's best address. He was living the life of a gentleman bachelor in rooms decorated by society interior designer Terrence Robsjohn-Gibbings. Drapes and fabrics were handmade in shades of beige and pink. The library walls were bleached teak; the carpet, celadon green. In the living room, the books in sight were out of reach near the ceiling and bound in colored linen to blend with the beige walls. Quality always mattered to Walter.

Moses wanted quality for his family. For his readers, he wanted action. The difference in priorities was obvious when Moses brought in Emile Gavreau from the Hearst organization, where he had been a top editor on the *New York Mirror* until Hearst fired him for writing a book that he felt cast the Soviet Union in too positive a light. Moses had state-of-the-art gravure color presses, and Gavreau's assignment was to redesign the *Inquirer*'s Sunday magazine, called *Picture Parade*, to help boost Sunday circulation to one million.

Tobias Annenberg with five of his eleven children soon after they were reunited in 1885 after emigrating from Kalvishken in East Prussia. Jacob stands behind his father. Moses is between his knees, and Max is seated to the right. (ANNENBERG FAMILY COLLECTION)

On August 20, 1899, twenty-two-year-old Moses—dark, wiry and bony—married Sadie Friedman, the kind, round, creamy-complexioned twenty-year-old daughter of a Chicago shoe and boot merchant. (ANNENBERG FAMILY COLLECTION)

Sadie and Moses had eight
daughters. Their only son,
Walter, was born in Milwaukee
in 1908 on Friday the 13th of
March. (ANNENBERG FAMILY
COLLECTION)

Through 1917,
Sadie, the girls and
"Boy" looked for-
ward to vacationing
at Paw Paw Lake
in Michigan.
(ANNENBERG FAMILY
COLLECTION)

In Milwaukee, the family grew, prospered and enjoyed more luxuries, including private schools and summer camp, where Walter learned to ride. (ANNENBERG FAMILY COLLECTION)

Moses was broke in 1906 when he came to Milwaukee, but by 1914, he was on his way to earning $1 million and dressed his family accordingly. (ANNENBERG FAMILY COLLECTION)

Moses sold William Randolph Hearst's *Chicago American* on the streets of Chicago at the turn of the century. Twenty years later, Moses was living in Milwaukee when Hearst (left) hired him to be national circulation director for all his publications. Famed Hearst columnist Arthur Brisbane (right) became a good friend, business partner and role model for Moses. (AP/WIDE WORLD)

In 1920, the Annenbergs bought a 36-acre estate at Kings Point, Long Island, from Broadway musician and showman George M. Cohan. (ANNENBERG FAMILY COLLECTION)

His sisters called him Beezie Binks when Walter turned fourteen and began wearing his first pair of long pants. (ANNENBERG FAMILY COLLECTION)

Hearst columnist and editor Arthur Brisbane thought Walter could more easily enter New Jersey's Peddie School as a Baptist. (ANNENBERG FAMILY COLLECTION)

In 1923, when Walter was fifteen,
Moses took the family to Europe,
visiting Kalvishken and tonier spots,
such as Berlin's Tiergarten.

Walter spent five of his
happiest years at Peddie,
where he graduated in 1927
and was voted the senior
class "best businessman."

Moses called him Walter, but he was always "Boy" to his mother and sisters. Middle row: Lita, Sadie, Esther, Jan, Enid, Polly. Front row: Harriet and Evelyn. (ANNENBERG FAMILY COLLECTION)

Taut, lean and bursting with energy, Moses also liked quiet time to read, listen to classical music or relax with his dog. (ANNENBERG FAMILY COLLECTION)

Although racing information made him a multimillionaire, Moses rarely wagered and had little interest in the sport, but he liked to ride, especially in the Poconos, and was a good horseman. (ANNENBERG FAMILY COLLECTION)

From the age of six, when he had to catch the family's supper in Kalvishken, fishing was Moses's favorite hobby, but only in lakes, not the sea, and preferably at the original Sunnylands, his retreat in the Poconos. (ANNENBERG FAMILY COLLECTION)

Always a snappy dresser, Walter was more a dandy in his twenties, even at his father's 2,000-acre Ranch A (for Annenberg) in Wyoming. (ANNENBERG FAMILY COLLECTION)

In the early 1930s, Moses bought Casa d'Oro, a palatial oceanfront estate on Miami Beach's Millionaires' Row, home to the rental car magnate J. D. Hertz and the tire manufacturer Harvey Firestone. (ANNENBERG FAMILY COLLECTION)

Bookie-parlor bettors pore over run-down sheets offering the latest information on horses, jockeys and track conditions. (UPI/CORBIS-BETTMANN)

At the *Miami Tribune* in 1934–35, Walter wrote a gossip
column titled "Boy About Town," which mimicked—down
to the tri-dot ellipsis between items—the style of . . .
(ANNENBERG FAMILY COLLECTION)

Walter Winchell (right), whose column "Man About Town" was a fixture
in U.S. papers, including the *Miami Tribune*, which Moses had established to
put distance between himself and the Nationwide wire.
(UPI/CORBIS-BETTMANN)

Moses and Walter often disagreed about the contents of the *Inquirer*'s Sunday magazine. Father wanted photos of actresses in lingerie and cannibal reptiles in action; son pushed for Audubon's birds and waterfalls. (W. EUGENE SMITH/ BLACK STAR. TIME INC. PICTURE COLLECTION)

Indicted with Moses and Walter in 1939 were Arnold Kruse (left), Cecelia's chief accountant, and bookkeeper Joseph Hafner (right), neither of whom had any formal financial training. (AP/WIDE WORLD)

U.S. District Attorney William Campbell had never litigated a case and was expected to follow orders when tapped by the White House to prosecute Moses Annenberg for tax evasion. (CORBIS-BETTMANN)

Moses mistakenly believed the political connections of his lawyer Weymouth Kirkland (center, in hat and glasses) would help him evade jail; he was unaware that President Franklin Roosevelt wanted him out of circulation. (AP/WIDE WORLD)

In 1938, Walter married Veronica Dunkelman, an Ava Gardner look-alike from Toronto. Her father was a prominent men's clothier, her mother, a Zionist activist, and her brother, an Israeli war hero. (ANNENBERG FAMILY COLLECTION)

Walter Hubert Annenberg was so eager for a son when Ronny first gave birth, in July 1939, that he named their daughter Wallis Huberta. (ANNENBERG FAMILY COLLECTION)

As the children grew and needed more room, Walter and Ronny moved from a Rittenhouse Square apartment to a 14-acre estate they called Inwood on the Main Line in Wynnewood, Pennsylvania. (ANNENBERG FAMILY COLLECTION)

Disappointed that his partial deafness made him unfit for military service, Walter was eager to see Europe after World War II. In 1946, he spent nine weeks visiting battlefields, Berlin and Dachau and covering a Paris peace parley, where he learned to dislike French leader Charles de Gaulle. (ANNENBERG FAMILY COLLECTION)

Ronny and Walter were together for nearly a dozen of his most difficult years, spanning Moses's trial and imprisonment and Walter's efforts to pay the $9.5 million federal fine and save the family empire. (AP/WIDE WORLD)

"Moe had definite ideas about the physiognomy of his new tabloid," said Gavreau, which included "blasting his way into a new field ... a path to the inarticulates of the primitive and the abysmal, the only way to bag a million readers quickly." But when Moses explained his plan, Walter was "timorous, almost fearful" about the effect it might have on traditional *Inquirer* readers. "His father silenced him. 'We're not going to do anything raw, and we can tone it down when we get the million.'"[34]

On occasion, Walter had his way about the photos selected, "but more often," said Gavreau, "his father roared his disapproval." For the first issue, Walter wanted a pictorial series on the world's biggest waterfalls, a color photo of the Taj Mahal, a spread on Audubon's *Birds of America*, and two color pages of glazed fruit in crystal and silver bowls as served in the Warwick dining room. "Audubon," Moses hollered. "What the hell did he ever do for circulation? And pictures of food, with millions starving! Do you want to start a revolution?"

Instead, Moses ordered a two-page photo series on the ritual slaughter of a cow by a rabbi, tracing the kosher ritual from the first incision of the shiny blade of the *cholof*. Only after he saw the proofs of the bloody ceremony and considered the impact on breakfast readers did he agree to print the photos in sepia instead of color. Another page was devoted to a Zulu wedding in which the happy warrior married his bride by standing her against a tree and ceremoniously knocking her teeth out with his fist to display his love. There were features on cremation ceremonies in India, German students dueling and a hypnotized man's cheeks being pierced by long pins. Nature lovers had a page called "Murderers in the Animal World," which featured a horned viper devouring a rat. Voyeurs were well served: actress Alice Faye swanned about in lingerie; ten photos were devoted to "The Psychology of the Peeping Tom," while "A Day in the Life of an Advertising Model" naturally included photos of her morning shower.

Moses was ecstatic. "There's not a monotonous page in the whole damn book," he exulted. "The hell with monotony! If we don't go over a million with this, I'll kiss my brother Max in Macy's window."[35]

Moses loved putting his personal touch on issues devoted to national holidays. He rejected Thanksgiving photos of families gathered around a dining table in favor of a farmer with an axe chasing a turkey through the woods, chopping off the bird's head in the final panel. For women readers and ogling males, he added two pages on "The run-in-the-stocking bugaboo, and how to prevent it." At Christmas, Walter managed to get in two pages on the "Adoration of the

Magi," at Christ's birth, but Moses turned to Gavreau for what he wanted: "Cannibalism among Reptiles," "the Night Stranglers of Paris," and fourteen pictures featuring "Hollywood's Longest Kiss."

Walter caught on, but he was not willing to pander to readers. Instead he looked for stories with which he was comfortable and which might also have mass appeal. Stories about wealth fit that bill. He liked a feature on millionaires who spent $30,000 a year commuting to Wall Street in $60,000 planes flown by $1-an-hour pilots. He promoted another series on the homes and fortunes of India's maharajahs, whose annual incomes he could rattle off like multiplication tables. The first pictorial ran on the Nizam of Hyderabad, whose annual income was barely under $33 million. "Jesus," said Walter. "Have you figured out what that comes to a day? That's what I call money."

With *Picture Parade* pushing Sunday circulation past the magic million mark, Moses had another profit-making brainstorm. His editors said he looked like a kid in a toy store the night before Christmas as he wandered through the *Inquirer* building, stopping and pledging them to secrecy and explaining his idea for *Click*. His notion was to cannibalize *Picture Parade*, which ran 32 pages a week or 128 pages a month by taking 64 of the best pages, putting on a fresh cover and sell it as a national picture magazine to compete with *Life* and *Look* and the dozen or so other photo magazines.

By the second issue, *Click* circulation was up to a staggering 1.6 million on a formula of Hollywood actresses Bette Davis and Hedy Lamarr and public service features explaining what a woman should do when in danger of being raped: "Keep calm, don't run, but scream whenever you can," was the final admonition in the three-page article.

Emboldened, Moses pushed to break the two-million circulation barrier by incorporating more sensationalism. He offered $50,000 for picture ideas. His own was to show the birth of a child by cesarean section. Gavreau thought Moses had lost touch with reality. He showed a film of the operation in his office. Walter emerged looking sick to his stomach and Moses changed his mind. "I guess the public wouldn't stand for it," he said.[36]

Moralists in the public were not standing for much in *Click*. Not when a typical cartoon showed a freshly divorced woman in Nevada saying, "Boy, do I feel like a new man." Articles like "A Bellboy Learns about Life," in which the bellboy was helping a woman bathe, created a storm of protest across the nation. Canada banned the magazine, and made it a crime to send it through the mail. The Catholic Church blacklisted *Click*, which was then targeted by the National League of Decency. Walter wanted to kill the magazine. Moses saw that he had a crisis on his hands and ordered Gavreau to tone it down. The editor in turn gave the publication a sturdy, patriotic look. There were illustrations by James Montgomery Flagg, who designed popular military posters during the First World War, and stories on Nazi Bund camps, the evils of the communist movement in the United States, and when Lindbergh accepted a Nazi decoration, an article denouncing his politics. Circulation dropped by half, but after delicate and diplomatic negotiations, the Catholic Church and the Canadian government withdrew their objections.[37]

Despite the troubles with *Click*, Moses's efforts to boost sales of the *Inquirer* were a rousing success. By the end of October 1937, only fifteen months after he bought the newspaper, circulation of the daily had climbed from 288,000 to 367,763. Circulation at David Stern's daily *Record* dropped during the same period from 314,544 to 274,815. On Sundays, the *Record* had climbed from 384,000 to 404,083, but the *Inquirer* had truly taken off, rocketing from 690,000 to 1,052,625.[38]

Increased revenues brought increased spending. More pages were added for news. More stories were covered; more staff hired. Promotions continued. Moses continued to pack the paper with comics, which he had learned from Hearst were sure-fire circulation builders in the pre-television era. At the one-year mark, the daily contained fifty comics. The Sunday edition carried one hundred comic strips, "more than any newspaper on earth," the *Inquirer* trumpeted on the first page of the section, where the number 100 was printed in three-inch-high black type.

Across the street at the *Record*, Dave Stern was feeling the pinch. The *Evening Bulletin* was the biggest paper in Philadelphia, but Moses and the *Inquirer* were the masters of the morning. Stern was vanquished and Moses, secure in his victory and feeling muscular, began to consider Stern and his *Record* as trivial and irrelevant. When Stern felt so strapped in 1938 that he advised the *Inquirer* and the *Bulletin* that he planned to raise the price of his daily to three cents from the two cents each of the papers charged, Moses agreed to go along. His executives were astonished. If the *Inquirer* stayed at two cents, no one would buy the *Record*. "We could not understand," said Dimitman. "It was providing a rest period to an opponent who had been knocked groggy but not out."[39]

Over the protests of his editors and business team, Moses offered an ill-considered rationale. "Stern is a whipped puppy," he said. "He cannot do us any harm now. We can knock him out anytime we wish. He might go broke if he doesn't get this added revenue, then we might get a real competitor, one with greater strength and more money than Stern. Let him have the extra revenue and piddle along."[40]

That was the voice of a contemptuous, disdainful Moses who looked at Stern the way Joe Louis might have considered a flyweight climbing into his ring. In his increasing arrogance, though, Moses made a serious error. Had he analyzed the situation better, he might have realized that there was no more dangerous competitor for him than a cornered David Stern. The foremost publishing advocate in the nation for Roosevelt and the New Deal, the liberal publisher had friends in the highest places whom he was not reluctant to call on for help. Democrats in Pennsylvania and in the White House were ready to respond because their political problems with Moses were suddenly bigger than Stern's circulation and financial woes. The immediate cause was the *Inquirer*'s decision to oppose the New Deal. Once that happened, the interests of the White House and of Stern blended better than the decor in Walter's apartment.

12

DONNYBROOK

————

M OSES HAD A BRAINSTORM. The *Inquirer* would run two pages of photographs of the nation's leading political bosses accompanied by critical biographical profiles. "It will look like a rogue's gallery," he bellowed. "Let's show the country who these bruisers are." Walter paled when he heard the plan, the political equivalent of publishing the cesarean birth photos in *Click*, and ran into editor Gavreau's office. "For God's sake, forget it. It's dynamite," he said. "I'll get my father to change his mind." Walter succeeded that time, but failed when Moses's next inspiration was to have the *Inquirer* print the least flattering photos available of President Roosevelt's closest cabinet advisers under the headline "The New Deal Handpicked Eleven That Dishes It Out but Never Takes It."[1]

With the *Inquirer* a financial and journalistic success, Moses was eager to plunge headlong into politics. The impulse was legitimate. Many conservatives in business and industry broke with the Democrats long before Moses. Indeed, a large number were never with FDR at all. In their complaints that Roosevelt was a "traitor to his class," there was a whining tone which implied their fear of a loss of status. There were military officers in uniform who refused to toast the president. There was poisonous gossip about the president and Eleanor and anti-Roosevelt calumny about That Man, That Fellow who was living off his mother's income and trying to destroy the American way of life. Moses, for whom assimilation — but not class — was important, never shared those objections. He did not get personal because his disagreement was over policy.

He had not actively opposed the 1936 second-term election of Franklin Roosevelt because he believed that the shock therapy in the New Deal programs was necessary to get the country back on its feet. In June 1937, however, he joined conservatives in business and finance who maintained that the New Deal and what they termed its "left-wing, power-mad bureaucrats" were creating a collectivist leviathan that was destroying the principles of individual initiative and local responsibility on which the United States was founded. According to historian Samuel Eliot Morison, "Soon it began to be whispered, then written, then shouted that the Roosevelt administration was becoming totalitarian, assimilating American policy to that of Hitler or Stalin."[2]

Moses's criticism would become more strident later, but initially he had several specific complaints. He was disappointed by the departure from the administration of FDR's more conservative first-term aides Lewis Douglas, Dean Acheson and Raymond Moley and by what he called the president's "deliberate choice of his closest personal advisers from among the leftist zealots," including Harry Hopkins, head of the Works Progress Administration, labor secretary Frances Perkins, agriculture secretary Henry Wallace, as well as Henry Morgenthau and Harold Ickes.

He strongly opposed Roosevelt's 1937 effort to "pack" the Supreme Court. The president, who had not had an opening to appoint a justice, was enraged when the "nine old men," as he called them, repeatedly struck down major pieces of New Deal legislation. Roosevelt's proposal to add as many as six justices and thus infuse the bench with new blood rocked the country before it was abandoned in mid-1937. The publisher believed that the president had lost his constitutional mind.

What angered Moses most was the strike-ridden labor situation around the country. In 1935, impatient with the leadership of American Federation of Labor (AFL) president Sam Gompers, the Congress of Industrial Organizations (CIO) seceded and chose to be led by John L. Lewis, the dynamic head of the United Mine Workers. Within two years, CIO membership had grown to 4 million workers. Reveling in his victory, the pugnacious Lewis called a long series of sit-down strikes in which workers took over company premises, not to improve benefits, but to secure the CIO's exclusive rights to represent them in collective bargaining. Rampant violence erupted and in Chicago ten people were killed at a Republic Steel plant.[3]

Convinced that the Roosevelt administration was appeasing strikers and at its core was antibusiness, Moses laced into the administration in a two-page editorial. He had a few positive things to say about FDR: "Consider his inheritance. He faced an unprecedented industrial and financial depression. Industries suspended. Bankruptcies innumerable. Banks closing their doors in the faces of frantic depositors. Security values shattered. . . . Give Mr. Roosevelt credit. He took off his coat and pitched in to do the job."

On the other hand, the editorial went on, "never before in the history of this country has there been anything to compare with the widespread, concerted flouting of law and order that we see today. Never before has class hatred been elevated to the status of an unctuous virtue. . . . It is the outstanding tragedy of our time that over against his record of accomplishment there must stand the irrefutable fact that when the country was on the verge of anarchy and the greatest of all his opportunities — the opportunity to save the nation from so grave a crisis — met him face to face, he turned aside and passed it by!"[4]

In months to come, the *Inquirer* kept up the barrage under such headlines as "The War Against Business Goes On" and "No Room for Fascism in a Democracy." "Government, by swinging its mailed fist at business, has not brought lasting recovery," the paper said in December 1937 in an editorial which endorsed efforts to curb monopolies but not competitive businesses. "Under its [government's] stern restrictions and oppressive taxes, millions of employables have failed to obtain work."[5]

The following day, the newspaper was back blasting the Roosevelt administration for "rising to superlative heights of vituperation and abuse to plaster all the blame on business and industry." Moses believed in naming names, so a personal element was introduced to the fight. "Jackson, Ickes, Wallace and the rest ought to conserve their breath long enough to realize that while it is unquestionably true that price fixing by industry wrongly puts many businesses at a disadvantage, price fixing by government and attempts by government to run all industry and all agriculture are ruinous."[6]

The president's message to congress in early January 1938 "indicates not the slightest retreat from a program and an economic philosophy which have signally failed, in five years of drastic and costly experiments, to establish the United States on a sound recovery footing."[7]

Having first criticized the national administration, Moses next decided to take on Pennsylvania's "Little New Deal." He attacked governor George Earle for being a pawn of the New Dealers, for raising state income taxes that drove industry out of Pennsylvania, for failing to stand up to labor's demands and "for closing the Johnstown steel mills to prevent men who wanted to work from working." The only way to effect a political swing to the right, Moses then concluded, was through the 1938 midterm congressional and state-wide elections. "As far as Pennsylvania was concerned," wrote Dimitman, "he felt that those who had the power to make their convictions effective should enter the battle with bugles shrilling."[8]

Moses brandished his bugle that January by publicly endorsing a former lieutenant governor and obscure superior court judge named Arthur James as the Republican candidate for governor. Throughout the contest, editor Dimitman acknowledged, "every ounce of the *Inquirer*'s influence was thrown into the campaign on his behalf."[9] James was a small man with shrewd eyes who had been a water boy in the coal mines and was happy to hitch his ambitions to those of the *Inquirer*'s publisher.

Moses, who understood promotion as well as circulation, was the only one who saw a parallel between the judge's rise and that of Abraham Lincoln. In an example of his internal contradictions — preaching the virtues of independent journalism while manipulating coverage for his personal ends — he instructed his editors to go all out to include any homespun similarities in a major Sunday magazine profile introducing James. *Inquirer* reporters found his old mining lamp and a photo from the rear of a group of boys picking coal which James's publicity manager assured them was Arthur at age twelve and another picture of him as Kiwanis Club president, but otherwise the Lincoln analogy was difficult to sustain. "We pointed out that like Lincoln, he understood the common people," reported Sunday editor Gavreau, tongue deep in cheek. "Moe was disappointed, but I could do no more. Lincolns are not uncovered by millionaires."[10]

Throughout the campaign, the judge was in and out of the office of the publisher, who told James where to campaign and which issues to pursue. *Inquirer* writers drafted his speeches. James was a bland and feeble speaker, but everything he said turned up on the *Inquirer*'s front page, such as the "No Sales Tax, James Pledges Here" story which ran with an inch-high, eight-column headline.

Simultaneously, Moses launched an aggressive attack against the Democrats, notably Governor Earle, who was running for the U.S. Senate, but whose slipshod management of the state made him an expedient target. "Millions Taken in State Graft; Earle and 13 Associates Named," read one five-column headline, while another battering was delivered in "James Denounces Earle Machine for Communist Trend." Sitting on the edge of the news desk, the publisher often wrote the headlines, or, as Gavreau described, "added some of his own paprika."[11]

The campaign was not entirely negative. Pennsylvania had genuine problems which Moses wanted to illuminate and fix. During the "Little Steel" strikes of 1937 and the collapse of the anthracite coal industry in 1938, Moses sent separate teams of reporters to investigate labor and management viewpoints, then published their views and recommended solutions side by side for a week at a time. That was solid journalism, objective and public-spirited. It is difficult to reconcile Moses's doing that at the same time he wrote distorted headlines without accepting the paradoxical duality within him.

One of his best journalistic efforts, although it contained a political hook, was a comprehensive look at the state's collapsing infrastructure. He did not travel within Pennsylvania much, but he spoke often to business leaders and knew that many factories were vacant. Debt plagued cities, counties and school districts. Purchasing power was shrinking. The burden of rising local and state taxes was being borne by a narrower base. "Something obviously was wrong," Dimitman noted. To find out what it was, the *Inquirer* sent teams of reporters throughout the state and published a thoughtful seventeen-day series titled "The Migration of Industry from Pennsylvania." It concluded that excessive state taxation was driving away industry and that a new administration less hostile to business was vitally needed. Fortunately, Arthur James was available.

The political campaign itself was bitter, and went beyond ignoring the issues to neglecting the candidates: James and his Democratic opponent, Charles Jones, a judge from Pittsburgh whom the *Inquirer* rarely deigned to mention. As the *New York Times* pointed out with some surprise, "Much of the venom of the campaign has been directed not so much at the candidates themselves as at their backers."[12]

Normally, when backers do come into the spotlight, it is because they come from deeply entrenched political families or "machines" with a track record of organization and influence. Despite Moses's casual use of the word "machine," Philadelphia had nothing resembling New York's Tammany Hall, the Kelly machine in Chicago or the Pendergast operation in Kansas City. Nor did it have the dynastic families with a strong interest in public affairs such as the Roosevelts in New York, the Daleys in Chicago, the Kennedys in Massachusetts and the Longs in Louisiana. In Quaker Philadelphia, political power accrued, but was rarely seized. Moses, however, lacked Quaker constraint. His predisposition to grab for the golden ring of political influence gave him a place at the insiders' table.[13]

As soon as he published his first anti-FDR editorial in 1937, Moses moved into the triumvirate of statewide Republican power alongside Joseph Pew, who owned the Sun Oil company, and Joseph Grundy, the state Republican boss whose strength derived from his presidency of the Pennsylvania Manufacturers' Association. On the Democratic side were *Record* publisher Stern, Albert Greenfield, a millionaire banker and real estate broker who helped finance the *Record*, and Governor Earle, who had been assisted into office by Stern and the *Record*.

Greenfield was a particularly clever and tenacious political operator. Moses first met him while sharing a club car on a train bound for New York. Recognizing him across the aisle, Moses walked over, smiled and stuck out his hand. "Greenfield? I'm Annenberg. I think you are a son of a bitch, but I wish you were my son of a bitch instead of Stern's." Without waiting for a reply, Moses walked back to his seat and resumed reading his newspaper, leaving the startled Greenfield open-mouthed.[14]

Within days, according to Stern, who was told the story by Greenfield, Moses invited the Democratic tycoon to lunch. They had a pleasant talk and seemed to be getting on well until the end, when Moses stood up and shook the banker's hand. "I like you, Al, but you're financing Dave Stern," he said matter-of-factly. "I've got to destroy you to destroy Stern."[15]

A week later, the *Inquirer* ran a story on the closing of Greenfield's bank, the Bankers Trust Company, after the 1929 crash, alleging that a Greenfield company had withdrawn $300,000 from the bank five days before it folded and suggesting that the banker knew the failure was coming and had left his depositors unprotected.

Greenfield countered by fabricating for the *Record* what he said were Moses's private plans: "I sold James to the Republican leaders and he will have to follow my bidding because after I get him elected, I have big things in store for him. While he is governor he can appoint some judges for me. We Republicans are strong for judges. They control the Constitution and that gives us control over everything. With Pennsylvania turned into the Annenberg column and labeled Republican, I can start work on New York and Illinois, where I know the ropes, and in a few years control the Republican national organization. It is badly in need of money and brains, both of which I have more than I can use in this sleepy town. Then I will nominate a Republican president, put him in and then I will really have something." Greenfield concluded his published comments by saying that that was Moses's five-year plan for taking over the United States. "There it is, the American plan for Moe Hitler-Annenberg."

Then Greenfield took to the airwaves. In a radio broadcast he accused Moses of having been a circulation thug for Hearst and a panderer of racing "dope" to gamblers from which he made millions to buy the *Inquirer* and wrap himself in a cloak of respectability. Calling Moses "a self-appointed evangelist of power," Greenfield claimed, "His greed for recognition and dictatorship is his ruling passion. He is ready to cut down and destroy everything that stands in his way."[16]

Sometimes Moses ignored what he called the "below the belt" attacks. On other occasions, he scanned diatribes in the *Record* and sighed. "It's the penalty of leadership."[17] Once he wrote, "Political skunks can wear themselves out directing their poison gas at me, but I shall continue to do my duty as I see it."[18]

After the bank withdrawal story and the Hitler reference, the two men sued and countersued each other before the cases were eventually dropped. Of greater significance than the words was the fact that the battle had escalated well beyond traditional political differences. Having started as a business competition between the *Inquirer* and *Record*, the fight had progressed to an ideological and political war between pro- and anti–New Dealers and had now become venomously personal.

The poison emanating from each camp could not fail to draw the attention of the Roosevelt administration. Moses, after all, was beating Stern's *Record* handily and the gubernatorial prospects of his candidate, James, looked considerably better than those of the Democrats' Jones. If the Democrats went down statewide, Earle's chances of making it to the Senate might go down as well. The Pennsylvania political equation was only one element of the concern felt in the White House.

Another was that the president was furious. Roosevelt hated criticism, whether it be directed at him personally, at his team or his New

Deal policies. Presidential historian James MacGregor Burns called FDR "remarkably sensitive to pinpricks from the right," despite the years of broadsides he had endured.[19] Hearst's front-page editorials regularly denounced the "Raw Deal." At Colonel McCormick's *Chicago Tribune,* switchboard operators answered calls in the months before the 1936 election by saying, "Good morning. Do you know you have only [number] days left to save your country?"[20] *Baltimore Sun* columnist H. L. Mencken called the New Deal "this dreadful burlesque of civilized government" and wondered when Republicans would wake up to the fact that they could beat Roosevelt "with a Chinaman, or even a Republican."[21]

"Why don't you just ignore those sons of bitches?" Senate majority leader Alben Barkley asked. But Roosevelt could not.

Every morning he would lie in bed, smoke, drink coffee and read all the major newspapers, some days growing more livid by the moment. Perceptive admirers, such as historian Arthur M. Schlesinger Jr., knew that Roosevelt's public cordiality and exuberance were real but also part of a carefully cultivated persona. "Underneath there remained the other man — tougher than the public man, harder, more ambitious, more calculating, more petty, more puckish, more selfish, more malicious, more profound, more complex, more interesting," was Schlesinger's analysis. "He seemed soft and complaisant, but he was terribly hard inside."[22] He had to have been hard to accomplish what he did — recuperate from polio and run the nation for twelve years through depression, recovery and world war. He would also be hard with Moses.

Criticism from reporters bothered him less because there was not as much of it and, for the most part, the president liked the White House correspondents who covered him. He knew most by their first name, showed an interest in their personal lives and problems and invited favored writers to picnics and teas. He understood the natural adversarial relationship between press and president and had the confidence and skill to work it to his advantage as well if not better than any other president.

When he could not charm the press, he went around it. One tactic was to modify the presidential press conference. Previous presidents had demanded that reporters write out their questions and submit them in advance. When his immediate predecessor, Herbert Hoover, was asked to take direct questions, he spurned the request saying, "The president of the United States will not stand and be questioned like a chicken thief by men he does not even know."[23] Roosevelt fielded the questions as they were asked and also went directly to the people through a few fireside chats, countless other radio talks and the newsreels.

Publishers and newspaper proprietors were another matter and he often referred to them as "boobs," which in the 1930s meant jerks or fools. He knew most were Republicans who loathed him and he referred to them as a group as "the Tory press." "As you know," he wrote to Claude Bowers, his ambassador to Spain, "all the fat-cat newspapers — eighty-five percent of the whole — have been utterly opposed to everything the administration is seeking."[24] Polls showed the figure was half that, but the point was that the president was less than delighted with his press support.[25] As troubling as that opposition was personally, it also made it more difficult to build unified public support at a time when economic recovery at home was not assured and war clouds were gathering in Germany and Japan.

The first public indication that Moses had registered on the White House political screen came in April 1938. Senator Sherman Minton, an Indiana Democrat and friend of the president, urged in the course of a speech denouncing newspaper propaganda and publishers who opposed the New Deal that legislation be passed making it a felony for a publication knowingly to publish a falsehood.

Asked about the proposal, Roosevelt joked, "I'm trying to pare expenses, so I don't want any more prisons," but he had deliberately instigated Minton's speech. The previous day, in an off-the-record interview with the American Society of Newspaper Editors, the president had slammed the editors for not reflecting the opinion of their communities and for contributing to a fear psychology which made economic recovery more difficult.[26] Minton continued the lecture, but the bad news for Moses was that of all the heavyweight owners — Hearst, McCormick, Patterson, Luce — vilifying the White House, he was the only one mentioned by name.

Suddenly, Moses was in the administration's crosshairs. Yet he had no idea how serious his situation was. There was no evidence that he stopped to analyze the implications of being attacked personally, this time not by Stern or Greenfield, which he was used to, but by Washington. On the contrary, he showed just how little he understood about the magnitude of the political forces lining up against him by leaping again to the attack.

Thirty-six hours after Minton spoke, an emotional Moses issued a long, rancorous signed editorial titled "The New Dealers Can't Muzzle the *Inquirer,*" which said, "For a considerable time they have been whimpering and writhing under the lash of just editorial criticism that has followed their arrogant actions and their inflammatory speeches." He asked who would be the censor to determine what was false and true in the newspapers, Minton himself, Secretary Ickes or Solicitor General Jackson, "or just some obscure little New Deal bureaucrat with a scent like a fox hound and a heart full of hate?"

Working up a full head of steam and choler, Moses wrote that he was honored to have been singled out by Minton, "this ranting, blustering person, a one-man pet, a perfect servant of an august master. Elected to the Senate with only one plank in his platform — blind, unquestioning support of Mr. Roosevelt." If Congress intended to gag the press, he asked, "Why should it not copy the whole Hitler system and move to suppress all criticism? That is the way of the dictators. . . . Here and now I serve notice on Senator Minton, his mentors and his followers — if he has any — that I will fight this scheme with every ounce of energy I possess. I will fight it with a total disregard of consequences to myself."[27]

The editorial was heartfelt and even brave. The Minton proposal was more than flawed. It was unconstitutional, which was somewhat ironic, as Minton was later appointed to the U.S. Supreme Court by Harry Truman. None of that mattered. What mattered was that the editorial was foolhardy. Moses dared the administration to stop him. And he told how to do it.

Deep in the editorial, Moses pointed out that as the chairman of a Senate subcommittee, Minton was "in possession of powers, extended by the president himself, which enable him to pry into the income tax returns of any citizens who oppose the administration with the scantily concealed purpose of putting some outstanding Roosevelt critics on the spot."

Three years before, when they were both living in Florida, Arthur Brisbane had warned Moses about taxes. "Because he and I were so closely associated, he knew about how well I was doing and he said, 'Annenberg, are you sure about your income tax?'" Moses later told prosecutors. "He said, 'If I were you, I would advise you to look into your accounting department and make sure your income tax is all right because,' as he said at that time, 'don't fool with whiskers,' meaning Uncle Sam."[28]

Moses had consulted Weymouth Kirkland, his Chicago lawyer. "I asked him to get me a highly experienced income tax man so that I would be sure everything was all right. I had no reason to believe it wasn't all right, but I wanted to make doubly sure."

Kirkland approached the Chicago manager of Price, Waterhouse and asked to hire an accountant. Three were sent to Cecelia headquarters. One said he did not want to leave the accounting firm. The other two, said Kirkland, "didn't think the business was stable and didn't want to go into it. They weren't questioned as to why they didn't think it was stable, but that was their excuse. So the whole thing was kind of dropped."

Moses conceded that he had taken no further steps to follow up. "I didn't think it was necessary," he said. "It [Cecelia] was closely owned. I had nobody else to account to excepting the government and I was given to understand that the government examined our books every year and how was I to know there was anything wrong?"[29]

Moses's situation could scarcely have been more perilous. He had hoisted a red flag next to the tax issue. Yet he never checked to make certain that his tax house was in order, even though, when Brisbane had offered his warning, Cecelia was grossing, according to Moses, ten million dollars a year. Instead, he had trusted his chief financial man at Cecelia, Arnold Kruse, and the company's senior bookkeeper, Joseph Hafner, although neither man was a trained accountant.

Yet he continued to battle a federal government which had been looking for years for a way to bring down his racing information empire. The business was unseemly and filled with characters who would never have been invited to the Union League for lunch, but the Justice Department had found that the interstate transmission of gambling information was not illegal. For the remainder of 1936 and all of 1937, the episodic investigation of Moses, launched after the 1932 *Baltimore Brevities* case, languished. There was no hook on which to snare him and no strong pressure to try other than from the Florida politicians and rival newspaper owners he had stirred up in Miami and the Stern-Greenfield group in Philadelphia.

On the federal level, Attorney General Homer Cummings had neither the temperament nor inclination to pursue the publisher. He was chairman of the Democratic National Committee in the late Woodrow Wilson years and had been slated to be governor general of the Philippines when the sudden death of Tom Walsh, Roosevelt's original choice to be his first attorney general, opened that slot for Cummings. A member of the president's inner cabinet circle, Cummings was nonetheless the product of an earlier era. He wore a pince-nez, was sixty-eight in 1938, nearly twenty years older than Hopkins, Morgen-thau and Wallace, a dozen years older than the president, and for years had been showing a distinct lack of energy.

"Jim [Farley] says Cummings is lazy," Harold Ickes wrote in his diary in July 1936. "He can't get him to make speeches. He even refused to make a speech before the state convention in Vermont and Jim had to go himself although, as he said, as a New Englander Cummings was much better qualified to handle that meeting than he was."[30]

In Pennsylvania, the political climate turned ugly in the final weeks before the 1938 statewide election, which Democratic congress-man Michael Bradley maintained had boiled down to "the Roosevelt candidate versus the Annenberg candidate."[31] As the outlook bright-ened for Republican candidate James to capture the statehouse, Dem-ocrats did everything they could to stop him by cutting the ground out from under Moses.

In response to a call by Governor Earle, a special session of the Democratic-controlled legislature in Harrisburg authorized in August the creation of a commision to consider "making illegal the use of devices or methods of transmission of information or advices in fur-therance to gambling." The Thompson Commission was named for its chairman, state senator Edward Thompson, an ardent New Dealer, while the bulk of its investigating was handled by counsel Lemuel Schofield, a former director of public safety in Philadelphia.

The hearings took place in October and produced fourteen hun-dred pages of testimony from more than eighty witnesses, including former bitter rivals who characterized Moses as a racketeer and associ-ate of mobsters who had ruthlessly fought his way to the top of the rac-ing wire information industry. Walter, who was subpoenaed with his father to appear, hated the proceedings. When testifying, he clenched his teeth, scowled, and visibly flinched at some of the allegations about his father, which ranged from his early circulation fights in Chicago to his political battles in Miami and the half million dollars a year he paid AT&T to lease the racing wire. Much of the testimony was embarrass-ing, but if election results were the measure, the Thompson hearings were not lethal.

The war of attrition continued. In Philadelphia, David Stern enlisted the help of the Federal Trade Commission to investigate whether the *Inquirer* was undercharging advertisers to win business from the *Record*. Senator Joseph Guffey assailed Moses in a radio address which even Stern's *Record* described as "one of the most unrestrained political speeches ever made."[32]

"In all the years that I have fought against Republican misrule, it never entered my mind that the day would come when I would be obliged to attack the leadership of the Republican party in Pennsylvania on the ground that it was allied with organized crime, that it was controlled by an associate of underworld figures, that it was degenerating into an instrument for the protection of gambling," Guffey said. "Yet, that is the situation. The once great Republican party today has sunk to the blackest of all depths, to the deepest pit of moral degradation, under the leadership of a man who is the kingpin of illegal pool room gambling from coast to coast, a man who brings to the Republican party the methods, the tactics and the morality of the underworld. That man is Moses L. Annenberg."[33]

Moses struck back immediately. He sued for libel and published Guffey's speech in full, along with a long article entitled "Who Is Guffey?" The major point of the story was that the Democratic senator had been indicted in 1922 on charges of fraudulent conversion to his own use of $688,652 of "the moneys and property of the United States," a result of his term as a wartime sales director for the U.S. alien property custodian.

A major problem for Guffey, Stern and the Democrats was that George Earle, who had looked so promising, had turned out to be a weak governor. Moses was beating him up daily in the pages of the *Inquirer* with stories about investigations into the diversion of federal highway and relief funds. But the governor's liabilities were well known in Washington, where syndicated columnist Joseph Alsop had written of Earle's "really nauseous government."[34] Gifford Pinchot, the respected former two-term governor of Pennsylvania, who was a Republican but also a friend and supporter of Roosevelt's, wrote the president and called Guffey and Earle "two utterly unfit men" for high state office. The president understood. "My dear Gifford," he replied, "you and I know from long public experience that time and again we cannot get just the men we would select."[35]

With only a week to go before the November 8 election and predictions mounting that the Democrats would be routed in Pennsylvania, President Roosevelt and his advisers concluded that stronger action was necessary. They decided to send Harold Ickes to follow up Guffey's assault. Secretary of the interior and director of the Public Works Administration, Ickes was born in Pennsylvania, but grew up in

Chicago, where, before becoming a lawyer, he spent four years at the turn of the century as a newspaper reporter on the *Chicago Record*. While there is no record that he ever met Moses, nor was there any reason that he should have, Ickes was the *Record*'s assistant political editor in 1900–01, the same time that Moe Annenberg and his circulation toughs from Hearst's *American* were battling Victor Lawson's sluggers from the *Record* for dominance on Chicago's South Side.[36] Ickes almost certainly would have had bad memories of the Annenbergs.

One of Roosevelt's closest and most trusted advisers, Ickes was also the president's hatchetman. "He is the Public Executioner, the Court Poisoner and the Bouncer," *Time* said of him in a cover story. "If there is on the docket a hard, nasty, grinding job, Ickes gets the assignment."[37] His second wife, Jane, conceded that "it was no secret that he did not like to pull his punches and that he did like a fight."[38]

Ickes discussed his Philadelphia plans with the president on October 29 and sat down the following day to work on the address. He might have used a White House or Interior Department speechwriter, but in this instance turned to Max Ways, the chief editorial writer for David Stern's *Record*, to draft the remarks. "I had decided from the beginning that the burden of my speech would be an attack on Moe L. Annenberg," Ickes recorded in his diary. Ickes said he crafted the introductory paragraphs of the speech, about Republican candidate James's criticism of his public works programs. "Then the speech took up Annenberg, and this section of it was written by Ways," Ickes wrote. Work on the address, which was to be delivered on November 5, the Friday before election day, took all week. "We had to be pretty careful," Ickes noted, "because practically every page of the speech was libelous."

He asked Henry Morgenthau, who played chess by telephone with David Stern, if he should worry about being too rough or libeling Moses. "No, go the limit," the Treasury secretary replied. "You can't libel him."

To be certain, Ickes called Francis Biddle, a corporate lawyer from a distinguished Philadelphia family who was Guffey's counsel in the libel suit Moses had filed. Biddle reviewed the speech for potential libel problems. A year later he was named an appellate court judge and in 1940 solicitor general. By 1941 he would be attorney general.

On November 1, Roosevelt aides Tom Corcoran and Ben Cohen came to see Ickes. "They had pretty cold feet," Ickes recalled. "They thought Annenberg might seek ways to do me real damage, even physical damage. I might even run the risk of being shot." The president asked FBI director Hoover to give Ickes special protection to and from Philadelphia. Five agents were assigned.

The *Record* the next morning described the "overflow rally" at the Shubert Theatre. Ickes said, "It wasn't a big crowd," but it was enthusiastic. Telling them that if the Republicans won, "the future of Pennsylvania belongs to Moe Annenberg," Ickes claimed the publisher "comes from the world and lawless tradition commonly associated with Al Capone.

"I come here to tell Pennsylvanians what I know about Moe Annenberg, curse of two cities, because the prospects of turning the public contracts of Pennsylvania and the whole law enforcement machinery of the state over to a man of the record of Moe Annenberg is the most alarming thing that has ever happened to my native state."

He insisted that candidate James was in Moses's pocket. "Judge James has informed me by telegram that it is he and not Moe Annenberg who is running for governor of Pennsylvania. Tush, tush, Judge James — that's only a technicality. Of course you are the candidate. But the point is — whose candidate are you?" The speech went on, mangling Moses's history in Chicago by mixing it indiscriminately with that of Max. He detailed the fight with Jack Lynch for domination of the racing wire and explained that Moses affiliated himself with newspapers so that he could give good publicity to his friends and bad coverage to his enemies. He concluded by berating Judge James for accepting financial support from Sun Oil chief Joseph Pew. "You can't stand the stench of Annenberg on top of the gold of Pew. See yourself as others see you, Judge. Stand downwind and just whiff. Pew — Annenberg. Or, if you like it better, Annenberg — Pew."

A hatchet job from start to finish, the remarks were so vicious and so personal that the administration referred to them afterward simply as "Harold's speech," no subject required for clarification. The *Record* ran the story on the front page and the full text of the speech over six columns inside. The *Inquirer* ignored it, but on page five ran a short story about Ickes's failing to answer questions about allegations of public works fraud.

In the final furlong of the campaign, Moses dismissed the speech as one more blast of poison gas, one more kick below the belt. Walter, though, could not dismiss it. He was horrified and infuriated by Ickes's personal attack. His father had been slandered and the family's name dragged repeatedly through the mud in a manner that Walter never forgot. He believed with absolute certainty that Governor Earle was crooked and that his father opposed him in a tough but legitimate manner, but it was clear to him that liberal Democrats in Washington and Philadelphia would do anything to keep their hold on power.

His anger festered. Moses, however, had forgotten the speech by the night of Tuesday, November 8, when the incoming election results showed that Pennsylvania's Republicans had triumphed with an across-the-board landslide. James won the governorship by more than 250,000 votes, abruptly reversing the Democratic win four years earlier. Earle's bid for the U.S. Senate was defeated by more than 300,000 votes.

There was pandemonium at the *Inquirer*. A cascade of red flares bathed the exterior of the massive white building. Cannons on the roof were fired, rattling windows up and down Broad Street as far as City Hall. In the publisher's office, the walls decorated with Victorian landscapes and the floor littered with wire service returns, champagne corks popped and bounced from the ceiling, while flutes of bubbly were passed to exuberant politicians, campaign workers, reporters, secretaries and a flood of hangers-on. Moses sat behind his desk "as if on a throne," wrote Emile Gavreau, surrounded by the cheering crowd, some of whom were pummeling him on the back and urging him to greater pursuits. He roared with laughter and defiantly shook his fists in the direction of the *Record* building. In barely two years, he not only had Stern on the run, but had turned Pennsylvania politics around and stood poised to play a larger role nationally.

A few hours later, a front-page *Inquirer* editorial summed up the results, saying, "By yesterday's vote, Pennsylvania has repudiated the New Deal."[39] For the first time since the beginning of the political campaign, the *Record* could not disagree. "Election Puts New Deal on Defensive," read the eight-column banner headline in Stern's paper.[40] That was not a posture Franklin Roosevelt and his advisers were prepared to endure.

13

INDICTMENT

I N HINDSIGHT, Franklin Roosevelt's mastery of the 1930s and
early 1940s was so complete that it is difficult to understand how
beleaguered the president and his top aides felt when the November 1938 results came in. Yet they felt huge pressure and at the time for
apparently good reason. Roosevelt's 1936 reelection with 61 percent of
the vote had been overwhelming, but by 1938 the New Deal was looking battered and dysfunctional. Its experimental, big-government programs produced such erratic results that there was a surging national
sense of frustration.

Twenty-five percent of Americans were out of work in 1933 when
Roosevelt took office; the figure dropped to 14 percent in 1937, then
shot up again. By late 1938, nineteen percent were jobless. The
attempted reorganization of the Supreme Court in 1937 was a debacle
of overreaching and prompted scathing criticism of the president. The
administration's unwillingness to take a strong stand against sit-down
strikers infuriated management of all political stripes. Republicans
were not the only ones urging that Roosevelt curb his liberalism. Democrats were also split. Wisconsin governor Philip La Follette, son of
"Fighting Bob" and brother of senator "Young Bob," launched the
National Progressives of America, a new party based on the conviction
that people had had enough of relief efforts and the economics of
scarcity and wanted real jobs.

Although the president was not on the ballot in November, his
policies were. They were roundly trounced, and not only in Pennsylvania. The national returns were far worse than Roosevelt had anticipated. Republicans did not lose a single Congressional seat. GOP

strength in the House almost doubled, from 88 to 170, while the liberal bloc was halved. In the Senate, Republicans gained eight seats. The administration's recovery policies faced stalemate. The new coalition on Capitol Hill of Republicans and conservative Democrats could not wipe out the New Deal because they could not produce a two-thirds majority to override a Roosevelt veto, but the new Congress could stop the extension of its programs and wreak havoc with its funding.

There was little the president could do about the situation on the Hill, but he could shake up the other two branches of government. He moved two prominent liberals — Felix Frankfurter and William O. Douglas — onto the Supreme Court in 1939, which, following the 1938 appointment of Stanley Reed, gave him a secure majority.

He acted more quickly to rejuvenate his cabinet, naming his close friend Harry Hopkins, a former social worker who had been running the Works Progress Administration, to be secretary of commerce despite objections from the business community. The earliest move, and one with direct implications for Moses, was Roosevelt's decision within days of the election to dump Attorney General Homer Cummings.

Cummings had overstayed his cabinet welcome. He had contributed to the bungling of the court reorganization and then had gone on holiday in the middle of the fight, which pushed back Roosevelt's effort.[1] By 1938 his reluctance to press certain tax avoidance cases had riled the president. In a May meeting with Treasury secretary Henry Morgenthau, Roosevelt gave new marching orders on taxes. "Henry," he said, pushing back his chair, "it has come time to attack and you have more material than anybody else in Washington to lead the attack."[2]

It was natural that the president would turn to Morgenthau and not just because the Treasury secretary was responsible for the collection of taxes. With the exception of Hopkins, no member of the inner circle was closer to the president than Morgenthau and no one more loyal. The Treasury secretary's thousand-acre country home, Fishkill Farms, was only twenty miles from Hyde Park, the president's family estate. They had been friends as well as Dutchess County neighbors since 1914. When FDR launched his successful 1928 campaign to be governor of New York, Morgenthau was his advance man. Their wives, who shared a name, were as close as the two men. When he sent Mrs. Morgenthau a photograph of himself with her husband in the Buick in which they drove seventy-five hundred miles campaigning through upstate New York, Roosevelt inscribed it, "For Elinor, from one of two of a kind."

While the two spoke in the Oval Office, the president summoned Cummings to participate in the discussion, which turned to the devices of an unnamed tax cheat whom Cummings did not want to prosecute, while Morgenthau did not want to settle with him out of court.

Roosevelt pounded his desk and asked Cummings, "Goddammit, Homer, why don't you prosecute this fellow? Why don't you call him a son of a bitch?" If he were prosecuting the case, said the president, he would refuse to accept a settlement, because a moral as well as a legal issue was involved. "I want him behind bars." That would teach cheaters a lesson.

"Through this whole thing," Morgenthau wrote in his diary, "Cummings was as white as a sheet and his eyes were as angry as I have ever seen them. . . . I hope as long as I work for the government that I never take a moral licking like the one Cummings took today."[3]

Morgenthau did not like Cummings, nor did he care for Michael Igoe, the U.S. district attorney in Chicago. He discussed both in a conversation about Moses that he had with Harold Ickes three days before the election.

"Henry told me that his investigators just about had a case against Annenberg for false income tax returns," Ickes wrote in his diary. "He is very confident that the case is strong enough to bring a penitentiary sentence. He asked me to suggest a lawyer in Chicago who could be appointed special attorney general to prosecute this case. He does not trust Mike Igoe, the district [U.S.] attorney at Chicago, and he does not trust the attorney general."[4] One reason Morgenthau did not trust Cummings was that the attorney general was a friend of Weymouth Kirkland's, the lawyer Moses had hired partly because of that connection.

Within a fortnight, Morgenthau had arranged the ouster of each. The president announced the resignation of his oldest cabinet member and soon after, the appointment of Frank Murphy who, at forty-five, became the youngest cabinet member. An ascetic perfectionist, Murphy had considered becoming a Roman Catholic priest, but instead joined government to be what he called a "social priest." He was an energetic New Dealer who had spent two terms as Detroit's mayor and two years as governor of Michigan before being turned out in November's anti-Democratic surge.

Murphy was actually Morgenthau's first choice to prosecute Moses. "He will out-Dewey Dewey," the Treasury secretary promised, a reference to New York's Republican district attorney, who was winning a national reputation for energetic prosecutions and racket busting. But putting Murphy at the head of the Justice Department, he felt, would work even better than installing him as prosecutor.[5]

Igoe was moved out at the same time and replaced by William Campbell, the Illinois director of the National Youth Administration, a division of the WPA set up in 1934 to create jobs for four million young people. Campbell was picked by Tommy Corcoran, the brash Brain Trust lawyer whose irrepressible antics as an Irish-American and White House joker could not disguise the fact that he was a powerful behind-the-scenes master of the bureaucracy. Corcoran's choice, in consultation with the president, Morgenthau and Ickes, was inspired and showed the extent to which the administration intended to control the legal pursuit of Moses.

Campbell was thirty-three, a graduate of Loyola University night school, and had never litigated a case when he was tapped by the White House. He had, however, been the attorney for the Catholic Youth Organization founded by Bernard Sheil, the Catholic auxiliary bishop of Chicago and the right arm of Cardinal George Mundelein, the archbishop of Chicago, who was himself a good friend of the president's. The Sheil connection mattered because normally at that time, big-city bosses had a considerable say in who was appointed federal district attorney in their city. Mayor Edward Kelly was an Igoe man and had his own strong ideas about a successor. Aware of Kelly's interest, the administration picked a protégé of the archdiocese whom Kelly could not oppose.

"The whole picture is changed since Igoe is out," Morgenthau told a staff meeting the morning of December 2, 1938. He wanted to meet Campbell. "I want to show him the horizon," said Morgenthau. "I want to explain to him that he can be an international figure in law enforcement, that he can be as good or better than Dewey in a year."[6]

That same day, J. Edgar Hoover sent a six-page memo about Moses to the president. Claiming that Moses was "reported to be worth between fifty and sixty million dollars," Hoover described how "Moe and Max" hired thugs and gunmen to intimidate newsdealers in Chicago, how Moe moved to Milwaukee and New York and expanded his racing news interests and how he dominated the racing wire nationally. "In dealing with his competitors, Moe Annenberg, through his gang of sluggers and gunmen . . . carried on an almost legendary warfare of vandalism," Hoover wrote. "Printing plants of rival publishers of racing news were invaded in Chicago, New York and elsewhere, equipment destroyed, rival employees attacked and beaten up and competitors put out of business by all kinds of gangster tactics and methods so that in 1927, Annenberg was, through his numerous corporations, in absolute control of the disseminating of racing wire news service in the United States." In Miami, Hoover wrote, "when city authorities attempted to close down all bookmaking establishments, Annenberg, through the medium of his *Miami Tribune*, endeavored to intimidate the authorities."[7]

For a report to the president by the nation's top federal law enforcement official, Hoover's effort lacked hard intelligence. His sole citations were "newspapers and periodicals." He included no agent reports in his account. He mentioned that feuding between the Lynch and Annenberg factions of General News Bureau "resulted in two gang murders" in Miami, but FBI agent reports contradicted him. Hoover missed by a decade the date of Tobias Annenberg's naturalization, which became a factor when the government later explored deporting Moses on the grounds that he was not a U.S. citizen. The last half-page of Hoover's report was devoted to brother Max, but all that the director uncovered was that Max had a good salary from the *New York Daily News* and paid his bills on time. His report that Max "is not known to have any children," missed the fact that Max had two daughters and a son. Max, though, had not been a public and persistent administration critic.

That political hands were guiding the noose around Moses's neck should have surprised no one. The president was not reluctant to use the FBI and Internal Revenue Service to advance his agenda and harrass political opponents who caused him less trouble than Moses. Roosevelt was hardly alone in the practice; many sitting presidents have done the same. But as David Burnham, author of *A Law Unto Itself: Power, Politics and the IRS*, noted, "it appears, in fact, that President Franklin D. Roosevelt may have been the champion abuser."[8]

(In 1934 the Department of Justice had sought the indictment of Andrew Mellon, Treasury secretary under Harding, Coolidge and Hoover, for income tax fraud. When a federal grand jury found insufficient evidence to indict him and Mellon applied for a refund, the IRS reopened the case before the Board of Tax Appeals. "It seemed further evidence of Roosevelt's vindictiveness," wrote historian Arthur Schlesinger Jr.[9]

Mellon finally went to see Roosevelt and, in a private meeting in 1936, while the tax case was still pending, offered to build and donate to the nation the National Gallery. The president agreed and plans for the art gallery went ahead amid widespread public belief that the gallery was a payoff. Three and a half months after Mellon died in 1937, the government dropped all criminal and civil fraud penalties which could have been pursued against his massive estate.

When an IRS investigation found questionable contributions of hundreds of thousands of dollars to Lyndon Johnson's 1941 failed Senate bid, Roosevelt agreed to see the young Texas congressman, who was a protégé of Speaker Sam Rayburn's, the man most responsible for passage of New Deal legislation in the House. Later that same day, the six IRS agents who had been working on the case for eighteen months were replaced by a single agent who had not been part of the investigation. A quick study, the new man decided after three days that there was not enough evidence to proceed. When the former team protested that there was much more to investigate, the IRS team chief "was ordered to drop the case — at once, and forever," wrote Johnson biographer Robert Caro. "There were of course no fraud indictments, no trial, no publicity." Johnson's career was saved.[10])

Moses instantly understood the implication of the dismissals of Cummings and Igoe and the realization terrified him. Not only was the federal government continuing its pursuit, they were intensifying the chase. On election night, he had been crowing about defeating the New Deal, but a month later, his exuberance was gone, replaced by a desperate anxiety to get out of trouble. Without informing his lawyers or Walter, Moses began calling in chits to avoid indictment. Just as quickly, the White House noticed what he was up to.

At a cabinet meeting on December 28, the president announced that he was under mounting pressure not to press action against Moses for cheating on his taxes and that he had doubts about what to do. He did not say then who was pressuring him. Diary entries by aides later revealed that Chicago's Mayor Kelly was one because Moses had been a hefty contributor. Another, surprisingly, was former governor Earle. He argued that the new Republican administration in Pennsylvania might send him to jail for past misdeeds, but that if Washington eased up on Moses, the publisher might have his friends in Harrisburg ease up on him. Postmaster General James Farley also had doubts about proceeding. Moses had told him that he was ready to dump the Nationwide wire. "He's so badly frightened that he will give it away if he can't get rid of it otherwise," Farley said. "He's moving heaven and earth to prevent federal action."

Roosevelt's aides would not be deterred. "I remarked that he was one of the biggest crooks in the country and we ought to proceed against him," Ickes wrote in his diary. "Henry Morgenthau put in that the treasury case against Annenberg was the strongest that had ever been prepared against anyone. Henry said it was complete and air tight, with astonishing business and underworld ramifications. In the end the president and Farley seemed to stiffen up and the general feeling was that the prosecution would go forward." Morgenthau pushed a note across the cabinet table to Ickes. "Dear Harold," it read, "I do not intend to let you down."[11]

Two weeks later, Moses was showing signs of terror when he asked to see William C. Bullitt, the U.S. ambassador to France, who was home in Philadelphia for the Christmas holidays. The two men could not have been more dissimilar, and the likelihood of their meeting under normal circumstances was nonexistent. A Yale graduate and political liberal who was prominent in Philadelphia's social circles, Bullitt had earlier been the first U.S. ambassador to the Soviet Union. Moses cared nothing about that. His only interest was that Bullitt was in direct touch with Roosevelt.

Had Bullitt known Moses, he would have been shocked by the publisher's demeanor when he arrived in the envoy's sitting room on January 11, 1939. Far from truculent or even confident, Moses was obsequious as he tried to ingratiate himself with the president's friend. He explained to Bullitt that he considered himself a Democrat, that he had supported the president until the issue of the sit-down strikes and that while he felt compelled to change sides then, he still "loved" the president and would shift the *Inquirer*'s affiliation from Republican to Independent.

He wanted nothing for himself, Moses said. He just wanted to pass on that "as a human being and father of a family, he felt extremely sorry that Governor Earle, who had a charming wife and was the father of four fine sons, should find himself in danger of criminal prosecution."[12]

The pitch for Earle was nonsense. The real message was that Moses too had a charming wife and many children and should not find himself on the brink of prosecution. Switching to his own case, Moses declared that the accusations against him by Ickes and others had been based on "hearsay and misinformation." His brother Max had been the Annenberg involved in the Chicago circulation battles. He was merely the victim of "a case of mistaken identity," which was true, as Moses had left Chicago for Milwaukee in 1906, years before the nastier spate of circulation fights in the teens segued into the gang warfare of the twenties. And all those charges that David Stern had leveled against him in Philadelphia were the result of Stern's fear that the *Inquirer* would put him out of business.

Part of what Moses hoped for happened. Immediately after he left, Bullitt wrote a six-page letter to Roosevelt relating the meeting and his conclusion that "there was no suggestion whatever from Mr. Annenberg that he was asking anything from the federal government."[13] That judgment was as accurate as Bullitt's finding in 1933, after the president sent him to Europe to analyze the German situation, that, "Hitler is finished. . . . His influence is waning."[14]

If Bullitt missed the message, Roosevelt and Morgenthau understood precisely what Moses was doing. The Treasury secretary kept up his pressure, and a month later, with federal agents swarming over his financial records, the pace of Moses's backtracking picked up. He told Senator Joe Guffey that he would withdraw the libel suit he had filed against him, Stern and Greenfield if the federal government did not proceed with a tax suit. Guffey informed Ickes of the offer. Ickes replied that there was no chance that would happen and that "unless Henry Morgenthau changes his mind, which I do not believe is possible, the prosecution will be under way shortly."[15]

Morgenthau was not changing his mind. But with the threat of war in Europe increasing and likely soon to demand most of the administration's attention, he was concerned about losing time. He worried too that Moses might pay the taxes and penalties and avoid prosecution. The key to the Annenberg case for Morgenthau was not simply penalizing Moses with a fine which, no matter how high, he was certain that the wealthy publisher could pay. The goal was removing Moses from the scene so that he could cause no further political trouble.

"They are not going to have the opportunity to pay the tax," Elmer Irey assured Morgenthau. The chief of Treasury's enforcement branch, Irey had had thirty-five agents working on the case for two and a half years. Significantly, that time frame did not extend back to when Moses became the czar of racing information, but only since he had become political in Miami, bought the *Inquirer*, tried to put Stern out of business and turned on the president.

ON APRIL 10, Guy Helvering, the commissioner of internal revenue, recommended to Morgenthau that Moses be prosecuted for attempted income tax evasion for the years 1932–36. The principal charges were: failing to report profits of $200,000 a year from the sale of wall sheets; omitting $30,000 a year from operations in Canada; failing to declare $100,000 he had received in cash by misstating what he had paid ($750,000 instead of $850,000) for the purchase of the General News Bureau; charging to various Cecelia corporations nondeductible personal expenses — including the wedding for one daughter and a trip with his mistress to South America; disguising $2 million in income as a shift of revenues from one company to another; concealing his ownership of nearly $1 million in additional stock in Cecelia by claiming it belonged to an employee who denied he had ever owned the stock.

Morgenthau forwarded Helvering's letter to Attorney General Frank Murphy, concurring with the recommendation and pledging Treasury's full assistance in prosecuting the case. Then he went to lunch with Roosevelt and asked if there was anything special he could do for the president.

"Yes," the president replied. "I want Moe Annenberg for dinner."

"You're going to have him for breakfast — fried," Morgenthau answered.[16]

Murphy and the Justice-Treasury Departments team on the Annenberg case assembled at Justice on April 25 and 26 for eleven hours of talks — the transcript ran 296 pages — with Moses and Walter, five of their lawyers, Cecelia's financial chief Kruse, the bookkeeper Hafner, and James Ragen, the boss of Nationwide, the racing news wire.[17] Moses had asked for the meeting in the last-ditch hope that he could answer enough questions to stave off criminal proceedings. He planned to admit that he had erred, but to claim that he had not done so criminally.

"In the event there is no criminal liability," Murphy asked, "what does the taxpayer have in mind that he would like to do?"

Weymouth Kirkland, Moses's lead lawyer, said immediately that if Moses owed money for 1932–36, he would pay it right away.

"There is no question about that," Moses chimed in, uncharacteristically eager to please.

Kirkland explained that if the Cecelia accountants had done anything wrong, Moses was unaware of it; that the gross income passing through Cecelia annually was some $20 million involving more than eighty different companies for which tax returns had to be filed, as well as the family's personal returns. Various businesses were turned over to Cecelia, a private company, Kirkland said, but Moses "considered them his properties and he did so act at times as if they were all his properties. He forgot the corporate structures." Moses's business had grown large, Kirkland conceded, but "his bookkeeping and accounting department is still run as though it were the old grocery store where he lived in Chicago."

Moses's justification for mingling the properties was that Cecelia was all family owned. Five hundred company shares had been issued: 240 for Moses, 92 for Walter and 24 for each of the seven sisters, an aggregate of 168 shares. Walter held the shares in trust for his sisters so that if any one of them died, the shares would not pass to outsiders. Because Moses was responsible for supporting the family, he felt justified in using family resources for business expenses. The only problem was, that was illegal.

"Undoubtedly there are sums not accounted for on the books of the companies that should have been. Personally, I think a lot of it was just due to carelessness and due to the fact the bookkeeping system was very poor and not an up-to-date system," Kirkland said. "Frankly, what we want to do and we make no bones about it, we want to convince you if we can that there is no criminal knowledge or criminal intent on the part of Mr. Annenberg or his son or Kruse or Hafner."

Moses explained that he never saw any tax returns, corporate or personal, and that Kruse had been authorized to sign everything. "What was the use of my looking at it," he said. "It was left entirely in their hands. I always advised them if they were in doubt about anything to consult an attorney. I don't believe I ever looked in any of the books."[18] Once Moses bought the *Miami Tribune* and later the *Inquirer*, he rarely even went to Cecelia headquarters. In the past two years, he had been so focused on the *Inquirer* and still so fearful of flying, that he had traveled only twice to Chicago.

The man who maintained the books was Hafner, a thirty-seven-year-old whose formal education stopped at eighth grade. His bookkeeping experience consisted of a noncredit commercial course taken in Brooklyn when he was fifteen. To oversee the books of this multimillion dollar corporation composed of eighty-four companies, Moses paid him $175 a week.

On the morning of April 26, before the second session with Moses, Murphy telephoned Morgenthau.

"He wants to settle his case," the attorney general said. "They're desperate." Kirkland had been trying to contact Homer Cummings and some old friends at Justice, but Murphy said, "Nothing can help them."[19]

Later that day, Edward Foley, assistant general counsel at Treasury, briefed Morgenthau on the meeting and concluded that very little more was needed "to satisfy the conscience of the government officers that a criminal case exists and that no adequate explanation has been made which would exculpate Annenberg."[20]

MURPHY GAVE THE CASE to U.S. attorney William Campbell on May 11 to present to the grand jury in Chicago, where Cecelia was headquartered. There was also an anti-trust investigation under way against Moses on the grounds that Nationwide represented a monopoly on racing information. That case, however, was "dishwater," according to Morgenthau, although he was concerned that the second investigation might get in the way of his own "one hundred percent well-prepared case."

The same day the case went to Campbell, Moses made a direct appeal by letter to Morgenthau. "It is my intention and desire that the treasury department shall receive payment for all income or other taxes due from me, any of the members of my family or any of the corporations with which I am in any way associated," he wrote. If Treasury would only tell him what he owed, he would pay immediately.[21]

"The case is no longer in our hands," Morgenthau wrote back.[22]

Moses was desperate for another reason that he had not mentioned to Walter or anyone in his family. He had been having excruciating headaches that caused him to lock himself in his office at the *Inquirer* with his lights turned off. One day he asked one of his lawyers, Hammond Chaffetz, "When I'm indicted, how long can you keep me out of jail?"

"About three years," Chaffetz replied.

"That's all right," Moses replied. "I'll be dead then."

Chaffetz had heard nothing before then to indicate his client was ill. Moses did not have a medical exam, but Chaffetz mentioned the comment to a friend at the Justice Department, where he had earlier worked, and that lawyer had passed it on to Treasury counsel Foley. "Apparently he's a sick man," Foley told Morgenthau.[23]

Morgenthau was dismissive. He had heard such excuses before. There was no evidence anything was wrong with Moses. He looked fatigued, but no more so than usual for a sixty-two-year-old who habitually slept only four hours a night. His family was not aware that Moses was ill. The claim seemed to be little more than another bid to avoid indictment. Moses did not allude to his health again but resumed contacting individuals he believed might help keep the case from going forward to trial. His own lawyers assumed he was offering money for help, but he never asked the Kirkland team to pay anyone off to quash prosecution.

"At this week's cabinet meeting the president said that he supposed there wasn't a man at the cabinet table who hadn't been approached to see if there was not some chance of settling this case," Ickes wrote on May 13.[24]

Neither Moses nor Kirkland was making any progress toward settlement because settlement was never in the cards. Moses believed Kirkland was sufficiently connected in Chicago to halt the case, but nothing was working. What Moses failed to realize was that Kirkland, a bright and capable attorney, was probably the last lawyer he should have hired. What had impressed him was that Kirkland knew Attorney General Cummings and had represented the *Chicago Tribune*. It fell to Walter to educate his father, reminding him that Cummings was gone and Roosevelt despised the *Chicago Tribune* because its owner, Colonel McCormick, was virulently anti–New Deal. Moses did not want to listen, especially to his son, who he believed knew little.

Walter also told his father that he had heard that the government had information linking Kirkland to Jake Lingle, a star *Chicago Tribune* crime reporter in the 1920s. Lingle was close to the police commissioner, but also to Al Capone, who had given him a diamond-studded belt buckle and put him on his payroll. Only after he was shot in the head and killed while reading the *Daily Racing Form* in 1930 did Lingle's editors begin to wonder how a $60-a-week reporter had three homes, a closetful of tailor-made suits, a chauffeur-driven Lincoln and was able to take his family on regular vacations to Cuba.[25]

Walter had heard that some payoffs to Lingle had gone to Kirkland, which sounded incredible. His accepting the reports at face value suggested that young Annenberg could not deal with reality. Nonetheless, Harold Ickes had spoken with Frank Murphy about Kirkland. "I told Frank that Bert [Colonel] McCormick had had his name at the head of the Kirkland firm for a number of years . . . and that he had in effect been a stooge for the firm. I also said to Murphy that at one time it was my understanding that Kirkland was on the verge of disbarment by the federal court at Chicago." Whether or not Kirkland had a more serious problem, it was clear that he had negative clout with FDR's inner circle.[26]

Although Moses was nervous that his efforts were going nowhere and Morgenthau was smug in May 1939 when grand jury subpoenas went out to more than a hundred witnesses, government investigators realized that they did not have an airtight case. Nils Tessem, the IRS agent in charge of reviewing the Annenberg records, had been cooped up in a small room at Cecelia headquarters for months on what finance chief Arnold Kruse told Moses was a fishing expedition through his books. Tessem was feeling both physically confined and frustrated because he could not fill in the remaining holes in the case. The books were almost impossible to decipher. Blank checks, as a matter of practice, were issued to Moses and Walter to pay bills or for whatever they wished, with records to be resolved later. Accounts did not balance. Personal and corporate accounts were intermingled. Some records looked erased and rewritten, but it was hard to say whether the changes were legitimate or fraudulent.

Tessem felt the pressure to produce convincing evidence. Elmer Irey was pushing him. IRS commissioner Helvering, a former Kansas congressman who had chaired the state's Democratic Committee when Roosevelt defeated Hoover and was as political as Morgenthau and Ickes, was pushing him. Tessem looked around the Cecelia room piled high with boxes and asked another agent why the room felt so claustrophobic.

"What's wrong with this dump today?" he asked. "It seems smaller than ever."

"It's probably those boxes over there," the agent responded, pointing to a pile of containers in one corner. "They brought them in this morning."

Tessem moved closer. Nineteen boxes, marked Private Records, had been shipped from the Kings Point estate. "Tessem took a quick look in the boxes and set off for the U.S. courthouse for a subpoena enabling the government to seize the boxes before Moe's lawyers realized that the records had been delivered to the right floor but the wrong office," Irey later wrote. "Those records were obviously for the private information of Moe's defense because they clearly explained codes and also showed canceled checks that Moe had denied were in existence. There were also cash books, bank statements, correspondence and ledgers which all together filled in the holes in the government case."[27]

ON JUNE 6, seven handcarts loaded with ledgers and correspondence were pushed into room 475 of the ornate old U.S. Post Office Building in Chicago. Three more carts arrived the next day. The jury was empaneled by Judge James Wilkerson, the magistrate who in 1931 had sentenced Al Capone to eleven years in prison for tax evasion. On the wall above the judge was a dark, grimy painting of the biblical Moses on the mountain holding the stone tablets of the law. Outside the chamber, three deputies patrolled, moving loiterers along and checking the adjoining bathroom to ensure that no reporters had their ear up against the connecting door. Inside the chamber, three special U.S. attorneys stationed themselves to witness the proceedings as "observers," an unusual presence the Annenberg lawyers later challenged, without success, as jury intimidation.

The grand jury sat for nine weeks and heard 50 auditors and 227 witnesses pour out 11,747 pages of testimony. When it rose on August 11, it handed down ten indictments totaling 65 pages against Moses, Walter, Kruse, Hafner, and Ragen. Moses was charged with criminally evading taxes on $3,258,810 worth of income from 1932 through 1936. Interest and penalties brought the total government claim against him to $5,548,384, nearly $65 million in current dollars, which made it the largest criminal tax evasion case in history.

The government tabulated the figures as follows:

YEAR	TAX DUE	TAX PAID	TAX EVADED
1932	313,506.10	308.43	313,197.67
1933	388,645.65	6,189.73	382,455.92
1934	812,163.55	72,969.61	739,193.94
1935	676,225.04	69,559.33	606,665.71
1936	1,692,848.89	475,552.16	1,217,296.73
TOTAL	3,883,389.23	624,579.26	3,258,809.97

William Campbell immediately sent telegrams to Frank Murphy and Tom Corcoran advising them of the indictments. To reporters, he announced, "These indictments are only the opening gun in the government's case against Annenberg." Moses, who was released on $100,000 bond, issued a statement saying, "The indictments have taken me by surprise," and that he looked forward to presenting his version of events at trial, which was set for the autumn. "I ask only that the public reserve judgment until all the facts are known."

The publisher was not surprised, but he was worried. He did not dispute that his books were a mess, or that he owed money, but he was adamant that he had not criminally evaded paying his taxes. Neither his story nor Walter's would ever change. Walter's out of blind filial loyalty; Moses's, of self-delusion. His own lawyers knew that Moses was guilty. The more they had looked at his books, the more they realized he had not even attempted to pay what was due. He was such a shrewd and crafty businessman, so relentless in his attention to details involving money, that his own legal team found it impossible to square that side of him with the notion of his simply being careless and naive about his taxes. Kirkland concluded that Moses had so much money his intention was to brazen or buy his way out if challenged.

Politics, though, had made the Annenberg case about more than taxes. Moses was correct when he told *Inquirer* readers in an October statement titled "Why I Was Indicted" that "it was important to the Democratic party that I be destroyed prior to the 1940 elections."[28]

If he had bought a newspaper anywhere other than Philadelphia, almost certainly he would have been allowed to pay a fine and carry on. "Oh, it was a vendetta," was the judgment of Richardson Dilworth, the Democratic district attorney in Philadelphia who was the *Inquirer* lawyer but was always objective about Moses.[29] That was also the feeling of Jane Patterson, a court reporter who recorded the grand jury proceedings. "I became a thoroughly disillusioned young woman who could not fathom that an administration would use our system of 'justice' to pursue a personal vendetta," she wrote decades later to Walter. "As the testimony rolled in, I became increasingly convinced of your father's innocence."[30] (William Hopewell, who worked for a year as an auditor on the Annenberg case, wrote Walter in 1981 claiming that there were serious flaws in three audits of Cecelia, but that the IRS pressed ahead because it feared ridicule if the case collapsed. "The tremendous injustice to him has been on my mind — on and off — for years," wrote Hopewell. "I am sure that your father was not 'guilty as charged.'" At the time, however, such dissent was unknown, and Hopewell, who was seventy-five when he contacted Walter and who offered no paperwork to substantiate his claim, asked that his letters be kept confidential while he was alive.)[31]

IF THE GOVERNMENT wanted him, Moses wondered, why did it have to indict Walter? What upset him most, he said, was that "the government has found it necessary to place the blot of an indictment on the name of my son Walter, who was never in a position to and who could not possibly have knowledge of any matters whatsoever pertaining to taxes."[32]

The Morgenthau-Murphy team had little interest in pursuing Walter. He was a Cecelia director and had knowledge of the company's cash flow and profits, so indicting him was understandable. At the same time, they knew that he did only what his father told him. He had never been shown to have been involved in tax preparations. Indicting him, though, ratcheted up the pressure on Moses. Everything Moses had done had been designed to build a business empire he could leave to his only son. If he and Walter went to jail, all would be lost. From Morgenthau to Campbell, the government knew that Walter was his father's Achilles' heel.

In Philadelphia, *Inquirer* editor Dimitman called Moses to ask how the paper should play the story. "You're the editor," Moses replied. "That's your job." The response was so uncharacteristic that Dimitman realized the publisher's situation was far worse than he had believed.

Dimitman suggested the top of page one. Moses, who sounded as if he had been kicked in the stomach, agreed. The *Inquirer* twinned a United Press story on the indictments with an Associated Press piece on the publisher's reaction. On Moses's orders, editorial attacks on the New Deal eased and more critical coverage was initiated of governor James's Republican administration in Pennsylvania. The Sunday magazine was changed overnight from a tabloid to a more respectable broadsheet in which the first issue featured a full-page photo of the Archbishop of Philadelphia, Cardinal Denis J. Dougherty, in his ceremonial vestments.

Moses and Walter had barely returned to Philadelphia from Chicago when several more of the government's guns detonated. Two weeks after the first indictments, the grand jury handed down an additional indictment, charging conspiracy to defraud the government of $77,883 in taxes for the same years, or $137,729 after the addition of taxes and penalties. A week after that, a second grand jury which had been examining the anti-trust aspects of Moses's control of racing information issued seven more indictments. Many were similar to the earlier ones, but two charged that when Moses sent run-down sheets through the mail he was illegally operating a lottery. The opening they had found was Moses's decision years earlier to use numbers rather than horse's names to report race results, and thus force bookies to buy the coded run-down sheet. To the grand jury, numbers on a horse were no different than numbers pulled from a drum.

If found guilty on each indictment, Moses faced a potential maximum jail term of one hundred forty-seven years. The prospect was so daunting that when reporters asked, he showed some of his old cockiness with a sarcastic crack. Echoing Nathan Hale, he said, "My only regret is that I haven't enough remaining years to give to my country."[33]

John Flynn of *Collier's* magazine asked Moses if the one big mistake he had made was neither horses nor taxes but going into politics. The publisher revealed how little he understood what happened by disagreeing. "I would do the same thing again," he insisted. "I was fighting for my state and for my country. I would do it all over again even if they put me on the scaffold for it."[34]

Which is what they were preparing to do. Several months of legal pleading and bickering followed the indictments. On November 2, Campbell tightened the noose and moved on Moses's income when he formally asked AT&T, Western Union and Illinois Bell to discontinue service to Nationwide. Failure to do so, he warned, would be considered tantamount to conspiracy to violate federal and state law, although there was still no statute that said providing racing information by wire was illegal. The companies, unwilling to fight or stay allied with a client who was going down, quickly complied. Moses sought a restraining order to keep the service operating, but after Campbell pointed out that Nationwide earned $7.7 million from 659 bookmaking parlors in Chicago alone between 1933 and 1936, Judge Wilkerson rejected the request. On November 9, the plug was pulled on the wire services.

Moses, making a virtue of necessity, walked away within days from Nationwide. The business had been his biggest cash cow but had caused him trouble from the moment he set it up. The government did not have a legal basis for pulling the wires, but he could no longer fight that fight. "Mr. Annenberg finds himself in a position where the government of the United States, although it is at best doubtful that any statute supports its position, strongly opposes this business," said Kirkland.

"He feels he does not want to be connected with such a business under those circumstances."

The closing of Nationwide prompted a flurry of headlines that Murphy and Campbell were ready to reach a deal with Moses. Campbell denied it, but Morgenthau was angry. "I'm disturbed that the attorney general is considering making a settlement with Mr. Annenberg," the Treasury secretary told his legal counsel Ed Foley on November 24. Foley tried to calm down his boss. The reports concerned only an unconditional guilty plea by Moses on all counts, which they would have to accept if he offered it but he had not.

Moses kept doing all he could to reach a settlement. On November 29, he had Kirkland offer to pay a $2.5 million fine and accept probation. IRS commissioner Guy Helvering called the offer "frivolous" and asked for $11 million. Morgenthau kept resisting any settlement. "As far as I'm concerned, there's no difference between Annenberg and Capone. . . . My position is unalterably opposed to any deal."

The following day Morgenthau lunched with President Roosevelt and Attorney General Murphy. "President said he wanted us to collect every dollar and put Moe Annenberg in jail," the Treasury secretary jotted down on a piece of White House stationery. "Frank Murphy said at cabinet he is going to send Annenberg to jail."[35]

When Morgenthau called Campbell for an update on December 4, the U.S. attorney said he was willing to let some of the smaller fry go, including Walter, but there would be no deal with Moses.

"If a deal is made, I'm ruined," Campbell exclaimed.

"Well, you won't be the only person who's ruined," said Morgenthau.

Campbell explained that Kirkland had come in "with this poor-old-man stuff, who can't stand going to jail. I said, 'Poor old man, hell, I'll give you the name of three people that he has had killed in the city of Chicago in the last five years.' . . . I said, 'you're representing a murderer and a thief.'"

"Good for you," interjected Morgenthau.

"And Kirkland said, 'Well, I'll admit he's done some things he ought to be sorry for. . . .' I said, 'Sorry Hell, he ought to be hung.'"[36]

Campbell was excited and was saying what Morgenthau wanted to hear. The only flaw was that, polemic notwithstanding, there was neither evidence or even a credible allegation that Moses had had anyone killed in the previous five years, or the previous twenty. They named no names. No charges had been filed. No credible law enforcement reports sustained what Campbell charged. And Hoover's suggestion that two men had been killed in Miami had been discounted by his own agents. Moses, though, was a Velcro suspect. He had been so demonized that every allegation stuck.

The case was to go to trial in January 1940, but Judge Wilkerson, and then his wife, became sick and the action was pushed back to April. The increasing tension affected Moses's health. The headaches he had earlier mentioned to Hammond Chaffetz had become more pronounced and forced him to begin canceling appointments. Walter did not know what was wrong with his father. His own stomach was churning. He could barely sleep and was smoking more than two packs of cigarettes a day. Some of his father's behavior seemed bizarre, such as ordering that the street-level windows of the the *Inquirer* be used to display weapons that had been used in infamous crimes, including a pistol of Al Capone's, bankrobber Willie Sutton's machine gun, and a blood-stained saw used by a mother to kill her infant. Some staffers wondered if the publisher was trying to suggest this was what constituted real crime.[37]

One Sunday, Dimitman came upon a glum Moses and Walter sitting silently side by side in their office at the *Inquirer.*

"I've made up my mind," Moses said. "I'm going to plead guilty."

The editor was shocked. Walter, staring at his perfectly polished shoes, looked mortified. "He was only doing it so I wouldn't have to suffer," Walter said later.[38] Pressure on Moses's weakness had worked.

"I am pleading guilty because the government has advised me that in the event I do so, the case against Walter and my other associates will be dropped. As you know, I've always had great ambitions for Walter. I purchased the *Inquirer* and built it up with his future in mind. That's the only thing I'm interested in and if I can spare Walter the trial, I won't mind doing a year in jail."[39]

He insisted that his name be stripped from the masthead as chairman and publisher and said he would sever all connections to the paper. Walter refused. He only accepted Moses's decision to plead guilty because his father was so determined to spare him from trial. The decision would imbue in Walter a sense of guilt and obligation to his father that would last a lifetime and be manifest in a continuing effort to reflect honor on Moses. "His mistreatment was the making of me," said Walter.

In April 1940, the deal was concluded with the government. Moses pleaded guilty to a single count of evading $1,217,296 in income taxes and agreed to pay a penalty of $9.5 million ($110 million in current dollars) over seven years. The fine was $8 million; the additional $1.5 million covered payment from 1940 to 1946 of 6 percent interest on the unpaid balance. The government put liens on all Moses's properties except the *Philadelphia Inquirer*, meaning that if the payment schedule was not kept, the government could seize his other publications, his theaters, offices and apartment buildings, the Long Island, Miami Beach and Philadelphia homes and the Wyoming and Poconos ranches. The other charges against Moses were eliminated. All charges against Walter were dropped. Hafner, the bookkeeper, pleaded guilty to a single count of aiding Moses in the 1936 evasion. Charges against Kruse, Ragen and several minor figures were settled later.

The government held firm on the matter of a trial. Moses still faced a civil trial and a possible prison term on the single count, which called for a maximum penalty of five years. Weymouth Kirkland was unable to reach any agreement in advance on a likely punishment with either the government or the judge.

"I am in no mood to bargain with anybody," Judge Wilkerson told Kirkland earlier. "If your defendant wants to plead guilty, let him plead. He has to take a chance on these things."

When Kirkland left, Wilkerson took Campbell aside. "Young man, you are doing all right. They have been trying to get the wires and bookies out of this town for fourteen years. Don't let them stampede you into anything on this income tax case. Tell the attorney general I respect him as a very reputable law enforcing officer. If he wants to tell me privately, or through you, of a recommendation, I will do my best to follow his recommendation. I'm all for you, my boy."[40]

According to Walter, Kirkland told Moses that if he pleaded guilty to one count and saved the government the trouble of a costly trial, he would likely get off with three years' probation. If that indeed was the lawyer's analysis, it meant that he and Moses completely misread the political situation and the determination of the government to lock Moses away.

The guilty plea to the single count, though, was the right thing to do. Walter believed forever after that his father might have beaten all charges if he had opted for a full trial, but beating the charges was never in the cards. Kirkland knew it and so did Moses's own lawyer at the *Inquirer*, Richardson Dilworth. "Pleading guilty to the one count wasn't bad [advice]," said Dilworth. "He would have been convicted."[41]

Walter could not accept that. Refusing always to admit his father's guilt, he decided that Kirkland had sold out Moses by pressuring him to plead guilty before resolving whether he had to serve jail time. Kirkland himself was under pressure, said Walter, because the government was threatening to investigate him on taxes and for his possible connection to the killing of crooked *Tribune* reporter Jake Lingle. "The government leaned on Weymouth Kirkland," said Walter, "and the next thing we knew Kirkland started to behave as if he hardly knew my father."

Officials at the Kirkland and Ellis law firm in Chicago deny that there was ever a threat to Kirkland, who died in 1965. But the papers of U.S. district attorney Campbell, who died in 1989, contain a draft letter from Campbell to Samuel Clark, the assistant attorney general, saying, "A basis, in my opinion exists, for an investigation, at least civil, of the affairs of Mr. Weymouth Kirkland and his law firm. There is some question whether fees received by this firm are properly accounted for."[42]

The fees paid Kirkland and his partners to defend Moses, Walter and the Cecelia team were colossal. Walter estimated them at $100,000 per month in 1939. The firm's sources did not specify the amount, but conceded they constituted "a tremendous amount of money" which was paid promptly. Perhaps in advance. Richardson Dilworth claimed that Kirkland created an unusual billing method for the Annenberg case. "God, he was smart, old Kirkland," said the *Inquirer* lawyer. "When the whole thing started, he said to Annenberg, 'Have you got any cash and Moe said I've got about $2 million. Kirkland said you better just deposit it with me in an attorney's account. So when the case was all over and the old man was really hard up, actually he was bankrupt . . . except for this enormous income he had, he was really busted, so he went to Kirkland to get the two million back and Kirkland said, 'Well, let me see, first we've got to make up a bill.' And the bill came to — now this is approximate and there's a little exaggeration here, but not too much — but the bill came to approximately $1,950,000. So the old man never trusted Kirkland again."[43]

THE CIVIL PENALTY had been resolved, but the hearings at which Wilkerson would determine Moses's punishment on the criminal charge opened in U.S. district court in the middle of a heat wave in Chicago on June 5, 1940. By then the fight had gone out of Moses. "Annenberg knew, and Kirkland too, that the presentation of any case for the defense was a futile and empty gesture," said Dimitman. "The wheels had long ago been set in motion for conviction and sentence."

Campbell, the lean, fresh-faced, thirty-five-year-old U.S. attorney, offered a 109-page statement of evidence. Kirkland — who had turned sixty-three the previous day and looked every bit the elegant corporate attorney he was in an expensive, pale gray suit and round gold-rimmed glasses — had a 138-page statement.

The prosecution claimed that Moses's net worth had grown from nearly $8 million in 1930 to just under $20 million in 1938 in part because he had evaded taxes through countless instances of financial trickery. Among the eighty-four companies operated by Cecelia were dummy firms which concealed tens of thousands of dollars of assets; bank accounts and Cecelia stock that was listed in the names of family members to lower his own higher-rate tax burden, all of which was controlled by Moses (various companies paid the expenses of his wife, Sadie) and to cover the living expenses of the daughters and his sons-in-law; an $8,250 vacation cruise to South America with his mistress, Gertrude Boze, charged as a business expense; Boze's weekly salary written off as a "track hustling" expense; dental bills and gambling losses disguised as "political contributions." Moses charged off as business expenses most of the costs of Ranch A, including riding clothes, blankets, guest cabins and trout food. The cost of the 50 percent share of General News Bureau was $750,000 but was charged as $850,000, with Moses failing to account for the $100,000 he pocketed. That may have been the $100,000 that had been paid to Frank Nitti. The most embarrassing revelation was that the gala wedding at New York's Hotel Pierre for his daughter Harriet, to which guests from Chicago were transported in two Pullman cars, was charged to the *Daily Racing Form* as a "racing convention expense."

Kirkland contended that Cecelia was less an actual holding company than a family operation in which dividends had been handed back so the family could accomplish various goals, such as buying businesses or property or settling living expenses. "It was a family settling family problems in the only way it knew," said Kirkland. "These people didn't want lawyers. It was their company and they didn't see why they couldn't do what they wanted."[44] What they wanted was irrelevant. The fact remained that they had written off personal expenses as tax deductions, a serious problem that future defenders could never explain away.

Hindering matters further was Kirkland's unimpressive defense. In trying to explain what happened to $100,000 listed as household expenses, the lawyer awkwardly explained, "My client has a very expensive habit. He likes to play roulette. He is not very good at it either. He has lost considerable sums. It is probable that some of this $100,000 was used for that purpose and not for household expenses." He babbled with grandiose oratorical flourishes about Moses's determination to pay taxes properly in future, about repayment schemes and the new accounting system that Cecelia was implementing and, to Walter's horror, turned on all the maudlin taps to discuss the father-son relationship.

". . . Public trial broadcast throughout the land would leave a scar, even a verdict of not guilty, that might forever ruin the son. His father would not take that chance. . . . And if mistakes the boy [Walter was thirty-two] has made, must not much be granted for his inexperience and immaturity? Perhaps his desire to please his father, to accept the responsibility without experience to back it up may account for any trifling mistake he might have made. . . . The relationship which exists between M. L. Annenberg and his son Walter is something different from any such relationship I have ever known. They have been constant companions since the boy left school. His father entertains for him the deepest affection and hope for his future. Everything was built with the son's future in mind. . . ."

Kirkland appealed for a suspended sentence. "Such a punishment should best satisfy the government," he said, whistling into a gale. "For a man like Annenberg, imprisonment may mean nothing short of the end. . . . Certainly the law does not demand as satisfaction that this man be completely broken and destroyed."[45]

That was precisely the satisfaction which was demanded. On July 1, 1940, saying that tax evaders cannot expect civil retribution to pardon criminal behavior, Judge Wilkerson sentenced Moses to three years in federal prison.

Bill Campbell called the judgment "eminently fair and impartial." Morgenthau wrote and congratulated him on his victory.

Two months later, Campbell was named a federal judge.

Attorney General Frank Murphy was named a Supreme Court justice.

The government did not initiate an investigation of Kirkland.

Judge Wilkerson retired six months later.

Two weeks after Moses was sentenced, less than a mile from Wilkerson's courtroom, in Chicago Stadium, Franklin Roosevelt accepted the Democratic party's nomination for a third term as president.

14

LEWISBURG

———

THE ATMOSPHERE at the *Inquirer* was somber when Moses and Walter returned from Chicago after the sentencing. The publisher had been an overpowering presence at the newspaper, and the thought of his loss was staggering. He had been a hands-on proprietor, decisive, combative, an exciting manager who connected directly with his troops. Walter, who was about to take over, felt dazed. He had shown no management capability. That was not all his fault, because his father's unschooled training technique was to have Walter observe everything but be responsible for nothing. As a result, the easily cowed thirty-two-year-old with the slicked-down black hair was a shadow on the edge of his father's aura. He was not unpleasant, nor did the staff dislike him, but he had been relegated to such a background role that he scarcely seemed to exist.

"M. L. was a powerful man, who knew he had power and knew how to use it, not unkindly," said *Inquirer* reporter Shirley Katzander. "Walter seemed terrified of power."[1] "Until all the legal troubles, Walter didn't even come in until ten or ten-thirty A.M.," said Marion Hoeflich, M. L.'s secretary. "And then he sat there like a log. He had very few friends here."[2]

There was no talk among the staff that Moses had gotten what was coming to him. On the contrary, the feeling was that Moses had done what many employees believed most rich men in the 1930s did — shave their taxes any way they could. They did not question that he was guilty of tax evasion. Enough examples of the foolish write-offs he had taken had been made public to erase any doubt on that score. And he had acknowledged guilt to the one count. But the diabolically willful evasion on the mass scale that the government had claimed? Given their own experience with him, few of the staff believed that.

Moses did not hand out extravagant salaries and he had an aversion to overtime, but he paid better than union wages and in four years he had never stinted in trying to produce a better newspaper. He had once decided on the spot to spend $600,000 for a new rotogravure plant and to spend hundreds of thousands more for the jack rabbit edition which boosted Sunday circulation over one million. The common belief around the newsroom, which Walter shared, was that Stern and the Democrats had snagged Moses for beating up the *Record* and President Roosevelt. Stern bore some responsibility, because he complained to Roosevelt and any high-level Democrat who would listen to him about the political and financial threat Moses posed.

Stern, however, put the blame on another Democrat deeper in Moses's past: James Cox of the *Miami News*, whose enmity Moses had incurred during their political and newspaper battles in Florida. Cox had headed the Democratic ticket in 1920 when Franklin Roosevelt was his running mate. "I can truthfully say that I had nothing to do with it," Stern said in response to suggestions he had persecuted Moses. "But I know who did. Cox told me how he had ribbed the President: 'Franklin, you ought to be proud of the way you're pulling everyone back to prosperity, including Moe Annenberg. Under your administration he's making more money than Mellon and Rockefeller combined.'"[3]

The truth was that Stern and Cox undoubtedly helped bring Moses down, but their efforts were less significant than those of Moses himself. Unprosecutable on racing-related allegations, Moses was pursued on a provable charge because he caused political trouble and indicted because he ran Cecelia unprofessionally, with unqualified subordinates, and illegally, as if the company were his personal piggy bank.

Now, with three weeks to wrap up his affairs, he sat silently behind the big desk in his office, staring at the Victorian pictures on his wall with their images of families strolling to church, of Broad Street in the 1880s, of an earlier, more-forgiving America which had offered him boundless horizons. He refused to feel sorry for himself. He was grateful for the support his friends and staffers offered, but he wanted no whining. Those who came to commiserate, he reprimanded.

When he strode through the corridors, his shoulders slumped and he seemed to have lost an inch or two in height, but his jaw jutted and his gaze was as piercing as ever. Stud Norton, a poker pal and crony from the Hearst days hired to run circulation for the Sunday pre-dates, approached with tears running down his cheeks and offered to serve the publisher's term. Moses almost lost his own composure. "Brace up, Stud," he said, his voice cracking as he pinched the circulation man's ear. "I'll serve my own rap. But don't forget the Sunday's got to hold the million. I'll have more time now to think up some more ideas."[4]

Yet day by day the strain increased. "I'm going to jail," he suddenly moaned in the middle of one editorial conference as his editors stared down at the table or at their shoes. "I'm going to jail."

Other days he was more upbeat. Analysts from the Gallup polling group arrived to review readership surveys. One explained that pictures of Hollywood starlets in bathing suits drew more women subscribers than men because women derived satisfaction by mentally transplanting their head onto the bodies of the starlets. "By God, that's something new," Moses snorted, "but I'll stick to the old theory." Referring to war in Europe, another Gallup strategist explained that readers still preferred racing information to dispatches from the battlefront. "See that," Moses barked. "People want to know all about the racetrack, and I'm going to jail for it." When he was told that premier Edouard Daladier had ordered French troops to put down striking workers, he ordered, "Give that guy good play."

Walter sat at his desk in a daze and walked as if he had lead weights in his pockets. When Emile Gavreau came to his desk with some cartoons to approve, Walter leafed through them without looking, then pushed them aside. "Take them away," he said. "How the hell can I laugh."

Overhearing the conversation, Moses walked over to peer at the pile of illustrations. He discarded most, then grabbed one and began to chuckle. "Here, print this one," he ordered. "It's funny and, by God, it's the truth." The drawing showed two cleaning ladies on their knees looking up at a group of elegant, bejeweled women escorted by tuxedoed men. One worker was saying to the other, "What did virtue ever get us?"

One day Moses wandered into the office of Gavreau, who lived on a farm the publisher had once offered to buy so the editor could move into the city and be closer to the office. Gavreau refused and Moses was just beginning to understand why. "You get home there every night and nobody bothers you and you can forget everything, no worries, and you can sleep. And when you wake up, the sun shines. Jesus!"

Moses sighed. He walked toward the door, utterly weary, then turned around. "You're not such a goddamned fool after all. What is money, for Christ's sake?"[5]

On July 15, he finished a thirty-page statement titled "So that the Public May Know the Truth," which he intended to have the *Inquirer* run on his last day. The first sentence read "There is always another side to every story." The remainder, a recapitulation of his defense and a bilious critique of the government's case, characterized him as a martyred political prisoner.

"Like many another man who has had the temerity to speak out against injustices of government, to voice his political views in his newspaper and to fight for principles in which he believed, I have received my punishment. In Russia, under the Communist regime, those who voice their disapproval of Stalin or his policies are lined up against a wall and shot to death. In Germany, under the Nazi regime, those who voice their disapproval of Hitler and his policies are placed in concentration camps to die. In the United States, the New Deal has its own system of punishing its political enemies and those who question its purity, its policies and its motives. The New Deal sends out vast numbers of agents and investigators to snoop and to spy. It uses the power of the federal grand jury to threaten and intimidate. It uses the entire structure of federal government to punish. The federal government has sent me to jail as a political prisoner, camouflaging its purpose with income tax indictments."[6]

After thinking it over, Moses withdrew the statement and substituted a four-page version which said that he had intended to talk about the causes of his trouble, but "this is not the time for such a statement. When I return to Philadelphia, after payment of the penalty . . . I hope to be in a position to make public all the facts that led to the indictments and to my incarceration."

What changed his mind? The day Moses finished the first statement, his appeal for probation was filed. The far more pragmatic Walter urged his father to stop poking sticks in the eyes of government. Inflammatory language would destroy any chance of mercy then or later.

The appeal for probation was Moses's and Walter's last hope. It was based on the examinations of three doctors who testified that Moses had arteriosclerosis, hemorrhoids, bad tonsils and sinuses and that Sadie Annenberg had suffered a heart attack from the strain of the investigation, had undergone a recent gall bladder operation and might well die if her husband were incarcerated. Judge Wilkerson rejected the appeal.

The Bureau of Prisons assigned Moses to the federal penitentiary at Lewisburg, Pennsylvania, a medium-security prison about a hundred miles northwest of Philadelphia on the Susquehanna River. No Club Fed, the minimum-security institutions to which white-collar felons with no previous records are often sent now, Lewisburg opened in 1932 and held 1,638 inmates, of whom 85 percent were white and 65 percent were first offenders. Built of brick in Italian Renaissance style, the prison sported a soaring tower that would have looked at home in Siena or on St. Mark's Square in Venice.

Moses was not allowed to give up at the prison gate. Instead, he was required to return to Chicago on July 22, 1940, and turn himself in. Moses hugged Walter, told him to take care of his mother and the girls, and was then driven back to Pennsylvania by a marshal and deputy. He arrived on July 23, was admitted, fingerprinted, assigned prisoner number 10197, given a short haircut and baggy blue prison garb and told to mail his clothes home. The following day he sent his three-piece black suit, garters, socks, underwear, ring and penknife to Walter at the *Inquirer.* When Marion Hoeflich opened the package, the reality that her boss was a convict struck home. She burst into sobs, her head buried in her arms on top of the clothing.

Walter wrote immediately to Warden W. H. Hiatt to learn how often the family could write and visit. The rules allowed a half-hour visit every two weeks or an hour once a month, weekdays only. Moses could receive seven letters a week and send no more than two himself. Letters were limited to three pages typed by family and one page handwritten by prisoners. Packages and clippings were prohibited. When Arnold Kruse sent Moses two sets of false teeth, the prison promptly sent them back.

The first thirty days Moses spent under evaluation in quarantine. Prison authorities wrote Sadie with several questions about their family situation. Moses's attitude before and after marriage, she explained generously, was "always perfect — lovable, sweet and dear." Toward the children, she wrote, he was "the most devoted father at all times. No man could be better to his children. Our children were sent to the best of schools, and as for religion, morals and discipline, my husband was always most desirous that our children were taught everything that would build fine character and make them fine upright citizens that we can at all times be proud of." His interests outside the home were exclusively business. "He had very little time for recreation. His main interest in life was to make his wife and children independent, so they would have a bright future and all the things he was not able to have and enjoy as a child."[7]

Because space was limited to five visitors, the family took turns going to see him. Walter drove over every two weeks; his mother and three sisters went every month. "We were angry with him because of that girl," said Walter's sister Evelyn, referring to her father and Trudy Boze. "But we went down out of pity. We'd drive or take the train from New York to Philadelphia, then motor to Lewisburg. It was awful. They'd bring him out into one of those visiting pens. It was all devastating."[8]

Moses had given all the daughters so much money that each had well over $1 million. They lived in such luxury that the sight of their father in his prison uniform, even to those whom he angered, invariably started them crying. Moses was initially not all that eager to see them either. "I many times feel that I would rather have our loved ones remember me as I was than as I am," he wrote. He was, however, good with women and he had great affection for his daughters. When they did visit, he jollied them with quips and caustic cracks, often about their husbands, past and present, few of whom he appreciated.

Moses wrote in pencil almost exclusively to Walter, who had copies typed and passed on to the rest of the family. In his first letter, July 25, he warned his son that "we all have a great deal to think about and do due to our obligations and I therefore hope you will more than ever apply yourself in every direction to helping my state of mind while here. Please try to remember all I told you before I left and conduct our affairs accordingly . . . and do not let adverse publicity discourage you."

His first weekend there he discovered that the New York Sunday newspapers arrived before his *Inquirer.* "Please investigate and make correction," he ordered. Walter wrote back that if he were worried about newspaper distribution at Lewisburg, "you must be feeling a bit more cheerful." Sadie's encouraging notes were spirit lifters. "I adore Mother's letters," Moses wrote. "She is in a class all by herself."[9] "If Walter makes good," he said, "it will not be necessary for me to go back to work as before which will give me more time for her, family and traveling."[10] (Trudy Boze never wrote Moses. The day after he was sentenced to prison and she was left without a "protector," she propositioned one of Moses's lawyers. He turned her down and she was not heard from again.)

Within ten days, Moses was giving Walter orders about the *Inquirer*. "As the political campaign progresses, you must increase your policy with more vigor and intensity," he wrote on August 2, signing his letters, as usual, "the Poor Old Guv." "Tell your news staff I said they must not let the paper become dull or lackadaisical in any respect or department. YOU must keep thinking and working and you will be amazed at your achievements." Some letters revealed character traits that had contributed to his fate. "Get more circulation for the *Inquirer*," he wrote, "and for that you may, with my blessing, disregard principal [sic] and ethics."[11]

Walter filled him in on everything from circulation figures, guild negotiations and manufacturing costs, to such news as that the three doctors who testified for his probation appeal had billed him $2,500 apiece. Walter sent them $500 each. Paying off Moses's fine at the rate of a million to a million and a half dollars a year now that there was no longer income from the Nationwide wire made Walter think in ways he never had about minimizing expenses. He began consolidating Moses's assets, especially his stock holdings, which he converted to cash. The 1935 Cadillac kept in Miami was sold to a jai alai player for a paltry $250.

Next, he trimmed staff. Arnold Kruse left amicably. Stanley Kahn, who was married to sister Jan, was fired. Walter never liked or trusted Kahn, who took the firing badly. He tried to blackmail Walter by threatening to launch a rival to the *Daily Racing Form* and to have Moses transferred from Lewisburg to Alcatraz unless he were rehired for a thousand dollars a week. There was no chance of that happening, but the very mention of Alcatraz made Walter's blood run cold. He asked the friend who told him of Kahn's threats to swear out an affidavit in case the former son-in-law tried to follow through. "My philosophy concerning these things," Walter wrote, "is that I would rather be impoverished than submit to blackmail or extortion."[12]

As soon as Moses went to prison, Walter's work schedule shifted dramatically. He was in the office by 8:30 A.M., transforming his father's orders into action in Philadelphia while trying to raise his spirits in Lewisburg. He urged his father to start writing an autobiography or at least jot down notes.[13] "As I pace the floor in my office I think, if I only had your ability and my health, what a combination it would be! I don't suppose I can ever work into that, but for your edification, I am going to try to."

Moses had learned the hard way about political coverage and gave strict instructions about the 1940 campaign. By ordering Walter to "handle news in a dispassionate manner; no mud slinging and do not deal in personalities," he was abandoning his old approach to news. It is clear from reading his letters that Moses spent much of his free time each day reading and comparing the New York and Pennsylvania papers. If Guffey attacked Wendell Willkie, the Republican challenger to Roosevelt, Moses wanted to know why the *Inquirer* had no story. "I don't want any pussyfooting in regard to our political policy and I want particularly all political news well covered," he wrote, carefully underlining each word.[14]

Moses constantly exhorted Walter about being a leader. "I wish you would also gradually assert yourself as a full fledged boss should," he wrote. On another occasion, he seemed uncertain that Walter ever would: "I hope please dear God, that you will make the grade."[15] Both letters Walter dutifully had typed and sent to his mother and sisters.

Walter frequently tried to cheer up his father, sometimes to inadvertently hilarious effect. "The blue outfit you had on looked well on you," he wrote about Moses's prison garb. "As a matter of fact, blue is your most becoming shade, so when I come up with the family . . . please don't be concerned about your appearance." There were "Don't get discouraged" admonitions and pleasure that he was looking like "your old self once again. Please view your present situation as an enforced rest which ultimately will do you a great deal of good."

After several months of receiving regular and detailed reports of circulations gains and promotional stunts, Moses began giving Walter more credit. "Your competitors must be green with envy," he wrote. "Your good business judgment and earnest attention to all details fulfills all my hopes in so far as you are concerned."

Walter was learning quickly. When a sales manager for International News Service went to see Walter after hearing that he might lease wire lines instead from Western Union, Walter described in detail his problems with International's service and how "I was not going to deal in sentiment," and wanted improved service. Then he made a small deal with the salesman to keep the negotiations on a positive note and closed the deal with Western Union as insurance. It was what he thought his father would have done. "The best impression that I have ever seen you make on people was when you first 'knocked them down' and then 'picked them up' and treated them like a long lost brother," he wrote Moses. "It was very good psychology."

Both Annenbergs were disappointed when Roosevelt trounced Willkie in November by 449 to 82 electoral votes. In spite of the two-to-one odds against Willkie, Walter had predicted a Republican victory on the basis of the war's being in a quiescent stage and his feeling that rural and Bible Belt voters and conservative Independents would be enough to sway the vote. When it failed to happen, Walter conceded that "my judgment on the outcome . . . was certainly bad and I shall henceforth abstain from prophesying on elections."[16] Moses consoled himself by saying, "I am merely one of the many that guessed wrong. . . . I felt all along we might go wrong but I did not expect to go so far wrong."[17]

Both had held out hope that if the Republican were elected, he might pardon Moses. They never discussed the subject in their letters, nor, according to reports by warden Hiatt, during their biweekly visits. But it would have been natural for them to feel that way. Secretary of the Interior Harold Ickes believed Moses was angling for a pardon. He had heard circuitously from a Lewisburg official that Moses was talking about Willkie's promising to pardon him. "Whether this was an outright promise or not, I do not know," Ickes recorded in his diary, "but I suspect that Annenberg has a very good reason to believe that this would be the result."[18]

With Roosevelt in the White House for the remainder of Moses's full term, Walter, unaware of the president's personal role in his father's case, tried for a Roosevelt pardon. On February 19, 1941, he and Joseph First, the savvy young general counsel Moses had hired the previous year to watch the business side of the *Inquirer,* took the train to Washington, D.C., for a 10 A.M. meeting at the Mayflower Hotel. They met two major Pennsylvania Democrats: Matthew McCloskey, a wealthy Philadelphia contractor with such Irish charm that John F. Kennedy named him ambassador to Ireland, and David Lawrence, governor during the Kennedy administration and later a senior aide to Lyndon Johnson. After a forty-five-minute talk, McCloskey and Lawrence walked to the White House for an 11 A.M. appointment with the president.

They returned in an hour and told Walter that Roosevelt was sorry, but because of the publicity the case had received, he could not pardon Moses. He knew the Cecelia companies were being run properly, that the tax payments were being made and that the *Inquirer* had been fair in the 1940 election. "He said that he would have [Attorney General Robert] Jackson pass the word along the line that parole should be granted at the first possible time, i.e., one year," read Joe First's notes. "Also to DL's specific request, he replied that DL could so tell the family. MMc pledged that he would follow this up and make sure that M.L. was out by 7\22."[19]

M. L was not out on July 22. His request for parole was denied a week earlier. Walter called the denial "a painful surprise" which was "especially painful since the president had sent us assurances of your parole at the end of a year." He began plotting revenge, then had second thoughts. "Revenge becomes a fixation of the mind which is unhealthy and only causes further troubles," he wrote his father. Then he noted that he had sought solace in something President James Garfield had said about the nation which he believed applicable to individuals: "This nation is too great for mere revenge. But for the security of the future I would do everything."[20]

Moses reacted with less emotion and more calculation. "I warn all of you against any panicky action. Plan carefully." He was certain that "I am definitely entitled to parole." He had pleaded guilty only to save his son and associates, he reiterated. He had run Cecelia with able legal counsel; he had not overseen the bookkeeping. The government had audited his tax returns yearly and never told him anything was wrong. When he was assessed a fine, he agreed immediately to pay it. He had disbanded his wire service and cooperated completely with the government. He had had no previous arrests and his prison conduct had been exemplary. "If I am not entitled to parole I wonder who is?"[21]

On July 25, the family filed an application for executive clemency, a presidential pardon. Cardinal Joseph Dougherty, the archbishop of Philadelphia, wrote the president to support the bid, as did entertainer Eddie Cantor, merchandiser Bernard Gimbel, Hollywood tycoon Jack Warner and others. The most significant letter was from Judge Wilkerson to the president stating that he had no objection to a parole or a pardon.

"In fact, I think that everyone who took part in the hearing, including the United States Attorney, believed that if the record of conduct of the defendant in the institution in which he was confined showed that he had observed the rules of such institution, he would be able to make a successful application for parole." His support for early parole, said the judge, "was an important factor in my mind in denying the application for probation and in reaching a conclusion as to the sentence to be imposed." Wilkerson was saying that he had sentenced Moses to three years and turned down the initial probation bid because he wanted him to serve one year, but that was all he believed Moses should serve. Judge William Campbell, the former prosecutor, concurred and also signed Wilkerson's letter.[22]

Francis Biddle, the Philadelphia Democrat who had worked with Ickes on "Harold's speech" attacking Moses in 1938, had by 1941 become U.S. attorney general. His unequivocal recommendation to the president on August 21 was to deny clemency, and none was granted.[23]

The family next sought a rehearing on the request for parole. That took place on September 4, with Walter, Sadie, and two daughters, Esther and Enid, rearguing the case for Moses's release. The parole board was struck by Wilkerson's recommendation and Campbell's endorsement, but promised only to consider their petition. A few weeks later, on a business trip to Chicago, Walter was overcome. On a cold, drizzly night, he walked to Grant Park. "Sitting myself at the base of the statue I had a good cry," he wrote his father. "During this spasm of melancholia I reviewed all the tough luck we had experienced in the past few years and I reached the definite conclusion that we had certainly been more sinned against than sinning. Things must turn."[24]

Things did turn. On November 1, Judge T. Webber Wilson, one of the three-member parole board, advised Walter that the board had unanimously voted the previous day to parole Moses on January 21, 1942 — the halfway mark in his term. The board had formally entered the decision, said Wilson, which would be publicly announced on January 12. Walter was given permission from Warden Hiatt for a special visit to Moses, which he made on November 4. His father was elated.

Other hands, however, were at work to have the decision revoked. Weymouth Kirkland called Walter on November 6 to inform him that James Bennett, the U.S. director of prisons, was trying to persuade Wilkerson and Campbell to withdraw their letter and recommendation. The following day, Bennett told the parole board that Attorney General Francis Biddle did not want Moses paroled. On November 13, the press was notified that the parole rehearing had been denied.

Three weeks later, Japan attacked Pearl Harbor, and on December 8, 1941, President Roosevelt declared that the United States was at war. British prime minister Winston Churchill arrived at the White

House on December 22 for three weeks of war planning and coordination with the president. In Asia, Guam, Wake, Hong Kong and the Philippines had fallen to the Japanese. In Russia, the siege of Leningrad was in its fourth month, thousands of Russians were dying of starvation every day, and the Red Army was trying desperately to launch a counterattack against the invading Germans. The White House may never have been busier.

Between Christmas and New Year's, David Stern, publisher of the *Philadelphia Record*, visited Harold Ickes to inform him that a campaign was underway to pardon Moses. "He admitted that he had a selfish interest because once out Annenberg would make things hot for him," Ickes recorded in his diary, adding that the three-year sentence was "all too small." "After all, gangsterism which was a disgrace to this country for so long originated in Chicago where it grew out of the circulation war between Hearst and McCormick, in which war Moe Annenberg was the principal figure, first for Hearst and then for McCormick after McCormick had bought him from Hearst."[25]

Whether Max might have helped resolve the confusion was moot. He died in February 1941 of complications from a stroke after a prostate operation. Moses said he was "heartsick at [my] brother's untimely end."[26]

After seeing Stern, Ickes wrote the president on December 30 that a campaign was underway to pardon Moses. "My opinion is that even if he spends the full three years to which he was sentenced . . . Mr. Annenberg will not come anywhere near atoning to society for the wrongs that he has inflicted upon it. And in saying this, I do not have in mind his violation of the income tax laws. . . . In his much smaller sphere, Annenberg has been as cruel, as ruthless and as lawless as Hitler himself."[27]

"I think you are right about Mr. Annenberg," the president replied. He had told the attorney general that the case should follow "the normal course — eligibility for parole, which is a matter handled by the parole board, followed by at least four years before he could receive any presidential pardon."[28]

IN THE MEANTIME, the government was examining the status of citizenship of Tobias Annenberg. If his father had not been naturalized, Moses faced possible deportation from the United States upon his release from prison. That prospect terrorized Walter more than Stanley

Kahn's threat to move Moses to Alcatraz. Kahn was merely a disgruntled brother-in-law, but government officials were involved in the naturalization scare.

The question of Tobias's citizenship had surfaced in December 1940 when José Espinosa, chief investigator of the Alien and Immigration Registration Service, visited Moses in prison and then went to see Walter. The visit was odd. Espinosa wanted to leave his address and suggested that he and Walter might have lunch in Washington. Walter could not understand why Espinosa wanted to have any social contact and concluded from that and other innuendos that the agent was trying to entrap him, possibly into offering a bribe. Espinosa told Walter that the department could find no record that a naturalization certificate had been issued to Tobias. "This information tied in," Walter noted in a protective affidavit he swore out after his meeting with Espinosa, "with the ugly rumors . . . that a very concerted and thorough effort was being made to attempt to prove that M. L. Annenberg was not a citizen."[29]

Walter had anticipated that the government might question Moses's legal right to live in the United States, so he had personally sought out Tobias's citizenship papers, which were on file in the clerk's office at Chicago's Cook County Superior Court. Fearing that the records might disappear, he had a copy made and notarized which he kept in his safe. When Walter produced the document showing Tobias had been naturalized in 1893, Espinosa was startled and demanded it be handed over. Walter refused, made a copy of the copy, and the agent departed, apparently satisfied. "I am reasonably certain that there will be no question as to your citizenship," Walter wrote his father after the meeting.[30]

The question did not go away. Thirteen months later, in January 1942, the immigration bureau in Philadelphia summoned Walter, asking him to bring whatever evidence he had of Moses's citizenship. He brought a court-issued legal copy of the original and the photostat he had shown Espinosa. The agent told him that he could be jailed and fined for having a photostat of government papers. Walter explained that he had been ordered by Espinosa to make a copy in the first place. The agent was satisfied with the original, confiscated the photostat and told him never to make a copy again. Walter left, certain that the government had a wide-ranging conspiracy underway to destroy his father and maybe even him too. "They were coming at us from every direction. I was terrified."

DESPITE President Roosevelt's statement that the parole board should deal with Moses, the board was not given full freedom to determine Moses's eligibility. Stern was back in Ickes's office on February 17, more panicky than he had been in late December that Moses might be released. Francis Walter, a Pennsylvania congressman who sat on the House Judiciary Committee, and New Jersey senator William Smathers were asking that Moses be paroled. "Stern said that even [senator] Joe Guffey now wanted Annenberg released, but Stern doesn't and I think Stern is right," wrote Ickes. "Two days later I told Biddle how I felt about it and he agreed with me. He told me, however, that the parole board had decided on a parole. He said he was doing his best to prevent it, but indicated that he didn't know how long he could hold out."[31]

When Smathers went to see Biddle, the attorney general told the senator in confidence that he should stay out of the case because the Annenbergs were paying or offering to pay people to intercede on Moses's behalf. Smathers told Walter, who was enraged by the allegation. "The injustice being done Father is further evidenced by such a mendacious statement," Walter told him.[32] But there were rumors about payments. One alleged that Moses, before he was sentenced to Lewisburg, had offered $1 million to contractor Matthew McCloskey to keep him out of jail.

In an April 1 meeting in Washington with Walter, Sadie and attorney Joe First, the parole board members said they had reversed themselves after deciding to parole Moses because they were told falsely that he had worked for McCormick and had participated in the later circulation wars. They also were told that Moses had been a fugitive from justice in the Baltimore Brevities case in the early 1930s, and were not informed that those charges had been dropped. As a result, on April 10 they again declined to grant him a parole.

At that point, Moses's physical breakdown began. "Without meaning to be pessimistic," he wrote Walter on April 27, "I find my ordeal has affected my mental equilibrium to a point where I cannot see any use in planning to do anything. I've lost faith which means I've lost everything."[33] The letter, with a shaky penmanship so unlike the clear, firm characters he had formed for the previous two years, was the last he would write himself.

Without parole but including days off for good behavior, Moses's earliest release date would come in November 1942. That was too distant for Moses, who by then was suffering from ill health, fierce migraines and organized harassment from prison guards who called him "Jew bastard." Moses "obviously suffered great mental harm as a result of petty persecution" at the hands of prison officials, said Russell Varner, a senior guard at Lewisburg who volunteered an affadavit to Walter about his father's treatment. Varner said that Myrle Alexander, the associate warden, "was very anti-Semitic and was particularly hateful toward Annenberg." Moses spent his first year working in the prison greenhouse and his second in the library, but the torment took place primarily in the cell blocks. "During the entire stay of Annenberg," Varner maintained, "it was quite obvious that instructions had been handed down that he should not be accorded the same treatment that other prisoners were to receive, but on the other hand, every opportunity was to be taken to ride him."[34]

The strain was taking a harsh toll on the sixty-five-year-old. On May 6 he was moved to the prison hospital, suffering from low blood pressure, malnutrition and vertigo. The family visited on May 15 and were horrified by his appearance. Sadie thought that he was suffering from pernicious anemia, which had killed his father, Tobias. Walter's sister Harriet cabled the parole board the following morning. "His condition is truly grave. He is thin as a wraith and so weak that he cannot stand, but even more alarming is his complete lack of physical co-ordination and the heartbreaking fact that he has lost his will to live. He can't live much longer. Surely his debt has been paid with his soul and his spirit."[35] The rest of the family cabled the board the same day: "We plead and pray for you to return our Father to us, so that we may save his life."[36] Walter wrote Roosevelt, imploring the president to free his father and reminding him that the board had voted in favor of parole, but that the order had been rescinded because the board had confused Moses with Max.

Prison officials were concerned. They did not want Moses dying in Lewisburg. Dr. E. C. Rinck, the prison physician, called in Dr. C. E. Irvin, an internist from Harrisburg, to examine Moses. In Irvin's opinion, Rinck wrote Walter on May 20, "your father's condition was not critical and volunteered that such temporary periods of disability he is now experiencing are not unusual or alarming."[37] But Moses's condition continued to deteriorate, and he lost all feeling in his legs.

The parole board announced on May 27 that because of "the prisoner's physical condition" he would be released on June 11. Moses dictated a letter to Walter from the prison hospital presciently explaining that "despite the encouraging reports from doctors here, my physical

condition requires very expert treatment, to be started without delay."
He had hoped to recuperate at Sunnylands but believed he might have
had a mild stroke and should check into Temple Hospital in Philadelphia. He was so ill that he told Walter he thought he might be released
a few days early. On June 3, 1942, he was.

He was too weak to sign his release papers and barely managed to
execute a wobbly x as his mark. He had to be lifted from a wheelchair
into Walter's car for the drive to Philadelphia. He was sixty-five, but
except for his eyes, which held a determined glint, he looked eighty to
his daughter Evelyn. His family formed a tight protective circle around
him.

Philadelphia doctors urged that he be taken to the Mayo Clinic in
Rochester, Minnesota. After arriving by train on June 20 and checking
into a large suite at the nearby Kahler Hotel, Moses underwent several
weeks of diagnostic examinations. Walter returned to work in Philadelphia and kept the letters coming. He had the Ranch A foreman send
eighteen trout for Moses to share with his fellow Mayo patients. He
had the law firm check whether his father's medical bills were tax
deductible: they were not. Walter dutifully sent the news to his father,
writing at least once and sometimes twice a day. Moses had lost much
of his hearing and eyesight and was constantly nauseated.

Mayo's chief neurosurgeon, Dr. A. W. Adson, diagnosed a brain
tumor and operated on July 14 at St. Mary's Hospital. On the operating
room gurney, Moses calmly and firmly told his son, "Please, Walter,
look after all the girls." During the four-hour operation, Adson discovered the malignant glioma in Moses's cerebellum. It was inoperable.
"We can't do anything about it," he told Walter when he emerged from
the operating room. "Pray for pneumonia to take your father."

The next day, Walter sent a telegram to Dr. Rinck at Lewisburg
and letters to each of the three members of the parole board informing
them that his father was dying. He wanted them to know what he and
his family had known, that Moses had indeed been ill and should have
been released from prison long ago. Six months later, in another bitter
letter to Rinck, Walter wrote that he could not believe the Lewisburg
medical department "was completely unaware that a serious neurological condition existed." "The pattern of happenings and incidents as I
review them in my mind all fit in with the general objective, the objective that was accomplished," he wrote. "My one sincere hope is that
the persons responsible have sufficient character to be troubled by
their conscience."[38]

Walter and Sadie and the girls sat by Moses's bedside for days. They discussed the *Inquirer* and politics, and the need for the family to pull together as one. Moses warned them to limit their confidence in their friends. "If you treat them as your enemies of tomorrow, you will save yourself many heartaches and regrets," he warned them with bitter cynicism. He chided himself for being so sour and disillusioned and said if he were to recover, he should have his gall bladder removed, as Sadie had, to remove all the bile he had stored up.

He did contract pneumonia and slipped in and out of consciousness. When awake, he worried aloud about what would happen to the family without him. The girls and Sadie sobbed quietly. He asked whether Walter had the capacity to run everything. Had he taught him enough? Could Walter be effective? Walter felt a knot in his stomach the size of a football. The figure on the bed was not just his father, but his mentor, best friend, and, no matter how alternately demanding and brutally dismissive he had been, the person who meant most to him.

Just before 9:45 P.M. on July 20, 1942, Moses motioned for Walter to come closer so he could tell something to him alone, a message that would tighten his hold on his son forever and ensure his everlasting sense of guilt. Walter put his left ear near his father's lips. "Walter, who knows what is the scheme of things," Moses whispered. "My suffering has all been for the purpose of making you a man."

Then he died.

15

BOY TO MAN

OSES WOULD HAVE loved the black-bordered, six-column obituary published in the *Inquirer* the next day. Written earlier by E. Z. Dimitman and edited by Walter, it portrayed him as a circulation genius and crusading publisher who had had no knowledge of any discrepancies in his income taxes, but who had gone to jail to save an unspecified number of business associates — no mention of Walter — from prosecution. If journalism is the first draft of history, Moses's legacy was in caring hands.

He also would have been pleased with the huge turnout for his funeral on July 23, 1942. More than twelve hundred mourners, including civic leaders and Arthur James, whom he had elected governor, braved 96-degree temperatures to pay last respects. He would have been less thrilled that the service was conducted by a rabbi, but Sadie had insisted that Nathan A. Perilman of Temple Emanu-El, her New York congregation, preside. The rabbi read the Ninetieth Psalm and then from John Greenleaf Whittier's masterwork "Snowbound." Given the date and heat, the latter choice may have seemed odd if not ridiculous to mourners unaware that Moses could recite Whittier, who had edited the *Pennsylvania Freeman* a century earlier in Philadelphia, where a mob protesting his anti-slavery editorials sacked and burned his office. Perilman drew no analogy, but he praised Moses as a "champion of public rights, a defender of the weak and helpless, a spokesman for those who had much to cry out against but were without lips to speak in their own behalf."[1]

At the funeral, Sadie and the seven sisters were disconsolate, holding tightly to each other in grief, their faces twisted in sobs. Walter, though, showed no emotion during either the services at the Bair Funeral Home on Chestnut Street or burial at Mount Sinai Cemetery in nearby Frankford. He was determined not to show what might be considered weakness, because he was acutely conscious that he was now the head of the family.

His father's will had seen to that. Moses had signed it on May 24, 1940, on the eve of Judge Wilkerson's hearing which had put him in prison. The nine-page document left Walter in total control of the Annenberg fortune by naming him sole executor and sole trustee for the estate, which comprised primarily Moses's 240 shares of stock in Cecelia, renamed Triangle while Moses was in Lewisburg to remove the notoriety attached to the old name. Two trusts were created. The first was composed of Moses's stock, all of which was to go to Walter. One-third of the dividends and income from those shares was designated for Sadie, and after her death, the daughters; the other two-thirds of the income was set aside for Walter. The second trust was comprised of the nonstock portion of the estate, which was divided even more in Walter's favor: two-thirds to him outright, while he also held the final third, from which he was to pay the net income for Sadie's support.

The will so overwhelmingly benefited Walter at the expense of his sisters that it was obvious that there would be trouble within the family if the document stood as written. Eldest daughter Aye was upset and Walter too recognized that the distribution was inequitable and inappropriate. On July 7, 1942, while Moses was on his deathbed, Sadie, Walter, Aye and lawyer Joe First had gathered in Rochester, Minnesota, with a one-page codicil changing the disbursement of the income from the stock trust. The revision, which Moses was too weak to sign but marked with a scratchy *x*, guaranteed Sadie $200,000 a year for life, with the balance to be distributed "in equal shares" to Walter and all seven daughters. The trusts would endure until the death of Sadie and Moses's last child, when the remaining principal ($2.2 billion in 1998) would be divided among the lineal blood heirs.

Even with the codicil, the will reflected the faith Moses had in his only son and his old-fashioned European attitude toward primogeniture. Walter was given "uncontrolled discretion" to hold or dispose of Triangle stock plus authority to vote the stock however he wished and to invest in any security he chose. He had control of the *Inquirer* and *Daily Racing Form*, the *Massillon* (Ohio) *Independent*, several pulp detective magazines, *Screen Guide*, *Radio and Movie Guide* and *Click*, the photo publication, but not Nationwide, as the news wire had been disposed of before Moses was sentenced to Lewisburg. And while the codicil adjusted the income stream, Walter retained full mastery over his sisters' future finances.

It was no surprise that Aye, or Esther, the eldest and sole daughter to attend college, was the sibling who had spoken out. The strongest-willed, she had always wanted to be more involved in business matters. A frustrated eldest child, she had repeatedly written her father about strategy and even offered unsolicited advice on the hiring and firing of personnel. Walter later blasted her for what he called her "superior attitude," but what really bothered him was that he considered her a meddler. "She tried to undermine me with my father," he maintained.[2]

Years later, unhappy with the way her brother was managing things, Aye became cantankerous at Triangle board meetings. By that time, Walter had had enough of her and, irritated, dropped Aye and her sisters from the board. "I can't blame him," said Ronald Krancer, son of Polly, the second-eldest sister. "Aunt Aye and the lot of them got on his nerves. Those board meetings came to be miserable, with the sisters all complaining about whether someone was getting paid more than someone else. There were outside board members there and it became very embarrassing. Walter didn't need any of that."[3]

Evelyn, the sixth sister, agreed that "Aye wanted to run everything," but that Walter had no intention of allowing her. "Walter with the family money was like Frank Sinatra. He wanted to do it his way. He didn't want anyone interfering, which was proper because Walter knew what he was doing." He would learn that so well that none of the sisters except Aye complained when he stopped including them at shareholder meetings. "We missed going because it was fun following the business," said Evelyn, "but nobody other than Aye really gave a darn as long as they got the money."[4]

There was other protection built into the will that guaranteed the sisters would get the money if Walter could earn it. It specified, for example, that their trust was a "spendthrift" type, meaning that their numerous husbands could get none of the principal, nor could creditors borrow against it. Whether the trust grew or diminished in value depended on Walter. He had sole discretion whether to advance funds. He was exempted from any statute which limited a trustee's freedom or from having to post bond as executor. The only restriction on Walter was the implicit burden of duty, and that he felt heavily. "I felt a tremendous obligation by virtue of my being the only boy," he said. Yet his sisters were never very appreciative.

Still, Walter had all the authority he needed, which made him more confident than he had ever been. Moses's secretary, Marion Hoeflich, who did not have a high opinion of Walter, noticed one change almost immediately. "After his father died, his stutter got much better," she said.[5] The speech defect did not go away and he continued thirty minutes of daily oral exercises, a reflection of the steely self-discipline he was capable of exercising. He would live with the stammer all his life, but the fact that it became less pronounced allowed Hoeflich, Sadie, and Walter's sisters to acknowledge the obvious. For all his energy and creativity, the presence of Moses had created enormous tension in the family. Walter, though, could not admit that, even to himself. Not only did he love his father, but because Moses had provided well for the family, had given him a start in business and then sacrificed himself in what to Walter was almost Christlike fashion, he was emotionally and intellectually incapable of criticizing his father. Doing so was more than disloyalty, closer to treason or blasphemy. For the remainder of his life, Walter would insist that his father was "wonderful," which was patently untrue. What was true was that the death of Moses marked the beginning of Walter's coming into his own.

HAD HIS FATHER DIED while still in full command, there probably never would have been a liberation. More likely, Walter would have been overwhelmed. Everyone — from *Inquirer* and *Daily Racing Form* editors to Triangle staffers, distribution agency salesmen and his own family — believed that he was in over his head. His mother was supportive, but the only one with any confidence in Walter was Walter. And that sense had come about only gradually during the two years he had been running the *Inquirer* and Triangle while Moses was in Lewisburg.

"The full realization of my responsibilities and the awakening to them only dates back to when you went away," he wrote his father in March 1942. "I have tried not to make any mistakes in judgment and I sincerely hope that some day you will be able to say you were satisfied with the net result of my stewardship during your absence. All in all, I do not feel that those of us in charge of the businesses have anything to be ashamed of."[6] His father knew Walter was right. "You are doing such a good job," Moses replied two weeks later, "that there is hardly any reason for me ever even thinking of coming back to business actively as before."[7]

His father had looked over his shoulder from prison for all but those final two months when he had become so ill. The 423 letters that they exchanged served as Walter's tutorial. Thus, when he took charge Walter felt more energized than inundated. "I knew what I had to do. I had a large responsibility, but I just handled it because I had no choice."[8]

His large responsibility included a wife and two children, about whom more in the next chapter, his mother and seven sisters, five of whose husbands worked for Triangle, and a substantial business empire which was producing revenues even as the family was essentially bankrupt as a result of the government's fine and property liens. Three months after Moses died, Walter filed an estate tax return which showed that his father left assets of $2,700,016 and debts of $5,582,747.

Five million dollars of the debt was the unpaid balance of his settlement with the federal government. Of the assets, all but $45,000 in two checking accounts, $2,138 cash on hand, one Cadillac and five cases of Old Taylor whiskey worth $802 was in real estate and his 240 shares of Triangle stock, though the last was technically nearly worthless. The stock, which had been valued at $100 a share when Moses capitalized the company in 1923 with $50,000 for five hundred shares, had paid $100,000 in dividends ten years later, and $1 million in 1936 on a gross income of $10 million. But Moses had poured all his money back into the company. In the wake of his prosecution, fine, imprisonment and wide-ranging government liens on the family's property, the value of the stock had collapsed. In figuring his estate taxes, the IRS fixed the value of each share at $1.04.

The estate tax return did not reflect the $4 million the Annenbergs still owed on the *Inquirer* mortgage. As the new owner and chief executive officer of the newspaper, Walter assumed that debt. The combination of government liens on the houses at Kings Point, Miami, Sadie's New York apartment, Sunnylands in the Poconos and in a depressed wartime real estate market meant that those properties could not initially be sold. The only property Walter might have liquidated was the *Inquirer.* Unsolicited offers were made. Walter, though, had no intention of selling the paper, whatever the price. He believed that his father had gone to jail and died so that he might run the *Inquirer.*

In effect, Walter and his sisters were broke when Moses died. They were not officially bankrupt, because revenues from the *Inquirer* and *Daily Racing Form* could cover their debt payments. If Walter were to rebuild the family accounts, he was starting with several good commercial properties, but no pile of cash. His success would be the result of his own brains and skills, not from managing his father's wealth, because there was none left. On a cash projection sheet he assembled for 1943, his first full year in charge, Walter estimated receipts of $58,815, from a $20,000 salary from Triangle, $36,400 in salary from the *Inquirer*, interest income and $160 in director's fees. In 1939, the year before his father was sentenced to Lewisburg, he had received $276,000 from the then Cecelia shares, but for 1943 that income was down to $2,255. His projected expenses, mostly taxes and surtaxes but including $6,000 in contributions, totaled $45,423.60. That left him a disposable income for the upcoming year of $13,391.40. Anyone else would have found the notion absurd, but that same year, Walter promised himself that one day he would be worth $1 billion.

With big responsibilities and little income, he had plenty to handle, none of which was made easier by his emotional state. A spoiled bachelor until he was thirty, he had been forced over the next four years by federal prosecutors and parental and business duties to grow up quickly. Thirty-four years old in 1942, he was an amalgam of characteristics inherited from his mother and father. He looked more like the softer Sadie than the crane-like Moses, who was all angles, with a sharply etched face, bulbous nose, and wire-rimmed glasses over eyes that glared. Sadie was full-figured, with translucent skin, a finely shaped nose and smiling eyes that made her children want to sit and tell her everything. Walter too had a thin nose, soft but penetrating brown eyes, a broad chest and an incipient double chin. He was not fat, but all his life he watched his weight. His hair was thick and glossy and his skin shone as if he had just stepped from a shower. His charitable instincts came from Sadie, who was pleased that, despite his financial pressures, Boy had given a full 10 percent of his salary that year to charity.

His father's fall had instilled in him a late-blooming drive and the instincts of a risk-taking loner. But for the few years he had worked with Hearst in New York, Moses had been an entrepreneur who had not run with the business pack. Walter would be comfortable operating alone, but he had spotted the dangers of too much isolation. Moses was too easily cut off. Walter would never let that happen to him. He had also inherited from Moses two traits he did not like to acknowledge: a fierce temper that could prompt vindictive rages and a deep-seated persecution complex.

The anger was understandable. He had largely come to terms with his disfigured ear, but the persistent stuttering was a simmering frustration that he would never escape. The anger pricked by Moses's persistent belittling had been dissipated by the respect his father had shown him in his last years and by the trust he had shown by turning over his entire estate. But that flame of rage in Moses burned in Walter too, and brighter, given his conviction that his father had been railroaded and was the victim of a political vendetta. Exerting the same discipline that pushed him to perform his daily verbal exercises, Walter forced himself to contain the rage, but for decades to come, he was prone to outbursts of temper. As he had written his father at Lewisburg, he recognized that revenge was not a feeling he could indulge if the family were to prosper, but he retained a deep sense of bitterness.

He needed to direct his emotions, but with his father gone he had no one to approach for personal guidance. Joe First and E. Z. Dimitman could help on business and editorial issues involving Triangle and the *Inquirer*, but he had no mentor and few friends. When he married in 1938, he asked Moses to be his best man. He had no better friend.

Never much of a reader as a student or young man, he began poring over history books, the classics and the sayings of political figures, poets and essayists, looking for guidance and the framework of a value system. He would not acknowledge that he had not found the answer in the way his father conducted himself because, again, that would constitute betrayal. Yet he was clearly looking to reinvent himself outside Moses's shadow. He sought out several old teachers from Peddie, where he had always felt the most nurtured and guided, and asked for their recommendations. He wanted to be strong and successful, to restore his family's tarnished name, accepted socially, caring but not a dupe, but these were odds and ends of larger goals and principles which he felt but found difficult to articulate.

Walter sought bits of applicable wisdom, ranging from Thomas Jefferson's musings on freedom and sacrifice to Rudyard Kipling's immortal poem "If," which seemed so apt that Kipling might have written it for him:[9]

> If you can keep your head when all about you
>   Are losing theirs and blaming it on you,
> If you can trust yourself when all men doubt you,
>   But make allowance for their doubting too: . . .

If you can meet with Triumph and Disaster
    And treat those two imposters just the same;
If you can bear to hear the truth you've spoken
    Twisted by knaves to make a trap for fools,
Or watch the things you gave your life to, broken,
    And stoop and build 'em up with worn-out tools; . . .
Yours is the Earth and everything that's in it,
And — which is more — you'll be a Man, my son!

Other aphorisms he wrote down, repeated them until he had them memorized, and had secretaries type them up. At one point, he had a folder with more than 1,450 inspirational sayings that he had accumulated over decades, including:[10]

Beware of despairing about yourself. *St. Augustine*

Fortune is not on the side of the faint-hearted. *Sophocles*

Diligence is the mother of good fortune. *Cervantes*

Cleverness is not wisdom. *Euripides*

Determine that a thing can and shall be done, and then
    we shall find the way. *Abraham Lincoln*

Learn to bear your ills without being overcome by them.
    Juvenal

There is a time of speaking and a time of keeping still.
    William Caxton

In the kingdom of birds, the parrot is the best talker and
    worst flyer. *Orville Wright*

Lack of money is the root of all evil. *George Bernard Shaw*

The first and final thing you have to do in this world is
    last in it, and not be smashed by it. *Ernest Hemingway*

There is always room at the top. *Daniel Webster*

For Walter, these were more than sayings or basic truths. They were ingredients for a blueprint. One cannot imagine Moses doing such a thing, writing down adages in an effort to build and articulate a philosophy. Moses was an instinctual character, unconsciously natural, who moved into a room or situation and took it over, for good or ill. Walter, who would prove himself to be far more complex, subtle, thoughtful and intelligent than his father, had few of Moses's instinctive gifts. To his credit, he recognized that. Not a natural student, athlete, speaker or leader, he found it necessary to order his life with the help of a carefully crafted behavioral master plan.

He did not have to do that. He could have let himself be crushed by the tragedy that had struck the family. But that was never an option. Driven to prove himself, he never considered shirking what he considered his duty. He was too determined to succeed, so he would put one hand in front of the other and crawl out of the abyss. One of the first things he did was reject suggestions that Moses had done anything wrong. "My father never dishonored the family," Walter maintained. "He was brought down by small men who were unwilling to tolerate his strengths and convictions."

It was not a credible defense, and even the family did not completely agree. According to Evelyn Annenberg, most of the daughters believed with Walter that Moses had been the victim of a vendetta, but they did not hold their father blameless. They conceded that the Annenberg name had been horribly scarred. Instead of rejecting his father, Walter moved to commemorate him. He listed Moses on the masthead of the *Inquirer* as chairman and publisher for the years 1936 to 1942. He had printed on the cover of each of the company's magazines the slightly curved letters of his father's monogram, MLA, a practice he continued for as long as he owned Triangle. Over the decades after his death, discreet reminders of Moses's life were published on billions of copies of Walter's publications.

On a visit to his father's mausoleum at Mount Sinai, he came across a small prayer book with a fragment of an invocation that struck him as more significant than any of the other sayings he was collecting. "Cause my works on earth to reflect honor on my father's memory," it read. He had the words engraved on an eighteen-inch mahogany-and-bronze plaque which he kept by his desk. "This," he maintained, "is my life's motivation."

He considered the plaque a constant reminder of what he had to do to fulfill his father's expectations. Whenever he was asked the secret of his success, Walter always responded, "Being born the son of Moses Annenberg." It was the treatment of his father that "turned me around and made a man of me. It was a whip on my back, a lash spurring me on." And yet the prayer's words, while estimable and a worthy inspirational instrument, also belied his denials that he felt no shame about his father's behavior. The very implication of the plaque was that Walter felt an obligation to redeem Moses's reputation. More than implication, Walter's entire life would be an act of redemption, an unending effort carried out with such care that Moses's legacy would be almost forgotten. Almost.

INITIALLY, Walter refused to move into Moses's office. He stayed in his own for several years before constructing a luxurious executive suite on the twelfth floor, where Colonel Elverson had lived. "He was leery about taking M. L.'s space," said Marion Hoeflich. He waited six months before assuming the title of publisher and another two years before designating himself editor.

He never tried to duplicate his father's style, which would have been impossible. They shared a name and certain core political beliefs about the rights and duties of individuals, but otherwise Walter's personality, interests, behavior and management techniques were profoundly different. Walter remained shy, private and aloof. He had little of Moses's exuberance and none of his flamboyance. He did not spend time in the newsroom or sit in the cafeteria with the staff at lunch eating and telling stories. Most days he ate alone at his desk. In later years, he would say that he considered lunches a waste of time and that people who invited him out usually wanted something from him. He was right on both counts, but the real reason was that, at heart, he was a loner.

He did not ride trucks with the drivers, shout over the roar of the presses with the printers, joke with the Linotype operators, play cards with the mailers, take secretaries out for drinks or host staff picnics at Sunnylands. He did not drop into offices, but summoned executives to his office. He designated an elevator for his own use which shot him from street level to his tower office. The others were marked "Local to 11" or "Local to 13." Few stopped at 12, where access from the inner stairwell was also restricted.[11]

To employees who did not know him, as well as to some who did, Walter seemed a haughty, high-and-mighty proprietor who wanted to have little to do with the masses. He did have too many protective shields up to mix easily with strangers. And one of the aphorisms he had copied from Confucius was "Have no friends not equal to yourself." Nevertheless, he was more private than pompous, more prone to sitting in silence, thinking and planning an answer carefully, partly to minimize stuttering, than he was to bellowing orders, more awkward than autocratic, and his thinking about equality was more progressive than that of many of his contemporaries.

Such thinking came from both his father and mother. Sadie was well known in her circle for universal generosity of spirit. Her children, shopkeepers, servants, the postman — she tried to treat all equally. Moses had favorites and powerful likes and dislikes, but he was open-minded on such issues as race. While in prison, Moses had recommended the book *Twelve Million Black Voices* to Walter and editor John Custis, who had discussed it together at length. Custis called the book "a terrific indictment of this entire nation which has stood by complacently while Negroes in the North, no less than those in the South, have been treated with gross disregard of the fact that they were human beings." Custis urged that the *Inquirer* "do everything that we can to bring about a better public understanding as to their inherent rights."[12]

Walter agreed. In June 1943 he ordered that the *Inquirer* stop accepting "any classified advertising which discriminates in the matter of color, creed or race."[13] He asked David Stern of the *Record* and Richard Slocum of the *Philadelphia Bulletin* to follow suit and both did.

There were no black reporters working at any of Philadelphia's major dailies at that time. The first, Bob Thomas, was not hired at the *Inquirer* until 1957, the year Arkansas governor Orval Faubus tried to prevent the desegregation of Little Rock High School. Acel Moore, who began five years later and became the *Inquirer*'s first black columnist, noted that "in the 1930s and 1940s, first the old man and then Walter were covering issues in the black community that no other papers were covering."[14] "It was a matter of common decency and good business," said Walter. "Why shouldn't they be covered? My father and I wanted everybody, whites, blacks and anyone else to read the *Inquirer*."[15]

When he was not overseeing the newspaper, Walter spent most of his time with Joe First, who was eager to consolidate the haphazard operations of the corporations that had made the holding company a mare's nest of convoluted record-keeping. First had tremendous influence on Walter. A man of firmness and probity who became the young publisher's closest counselor, he shared Walter's determination to cut and cauterize immediately any ties Triangle had to shady businesses, managers or employees, especially those that were the legacy of Nationwide and the run-down sheet operations.

He followed most of First's advice. As Moses lay dying, Walter had been informed that his father's friend Walter Howey, a Hearst editor and model for a lead character in *The Front Page*, was ripping off copyrighted information from the *Daily Racing Form* and reprinting it in a racing edition of the *Boston Daily American*. When the son complained, Howey phoned back, called him "laddie boy," refused to stop pirating the racing news and threatened to have legislation introduced to bar distribution of the *Daily Racing Form* in Massachusetts.

Joe First suggested that they make affidavits of the conversation and sue. Walter, though, considered Hearst a family friend and a gentleman who would respond to a personal appeal. With the excessive civility that became a trademark of his Victorian writing style, he wrote Hearst a letter complete with affidavits, details of the theft, Howey's unrepentant and belittling behavior and an explanation that he was contacting him directly, "because of the high personal interest in which I hold you, and I am happy to conclude this letter with the hope that I may not long be deprived of the pleasure of paying you the personal visit which I had so much anticipated."

Walter was certain that the letter would do the trick and he was shocked when Hearst's dismissive reply all but called him a naive young fool. "My dear Mr. Annenberg," Hearst wrote back. "Pardon me if I say your affidavit is a lot of nonsense. I have always been a good friend of your father's and nothing could induce me to say or write or do anything that would injure him. Moreover, I do not for a minute believe that Mr. Howey made the statement attributed to him. Sincerely, W. R. Hearst."[16]

The repudiation was a glass of ice water in the face and drove home a lesson about trust that Moses had tried to impress on him from his deathbed, to treat today's friends and associates as tomorrow's potential enemies. In the big leagues, Walter reminded himself, players filed their spikes, threw spitters, corked their bats, stole signs and seized every competitive edge. First suggested once again that the *Inquirer* sue Hearst. Walter gave the go-ahead and soon after, the *Boston American* stopped stealing the material.

First had come from the Philadelphia law firm of Paxson, Kalish and Treen, which also employed Richardson Dilworth. Moses had hired First in 1939 to help Walter manage the business, which he did for nearly half a century. A short, plain-looking, soft-spoken man with little charisma, First was a corporate lawyer's lawyer, coolly rational and cautious. Called "the abominable no man" behind his back, First's immediate inclination was to say no to anything that involved spending money. A suggestion that the company purchase new equipment, hire more staffers or buy another enterprise all elicited the same response from First: "No, we're getting along without it."

Little escaped his attention. An executive who sent First a careful cost analysis of a project bound in a cover folder, found the empty binder returned with a note, "I want the meat, not the frills." In search of meat to cut, First and Walter culled the Triangle holdings to line up sales.

When independent magazine publisher John Cuneo asked to inspect Triangle's printing operation in Chicago with an eye to purchasing it, Walter was concerned that his visit might suggest to other potential buyers that he was dumping properties. Cuneo suggested that his foreman "call someone at our printing plant and ask if they could, as a courtesy, look at the equipment because they had heard so many interesting things about it," Walter wrote Martin Tveter, one of his Chicago managers. "I agreed with him that this would be a disarming way of handling it and should certainly give no cause for speculation."

An added problem in the early 1940s was that the onset of war so depressed property values that Walter worried whether he would ever be able to raise enough money to get out of debt. He asked the government to lift the lien on the Kings Point estate and the IRS complied. But when the magnificent property was offered at auction, it attracted a single bid of $25,000, which he rejected. Too few people had the means or inclination during the war to maintain and staff major properties, especially oversized summer homes.

Walter did slightly better two years later when he sold Sunnylands in the Poconos for $100,000 ($945,000 in current dollars). He had little choice. In addition to raising income, he needed to reduce overhead, and the yearly upkeep, taxes and staff costs of the property amounted to tens of thousands of dollars. He was unsentimental about letting it go. He had enjoyed the retreat, but it did not appeal to him in the same way it had to his father. Moses loved Sunnylands because there he could fish, ride and be outdoors. Walter had liked it as he had Ranch A, because he could be with his father. He never went back after Moses's death.

The lack of a decent offer was not the only problem with the Long Island property. Ranch A and Sunnylands meant little to Sadie and the daughters, but Kings Point had been home to all of them. It was also the symbol of the family's early success. Now it had become a deadweight, an embarrassing encumbrance that made Walter more aware that every dollar would come hard.

"I don't want you to get the impression that I am becoming hysterical in my desire to liquidate properties," he wrote Tveter, but he was close. "I tell you quite frankly that if I can get a reasonable amount for the books and the printing equipment, I want to get out.

"Regarding the Milwaukee properties and the *Massillon Independent*, I would also be glad to let these go, providing the price was right," he went on. "After all, I have no sentimental interest in them and looking at it quite coldly, I do not know whether I have the right to possibly jeopardize our whole picture by trying to hold on to properties which are not directly related or needed in our real business."[17]

Some businesses that he wished to sell he gave away on his father's final instructions. Moses wanted to reward his most loyal friends and employees. A few — including Joe Ottenstein, who ran the news distribution agency in Washington, D.C., had loyally taken the fall in the Baltimore Brevities case and was one of the few associates Moses was willing to see while in Lewisburg — were given title to the companies they were running. When Walter told Ottenstein of his father's gift, both men were so overcome with emotion they broke down in tears.

Such generosity was touching but also left Walter less financial margin for error. In Philadelphia, strict procedures were instituted to wring out every saving. Orders that thermostats in the *Inquirer* building be kept at 68 degrees in winter had some reporters working in sweaters, jackets and hats. Salaries and pensions were lean; bonuses, nonexistent. Expense accounts were minimal and carefully scrutinized. Reporters took buses instead of cabs. Walter offered no apologies. "The government was trying to wreck us in those early days and we had to battle to save everything."[18]

The government was rarely far from his mind. Not only was the thought of paying his father's fine a constant burden, he was concerned that if he made the slightest wrong move, Washington was watching and ready to strike. He reviewed editorials to insure they were not incendiary. "I wanted the paper more in the middle of the road," he said. "I was very anxious to make sure that we were fair in the political writings. Editors have a tendency to favor one side or the other, but I wanted both sides to feel they were being adequately covered."[19]

After writing the critical note about his father's health to Dr. Rinck at Lewisburg, Walter drafted a letter to Judge Arthur Wood, head of the parole board, in February 1943 on what would have been Moses's sixty-sixth birthday. "How large looms the part you played in causing his premature death. You signed his parole because you knew that he had earned it, and then for personal and practical reasons you revoked it, causing him to become critically ill. What black and bitter irony that you are set up in judgment upon far worthier mortals. When we appealed to you repeatedly for mercy because of his illness, you were at all times prejudiced, intolerant, inhuman and openly antagonistic. You were dishonest and prevaricated in front of your colleagues to influence them. You used your public office for personal and political advantage. Yours is a terrible crime, the crime of sacrificing a human life. If there is any justice, you will one day be visited by the deep sorrows you have caused so many others."

Having written the letter, Walter decided not to send it. Rinck was no threat, only a prison doctor. Wood was a federal judge who could cause trouble. Walter stepped back.

The government was watching Walter and Triangle. The IRS routinely audited their personal and corporate taxes. In 1943, the IRS discovered that while at Lewisburg, Moses was paid $30,000 a year each from the *Inquirer* and Triangle for giving consultative guidance to Walter and First. "The IRS is questioning how a man serving a sentence in a federal prison could be earning $60,000 a year," U.S. prison director James Bennett wrote in a blistering letter to Warden Hiatt. "This certainly looks very bad."[20]

In 1943, Joe First wrote a thirty-two-page letter to the IRS detailing the services Moses had provided through his letters to Walter to earn the salary in 1941.[21] Two years later, the IRS was still curious and First provided an additional twenty-nine-page recapitulation of Moses's advice during 1942.[22] Nothing came of the inquiry, but Walter recognized that it would be a long time before he and his family were out from under the federal microscope and thumb.

Walter felt so vulnerable that he developed a sensitive internal warning system. When he heard that J. Edgar Hoover thought that a Triangle publication was about to publish an article critical of the FBI, he immediately sent a letter to Hoover. "Rumors have reached me to the effect that publications which I direct are supposed to be critical of you and your efforts," he wrote. "Mr. Hoover, if it is true that you have been so informed, then I wish to take this opportunity to deny such allegations." Then, in an attempt at ingratiation that recalled his father's laudatory telegram to President Roosevelt, Walter added, "as a matter of fact, if it should interest you, I consider your success phenomenal and a truly brilliant performance. . . . I gain great comfort out of the knowledge that the Federal Bureau of Investigation is headed by so able an individual as yourself."[23]

Extreme caution prompted Walter's flattery. He knew that the FBI had participated in the investigation of his father, although he did not know the details of the director's involvement. He understood that Hoover was extremely sensitive to the slightest censure of the bureau, so all it took to set every self-preservation synapse tingling was a suggestion to Walter that Hoover might be upset. Walter understood his own reaction and drew from it a larger lesson that profoundly influenced his future relationships with U.S. presidents and other powerful figures. From the scars inflicted from 1938 to 1942, "I ultimately came to the recognition that the greatest power is not money, but political power," he said. "Political power is more direct, more sensitive, more pervasive than dollar power." Cultivation of access to high political power would become an important part of his agenda. Some was natural, the result of becoming more involved in politics through the *Inquirer* and getting to know personally governors, senators and presidents; other strategic aspects were pure defense mechanism.[24]

NINETY EMPLOYEES left the *Inquirer* and Triangle during 1942 to enlist in the armed forces. At the age of forty-four, counsel Richardson Dilworth had rejoined the Marine Corps, fought on Guadalcanal, where he earned a Silver Star, a Purple Heart and the rank of major. Walter was torn by conflicting pressures. He felt savaged by the Roosevelt administration, yet held a strong sense of civic duty to his country. He had registered for the draft in October 1940, but that was so soon after Moses's imprisonment that a call-up would have caused major management problems. He hoped then that he would be passed over and he was. Fifteen months later, the attack on Pearl Harbor pulled the United States into the war and Walter's feelings about serving changed. He still felt the weight of running his businesses, but he also believed that Joe First could handle Triangle without him for a while. The *Inquirer* posed a bigger dilemma, but E. Z. Dimitman, who at forty-five was ten years older than Walter, was capable of holding the newspaper together.

It seemed obvious to everyone else that Walter was unlikely to be accepted by any of the services. He was stone deaf in his right ear. Yet his country was at war, and it was a point of honor and a matter of duty to Walter that he try to serve.

He first attempted to join the Marines because they were the toughest and most demanding and that was where Dilworth, whom he admired, served. The examining doctor rejected him. Walter appealed up the chain of command until General Clifton Cates told him brusquely to forget it. "We have rules and we're not going to break them for you," Cates barked. "Marines count on each other. We can't count on someone who can't hear." Undeterred, Walter tried the Navy. "Suppose you were on the bridge and you couldn't hear an order or a hissing sound from an incoming shell," the chief of medical affairs told him. "You would be jeopardizing the lives of everyone on board."[25]

Walter abandoned his quixotic pursuit. He regretted not being accepted, but he could not be accused of trying to avoid service. Joe First and E. Z. Dimitman did not share his regret. The perils of war were one thing; Triangle under the gun was another. With Walter in the *Inquirer* building, the business of restoring the business could continue.

Sadie was relieved that her Boy had not gone off to war. The prospect of losing her son was too dreadful to consider. The one who would have had to bear the biggest burden was his wife, Ronny, who, four years after she married Walter, already had her hands full.

16

MAIN LINE

———

R ONNY DUNKELMAN was so beautiful and such fun that she
sparkled. An Ava Gardner look-alike, she was a sloe-eyed
stunner with lustrous auburn hair, high cheekbones, a daz-
zling smile, a voluptuous figure and a warm and easy sense of humor.
Walter was attracted the moment he saw her in early 1938 gliding
across the Waldorf-Astoria ballroom in the arms of David Werblin.

Werblin was twenty-eight, two years younger than Walter, when
they crossed paths at the hotel. Nicknamed Sonny by his mother —
"Sonny as in money," said sports broadcaster Howard Cosell — Werblin
was a formidable competitor for Miss Dunkelman's favor. An agent with
the Music Corporation of America, he went on to transform MCA's television division into a behemoth, to run Madison Square Garden, to
build the Meadowlands sports complex and found the New York Jets
football team.

For all his entrepreneurial skills, Werblin was no match for Walter
when it came to the pursuit of his dance partner. He ignored Walter,
who came by and said, "Hello, Sonny," time and again hoping to be
introduced. "Sonny was crazy about her," said the beauty's sister,
Zelda. "He wouldn't introduce her because he was afraid of what
might happen."[1] As well he should have been. Returning to his seat,
Walter told his sister Jan, "That's the girl I'm going to marry."

"You're nuts," Jan replied. "You don't even know who she is."

The next day, Walter bet his friend Rhea Levy $100 that she could
not learn the name of Werblin's date. Rhea claimed her winnings in less
than an hour. The woman was Ronny Dunkelman and she knew her.
Walter asked Rhea to organize a party and invite her, which she did.[2]

Bernice Veronica Dunkelman was the fourth child of David Dunkelman, one of Canada's most affluent businessmen. A pioneering merchant who had emigrated as a child from Poland and eventually was inducted into Canada's business hall of fame, Dunkelman was known as the Henry Ford of the Canadian men's clothing industry. He established Tip Top Tailors, the first Canadian firm to mass-produce and sell ready-made men's suits for a single price — $14 — as well as manufacture uniforms for the police, armed forces and Mounties. Starting with a single retail store on Toronto's Yonge street, Tip Top expanded to sixty-five stores nationwide with a sales force of three thousand.[3]

Ronny's mother, Rose, was equally prominent. An indefatigable charity worker, she supervised the immigration and adoption of refugee war orphans from the pogroms and First World War. She adopted into her own family a young Polish refugee named Ernest whose parents had been killed before his eyes. She was a Canadian Red Cross officer, was awarded a 1937 coronation medal by King George VI for her humanitarian work and was an outspoken champion of Zionism and the colonization of Palestine.

Ronny grew up on the outskirts of Toronto in a cheery, tight-knit family of seven that lived in a sprawling English-style mansion on a ninety-acre estate known as Sunnybrook Farm. The house, which stood at the end of a thousand-yard driveway, had three stories of living and servant quarters on one side, a living room, billiard room, library and two stories of guest rooms on the other. The living quarters opened onto a broad patio and thirty-five acres of lawns and gardens which spilled down to the banks of the Don River. On the other side of the house was the oak hunt room with its double cathedral ceiling, period furniture, gigantic banquet table and a fireplace big enough to stand in which accommodated five-foot logs.[4]

Comfortable and usually full of guests and with children racing about, the house had the feel of the Annenberg home at Kings Point. The parklike grounds were the stuff of children's fantasies. A secret panel in the bar led to a tunnel that cut under the gardens to a thickly wooded ravine, and on weekends the family rode on trails which crisscrossed the land.

In summer, the family moved to Roche's Point on Lake Simcoe, north of Toronto. Rose Dunkelman had purchased the land because much of the best weekend property was being bought up by gentiles and turned into WASP enclaves that excluded Jews. Using a middleman to conceal her family's identity, she purchased a hundred acres of lake-front land, built a dozen homes, and created one of Ontario's loveliest retreats. She named the compound Balfour Beach after Arthur Balfour, the foreign secretary whose 1917 declaration pledged British support for a Jewish national homeland in Palestine. Each time she had a baby, she added a house to the grounds.[5]

After high school in Toronto, Ronny went to Smith College for a year, then transferred to art school in Boston. "She was very popular and dated a lot, but she was also very choosy," said her sister, Zelda, who was eighteen months older. Part of the choosiness stemmed from Rose's insistence that Ronny and Zelda not date gentile boys. They cheated on occasion, but 90 percent of the boys they went out with were Jewish.

When she met Walter, Ronny was twenty-one and attending the New York School of Interior Design with her sister. "I don't know how we made it to class," Zelda recalled. "We were out every single night. Never with just one boy, because then you became engaged, and we wanted no part of that. Whenever a boy asked Ronny to marry him, which happened quite often, she stopped going out with him."[6]

Walter was eight years older than Ronny and, at their first meeting, at the party arranged by Rhea Levy, he informed Ronny that she would be calling him often. She laughed out loud. Men called her all the time; she did not call men. Walter asked her out for the following weekend. She turned him down. She had a date at Princeton. Yet his directness intrigued her. "Walter wasn't like the other boys she was seeing," said Zelda. "He didn't look or act like them. He was nice-looking and polite, but he looked more mature and was much more serious."

Ronny knew he was wealthy, but, according to Zelda, she did not know or care how rich he was. She paid little attention to money because she had plenty from her father. She finally agreed to see him, but on their first date she blushed beet red when Walter told mutual friends that he and Ronny would marry in June — which is exactly what happened. Like his father, Walter was capable of moving quickly when he made up his mind to do something.

In Ronny, he saw just what he thought he wanted. She was beautiful, outgoing and came from a respectable, affluent family with strong parents. Walter was an executive in Philadelphia, a city which did not easily welcome Jews, especially in the racetrack information business. He was looking for a wife who would be an attractive and supportive companion, one who could mix comfortably and visibly on the social circuit and be a good mother to the four or five children he wanted to have. It was not imperative to Walter that his wife be Jewish, though Sadie was delighted that she was. Ronny, however, could only marry a Jew, although her family was more interested in Jewish political causes than in religious practice. Ben Dunkelman, Ronny's brother, was so involved that after serving as an officer in the Canadian army during World War II, he fought in Israel's 1948 war of independence. His bravery and military skills were such that Prime Minister David Ben-Gurion appointed him commander of the armored Seventh Brigade, which he led in the crucial fighting that freed much of Galilee.

Ronny's mother liked Walter and her father adored him. Both were very pleased that their first daughter to marry was joining a successful Jewish family. The fact that Moses had made his fortune with the racing wire and *Daily Racing Form* did not trouble them at all in the spring of 1938, when the Annenberg problems had yet to accelerate. Walter's parents were equally enthusiastic about Ronny. After eleven sons-in-law, Sadie was thrilled to welcome a new daughter-in-law. Moses, who loved beautiful women, simply gazed at Ronny the first time they met. "I like you," he said, finally breaking the silence.

The courtship was frenetic. Walter was older and more mature, but he was also great fun in 1938 in the months before the Annenbergs began to feel the full weight of tax investigations and federal prosecutions. He often drove up to see Ronny in New York, where they danced, shopped, went to parties, dinners, movies, and before long, Ronny — who loved a good time — realized that she had fallen in love. When he returned to Philadelphia, instead of writing letters she cabled him tender rhyming couplets: "Glad you called again tonight, / For if you don't, I don't feel right. / In New York please think of me, / and soon again together we'll be."[7]

Other rhymes revealed a perception about what she was getting into. "I share your time with politics, / I share your time with news; / I hear about elections, / and have to share your views; But when the fight is over, / and the battle it is won, / I hope to have you to myself, / and boy, won't that be fun."[8]

Walter shared Ronny's lack of higher education, but at about the time he met her and started thinking of settling down, he began a conscious effort to broaden his knowledge. She could not resist teasing him: "Your grand allusions historical, / your praises metaphorical; / your reference to mythology, / and Haley's pure astrology; / to [British War

Secretary] Leslie Hore-Belisha, the head of the militia; / to kings and queens that time and fate, / have long since sent through the pearly gate; / can make me feel so nice inside, / but I'd still rather be your Yankee bride."[9]

Ten days before their wedding, she cabled from Toronto, "Left hand ring finger size five. The rest I leave to you." Walter already knew her ring size. Three months before, he had bought her a sixteen-karat marquise diamond engagement ring. "She could barely hold her hand up," sniffed Marion Hoeflich, who thought the stone ostentatious.

At Moses's insistence, Walter had Ronny sign a prenuptial agreement which denied her access to his ninety-two shares of the family company, then worth some $5 million. His father was pathological about ensuring that only lineal blood descendants should inherit shares and had demanded and received similar pacts before the weddings of each of the daughters. This agreement made clear that if he and Ronny divorced or Walter died, the shares would revert to Walter or go to his sisters or children.[10] If Ronny had objected, Moses made clear, the wedding would have been off, but, according to Morton Wilner, who married Zelda, "She didn't give a damn. Her father had plenty of money and she wasn't after Walter's."[11] Ronny would have agreed to anything. She had become besotted. "The thrill of your love from the very start, / has made my footsteps light; / and filled to the brim my singing heart, / so that all the world seems right," she wrote in her final pre-wedding telegram.[12]

The marriage ceremony took place at the Dunkelman home in Toronto on June 26, 1938, the beginning of a fateful period. Three months earlier, Hitler had annexed Austria; two months earlier, Moses had come under attack for the first time in Washington for opposing the New Deal. The ceremony was a relatively small affair for a hundred guests, most of them family. Moses was his son's best man because Walter had so few close friends his own age that he had no one else to ask.

The friends issue would be a factor all Walter's life. He would have colleagues, associates and respected employees, but until late in life few friends whom he trusted unequivocally and liked nonjudgmentally. Respect and extreme caution held him back. "He wanted to respect someone before he played with them," said Wilner, who had known Walter at Penn.[13] The caution came from a fear of being hurt, taken advantage of or used, initially as a child with a stutter, later when he felt persecuted by federal agents and still later when trying to determine if people liked him for himself or for his money.

Ronny and Walter spent two months on their honeymoon, first at Lake Louise in western Canada and then in Hawaii. Moses must have hated to see Walter go. Scarcely had the newlyweds left their wedding reception when he sent two telegrams.

The first was tender and revealed the sentiment that Walter knew existed in his father and loved, but which Moses rarely revealed in public. "Until you did the one and only great thing in your life last Sunday in acquiring as fine a girl as there is on earth and for which you are deserving of no end of compliments and credit it had not dawned on me that you suddenly grew into full manhood and I confess that I had continued to look upon you as my little boy Walter. Now with the full realization of your maturity and your many fine qualifications and characteristics I look forward to your future with much happiness and satisfaction."[14]

The second telegram, sent the same day, was all business. "Before you left I told you you had better hurry back and attend to your paper otherwise you may not recognize it on your return if you remain away too long." He described story conferences, new columnists and features in such detail that he seemed to have forgotten that they had been together in Toronto only three days before. Moses was missing his son, but he also seemed to be establishing early in the marriage that Annenberg business came before family matters.[15]

Walter was so eager to begin a family that he was concerned to learn that Ronny was not pregnant when they returned to Philadelphia from Hawaii. He asked her to see a gynecologist to make sure nothing was wrong.[16] Nothing was, and two months later she told Walter that she had some good news for him. On July 15, 1939, while the grand jury sat in Chicago to hear evidence against Walter and his father, Ronny gave birth to a girl. At Walter's urging, they named her Wallis Huberta, the closest approximation he could find to Walter Hubert. She was a healthy child in all respects but one. Like her father, she had a severe hearing loss on the right side, although the problem would not be discovered for several years.

Wallis was the tenth grandchild for Sadie and Moses, but she came at just the right moment to give a much-needed lift to the family. Ronny was pleased to be a mother and Walter was thrilled. He still wanted a son, but said he was happy to have a daughter.

A year later to the day, Ronny gave birth in Bryn Mawr Hospital to a son, Roger, the male heir who would insure the continuation of the Annenberg line. The child was born with a severely cleft lip and palate. Over the next three years, five operations would be required to repair the disfigurement. Exactly one week after Roger's birth, Moses entered Lewisburg Penitentiary.

When the Associated Press announced the birth of Moses's twelfth grandchild, and Walter's first son, the news story reported that the infant had been named M. L. Annenberg II. Walter said later that the story was incorrect, that he and Ronny had never intended to name the child after his father. There was no suggestion in available family documents that other names had been considered.

Ronny, her mother, Rose, and her brother Ben were upset and angry about Roger's deformity. Not at Roger for having it, but at Walter for not mentioning the possibility. "Ronny was very upset that she had not been told," said Zelda. "By rights she should have been told that the family had a genetic flaw." The flaw, though, was in Ronny's thinking. No one knew whether the family actually had a genetic problem or just bad medical luck. Walter had a deformed ear, which Ronny could see as well as anyone, but they were unaware when Roger was born that Wallis too had a hearing problem. At that time, there were neither genetic screening tests nor such prenatal procedures as amniocentesis, which might have revealed Roger's problem. Ronny had told friends and her siblings that she wanted a family as large as the five she grew up with, but after Roger's birth she decided against having more children. Walter did not try to change her mind.

He discussed the children in an exchange of letters with his father six months after Roger's birth, when he sent photos of them to Lewisburg. "Wallis is now at an age (eighteen months) when I cannot see enough of her. She is developing a remarkable vocabulary and is extremely bright, although somewhat temperamental. She is a typical Annenberg and her biggest delight is to tease somebody," Walter wrote. Roger, he said, was undergoing a second operation on his lip, which he hoped would produce "a result that will be perfectly satisfactory to me."[17]

Moses commiserated. "To expect one continuous round of pleasure from children is just expecting too much," he replied. "As an average, our family is pretty good, but the heartaches Mother and I endured during the development period prompts me to advise not to expect too much and not to be burdened with too many."[18]

When he responded the following day, his own thirty-third birthday, Walter agreed and suggested that the growing likelihood that the United States would join the war then under way in Europe had also influenced his thinking about family size. "While I once thought it might be a fine thing to have four or five children, I now believe that the two children I have is sufficient family. . . . I don't want to be the one to bring additional children into this world to face a possibly difficult future. No doubt I will have my hands full in properly raising my son and daughter and if I can do a good job with them, I will feel satisfied."[19]

The first thing they needed to raise the children properly was more space. Roger was walking and Wallis was running, but they had no place to play except Rittenhouse Square, which was a crowded urban park surrounded by traffic. Ronny had endured Walter's $500-a-month duplex in the Rittenhouse Plaza, although she found it too masculine for her taste. Now it was too small for the four of them. She wanted a house with a big yard and Walter agreed. He wanted to raise his children in the best environment and he also was ready to put some distance between his office and home.

Ronny found a beautiful Georgian mansion on fourteen wooded acres in Wynnewood, about twenty minutes by car and fifteen by train from the city center. The property, called "Inwood" and surrounded by other fine estates, had fallen into disrepair and needed major renovation. Walter purchased it for $45,000 after first checking with Moses. His father wrote his approval from Lewisburg, warning him not to let his sister Enid "drag around one of those artistic designers with morphadite [from hermaphrodite, or bisexual] characteristics to leave you with so much wormy second hand furniture and alleged antiques that you'll never get out of debt."[20]

WYNNEWOOD was on Philadelphia's Main Line, which for decades had been as much a state of mind as it was a location. Taking its name from the double-track rail route built in the 1860s, which stretched from Philadelphia twenty-five miles west to Paoli, the Main Line became one of the nation's most exclusive addresses and shorthand for its singular brand of WASP aristocracy. Beginning just beyond the city limits of Philadelphia, known then as the "Workshop of the World" for the textiles and steam engines that were produced in its belching factories, the Main Line was an early planned preserve, designed and promoted by what was then the nation's biggest corporation, the Pennsylvania Railroad.

To boost development in the 1870s, the railroad had bought large tracts of land near what is now Bryn Mawr, established stringent residential zoning laws and built mock Gothic stations near which railroad executives were expected to live. Communities along the line were rechristened with more elegant Welsh names — Merion, Ardmore, Haverford, Berwyn — and the rail executives and other worthy tycoons built sprawling estates with names like Ravenscliff, Androssan and Cheswold, featuring white-gloved servants and formal gardens.

In both appearance and attitude, the Main Line was the English countryside, right down to its fox hunts and cricket teams. Children rode ponies from estate to estate and adults in hunters' pink coats and silk top hats thundered across rolling meadows on the trail of yapping hounds or raced point-to-point, then returned to fifty-room mansions and martinis, black-tie dinners and dancing until dawn. Ronny and Walter loved the area's beauty, elegance and convenience. Inwood was smaller, but reminded Ronny of Sunnybrook Farm and Walter of Kings Point.

The Main Line was as insular and inbred as it was lush and well maintained. The social structure was based on the ideal of the aristocratic English gentleman. By definition he did not work, at least not hard, but had lived comfortably in those years before the Great War and income taxes by doing business with his friends or living off his inheritance. Upper-class Quakers who emulated English aristocrats shared some of their traits. They were not aggressive workers either, but they were inheritors and thrifty savers who kept a great deal of money in the local banks.

Social conventions were as scrupulously maintained as the lawn bowl courts at the Merion Cricket Club. The elite cultural institutions included the Philadelphia Museum of Art, the Academy of Music and the venerable ball, the Assembly, which dated to 1748.

Acceptance to the inner social circle was based on a complex formula of bloodline, money earned in certain acceptable ways — law and banking, not trade — and upbringing in the appropriate institutions and summer places: St. Paul's or Groton; Harvard, Yale or Princeton; Northeast Harbor or Hobe Sound.[21] Rarely did a Philadelphian or Main Liner ask what a newcomer did. They wanted to know where he went to school and who his parents were.

Sociologist Digby Baltzell, who popularized the term WASP — for White Anglo-Saxon Protestant — captured the local upper-class ethos in his book *Philadelphia Gentlemen* by contrasting typical letters of introduction for three young East Coast gentlemen seeking employment. The letter for the Bostonian stressed his honors degree in classics at Harvard and fluency in French and German. The New Yorker was described as a hustler who had boosted revenues for his firm. The Philadelphian's attributes were rather different.

> "Sir, allow me to introduce Mr. Rittenhouse Palmer Penn. His grandfather on his mother's side was a colonel in the Revolution and on his father's side he is connected with two of the most exclusive families in our city. He is related by marriage to the Philadelphia Lady who married Count Taugenichts and his family has always lived on Walnut Street. If you see fit to employ him, I feel certain that his very desirable social connections will render him of great value to you."[22]

Walter and Ronny moved to the Main Line in 1941, a year after Katharine Hepburn, Jimmy Stewart and Cary Grant starred in *The Philadelphia Story*, the hugely popular movie about class and privilege on the Main Line. Stewart won the 1940 best actor Academy Award for his portrayal of a happy-go-lucky journalist who fell in love with Tracy Lord, the vivacious young aristocrat played by Hepburn, but could not marry her because he was not her kind and would never fit in.

It was far from certain that Walter and Ronny would fit in when they took up residence in Wynnewood, although Walter was about to be the powerful owner of the *Philadelphia Inquirer* and was becoming more involved in civic and social affairs. "At that time," said Robert Montgomery Scott, the former president of the Philadelphia Museum of Art, whose family was a mainstay of the Main Line and whose mother, Hope, was the model for the Tracy Lord character, "my ilk didn't have any respect for people like the Annenbergs at all."[23]

Ronny and Walter had two strikes against them. They were Jews and Moses was a convict. Philadelphia suffered a strong element of anti-Semitism and simply being Jewish, especially an arriviste, was a towering hurdle to social acceptance. The notion that a bright, accomplished, attractive Jew could appear in Philadelphia and be invited in merely because he had a lot to offer was unrealistic before World War II.

There were Jewish members of the Philadelphia aristocracy, descendants of predominantly Spanish Jews who arrived in the 1730s, before the Revolutionary War. Haim Solomon, a Polish Jew, had helped finance the revolution by mobilizing Philadelphia's financial resources to carry the Continental army through its final campaigns against George III's troops.[24] For these early Jewish families — the Rosengartens, Fleishers, Madeiras and Gratzes — acceptance and membership in the exclusive clubs was possible.

"In the midst of this snobby attitude that Philadelphia had against people that were not its members, if you were Jewish and had been a member for years, your Jewishness was not held against you at all," said Thacher Longstreth, a city councilman and veteran political gadfly whose autobiography, *Main Line WASP*, is insightful on the subject. "You were protected just like everyone else. If someone insulted you, one of your Protestant friends had whoever did it thrown out of the club."[25]

Member "for years" actually meant "for a century or more." German Jews who arrived in Philadelphia in the mid-nineteenth century were on occasion able to assimilate, but those like the Annenbergs who came to the United States in poverty from farther east on the Russian border in the third wave in the late nineteenth and early twentieth centuries discovered that access was all but impossible. The WASP hierarchy in Philadelphia, with its myths and Anglophilic pretensions shut out Jews as it did blacks, excluding them from clubs, law firms, banks and neighborhoods. The doors slammed with such finality against the last wave that even the long-assimilated families felt the impact. "Philadelphia's Protestant establishment, in a cool, patrician manner, built an inviolable caste system," explained social historian Murray Friedman. "Upper-class and seemingly well-integrated German Jews learned the painful lesson that to the gentile peers a Jew remained a Jew and as such an outsider."[26]

Acceptance for Walter and Ronny hinged more on Moses Annenberg, who posed a formidable problem. "The establishment would never say they were freezing Walter out because of anti-Semitism," said Digby Baltzell. "They would blame it on his father. Moe Annenberg was a much bigger reason for the snobbishness directed at Walter. It was why Walter was shut out for so many years."[27]

Digby Baltzell and Thacher Longstreth were not alone in believing that Philadelphia was probably the single most difficult city the Annenbergs could have picked in which to work and live. "There's probably not a town or city in this country at that time where Moe Annenberg would have been less likely to have been accepted," said

Longstreth. "He would have been taken in in Chicago and more than accepted, probably lionized, in New York. But in Philadelphia, he was ostracized."[28] When Walter was prevented in those early years from joining Gulph Mills or any of the Main Line's most prestigious country clubs, he built a three-hole golf course on his Inwood property.

WALTER WAS determined to restore the family name and finances, to pay the federal fine, to preserve the *Inquirer,* the *Daily Racing Form* and the rest of the Triangle stable of smaller publications, and to be a good father. Ronny settled in to a new and less than completely welcoming community, eager to renovate Inwood, raise two active children, one of whom needed medical care, and support a busy husband. It was not an easy undertaking. Overshadowing everything from her marriage in 1938 until Moses's death four years later were the legal case and Walter's unceasing effort to secure his father's release from prison. "She felt like she was in the middle of a tornado," said her sister, Zelda. "Those years were hell."[29]

Ronny rarely went to the *Inquirer* office unless she were meeting Walter for an evening function, but the staff loved her. "She was a wonderful girl," said Marion Hoeflich. "She never complained. She was pretty, came from a delightful family and was a lady to her fingertips. And her brothers. So handsome. Any one of them could have gone to Hollywood."[30]

Ronny loved her brothers, her children and Walter. She had a more difficult time with her seven sisters-in-law. "Walter's sisters were very, very difficult for Ronny," Zelda said. "She was from Canada and she just was not as sophisticated as these New York girls. They adored their brother, who had taken on all these responsibilities and who could do absolutely no wrong. He was like a god to them, so whenever there were any problems, it was always Ronny's fault."[31]

Walter's family confirmed that he always got the benefit of the doubt. "What Uncle Walter did for the family was phenomenal," said Cynthia Polsky, daughter of Lita Hazen, the fifth sister. "My mother certainly felt that the sun rose and set on him."[32]

Raised as princesses, the Annenberg daughters reminded some people of Cinderella's stepsisters. "The most dreadful women," Richardson Dilworth called them. "My mother and my six aunts, with a few exceptions, were probably the most difficult people I ever knew," said Ronald Krancer, son of daughter Polly. "All of them were spoiled and a number were totally unreasonable."[33]

"They had the money and the upbringing," said Marion Hoeflich, who knew most of the daughters from her years as secretary to Moses. "But they were also the kind that my diamond has to be bigger than your diamond. Some were nice, but most were terribly difficult. So imperious. They were nouveaux riches and always giving orders, telling you to drop everything and take care of their train tickets or hotel reservations. Do this, do that and do it yesterday. And they had the worst taste in men you ever saw. Imagine bringing a fellow home and telling your father he's got to support him."[34]

One of the many who needed support was Leonard Howard, Lita's first husband, who was making $40 a week in a stock brokerage when he met her. Moses hired him at $200 a week and continued to supplement the allowances of Lita as well as her sisters.

"They were all spoiled," Howard complained in a deposition to prosecutors who were trying to determine how much money Moses had. "My wife was brought up, as the other children were, in a very extravagant manner. They did not know the value of a dollar because they always got whatever they wanted. I never saw those sisters denied anything."

In his mind, they all had exorbitant clothing, manicure and hairdressing needs. "One summer my wife bought 14 white dresses at Best & Co. for the season at Great Neck," he said. "And because she had a phobia about going into hairdressing salons, the hairdresser had to come to the house and instead of costing $5 or $10, the hair cost twenty. I thought it was too much."[35]

Lita told her family that Howard was too much — of a petty jerk — and divorced him in 1934 after four years of marriage.

The other sisters liked Aye, the eldest, who was Walter's least favorite. He claimed she was "too aloof," but his problem with her was that she was the most competitive for Moses's attention. It did not help that Walter could not stand her husband, Leo Simon. He owned a chain of women's clothing stores and made the mistake of demanding that Walter give him a discounted advertising rate in the *Inquirer*. When Walter refused, Simon advertised in the rival *Evening Bulletin*. However, Evelyn, sister number six, called Aye "my absolute favorite." Aye was the brightest of the girls. An artist, she never showed her work, but was a serious painter and a founding member of the Skowhegan School of Painting and Sculpture in Maine. Aye played carefully selected classical music over the crib of her adopted son,

Steven, who went on to found and conduct the Washington Chamber Symphony.

Polly was the odd sister out. Not as pretty as the others, she was the family mimic and clown, the leader of the faction that skipped school for hair appointments. She once attended a Christian Science service where she stood up and proclaimed that prayer had healed her broken arm and two legs. She had, of course, never been injured. There was also a dark, temperamental side to Polly. "She could be very odd," said her sister Evelyn. "Extremely difficult," said her son Ronald. "She was always angry about something, never at peace with anyone. She really needed care, a good therapist."

Polly first married Herbert Krancer, a handsome man who worked for Moses at the *Daily Racing Form* and *Radio Guide*. Krancer reciprocated by physically abusing Polly. "A stormy life," she admitted before divorcing him for cruelty. She then married a Chicago ear, nose and throat specialist named Benjamin Levee and saw much less of her sisters in New York or Ronny and Walter in Philadelphia. "One day she called me up and I said, 'Yes, Mrs. Levy,'" recalled Richardson Dilworth. "And she said, 'Are you trying to insult me?' I said 'No, what do you mean?' And she said, my name is Le*vay.*" Dilworth howled with laughter.[36]

Jan, number three, was the family beauty. Called "Empress Justina" by her sisters because she once appeared in a local opera where her dress cost more than the production, she had long red hair, gorgeous clothes, marvelous flair and wanted to be an actress, a career that never materialized. "Men were crazy about her because she was so beautiful," said Evelyn. Her first husband was Stanley Kahn, who worked for Moses and whom Walter came to hate. "An unscrupulous chiseler" who stole from the company and double-crossed the family was Walter's judgment. Later married to Stewart Hooker, a *Daily Racing Form* and *Morning Telegraph* executive, Jan did not have the volatile, edgy and highly sarcastic disposition that her sisters seemed to have inherited from Moses. Calm and composed, Jan was unflappable, her mother's daughter.

Enid, the fourth, was one of the more intelligent sisters and the only daughter to hold a full-time job, as editor of *Seventeen* magazine. Her first marriage ended in divorce; then she married Norman Bensinger and adopted a daughter, Pamela, who broke Enid's heart. Pamela became fixated on learning the name of her natural parents, which Enid did not know and in the 1940s could not learn. When Enid invited her to New York for her birthday party, Pamela cabled, "Sorry can't make your birthday, have to go to a dog show."

"That was as bitter a repudiation of a mother who gave her everything as I'd ever heard," said Walter.[37] In the 1970s, Walter and the family fought and won a bitter legal case to prevent Pamela from inheriting a full family inheritance on the grounds that Moses had intended the Annenberg fortune to pass only to blood descendants. Pamela settled for $4 million; the family said good riddance. Willowy, elegant and chic, with exquisite taste, Enid later married Ira Haupt, an investment banker, who was happy to see his wife channel energy outside the home, especially into gardens and horticulture, her passion.

After divorcing Leonard Howard, Lita, who was often the mediator among the sisters, married Joseph Hazen in a 1936 double ceremony with Enid and Ira Haupt. An inordinately intelligent man — and, according to several family members, "the best of the sons-in-law by far" — Hazen was a loving husband and father and kind lawyer and film producer who wrote the Warner Brothers contract that enabled the studio to produce *The Jazz Singer*, the first movie with sound. In partnership with producer Hal Wallis, Hazen made *Come Back Little Sheba*, *Gunfight at the O.K. Corral* and *True Grit*. Their daughter Cynthia, a painter and philanthropist, would become the brightest star of the next Annenberg generation.

Evelyn, the sixth sister, was an athlete who eloped at nineteen with Kenneth Friede and was accompanied by her mother on her honeymoon to France and Italy. "We had a wonderful time," said Evelyn. "We both adored my mother." Friede was yet another son-in-law to whom Moses gave a job, on the *Morning Telegraph*, where he stayed even after Evelyn divorced him and married William Jaffe, an art partron and lawyer who represented Columbia pictures.

Harriet, the youngest sister, played the piano by ear, loved to sing and dance and wanted to go on the stage. "She was mad for the theater," said Evelyn. (The passion, along with the means to indulge it, allowed her to buy the diamond that Richard Burton purchased for $1 million and gave to Elizabeth Taylor.) She appeared in two road shows before marrying Bert Friedlob, a film producer and playboy whom she divorced. She then had a happy marriage with Sadie's fourteenth son-in-law, New York stockbroker Paul Ames. Together they became Broadway angels and, starting in the 1940s, invested in a string of musicals, among them *Brigadoon*. "She was a little naughty," said Walter,

"but a good scout at heart." A brave woman who was unafraid of anyone or anything, Harriet dropped dead of a heart attack in her early
fifties.

Even discounting Dilworth's "dreadful" and Krancer's "most difficult" characterizations as perhaps excessive, the sisters were nonetheless an awesome assemblage of powerful personalities. Composed or
volatile, they had trenchant likes and dislikes which they were rarely
reluctant to express. By the middle 1940s, Ronny had become one of
the dislikes. "She was a bitch," said Evelyn.

Actually, she was unhappy. Ronny did not know many people in
Philadelphia. She was lovely to look at and fun to be with, but had little drive to do more than enjoy herself. Never much of a student, she
had few intellectual interests. Walter and she were similar in that latter
regard when they first met and married. But once he began trying hard
to improve himself and Ronny did not, friends, family members — and
Walter — realized that he was significantly more intelligent than she.
Unable to keep herself entertained or involved and with a nanny
responsible for the children, she became bored on the Main Line.

In the meantime, Walter was a workaholic, putting in fourteen-
hour days on *Inquirer* and Triangle business as well as paring every
expense to the bone to make the multimillion-dollar installments on
Moses's fine which were due through 1946. He was so nervous about
the government catching him out that he had refused to let Ronny ship
anything from Canada to Philadelphia, including their wedding presents. He was apologetic, though, and tried to explain by equating his
behavior with that of wartime shell-shock victims. "I too have developed an anxiety neurosis because of the feeling I have of once again
getting enmeshed with federal trade authorities, Treasury snoopers,
agents, immigration officials, customs officers and various and sundry
other official (and officious) individuals who have and still would like
to make life miserable for me."[38]

Walter was attentive when he was home, but Ronny chafed at his
exceptional tidiness and nitpicking perfectionism. She laughed when
he lined up his socks and underwear in his bureau drawers and his
shirts and jackets in his closet and bristled when he criticized her
sloppy penmanship on bank checks. Ronny also liked a good time, but
good times seemed few and far between with the family under siege
by the government. She visited home often, but her own family in
Toronto seemed far away. Walter's sisters did not like her. Her son had
problems. Her husband's seriousness and what she considered his

penny-pinching were getting to her. Although it was 50 percent higher than the average *Inquirer* reporter's salary, she was not pleased with the $75-a-week allowance — later upped to $85 — that Walter deposited in her account at Tradesmen's National Bank.

"I have at hand a bill from Simon August in the amount of $237 representing charges for the 'few scatter rugs' that are in the baby's room," Walter wrote her in December 1940. "To say that this appears superfluous and ridiculous is superfluous. In the future, please exercise some degree of judgment in your purchases."[39]

"For pure unadulterated waste, the enclosed Western Union telegram to the *New York Times* cost $1.81," he wrote eighteen months later. "You could have sent all this in a letter with a three cent stamp — these are the things you will have to learn."[40]

When Ronny had a charge at Elizabeth Arden sent to the office in July 1943, Walter's secretary wrote her that he was paying the bill but, "We will deduct this sum from the next allowance check which we deposit to your account."[41] Six months later, when Ronny complained to Walter about his refusal to pay the sales tax on securities she had sold, he sent her a two-page, single-spaced accounting of what he had spent on her over and above her normal allowances. The total was $4,341.35 for such items as a mink coat, Persian lamb muffs and a $375 donation in her name to the United Jewish Appeal. In addition, while they were scrimping at the *Inquirer,* he had bought her $17,495 worth of jewelry, including gold bracelets and ruby and diamond pins.

Beyond that, he spent another $13,916 on her personal and household allowance, and salaries for maids, a nanny, and Rose Babos, his father's old cook, not to mention the $7,900 he gave away in contributions during the first six months of 1943. "Please understand that there can be no extras during the year 1944," he wrote her. "I trust the above figures will clearly indicate why this is necessary."[42]

She fought back, impishly but with a bite. "Dear Sir," she wrote him at the *Inquirer.* "Because of obvious rise in cost of foodstuffs and lack of increase in budget to meet same, I find that I am no longer able to make ends meet. You will recall I have brought your attention to these facts before and they have received nought but scorn. I have therefore but one path to follow — I hereby relinquish my post as family exchequer."[43]

Walter's sisters had expensive tastes, but he was not responsible for their personal bills. Ronny's prompted more complaints. "With the many expenses we have these days, I cannot afford monthly floral bills of $50," he wrote in April 1945. A week later, he was back with "You are breaking me — bills, bills, bills." In 1946, he was trying to bring her into financial line again, complaining that "your insatiable appetite for spending is a disease that I hope you will be able to cure." When she overdrew her checking account by $30.50 in 1947, he was horrified. "While this might not be embarrassing to you, it is extremely so to me."[44]

Ronny said he was nickel-and-diming her. Walter was annoyed that she showed such little self-discipline. Yet when she took the children and went to Lake Simcoe each summer for three or four weeks with the Dunkelmans, he missed her terribly. He joined them for a few days midway through their visit and otherwise kept in touch by telegram. Some cables involved logistics; others were more telling.

"Pretty, occasionally graceful, girlish, disposition spectacular and sometimes alarming, her nature calls for domination, experiences great difficulty masking true likes and dislikes, fits neatly into the category of old fashioned mother," he wired her. "Has been known to take an extra move in backgammon, also failing to count all cards in gin rummy defeats, gets rather standoffish about paying gambling losses, generally maneuvers with native shrewdness cosmetics on husband's charge account. Great believer in charity especially if husband foots the bill. Yes, yes, a devoted wife, leaves packages almost anywhere, engages dummy dressmakers, spills food on her clothes, breaks dishes and has ninety negligees. But it all adds up to the woman I love. [Signed] Double Big-Mouth."[45]

Six weeks later, he sent a half-joking cable to their home signed Metro-Goldwyn-Mayer. "Am going to make another version of Dr. Jekyll and Mr. Hyde. (This time) Dr. Jekyll is going to be a female and we have learned on good authority that your abilities qualify you for the role. Would you be interested?"[46] Her evil twin was getting under his skin.

While the expenses were a continuing source of aggravation at a time when Walter felt under the gun financially, they were not what eventually undermined the marriage. There were larger problems.

One had little to do with Ronny and everything to do with her being married to Walter during the worst years of his life — the legal battle, Moses's imprisonment and death, the gigantic fine, taking control of the *Inquirer* and Triangle, the first years of marriage, a newborn with physical problems — all the while trying to sort out his own persona, perhaps the most difficult challenge of all. "I have been under a tremendous strain," he had written his father at Lewisburg in April 1942, "and considering my inability to sleep these days and constant source of business aggravation and irritation that I have each day, my nerves are not as good as they used to be."[47]

He had been a smoker since attending the Wharton School at Penn, and tension over what the government might do next had pushed him up to three packs a day of Philip Morris cigarettes. One morning he awoke with a throat so raw he could barely speak. The specialist he consulted blamed the smoking. "Keep it up for a few more years and you'll have no problems at all," the doctor said. Walter got the message, quit cold turkey and never smoked again, a feat in itself considering that Ronny continued to smoke. Quitting added stress in the short term, but also revealed his capacity for self-discipline. A moderate drinker, he gave up liquor too, although only temporarily.

The other problem involved the profound difference in Ronny's and Walter's personalities. "Ronny liked a good time," said her sister Zelda. "With Walter, everything had to be just so." Ronny was vivacious and warm. Walter had been charming and fun when he met her and he warmed up again when he became a successful ambassador. Yet during these years of struggle and adjustment, he was stiff, reserved, formal and defensive. When the mayor asked the Annenbergs to give a greeting at one New Year's parade, Walter offered dutiful best wishes to the crowd, then handed the microphone to Ronny. "Kung Tsi Fat Choi," she shouted. Any Chinese listeners might have understood the traditional Cantonese New Year greeting "May you have a prosperous life." Everyone else was baffled. "They were very, very different," said Wallis Annenberg. "My father was serious and interested in making a name in the business and political world. My mother was emotionally immature and wanted to party and have fun. I think they were total diametric opposites."[48]

In short order, their different approaches to socializing led to complaints about her flirtatiousness and his jealousy. "She was a bit of a flirt," Walter conceded. His sister Evelyn put it more bluntly. "She was boy crazy." Daughter Wallis conceded, "My mother wasn't promiscuous, but she was definitely a flirt and she had more men chasing her."[49] According to Zelda, "Walter was insanely jealous." No one accused her of having an affair, but Ronny's head was turned. "Men were after her all the time and she didn't know how to handle it," said Evelyn Annenberg.

Ronny recognized that she and Walter had a problem. In August 1944, she wrote him from the Dunkelman summer home on Roche's Point asking for "your forgiveness and understanding." "Darling, I admit that you have many reasons for being disgusted with me and feel like throwing in the sponge, especially in view of the consideration and sweetness you have shown me. There are innumerable examples of your sweetness and generosity and sincere effort to show your fondness for me.

"I love you. Not in the way that caused me to stamp out of taxi cabs in jealous rage. I don't think that kind of being in love was intended to last in marriage. The real thing is a deeper unity, something concerned with our home, our children, our futures.

"As for Bob Kerdasha, the whole idea of your jealousy toward him seems to me absurd. I have not as yet reached the age where I no longer require companions my own age — male or female. The fact that he is young and unmarried is immaterial. To me, your friendship with Mrs. Earle, an attractive divorcee, is on the same basis. Actually I feel hurt that you no longer trust me and are resentful of my friendship with Bob or anyone else." Ronny ended the letter by apologizing. "Sorry, Wally. I will try to be more understanding (and respectful) in the future."

Yet the seeds of mistrust had been sown and the gap continued to widen over their separate interests. As he became more comfortable running the *Inquirer* and Triangle, Walter edged more into Philadelphia's civic and social mainstream. It troubled him that Ronnie was having difficulty keeping up and that she shared so few of his soaring interests in business, politics and current affairs. "There was never any teamwork," said Wallis. Walter would not say so himself, but he also wished she were smarter and not so perpetually flighty.

At the time of their eleventh anniversary in 1949, Ronny's card "to my sparring partner" signaled the beginning of their final rounds. "For tho' we're not like turtledoves," it read, "at least we haven't put on the gloves." No, there had been no violence, but the marriage had irretrievably broken down. Walter was willing to keep trying. Ronny was the instigator of the split which, with some initial exceptions, was amicable.

In September, three months after sending the card, she moved to Florida and filed for divorce on the grounds of "extreme cruelty." In what was a mild formal complaint, she charged that Walter preferred his own family to hers, that he considered her family "chowderheads," that he refused to socialize with some of her friends and that he "always demanded the plaintiff keep the home to perfection and that their children likewise always be in the best of order."[50]

Walter denied all charges except the one alleging perfectionism. "Defendant admits that he desired his home to be kept in good running order; [and] that his children should be brought up properly."[51]

In Miami Beach, Ronny also told friends that Walter had objected to raising Wallis and Roger as Jews. That was inaccurate. Walter had no interest whatsoever in organized religion himself, just as his father had not, but he had no objections to the religious training of his children if Ronny wanted to take on the assignment. But he would not pursue the training himself. The children were not raised as Jews during the marriage or after the divorce, when they spent most of their time in Ronny's care. She could have sent either child or both to Hebrew school but chose not to, which was fine with Walter.

Other stories filtered up to Philadelphia from Florida. "One report is that R. [Ronny] has been drinking heavily and looking badly," Joe First wrote to Morton Wilner. "If true," First underlined, "it may be something that you or Zelda may sometime be able to advise me on. I know people are very happy to gossip and I am discounting most things I hear."[52]

In the divorce settlement, Walter agreed to pay for Wallis's and Roger's education, $5,000 a year ($34,000 in current dollars) for each in child support, a $100,000 lump sum ($672,000) payment to Ronny and $35,000 ($235,000) annually in alimony, which she collected for only three months.

While in Florida waiting for the divorce, Ronny met Ben Ourisman, a wealthy auto dealer from suburban Washington, D.C., who had been a widower for twenty years. Just as Walter had, he too fell instantly in love with Ronny. "She was very vivacious and knocked Dad off his feet," said his eldest son, Mandy Ourisman.[53] They wed quickly. "Too fast," said Zelda, explaining why the Ronny-Ben union lasted only four years.

When Ronny left with the children, Walter said he felt no remorse, but thought hard about how he wanted to spend the rest of his life. He was forty-two. His father had been dead for eight years. The fines were all paid. He had gone beyond being Moe's son and was starting to come into his own as the proprietor of the *Inquirer* and of Triangle. At the office he was curt, distant and demanding, but socially he was engaging and courtly. He was powerful, rich and good-looking and women liked being with him as much as he enjoyed them. But he had learned from Ronny, who appeared to offer everything, that the right woman for him had to be more than physically attractive or come from a good family. She had to be smart and share his interests, and, because he had been the favorite child and was doted on forever, she should also be prepared to defer to his every iron whim, boyish or otherwise. He wanted to marry again, but to such a partner. He had thought Ronny would fill that bill, but she had turned out to be, in his words, "terribly wrapped up in herself." What Walter wanted was a wife who would be wrapped up in him. If he could find the right one, they could make quite a team.

17

SEEDS OF EMPIRE

WALTER WAS WALKING on Fifth Avenue with his sister Enid, enjoying the sun in early April 1944 and gazing idly into shop windows, when she stopped to take a closer look at several mannequins showing the latest teenage fashions. "You know there's no magazine for teen girls," he remarked. As they continued their walk north toward their mother's apartment, Enid said that he was right. She read *Vogue,* wore fine clothes, and followed fashion and the arts, but for the younger generation, including their own teen nieces, she had to admit there was nothing.

On his return to Philadelphia, Walter scanned the latest copy of *Editor and Publisher,* the trade magazine for the newspaper industry. One article related the impact of the 1943 decision by the War Production Board to ration newsprint. Under wartime rules, the armed forces received all the paper and pulp they needed, but stringent restrictions limited the amount of paper a publisher could use and prevented wildcat newcomers from entering the magazine publishing field.

There were, however, modest loopholes. Publishers already putting out two or more magazines were allowed to redistribute their paper to take advantage of the fact that demand for all publications far outstripped supply. The article started Walter thinking about another snippet of publishing intelligence he had heard — that the paper quotas had forced some of the fashion magazines, including *Vogue* and *Harper's Bazaar,* to turn down as many as 150 pages of advertising per issue.[1] This was a torrent of money waiting to be mopped up. "I knew there was a market," he said, "and then when I heard about the other books rejecting all that advertising, my appetite was whetted."[2]

He checked with Lit Brothers and other clothiers in Philadelphia for suggestions on who best knew the fashion industry. The consensus was that Helen Valentine, the merchandising and promotions director for *Mademoiselle*, was the person to see. Walter immediately called her in New York and asked her to come to Philadelphia to discuss a business idea. When Mrs. Valentine arrived, he told her that he was thinking of publishing a fashion magazine to tap the advertising overflow. His one criterion was that it be "wholesome" because he wanted it to be respected, but he was uncertain where to position it editorially.

She knew instantly. "Teen-age girls," she told him. "There are eight million of them. They have their own spending money, buy their own lipstick and makeup. Clothing lines are being designed for them and advertisers are ready to buy space, but there is no publication aimed at that market." Walter sensed that she was right. He had only just said as much himself to Enid. That teen girls were a vast, untapped market was true in part because the whole concept of being a "teenager" was new. The term had been introduced in 1938 and the broader notion of adolescence had only been defined in 1904 when psychologist G. Stanley Hall recognized that the teen years were a distinct stage of life and not merely an interim between childhood and adulthood.

Demographic studies were an integral part of marketing in the late twentieth century, not during the 1940s, but Walter always operated on instinct. "He's the man with the golden gut," said David Sendler, later one of his top editors.[3] With the ad overflow and Helen Valentine's reaction, he had a market opening and the idea to fill it. He would advance a theme that Sadie and Moses had tried to instill in the Annenberg children, to respect elders, behave responsibly and look presentable. Parents would appreciate the message, which he believed would translate into added business.

Walter reviewed the Triangle stable. He had two detective magazines, including *Official Detective Stories,* which sold for a dime and was earning up to $50,000 a month. *Screen* and *Stardom,* two movie fan magazines, were making a comfortable profit. He had moved *Click* up-market, away from the Hearstian formula of sex and sensationalism that Moses liked but which troubled Walter. As a result — or maybe in spite of the change — *Click* had become the nation's third-largest photo magazine, behind *Life* and *Look.*

Although its circulation was over a million, *Click* was unlikely to overtake the Luce and Cowles publications. The detective "books" were great sellers on the army bases, but demand was bound to drop after the war. He saw no reason to keep two fan "books." *Stardom's* paper quota could easily be put to better use. He saw two advantages to launching a teen magazine while the war was on: no start-up publisher could challenge him and he would have a head start on the postwar boom. He called Helen Valentine and offered her the editor's job. There remains a dispute over who suggested the title *Seventeen* to catch the upper middle of the bobby-sox brigade.

Walter liked the name but, scrupulously careful, he wanted clearance from Booth Tarkington, whose 1917 novel *Seventeen* was a bestselling classic. Stressing the wholesome theme, he asked the novelist if he had objections. Tarkington said the formula sounded so constructive that he urged Walter to use the title.

On September 1, 1944, the first issue of *Seventeen* rolled off the presses — thick, slick and oversized, featuring forty-five pictures of Frank Sinatra and advice on fashion, beauty, etiquette, school problems, movies, music and behavior. Priced at fifteen cents, the magazine had a press run of four hundred thousand which sold out and prompted 500 letters on general content and 425 more on a knitting article by Helen Valentine. The October run was increased to five hundred thousand; November's by an additional fifty thousand.[4]

Advertising kept pace with circulation. The December holiday issue comprised 120 pages, 66 of which were ads. Walter could have printed more pages of each, but the quotas prevented him. *Seventeen* was such a successful start-up that he decided to shut down *Click* even though its projected revenues for 1945 were $1 million. "The demise of *Click* was brought about by the fantastic success of *Seventeen*," Walter told Wade Nichols, a former *Click* staffer who was in the army and wrote to ask what had happened. "The company was faced with either carrying along everything skimpily or sacrificing a publication to more fully realize the possibilities offered by another." In January and February, *Seventeen* went to 160 pages, 95 of them advertising, and Walter was still forced to reject 20 pages of ads.[5]

Pegged as a hot book by Madison avenue, *Seventeen* would have been even thicker if Walter had not adopted a conservative advertising policy. The magazine accepted no liquor, beer or cigarette advertising. Even background figures could not be shown holding cigarettes or beer. To avoid potential criticism that the magazine promoted early marriages, it refused hotel ads featuring honeymoon suites or bridal gowns. Because Walter found the word distasteful, he forbade use of the word "pimple" in headlines, yet he could not stop jokers calling his magazine "The Acne and the Ecstasy."

The cosmetics industry was a major advertiser and some young models appeared elaborately made up, but *Seventeen* refused to accept ads for hair coloring. Walter's rationale was that a parent could tell a child to wash her face, but he did not want a fourteen-year-old brunette showing up at the breakfast table as a blonde and telling her parents she had been inspired by *Seventeen*. "To me, not having that advertising was a matter of character," Walter said. "And it was good business. Parents, especially mothers, liked having their daughters reading *Seventeen*."[6]

The mother he had in mind was his own. In any examination of Walter's life, Moses gets the lion's share of focus as the parent who most shaped the only Annenberg son. Yet in her modest, retiring and very different way, Sadie influenced Walter every bit as decisively as his father. When Moses belittled, Sadie encouraged. "My sweetheart Boy," she wrote him soon after *Seventeen* was launched. "I am so very proud of you my dear because you do use your head."[7] Sadie's strength had taught him to use his heart as well. Because he was the product of parents who were very different from each other, Walter's temperament often alternated between their two poles.

Moses had been tall, lean, rock-hard and tenacious; Sadie was short, soft, nurturing and intuitive. Moses wanted Walter to seize opportunity; Sadie wanted Walter to offer others opportunity. Moses showed Walter how to make money; Sadie taught him to give it away. Moses's fall inspired Walter to restore honor to the family name; Sadie's goodness showed him the way to do it. "My mother was very concerned that we be good citizens," said Walter. "We were brought up to understand what was expected of us."[8] Sadie had taught her children that whatever their troubles, they were a fortunate family on whom God had smiled. It was her philosophy that the family had a duty to help others less fortunate that later inspired the Annenbergs' philanthropy. But well before that, Sadie's decency, and Walter's idealistic respect for her as an Everywoman role model, contributed to *Seventeen*'s underlying philosophy.

Seventeen was aimed at daughters, not mothers, but in many ways, the magazine was as much about respect as it was about teen fashion. Children and parents respecting one another. Readers and advertisers respecting *Seventeen*. The business community respecting Walter, the once-weak son who was creating, as had his dynamic father, a successful company of quality. And, most of all, Philadelphia and the nation coming to respect the name Annenberg because it was affiliated with good works, reputable issues and honorable people. Financial success alone was not enough. Because his father had been hurt by ties to a disreputable business, it became increasingly important to Walter that his businesses do "good" and that he associate himself with people of "character" whom he called "decent citizens." Raising decent citizens was an important theme in the *Seventeen* formula. Walter wanted his young women readers to buy his advertisers' products in the context of looking presentable and behaving responsibly.

Helen Valentine was a talented editor, not an evangelist like Walter, but she recognized the merit in her owner's vision and promptly incorporated it into *Seventeen* so that readers, parents and the ad sales department all benefited. She set the tenor of the magazine for years, but after the war, she and Walter clashed over its target audience. She wanted to stay focused on teenage girls; Walter pressed her to include an older group called juniors who ranged in age up to about twenty-four, whose style sense was more sophisticated and who had more spending money. By 1948, more confident about his instincts, he was insisting that she devote half the magazine's editorial content to each of the age and style groups. Valentine called the decision "drastic," but conceded that "you are probably right that including juniors will bring an immediate gain in advertising revenue."[9]

He was right. Circulation climbed to one million and advertising revenues to $3.4 million, but Valentine was uncomfortable with the change. "More teenagers wanted junior clothes and the junior advertising was far more profitable, but she disagreed with me rather violently," said Walter. When she tried in 1950 to persuade him to fire publisher Alice Thompson, Walter instead fired Valentine and replaced her with Thompson, who had been the founding editor of Condé Nast's *Glamour* magazine. Walter and Thompson got along well for five years until the editor one day made the same mistake as her predecessor and forgot who was actually in charge. Walter was testing another magazine and asked Thompson if he could borrow a few of *Seventeen*'s unused offices.

"We can't do that," she responded. "I don't think we ought to be engaging in tenement journalism."

"Tenement journalism?" Walter erupted with a temper like his father's. Usually he kept it under courtly wraps, but when unleashed, his rage was formidable, as it was this time. He did not have to ask her at all, "but I was trying to be polite. She missed the signal so that was the end of her. Good-bye Alice."[10]

Into the publisher's job went sister Enid, who had written features for the *Inquirer* and its Sunday magazine until she became annoyed with copyeditors rewriting her stories and asked her brother for a more challenging job. "What the hell, she knew enough about journalism to let her try," Walter said. "Turned out she was damn good."[11]

At first, Enid did not want the job. She could write and had an exceptional sense of style — she was in the fashion hall of fame, grew prize-winning orchids and was the nation's leading benefactor of horticulture. But she knew nothing about running a magazine and did not want to look foolish. Walter insisted.

Of all his sisters Enid was closest to him in age and temperament. Watching her work at the *Inquirer,* he had seen that she had real ability. He trusted her and promised he would always be available for advice. She was persuaded because her regard for her brother was high. *Seventeen* was doing well and Walter was proving to be a wizard at making money as a result of his "epiphanies," as the family called his seemingly divinely inspired business decisions.

"My brother always had these brilliant ideas that nobody else thought were going to work," said Enid. In hindsight, she turned out to be one herself, but at that moment, she was terrified. "Everyone must have been laughing to high heaven at my brother's nepotism, and I vowed I would not embarrass either myself or him."[12]

She never did and she was not terrified for long. She held the publisher's job from 1954 until 1962, when he named her editor in chief. Within a half-dozen years, advertising revenues had risen to $18 million and circulation to nearly two million, which was a hundred thousand ahead of *Glamour* and nearly double that of *Mademoiselle. Reader's Digest* said that more college girls read *Seventeen* than any other women's magazine. Surveys showed readership at 6.5 million, more than half the nation's population of teen girls. The magazine claimed that "five times as many high school and college girls buy from *Seventeen* [as from] all the fashion magazines combined."[13]

Enid's talents turned out to be a perfect match for *Seventeen.* No one worked harder or proved a quicker learner. She knew how to delegate and had enough self-confidence to admit when she did not know something. She understood her audience, both teen and parent; she was highly organized, had an excellent eye for stories, great curiosity, a powerful common sense and a resolve to do good works.

She was tough and a stickler for proper behavior. When, shortly after she took over, a woman executive said she was "too busy" to show her around the offices, Enid smiled sweetly and said, "You have written your epitaph." The woman was gone before lunch. While vacationing in Paris with her husband, Ira, Enid came across a *Seventeen* editor who was also on holiday and invited her for dinner. During the meal, the woman inquired whether she was being promoted to an editorial job that had just opened. Enid said they would discuss it back in New York. After the editor persisted, Enid told her, "I'll remember to look for someone else."[14]

When Enid became editor, there were 10.5 million teen girls in America, with an estimated annual allowance of $5 billion. "And they don't put it in piggy banks or gilt-edged securities," she said. "Teenagers have no tomorrows, only todays." They accounted for 25 percent of cosmetic and toiletry expenditures and 20 percent of spending on women's apparel and shoes, and Enid knew just how to deal with them. "Don't talk down to them and don't promise what you can't produce because a teenager who is disappointed never forgets. They really believe what they read," Enid said. "In ads, use young models and place them in real situations, perhaps slightly idealized, preferably centering on their social life, like dates or pajama parties. And keep in mind that for teenagers the picture is mightier than the pen."[15]

Elegant in her Chanel suits and, unlike some of her sisters, her judicious displays of jewelry, Enid edited *Seventeen* until 1970 from her pink swivel chair under the old master paintings in her pink office overlooking Park Avenue. She hated to waste time, avoided lunches, and was often spotted on her way to an appointment sitting ramrod straight in the back seat of her black Rolls-Royce, nibbling on a chicken sandwich plucked from her designer purse.

She stayed trim. *Seventeen* grew plump. The fall fashion issue in 1967 weighed three pounds and contained 456 pages, 336 of them ads. It suffered no paper rationing, but Enid still turned away ads. Throughout the flower-power hippy era she published little psychedelic art and few photos of long-haired bearded young men. "I love teenagers," Enid said, "but when it comes to standards, I'm an awful square."[16] Square, but no old fogy. Her feelings about content ensured a tasteful tone, but she moved *Seventeen* from stories about kissing and petting to information on menstruation, drug addiction, homosexuality and teen sex and marriage.

She never wrote or talked about it, but Enid must have felt especially qualified to have *Seventeen* discuss teen marriage because she had run away herself at seventeen in 1924 and married thirty-nine-year-old Norman Bensinger. Moses had been furious and she later divorced Bensinger, but as most editors understand, experience makes the most penetrating magazine articles. A letter from a girl explaining how she could not discuss certain issues with her mother prompted a health series incorporating "How to Get Sick on Pills and Capsules" and "What Makes Boys Different." Dinner party conversation led to "A Girl's Guide to Sailing" and "Teen Life in India." Reading about a civil rights march caused her to commission "What You Can Do for Human Rights in Your Own Home Town."

In speeches and articles she urged teens to get all the formal education possible. "If you can't go to college, be curious, get the reading habit," which was how her father, Moses, had educated himself. She wrote about the value of teens' belonging and conforming and also about how teens revolt, join gangs and become delinquents. Dignity and respect were constant themes for parents as well as children. "Maintain parental dignity. A girl wants to be proud of her parents at all times. She wants to present a neatly dressed father to her friends. She wishes Mother would 'act her age' instead of showing a boy how well she jitterbugs," Enid wrote. "Criticize less; criticize privately; give graciously — or not at all. Establish rules together." Once she became comfortable in the job, Enid sought little guidance from Walter. The editorial formula came from her heart and was reflected in her activity away from the magazine as well.

In the belief that flowers and wildlife were curatives, she donated a greenhouse and solarium to New York University's Institute of Physical Rehabilitation, which the staff promptly dubbed "the Garden of Enid." So blind teenage girls could learn about fashion, she inaugurated a "Please DO Touch the Merchandise" program of special fashion shows in major cities around the United States and produced a special braille edition of *Seventeen* which she donated to a thousand girls each month. Walter was delighted with the job she was doing, though he did wish that she'd stop calling him Boy.

WITH *Seventeen* well launched in New York and a national success, Walter threw himself into the kind of civic works in Philadelphia that he believed "decent citizens" should perform. Eager to be part of the war effort, he was delighted when he was invited to join a secret unit of the Philadelphia Police Department to investigate radicals and espionage activity. The FBI and police departments had been swamped with tips about subversives and fifth columnists, all of which had to be investigated, and Philadelphia had particular reason for concern. The Philadelphia naval yard's sixty-five thousand workers labored around the clock on triple shifts building and repairing warships, the Frankford arsenal manufactured ammunition and the Philadelphia quartermaster depot was the central disbursement point for military uniforms, boots and supplies.[17] Each was a potential target for saboteurs. Walter was deputized and given powers equivalent to those of city detectives. Initially assigned two cases which he could not talk about, which was "pretty tough for a big-mouth like myself," he did his snooping at night, which did not delight Ronny. One part of the assignment he particularly liked was riding around the city in police cars. That became a long-term fascination as well as an education into how Philadelphia worked, and the source of story tips which he enjoyed passing on to *Inquirer* editors.[18]

One night a week he reported, along with other prominent Philadelphians, for work as a waiter, serving meals to military men and women at the Stage Door canteen in the basement of the Academy of Music. He assigned writers from the newspaper to the Office of War Information, where Enid had worked before coming to the *Inquirer*, and was active in the Pennsylvania Defense Council, which coordinated statewide civil defense activities.

To support the Army Relief Society, he had the *Inquirer* organize and promote a football game in Memorial Stadium between the U.S. Army and the Philadelphia Eagles, the local professionals. On the masthead of the *Inquirer*, he published a wartime platform which pledged "to publish the war news graphically and accurately, not exaggerating our victories nor minimizing our defeats; patriotically to commend or to criticize our country's war efforts and policies as the public interest may require."

For his news columns, he bought analyses of battles and strategies by senior military officers and published, sometimes over a period of weeks, excerpts from the latest military books. He assigned lengthy profiles of senior generals and admirals, many of whom came from Pennsylvania, including army chief of staff George C. Marshall, Henry Harley "Hap" Arnold, chief of the army air forces, and his deputy Carl "Tooey" Spaatz, who commanded the allied bombing effort against

Germany, and admiral Thomas Kincaid, Pacific commander of the Seventh Fleet.

Walter was having problems with managing editor E. Z. Dimitman. The editor had been his father's alter ego for years. E. Z. and Moses had thought the same way, treated staffers the same, walked and talked the same, even looked the same — tall, angular, wiry. In many respects, Walter respected Dimitman's management of the *Inquirer*'s war coverage. Dimitman sent two of the *Inquirer*'s top reporters overseas with superb results. Reports from Alexander Kendrick in Moscow on fighting on the eastern front and the difficulties the Soviet people were having were exceptional. So were those from Cy Peterman, who brought the D-day invasion into the living rooms of *Inquirer* readers after he flew behind German lines into France aboard an air corps glider.

Walter's trouble with Dimitman stemmed directly from the fact that it was he and no longer his father who was running the paper. Moses had been as strident as he was dynamic as an editor and publisher. Walter was neither. He had clashed with his father and Emile Gavreau over the contents of the Sunday magazine, trying to tone it down, and he now found Dimitman balking at his directives. Walter pushed for more cultural stories on the art museum and Academy of Music and more thorough coverage of social events. Such stories bored Dimitman, who often failed to assign them. One day in 1943, Walter called the editor to his office, recited a list of unpursued stories and told Dimitman that if he continued to ignore orders, he would have to find other work. Dimitman was astonished at the ultimatum and found it difficult to accept, coming from a man he had not yet grown to respect. "I forgot the old maxim," said Dimitman. "The king is dead, long live the king."[19]

"Dimi couldn't work with Walter, so he quit just as Walter was about to fire him," said his wife, Marion Hoeflich.[20] The publisher had been in nominal charge for three years, but Moses had not been dead a year and Walter had already done what few thought was possible: evolved from a pampered playboy whose suggestions were easily dismissed to a decisive executive. Somehow Marion's husband had missed the transformation.

When the war ended in Japan in August 1945, Walter slammed a single three-inch-high headline — PEACE — across all eight columns of the *Inquirer*'s front page, printed a prayer of thanksgiving beside the nameplate of the paper, and began planning his next move. He wanted to go to Europe to see what had happened to the continent he had known as a youth and which was rapidly being reshaped by postwar political and economic forces. Leaving Ronny and the children behind on Lake Simcoe, he spent the following August and September traveling through Germany, Austria, France and England. Since his days in Miami writing "Boy About Town," he had wanted to be a foreign correspondent, and while he would not have qualified otherwise, now that he owned his own paper, he could fulfill his ambition. He could not type, but every few days he sent long handwritten letters to Joe First, who had them edited into stories that ran under Walter's byline.

The government and U.S. military were pleased to escort senior journalists around in the former war zone because the printed word was still the way most Americans received their news. As publisher of the *Inquirer,* Walter was a VIP and was given preferred treatment once he checked into the Frankfurt headquarters of U.S. forces. Orders were issued authorizing him army escorts and transportation by military aircraft and government vehicles, the most efficient means of getting around, as the bomb damage to roads and railways was severe and would take years to repair. "The carnage is complete," Walter wrote from Frankfurt. "Atomic bombing could not have accomplished more."[21]

One of his first stops was Zeilsheim, an all-Jewish displaced persons camp of 3,300 exhausted souls near Frankfurt. He explored the kitchens, examined children suffering from malnutrition and spoke — "My German's not too bad," he told First — with survivors of Dachau and Buchenwald. "Same vile, sad story — starvation, overwork, torture, abuse, bullying and cold, meaningless murder." The great majority of the former prisoners, he discovered, were "ardent Zionists who want to go to Palestine."

His brother-in-law Ben Dunkelman was in Palestine at that moment, a Zionist helping to establish a Jewish state. Two weeks before, on July 22, Irgun forces led by Menachem Begin, who was to become prime minister of Israel, had protested British rule in Palestine by detonating a bomb in Jerusalem's King David Hotel, killing ninety-one people. Walter, however, made no reference in his dispatches to Ben or to the dramatic events in the Middle East, nor did he give any hint of his own thoughts about Zionism. If anything, his reports were bland, dispassionate, superficial and pedantic and revealed a lack of real curiosity and of solid journalistic training. He was on the certified tour and recording dutifully what he saw with the kind of detail a touring student might have included in a trip report for a teacher. Yet there was no evidence that he was emotionally connecting with what he saw and no contextual analysis that related anything he was experiencing to what had happened in the war.

In Heidelberg, he found the demand from Germans for cigarettes so strong that he resumed smoking for the duration just so he could share a pack and give some away. In Munich he was housed at the palatial former residence of Herman Geisler, the district's deputy administrator, which reminded him of the designer of his apartment on Rittenhouse Square. The furnishings were "the closest thing to Robsjohn Gibbings imaginable," he wrote to First. "These krauts, at least some, had wonderful taste, but I can't get away from the feeling that this place was built on blood."

The next morning he visited Dachau, the concentration camp where 280,000 victims had died and which was being used to detain Nazi prisoners. To his astonishment, the first solitary cell he came to bore the name Herman Geisler. Walter slid back the viewing screen and unable to resist the impulse, shouted, "Herr Geisler, achtung" into the cell. "Up he jumped, trembling," Walter recounted. "He probably figured the Americans were going to forgo trial and his day was here." Pleased with having frightened a ranking Nazi, he went down the row of cells, peering into each one. "Never have I seen a meaner, wilder, more sadistic-looking collection, even the few women looked like beasts." The morgue had been repainted four times since the end of the war but there were still bloodstains around the base of the walls. He found the room still smelled so much of death that he ran out after a moment.

Dachau reeks of evil and leaves a horrific impression, but Walter's reaction was muted. In a sixteen-page letter to Joe First, he described everything he saw and heard, down to and including such facts as that it took fifteen minutes for the crematorium ovens to consume a fat corpse, but up to an hour for a thin, emaciated one.

The details were all there with a claim that he had been powerfully affected by the experience. "Impressions and scenes here will never leave me," he wrote. "One cannot gain a true impact of this national conduct unless one has an opportunity to personally inspect one of these monstrous camps. If I have gained no other knowledge on this trip, my visit and study of Dachau was worth the time spent."[22]

Yet there was little evidence that his feelings matched his words. There was no mention in the letter of his Jewish origins, or musings that he might have lost relatives at Dachau or in other camps or even that he might have suffered such a fate had the Annenbergs not fled East Prussia. It is common during tours of the death camps for Jews and gentiles as well to break down crying, to yell out in rage or at the very least leave the sites emotionally drained. But there was little or no hint that Walter had been so affected. Several inferences can be drawn: one, that he had thoroughly discounted much of his own heritage; two, that his experience with his father's prosecution had so seared him that he was incapable of emotional introspection or of baring his feelings; three, that he was a remote man who observed dutifully but clinically some of the greatest evil and destruction in human history; or four, that he simply could not put his emotions on paper.

From Dachau he was driven to Berchtesgaden, Hitler's Bavarian mountain retreat, where he had his picture taken at the fifty-by-twenty-foot window in the fuhrer's living room. Another three thousand feet up the mountain was Hitler's tea house on the Eagle's Nest peak, a peak from which he could see Austria.

At the Nuremberg war trials, Walter sat in the front row, studying what he called in his best recruiting-poster prose, "the beasts who are very much real, loathful and despicable." He found Hermann Goering, Hitler's deputy and the chief defendant, "still full of fight." Within weeks the tribunal sentenced to death twelve leading Nazis, including Goering, who cheated the executioner by taking poison two hours before his scheduled hanging.[23]

From Germany, Walter went to the French Riviera, where his writing picked up a freshness and animation that until then had been missing. The introduction in July of the bikini swimsuit may have boosted his mood. Walter checked in for a week at the Hotel du Cap at Cap d'Antibes, a glamorous resort which drew "practically all the smart good-looking people wearing absolutely the most attractive sport clothes I've ever seen, especially the women . . . [who are] so lovely and chic that opinion is that few wives are among them." They were tempting, but he insisted that he limited his fun to the roulette table, where he dropped 10,000 francs, then about $8,400 dollars or $68,000 in current dollars. Valentina, a well-known dress designer whom he called "a brainy woman, wonderful personality and much fun," invited him to drive with her to Zurich because her husband was traveling in Sweden with actress Greta Garbo. Walter said no thanks and stayed in Antibes to dine with couturier Elsa Schiaparelli and friends. "Career women, seven in all," he reported, "very feminine, yet fight and scratch each other to beat hell."[24]

Firsthand impressions matter, and having been rejected by the military services, he was somewhat mollified by observing the ravages of war and the initial steps toward recovery. But he was also interested in the politics of the postwar, which were evolving rapidly worldwide. In 1946, the United Nations General Assembly and Security Council each held their first meeting in London. Italy threw out its monarchy. Civil war resumed in China between the nationalist forces of Chiang Kai-shek and Mao Tse-tung's communist followers. A new constitution drawn up by General Douglas MacArthur relieved the emperor of sovereignty and introduced democracy to Japan. The most dangerous threat to the fragile postwar order was the Soviet Union. In Fulton, Missouri, that March, ousted British prime minister Winston Churchill warned that "from Stettin in the Baltic to Trieste in the Adriatic, an iron curtain has descended across the Continent."

Ideologically, Walter had shared an anti-union bias with his father, but otherwise he had never shown himself to be anything other than a cautious centrist. Nor had he ever thought much about foreign policy. On this trip, though, he learned that the United States had to play an active role in Europe's recovery. Germany could not rehabilitate itself. It could not feed its displaced persons, let alone rebuild cities and stand up to the Soviets. U.S. forces were well supplied — thick steaks, potatoes and plenty of beer, whiskey and cigarettes — but the ration for German citizens was one thousand calories a day. Germans working for the occupation forces were given one meal a day and, said Walter, "they shovel during that meal much as I do when I'm turned loose in front of a large bowl of spaghetti." Back home, he would become an early and powerful editorial advocate for the Marshall Plan.

He had had a couple of fleeting opportunities to assess the Soviets. While visiting Berlin, it was probably appropriate that a visitor so attuned to quality furnishings was shocked to see that Red Army troops had stripped the interior of the Reich's chancellery down to its doorknobs. In Paris, he dined and talked into the night with Walter Bedell Smith, the American general who was ambassador to Moscow, who persuaded him that Stalin's army had to be contained at all costs. "I leave this continent with one definite conclusion," he wrote to First. "Our only hope of peace is arms, arms and more arms. Peace through a show of force. The United Nations is something vaguely distant to these people. We must have defense in depth . . . otherwise the Russians will continue to move in and someday be in a position to outproduce us."[25]

In Philadelphia, editors transformed the letter into a front-page column under the headline "U.S. Must Arm and Rearm to Keep the Peace." "If this country were to abandon Europe," it read, "we would merely be hastening the day when the dictator of the Kremlin could set in motion combined production facilities greater than ours, designed to defeat ours." On East-West issues, Walter had become a hard-liner and would remain one the rest of his life.

The Russians were not alone in having a negative effect on Walter. While in Paris observing the peace conference and opening an *Inquirer* European bureau, he came across Charles de Gaulle and developed an irrational hatred of the French leader that would persist for decades after the general's death. The problem was de Gaulle's ultranationalism, which Walter saw as anti-Americanism and which upset him out of all proportion. Thousands of U.S. and allied soldiers had died for France, an effort the Frenchman dismissed by claiming inaccurately that the French essentially had liberated themselves. Winston Churchill and Franklin Roosevelt tolerated his hauteur and delusions of grandeur, recognizing that he was trying to repair the psychological as well as military damage that the humiliated France had suffered. But his attitude was too much for Walter, who considered him an arrogant ingrate.

"Eisenhower let him lead the troops into Paris as a gracious gesture and de Gaulle took it seriously," he said. "He felt as if he were the most important figure in freeing Europe from the Germans. Without Ike and Churchill, he never would have made it out of London." Walter attended several de Gaulle press conferences and was staggered to see the imperious Frenchman holding court from an outsized, throne-like chair on a raised platform. "The higher he sat, the lower went my opinion."[26]

(His antipathy toward the French president endured for years. There is no indication that de Gaulle knew Walter existed, let alone harmed him personally. And while de Gaulle annoyed a host of American leaders — as did any number of other pompous, nationalist politicians around the world — his leadership of France never posed a threat to the United States, as did, say, Soviet leader Leonid Brezhnev, about whom Walter could not have cared less. On the contrary, what troubled Walter most about de Gaulle was that he was an ally, but not a team player. When de Gaulle vetoed Britain's entry to the Common Market in 1962, ordered the removal of American nuclear weapons from France and, in 1966, withdrew France from NATO's military command, super-patriot Walter considered each act a disloyal outrage and an affront to the United States. A more sophisticated student of international affairs might have examined de Gaulle's motives and style and discovered that his hauteur was overcompensating for insecurity. In fact, the same has been said correctly of Walter's public formality. Walter, however, was not curious about de Gaulle's motives, strategic or psychological. A visceral man whose reactions were instinctual, he concluded that the French leader was a disloyal ally and thus worse than an outright enemy. A heartfelt yet shallow assessment that otherwise made little sense ended up revealing more about Walter than about de Gaulle.)

When he returned from Europe to Philadelphia, Walter paid the final $1.5 million installment of his father's fine with an enormous sense of relief. There had been times when he was not sure he could keep the *Inquirer* and Triangle financially above water and maintain the payment schedule. He was so pleased to close out the debt that he went to IRS headquarters in Washington and presented the check personally to chief counsel James Wenchel. At the end of a friendly meeting, Wenchel asked Walter if he knew that the headquarters they were in was built on what was known during the Civil War as Hooker's island, for the Union general whose camp followers were known as Hooker's girls, or hookers. Wenchel did not elaborate, but Walter thought about the remark and concluded that the IRS official was conceding elliptically what he had long assumed was true. Like the Union soldiers, his father too had been screwed on the premises.[27]

The payment did not quite end the chapter on Moses. What finally did was David Stern's decision in February 1947 to sell his paper, the *Record*, after a bitter three-month strike. The newspaper guild had targeted the *Record*, figuring that the liberal Stern, a self-proclaimed labor supporter, would cave in to its demand for $100-a-week base salary for experienced reporters. The guild made the same demand of the *Inquirer*, but Walter rejected it and the union left him alone.

To the guild's surprise, Stern fought back hard. He increased his $68 offer to $75, but the two sides never moved closer. Finally, claiming "the people I thought were for me were against me," the New Deal publisher stunned the union by selling out to Robert McLean, the wealthy and conservative owner of the *Evening Bulletin*. The *Bulletin* took over several *Record* features and picked up its Sunday edition, but closed the daily. Walter figured that Stern got what he deserved. The once-dominant publisher who had hounded his father was hoist with his own petard, ruined by those he had championed, in a twist of fate that left Walter feeling especially gratified.

The *Record*'s demise left the *Inquirer* with a monopoly in the morning and total editorial and business-side freedom for Walter. One of his first moves was to order a hard-hitting series on the notorious Republican machine which had controlled Philadelphia since 1884 in concert with conservative businessmen. Muckraker Lincoln Steffens, writing in 1903, branded Philadelphia "the worst-governed city in the country." Since then the situation had only deteriorated. City hall and the city water supply each gave off a distinct and foul smell.

Under pressure from reformers, incumbent Republican mayor Bernard Samuel had been forced to set up a committee to investigate municipal malfeasance. The group found a "huge catalogue of haphazard and crooked practices," including the fact that $40 million in city funds was missing. The director of the city's tax collection unit and the head of the vice squad each committed suicide; the fire marshal went to prison.[28]

The *Inquirer* reported daily on the graft and corruption rampant in virtually every city office and pressed for a thorough housecleaning. When little happened, Walter upped the ante with a 1949 announcement that tore into the Republicans and won him national attention. The paper, which had not backed a Democrat since Andrew Jackson, ditched the GOP and reaffirmed the independence Moses had declared a decade earlier.

> "The political misrule of the present [Republican] administration in Philadelphia cannot be condoned," [the *Inquirer* said in an October 27 front-page editorial Walter dictated.] "It is time for a change. It also appears to be the logical time to declare our journalistic independence.
>
> "No political party should be able to take any newspaper for granted. On October 14, 1939, my father, M. L. Annenberg, put on our logotype the slogan 'An Independent Newspaper for All the People.' He meant exactly what he said. I am sure that if my father were alive today, and had the same opportunity, he would have done as I have done.

"Unfortunately, he could not take the action I did because of a competitive newspaper situation in Philadelphia and the Federal government's campaign of using every resource against him. Fortunately, through the mills of the gods, I have been completely free to take whatever stand is necessary in the interests of all the people.

"There is no question of the *Inquirer* going Republican or Democratic. As far as our editorial approach is concerned, we are going to continue to support an individualistic philosophy as against any collectivism. . . . This election is solely a Philadelphia situation and party labels mean very little on a local level. The conditions which exist here can only be corrected by a more suitable division of political authority."[29]

The editorial prompted a flood of letters. Most were favorable, though a few came from shocked Republicans who accused the *Inquirer* of betrayal. He ignored the criticism. He wanted good government and felt certain that, with the war over, the sleepy old town was ready to shake off its torpor. In a record off-year turnout twelve days later, Philadelphia voters proved him right, booting out four Republicans and replacing them with Democrats in four key city slots. Leading the charge were ex-marine major Richardson Dilworth and his patrician ally, Joseph Clark, a Chestnut Hill socialite. The former Republican leadership was so widely recognized as corrupt that the *Inquirer*'s potential conflict of interest in supporting its own attorney, the Yale-trained Dilworth, never became an issue. As treasurer and controller respectively, the candid, dashing Dilworth and the cool, analytical Clark took control of the city's much-abused purse.

Walter could not have been happier with the results. After the votes had been counted, he reiterated that party politics had nothing to do with his call for change. "It was a matter," he said in a follow-up editorial, "of trying to redeem the city from those who had sunk it in the mire."[30]

Like Batman and Robin, Dilworth and Clark exposed widespread wrongdoing until in 1951 they completed their takeover of city hall, with Clark becoming mayor and Dilworth district attorney. Together they gave Philadelphia its best governance this century and in those glory days Walter's wealth, power and influence soared.

18

LEE

EONORE ROSENSTIEL was at her rented house in Palm Beach
in February 1950 when her best friend, Harriet Simon, invited
her to Boca Raton for lunch. Lee, as she is known, drove down,
spent the afternoon and, at the urging of Harriet and her husband, Sylvan, a Columbia pictures producer, decided to stay for a cocktail party
in honor of Henry Crown, one of Chicago's most prominent financiers
and businessmen. She was happy to have more time with Harriet,
whom she had known for a dozen years, since they had met in Los
Angeles while she was at Stanford and Harriet at UCLA.

The party was held in the penthouse suite of Hildegarde and Myer
Schine, a hotel tycoon whose daughter Renee married Henry Crown's
son Lester later that year. A friend of the Schines from his Miami
Beach days, Walter happened to be in Florida and was also invited to
the party, where Hildegarde introduced him to Lee, a slender redhead
with an alert mind, sophisticated style and beautiful smile.

After cocktails, the guests adjourned downstairs to the dining room.
Lee and the Simons were to sit at the Crowns' table; Walter was joining
the Schines. But an orchestra was playing, and before being seated,
Walter asked Lee to dance. "We started to dance and we just kept dancing," said Lee. "We never sat down for dinner." Henry Crown was furious. "He had every right to be," said Lee. "I wasn't very polite."[1]

The dinner group was agog. "Everyone could see something definitely was happening," said Harriet. "They connected right away and
then they danced all night. It was magic and magnetic."[2]

Walter was returning to Philadelphia the next day but asked Lee if
she would have lunch with him if he came to Palm Beach and left from

there. "I said, 'Sure.' He drove up and we had lunch. By the time I put him on the train we each knew our worlds had changed. I thought he was handsome and fun and wonderful." Walter felt the same. "From the moment I met her, I was crazy about Lee." Which was fortunate, because had they not felt so strongly about each other, they might never have endured the next tortured stage in their romance.

When they met, Walter had been separated from Ronny for four months and was on the verge of divorce. Lee, however, was married, with two children, the younger barely a year old. Her husband, Lewis Rosenstiel, was the dictatorial founder and chairman of Schenley Distillers, the nation's second-largest spirits concern after Seagram's, which was owned by the Bronfman family. Consumed by his business, the fifty-eight-year-old liquor baron had returned to his New York headquarters and left his thirty-two-year-old wife in Florida. He had done it often before. Lee did not smoke or drink, and while she enjoyed people and liked to socialize — her school chums called her Lively Lee — she was not a flirt. Despite her liveliness and charm, she was a lonely woman at that point.

Ten years younger than Walter, Lee was born in February 1918 in New York. Her mother, Clara Henle, was the eldest of four sisters; her father, Max Cohn, the eldest of four brothers. Clara and her family had emigrated from Berlin. Max's parents were also immigrants. His father was a German Jew who ran a tailor shop on Manhattan's Upper East Side; his mother, a Russian Jew from the Pale of Settlement near the Polish border. Max was the only Cohn boy to attend college. He was also the least successful.

When Leonore Cohn was seven, her mother died at the age of thirty-two. Her father, Max, collapsed. A weak man, he sobbed uncontrollably. He did not know what to do with his life, his textile business was failing and what would he do with two young daughters? Max's younger brother, Harry Cohn, the head of Columbia pictures, stepped in and offered Max a job making short subjects for the studio. Max left immediately for the West Coast. Three weeks later, Lee and Judith, her sister, crossed the country by train with their Aunt Jen, a spinster sister of Clara's who hoped to marry her widowed brother-in-law if he could stop crying long enough to ask her.

After eighteen months Jen realized that Max was not going to propose. She became sick and Lee and Judith were sent off to the Page boarding school for girls in Pasadena. "Nobody knew what to do with us and we had no place to go," Lee recalled. It was a good school, not an orphanage, and while she had a satisfactory time there, she felt terribly insecure. Her most enduring memory was a prayer the girls said before dinner which she recited without hesitation more than seventy years later: "Let the words in my mouth and the meditations in my heart be acceptable in thy sight, oh Lord, my strength and my redeemer." The prayer was a source of solace at school and in later years when she sought support or relief from sadness.

Max felt guilty about not seeing the girls and decided to try again. He rented a bungalow in an apartment court near Sycamore and Melrose Avenues and hired an older woman, a grandmotherly type, to live in and take care of them when they were not at the neighborhood school. Although the family was Jewish, no one practiced the religion. Instead, the nanny took them regularly to Christian Science Sunday school.

After two years, Max could no longer tolerate the living arrangement. He turned the girls over to his brother Harry and his wife, Rose. "My father gave us away," said Lee. After that, she and her sister saw little of him until he lay dying and asked forgiveness for abandoning them. "He just couldn't manage it," Lee said, more in resignation than in anger. "A sweet man, but very weak."[3] "A schnook," echoed her sister, Judith.[4]

At the age of eleven, Lee moved to Harry Cohn's home at 135 Fremont Place, off Wilshire Boulevard, first to an empty maid's room, then into a bedroom built over the port-cochere from which she and Judith peered to watch the stars arriving in their Duesenbergs and Hispano-Suizas. There was plenty to see. During the thirty-five years Harry Cohn *was* Columbia pictures, from its founding in 1923 until he died of a heart attack in 1958 with forty-five golden Academy Award statuettes arrayed behind his desk, the road to and from Harry's home and office was Hollywood's fast lane.

His triumphs included *It Happened One Night*, which swept all four top Oscars in 1934; *You Can't Take It with You*, best film of 1938; *Mr. Smith Goes to Washington*, Jimmy Stewart's 1939 star vehicle; and the 1940s and '50s greats *All the King's Men, From Here to Eternity, Picnic, On the Waterfront* and *Bridge on the River Kwai*. But he was also the toughest and most ruthless of the studio bosses, the last of the despots in an era when cinemoguls Sam Goldwyn, Louis Mayer, Jack Warner and Cohn were as well known as the stars and directors they managed. Gossip columnist Hedda Hopper called him "a sadistic son of a bitch." When he died, more than two thousand people showed up for his funeral, prompting comedian Red Skelton to utter the most quoted epitaph in movie history: "It only proves what they always say — give the public what they want to see and they'll come out for it."

For every star or director he drew to Columbia, which he spelled "Colombia," twice as many fled, terrified of his abuse, his vulgarities, and an elaborate spy system he developed to dominate the personal and professional lives of his employees. There may have been another side to Harry Cohn which explained how he wooed some of Hollywood's greatest talent to make such fine films, but if so, it largely escaped the notice of his family as well as his contemporaries. "He was very difficult," Lee said. "Brilliant in the movie business, but his character was third-rate."

The first-rate character was Harry's wife, Rose. Unable to bear children, she had insisted to Harry that they take over the upbringing of Max's daughters. "All right, goddammit, but it's your decision, not mine," Harry said. "I'll pay their bills but I won't be responsible for their problems. Keep them away from me. Is that understood?"[5]

Rose said that it was. She did the best she could, although her effort fell short of raising the two girls as their own. The girls had a cook, a chauffeur and a governess, but nothing was theirs. They were always treated as wards, never as family members. Harry was no family man. He had little idea how to deal with girls other than trying to hustle them into bed, one thing he did not try with his nieces. On fall Saturdays, Rose packed him a lunch and sent him off to watch football, on which he bet huge sums. The wagers, though, were placed through a bookie. Harry rarely saw games because he picked up his latest girlfriend and spent the afternoon at her apartment instead of at the stadium.

Rose put up with his abuse for years. She had been married before, to a wealthy New York attorney, but Harry had pursued and won her with an intensity and charm that seemed out of character for an insatiable womanizer with a worn-out casting couch. Rose was short, stocky and not a beauty. She was, however, intelligent, ran an excellent house, and was kind to her two young charges.

There was little or no talk about school and they rarely ate with Rose, but the girls were often swept up in what was going on in Hollywood. Irving Berlin, Rita Hayworth and Clark Gable came to the house for meals. As a teenager Lee used to press her ear to the door to hear Rose commiserate with Rita Gable about her husband, Clark's, skirtchasing. Rose let them watch her play mah-jongg with her lady friends in the afternoon. During the Depression, she took them in her yellow Rolls-Royce to Ocean Park to see flagpole sitters and marathon dancers staggering around, to amusement parks and the Santa Monica pier. Watching filming on the set and viewing daily rushes were special treats. When Harry hired Lee's Aunt Jen to run the Columbia wardrobe department, dress-up games became part of the girls' entertainment.

Rose was more than a babysitter and housemother. She provided the basics for two important aspects of Lee's life: her sophisticated ability to entertain everyone from childhood friends to royalty and presidents, and her religious upbringing. Rose had developed her entertaining talents during her first marriage to Oliver Cromwell, an attorney who owned a 125-foot yacht, the *Zama*, and a large house in Larchmont, New York, which was always filled with guests. In Los Angeles, notwithstanding his behavior at the office, Harry could turn on the charm when he wished, and the Cohns often entertained Hollywood's brightest stars at their home. In later years, Rose directed the hospitality committee for the Hollywood Bowl and hosted after-concert buffets for the performers and VIPs. "She set a great table and had a wonderful sense of style," said Lee.

Harry's shenanigans helped broaden Lee's horizons. In the summer of 1936, "Uncle Harry was in love with some young girl and he was so eager to get Aunt Rose out of town," she said, "that he sent us first-class through Europe." They sailed over on the *Berengaria*, back on the *Normandie* and traipsed from one great city and hotel to the next. Staying in London at the Dorchester for a month and spending weekends in English country homes, she read everything she could about King Edward VIII's ongoing romance with American divorcée Wallis Warfield Simpson, for whom he gave up the throne that December. She and Judy were in a crowd in Green Park waving at the king, who was crossing Constitution Hill, when an assassin's shot nearly made the whole abdication crisis moot.

From the Ritz in Paris, they made forays to a couturier friend of Rose's who introduced Lee to exquisite custom-made clothes. Thanks to Harry's guilt money, Rose had bought each girl a new traveling wardrobe before they left for Europe, and once there she treated them to dresses and blouses in Paris and stylish shoes in Rome. The experience delighted Lee and sparked an enduring fascination with expensive clothes and jewelry.

The other lifelong interest that Rose encouraged was Lee's interest in Christian Science. Although Harry's wife smoked and drank whiskey sours and champagne, which violated church dogma, she was nonetheless, like the interim nanny, a serious Christian Scientist. Born and raised a Christian, Rose sent Lee and Judy to Sunday school and took them to meetings every Wednesday evening. Judy later gave it up, but it is hard to overestimate the significance of Christian Science to Lee. "It's a very important part of my life," she explained, "and even though I go to doctors from time to time, it has meant *everything* to me. It's been a real source of strength and sustained me through many, many problems."

The spirituality in her faith offered refuge in a life that for many years held no other anchors. Christian Science also had a profound effect on the formation of her personality. One reason she was considered lively and upbeat was that while Lee had strong likes and dislikes, she would go to extremes to avoid speaking ill of anyone or anything. A firm believer that thoughts take wing, she was never comfortable speaking of illness or negative rumors. Whenever she faced a bad situation, she grasped for her faith and an uplifting element on which to structure something better.

That foundation stood her in good stead at school, where she was unhappy for years. She was a good but not great student. She liked math, history and all things political, but writing and expressing herself were daunting. She had no boyfriends, no prom dates and then, just as she finished high school, Uncle Harry dumped Aunt Rose. Lee had been accepted at Stanford and had a place to go. Sister Judy, who had no one to take care of her, was shipped off again to boarding school.

Harry did not cut Lee off. He gave her a $50-a-month allowance and a small roadster to get around. She joined the Christian Science society and checked out sororities, but she was not asked to join because she was born a Jew with the name Cohn. "I didn't like having the name Cohn at Stanford. Being Jewish there was a big factor in 1935 and it annoyed me terribly."

While her friends did their best to push her off the straight and narrow, she went to church regularly, still did not smoke or drink, and was very careful with the Jewish boys who asked her out. Harry had put the hex on sex for Lee just as Moses had frightened Walter. "Uncle Harry made a movie about a teenager who got pregnant and died and made me come down to the studio and watch it all by myself in the projection room. It scared the daylights out of me."

After two years at Stanford, she was very lonely, dropped out for a year, returned to Los Angeles and moved in with Aunt Rose. After four months in secretarial school, she spent a semester at the University of Southern California and then returned to Stanford for her final two years.

When she graduated in June 1940 — on the day Moses was sentenced to prison — Lee had no idea what to do with her life. "I had no place to live," she explained with a shrug, "so I got married."

While at college she had met Beldon Katleman at the Hillcrest Country Club, the Jewish golf club in Los Angeles. He was a UCLA graduate whose family owned real estate in Los Angeles and the Circle K national chain of parking lots. "He was not drop-dead gorgeous, but he was tall, nice looking, and his father was very, very successful," said Harriet Simon, who double-dated with Lee. Lee had no money of her own, but she was surrounded by wealth and it was natural for her to marry someone well-to-do. Beldon's wealth was not enough to endear him to Harry. Her uncle absolutely forbade her to marry Beldon. "He just didn't like him," said Lee. "He didn't think he was good enough for me."

Rose did not like Beldon either, but Lee didn't care. She enjoyed his parents, who were warm and seemed to offer the kind of wholesome home environment she had seen in films about storybook families and longed to have herself. Harry finally offered to pay for a wedding, but insisted on bringing his new fiancée, a bit actress and model named Joan Perry. Rose Cohn said if Joan came, she would not show up. Lee decided against any ceremony, married Beldon in January 1941 and almost immediately determined, "It was a big mistake."[6]

When war was declared in December, Beldon joined the Signal Corps, went to officer candidate school, was commissioned a lieutenant and was transferred to the motion picture division. Lee, who was by then pregnant, moved in with his family, gave birth to a daughter, Diane, in 1942 and after two and a half years of a deteriorating marriage, left her husband. His parents sympathized. Beldon was their only child and they had spoiled him terribly. "My first mistake was breast-feeding him until he was five," his mother told Lee in an effort to cheer her up.

Housing was tight during the war and Lee could not find a place to live for herself and Diane. Aunt Rose was living alone in Hollywood at the Chateau Marmont; Harry and his new wife, Joan, were in a rented house. Harry, who was thrilled that her marriage to Beldon had broken up, let Lee move into a tiny bungalow complex that Columbia maintained for visiting screenwriters. To support herself and Diane, Lee worked for Joan for $75 a week. When Joan became pregnant and went house hunting, she found a lovely home at 1000 North Crescent in Beverly Hills. It belonged to Lew Rosenstiel, the Schenley chairman, who had bought it when his first wife was ill in hope that the southern California climate would improve her health. After she died in 1944, Rosenstiel would not set foot in the house, but neither would he sell it.

Harry's lawyer knew Lew's lawyer, however, and arranged for Rosenstiel to have dinner with the Cohns when he came out west so Harry could try to buy the house. As they often did, they invited Lee, living in what she called "this little dump," to join them. "So I had dinner," said Lee, "and this man fell in love with me."

The next morning the lawyer called. "Lee, are you sitting down? Lew wants to take you to dinner."

"I'm sorry, I can't," she replied. "He's too old." She was twenty-eight; Lew was fifty-four and had been a widower for a year.

Uncle Harry called. "Lee, don't be ridiculous. We want to buy the house. All you have to do is go to dinner."

Lee went to dinner and found Lew pleasant but boring. Two weeks later, in February 1946, he proposed. Lee laughed. She was not even divorced and would not be until June. Furthermore, she knew nothing about him.

Harry was happy because Lew sold him the house. He did not care what happened next. Over the garage was a small apartment. Lee moved in with her four-year-old daughter. Lew kept up his pursuit, with the help of Joan Cohn. A beautiful woman, she also knew her Harry. Lee might be his niece, but the last person Joan wanted around the house was an unattached redhead as attractive as Lee. She promoted Lew to Lee at every opportunity.

Lee talked it over with her friend Harriet, who told her anything had to be better than relying on Harry Cohn, especially with Rose gone. Lee herself had warned Harriet's husband, Sylvan, not to work for Harry, that her uncle would destroy him. But Harry had been a mentor to Sylvan, whose own father died when he was thirteen, and had promised the director that he would one day run Columbia. Instead, Harry killed him, according to Harriet, by loading so much stress on Sylvan that he eventually had a heart attack and died at forty. "Harry was an evil man," said Harriet. "Lee had to get away."

Harriet's mother also urged Lee to marry Lew. "Lee, how can you be so stupid," she told her. "Here you are, living over a garage, depending on an ogre. You have nothing and Lew, a nice man, can give you everything." That was Lew's pitch too. "He was a great salesman," said Lee. "He never gave up."

She was not in love, but she was growing to like him. He was kind to her, wonderful to Diane and as she toted up the plusses and minuses, the benefits of marrying the wealthy executive far out-weighed any rationale for staying over the garage and working for Joan. So on June 29, 1946, as soon as her divorce from Beldon Katleman was finalized, she married Lew and moved to Conyers Farm, his fifteen-hundred-acre Greenwich, Connecticut, estate with its lake, boathouse and four hundred acres of apple and pear trees.

At that moment, Lew was one of the most successful businessmen in America. A solid six feet four, with the build and temperament of a middle linebacker, he had created Schenley during Prohibition and made it the premium U.S. brand after repeal. He lost the top spot to Seagram's, then regained it during the war when he pushed expansion so quickly that Schenley was marketing 152 brands on products from anisette to zinfandel. Driven by his fierce competition with the Bronf-man family, who ran Seagram's, Lew began to take a beating in 1947 when he figured wrongly that drinkers would return to straight whiskeys after the war. He pushed bourbon, but buyers preferred Sea-gram's blends. When bourbon sales slumped to 10 percent of the mar-ket, Lew's health fell with them — into a clinical depression.

"Eighteen months into our marriage, I learned Lew was manic depressive," said Lee. Despite electric shock treatments, in the days before lithium, he suffered rapid and profound mood swings. When he was well, Lew was a robust delight. When he took time off to relax, he was an affable Renaissance man who painted oils, played and com-posed music for the piano, loved choral music and poetry and was fasci-nated by politics.

When he was depressed, though, life at the office and at home was a nightmare. Lew understood the situation was not easy for Lee, but he adored her. Two and a half years after their marriage, Lee gave birth to their daughter, Elizabeth. Lew was ecstatic and did all he could materially to make Lee happy. She loved pretty things, expensive things, and he bought her everything she wanted, but his depressions and workaholic habits left her anguished.

He rented an elegant waterfront home in Palm Beach, put a yacht and crew at the end of the pier, and flew back to New York, leaving Lee alone in Florida for weeks at a time. When she lived with him, Lew worked all night, slept from 8 A.M. until noon, then returned to the office. He had no girlfriends. He was not cheating on Lee, just working. "Lew set her up with a yacht and a house in Palm Beach and all the charge accounts she could ever want and then left her for work. Plenty of women would consider that an ideal situation," said her friend Harriet, "but Lee didn't want to be a well-kept, beautiful toy. She really wanted to be a wife."[7]

That was her life when she met Walter at the cocktail party for the Crowns at Boca Raton. By chance, only a week before, Lee had met Ronny Annenberg, who had come to the Rosenstiel's house for cocktails while in Palm Beach waiting for her divorce from Walter. Lee took Ronny and Ben Ourisman out for an evening sail on the *Holiday*, found Ronny "very attractive" and the chance meeting with his ex-wife helpful in understanding Walter when she was introduced to him.

Returning to New York, Lee was invited to lunch at the Colony restaurant by Jan Annenberg, one of Walter's sisters whom she knew slightly. Jan had been present when Walter met Ronny, and now she wanted to take a closer look at the woman her brother could not stop talking about. When she showed up to meet Jan, Walter was with his sister. Over the next two weeks they saw each other three more times. On the third occasion, Walter said he wanted to marry her if she could get a divorce.

His attorneys researched divorce law in Connecticut and Florida and determined that in 1950 the primary grounds were adultery, natural impotence, desertion, insanity and extreme cruelty. Neither, however, wanted a contested divorce or a public airing of their situation. Walter wanted to avoid any publicity. It was up to Lee to make the approach. When she went back to Palm Beach, Walter egged her on.

"As in checkers sacrifice is necessary for achievement," he cabled her on Valentine's Day. Lee was frightened about breaking the news to Lew. Walter cabled again to tell her of the most important maxim he had learned from his father's troubles. "Adversity tests character and determination," he wrote. "In the race of life there are always elements of gamble but our basic ingredients are the necessary honorable requisites on which better things are built. The earned right to reconstruct should not be denied or allowed to fail by default. It is my shame that you must fight single-handed nevertheless courage, courage and still greater courage will faithfully support you in attaining your legitimate ambition."[8]

Sylvan Simon died and Lee flew to California to be with Harriet. Walter cabled her in Beverly Hills to keep her from losing courage.

"The drive determination resoluteness of purpose to bring about the fulfilment of our ambitions rests in your hands. God grant you the strength to fight off the temptations of surrender," he wrote. "I recognize the obstacles facing you but take courage and assurance from the knowledge that I love you deeply. . . . These are the hours of decision."

Lee trusted Walter, but she was also nervous. She had no mother, no father, two small children and was about to launch what could be a titanic struggle with Lew, the only man who had given her financial security. Walter's constant reassurances were an important boost. "You have given me the inspiration to go forth into battle," she wrote him back. Harriet helped too, and when Lee returned east she acted. "I didn't want to be dishonorable, so I went to Lew, told him I had fallen in love with someone else whom I wanted to marry and asked him to give me a divorce."

Lew, who had a monumental temper, responded just as she had feared. "I'm not going to give you a divorce," he replied in a fury. "I love you. I don't want to be divorced and I don't want you to marry anyone else."

She pleaded with him to consider the troubles they had been through in the previous four years, his rages, depressions and all the times he had left her to return to work.

"I've been a terrible husband. I know that," he conceded, according to Lee. "But we have a baby and I promise I'll be a better husband. You have to give me another chance." He begged and badgered her until Lee agreed. "I said good-bye to Walter. We didn't see each other, or write or talk. From time to time I read about him in the gossip columns linked to some girl. It was awful."

Lew did try harder to make the marriage work. And so did Lee. But a year after she had given him up, she ran into Walter in the gift department of Bergdorf Goodman's on Fifth Avenue. Lee said the meeting was strict happenstance. Walter said a sister tipped him off that Lee was there. He asked her to come across the street to the Plaza Hotel lobby to talk. They decided they were still in love, that Lee would sue for divorce on grounds of "extreme mental cruelty," that sister Evelyn's lawyer husband, William Jaffe, would handle the lawsuit, and the hell with any publicity.

Lew battled back, angry and vindictive. He also attempted to undermine Lee's affection for Walter. He had Walter followed and hired Ben Javits, a lawyer who was the brother of New York senator

Jacob Javits, to try to dig up dirt on the young Philadelphia publisher. Because Walter had nothing to hide, he was amused by Lew's tactics. He knew and liked Javits, so when the lawyer called one of his friends, Walter had him say that Walter was keeping three different mistresses. When he found that Lee could not be swayed in her determination to leave, Lew resolved to make the divorce cost her dearly. She had to leave behind everything he had ever given her. She could leave with the clothes on her back and nothing more. All her jewelry, including a 10-karat emerald-cut diamond ring, a diamond necklace, a diamond locket and other diamond pins had to remain behind. The harshest demand was that she could not take their daughter. Lew refused to give her custody of Elizabeth.

"Lew, this is the most terrible thing you could possibly do to our daughter," Lee said. Everyone, even his own lawyer, Sam Rosenman, who was Franklin Roosevelt's and Harry Truman's White House counsel, tried to talk Lew out of holding Elizabeth ransom. He would not budge. "He never stopped being angry," said Lee. "He was determined to make me pay."

Walter told her to walk out. He would make sure she lacked nothing. His pretax income that year was $1 million. His assets at age forty-three, said his then attorney, Harold Kohn, were "conservatively valued at substantially in excess of ten million dollars."[9] Because Lew had put Lee's jewelry into a Greenwich bank vault to be held for Elizabeth and Diane, as a wedding present and to replace what she left behind, Walter bought from Harry Winston a $250,000 diamond necklace and a 26.8-Karat emerald-cut diamond ring. The certifications, he told her, she should lock in her own safe deposit box. "The deep love and affection" which came with it, he added, "you can lock away in your heart." Elizabeth, he assured her, would be recovered as well. Through Jaffe and Rosenman, Walter pressed Lew to relent. Yet while Lee would ultimately gain more time with her daughter, she never regained legal custody.

In June 1951, Lee flew to Los Angeles to be with Harriet and to see her uncle Harry and Beldon's parents. The separation agreement had not been finalized and Lee was frantic. "Not one person here feels I have a chance to get rid of Lew," she wrote to Walter.[10] What made the moment more traumatic was that Walter had just gone overseas for two months. Given a postwar exemption for his hearing disability, he was serving in the naval reserves as a lieutenant commander on the USS *Missouri,* cruising around northern Europe and the West Indies.

The prospect of returning east to make the final break with Lew left her barely able to sleep. "I just don't think you realize to what lengths this madman, who is so vitriolic, will go," she wrote "my dearest, dearest darling." "He is going to do everything he can to ruin us."[11]

Walter was mindful of her anxiety, but he was overjoyed to be on the *Missouri* after being disappointed for years that he had been unable to serve during the war. He also believed that the worst of the troubles with Lew were behind them. From afar, he tried to calm Lee down. He sent her a copy of a 1913 lecture by Sir William Osler, a renowned professor of medicine at Oxford, and underlined a portion of his thesis that "the failure to cultivate the power of peaceful concentration is the greatest single cause of mental breakdown."

Osler's prescription for inner harmony, a formula that Walter tried to follow himself, struck a chord. Despite the importance she had placed on Christian Science as a young woman and would again, she had abandoned the religion for most of the years she was married to Beldon and Lew. Now she returned to her lessons. On August 7, 1951, she and Lew signed their separation agreement. Immediately after, Lee flew west. With Harriet she moved into a cottage on the Nevada side of the Cal-Neva Lodge on Lake Tahoe's north shore to wait out her six-week residency for divorce. Lee wrote "my dearest husband-to-be" almost daily.

In September, Harriet left and Walter arrived with his sister Jan to spend the final weeks at Cal-Neva. The three of them hired boats and hiked around parts of the lake during the day, gambled in the casinos at Tahoe and in Reno and watched the entertainment in the Celebrity Showroom and Indian Room of the log cabin main lodge, which in the later fifties and sixties was a hangout for Marilyn Monroe, Dean Martin, Frank Sinatra and Sinatra's "rat pack." While in Nevada, Walter asked Lee to sign a prenuptial agreement. Thirteen years earlier, Moses had been insistent and Ronny had agreed. But with Moses gone, Lee refused. "I just said 'No,' and Walter said, 'Fine.'"[12]

When the divorce came through, they flew to New York, celebrated by seeing the new musical *Guys and Dolls,* and two days later were married in Sadie Annenberg's apartment at 2 East Eighty-eighth Street. There was no rabbi. Lee was even less interested in her Jewish heritage than Walter was in his. Instead, the service was conducted by Dr. Carrol Oscar Morong, the Baptist headmaster of Peddie, the school to which Walter gave increasing credit for having developed his character. Their time together in Nevada had served as an interim honeymoon, so they took no trip then. After the wedding ceremony, they spent the night in New York, then drove to Philadelphia, where Lee had only visited once. Her first look at Inwood convinced her that Walter's house had to be totally redone. Indeed, with a new partner on board, his whole life was about to be made over.

LEE PLUNGED into renovating the house, but concentrated more on getting her marriage off to a solid start. Divorced twice, she was not going to let it happen again. She and Walter were in love, which is the key ingredient in marriage, and had an intensely physical relationship. No matter how many grand homes they owned, fine hotels they stayed in or yachts they cruised on, they always slept in the same bed. Both were touchers and holders of each other's shoulders, arms and hands. In later years, if Lee were elsewhere in the house, Walter would often go to look for her, just to see her or hear her voice. Such behavior stemmed from her complete focus on her new husband. "I'm a pleaser," said Lee, "and my first goal was to please Walter." That was the kind of spouse Walter wanted. He had revealed as much a few months earlier in a note he had sent to Sadie on Mother's Day: "Your aid and comfort during tribulations certainly highlight that the essence of motherhood is submission and sacrifice."

His schedule became Lee's. She joined him for lunch at the *Inquirer* building, began learning the local political and cultural landscape and threw herself into charities and civic affairs, including volunteer and later board work for the Academy of Music, Philadelphia Museum of Art and the University of Pennsylvania. They did everything together — planned strategy for gaining greater custody of Elizabeth, pored over architects' and landscape designers' plans, hosted dinners for city officials and corporate executives, organized visits of their children, discussed each other's clothing, played golf and bridge, danced together at fund-raising balls and started traveling, initially to Europe on a second honeymoon.

Anyone marrying Walter gained Sadie and seven sisters-in-law. Ronny had had her own supportive family in Canada, could always go home, never had to come to terms with Walter's sisters and did not. Lee had no family and no other place to go. There was no question that, one way or another, she was going to do all she could to get along with Sadie's daughters. She was helped by the fact that, unlike Ronny, she had a college education, considerably more sophistication from her years in New York and Palm Beach with Lew and Los Angeles with

Uncle Harry, and plenty of experience in dealing with difficult relatives. She also had an innate sense of diplomacy. No matter how anyone pressed her, Lee refused to identify a favorite sister. "I tried to like them equally," she said, adding with a laugh, "although that wasn't always easy."

With Sadie living alone in New York in an apartment overlooking the future site of the Guggenheim Museum, Walter and Lee often drove up to stay with her on weekends. Most of his sisters lived nearby, some in apartment buildings along Park Avenue where they waved to each other from their terraces. The visits in the 1950s pulled the Annenbergs closer than they had been since 1936 when Moses moved to Philadelphia and split the family. Lee and Walter spent Saturdays in New York exploring art galleries, an adventure that would have two important results: instigating a pattern of teamwork and, ultimately, creating one of the nation's best private art collections. Each decision they made to add or subtract a piece, they determined to make jointly. Decades later, neither could recall a single case of disagreeing on an acquisition or sale.

UNTIL THEY BEGAN exploring galleries together, neither had had a particular interest in pictures. Each had an eye for quality, but fine pieces of art had not figured in their upbringing. Sadie Annenberg's masterpieces were her children. Moses had no time for art. "I wouldn't give a dollar for all the old masters in the Metropolitan Museum," he boasted. Walter, who well into his eighties was able to remember almost everything else about his childhood, recalled nothing of what had been on the walls of his family's homes. During the forties he was too busy salvaging Triangle to consider buying art, particularly as his and Ronny's interests diverged. On Lee's side, Harry Cohn preferred starlets to paintings, while Lew Rosenstiel's nonbusiness interests had been music and politics.

The catalyst for the Annenberg family fascination with fine art was sister Evelyn's second husband, William Jaffe. A talented lawyer who became chief legal counsel for Columbia pictures, Jaffe had grown up in New York, where his mother had taken him to museums and nourished an interest that developed into a knowledgeable passion. After the war, he began "arting," as the family called it, with Evelyn, eventually inviting along several of her sisters and brothers-in-law. Enid and Ira Haupt and Lita and Joseph Hazen arted with the Jaffes on Saturdays and began collecting in the late 1940s.

In the early 1950s, Lee and Walter joined in. Unlike some permutations of Annenbergs and in-laws, this group was bright and congenial. Of the nearly two dozen in-laws who joined the family, Lee, Joe and Ira were the class of the lot. And while the couples were serious about their collecting and shared an interest in similar works, they did not compete for pictures. There seemed to be plenty to go around. The art world in the immediate postwar period was small, with few active collectors despite prices that later were considered laughably low. Evelyn bought her first Picasso, a cubist oil, in 1948 for $2,700.[13] Enid once bought two nearly identical Monets because she liked them both and they were so inexpensive.

Walter and Lee were not interested in buying occasional pieces. From the outset, they wanted to build a collection. "We thought the sisters' collections were wonderful and we wanted to do it, too," explained Lee.[14] They approached the project with the same strategy they would apply to all serious endeavors. They did extensive research, paid meticulous attention to detail, restricted their interest solely to pieces of high quality and reached out to experts they could trust who would guide them. There was never any manic or obsessive collecting. "Never buy four C-plus paintings when you can buy one A," was Walter's philosophy.[15]

Nor did he and Lee ever buy art as an investment. Walter had a great capacity for figures and years later remembered the original purchase price of most of his pieces. But while he appreciated their worth, his interest in their spiraling potential market prices was mostly limited to making certain the works were properly insured. "I couldn't care less about their dollar value," he said. "People who think about art as an investment are rather pathetic. They should put their money in real estate and stocks. We set out to get things that we genuinely loved and respected and wanted to live with."

"This was purely art for enjoyment," said Lee, "paintings that we wanted to have because we loved them." Walter's selection sense was straightforward. "Unless I am excited by something, I don't want it in my house. Whether someone called it the best example or someone else considered it mediocre did not matter. If it moved me, that was enough. Being moved is what collecting is all about."[16]

Sam Salz, a New York dealer whom he heartily disliked but appreciated professionally — an unusual combination for Walter — sold them their first two paintings the year they were married. *Les Oliviers*, or *Olive Trees: Pale Blue Sky*, painted in 1889 by Vincent van Gogh ("Van

Hoch," Walter insisted gutturally, stressing the proper pronunciation of the Dutchman's name) was their initial purchase, for $68,000, a princely sum in 1951.[17] "Twice I have been to that same place near Arles and have seen that exact purple afterglow," he said. "Van Gogh, I find, never exaggerated. And that sky with those blues and pinks. Those pinks are wild!"[18]

Their second, a bargain at $27,000, was Claude Monet's 1887 *Femme a L'Ombrelle*, later known as *The Stroller*, a portrait of the artist's stepdaughter Suzanne Hoschede deep in his Giverney garden.[19]

As they wandered through the New York galleries, dealers showed selectively what they wanted them to have and held back that which they wanted to keep for other collectors. Eventually, the Annenbergs returned time and again for tutoring to two dealers, Knoedler and Wildenstein. Enid had built her collection with the latter and took Walter and Lee to meet Daniel Wildenstein, whose father, Georges, had begun the family's international art dealing business. Georges had once incurred the wrath of Charles de Gaulle by selling a French masterwork — Georges de la Tour's *La Bonne Aventure* — to the Metropolitan Museum in New York. De Gaulle, who wanted the piece for the Louvre, retaliated by barring Georges Wildenstein from the French Academy. After the French president's death in 1970, Daniel avenged the family by naming one of his best foals "Goodbye Charlie." The joke was not lost on Walter, who later bought from him a modern painting, *Palais Gruyère*, which portrayed the Elysée Palace in cheese surrounded by mice.[20]

"Wildenstein was just wonderful," said Lee. "The gallery knew what was good for them and for us and they really wanted to help us make a collection." Daniel and the Annenbergs became friends. "They were always buying together," he said. "I don't think he would have bought a picture that Lee did not like." Their taste was originally unschooled, but natural, the dealer explained, and became increasingly sophisticated as they spent more time viewing paintings in museums and galleries. They often called to inquire about the condition of a particular piece and whether it was a good or bad buy, but never asked about the subject matter, the artist or the history of the painting. "Walter never let himself be influenced by anybody," said Wildenstein. "I was trying to, but he is a very strong man and it was all his own taste. He is the only collector I know who does not have an adviser. Even museum directors bring along a curator, but with him there was nobody."[21]

Wildenstein once called to offer Walter a *Mont Saint-Victoire* by Cézanne. "You don't have a Cézanne," he told Walter, who had admired the 1902–06 painting at a time when the dealer would not sell it. He was holding it for Robert Lehman, but the investment banker had taken so many months to decide that the dealer tired of waiting. Walter snapped it up for $550,000. Within days, Lehman called, pleading with Walter to sell "because I love it." "So do I. That's why I bought it. You blew it," Walter chuckled. "He hesitated and lost," added Lee.

The Annenbergs were doing neither. Working closely together, huddling over soup, sandwiches and architects' plans and speaking on the phone three and four times a day when Walter was at the office, they were turning Inwood into a show piece of art and furnishings and themselves into fixtures on Philadelphia's civic affairs and charity circuit. Walter's personal life was coming together. He had survived a discomfiting divorce. He had a firm hand on the *Inquirer. Daily Racing Form* and *Seventeen* revenues were climbing in the postwar expansion. There was a new brightness in his eyes and a slight swagger as he walked chin high and barrel chest first into the *Inquirer* building each morning. He felt confident. And lucky. It was no time to be hesitant.

19

TELEVISION

MERRILL PANITT was ready for bed in late November 1952 when his telephone rang. Walter was calling his young administrative assistant, who, more as a hobby than as an assignment, also wrote a television column for the *Philadelphia Inquirer.* Panitt was not surprised by the call. Walter often telephoned editors and assistants at home at night and early in the morning, although he was careful not to call after midnight or before 7:30 A.M. What did startle Panitt was how irate Walter sounded.

"Why was that full-page ad for *TV Digest* in tonight's *Bulletin* instead of in our newspaper?" he demanded.

Panitt replied that he did not believe the publication had anything against the *Inquirer.* He figured that it probably had only enough money for a weekday ad and decided to spend it in the evening newspaper, which had a slightly larger daily circulation than the *Inquirer.*

The response seemed to mollify Walter.

"The ad says *TV Digest* has a circulation of one hundred eighty thousand," he went on with less edge in his voice. "Is that possible?"

Panitt was used to such questions from his employer. Walter read newspapers closely and often spotted small items which piqued his interest. Panitt had been keeping an eye on *TV Digest*, which was published in Philadelphia and carried listings for the local television stations. The *Digest* had bought the ad in the *Bulletin* to attract advertisers by touting its reach with readers. The ad copy pointed out that *TV Digest* was more than a reference book of listings, that it was "loaded with editorial matter that keeps 577,244 faithful cover-to-cover readers" coming back for more each week. In its fifth year, the ad claimed, *TV Digest* was outselling every national weekly in the Philadelphia area, including *Life* and the *Saturday Evening Post*. Panitt told Walter that the circulation figure had been verified by the Audit Bureau of Circulation, so the claim was reliable.

There was such a long silence on the phone that the connection seemed to have been broken, but Panitt knew enough not to fill the dead air. Walter typically took time to listen intently while he marshaled information and evaluated a response carefully rather than racing ahead to the next question. "When you talk to Walter Annenberg on the phone, you get used to long pauses," Panitt said. "You let him think. Quietly."

Walter finally stirred. "Aren't there some other magazines like *TV Digest* around the country?"

There were. "There's one called *TV Guide* in New York with a circulation of about four hundred thousand," Panitt replied, "and one in Chicago called *TV Forecast* that has about a hundred thousand."

After another long pause, Walter asked if they had anything in common.

Panitt did not think so. "Editorially, *TV Forecast* hates television; *TV Guide* is a fan magazine; *TV Digest* can't seem to make up its mind."

There were a few other such magazines. Each did its own listings and stories. If one had a good story, put it on the cover and sold extra copies, the others often followed suit. Generally, they were independent.

The pause was so long this time that even Panitt thought he had been cut off.

"How would it be," Walter finally came back, "if we were to print a color section with national articles in our Philadelphia rotogravure plant, ship that section around the country, and in each city we'd print the local listings and bind them inside the national color section?"

Four years earlier, Walter had built the gravure plant, for high-quality color printing of magazines, on a lot next to the *Inquirer* building. Now it was Panitt's turn to pause and think. The idea was huge, the logistics daunting and the financial stakes high, but he knew that interest in television was booming. "It's possible," he said cautiously.

Walter began musing aloud. Staffs in each major city. An emphasis on network shows. Advertising sold on a national or local basis the same way radio and television sold time. The formula — national stories wrapped around local news — was similar to what his father had done four decades earlier when he had bought the *Daily Racing Form* and published eight regional editions.[1]

Over the next few weeks, as his father had before him, Walter did his own legwork. Bundled up in a cashmere overcoat, scarf and galoshes, he walked streets in December's wind and snow, introduced himself to newsstand operators in New York, Chicago and Philadelphia, buttonholed customers and asked why they were buying TV magazines when the information was free in their daily newspaper.

"I was amazed that they all said the same thing," Walter explained. "They liked this small book that they could keep on top of their TV. The listings were far more complete than the coverage in the newspapers and they liked reading the stories about what was happening in television."

THE CONCEPT was coming together in his mind, another "epiphany," like the one he had had in 1944 with *Seventeen* magazine, and again in 1945 when he had decided to buy WFIL radio in Philadelphia for $190,000 from the Lit Brothers department store.

"The medium to be in was television," said Walter. "I had no doubt it was going to be the most powerful tool we'd have for communicating." When he had purchased WFIL, it was an AM radio station, but what made it attractive was that the station had a permit grandfathered in to build a television station. "That's why I bought it. I knew they had the right to proceed from the FCC [Federal Communications Commission] and I felt the time was ripe."[2]

He had called together his top Triangle and *Inquirer* executives, twenty in all, told them his thoughts about exercising the option to build a TV station and asked their opinion. Although he made all the final decisions, he liked advice unvarnished. He was surprised by their response. "They were all against it because it would mean losing too much money for several years," Walter recalled. Intuitively, the way he made most decisions, he disagreed. He doubted it was that risky. "I told them, 'Gentlemen, I appreciate your viewpoint, but I am filing the license application. It's only going to cost me a three-cent stamp. We are not going to miss out on television the way we did on radio. Full speed ahead.'

"I was willing to gamble that it wouldn't lose that much money. And it didn't cost me much. It operated in the red for only six months. But my instinct told me this was an opportunity. How could it fail?

WFIL had authorization for television and I knew Philadelphia was going to be entitled to three stations. I would have one of three in an area that served more than five million people. I knew the advertising potential. It had to be a bonanza!"[3]

When the license application was approved in 1948, WFIL became the thirteenth television station, his lucky number, in the United States. Walter was in on the ground floor. By 1952, he had learned enough about television as a station owner and viewer to recognize that there was a market for more information. "TV is like the theater," he had discovered. "You can't enjoy it without a program."[4]

WITH THE IDEA for the publication in hand and certain that viewers and advertisers would respond, he decided to buy out the digests already being published instead of competing against them or facing a copyright challenge if he published and ignored them.

In New York, *TV Guide* had been founded in 1948 and was published by Lee Wagner, a lawyer who had been circulation director for several movie magazines. By the time Walter asked Joe First to approach him, Wagner was having financial problems with the magazine and the two regional editions he was publishing in New England and the Baltimore-Washington area. Wagner sold all three to Walter for $1.5 million and remained a Triangle consultant for a decade.

In Chicago, *TV Forecast* had been launched in 1949 by Les Viahon and three other ex-GI buddies. They had each chipped in $250 and started publishing in the basement of a classroom building on the Northwestern University campus. They bound their first issue with staplers borrowed from professors upstairs. By Christmas 1952, the magazine was so successful that they flew the staff to New York for a party at the Rainbow Room. They had just returned to Chicago when Joe First called to ask if they would sell. Lee Wagner, he informed them, had sold the New York listings. Figuring that holding out against Triangle was foolhardy, the four flew to Philadelphia, planning to ask for a half million dollars. After several drinks each on the plane, they decided to try for a million and could hardly believe their ears when First agreed.[5]

TV Digest was run by two brothers in Philadelphia, Irvin and Arthur Borowsky, who were in the commercial printing business. In 1948, they teamed up with a local Philco television distributor, who provided the names of TV set owners, and began publishing a program guide to increase television sales and boost their own printing operations.

Walter, who knew Irvin, had Panitt pose detailed questions about the *Digest* and then tell him Triangle had bought the New York magazine. Walter then asked what he wanted for it. Irvin said $600,000: $150,000 up front for the name and $15,000 per brother per year for fifteen years. Walter said fine. "There was no haggling at all," said Borowsky. "He's not the type to haggle."[6]

After buying the three, Triangle approached publishers of television magazines in Boston; Davenport, Iowa; Minneapolis; Pittsburgh; and Wilkes-Barre, Pennsylvania, to change the names of their magazines and serve as franchisees. They bought twenty-four pages each week of the new magazine's national editorial copy and later were purchased by Triangle. Editorial and advertising teams were sent to Los Angeles and Cincinnati, part of the effort to launch ten editions nationally at once. "I wanted to preempt the whole country to keep anyone else from copying my idea," Walter explained.[7]

He was the only one worried about being copied. Everyone else told Walter he was crazy and that his idea was doomed. The cautious and tight-fisted Joe First had been opposed. He knew the start-up costs alone would total millions of dollars for what was at best a chancy operation. Norman Chandler, publisher of the *Los Angeles Times*, warned Walter that Sunday papers would soon carry more comprehensive television listings, probably in small format, which would drive him out of business. Gardner Cowles, whose company owned *Look* magazine, newspapers and television and radio stations, told him it was impossible to publish a magazine that was both national and local. "Cowles told me I had rocks in my head," Walter recalled.[8] None of their objections deterred him. "I trusted my instinct, and it turned out to be the best business move I ever made."[9]

The team he selected to produce *TV Guide* — the name was a narrow choice over *TV Digest* — gave the doubters little reason to alter their opinion. Michael O'Neill, who managed the *Inquirer*'s charity programs in Philadelphia, was named advertising director, although he had no previous advertising experience. James Quirk, former press chief for General Matthew Ridgway in Korea and Japan, was promotion manager of the *Inquirer* and kept that job while assuming the same position for *TV Guide*. Roger Clipp, director of WFIL, was named general manager. TV critic Panitt, whose only previous editing job was his high-school yearbook, became managing editor.

"Annenberg always seeks to operate within interior lines, stressing economy," said Panitt. Hiring everyone from in-house to save money had its drawbacks. "There wasn't ten minutes of solid magazine experience in the lot," Panitt conceded. Walter did not mind. He was a shrewd judge of character and had decided that the team he picked was sufficiently smart, creative, driven and "decent" to do a good job. His formal business education had been slight, but he recognized the merits of Alfred Sloan's delegation of operating authority and the General Motors president's emphasis on managers of good character. The unschooled Moses had tried to do too much himself and too often had relied on unqualified and even sleazy subordinates. Walter would not make the same mistake. One of the major reasons for his business success was that in most areas he delegated work to strong lieutenants. "Quality of management is everything," was a regular Walter refrain, "quality, quality, quality."[10]

Walter already knew what he wanted: another industry bible, much like the *Daily Racing Form*. Newspapers carried television listings just as they carried race results, but they did not extend themselves to cover the industry. That was a result of condescension and the fact that television was beginning to be seen as competition to the daily press. *TV Guide* would cover the television industry with more enthusiasm, detail and accuracy than any newspaper or other periodical could match. "No one on a newspaper is vitally concerned about Milton Berle's guest next week," said Panitt. "We care."[11]

The first issue covered the week April 3–9, 1953, and featured a cover photo of Desi Arnaz IV, the newborn son of comedians Lucille Ball and Desi Arnaz. Selling for fifteen cents and measuring five-by-seven-and-a-half inches to fit on top of the set, the magazine appeared in ten cities and sold 1,560,000 copies, the biggest start-up in history. Cheers broke out in *TV Guide*'s offices above a wholesale popcorn distributor on South Broad Street in Philadelphia. The next week circulation dropped 70,000 copies; the following week, another 7,000. Throughout the long, hot summer of 1953 circulation continued to slide. Advertising was slow. Salesmen found it difficult to sell the national-local hybrid. New editions were introduced in Rochester, Pittsburgh, Cleveland, Detroit and San Francisco, and still the decline continued. By mid-August, circulation was 200,000 lower than for the first issue. Triangle was losing hundreds of thousands of dollars a week. In the midsummer heat, the gloom in the office was as heavy as the acrid smell of burning popcorn wafting up from the first floor.

Walter was not among the doubters. He remained certain that his instincts were right and that it was just a matter of time before the magazine caught on. "We editors consoled ourselves by saying that television viewing *always* dropped in the summer and that things would be better in the fall," Panitt recalled.[12] The editors planned a thick fall preview issue of the season's best new shows and profiles of the stars.

Circulation for the regular September 4 issue soared to 1,600,809, an increase of 250,000 copies over those produced during the August doldrums. The special fall preview was published the following week and sales climbed another 150,000. Advertising was still a struggle. *TV Guide* expanded to sixteen editions after a year, but ad revenues totaled only $760,000. It was three years before the back cover was sold to a national advertiser. With the exception of modest seasonal dips, though, circulation never again posed a problem. By the fall of 1955, two and a half years into the venture, *TV Guide* was producing thirty-nine editions and guaranteeing circulation of 3 million weekly.

When the magazine moved in 1957 from the old *TV Digest* offices in Philadelphia to a modern industrial building in Radnor, a few miles west of the city and minutes from Walter's home in Wynnewood, Panitt installed a small replica of the Liberty Bell. Each time circulation jumped by 100,000 copies, the bell was rung. The sound echoed through the building, mixed with applause. Before long, the clapper broke from overuse. For a quarter century, *TV Guide* continued to grow until, in 1978, the magazine hit its peak and was publishing ninety-four editions and 21 million copies a week, or a billion copies a year, the only magazine ever to reach that level in sales. Walter estimated that *TV Guide* was netting $150,000 a week, or nearly $8 million a year for him and his sisters, Triangle's sole stockholders.[13]

IN THE PRECOMPUTER ERA, producing multiple editions of what was essentially two magazines — local listings plus national copy — was complicated. The listings were printed in large type so they were more easily read in the dim light of a television. For an inside touch, light gossip was added: "Sheree North was tossed off a coast-to-coast interview program when she arrived sans makeup when the show was one-third over." The key to the magazine's early success was the "logs." Drafted by reporters who scoured the studios for news, talked to directors and casts, they were a two- or three-sentence plot summary to tell enough, but not too much, about each program. This summary of every film and series meant that only *TV Guide* buyers or subscribers would know ahead of time during reruns if they had already seen a program.

Producing these logs was exhausting and called for absolute accuracy. The concept was based, as the regional editions had been, on the *Daily Racing Form*, which handled prodigious amounts of data in multiple editions with exemplary precision.

While each edition of *TV Guide* was handled as a separate, local magazine, the national editorial material was assembled in Radnor, originally by a staff of nine writers. The twenty-four-page, four-color wraparound was printed at Triangle's gravure plant, then shipped around the country to each city, where the local sections — thirty-two to eighty pages — were job-printed. To produce the thirty-nine editions in 1955, Walter and Panitt had assembled a total staff of 367 reporters, editors, circulation and ad salesmen, an average of about 10 per magazine. Panitt hired the great sports columnist Red Smith, who was then writing for the *New York Herald Tribune*, for occasional pieces and kept his eye open for more top-flight writers.

FROM THE OUTSET, Walter's goal for *TV Guide* was to cover and critique a communication medium that was becoming increasingly important in American lives. "Whether we like it or not," said Panitt, "television affects not only our mores, but just about every other aspect of our society — business, education, politics, government, international affairs and human relations."[14] That was true in the *Guide*'s peak years in the 1970s when Panitt made the comment, but less obvious when the magazine was launched. In 1952, when Walter saw the *TV Digest* ad in the *Bulletin*, sixteen million sets had been sold in the United States, a figure that would double in less than three years as television became the centerpiece of American homes.[15] While he was checking newsstands and interviewing *TV Digest* buyers, Lucille Ball was pregnant in real life and drawing huge audiences to her popular *I Love Lucy* show. When she featured a fictionalized version of the birth on January 19, 1953, the show drew 68 percent of the nation's viewers, the highest-rated program in the 1950s, and clinched both Walter's decision to proceed with his new magazine and his choice of Lucy and her new baby as the illustration for its first cover.

Walter wanted to produce more than another fan magazine. Those magazines offered frothy stories, and their circulation tended to peak at a million or two at most. Walter was aiming higher for economic and philosophical reasons. He spoke of giving readers the ability to choose wisely and of influencing programmers to create better shows. He wanted quality coverage of the industry and medium — "authoritative, but not authoritarian" — that would be essential reading for what he expected would ultimately be tens of millions of viewers.

In its early days, little effort went into lobbying for better shows. The magazine at first was an industry booster, aimed at creating viewers and readers. It relied on publicity offices for story ideas and photos and there was little edge to its articles. "We can't go as far as the *New Yorker* in a profile because it has a select audience and we have a mass one," Panitt explained. "Our readers don't want to know what heels the stars are. We don't take TV apart because the people who buy the magazine like it, and so do we."[16]

There were articles on the technological innovations that were transforming television, such as the prospects for color broadcasts and the miniaturizing of equipment. "In the Cast" was a regular feature which dealt with the lives of supporting actors in shows. Because 60 percent of sales were at supermarkets, *TV Guide* included a food column which featured easy-to-prepare meals that housewives could serve in front of a television set. Markets loved to sell the magazine because *TV Guide* was designed to fit their merchandising practices. "We offer food stores a 26 percent markup on a small-sized, fully returnable product that turns over fifty-two times a year," said publisher James Quirk. "There's no price stamping, no use of shelf space. No one has to break open a case; our wholesalers service each store and we bill direct to chain headquarters." For the predominantly female buyer, the magazine covers featured a preponderance of male stars. For male readers, there was usually a photo and brief sketch of a pretty female star.[17]

Personality profiles were "factual pleasant accounts which acquaint the reader with the stars without trying to disillusion him," according to a 1960 self-study by the editors. There was room for a homily or a parable, but not for negativism. The underlying theme of a profile was often how a nice guy or gal could finish first. Readers learned from a 1954 "Close-Up" how, as a child, Eddie Fisher helped his father with his grocery wagon, and then as a singer earning millions, bought his parents a house and lived an exemplary life. Donna Reed was an all-American model mother. Families who watched her show together would probably stay together.

If a star had strayed, there was inevitably a moral to be found in his return to the straight and narrow. Phil Silvers's life had revolved around the racetrack and leggy women, his profile acknowledged, but the once prodigal actor had settled down with his new wife and was becoming a model husband. "Close-Up" denounced the busybodies who wondered why Liberace had not married, reporting that he nearly had wed twice, but held off because he did not want to leave his dear mother, who was working two jobs to pay for his piano lessons.[18]

A moderate amount of violence was acceptable as long as there was no blood and wholesome straight shooters like Hopalong Cassidy or Roy Rogers were pulling the triggers. *Dragnet* was good because every week Sergeant Joe Friday taught how crime did not pay. Just as *Seventeen* refused liquor ads, alcohol was not fit for discussion or advertisements in *TV Guide*, although that later changed. There were no ads for funeral directors (too depressing), astrologers (too cheesy) or guns (too dangerous). Sex and titillation were banned. Lucille Ball had a baby, but the word "pregnant" did not appear in the magazine. If a show involved a pregnant teenager, the program notes said that she had "trouble with high school graduation." The slightest hint of a nipple on a proof brought out the airbrush. A cover photo of dancer Fred Astaire was yanked at the last moment because of "a crotch problem."[19]

After the first few years, the novelty of *TV Guide* began to wear off, and critics started sniping that the magazine was mushy. "It is the bland, fat princess of the TV-log magazines [which feeds readers] an exclusive diet of pablum and prune juice," the *San Francisco Chronicle*'s respected television critic Terence O'Flaherty wrote in 1958.[20]

Walter considered the criticism unduly harsh, but he took it to heart. He and Panitt would never ease their vigilance in keeping suggestive or offensive material out of *TV Guide*, but he refused to produce a bland magazine. High circulation was not enough. Pablum was unacceptable. Top quality was imperative. He wanted a publication that informed and instructed readers intelligently. On occasion, when it was appropriate, he even wanted *TV Guide* to try to alter the values and tastes of Americans who were being influenced by what was becoming the most powerful medium in history.[21]

To find the appropriate voice for the magazine, he gave increased authority to Panitt, who was nine years younger and always deferred to Walter, but who also had an uncanny ability to intuit precisely what his boss wanted. Born in Hartford, he had been a United Press reporter before the war and had come to Walter's attention when he was a young major serving on the staff of General Eisenhower. Walter had heard that he could write and had "good character." "This is a combination which naturally interests me," Walter cabled, asking Panitt if he had postwar plans.[22]

When the war ended, Panitt came to work immediately for Triangle and became Walter's administrative assistant. At *TV Guide*, Walter submitted story ideas and closely monitored tone, content, graphics and photo quality. He would ask Panitt to send a complimentary note to a writer if he spotted a particularly good story. Typographical errors enraged Walter. Sometimes he complained that a cover was awful. "But don't worry about it," he often added. "Babe Ruth struck out on occasion too." Panitt said, "I wished I had a dollar for every time I've heard that."[23]

The tweedy, professorial Panitt was the magazine's editorial nucleus. He improved the editorial staff, hired better freelancers, and gave contracts to such photographers as Yousuf Karsh. He allowed writers more license to be tougher about the industry and, in the 1960s, more skeptical and critical of mediocre programming. Profiles took on a sharper edge:

Singer Bobby Darin "in person is fully as offensive as he is in public. . . . He does not merely talk rudeness, he lives it."

Actor Robert Goulet's "abandoned nonsense as a conversationalist is offset by his monastic restraint when it comes to expressing a straight opinion."

Broadcaster Hugh Downs's image "is one part Honest Abe, one part Tonto and one part Leonardo. It's not an entirely true image, for Downs is more skilled pitchman than open-hearted, more yes-man than critical friend, more memorizer than thinker."[24]

More tang and incisiveness in major stories increased *TV Guide*'s credibility, but Panitt, with Walter's encouragement, also wanted to raise its intellectual quotient. Next to pieces on cop shows like *Starsky and Hutch* appeared essays by Margaret Mead, William Saroyan, Arthur Schlesinger Jr., and John Updike. There were articles on Theodore Roosevelt and Huckleberry Finn. Politically, the magazine was middle-of-the-road conservative, reflecting Walter's outlook, which was never as right-wing or partisan as some critics later charged. His friend Ronald Reagan wrote a commentary, but so did John F. Kennedy. Staff writers Edith Efron and Dwight Whitney could make allusions to Kafka and Freud without fear that the editor would strike them out.

In "As We See It," Walter and Panitt had an editorial platform from which they could discuss the industry, the medium and everything that television touched, including social and political trends. They were careful how they used it. "Together Annenberg and Panitt sought to make their magazine a conscience for the industry, an arbiter of taste, public morality and, occasionally, private ethics," wrote Glenn Alt-schuler and David Grossvogel in their comprehensive history of the magazine, *Changing Channels: America in TV Guide.* "Only boosters, they believed, were qualified to be critics, for they would be caring, con-structive and balanced."[25]

Panitt often urged readers to view programs about Shakespeare, the ballet or symphony. When ratings showed that they had ignored his advice, he scolded them for not aiming higher. A writer could always get stories in about programs on National Educational Television and its successor, the Public Broadcasting System, because Walter and Panitt felt that they were producing high-quality programs that Ameri-cans would be wise to watch. On the commercial networks, Ed Sulli-van was praised for showcasing opera singers, dancers and excerpts from Broadway shows on his Sunday variety show. So was NBC presi-dent Pat Weaver for putting such intellects as Arnold Toynbee and Bertrand Russell on the air in the *Wise Men* series. Viewers were impor-tuned to give the show a chance and to resist the impulse to switch the dial.

TV Guide took the lead in lobbying to improve television. An April 1961 "As We See It" editorial signed by "The Editors," meaning Wal-ter and Panitt, was an open letter to Newton Minow, whom President John F. Kennedy had recently appointed chairman of the Federal Communications Commission, which licensed broadcasters. The edi-torial noted that one requirement for renewal of a license was that a station broadcast "in the public interest," a standard *TV Guide* argued was not being met. The editorial argued that the networks controlled program quality during peak viewing hours; that they often demanded part ownership of programs selected for broadcast; that too much vio-lence was "making our youth callous and damaging America's image abroad"; that local stations did not use enough of the higher-quality informational shows being produced; that ratings were the sole criteria for program selection; and that a few talent agencies exercised "almost dictatorial control" over programming.

TV Guide demanded that the FCC investigate, speak to industry leaders and report to Congress. Minow responded with his own open letter in the magazine in which he called television "the most powerful instrument ever devised for reaching the minds and hearts of men" and *TV Guide* "a distinguished and influential voice in broadcasting." Pledging action, he agreed that television had a responsibility to "serve the nation's needs as well as its whims; that television must assist in preparing a generation for great decisions; that television has a deep obligation to guide our country in fulfilling its future."[26]

Two weeks later, in a May address to the National Association of Broadcasters, Minow offered a devastating critique of television which endeared the thirty-five-year-old lawyer to Walter and decades later would lead to their collaboration in a television venture. "I invite you to sit down in front of your television set when your station goes on the air and stay there. You will see a vast wasteland — a procession of game shows, violence, audience participation shows, formula comedies about totally unbelievable families . . . blood and thunder . . . mayhem, violence, sadism, murder . . . private eyes, more violence, and cartoons . . . and endlessly, commercials — many screaming, cajoling and offending."[27]

Minow's "vast wasteland" speech, as it became known, was a bomb blast over the landscape of television, which was entering its own adolescence. The assessment of the FCC chairman did not affect the tenor of programming as a whole. The sins he cited continued to be committed decades later, in many cases far more egregiously. But he created an awareness among some viewers, programmers and industry executives that television could also be more *See It Now* and *Omnibus* and less *Have Gun Will Travel* and *Wanted — Dead or Alive*.

WALTER HAD BEEN an advocate of high-quality programming since his television license application was approved in 1947, and he began thinking of ways to fill mostly empty air time with worthwhile shows. Two of his most innovative creations were *Wiffil Schoolhouse* and the better-known *University of the Air*, which were precursors to his gifts in the 1980s and 1990s to public television. Both programs resulted from Walter's 1950 order to WFIL director Roger Clipp to schedule primary-school and college-level courses during the day, when there was virtually no programming.

In the 1940s, his own children were in grammar school and *Seventeen* magazine had focused his attention on teenagers. He thought often about his father's education. Moses had had almost no formal schooling, but he had transformed himself into a well-read adult through perseverance. As his father had predicted, Walter regretted dropping out of Wharton. As head of Triangle and publisher of the *Inquirer*, he dealt every day with business executives, cultural leaders and politicians. He recognized his own shortcomings in education. He also knew that World War II had interrupted the schooling of many teenagers and young adults. In the postwar period, a large number had been unable to return to school. Some could not afford it; others were embarrassed to join classes with much younger students, had to work, were married, or all of those. "He's been very consistent in his goals over the years," said Bill McCarter, program director of WFIL's *University of the Air* in the 1950s and later president of WTTW, Chicago's public television station. "He had a passion for wanting to educate young people, especially those with limited means."[28]

Broadcasting school programs was an innovative approach to both television and education, but Walter's motives were every bit as pragmatic as they were altruistic, just as they had been when he launched *Seventeen*. "I was trying to get to young people and at the same time win the support of their parents," he explained. "I thought anything to do with school and training the young, or even the not so young, would be appreciated by older people, especially parents. I thought it would be good for the children, good for the family, and also good for business, including advertising."[29]

That was the intended guiding philosophy behind all of Walter's business behavior. There was always an element of idealism in what he did, thanks to his mother, Sadie's, influence and his own determination to associate the Annenberg name only with ventures of quality and excellence. But he was no dewy-eyed dreamer. He was a businessman, and with Moses peering metaphorically over his shoulder, Walter never strayed far from enhancing his personal interests. And why not? His feeling was that if he could do well by doing good, everyone benefited.

Characteristically, he ordered no feasibility study of educational TV. He did not draft a budget. He did not consult at length with educators or other broadcasters. He believed the idea made sense, so he ordered that it be implemented.

The experiment began at 11:10 A.M. on January 2, 1951, when WFIL began broadcasting college courses to 121,000 television sets in eastern Pennsylvania, Delaware and southern New Jersey. Presented Monday through Friday for fifty minutes a day with the cooperation initially of twenty-two colleges and universities from the tristate area, *University of the Air* offered two courses a day — one for twenty minutes, the other for thirty — or ten courses a week for thirty-four weeks a year. WFIL program director Jack Steck said that educators had been critical for years of what radio and television had or had not done. "They now have the chance to prove they can use the medium for their purposes. This is their program."[30]

It was their program in more ways than one. Walter and Roger Clipp, the director of Triangle's television properties, convinced the universities and colleges that participating in the show was good advertising for their schools. The educators concurred and appreciated their freedom to design the courses. What pleased Walter, in addition to airing programs he respected, was that the entire venture cost him next to nothing. Institutions found it gratifying to bask in the light of the bold new medium. They offered their best instructors, who received a tiny stipend and the fame that went with being on the air.

Professors, few if any of whom had had previous broadcasting experience, were filmed in a WFIL studio furnished with a desk, podium and blackboard. "You can't interrupt me to ask questions, but if you write me letters with specific queries, I'll try to answer them," Russell Erb, a chemistry professor from Pennsylvania Military College, told his unseen class the first week.[31]

Called by the *New York Times* television's "most ambitious program of mass education," the *University* first offered courses for credit in nuclear physics, Spanish, the menace of Soviet aggression, understanding economics, the art of thinking, governments around the world and more. In later years, the educational program increased to hundreds of courses which were taught over the airwaves of five other Triangle television stations that Walter bought in the 1950s: WNBF, Binghamton, New York; WFBG, Altoona-Johnstown, Pennsylvania; WNHC, Hartford-New Haven, Connecticut; WLYH, Lebanon-Lancaster, Pennsylvania; and KFRE in Fresno, California.

University of the Air won accolades from across the country: educational awards, broadcasting commendations and the first of dozens of honorary degrees. Presented with two duPont awards for public service, the first to receive the honor more than once, and later with a George Foster Peabody Award, broadcast journalism's highest honor, Walter was widely recognized as its inventor and guiding spirit. He was thrilled at having been recognized for doing something worthy and delighted that another hunch had proved to be a triumph.

A YEAR AFTER launching *University of the Air*, he promoted a different kind of program for young viewers that became one of the most successful and enduring shows in television history. In this case, another man made it famous and built his own fortune. Walter did not mind. The program was wholesome, cheap to produce and fabulously lucrative, a much bigger hit than he or anyone else could have predicted.

WFIL was filling afternoon air time in 1951 by showing third-rate movies. Hollywood considered television competition, just as newspapers did, and had no intention of selling networks or local stations anything good to air. The television movie reruns were driving away viewers and were canceled. Station manager George Koehler was desperate to find a replacement. WFIL was receiving little from its network, the American Broadcasting Company. ABC had only fifteen stations compared with NBC's sixty-four and CBS's thirty-one and offered no daytime programming. Koehler asked a WFIL disc jockey named Bob Horn to transfer to television his popular radio show "Bandstand," which played pop recordings.[32]

Horn went on the air on October 6, 1952, with a partner, Lee Stewart, the show's designated comic. They quipped and played records and teenagers danced, a formula that had originated on radio in 1945 on the "950 Club" on WPEN, another Philadelphia station. Heavyset, with a big, bulging nose and slick black hair, the thirty-seven-year-old Horn had the looks of the radio personality he had been, while Stewart proved distinctly unfunny and would be gone within a year. But the program was an immediate success. Sixty percent of Philadelphia's afternoon television audience was tuning to WFIL to watch *Bandstand.* To mark its second anniversary, *TV Guide* commended the show as "the people's choice" for a 1954 *TV Guide* award. The Triangle publication did not mention that Triangle owned the program.[33]

The flamboyant Horn became one of Philadelphia's most famous personalities, cruising town in his green Cadillac Eldorado. But his world came crashing down in 1956 when he was arrested and charged with drunk driving and statutory rape. He was dropped from *Bandstand* immediately, which left WFIL in desperate need of a quick replacement. "We had this clean-cut kid working down the corridor who looked like a teenager himself," said Walter. "So we put him in and forty years later he still looked astonishing."[34]

The "kid" was twenty-six-year-old Dick Clark, who was emceeing the radio version of *Bandstand.* "Hooo, yeahh," he said when station manager Koehler asked him if he wanted the TV job. Youthful, polite, telegenic and with the well-scrubbed, all-American looks of a Campus Crusade for Christ solicitor, Clark was the perfect choice to succeed a brash older man arrested on lurid vice charges. "Dick was wholesome and that was important," Walter acknowledged.

Clark did more than inject a wholesome image into *Bandstand.* After repeated tries and finally by offering it for free, he persuaded

ABC, still a distant third in size and ratings to NBC and CBS, to put *Bandstand* on the network. In August 1957, a ninety-minute version of the show, which had expanded in Philadelphia to two and a half hours each afternoon, was renamed *American Bandstand* and broadcast nationally for a seven-week test. By the fourth week, it had become the number one daytime show, a savior for ABC, and Clark was on his way to becoming a national celebrity.

"Mr. Annenberg," said Clark, was "the Wizard of Oz, and I say that as a compliment. He was the boss. You knew he was there, watching, listening and, you hoped, approving." Walter did approve, but there was a moment during the payola scandals of 1959 and 1960 when he needed reassurance that his golden boy Clark was not accepting payoffs for playing certain records.

The face and spirit of *American Bandstand*, Clark was by then a huge success. The most influential music host in the world at the very moment when rock 'n' roll and Elvis Presley were driving a pop-culture boom, he had interests in record and music companies, disk pressing plants, record distribution companies and talent management agencies. "I had a lot of conflicts and potential conflicts of interest," said Clark, who turned out to be one of broadcasting's canniest businessmen. "I never took money to play records, but God almighty, I took some gifts. I also owned everything in the world I could get my hands on. I was an entrepreneur and while I'm not as pure as the driven snow and never purported to be, I was not a thief. I didn't do anything illegal."[35]

When the federal government began investigating the payoff scandal, Clark confessed his conflicts to his WFIL superiors and swore that he had taken no money. ABC insisted that he divest himself of his music business interests, and the House of Representatives subcommittee investigating payola summoned him to Washington. Before testifying, he was invited to Inwood for a birthday party for Walter's daughter, Wallis. When Clark arrived, Walter took him aside.

"Is there anything at all that you haven't told us that could possibly be an embarrassment to anybody?" Walter asked.

"Mr. Annenberg," Clark replied, "I've told you everything."

"In that case, my boy, don't worry," Walter said, smiling and draping his arm around Clark, who survived the probe with his reputation bruised but intact. "A federal investigation is like a crucible. They're going to put you in it and they're going to boil you and it's going to harden you for the rest of your life. Now let's go and enjoy the party."[36]

20

THE CHILDREN

———

ALTER'S CHILDREN, Wallis and Roger, were living with their mother, Ronny, in Washington in 1951 when the newly married Lee Annenberg moved to Philadelphia. With Lee came Diane, her nine-year-old daughter from her first marriage, to Beldon Katleman. Two-year-old Elizabeth remained in Connecticut and New York during the week with her father, Lew Rosenstiel. Lee saw her younger daughter only on weekends and alternating holidays when a governess brought her by train to visit. Each time the child left, Lee retreated to her bedroom in tears and turned to her Christian Science lessons for solace. By constantly pressing Lew, who married three more times, Lee managed to adjust the regimen. If Lew wanted to take Elizabeth to Florida in the winter for two months, for example, then Lee was able to have her in Philadelphia for the same amount of time. By second grade, Elizabeth was living with her mother for the whole school year and Lew had her for most vacations.

Walter had a good relationship with both of his stepdaughters. He welcomed them into his house and helped raise them, while always being careful to avoid interfering in their relationships with their own fathers. He gave them advice, presents, trips, birthday parties and debutante dances, but Lee took the lead in their upbringing. "Walter was always there, ready to help me with my homework, especially my Latin and any essays I had to write," Diane recalled. "He was terrific."[1]

Elizabeth, the youngest of the four children, remembered her years at Inwood as having been "fun"— swimming in the pool, running around the courtyard in pigtails and Sunday dinners with Diane, Lee and Walter. When she was grown and her own marriage collapsed, Elizabeth found that she could count on Walter. "He was extremely supportive of me, and very, very supportive of my mom, who was trying to deal with me. Big time," she said. "He's good with women. He grew up with a lot of strong women and that may explain why my experiences with him, and my own daughter's, have been so good."[2]

With his own two children, Walter's involvement was more intense. He supported them financially, sent them to camp and on trips, scrutinized every aspect of their education, behavior and appearance, brought them to Philadelphia every month, sent them presents and wrote them regularly, sometimes twice a day. Wallis and Roger developed close and warm relationships with Lee, but from the clothes they wore, and the words they misspelled to their spending habits and the schools they attended, Walter considered himself — as Moses had with him — ultimately responsible for every aspect of their upbringing.

That is how he behaved after Ronny left in 1950 with the children, married Ben Ourisman and moved to Washington. During the years he and Ronny lived together in Philadelphia and on the Main Line, Walter had been less attentive. Wallis and Roger saw little of either parent. Throughout the 1940s, nanny Marjorie Voyce was primarily responsible for raising the children. Ronny was adjusting to Philadelphia and trying to develop a social life. Walter was busy trying to save his father's empire and building up the *Inquirer* and Triangle. After receiving Wallis's first-grade report card from the Montgomery Country Day School in 1946, Walter wrote the headmistresses to say how "gratifying" it was to see that his daughter, described as "shy" and "thoughtful," was improving. "In the near future, I am going to avail myself of the opportunity to discuss the youngster with you — something I should have done long before this," he wrote. "Please be patient with an extremely busy father."[3]

When they lived in the Rittenhouse Plaza in downtown Philadelphia, Wallis and Roger stayed with their governess in a separate apartment from their parents. After Ronny and Walter moved to Inwood, the children lived closer, just down the corridor from the master bedroom on the second floor of the elegant home. Once they were older, Walter took Wallis and Roger to Penn football games and to the Army-Navy game every year, when they would sit all dressed up in the mayor's box, snow often falling softly, excursions that gave Wallis an enduring love of sports. He took them to Rodeo Ben's, a fancy western store in Philadelphia, and bought them cowboy outfits. On holidays like Christmas, although not Jewish holy days, which were ignored, Ronny did all she could to make the occasion festive.

Day-to-day contact and overt affection, though, were limited. The children were occasionally bounced on a knee, tickled or told a story, but more often were kept at a distance like the offspring of the English upper class: seen but not heard; written to, but rarely embraced. Grandmother Sadie could not stop showing her affection, but Ronny was no Sadie and neither was Walter. Except for Sundays, when Walter carved a roast and they sat together around the dining room table, the family shared few meals. When Lee arrived, dinners together became more common, but by then, Wallis and Roger had moved to Washington and only experienced the family meals on visits.

"My father was working all the time and my mother wanted to hang out with her girlfriends or go to a party and have a good time," Wallis explained. "My first memory of my mother was of her sitting at her dressing table with an eyelash curler in each hand getting ready for a party." She smiled at the remembrance. "My friends called me Summertime because my daddy was rich and my momma good-looking."[4]

Wallis was ten in 1949 when her mother brought car dealer Ben Ourisman to her room, introduced them and said he could help with her spelling. He quizzed her, then left the room, and Ronny casually announced that she was going to marry him. "The next thing I know," said Wallis, "we're on the train to Washington, she hands me the lyrics to the Ourisman Chevrolet advertising jingle and I was told that I was going to sing this at the wedding. My mother was way out there in her own ding-a-ling world. Emotionally immature, mostly interested in herself, but lots of F-U-N."[5]

Both children went to private school in Washington: Wallis to the National Cathedral School and Roger to the only slightly less Waspish Landon School. At home, the children were lonely. Ben Ourisman was kindly, but he had been a widower for twenty years. He was captivated by Ronny but had little interest in her two youngsters. His elder son, Mandy, was twenty-three and married. Second son Florenz, named for his mother, who had died within days of his birth, was a twenty-year-old who became close to Ronny, an exuberant Auntie Mame in her mid-thirties. When he came home from college, they would sprawl like a couple of teenagers in Flo's bedroom and discuss his dates.

Wallis and Roger, jealous of the time their mother spent with their stepbrother, put itching powder in Ronny's bed and regularly set Flo's alarm for 6 A.M. They rolled on the floor giggling when they heard Ronny yelling and Flo thrashing around blindly looking for the clock.

Only a year apart in age, Wallis and Roger were allies. They played together, hugged and shared their loneliness. "He was my partner," said Wallis. "He was my best friend and the person I was closest to."[6]

He was also emotionally troubled and his cleft lip and palate continued to require surgical repair well into his teens. "Today they could put it right quickly, but his was never completely fixed and it changed his look," said his aunt, Zelda Wilner.[7] Roger did not think so, but in spite of the lip problem, he was becoming a good-looking young man. "He looked like a Dunkelman, tall and slim like a flamenco dancer," said Wallis. "He was beautiful. He had the most gorgeous eyelashes. Oh, you could fall for those eyelashes." Roger went to the beach dressed in white, looking as though he had stepped from a Seurat painting. All that was missing was a butler in tow with a picnic basket, and shading him with a large parasol.

Unlike Wallis, who was partially deaf, Roger's ears connected him to the world. He played the piano by ear. He wrote touching poetry. He spoke in rhyming couplets. "Our blood will turn from red to blue, although our money is but new," he once told Wallis, who considered him a savant.

Roger never got along with his mother. Ronny treated her daughter as an equal, not a child, and spent hours telling her about her own social life and talking about clothes. After she divorced Ben Ourisman — too stodgy in his widower ways, she claimed, which his sons confirmed — Ronny would discuss her love affairs with her daughter and even took Wallis along on dates. But she had little to say to her son. "Roger got the short end," said Mandy Ourisman. "Wallis was a cute gal. She was fun and eager to please and much easier to be with than Roger."[8] "Wally was a ball of fire," added Flo Ourisman. "Roger was much more serious."[9]

In their early years, both children had trouble at school. Wallis was a steady worker and verbally astute but could not grasp geometry or algebra, although Walter arranged a tutor. She was well liked, but felt out of place at the National Cathedral School. Grandmother Sadie Annenberg said nothing about her attending the nation's foremost Episcopal girls' school, but grandmother Rose Dunkelman, a founder of the Zionist movement in Canada, begged Ronny to send the children to Hebrew instruction. Wallis's uncle Ben Dunkelman was a hero of Israel's 1948 war of independence. "And here I was at NCS, the only girl who couldn't say the Apostles' Creed when everybody stood up to recite it," said Wallis. "Throughout, I felt this tremendous dichotomy. Who was I?"[10]

Roger also had academic problems. He could write well, but as his teacher Jack Barker pointed out in primary school, "Roger does not always take his oral work seriously; instead he is inclined to clown to get laughs. . . . he is generally inattentive in music class."[11] Walter promptly wrote Barker to ask if he could help his son, the first of a series of attentive letters he wrote for years to various school heads and university deans.

Roger's behavior remained a persistent problem. He was sometimes hyper and at other times passive, but no clinical diagnosis determined that he was a manic depressive. He was teased at school about his lip and lack of athletic ability. Some days he came home and, refusing to talk, played the piano for hours or stayed in his room and cried. After clearing it with Walter, Ronny consulted a child psychologist when Roger was thirteen. She kept Walter informed, telling him that, "accepting with whatever calm you can muster will be the wiser course to pursue in the face of these flare-ups, bouts of unreasonableness and clashes of temperament that are positively bound to occur, and occur frequently, I fear."[12]

Landon School was only a few minutes drive from home, but when he entered seventh grade later that year, Roger was enrolled by Ronny as a five-day boarder in an effort to help him make friends and adjust socially. His grades and his ability to get along improved dramatically. "He has become a much more likeable and considerate person," adviser Paul Oakley wrote at the end of Roger's first boarding year.[13]

Yet he remained agitated. "The divorce had had an effect on him. It troubled him that his parents had split and that he didn't have a single home," said Mallory Walker, who was Roger's roommate at Landon. "He didn't just push past what had happened. He was candid and open and vulnerable. He was very self-conscious of his looks and he felt that because of the cleft palate he spoke differently. He was not athletic, not a graceful person, and I had the impression that he was troubled, filled with emotion and insecurity."[14]

Like Wallis, Roger was also suffering an identity problem. "He was trying not to be Jewish, but he obviously was, and he was having trouble dealing with it," Walker recalled. "Once he kind of barked out, 'I don't know who my father is trying to kid; he has the map of Israel on his face.' It made such an impression that I've remembered the words all my life."[15]

Walter did not believe that he was trying to kid anyone. Despite what Roger allegedly said, he did not look particularly Jewish at all. It was true that he did not go to temple. But that was because he did not care for organized religion. As he explained to Simeon Maslin, rabbi of the Keneseth Israel congregation in north Philadelphia: "I do not question that formalized religious beliefs theoretically stand for justice and peace, but from a practical standpoint I see no end of divisiveness and bitterness . . . and limited concern for true brotherhood among men."[16]

He would visit Israel only once — with his mother. But Walter never denied his Jewishness. In the 1940s, most of his and Ronny's friends in Philadelphia were Jewish, as were his and Lee's in the early years of their marriage. He gave to Jewish charities, he told Maslin in 1987, "to aid those who are seeking a better way of life and to gain a measure of dignity for themselves." Back in the 1940s and 1950s, however, local Jewish community leaders in Philadelphia believed that Walter was contributing more in an effort to vindicate his father's name than from any real interest in the work of the charities. Later, as he did more for the community, that attitude would change.[17] Walter looked coolly upon Jews who changed their names to appear less Jewish. He argued that it was not he who was keeping Wallis and Roger from attending Hebrew classes. According to Wallis, she and her brother went a few times, then chose to drop out. Ronny never objected.

Walter's disconnect with his Jewish identity was more the result of the way he had been raised. Moses, whose father, Tobias, had been very religious, forcefully rejected his Judaism, which had a palpable effect on Walter. Once Moses made his break — which actually took place when he fended for himself as a boy in Chicago, long before he threw the rabbi out of his Milwaukee office — Sadie never nudged, let alone pressured Walter to consider his origins. She went along with enrolling her Boy at Peddie as a Baptist, although there was no evidence that the charade was necessary. By every account, Walter's five years there were fun, fulfilling and friction-free.

Those were passive reasons for his attitude. There were active ones as well, although Walter did not like to discuss them. It was not easy being a Jew in his day and age, especially in Philadelphia. Jews were too easily slighted, and he had already had his fill of slights, about his ear and stutter, his lack of athleticism, lack of friends, and the widespread perception that he was a dim, pale, soft replica of his dynamic father. Then there was the matter of persecution. Most Jews felt persecuted, unfortunately for good reason, but Walter could not tolerate additional persecution. He had had enough for a lifetime when the family was targeted by the IRS, federal prosecutors and the century's most powerful presidential administration. The feeling did not go away after his father died. Walter would always be Moe's son, and for decades as he became more successful and prominent — a much-improved version of Moses — he was featured in newspaper and magazine stories. Even articles that had nothing to do with his history or family background often gratuitously reminded readers that his father had gone to jail, which infuriated him more.

Thus, with no feeling of religious, historic or psychological commitment to Judaism, Walter saw little reason to embrace a cultural identity that would probably do him no good and might even lead to more pain. What mattered as his wealth, power and influence increased was being in the company of powerful and influential achievers, the more successful the better. To be sure, there were well-to-do Jews in Philadelphia, but some of the most prominent, including David Stern and Albert Greenfield, had tried to destroy his father, while others had frozen out the Annenbergs socially. The result was that Walter found himself most comfortable with politically centrist, prosperous WASP Republicans. "It had nothing to do with anti-Semitism," said Wallis. "It's just that the people my father admired were achievers in government and business and they were always of another religion."[18]

IDENTITY PROBLEMS were merely part of Roger's troubles. He was not getting along with his mother or stepfather. Having started out well as a boarder at Landon, he turned rebellious in his second year. "The maturation of Roger Annenberg," headmaster Paul Banfield wrote on his report card in June 1955, "is a tortuously slow process which is a source of much discomfort both to Roger and his teachers. . . . Each of the boy's masters reports disappointment at his limited progress."[19] That summer, when he turned fifteen, Roger attempted suicide by slashing his wrists. Walter, distraught, urged Ronny to let Roger move back to Philadelphia.

Unable to cope with her son, Ronny agreed. Walter first considered sending him to board at Valley Forge Military Academy with the idea that discipline was what he needed. On further thought, he opted to have him live at home and attend nearby Episcopal Academy, the excellent prep school founded in 1785. Lee, who felt Roger might benefit from more family contact, was instrumental in the decision. Having been married to a manic depressive, Lew Rosenstiel, she was patient and caring with her stepson. Roger responded to her kindness and wrote her letters addressed to "Sweets." "Mom used to spend hours with him, hearing him perform on the debating team, working with him on his homework, just being with him," said Diane, who was two years younger than her stepbrother.[20] "He was a darling boy and we had a wonderful relationship," said Lee, "but he was obviously unwell."[21]

Although the cause continued to elude them, the move to Philadelphia had an immediate positive effect on Roger. He missed Wallis, but he loved Lee's sensitivity and the greater attention he received from his father. When he was sixteen and a maid found a *Playboy* magazine under his bed, Diane recalled, "Mother said, 'For God's sake, put it back and don't say a word.'" Six months after he had arrived back, he wrote a note to his father saying how grateful he was to be home. "Please you must never tell me to go to Washington," Roger wrote. "You must never forget that I am a son who belongs to you and needs very much your parental guidance and help and love."[22]

His schoolwork improved greatly. "Roger is doing splendidly," read his tenth-grade report card. "He deserves commendation for the superior showing he is making. He certainly has a fine attitude."[23]

A proper attitude was important to Walter. He did not understand what was troubling Roger, but whatever it was he believed could be helped if only his son could exhibit greater self-control. He continually tried to instill the importance of attitude and order in each child, almost exclusively by letter. The practice held plusses and minuses. "I always knew where I stood with my father. It was cut and dried. This is how you dress, how you speak, how you act," said Wallis. "But no one really said anything. From letters and what was unspoken, you learned the rules."[24]

Walter in these years rarely communicated anything of a personal nature by telephone or, for that matter, face to face. It made him uncomfortable. He felt more vulnerable when speaking. Writing gave him greater control over situations, allowed for more precision and insured he would not be interrupted or challenged. It also reflected his deliberate remoteness from most things emotional. He had been seriously hurt in his life and one method he adopted to keep it from happening again was to shield his emotions under a protective carapace of formality and distance, both psychological and physical. He was not emotionless. On the contrary, he had strong feelings and could be frighteningly mercurial. Calm Walter's emotions included a patriotism that was intensifying as he became older and more successful. At the core of fiery Walter were a quick temper and an array of hot buttons, the hottest of which was any criticism of himself or his father. That button was toggled easily and often. It did not always work, but distance translated into more control of his environment. The price, though, was standoffishness and a formality which some mistook for stuffiness.

AFTER A SPRING VACATION in Palm Beach, Wallis wrote to thank her father for the holiday and admitted that it was hard getting back in the swing of school, but that she knew too much vacation was not good. Walter was "enormously pleased" with her note. "It certainly indicates an intelligent understanding and I trust that all your life you will recognize the necessity of balance and moderation in all things," he wrote the eleven-year-old. "Too much work, too much vacation, too much of any one thing is unsound."[25]

When both children went off to summer camp in Maine, after saying that they felt they were being sent away for punishment, Walter wrote that he wanted them to go because "the many activities and the team play participation will give you both a training that will prove invaluable later in life." Soon Wallis admitted she was having fun, especially scoring points for her camp team. "That's the proper camp as well as school spirit," he wrote. "As a matter of fact, that is the spirit you will find necessary in life to be a successful citizen."[26] In his desk drawer, he told them, he kept a slip of paper which read: "Back the Team! Get on the Team!"

There were letters when she was ten correcting her spelling. "Incorrect: tring to loose wait; Correct: trying to lose weight."[27]

The letters, most of which were just a paragraph or two, were often signed P.O.D., or Poor Old Dad, an uncanny reminder of Moses's trademark signoff The Poor Old Gov. Almost invariably, the contents nudged and sermonized with wisdom that sounded clichéd, but was real for him: "The fact is that if you want to make a success out of your life, and take advantage of all the opportunities that are yours, you have to concentrate on succeeding at your job. Your job right now is to apply yourself diligently in the classroom," he wrote thirteen-year-old Wallis. "There are other things that go to make up success in life, such as good judgment and wholesome characteristics — fortunately, you start off with these."[28]

When Roger was thirteen, Walter warned him, "Whatever you may fall heir to in the way of security someday, may or may not be permanent." With that in mind, he had an aphorism for him to ponder: "Man leaves to his fellow man nothing that endures except example."[29]

Wallis was warned about her personal appearance: "Inasmuch as you have no personal maid, and I might add that it is good training that you don't, it becomes mandatory upon you to make sure of your own appearance when you are out in public. I admit I was a little surprised that you arrived here for your big weekend date with two buttons off your polo coat [and] a broken button which was hastily repaired with scotch tape." He had taken the coat in question to be repaired, he told her, and was sending her a new one as well, with slightly longer sleeves.[30]

Wallis remembered no talk of the buttons during her Philadelphia visit, though she might have missed the unspoken message. In case she did, the letter delivered the lesson. On other occasions, Ronny heard the complaint. When Wallis once arrived in Philadelphia with her hair ribbons unpressed, something Sadie would never have allowed, she was not criticized, but Walter wrote Ronny to say how he hoped the ribbon problem would not be repeated.

Lifestyle offered rich opportunities for sermons, delivered always with a prim, Victorian phraseology: "If you sense I am about to preach to you," he wrote Wallis when she was seventeen, "it is only to tell you again how happy I am that you don't drink, because indulging in alcohol, especially in a woman, brings on a looseness in tongue as well as in character, and it naturally follows that the most desirable kind of man shuns such a woman."[31]

Wallis, who was close to her mother, but more like her father in terms of being careful, frugal and hard-working, usually received the more personal, tailored advice. Walter loved the fact that when she was ten and he began sending her two dollars a week, Wallis called a half-dozen banks to determine the best savings interest rate before opening an account.

Roger was more like his mother. When his allowance arrived, he ran to the dime store and, Wallis recalled, bought toys and trinkets. Walter's advice to him more often came from his portfolio of aphorisms from great men. "A man must stand erect, not be kept erect by others," he wrote the fifteen-year-old, citing Roman emperor Marcus Aurelius. "I send you this not to criticize you but rather to encourage you." In that same letter, he also advised Roger to consider the words of British

prime minister Disraeli, "The secret of success is constancy of purpose."[32] One can only imagine a teenager's reaction to such notes.

Not every letter was a lesson or sermon meant to be carved in marble or on the psyche. Some were fun: how he had booked a table so
they could shoot pool together and to wear suitable "pool shark" clothing; others enclosed presents, sometimes monogrammed. "I am glad
we have the same initials so you can send me things you consider dog
meat," Wallis noted perceptively.[33]

Encouraging letters were a staple, and frequent: "Please make
every effort to do a good job on your final exams," he wrote Wallis
before her graduation from National Cathedral School in 1957. "I could
say many things to try to inspire you, but I shall summarize them. . . .
'Luck is Infatuated with the Efficient.'"[34]

Wallis had poise and personality, but her C average ruled out a
number of colleges Walter hoped she might attend. He asked several
well-known people to prepare letters of recommendation, including
Mrs. Wendell Willkie, who wrote to Skidmore, where she was a trustee,
and Mayor Richardson Dilworth, who wrote to Bradford Junior College.
Ronny suggested Rollins, but to Walter, Florida was for vacations, not
school. When her adviser at National Cathedral School told her that she
lacked the credentials to apply to any four-year college, Wallis was
despondent and asked her father if it was necessary that she go at all.

Walter insisted that it was. "In the world in which we live today, a
young lady who does not have a college education just is not educated," he wrote as the rejections came in. ". . . it's par for the course in
the circle in which you will be operating, at least in which I hope you
will be operating. It is my earnest hope that you will not be satisfied
unless you are contributing something to or for the benefit of others."[35]

When she was accepted at Pine Manor Junior College in Welles-
ley, Massachusetts, the whole family was pleased and relieved. To get
her started on what he felt was the right foot, Walter wrote to explain
his philosophy of constructive endeavor, which he summed up in
the axiom "I shall participate, I shall contribute, and in so doing I
will be the gainer." He asked her to keep the letter and to reread it
periodically:

> Have you ever stopped to ask yourself why some people
> are dull, negative, even bitter, and others alive, affirma-
> tive and happy? They weren't just born that way. Some
> were too lazy to release the creative energies that are in

all of us and their happier friends thrust all of those energies into *accomplishing something* every day of their lives.

Now it is not easy to find something to do that will intrigue and bind your interest and enthusiasm. This you must seek for yourself. Some people find an interest in making money, and although they appear to be slaving, many actually enjoy every minute of their work (or there would not be so many people devoting their lives to this end). For others, (sometimes fortunately and sometimes unfortunately), this is not always a must in their lives and too many of this privileged group become aimless, useless, bored and boring. Yet what an opportunity these privileged people have for doing good for the world and achieving for themselves a greater happiness if they are not too lazy to think beyond their own skins.

What I am getting at, dear daughter, is that during these years of opportunity for you that are starting now, you will find that the greatest happiness comes from being vitally interested in something that excites all your energies. This can be your school work, extracurricular activities at school, or social service work outside school. But find something that stirs you to exerting your best efforts and give yourself to it wholeheartedly.

For when we hold back out of laziness or selfishness we tie ourselves into knots of boredom, and when we give everything that we've got to *achieve* the best job possible, without any holding back, that is when we win the greatest success, not only in the *achievement* but in *personal satisfaction and happiness*. This is the road to take.

An applicable example that I can give you is that of the duPonts. The motto of that family has been *achievement* and every member of that family with this ideal has gone out and made his own distinctive mark in a field of his choosing, whether it was horticulture, athletics, chemistry or farming. Find yourself a field which you can make your own and try your darndest for the best achievement in that area. God bless you.[36]

Pine Manor was the right place for Wallis from 1957 to 1959. It offered her a nurturing two-year program. Wallis loved it and excelled.

When she made the dean's list, Walter was as elated as his daughter. He congratulated her, then wrote the school president, Frederick Ferry. "I can't tell you how pleased I am," he exulted. "This was an especially good week for me because I was notified of my son's election to the Cum Laude society at Episcopal Academy, so you can see, at the moment, I am a proud father."[37]

When Wallis graduated a year later with honors, fourth in her class academically, and was accepted for her final two years at Columbia University, Walter was even prouder. He gave her a $2,500 check as a graduation gift, took her to Europe for a month, and could not resist crowing slightly to the National Cathedral School, which he believed had failed to recognize his daughter's potential. It was "no shock" at all that Wallis had done so well, headmistress Katharine Lee responded sweetly. "She certainly has come into her own and we are delighted."[38]

Roger had also come into his own at Episcopal. He became president of Junto, the debating society, feature editor of the *Scholium*, the school newspaper, and was active in the music and glee clubs. "He was a hard-working student with a good sense of humor," said Anthony Wayne Ridgway, who was Roger's English teacher.[39] Morrison Heckscher, one of Roger's closest friends, called him "imaginative, impetuous and intellectual." "He was like a hero to me," said Roger's stepsister Diane. "He was fun and a fabulous student. I adored him." Walter was so pleased with his son's involvement and success that he donated $5,000 toward a new school chapel and when Roger was elected to the honor society, gave his son a check for $3,500.[40]

He was particularly proud that Roger was more than a student concerned with grades; he was a thinker with serious interests. "What set Roger apart from many of his classmates was a true appreciation of some of the more intellectual aspects and pleasures of life, music and art in particular," read his senior yearbook entry. "Roger probably has more knowledge, appreciation and love of the arts than any other member of the class . . . a trait for others to try to emulate."[41]

Roger graduated with highest honors in 1958 and was accepted early by Harvard. Walter was overjoyed that Roger was finally living up to what he was certain were his talents and potential. As it turned out, though, Harvard could not have been more wrong for Roger, who began to unravel soon after the chauffeur dropped him off in Cambridge. His first set of grades — a B minus, three Cs and a D — shocked Walter. He immediately wrote Roger's adviser Donald Felt asking how he and Lee might help. "I do believe that for a cum laude student of Episcopal Academy, Roger's initial efforts have not measured up to his capabilities."[42] The same day, Walter wrote Roger: "Unless there is an improvement I will have to employ sanctions against you, quite possibly affecting your purse, which may be the only means of properly impressing upon you what has got to be done for your future, not mine, but yours."[43]

When there was little improvement by the end of his freshman year, Roger was repentant. He sent his father a letter entitled "Discipline" in which he confessed that he had squandered "many a wasted hour [on] basically worthless purposes," and promised to be more responsible. "To reinstate myself, I must work and study always building, driving and creating. I was born into an optimum situation and am by birth part of a productive, orderly and disciplined way of working and living that inherently possesses immense purpose."[44] He may not have been making grades, but he had clearly picked up his father's style of letter writing.

Walter attributed Roger's academic problems to insufficient willpower, never to a lack of ability. "Perhaps the freedom permitted freshmen at Harvard was a little too heady for him to embrace," he wrote to Roger's sophomore tutor.[45] But during his second year, Roger's difficulties accelerated. He had wanted to live at Eliot House, the dormitory which attracted Harvard's WASPs, preppies and oarsmen. Thinking it might help his chances, he sent a telegram in March of his freshman year telling his father that he planned to be baptized as an Episcopalian on Easter eve. Despite his own disinterest in religion, Walter was horrified at the prospect of Roger's converting. He fired back a plea to hold off until they could discuss the matter. When they did, Walter talked him out of it and Roger made it into Eliot anyway as the roommate of two rowers, Lloyd Dahmen and Philip Olsson, having met the latter at a Young Republican campus function during his first year.

"Roger had a brilliant mind and I could have seen him as the curator of a museum and he would have been totally fabulous," said Dahmen. "But his father wanted him to take over the reins of Triangle. Roger tended toward the artistic, though, not business. He once showed me a letter from his father and the phrase that jumped out at me was, 'I hope you are preparing yourself to take over Triangle publications.' That's exactly what Roger did not want to do, at least that's what he told me. If he could have studied art or music and never set foot in a business or a lawyer's office, that's what he would have done. But he was feeling pressure."[46]

Roger was definitely feeling pressure, but despite what he told and showed Dahmen, it was mostly academic and social combined with an inner tension that was beyond his control. There was no other evidence that Walter at that time was pushing Roger toward Triangle. In fact, unlike Moses, Walter had serious misgivings about involving his son in his business. "It was never in the cards that Roger take over the business," insisted one family member. One reason was that Walter did not want a battle with his sisters and their children over who succeeded him. Walter was the majority shareholder, but he had no intention of riding roughshod over his siblings when he had his own doubts about Roger's suitability. His son had never shown any interest in the *Inquirer* or in the holding company. He rarely came by the offices and Walter never asked him to work summers at any of his businesses. Based on his record at Episcopal and admission to Harvard, he seemed to have the brains for succeeding him, but Walter was prepared to give Roger time. Moses had given him leeway when he dropped out of Wharton and turned to stock speculation, a flexibility Walter had not forgotten. Once Roger's grades began plummeting and mindful of his son's earlier attempt to kill himself, Walter recognized that any longer-term plans ought best be put on hold.

Roger took an economics course, but rarely went to class. Instead, he borrowed Dahmen's notes two days before exams and earned a higher grade. He did very little socializing. He had no girlfriends and did not date, but, according to his roommates and relatives, he was not gay. He was, though, still self-conscious about his lip and grew a thin, wispy moustache to cover his scar. At night in his room he drank Courvoisier cognac, at first a shot "to help me sleep," then later as he withdrew more, as much as a half bottle at a time.

Two things seemed important to Roger. "He was tremendously proud of his father and grandfather," said Philip Olsson. "He always spoke of them with immense respect." And long and often about what his grandfather had had to overcome, how the Jewish publisher of the *Daily Racing Form* had managed to buy the *Philadelphia Inquirer*, of his father's genius in creating *TV Guide* and running the empire, and of his Uncle Ben's bravery in Israel. What is not clear is whether, or the extent to which, their accomplishments might have prompted any sense of inadequacy.

The other important issue was acceptance. "Roger had this terrible difficulty reconciling how he came from so much, and how in Philadelphia he was accepted and would be invited to all the right parties and places," said Olsson, "and yet when he arrived at Harvard, which can be impossibly snooty, he wasn't easily accepted into anything."[47]

Roger might have enjoyed greater acceptance had he stayed involved with the Young Republicans, but he dropped out. It is facile to say that instead of going to Harvard, he should perhaps have attended a music conservatory or been a music instead of an English major. But he was not even active in Harvard's rich music community. He was troubled and increasingly isolated, although that did not keep him from unrealistically setting his sights on gaining acceptance to one of the exclusive "final" clubs. Little of significance went on in them, but they were fun and social and the important thing to some students was to belong solely for the sake of belonging. Porcellian was the most selective, but Roger, with no academic, athletic or local social credentials, did not have a chance of getting in. (Porcellian had rejected Franklin Roosevelt, which some historians maintained was the bitterest moment of his life and explained the anti–upper-class theme of his New Deal.)[48]

"Out of all reason and proportion, a final club became very important to Roger. He was the type who wanted to be the best he could be because his family had been the best, but the clubs were reprehensible," said Dahmen. "The top final clubs would have nothing to do with him and the lower tier behaved worse. They played him along because they knew he wanted in very badly. The more he tried, the more it hurt and the more it hurt, the deeper he got into it."

Walter knew none of this. There were no references to the harsh club situation in the letters they exchanged. The social lay of the land at Harvard was foreign to him. He had no personal ties to the university as he had at Penn. As far as Walter was concerned, as evidenced in his letters, Roger simply was not applying himself. He spent most of his sophomore year on academic probation. Walter was concerned; he maintained a regular flow of correspondence with Roger's tutor and flew to Boston to consult. But the tone of his advice to his son remained even. "You know, Roger," he wrote in April 1960, "I have asked very little of you — just the determination to properly prepare yourself for later in life."[49]

In July 1960, while attending a Harvard summer session, Roger asked to consult a psychoanalyst. Walter promptly agreed. In order for Roger to feel in greater control of his own choices, he urged that his son pick the doctor, and he established a special bank account from which Roger could pay the bills himself.[50] Roger began the consultations in

August with a Cambridge therapist named Jerome Weinberger and continued until December when, never having paid a single bill, he suddenly quit, citing "pressures of the hour, examinations and work." The concerned therapist wrote Walter on New Year's Day to fill him in: "I am calling this to your attention because of your concern for your son. I would strongly recommend that he have intensive treatment."[51]

Only days later, in January 1961, Roger attempted suicide again, by overdosing on the sedative Seconal. Walter immediately flew to Boston, withdrew him from Harvard on medical grounds and brought his son to Philadelphia for treatment at Temple University Hospital. "His condition is not good," Dr. O. Spurgeon English advised Walter soon after Roger arrived. "He is mentally further away from life and reality than he was two and a half years ago. . . . He is unable to do any constructive thinking about the future at all."[52]

In mid-February, after exhaustive testing, Roger was diagnosed as psychotic and schizophrenic.[53] The disease was a treatable but incurable mental illness that struck typically between the ages of fifteen and twenty-five. The first signs were often feelings of tension, social withdrawal and an inability to sleep and progressed to introversion, a loss of drive and motivation and distorted thinking.[54] At the time, its cause was not known. Recent research suggests that it may be a brain disorder that runs in families but is not necessarily genetic. What was known was that drugs and psychotherapy could provide effective treatment. Walter was shaken by the diagnosis, although relieved that the doctors finally understood what was wrong with his son and could begin a course of treatment. In gratitude and to ensure Roger's continuing first-class care, he gave Temple funds to buy a piano for its psychotherapy patients.

Roger never returned to Harvard. Dr. English saw him as an inpatient five days a week through September 1961. Each week he wrote long updates of Roger's condition to Lee and Walter, who agonized over his son's anger, which was intermixed with flights of fantasy. In October, Roger moved from Temple to an exclusive sanitorium in Bucks County, Pennsylvania, run by a Dr. John N. Rosen and patronized by various DuPonts, Rockefellers and other wealthy families. Walter chose the clinic because it came well recommended and offered a homelike environment for patients who needed constant supervision.

Roger seemed happier there. He played the piano, often up to six hours a day, learning Chopin and Rachmaninoff and "pursuing my study of Beethoven's first piano concerto, which is very difficult, exciting and challenging," he wrote Walter and Lee in July 1962. Confident that Roger was relatively stable, under twenty-four-hour observation and accompanied everywhere by a full-time minder, they had decided to spend a month in Europe. Roger, who had been allowed to see them off at the airport, teased his father gently in a letter for grousing that the golf course at their Swiss resort had been better the year before.

Walter was corresponding regularly, and on July 20, Roger wrote again. He had thrilling news. He had been invited by the local orchestra to write commentaries for their upcoming performances. He was excited and could not wait to tell them the details. "I am looking forward to your return very much."[55]

When their plane touched down in Philadelphia on the afternoon of August 7, Walter was baffled when he and Lee were ushered without explanation from their plane into a small office at the airport. His counsel Joe First and editor E. Z. Dimitman met them there with terrible news. Roger had committed suicide earlier that day, soon after their flight had taken off from Paris. An autopsy would later show that the twenty-two-year-old had swallowed the equivalent of twenty-eight one-and-a-half-grain capsules of Seconal. Walter slumped and could barely breathe. He and Lee sobbed. Then he became angry. Dr. Rosen had known about Roger's suicide attempts. There were hesitation scars on his neck as well as his wrists. How was it possible that at a high-security clinic, with his own minder in attendance, Roger had got hold of drugs? They never discovered the answer.

"It was so tragic, we didn't know how to deal with it," said Lee.[56] They returned to Inwood, crying all the way. The funeral was held the next day for the family only. After the service, Walter went to his office, where several editors had heard the news but waited to take their cue from Walter before saying anything. He did not mention the tragedy. He had already begun to internalize his grief and for years he refused to speak of Roger's death. Decades later, he continued to become emotional when discussing the basic elements of his son's brief life. Nor did the passage of time lessen his and Lee's anger about the circumstances of his death. Although about 15 percent of schizophrenics kill themselves these days, fewer than in the 1960s, when medication was less effective, they continued to believe that somehow the suicide could and should have been prevented.

The *Inquirer* waited a week before disclosing Roger's death. The notice made no mention of suicide, saying only that the publisher's son had died "after a long illness" that had interrupted his studies at Harvard. Walter claimed that he had the story held because Sadie was traveling and that he wanted to tell her in person when she returned home. After he informed her, his mother's first concern, as always, was for her own son. "How could he have done this to you, Boy?" she asked. The unsaid implication was, After all you did for him.

Already hurt, already withdrawn, Walter pulled further into himself. "His death was a permanent body blow," said Walter, an only son, of his only son. Walter loved Wallis, but Roger had been the embodiment of his hopes, as Walter, and not his sisters, had been for Moses. Walter was not certain if Roger would ever have run Triangle, but he had never doubted that he eventually would be cured. "I realized the odds," he said. "I knew it was a long shot with an illness like that, but a father cannot abandon hope."[57] Instead, he was gone at the age of twenty-two and Walter, then fifty-four, would have to reconsider the long-term consequences of his legacy.

Wallis was never a candidate to take over the business, although she would have appreciated being considered. She was not. Walter, like most of his peers in 1962, was too old-fashioned to train a daughter for the executive suite, although much later he would hire strong women to manage several of his most important interests. Even if he had felt differently, he believed that Wallis too might have provoked a succession battle with his sisters. And besides, by then Wallis was married and headed on another track. During her Pine Manor graduation trip with Walter and Lee, she had fallen in love in Venice with a Princeton graduate named Seth Weingarten, who was about to begin Yale Medical School. She had dropped out of Columbia and married him in 1960. At the time of Roger's death, which left her inconsolable, Wallis already had one child. She would have three more before her marriage turned turbulent and left Walter with a new set of emotional challenges.

21

PRESS LORD

W ALTER'S SUCCESSFUL EFFORT to boost Joseph Clark into the mayor's office and to make Richardson Dilworth district attorney in 1951 made the publisher a kingmaker in Philadelphia. At the urging of the *Inquirer*, thousands of Republicans had crossed party lines to vote for the two and give Democrats control of city hall for the first time in sixty-seven years. Walter received credit for their triumph in the national media and *Newsweek* even asked whether he had political ambitions himself. "I would never run for elective office," said the publisher. "I believe I can be far more effective in public service through journalistic enterprise."[1]

It was a good decision. He was fascinated by political power, but he would not have made a good politician and Walter knew it. Too much a loner, too thin-skinned, still angry, driven by conviction not consensus and uncomfortable as a public speaker, Walter was a visionary businessman who would later become very effective in public service through his philanthropy. If never tempted to run for office, he still relished the power he had exerted and the result it produced. The 1951 victory, combined with what he had learned from his father's experience with the Roosevelt administration and the knowledge he gained as the owner of the *Inquirer*, gave him a more refined appreciation of power. "I got around to the recognition that the greatest power is not money power, but political power," he said. "Political power was more direct, more sensitive than dollar power."[2]

Throughout the 1950s and 1960s he would exercise both kinds of power, always after assessing the stakes and the lay of the political and financial landscape, and after ensuring that whatever move he made would not leave him beholden. When Clark and Dilworth came to his twelfth-floor office after their election to thank him and ask what he wanted, Walter said he wanted the opportunity to buy four good seats a year for the Army-Navy football game, played in Philadelphia. "That's it, and I insist on paying for the tickets," he said. He wanted to take Wallis and Roger, but would never have it suggested that he had accepted anything for the *Inquirer*'s support.

Happy for the time being with the local political situation, Walter plunged deeper into business and community affairs. He was newly married to Lee. *Seventeen* and WFIL were doing well. *TV Guide* was soon to be created. With David Stern's newspaper closed, the *Inquirer* and *Evening Bulletin* were competing collegially as the two major dailies in town. The *Inquirer* was the livelier paper, more colorful and aggressive, more blue-collar, working class, the morning voice of the neighborhoods and of the large and active Catholic community for which it made a point to print the Pope's Christmas and Easter messages verbatim on the front page. The *Bulletin*, also traditionally Republican, was moderate, staid and noncombative, read in the evening by executives on the Main Line train. In a signature 1960s ad that ran regularly in the *New Yorker*, the *Bulletin* claimed, "In Philadelphia, Nearly Everybody Reads the *Bulletin*."

About 50,000 more people read the *Bulletin* daily than the *Inquirer* during the 1950s, a gap that doubled and eventually tripled in the 1960s. The *Inquirer*'s Sunday circulation in the 1950s, however, was 1,230,000, nearly twice the *Bulletin*'s 650,000. The discrepancy gave Walter an idea. He got along well philosophically with *Bulletin* publisher Robert McLean and approached him to propose a merger. Each paper was profitable, but costs were climbing, the number of cities with multiple competing papers was declining, and Walter believed each paper would make far more money if the *Inquirer* and *Bulletin* could reach a joint publishing agreement and split the profits fifty-fifty.

With McLean's go-ahead, Walter discussed the details with Richard Slocum, the *Bulletin*'s general manager. Plan A, as they called it, would have embraced one morning, one evening and one Sunday paper. Slocum was enthusiastic, but a few days later appeared in Walter's office, clearly distressed. McLean, he said, insisted on a sixty-forty split.

"On what basis?" Walter asked. "Certainly not on circulation and advertising linage."

"McLean said he brings more prestige to the deal," Slocum replied.

Walter's head jerked as if he had been slapped. Almost any reason except this one might have been negotiable, but McLean's words were a personal affront. "Dick, the deal is off," Walter said. "Pigs, you realize, go to the slaughterhouse."[3] Slocum nodded glumly.

Years later, when he no longer owned the *Inquirer* and the *Bulletin* folded, he took great satisfaction in having been proved correct. "While your team is entitled to take a bow, the people who should be credited are the pathetic executives of the *Evening* and *Sunday Bulletin*," Walter wrote *Inquirer* promotion manager Leonard Bach in 1980, recounting the McLean story. "Arrogance and greed are a paved highway to disaster."[4]

POLITICALLY, Walter called himself an "independent Republican," meaning that he tended to support Republicans and GOP issues, but he always reserved, and on more than a few occasions exercised, the right to jump ship. His alliance with Clark and Dilworth was one example. Backing them had given him a bridge to Democrats which he used in 1952 to try to attract the national political conventions to Philadelphia. His chances were almost nonexistent, because the city had hosted both conventions in 1948 and the likelihood that the two parties would return was small. The accommodations had been disappointing and for Republicans, Philadelphia seemed jinxed. The nomination of New York governor Thomas Dewey to challenge President Harry Truman had seemed likely to produce an easy winner. "After sixteen years of Democratic rule, Republicans were almost certainly choosing the next president of the United States," said *Time* when the delegates convened in Philadelphia.[5]

Dewey failed, but four years later, Walter was undeterred and eager to play a larger civic role. He was by then one of the biggest civic boosters in a city that needed boosting. Once the national capital for politics and finance, Philadelphia at midcentury had a well-deserved reputation for being stodgy and uncreative. Walter hoped to draw more attention to the area, for reasons of pride as well as for promoting his publishing and broadcast interests. He coined the phrase "Delaware Valley, U.S.A." to describe the Wilmington, Philadelphia, Trenton and Bethlehem business and industrial basin and began a weekly column in the *Inquirer* called "Delaware Valley, U.S.A." to highlight growth potential in what he called "the world's greatest industrial area."[6]

Awards had poured in from various business and civic organizations. It was natural that he be given a leading role in the city's effort to attract the conventions, but the fight was uphill. Senator Robert Taft of Ohio and Colonel McCormick of the *Tribune* were pushing hard for Chicago, which easily drew the GOP. When President Truman dropped by the Democratic National Committee meeting in Washington as Walter was making Philadelphia's case, the president cut him off. "You're a nice young man and you've undergone a lot, but forget it," Truman said. "You're wasting your time."[7]

Rather than feeling rebuffed, Walter became a bigger fan of Truman. "You had to admire his directness," Walter said. "Truman was realistic and he gave it to you straight." Walter identified with that trait. "I fancy myself as a rugged individual," he said, "and a straight-shooter."[8]

Walter was such a straight-shooter that there was little doubt about where he stood on any issue or on anyone. He was unfailingly judgmental. If he liked or respected a person or an institution, he gave his total support — editorial, financial, or whatever was appropriate. And the person retained that backing until or unless he gave Walter reason to change his mind. Conversely, crossing Walter was dangerous. The Coleman case displayed both behavioral facets.

William Coleman was a lawyer who in 1953 could not get a job in his native Philadelphia, although he had graduated summa cum laude from Penn, finished first in his class at Harvard Law School, was selected for the law review and clerked for Supreme Court justice Felix Frankfurter. The reason: Coleman was black.

When Walter heard that Coleman was commuting to New York because he could not work in his hometown, he urged that his own law firm, Dilworth, Paxson, hire him. "In fact, if you don't hire him, I'll take my business and that of the *Inquirer* elsewhere." The law firm, which had previously turned Coleman down, quickly brought him on board. When several staffers protested, Walter heard and became so angry that he informed the managing partner that if the objections did not cease, he would insist that the employees be fired and then make certain that they would find no other jobs in Philadelphia. The complaints stopped, and Coleman began what would become a highly distinguished career, including service as secretary of transportation in the Ford administration.

How well did he know Walter when the publisher interceded for him? "I didn't know him from Adam except by reputation," said Coleman. "I had never met him or spoken to him, and it was another five years before somebody else told me how I happened to be hired."[9]

Why did Walter stand up for someone he had never met? "I'd heard he was good, and what the hell sense does it make not to hire somebody because of their color?" replied Walter, who has sensitive antennae for discrimination. "I'd say we were lucky to get him." And why did he then land with both feet on the few employees who complained? Because they were wrong and he would not tolerate a hostile work environment for Coleman.

Walter did the right thing for the right reason, and yet the incident revealed the two sides of his personality that were often in conflict: idealism and magnanimity, a product primarily of his mother's influence, combined with the tough, bullying tactics frequently employed by his father. A friend of Walter's for many years described the duality succinctly: "If you're a friend of his, anything goes. But if you're on the other side, watch out. You're a dead man."[10]

WALTER'S GENEROSITY, which assumed colossal proportions in later years, was much apparent earlier on the retail level. If someone had financial problems, was ill or faced a sudden emergency, Walter often intervened directly. He had a soft spot for underdogs and people who needed an extra hand and approached such matters like a lord of the manor, with a strong sense of paternal responsibility. He kept loyal employees at work past retirement age if they were not ready to leave. To ease bitter feelings after a 1958 strike, he offered double severance pay so strikers would not feel compelled to return to work. An aged newsstand operator whom he passed each day was given a pension because Walter felt he was too old to be working outside in the cold and heat. After one worker's daughter was injured in a car accident, Walter summoned the city's best plastic surgeon and paid all the girl's bills. When he heard the *Inquirer*'s library staff had canceled its Christmas party to spend the money it had collected on a coworker's child who had been burned, Walter paid for the treatment and the party.[11] After *TV Guide*'s assistant promotion manager Jules Hoffman died helping his wife and three sons flee their burning home, Walter quietly paid for medical care for his wife, who had shattered her spine jumping from a window, and for college for all three boys.[12]

If he opposed something or someone, Walter did not do so gingerly. He made his position clear. He broke ranks with Republicans, including Henry Luce, the founder of Time Inc., over their support for Chiang Kai-shek, the "generalissimo" defeated for the leadership of China by communist leader Mao Tse-tung. Walter held no brief for Mao, but he believed, rightly as it later became clear, that Chiang was a corrupt and weak leader who had also misused American aid.

(Luce never forgave Walter. Years later, he picked up a telephone extension and heard his wife, Clare Boothe Luce, who played backgammon with Walter, talking with the publisher. She had nicknamed him Lorenzo, as in de Medici, for his philanthropy to the arts. When he overheard the endearment, Luce was enraged and falsely accused Clare of having an affair. Clare told Walter and they both had a good laugh. Walter relished having provoked Luce's ire, but until Luce died in 1967, Walter paid a price for his friendship with Clare. "Luce never missed an opportunity to pan me and make certain nothing favorable about me ever appeared in *Time*," said Walter, who had little respect for the magazine publisher. "[Co-founder Briton] Hadden was the brains behind *Time*.")[13]

Walter was also an early opponent of Joseph McCarthy when the Wisconsin senator charged in 1950 that the State Department had been infiltrated by communists and subversives. The *Inquirer* demanded proof. "This newspaper has criticized Senator McCarthy's failure to back up his sensational charges with evidence and his irresponsible use of smear tactics," the *Inquirer* said that April.[14] Walter considered McCarthy personally despicable. "He was a ruthless son of a bitch, an evil person. Those stooges of his, [Roy] Cohn and [David] Schine, were lice."[15]

He was pleased to have been proposed for membership in the Union League club, founded in 1862 to support President Abraham Lincoln. Despite his prominence in the community, club memberships were not easy to come by in Philadelphia in the 1950s for the Jewish son of Moses Annenberg. This opening would have allowed him to mix more easily with the city's business upper crust. But when he saw that the pro-Lincoln charter required him to support the Republican party, he immediately withdrew the application. "I have supported Democrats before and I may well again," he said. "I cannot compromise or inhibit my independence."[16]

SOME OF the "other side" or dark side of Walter showed up in the *Inquirer*. Propelled by strong convictions, plus fury over the injustice he believed had been done to his father, attuned to anti-Semitism in

Philadelphia, and sensitive about his stutter and hearing difficulties, Walter was prickly about criticism, social distinctions and snobbery, especially of the old-family, East Coast variety. Rarely hesitant to strike back at or punish those who he believed had erred or abused him, he could be editorially vindictive.

In this regard, his role models were the publishers with whom he had grown up — William Randolph Hearst, Colonel McCormick and Moses Annenberg, not Arthur Sulzberger of the *New York Times* nor Bernard Kilgore of the *Wall Street Journal*, whose papers he read daily and admired, but did not imitate. This avenging trait was manifest in Walter's blacklist of names of individuals and groups which were not to appear in the pages of the *Inquirer.* That blacklist was infamous, capricious and unworthy of a major metropolitan newspaper and a man who put such stock in an individual's decency and character.

It was the sorriest blot on Walter's record as a newspaperman and a manifestation of the anger and insecurity that bedeviled him from the 1940s through the 1960s. Oddly, the trait surfaced at the same time he was displaying great creativity and idealism in other areas. There were two links between the contrasting behaviors. One was that Walter, among his many legacies, was a spoiled child. He'd had tough times with his father and the government, but essentially, as the only son and brother, his mother's darling "Boy" who could do no wrong, Walter was both used to getting his own way and insistent upon it. When he did not, it was not uncommon for him to have a tantrum. Another close friend of Walter's for decades, who had the highest respect for him, said that "for all Walter's skills and accomplishments, he is still a boy in many ways, still a baby. Combine that with his extremely strong opinions and fireworks can result."[17]

The second link was his impetuous nature. In non-*Inquirer* matters, he melded intelligence, intuition and impetuosity to make snap, brilliant business moves. But in his newspaper pulpit — significantly, not at *TV Guide*, where he rarely interfered on editorial matters — his strong likes and dislikes, coupled with that same impetuosity, had a different result.

The blacklist was not written down and it frequently changed. E. Z. Dimitman, the executive editor who had returned to the *Inquirer* after several years in Chicago, maintained it in his head, hearing directly from Walter or knowing intuitively that someone or something was not to be mentioned. Certain folders in the morgue, the *Inquirer*'s clip library, were red-flagged with tags advising reporters or deskmen to check first with Dimitman before writing a story on that subject.

Dimitman's first job in journalism had been on the *Philadelphia Press* in 1919. His journalistic sensitivities were deeply rooted in the 1920s, and his editorial style had evolved little from those years. More attuned editorially with Moses Annenberg and more conservative politically than Walter, Dimitman was more likely to use a hatchet than a scalpel. When he was not choosing what went in or stayed out, the decisions were made by his alter ego, Morrie Litman, the *Inquirer*'s unpolished city editor, who was also wedded to the Hearst formula of sex, lurid crimes and banner headlines to sell newspapers.

These two decided what they thought the publisher wanted in the paper on the basis of their own preferences, which were often predicated on what they believed Moses Annenberg would have wanted. Walter, consumed by Triangle's business affairs and expanding his holdings, spent little time on the paper's small fights. Weeks often passed between his visits to the newsroom. Yet as a hands-on proprietor, he rightly took responsibility for being the final arbiter on who or what appeared in the paper or who disappeared. There was never any question but that the blacklist was Walter's. "I respected Dimitman," Walter said, "but if I wanted the paper to say something, it was my view that was involved."[18]

When Rose DeWolf turned in a column about the Philadelphia-Baltimore Stock Exchange quoting its president, Elkins Wetherill, she was told his name could not be used. Wetherill told her to source the quotes to an exchange vice president. Sometime later, Wetherill was removed from the list and mentions were once again allowed.[19]

When Thacher Longstreth, a perennial Republican candidate for mayor, was quoted in another newspaper calling the *Inquirer* "a mediocre paper which the publisher uses for his own political ends," his name was banished for years.

No references were allowed for varying periods to entertainers Zsa Zsa Gabor and Imogene Coca. No reasons were given.

Sonny Liston, the heavyweight champion from Philadelphia, was banned from front-page mention because of his criminal past and unsavory companions. "He was a bum," said Walter, a lifelong boxing fan. "I didn't want to give him publicity."

Although he was a friend of the Annenbergs', the name of University of Pennsylvania president Gaylord Harnwell disappeared temporarily after a dispute. Widely viewed as a windbag, Harnwell was referred to as a "university spokesman" or "the speaker." In one case, when it was imperative to publish a picture of a Penn award presentation, Harnwell was airbrushed out.

Nicholas Katzenbach, who was attorney general during the Johnson administration, inquired why references to him in the *Inquirer* during the 1960s were invariably critical. "A guy at the paper said I was on Walter's blacklist, but to this day I have absolutely no idea why." A native Philadelphian, Katzenbach never met Walter, although he was introduced to Lee at a dinner. "She was lovely, but did I spill soup on her dress? I'd pay money to find out why he was so upset with me."[20] Walter did not recall that he was.

When he heard he was temporarily on the blacklist, builder Matthew McCloskey tested it by inserting himself between two politicians in a photo situation that he knew the newspaper would have to use. The following morning, the picture appeared, but McCloskey was nowhere to be seen.

After Ralph Nader wrote "Unsafe at Any Speed," his bestselling critique of the Chevrolet Corvair, which had a tendency to flip over, he became a nonperson in the *Inquirer*. There would be no such criticism of General Motors, one of Walter's favorite companies, in his paper.

Another quarrel involved the Philadelphia Warriors and the Triangle-owned arena in which the team played. When Triangle was unable to reach agreement with the team on a lease renewal, for the remainder of the season the *Inquirer* eliminated coverage of the basketball team. There were no game stories, no features, no line scores, no mention in the NBA standings box and promotional ads were rejected. Game attendance plummeted. It was as if the team had ceased to exist.

Other publications crossed Walter at their peril. In a 1964 article on the Main Line, *Holiday* magazine took a gratuitous swipe at Walter. "On the surface," it said, "Walter Annenberg might seem to have everything against him as far as society is concerned. . . ." Walter, who avenged real or perceived slights, retaliated with a smarter, more targeted response a few weeks later when several staffers quit *Holiday*. He ordered a story on the dissension and financial woes besetting *Holiday*'s parent company, Curtis Publishing. Then, each time anyone quit the *Saturday Evening Post*, Curtis's flagship, the *Inquirer* rubbed salt in the wound by running an item about "further staff turbulence." Walter turned loose reporter Joe Goulden to do a weeklong series on Curtis, which was indeed so troubled that the *Saturday Evening Post* eventually folded in 1969.

ONE OF THE MOST celebrated *Inquirer* crusades was Walter's decade-long campaign to open the Barnes Foundation art collection to the public. Dr. Albert Barnes, an eccentric who made a fortune manufacturing antiseptics, had put together one of the world's great art collections — 713 masterpieces and mediocrities, including 180 Renoirs, 69 Cézannes, 60 Matisses, 44 Picassos and 18 Rousseaus — which he housed in a sprawling twenty-three-room, orange limestone gallery on his Main Line estate in Merion. Founded as a tuition-free, nonprofit educational institution, the foundation had tax-free status to advance art appreciation. The problem was that Barnes only allowed a few students whom he chose and a few visitors that he judged worthy to view the collection. When he died in 1951, his will decreed that the gallery remain closed to the public, contravening the legal grounds for a foundation.

Walter, who was then in the early stages of building his own Impressionist art collection and, given his past trauma, always eager to expose tax dodges on the part of others, was incensed that the Barnes should be closed to the public yet enjoy tax-exempt status. For nine years without letup, the *Inquirer* attacked the restrictive policies as an affront to the tax-paying citizens of Pennsylvania. Throughout, rumors swirled in art and social circles that Walter sustained the campaign because Barnes had personally insulted him, perhaps by refusing him admission. The story went around the paper that Walter had managed to secure an invitation and that when he arrived the butler said, "Right this way, Mr. Annenberg," took him down a corridor and ushered him out the back door, humiliating him on Barnes's orders.[21] The tale was fiction. Walter did not know Barnes well, but they had met several times and had a pleasant superficial relationship. Barnes never affronted him, but the rumors seemed credible because the erratic and vindictive Barnes insulted and dismissed almost every art critic or connoisseur who asked to see his collection.

Finally, state supreme court justice Michael Musmanno ruled that if the gallery were open only to "a select restricted few, it is not a public institution and the foundation is not entitled to tax-exemption as a public charity." Walter and the public, which could now see a great collection, were delighted. "Philadelphia and art lovers owe you many thanks for your tireless efforts," local plutocrat George Widener wrote him.[22] "I must admit," Walter responded, "that I do get an eminently satisfying feeling from accomplishing an affirmative result that is in the public interest."[23] Among those most pleased with the outcome was

Judge Musmanno. An inveterate public speaker, he found that his Columbus Day speeches and talks to civic groups suddenly began receiving respectful attention from the *Inquirer.*

LATER, Walter had second thoughts about the blacklist. "There was a time when I left out certain things. But I did not attack those people. I just ignored them," he said in his eighties when he had mellowed. "I rarely did it, but on thinking about it, I should not have done that."[24] But he had no regrets over such efforts as the Curtis series or the Barnes crusade. Some *Inquirer* staffers felt Walter had overreacted on Curtis, but the story was a fair, if tough, account of a major company in a financial and management morass. To have ignored the Curtis situation would have been shoddy journalism. Similarly, some Philadelphians criticized the unrelenting *Inquirer* campaign to overturn Barnes's will. Walter, though, was ahead of his time. Exclusionary private clubs were given tax breaks as a matter of course up to and throughout the 1950s, a practice that began to erode with the 1960s civil rights legislation. The Barnes would have been unable to maintain the status quo. "The Barnes could have stayed closed if it paid taxes," said Walter. "But having it both ways was undemocratic."

Walter believed most of the criticism directed at him was the result of competitive carping or jealousy, a common reaction among successful men and women. Although some censure came from *Inquirer* staffers — "We get crank letters from our own reporters," said a newsroom veteran — Walter personally was convinced that he ran a balanced and honest news operation. In some instances, he took extraordinary steps to maintain balance and sometimes to avoid rendering any opinion. The maneuvers were awkward and the journalism flawed, but Walter believed the approach would stave off potential criticism that he was playing favorites.

In the 1952 presidential campaign, well before it became required television news practice, he ordered that equal *Inquirer* coverage be given to Republicans and Democrats so that neither side could complain of unfair treatment. Adlai Stevenson, the former governor of Illinois, headed the Democratic ticket that year. His running mate was Senator Estes Kefauver of Tennessee, who chaired the televised 1950–51 congressional hearings into organized crime and became the nation's most recognizable crime buster. The Republican ticket was headed by Dwight D. Eisenhower, the war hero and general, with California senator Richard Nixon as the GOP's vice-presidential candidate.

Walter had great innate respect for Eisenhower, but it was through his mother, Sadie, that he became friendly with Nixon. She had met the young Californian when he was a congressman and had been impressed by his comments about his mother, Hannah, whom Nixon called a "saint." On the evening Sadie met him, Nixon had described his mother's devotion to her sons and how she had instilled in them a drive to grow up and be somebody and to do something.[25]

That was enough for Sadie, who became a small yet faithful contributor to Nixon's campaigns and political career. Before his mother introduced them, Walter had been impressed by Nixon's energy and persistence on the House Committee on Un-American Activities, or HUAC. The committee was investigating the spread of communism and its sympathizers, a palpable fear at the time which spawned the excesses of both McCarthy and the reactionary committee itself, which Walter considered a patriotic body attempting to defend America. He also had a special fondness for one of its leading members, Representative Francis Walter, the conservative congressman from eastern Pennsylvania who had been helpful in pressing the Roosevelt administration to parole Moses.

The most dramatic moment in an otherwise pedestrian presidential campaign came in September when it was discovered that a group of wealthy California businessmen had created a fund of about $16,000 to help the financially strapped Nixon pay his campaign expenses. Nixon was straightforward when asked about it, saying it was not a salary or money that he could use for himself. Many newspapers carried the story inside, including the *Inquirer*, which ran its article on page two under the headline "Friends' Gifts to Nixon Draw Demands." The liberal *New York Post*, however, which was hostile to Nixon, went on the attack. "Secret Nixon Fund," screamed the front-page banner headline on September 18. "Secret Rich Men's Trust Fund Keeps Nixon in Style Far Beyond His Salary," read the subheadline, which was incorrect. Whatever Nixon's faults were in 1952, high-style living was not among them.

The second day, when the story received more attention nationwide, the *Inquirer* moved it onto the front page under the headline "Nixon's Explanation of Fund Accepted by Eisenhower; Public to Get Accounting." A second story reported Adlai Stevenson's reaction that it would be improper to draw a conclusion about Nixon's behavior "without all the evidence." Over the next several days, until Nixon's famous "Checkers" speech on September 21 saved his place on the ticket, a list of the contributors was made public and shown to be mostly small businessmen, not millionaires. The disbursements were also released, revealing that he had spent none of the money on himself. Nixon's critics were not appeased. A *Washington Post* editorial demanded the candidate's resignation. Later, some of Walter's critics, including biographer Gaeton Fonzi, accused the *Inquirer* of "looking the other way" on the accusations.[26]

But neither the paper nor Walter had done that. The *Inquirer* did not play the story as dramatically as the *New York Post*, but gave it coverage comparable to that in other big-city papers. There was no evidence, then or later, that Walter had told his editors to give the story special treatment. "All I said was to play it straight," he maintained. At the end of the campaign, the *Inquirer* was so proud of its balanced coverage that the paper reported in a full-page ad that it had devoted 764 column inches of articles to the Democrats and 737 inches to the Republicans.

TWO WEEKS AFTER Eisenhower won the White House in 1952, Walter made his late-night call to Merrill Panitt that led to the launch of *TV Guide* in April 1953. As the *Guide* hit newsstands that month, publisher Gardner Cowles of Cowles Communications announced that he was folding *Quick,* a pocket-sized magazine that he founded in 1949 and whose circulation shot up to 1.3 million in four years. *Quick* looked successful, but it took no ads and failed trying to earn a profit on circulation alone. For $250,000, Walter bought the name and in September 1953 launched his second major venture within six months — a *Readers' Digest*-sized, biweekly news and picture magazine. Walter's *Quick* did not take ads either, but by printing it on the *Inquirer* gravure presses, he believed he could avoid the overhead costs that killed Cowles's *Quick*. His version, Walter figured, could break even with a circulation of a million sold strictly from newsstands.

Nine months later, in February 1954, Walter determined that he was wrong and that Cowles had been right. He could not make *Quick* work editorially or financially. He was not happy with the journalistic content, provided mostly by freelancers, nor could he sell enough copies to make a profit or attract advertisers without investing money that he preferred to spend on *TV Guide*. *Quick* was quickly forgotten, but not its lesson. With *Seventeen,* WFIL-TV and *TV Guide,* he had discovered how to start ventures. *Quick* showed that he knew when to shut one down. With a fresh understanding of how to cut losses and exit an enterprise unburdened by fear of failure or excessive conceit of ownership, Walter was becoming a complete entrepreneur and businessman.

THE QUICK EXPERIENCE had an impact on another 1954 decision. Colonel McCormick of the *Chicago Tribune* was ill, suffering from a diseased liver that would kill him within a year. Equally painful was the financial beating he was taking at the *Times-Herald*, his Washington, D.C., newspaper, which in 1953 had lost $592,000, or nearly $50,000 a month. McCormick contacted Walter to see if he would take it off his hands for $5 million. Walter had known the Colonel since he was twelve and had accompanied his father and uncle Max to McCormick's 1920 Christmas lunch at the *Tribune*. The *Tribune* publisher was so taken with the youngster that he sat next to him, an honor Walter never forgot. After Walter took over the *Inquirer*, the two men saw each other regularly in New York at annual publishers' meetings and kept in touch by letter and occasional visits to McCormick's home in Florida, where he made the offer.

Walter knew the Colonel's price tag was a bargain, but he was also aware that the *Times-Herald*'s losses were projected to rise to $60,000–$80,000 a month. There was no end in sight to the competition between the *Times-Herald* and Eugene Meyer's *Washington Post*. "I said, 'Colonel, I'm the head of a family company. I can't afford to lose that kind of money. It could go on for fifteen or twenty years and my sisters would harbor a tremendous resentment. You ought to sell it to Eugene Meyer.'"

Meyer had tried to buy the paper in 1948 after the death of the Colonel's cousin, Cissy Patterson, who had been its editor, publisher and sole owner. Meyer made a $4.5 million bid at that time and offered to purchase Patterson's nonvoting shares of *Chicago Tribune* stock, which doomed rather than enhanced the bid. Alarmed by the prospect of the Meyer family's owning a piece of the McCormick-Patterson trust, McCormick stepped in to buy the *Times-Herald* himself. He said that he wanted the paper to be "an outpost of American principles," meaning isolationist and conservative like his *Chicago Tribune*.[27]

When Walter told McCormick that Meyer was unquestionably his best buyer, the Colonel balked. Meyer and the *Post* were too liberal, he said. Also, he told Walter that while he had no personal objections to Meyer, he had strong reservations about Philip Graham, who was married to Meyer's daughter, Katharine, and was running the *Post*.

McCormick called him an emotionally unstable left-winger with a drinking problem.

"I'd have to hold my nose before I'd sell Meyer the paper," the Colonel told Walter.

"He is still your best buyer," replied Walter, who had a good relationship with Meyer. "He needs the *Times-Herald* to make the *Post* whole in Washington."[28]

McCormick did sell the paper to Meyer, for nearly $10 million — $8.5 million plus more than a million in severance to *Times-Herald* employees who did not want to work for the *Post.* Eugene Meyer and his strong-willed wife, Agnes, called separately to thank Walter for making it possible for them to buy the *Herald.* Eugene Meyer asked what Walter would have done if he had bought the paper himself. "I said I'd take all the features from the *Times-Herald* and put them in the *Post.* That will drive the *Evening Star* out of business, because there's no way they'll be able to match you. And that's exactly what happened."[29]

In 1954, the year the Meyers and Grahams bought the *Times-Herald,* the *Washington Post* lost $238,000. Over the next three years, the *Post*'s profits exceeded $2 million a year and its circulation doubled, to four hundred thousand. The transaction put the *Post* on its way to becoming one of the nation's most influential dailies, one ultimately capable of toppling a president. Later, when the *Post* was critical of him or took cheap shots at his father, Walter would be particularly incensed that Katharine Graham, who took charge of the paper in 1963 after her husband, Phil, committed suicide, did not treat him with greater consideration. His feeling was that the *Post* would never have become so rich and powerful had he not stepped aside and made it all possible.[30]

(Katharine Graham acknowledged in her bestselling 1997 memoir, *Personal History,* that the *Post*'s unexpected acquisition of the *Times-Herald* was "the defining moment for the company."[31] The deal, she wrote, involved Kent Cooper, former general manager of the Associated Press and a friend of her father's, as his go-between with the Colonel. Unaware of Walter's discussions with McCormick, she was dismissive of his claim to have played a role in the process which enhanced the *Post*'s success. Her reaction predictably angered Walter, who added it to what had by then become a thick mental file he maintained of personal slights by the *Post.*)

BY DECEMBER 1957, circulation at *TV Guide* was more than 5 million a week. *Seventeen* was selling a million copies a month. The *Inquirer* was selling 610,000 papers a day, up 50 percent since he had assumed control. The *Daily Racing Form* was an ever-reliable cash cow, and Walter was ready to expand again. For $3 million he bought the midday *Philadelphia Daily News* from builder Matt McCloskey, which gave him control of two of the city's three dailies, and an afternoon opening to compete with light features and news updates against the evening *Bulletin.* In the three years he owned it, McCloskey had pumped $5 million into the paper and cut its losses from $225,000 to $40,000 a month. But the *Daily News* remained a sinkhole, or "an expensive luxury," as McCloskey put it, with little chance of turning a profit soon.[32]

Walter moved quickly to consolidate the *News,* which continued to publish under its old name, into the *Inquirer's* operations. Within days he had eliminated its pallid Sunday edition, which went to press on Fridays, cut back the daily from six to two editions, shifted its editorial tilt from pro-Democrat to the independent-Republican flavor of the *Inquirer,* and fired seventy-seven staffers. Among the first to go was the startled J. David Stern III, the forty-eight-year-old son of Moses's old nemesis and the publisher of the *Daily News,* who had been told only four days earlier by McCloskey that the paper was not on the block.

By filling the paper with wire service copy and local human interest stories featuring crime and violence, Walter made the *Daily News* must reading among construction workers; it became profitable in two years, and doubled its circulation in five.[33] Accepting the younger Stern's resignation, however, was the most satisfying aspect of the purchase, as gratifying as driving Stern's father out of the newspaper business had been a decade earlier. Stern III, who was a year younger than Walter and known as Tom, had been as critical of Walter as David Stern had been of Moses. Not long before the sale, the *Daily News* had published an editorial headlined "Gutter Newspapering" which charged that "Philadelphia these days is being subjected to some of the dirtiest newspapering in recent history. The muck is being hurled by Walter Annenberg and his unhappy *Inquirer. . . .*"[34]

The charge was prompted by an *Inquirer* series which had found abuses on the part of key Democrats on Pennsylvania's parole board. The story was of natural interest to Walter because of his certainty that there had been Democratic tampering with Moses's parole. Tom Stern's *News,* like his father's *Record,* defended Democrats and reveled in attacking the *Inquirer.* A year earlier, in 1956, the *News* had claimed that an *Inquirer* truck driver was killed in the newspaper's parking lot, not by a mugger as the *Inquirer* and police determined, but by loan sharks "believed to be minor executives" of the *Inquirer.* Walter was furious about the allegation and demanded a police and *Inquirer* internal investigation. Neither found substantiation for the charge. That was the transgression which prompted the blacklisting of McCloskey, although over the years he was more friend of Walter's than foe. The Sterns, however, had always been foes. From Walter's perspective, they had started the feud the day his father came to Philadelphia in 1936 and bought the *Inquirer;* all he did was win it.

IN THE 1960 presidential race, which paired Nixon against Democratic senator John F. Kennedy, Walter again took care not to play favorites, although he had by then become friendly with Nixon. In 1956, they sat together when the vice president visited Philadelphia to address the Poor Richard annual dinner. Speaking with him and hearing his remarks, Walter realized that from tax policy to Nixon's anti-communism, he agreed with the vice president on virtually every substantive issue. Equally important, he appreciated that Nixon was not a stuffy, upper-class, Establishment Republican, but a gritty, self-made man who stood up to vilification and attack without cracking. Walter had come to the conclusion that life was a series of never-ending tests, including some — his stuttering, Moses's prosecution, his family's early social alienation, Roger's health problems — that were cruel and unreasonable. Nixon, who was every bit as sensitive to criticism and challenge as Walter, was in complete agreement. The key, they agreed, was never allowing the bastards to grind them down. There was another, related trait in Nixon that Walter appreciated: he did not appear to care if he were loved, but, like Walter, he was determined to be respected.

Lee's opinion of Nixon was also a factor. She liked the fact that he was a Californian, but she also agreed with his positions, which she had examined closely. She had first been interested in politics while married to Lew Rosenstiel, but became more so after moving to Philadelphia, where Walter was so involved. More conservative than Walter, Lee was such a Republican activist that she was appointed vice president of the electoral college of Pennsylvania in Eisenhower's second term.

Nixon enjoyed both Annenbergs. He appreciated Walter's blunt candor and the fact that the publisher asked for nothing. He respected Walter's explanation that he would not be a financial contributor to a politician about whom the *Inquirer* was writing. Nixon considered Lee informed and exquisite. "She never ceases to amaze me with her understanding of how the real world works and by her upbeat captivating personality," he wrote Walter years later. "As you can appreciate, I've been seated by some pretty sad dogs in my travels over the years. Lee is a thoroughbred in every respect."[35] The vice president also appreciated the warmth and backing of Sadie. When the Nixons invited Sadie to a dinner for them in New York, the loyalty of Walter and Lee was sealed. By 1958, Nixon had become so comfortable with the family that he came to Inwood to recuperate after a grueling trip to South America that had ended in Venezuela with leftist mobs assaulting the vice president.

As in 1952, Walter again ordered Dimitman and his *Inquirer* editors to play the 1960 campaign straight in the news columns. He refused to assign reporters to travel regularly with either candidate, but instructed that the *Inquirer* make do with wire-service copy from the Associated Press and the United Press, which filed straight news. His decision that one of the nation's largest dailies would not cover a presidential campaign independently made no journalistic sense. Walter, though, insisted it was the best way to guarantee balanced coverage, as he was known to be Nixon's friend. The *Inquirer*'s editorial page, run for many years by Paul McCurdy Warner, favored Nixon, as did the majority of the nation's newspapers.

When Dr. Norman Vincent Peale, the best-known Protestant clergyman in the country, issued a statement questioning whether the Roman Catholic Kennedy could properly separate church and state and govern independently from the Vatican, Walter dropped Peale's popular weekly column from the *Inquirer*, even though both he and Nixon were friends of Peale's. The paper regarded the column as "a nonsectarian feature, strongly inspirational to men and women of all faiths," said a statement by the publisher in September 1960. "To our regret, Dr. Peale has impaired this public image and distorted the nonsectarian character of his writings by his approach to the so-called 'religious issue' in this political campaign."[36] The next day, the *Inquirer* broadened its stance that religion should be a nonfactor. Praising Kennedy for having been "laudably frank" about his Catholicism, the newspaper declared, "There should be no room in our country for bigotry or intolerance concerning the manner in which any American worships God."[37]

WHEN THE CAMPAIGN ENDED, Walter was disappointed that Nixon had narrowly lost, but again he felt that the *Inquirer* had covered the campaign fairly. He had every intention of supporting John Kennedy as best he could because, whatever political differences he might have with the new president, he wanted to maintain good relations with the White House. He was apprehensive about Kennedy because he could not stand the president's father, Joseph P. Kennedy, and worried about the extent to which the son might share his character. Walter's hostility had its origins in the senior Kennedy's disreputable and pro-Nazi past. An Irish-American financier, Kennedy was ambassador to Britain from 1937 until 1940, when President Roosevelt pulled him out after Kennedy's repeated predictions that Germany would defeat Britain. "He was a miserable human being," Walter said of the senior Kennedy. "He was all rat. It was shocking how he was openly supporting Hitler."

Before he was recalled from London, Walter claimed, Joe Kennedy was illegally using embassy facilities to ship inexpensive Scotch whisky to the United States. The idea that Roosevelt could have condoned such behavior by Kennedy at the same time the president was pursuing his father, Moses, angered Walter terribly. How could Roosevelt honor the kind of man who had his mistress, the actress Gloria Swanson, living in his home? "This was a man," he said of Joe Kennedy, "who because of his financial expertise was given one hundred thousand dollars to examine Paramount studios after they were coming out of receivership. His recommendation was that there were too many Jews in the motion picture business and that the studio should be sold to him."[38] And yet the Kennedys were considered acceptable and the Annenbergs were fighting to emerge from under a cloud. The situation, it seemed obvious to Walter, was not fair. It was appropriate that John Kennedy conceded famously that life was not fair.

As a moderate Republican, Walter had no serious objections to the new president on policy matters. He decided to withhold judgment on his character until he saw more of him. He was very pleased when Kennedy contacted him soon after moving into the White House and asked for help. The president intended to name Matt McCloskey ambassador to Ireland and wanted to know if the *Inquirer* would oppose the nomination. Walter said he understood the value of "sentimental appointments" and was eager to be helpful. Kennedy chuckled at the gentle dig and asked if Walter knew how he could get around the opposition to McCloskey of Iowa senator Bourke Hickenlooper. Walter said he would see what he could do and called Gardner Cowles, who had sold him *Quick*, but who also owned the *Des Moines Register,* Iowa's most influential newspaper. Cowles spoke to Hickenlooper, who withdrew his objection, and the nomination of McCloskey, a professional Irishman with Kennedy-like charm, sailed through.[39]

Soon after, Jacqueline Kennedy called to explain her plans to renovate the White House and display the nation's artistic heritage. She praised Walter's art collection, which she had been discussing with Henry duPont, a trustee of Winterthur Museum.

"Harry tells me that you own the definitive painting of Benjamin Franklin," she purred, "and the president and I think it would be a wonderful idea if you, a great Philadelphia publisher, would consider giving the definitive portrait of the greatest Philadelphian to the White House as our first major acquisition."

"Mrs. Kennedy," Walter said, "that's about the most astute arm-twisting I've ever been up against. Let me think about it for a few days."

The portrait, by the Scottish artist David Martin, painted from life in 1767 when Franklin was sixty, showed the statesman seated at a desk, reading a manuscript with his thumb under his chin. Walter had bought it in the early 1950s. When Mrs. Kennedy telephoned in 1961, it was worth $200,000. He called the First Lady back in an hour.

"Much as I love that painting, you are correct. It is more appropriate that it be displayed in the White House than in my home. It will be delivered to you tomorrow morning," he said, honored to have been asked and relieved that she had not requested his even more spectacular Anne Rosalie Bocquet Filleue portrait of Franklin.[40]

She wrote immediately, saying she was "speechless, overcome by your generosity and by the power and beauty of the picture."[41] To thank the Annenbergs and to show them the painting, which she had placed over the mantel in the Green Room, the president invited Lee and Walter to the White House for a small private dinner. They found the Kennedys so charming, bright and welcoming that Walter rarely thereafter criticized the young Democrat editorially, unlike some conservative publishers who rebuked him for his civil rights activism, for rolling back steel prices and for negotiating with the Soviet Union.

The other Kennedy who impressed Walter was the president's mother, Rose. He saw a surprising number of similarities between her life and that of his mother, Sadie. Both women had nine children, including some who had been very successful. Both had suffered the loss of at least one child. Both were married to — and led quite separate lives from — crude, abusive, strong-willed husbands who made huge fortunes, experienced sharp public criticism, and maintained long-standing, indiscreet extramarital affairs. Both had sought strength in religion.

With the president's approval, Walter wrote to Rose Kennedy in 1963 and asked if she would work with an *Inquirer* writer to produce up to a dozen articles of two thousand words each about her children for whatever sum she considered "worthwhile." "The breadth and depth of their activities and their achievements are indeed remarkable," he said.[42]

Mrs. Kennedy never wrote the series. Four months later, her son was assassinated in Dallas. Walter, who had yet to come to terms with the death of his own son fifteen months earlier, sat in his twelfth-floor office and sobbed. Bells announced bulletins on the *Inquirer* wire service machines. The story, however, would unfold on television. After November 22, 1963, it was television, the medium in which Walter held such an influential position, which would be the primary conduit of news and shared experiences to the world.

Walter was not thinking then about news or what the television revolution might mean for him. He was worried about the future of the country. He was so out of touch with the biggest story of the decade that his *Inquirer* reporters were frustrated and furious. He refused to send anyone to Dallas to work on the story, not even Joe Goulden, a Texan who had worked there for years and knew many of the officials involved in the case, including the district attorney and lawyers appointed to defend Lee Harvey Oswald. "I got so mad I came down with an attack of gout," said Goulden. "He was thinking like a philanthropist, not a journalist."[43]

Walter ordered the *Inquirer* to use wire service copy and feature stories from the supplemental news services. There was so much information available that Walter felt there was no need to send his own people to produce more. He came to the same conclusion in 1967 when the *Inquirer* did not send staffers to report the Six Day War between Israel and the Arab states. "The coverage was so broad and deep. There was endless material coming in from every conceivable outlet, from columnists and syndicated material. And strange as it may seem, I have a thrifty side to me," he explained after the JFK assassination. Although not staffing the story made sense to him then, he later conceded that his thriftiness had been wrong. "In hindsight, I wish I'd sent him," he said of Goulden. "The story was of such importance to the country it was a mistake not to."[44]

Instead, to pay off her mortgage, Walter sent a check for $12,500 to Mrs. J. D. Tippett, the wife of the police officer shot and killed by Oswald after he fled the Texas Book Depository building. He did it without telling his own newspaper, which learned the news from the Associated Press. "Scooped on our own story," grunted Goulden. Walter had not wanted the *Inquirer* to break the news of his donation. He wanted no one suggesting that he had used the *Inquirer* to take credit for his gesture. After the Six Day War, he wrote a $1 million check to the Israeli emergency fund. He told no one until the story leaked from Israel. Then he acknowledged that he had made the donation in honor of his mother.

WHEN LYNDON JOHNSON succeeded Kennedy, Walter was impressed by the way the vice president picked up the slain president's mantle. He had met the Texan in the 1950s when he was Senate majority leader and kept in touch with periodic letters; although he did not know Johnson well, he appreciated his earthy practicality and decisive leadership style. LBJ in turn courted Walter and in his first months in office invited him to several White House gatherings with publishers. Few presidents were as aggressively seductive as Johnson. Walter, whose old scars gave him a keener sensitivity than most men to presidential esteem or disapproval, relished the attention.

He also discovered that he liked Lady Bird Johnson, whom he praised in editorials for her involvement with the early-education program Head Start. After purchasing rights to Ruth Montgomery's biography *Mrs. LBJ* and publishing three excerpts in the *Inquirer*, Walter wrote Lady Bird to say, "I admire and respect your capacity for diligence, determination and dedication."[45] She promptly responded and complimented him for giving the Franklin portrait, which she said made her "simply glow with pleasure" every time she passed it.[46]

The fact that Johnson was married to such an intelligent and caring woman as Lady Bird elevated the president considerably in Walter's estimation. He always judged the character of men and women he met in part by the caliber of those close to them, especially a spouse. The challenge to LBJ in succeeding Kennedy also held echoes for Walter of what he had undergone in assuming control of Triangle and the *Inquirer* from his father. Moses, like Jack Kennedy, had been much loved and admired by his staffers and supporters. Walter, like Lyndon Johnson, had been considered out of his depth as a successor. Acceptance by the Establishment was a challenge to each man.

Walter found himself in considerable accord with Johnson. He backed Johnson's efforts to pass civil rights legislation and to cut taxes. By the time LBJ ran for a full term in 1964, the publisher found that he had a real choice to make. He could not stomach Arizona senator Barry Goldwater, the Republican front-runner. "He was a smart aleck, a dope and he drank too much," said Walter. "He wasn't fit to be president."[47]

Goldwater was an ideologue, picked by the party's conservative activists who wanted, as their bumper stickers made clear, "A Choice, Not an Echo" of moderate Republicans. Walter agreed with some of Goldwater's maxims and ethical certitudes about patriotism and individual initiative, but he was concerned about the right-wing extremism and its lack of conciliatory public spirit. He joined other moderates in an effort to draw Pennsylvania governor William Scranton into the primary campaign to challenge the Arizonan, but Scranton declined. When Goldwater defeated New York governor Nelson Rockefeller for the nomination and deepened the divisions within the GOP by claiming memorably that "Extremism in the defense of liberty is no vice," Walter endorsed Johnson, the first time since the Civil War that the *Inquirer* had backed a Democrat for president.

Walter advised Richard Nixon promptly of his decision. "This [decision to back Johnson] is based largely on our judgment that he has indicated a stability in the office that we do not believe Barry Goldwater would manifest," Walter wrote. "Additionally, it is our belief that Goldwater's judgment did not register too highly in the selection of his running mate. I know I do not have to remind you about Bill Miller's callous and unfair attacks on you when he was the Republican party chairman."[48]

The week before the election, President Johnson came to campaign in Philadelphia and to thank Walter for his support. The publisher was honored and nervous. He ordered reporter Goulden, entrusted with writing the story, to stay downtown overnight so as not to miss the 8 A.M. appointment. Walter slept at his office. When Johnson's limousine pulled up outside the *Inquirer* building, Walter leaned in and greeted the president. Goulden could hear nothing, which satisfied Walter, who had decided he wanted only a two-paragraph story on page three to avoid drawing too much attention to his public embrace of the Democrat. "Never have so few lines caused so much mental anguish and angst," said Goulden. "After about the seventeenth rewrite the deed was done. No quotes, no color and no problems for Walter of criticism from fellow Republicans."[49]

BY THE MID-1960s, Walter Annenberg had become one of the nation's most powerful media barons and, with a net worth exceeding $100 million, one of the richest. His professional and financial activities were proceeding smoothly, but his personal life suffered two further major blows.

The worst came on July 6, 1965, when Sadie died in New York after a long illness at the age of eighty-six. To the very last, fifty-seven-year-old Walter had remained "Boy" to his mother. He had never been anything but her darling. He telephoned Sadie daily and wrote her often, addressing her as "Dearest Mother," and sometimes jokingly as "Dearest Celestial." Throughout the turbulence of life with his father, the difficult succession, strained relations with his sisters, his troubled first marriage and Roger's death, Sadie had provided his greatest stability. Adoring and nonjudgmental, she was Walter's rock.

Over the decades he had chided her for allowing his sisters to charge bills to her accounts, upbraided her two days after Pearl Harbor for being "not only extravagant but downright un-American" for spending $35 on a hat, given her a Rolls-Royce and loved her always with his whole strength. In his office and at home, Walter kept large framed copies of a favorite color portrait of her, a five-foot-tall vision in pink — pink suit, broad-brimmed pink hat, pink purse on her arm, a triple strand of pearls, a diamond brooch and white gloves. Wherever he went throughout his life, whether for a month to Europe or an overnight trip to Chicago, he carried a framed traveling version of the photo, which he set on his bedside table.

"My mother was marvelous, and a nut on decency," said Walter. "She was all goodness, and we weren't the easiest to raise."[50] Said with a son's pride, but undisputed. Each daughter thought she was Sadie's favorite. "She was a fabulous mother hen," said sister Evelyn. "Fantastically warm." A much finer person, the daughters felt, than their father. "We all adored her."[51]

At her funeral at Temple Emanu-El in New York, Dr. Lester Tuchman, a physician friend of thirty years, eulogized her as a "lamedvovnik," a Jewish saint, "characterized by modesty, inner strength, radiant goodness, self-effacement and involvement in life." Eulogies spring from hyperbole, but in this instance, Tuchman was not exaggerating. Of all the Annenbergs, Sadie was the least complex, the most genuine and most loving. Her affection for her family and friends was abiding, deep and honest. She showed strength in refusing to move to Philadelphia, where she would have been humiliated by Moses's living with Trudy Boze. Yet she stood by him in harder times when he was prosecuted and jailed. She was also the only one of the Annenbergs who kept alive a Jewish sense of identity, which may well explain why she, more than any of her children, seemed, too, to have a better sense of self.

Seven hundred condolence letters were received and logged, from little-known priests and nuns to Golda Meir, J. Edgar Hoover, RCA founder David Sarnoff, conductor Eugene Ormandy, jeweler Harry Winston and the Nixons. "Pat and I will always remember the last evening we saw your mother in California when she was the belle of the evening as she regally 'held court' to the delight of all the guests," wrote Nixon, who also made a contribution in her memory to Mount Sinai's medical school.[52]

"Sadie Annenberg thought that love was the sovereign cure for all things," said Rabbi Nathan Perilman, who had presided over Moses's funeral twenty-three years earlier. "Her generosity went out most to those who needed it most, to those who were neglected or forgotten or rejected. Her joy was to help educate, to hold a lamp for those who wanted to find their own way and who might someday bring important values to life."[53]

Walter saluted her casket and said, "Goodbye, pal." No one had ever been kinder to him or offered such unquestioning love. In his eyes, she had been the model mother. His appreciation for fine arts had come from Sadie. She had been the inspiration when Walter suggested that his father run in the *Inquirer* magazine a spread on *Birds of America* by John J. Audubon instead of a lingerie-clad model. His father loved music, but it was Sadie who hated to miss a performance of the Metropolitan Opera, attending well into her eighties with her faithful companion, Ida Tomber.

Sadie had been the first of the Annenberg philanthropists. "If you love something," she said, "you will find a way to care for it, whether it's a person or an institution."[54] Much of her giving was anonymous. She supported the home and hospital of the Daughters of Israel and the Rusk Institute of Rehabilitation at New York University. She gave several gifts to Israel, including to the Soil and Irrigation Institute at Gilat, near Beersheba, which was named for her, and to the American Friends of Hebrew University. She was active in the Williamsburg Settlement of the Brooklyn Philanthropic League.

When given its gold medal as an "outstanding friend of the underprivileged" by financier Bernard Baruch — an award previously given to Eleanor Roosevelt — fifteen hundred people attended the ceremony at the Waldorf-Astoria. The family gave $1 million in her name in 1962 to the Albert Einstein College of Medicine at Yeshiva University, where she was a volunteer worker. Just a month before Sadie died, each of her eight children gave $1 million toward construction of a twenty-three-story School of Medicine at New York's Mount Sinai Hospital.

SEVEN MONTHS after Sadie died, the family suffered another shock. New York's newspapers on February 7, 1966, carried a horrifying story. "Society Girl's Body Found in Heir's Car on East Side," read the *Daily News* headline. "Frozen Body of Girl Student in Car of Annenberg Heir," said the *Daily Mirror.* Even the *New York Times* had the news on the front page, headlined, "Publisher's Heir, 25, Held in Girl's Death." When the story came in over the AP wire, editors rushed it upstairs to Walter and waited to learn if he would print it. The *Inquirer* published it the following morning.

Walter's nephew Robert Friede, son of sister Evelyn, had been arrested and charged with homicide after the body of a nineteen-year-old girl was found in the trunk of his car. Friede, an unemployed graduate of Choate and Dartmouth, was living on New York's Upper East Side on a $27,000-a-year income ($135,000 in current dollars) from a trust fund set up by Moses that was to jump to $100,000 a year when he turned thirty. The young woman, who had died two weeks earlier of a heroin overdose administered by Friede, was Celeste Crenshaw, an attractive high-school dropout whose affluent family owned the Crenshaw Company of Raleigh, North Carolina, a manufacturer of lighting fixtures.

They had discussed marriage, but both Friede and Crenshaw were already on probation for felony narcotics violations when two policemen noticed a parked red Chevrolet Impala idling at 3 A.M., its dazed driver wearing filthy jeans and a dirty shirt. When they asked Friede for his license, two packets of heroin fell from his wallet. Was he on drugs? one cop asked. He was, Friede mumbled. While searching the car, they found Crenshaw's body in the trunk.[55]

The Annenbergs and Crenshaws were devastated. "It was terrible, horrible," said Lee Annenberg. Walter's sister Evelyn found her son's crime incomprehensible. Her Park Avenue apartment was filled with Picassos, Légers and Modiglianis. Hers was one of the nation's richest and most productive families. "There isn't anyone in this family who even stays up beyond the eleven o'clock news," she said. "We have tried to have a motto of doing everything for the good of others." Her name was often in the papers as the chair of a fund-raiser for the Musicians' Emergency Fund or the Children's Cancer Fund. Evelyn was a Mount Sinai volunteer who appeared at the hospital twice a week for decades. "I don't know quite how to fit this arrest into the puzzle of my life. We're as divorced from this world of drugs as from what's going on with the astronauts."[56]

Indicted when he was arrested on eight counts of manslaughter, assault, illegal drug possession and improperly transporting a body, six weeks later Friede pleaded guilty to second-degree manslaughter and unlawful posession of heroin. He had not intended to kill Crenshaw when he injected her with heroin, Friede's lawyer said, but had "hopes of marrying her and living a life free from narcotics." Sentenced to two and a half to five years in jail, Friede served the maximum, initially at Sing Sing, then at Dannemora in upstate New York. When he finished his term, he relocated to the Pacific Northwest to rebuild his life.

Walter was saddened for his sister, distressed that the family name had been tainted again, and livid at how the press had covered the crime. He understood that the story was legitimate news, but he was furious that so many articles had referred to Moses's indictment and imprisonment. "What I resented," he complained to one publisher, Kingsbury Smith of the *New York Journal-American*, "was the relish with which [your reporter] ripped into the unfortunate incidents in my father's past."[57]

IN THE SUMMER OF 1966, just months after the Friede case was closed, Walter became embroiled in a vicious political battle to replace the retiring Pennsylvania governor, William Scranton, a moderate Republican whom he regarded highly. The candidates were Raymond Shafer, the Republican lieutenant governor, and liberal Democrat Milton Shapp, an electronics magnate. Shapp had made millions in the cable television industry, which made him a competitor with certain of Triangle's TV interests. Walter had an intense, visceral dislike of Shapp. "An oily windbag and a faker," Walter called him. "A sleazy son of a bitch with bad character."[58]

Shapp was born in Cleveland. His parents were immigrant Jews from Lithuania, not far from Kalvishken. Although it sounded disingenuous to people who observed his own WASP style, Walter disapproved of Shapp's name change from Shapiro to sound less Jewish, and took greater exception to what he considered Shapp's incessant self-promotion. When Shapp spent $1 million of his own money to win the Democratic primary, Walter accused him of buying the election. But what annoyed Walter most was Shapp's opposition to the merger of the Pennsylvania and New York Central Railroads. Shapp criss-crossed the state calling the merger "a systematic sellout of Pennsylvania's future" and "a legalized multi-million dollar swindle that would put the robber barons to shame."[59]

The Johnson administration disagreed. In May 1966, a month after the Interstate Commerce Commission approved the merger, commerce secretary John Connor came to Philadelphia. "I disagree very sharply with Milton," Connor said. "I think this merger will result in a more efficient railroad transportation system." That was Walter's position. Like many Philadelphians who accorded the Pennsylvania a special prestige and respectability, he considered the railroad a national institution as well as a great company. An important factor was that the company was chaired by his friend and Main Line neighbor the socially prominent Stuart Saunders. Indeed, his friendship with Saunders had helped break down some of the aloofness the Annenbergs had encountered from other Main Liners.

The 1960s, though, were bad years for railroads. Millions of passengers deserted trains as automobile sales soared and the price of airplane tickets dropped. The merger was supposed to lure them back with better equipment, greater efficiencies and improved service. The new Penn Central would operate 35 percent of the nation's passenger trains and carry 74 percent of long-haul riders, while its freights served 55 percent of U.S. manufacturing plants.[60]

Walter went all out editorially for the merger. He was criticized later for not disclosing during the governor's race that he was the railroad's biggest individual stockholder, with 177,000 shares valued at about $13.3 million.[61] But during the campaign, Walter had not owned stock in the railroad. He had bought his shares after the election when he joined the railroad board in 1967. Saunders, who became chairman of the merged Penn Central, confirmed the timing.[62]

"I'm not going to let that bum Shapp destroy the railroad," Walter told Dimitman, giving the editor a green flag to train heavy editorial guns on the Democrat.[63] He would do whatever was necessary to insure that the merger was not derailed by a would-be politician who had called his friend Saunders, and Walter by implication, a "robber baron." He started by dictating an editorial titled "Rabble-Rousing

Irresponsibility" that claimed Shapp's charge was "disgusting" and had overstepped "all bounds of decency and honesty." What followed turned nasty.

Joseph Miller was the *Inquirer*'s political editor, a job he had held since the 1930s. An unpleasant toady and hatchet man, Miller's political philosophy was founded on the conviction that the sun rose and set on the GOP and that anything any Democrat did was suspect if not outright illegal. At a news conference, Miller employed a sleazy stunt perfected by Hearst reporters a half century earlier, but which in the modern era was no longer acceptable behavior by reporters from major newspapers. He had heard that the Democrat had been treated for depression and so asked Shapp if he denied ever having been in a mental institution. If he said nothing, Miller could write that he did not deny. Because the charge was false, Shapp did deny it, but he could not win. The next morning, Miller's story declared that Shapp denied he had ever been treated in an asylum. A week before the election, the *Inquirer* ran a reminder of the denial.

Another story described how Shapp had employed a known criminal to handle his public relations, although the man was actually a messenger boy who had been fired when his background became known. After a front-page series linked Shapp to an eccentric white supremacist, who had also been fired from the campaign, the *Inquirer* charged that Shapp had paid one hundred black ministers for their support. One way or another, he was doomed to be tagged a racist. "Walter was so hard on Shapp," a high-level Shafer campaign aide said, "that Shafer and I were embarrassed."[64]

So were some *Inquirer* staffers. "The coverage of the Shapp campaign was clearly unbalanced, a classic example of editorial bias and how not to cover a political campaign," said Acel Moore, a columnist and associate editor of the *Inquirer* who joined the paper in 1962. "It wasn't ideological; it was personal."[65]

A mid-October editorial made clear how tough Walter was. The choice, it said, was between "the prudent and capable administration of state government by Raymond Shafer and the reckless irresponsibility of Milton Shapp. . . . The people of Pennsylvania are not stupid. They know that a Milton Shapp as governor contains the promise only of erratic and unstable management of their affairs. It is beyond belief that they would take this road to disaster."[66]

Shafer won by 214,000 votes and Shapp was left to complain, "We would have won if it hadn't been for Annenberg." Four years later,

Shapp tried again and did win. By then, neither Walter nor the railroad were factors. The publisher was in London and the Penn Central was essentially out of business, having filed for bankruptcy in June 1970. Finalized in 1968, the biggest transportation merger in history had been a bust, a victim of poor management, high interest rates, rising costs and an economy deteriorating as the U.S. involvement in Vietnam escalated.

Walter, who was on the Penn Central board until 1969, lost $9 million as the railroad's stock price plunged. When he left the board to move overseas, he named Gustave Levy, senior partner of Goldman, Sachs, as trustee for his portfolio.[67] Walter had continued to believe that the merger was a good idea. The latter was a rare business miscalculation, but less costly than the campaign against Shapp, which had given him a reputation beyond Philadelphia as a resentful, vindictive and autocratic publisher. "He was dictatorial and self-serving," said Ben Bagdikian, author of *The Media Monopoly* and one of the nation's foremost press critics. "If anyone had any doubts earlier, it was clear after the Shapp race that the *Philadelphia Inquirer* was Annenberg's personal weapon to pursue his own likes and dislikes socially and his own financial welfare."[68]

THROUGHOUT THE 1950s and 1960s, the *Inquirer* covered Philadelphia the way Hearst's *American* reported and wrote about Chicago in the teens and twenties. Sixteen reporters covered Philadelphia's police districts; three covered City Hall; one reporter watched the courts. There was minimal coverage of New Jersey or the suburbs. No reporters were stationed overseas. The only bureaus beyond Philadelphia were a one-man operation in Harrisburg and two in Washington, D.C. Its own reporters and editors had little good to say about the paper in those years. "The *Inquirer* wasn't much of a paper in the 1960s," said Robert Greenberg, who was hired in 1958 and became a night city editor under Walter. "He knew how to make enormous amounts of money, but he did not know how to put out a good newspaper. The people he had in charge weren't up to publishing a modern paper and they constantly did things they thought he wanted without asking him."[69]

Nor had it been much of a paper in the 1950s. A 1957 assessment in *Newsweek* applauded Walter for pursuing "a vigorous policy of civic crusades, exposés and solid news coverage," but the judgment of his fellow publishers was less flattering.[70] A 1960 survey of 311 publishers in *Editor and Publisher*, the trade magazine of the news industry, ranked the *Inquirer* twenty-fourth nationally in quality, five slots below the *Philadelphia Bulletin* and well behind such smaller papers as the *Milwaukee Journal, Baltimore Sun, Arkansas Gazette* and the *Portland Oregonian*.[71]

A prolonged strike by the reporters' guild almost crippled the *Inquirer* in 1958. Editors and nonguild workers continued to publish for a fraction of the paper's usual circulation, though the effort was complicated by the Teamsters. Union delivery drivers began a wildcat sympathy strike, which included scouring the city, intercepting teenage delivery boys and, shades of Chicago, dumping their papers into the Schuylkill River.

So many staffers accepted the buyout offers and departed that the newsroom was left with a vast number of empty desks, all equipped with typewriters and in-boxes. "When I arrived for a tryout in April 1961 and saw all those desks, I thought there must be a helluva crowd of reporters out working on beats," said Goulden. "The thought never occurred to me that the desks were in fact empty."[72] The skeleton staff of rewrite men filled editions by picking up stories from the *Bulletin* and other papers, and fleshing out wire copy and story tips by telephone. For a big-city daily, the reporters who remained after the strike were a weak lot. The *Inquirer* took pride in hiring locally and promoting from within, but too many reporters had been copyclerks before the strike.

The paper had a few big hitters, including society columnist Ruth Seltzer, an institution among social Philadelphians, whom Walter lured away from the *Bulletin* with a fifteen-year contract and a fat expense account. Another was Joe McGinniss, whose fine coverage for the *Inquirer* of the 1968 assassination of Robert F. Kennedy was widely praised.

The *Inquirer*'s star, though, was an investigative reporter named Harry Karafin, who started as an $18-a-week copyboy in 1939. Karafin was brash and cocky and swaggered his way up the ladder. He poked, probed, made friends with the city's major players and developed countless sources. Friendly prosecutors let him browse through confidential files in the district attorney's office, giving him leads to exclusive stories that the *Inquirer* bannered all over page one. He was Philadelphia's muckraker, the originator of the *Inquirer*'s best stories exposing corruption as well as the source of the most damaging information directed at *Inquirer* targets like Shapp and others.

He was also a liar and a thief. Exposed by *Philadelphia* magazine in April 1967, the city's best-known reporter was discovered to have been a shakedown artist who for years had been extorting money from people and businesses not to write about them. His victims ranged from dance studios, loan sharks and shady home repair companies to the city's biggest bank, First Pennsylvania Banking and Trust, which paid $60,000 to a public relations agency in which Karafin had an interest.

Until *Philadelphia* magazine broke the story, no one had asked how the reporter, on an $18,000 salary, paid cash for a pair of red Buick Rivieras, lived in a $45,000 house with $25,000 worth of furniture, dressed his wife in furs and vacationed in Europe.[73]

His editors should have questioned him, but he was not supervised. They liked him, his friendships with the city's power elite and the fact that on deadline, Karafin delivered. What astonished some Philadelphians was that no one had complained. Even the chairman whose bank was extorted from did not blow the whistle. The reason, *Inquirer* critics claimed, was that Walter and his editors knew and condoned the reporter's behavior because, after all, wasn't Karafin an *Inquirer* hatchetman?

Karafin was not fired until *Philadelphia* was almost on newsstands. Two weeks later, the *Inquirer* wrote its own ten-column report under the headline "With Sadness and Regret." It insisted that Karafin had no accomplice and that no superior had known of his activities because he had been "a remarkably adept liar."[74] Walter was mortified. He ordered that a box run with the Karafin story asking readers to speak up if they knew of any "improper or unprofessional acts" by *Inquirer* employees. "The fact that Karafin was not detected sooner," he said later, "caused me great distress and humiliation."

The reporter was found guilty of blackmail and sentenced to jail, where he died. Walter took a broom to his newsroom. Out went Morrie Litman, the city editor supposed to supervise Karafin. Out too went Philip Schaeffer, a respected deputy city editor who had had no oversight. Soon after, Schaeffer applied for a job at Temple. The university called to determine whether Walter, a major donor, would object if it hired someone he had fired. "Schaeffer, he's wonderful," Walter enthused. He had no intention of hurting his editor elsewhere, but he wanted a clean sweep at the *Inquirer.* He could not keep a supervisor who should have known.[75]

THE PAPER never won a Pulitzer prize under Walter's stewardship, but it had done some things well, including trying to explain the Vietnam buildup. Walter supported Johnson's escalation of the war because he backed the U.S. government. But he conceded that he did not understand the issues behind the conflict and ordered a long series beginning with precolonial Vietnam and describing how the United States became involved and the stakes. "Just lay it out objectively," he ordered Goulden. "I don't want an opinion. I don't know, myself. Educate me."[76]

At a time when few mainstream newspapers were distinguishing themselves, the *Inquirer* did a relatively good job of covering the local black community. "The *Inquirer* was always ahead of the curve in race matters," said William Coleman. "It was often more liberal than the *Bulletin*," confirmed Judge A. Leon Higginbotham. "The *Bulletin* wanted a better city, but did not want to fight for it. The *Inquirer* was willing to get into the fray."

ONE WAY the *Inquirer* and Walter got into the fray was by using its squadron of police reporters to promote a tough-talking former vice cop named Frank Rizzo. The son of a policeman, Rizzo had joined the force in 1943, won notoriety in the 1950s for leading raids on strip joints and coffee houses, and worked his way up to captain of the vice squad. Walter got to know him well in the 1950s when he called Rizzo and asked to learn more about Philadelphia. The ambitious Rizzo, who understood what it could mean to have a powerful newspaper proprietor as a friend, had plenty of time to show the publisher how the police department really worked. His cruiser siren screaming, Rizzo took Walter around town and with him on Saturday night vice raids. "It was a hell of a lot of fun," Walter admitted. Afterward, the cop would indulge the publisher's passion for spaghetti by taking him to one of his favorite Italian restaurants in South Philadelphia.

When the *Inquirer* was struck in 1958, Rizzo maintained security at the newspaper. Walter was grateful and became an enthusiastic supporter of Rizzo, who in 1967 became police commissioner. When race riots broke out in Washington, Newark, Detroit and other cities after the 1968 assassination of civil rights leader Martin Luther King Jr., Rizzo kept Philadelphia calm by having tough tactical units patrol black neighborhoods. The civic order made him a hero to the white working class and earned the admiration of Walter, a law-and-order maven who considered anarchy the greatest threat to the nation's security in the 1960s. Admiring profiles in the *Inquirer* characterized Rizzo as "the toughest cop in America," a reputation he rode to election as mayor in

1971, delighting reporters with such vivid promises as, "I'm going to make Attila the Hun look like a faggot after this election's over."

Rizzo, who won two terms as mayor, lost Walter's support as he became increasingly racist and tried to change the city charter to run a third time. "Annenberg was a law-and-order guy who was prepared to be firm, but there's a fairness to the guy. He's no extremist," said William Green, the Democrat who succeeded Rizzo as mayor. "Rizzo crossed the line with racist statements and trying to change the charter. Annenberg would never go for that."[77]

By 1968, Walter had begun to lose interest in the *Inquirer.* The Karafin affair had been a terrible embarrassment which tainted his reputation and that of the *Inquirer* and demoralized the staff. Major capital investment was needed to modernize the plant. There was a desperate need for an entire generation of fresh editorial talent. Walter had lost confidence in editor Dimitman, whose day had long passed, but he had no ready replacement. The main attraction which kept Walter involved was Richard Nixon's second run for the presidency, this time against Democratic senator Hubert Humphrey of Minnesota.

Walter had remained in frequent contact with Nixon throughout the 1960s. The publisher sent the politician copies of supportive editorials, columns and cartoons; Nixon sent Walter speech texts and autographed photos. Walter also kept in touch with other Nixon backers. "Had you been at the Gridiron Dinner last Saturday you would have been pleased and proud of Dick Nixon's response for the Republican party," Walter wrote Elmer Bobst, the chairman of Warner-Lambert pharmaceuticals and a Nixon supporter since the early days of his vice presidency. "There was a spontaneous round of standing applause given him at the end of his remarks. I had never heard him in better form."[78]

He also gave Nixon his legal business in California and, when the former vice president moved east, a retainer to handle some of his and his sisters' affairs in New York. In 1962, when Nixon failed to win the California governorship, he had claimed famously to reporters, "You won't have Nixon to kick around any more because, gentlemen, this is my last press conference."

A month later, ABC television aired a program titled "The Political Obituary of Richard Nixon" but Walter refused to allow his ABC affiliates in Philadelphia and New Haven to run it. The half-hour documentary included interviews with four key people in Nixon's career: Jerry Voorhis, the first opponent he had defeated; Gerald Ford, a fellow congressman who ultimately succeeded Nixon in the White House; Murray Chotiner, a long-time Nixon aide; and Alger Hiss, the former State Department official convicted of perjury in 1950 after he denied turning over classified documents to a communist spy ring. As a member of the House Committee on Un-American Activities, Nixon had been Hiss's principal interrogator, a role which had simultaneously vaulted him to national prominence and made him anathema to liberals, who maintained that Nixon was framing the polished one-time protégé of Oliver Wendell Holmes, aide to FDR at Yalta and president of the Carnegie Endowment for International Peace.

Walter hated the idea of Hiss — who served forty-four months in Lewisburg penitentiary — judging Nixon's career on a program airing on Veterans Day. "TV Show Is 'Killed' " was the headline on a small front-page box in the *Inquirer* the day the program was scheduled to run in Philadelphia. "I cannot see that any useful purpose would be served in permitting a convicted treasonable spy [sic] to comment about a distinguished American," read the explanation for the publisher's action.

The cancellation caused a furor, but Walter was unrepentant. He had every bit as much right, he believed, to decide what his station broadcast as he did in determining what went into the *Inquirer.* He did not see the issue as a matter of censorship, but of judgment. An ABC executive had decided to air the Nixon show; he had decided not to on the basis of what he felt was good for his audience. Many people would have called that arrogant or disingenuous or both. In Walter's universe, where one acts on one's beliefs, not on what others think, his response was perfectly valid.

Because of the torrent of mail and calls, he published a page-three "Letter from the Editor" three days after the show, acknowledging that as a result of the messages, "I feel that an amplification is in order." The use of Hiss "to sit in judgment," he thought, "would be repugnant to most viewers." Those who accused him of favoring a friend were wrong, he went on. Less than a week before, he reminded readers, the *Inquirer* had sharply criticized Nixon for his attacks on the press following his loss in California.[79] The problem was Hiss. "Hiss was a damned spy. Even the Russian record shows that," he said later. "I wasn't going to let a traitor sit in judgment on a veteran and a senator and a vice president on Veterans Day."[80]

The mail, however, also convinced him that the public had little knowledge of the Hiss case. "I want a full takeout for Sunday's paper," he ordered Goulden. "Be objective, report both sides and tell everything the public should know about the case no matter how much space it takes." The story ran on page one and jumped to a full page inside and laid out the charges and countercharges objectively. To outsiders, it looked as though Walter had been high-handed one moment and even-handed the next, in other words, more gyrations between Good Walter and Bad Walter. In fact, this Hiss controversy was a clear example of Walter's behavior pattern. When he was crossed or perceived himself threatened or treated shabbily — which included disrespect directed at Moses — he could react venomously and vindictively like his father. But when nothing particularly was at stake personally, he could behave with impartiality.

When Nixon had moved east in 1963 to join the Mudge, Rose law firm in New York, he had told Walter and the *Inquirer* had broken the story. But it broke nothing during the 1968 campaign. The newspaper staffed the Republican convention in Miami which nominated Nixon and Spiro Agnew, but political columnist Joe McGinniss was called on the carpet for writing snidely about the GOP.[81] When he was not assigned to cover the riot-marred Democratic convention in Chicago, McGinniss quit to follow Nixon and write *The Selling of the President 1968*, his bestselling examination of the Republican team's advertising techniques.

Once again Walter decided against covering the fall campaign. Convinced that whatever the *Inquirer* wrote about either Nixon or Humphrey would result in his being criticized, Walter opted out and ordered that the *Inquirer* stick to running wire service copy.[82] *Inquirer* editorials strongly backed Nixon and his "secret plan" to end the war, but the news columns played the race down the middle. There were no attacks on Humphrey nor attempts to dig up dirt on Johnson's vice president. His determination to avoid enterprising coverage would have been anathema to a serious journalist or editor, but at the *Inquirer* he was neither. He held the title of editor, but at best he was an old-fashioned proprietor with editorial urges, some good, others awful. Controlling his urges in this race, he had the paper offer a bland headline daily with equal space given to each candidate.

It is hard to understand how he could have bashed Shapp with such enthusiasm only to have been so punctilious in the presidential campaign. One obvious reason was that he hated Shapp — and took great delight when the multimillionaire later revealed that he paid no federal income taxes from 1967 to 1969 — while he liked Nixon and had nothing against Humphrey.[83] Another was that he did not mind being criticized for what he published about the Pennsylvania campaign. That went with the territory. But he was wary about being caught out in the national contest. Critics and some of his own reporters wondered if he held back in the 1968 race because he suspected or knew that he might be offered a post if Nixon won. Yet Walter denied that he had any idea he would be awarded anything and there was no evidence to contradict him. He did not even give money to the Nixon campaign. He could have donated, probably without being discovered, as there were no stringent financial reporting requirements in 1968. But he believed, and properly, that it was inappropriate for a newspaperman to contribute financially to a candidate. Lee gave $2,500 to the campaign and his sisters contributed as well.

On October 31, President Johnson ordered a halt to the bombing of North Vietnam in an effort to advance the peace talks underway in Paris and to boost Humphrey's chances of succeeding him. The gesture fell short. Five days later, in the second tightest presidential race of the century — only his 1960 finish against John Kennedy was closer — Nixon edged Humphrey. Walter finally had a real friend in the White House.

22

DREAMWORLD

FROM THE AIR, the lush emerald patch surrounded by raw desert looks like a Persian carpet dropped on a moonscape or one of those verdant Israeli farms carved out of the Negev's sand and rock. No clouds block the sun over the Coachella Valley and the twelve man-made lakes on the property below shimmer like a brooch on a velvet gown.

From the ground, the first view of the property is a green row of thirty-foot eucalyptus trees and oleanders reaching up behind the long, soft pink wall that surrounds the 240-acre property at the improbable intersection of Bob Hope and Frank Sinatra Drives.

There are numerous walled compounds in Rancho Mirage, a two-hour drive east from Los Angeles and about ten miles south of Palm Springs. Some enclose luxurious country clubs named Thunderbird or Tamarisk; others are sumptuous condominium communities built around their own golf courses. None is like Sunnylands, the private dreamworld and winter home that Lee and Walter began building in 1963 and named after the retreat Moses had owned in the Poconos. Even the White House would be secure behind the walls, barbed wire, sensors and the electronically controlled gate guarding access to the estate which houses the Annenbergs' billion dollar art collection. Armed guards in blue uniforms man the roomy gatehouse and patrol a concealed security road. They are part of the staff of sixty groundskeepers, cooks, maids, butlers and gardeners who maintain Sunnylands.

Nothing but the guardpost and trees is visible from the street. Inside the gate, the half-mile driveway appears to have been just scrubbed clean. The surrounding desert is flat, but the drive immediately begins to climb gently past gnarled olive trees, lakes with ducks, and manicured lawn. Within seconds, the world outside the estate has disappeared and a visitor feels transported to the greenery of the English countryside.

At the top of the rise, the drive is split by an island of pink and white petunias in which the flagpole sits. The Stars and Stripes flies daily, but, like the monarch's standard over Buckingham Palace, the white and yellow Mayan sun god flag of Sunnylands is raised only when the Annenbergs are in residence, usually from early December until mid-April. The single-story main house is visible to the left, appearing to hover over one of the larger lakes. Beyond the house, and appearing to extend in the clear desert air to the foothills of the majestic San Jacinto mountains, is the golf course, nine divot-free fairways artfully designed with triple tees so that golfers can play the equivalent of twenty-seven different holes. Beside the entrance to the house, in the center of the cobblestone courtyard, rises a thirty-foot Mayan column, a replica of the central column of Mexico's National Museum of Anthropology in Mexico City, from which water courses onto a pool of smooth rocks.

The large double doors are open. Either Lee or Walter usually waits to greet guests near the large pots of cymbidium orchids grown on the estate and which line the entrance hall. Inside, first-time visitors tend to stare wide-eyed at the 6,500-square-foot living room with its pale pink marble floors and soft green sofas, carpets and walls of cinder-brown lava rock, backdrop for their collection of Impressionist and post-Impressionist paintings. In the vaulted center of the room, light pours in from a raised cupola onto the dark green bronze of Rodin's "Eve." Nearly six feet tall, the sculpture stands by a reflecting pool surrounded by hundreds of bromeliad plants. Through the window, next to a swimming pool that cascades down several levels like a natural pond and stream, is a huge and rare beaucarnia palm estimated to have been eight hundred years old when Walter purchased it from Estelle Doheny's Beverly Hills estate.

WALTER FIRST VISITED the desert in the late 1930s to gamble on weekends while visiting Los Angeles. At that time there were only a few southwestern-style adobe villas, including one where Greta Garbo came to be alone, in the sandy basin at the foot of the San Jacinto and Santa Rosa Mountains. The Hollywood crowd had begun arriving in greater numbers after 1934, when actors Ralph Bellamy and Charles Farrell built two tennis courts and opened the Palm Springs Racquet Club. Soon, Errol Flynn, Clark Gable and Claudette Colbert could be found by a swimming pool while Spencer Tracy and Jackie Cooper headed for the golf course.

Drawn by the valley's proximity, beauty and perfect winter weather, film and business executives built weekend homes with views of snow-covered peaks that rose to 10,800 feet above the desert floor, where temperatures in summer often reach 110 degrees. They sank artesian wells into the aquifer which gave Palm Springs its name and the desert began to bloom. Championship golf courses and luxury hotels sprouted. Air conditioning transformed living habits and after World War II, population in the desert doubled every decade. Before long the valley was boasting that it had more swimming pools per capita than anywhere else and was the Winter Golf Capital of the World.

Bing Crosby, Frank Sinatra, Bob Hope and director Frank Capra all built homes and entertained friends. Eddie Fisher honeymooned there with Debbie Reynolds and with Elizabeth Taylor, who also spent honeymoons in the valley with Michael Wilding and Mike Todd.[1] Jack Warner and Frederick Loewe negotiated the film rights for *My Fair Lady* at the Palm Springs spa. President Dwight Eisenhower, who built the first White House putting green and practiced his short irons by the hour on the south lawn, brought his fifteen handicap to the desert and moved into a bungalow overlooking the eleventh fairway of the El Dorado Country Club. Thirty years later, President Gerald Ford built a home in Rancho Mirage and became an Annenberg neighbor and friend. A mile down Bob Hope Drive from Sunnylands, Betty Ford established her substance abuse clinic at the Eisenhower Medical Center, which Walter helped found and fund.

After he married Lee in 1951, Walter began returning to the desert. Lee missed California during the Philadelphia winters. She also missed her friends, especially Harriet, who had remarried after the sudden death of Sylvan Simon, the Columbia studio director. Within months of Lee and Walter's wedding, Harriet had wed Armand Deutsch, a grandson of Julius Rosenwald, the Chicago philanthropist who had founded Sears, Roebuck. Deutsch had joined a brokerage firm after college, but soon discovered that he hated the work, got into show business as a talent coordinator for the Rudy Vallee radio show, moved to RKO studios and eventually became a producer for Metro-Goldwyn-Mayer.[2] Harriet and Ardie, as he was known, knew everyone in the industry.

Ardie and Walter's first meeting, at the "21" club in New York, had begun inauspiciously, with the women trying too hard to ensure that their husbands would get along. Halfway through dinner, Walter put his hand on Ardie's. "Let's make it a point to get on together. It certainly is in our best interests and it will make our lives easier." In thinking later about the gesture and remark, Ardie concluded that he had experienced "Walter's preferred way of dealing with a problem, which is to recognize it and whenever possible, move decisively to end it."[3]

THROUGHOUT THE FIFTIES, when their children left Philadelphia to spend March vacations with their other parent, Lee and Walter flew to the desert for a winter break. They stayed twenty miles south of Palm Springs at the La Quinta Hotel. Known as a discreet hideaway, La Quinta was long a favorite destination for Flynn, Gable and Dolores del Rio.[4] When the Tamarisk Country Club opened in 1952 in Rancho Mirage, the Annenbergs joined and played golf with the Deutsches and Frank Sinatra. "Every time we came down the fourteenth fairway, we could see this big mound of sand because there was nothing here then, nothing," said Lee. "I told Walter that if we ever built a house, wouldn't it be fun to have it high enough so we could look over the trees at the mountains."[5]

The mound of sand was sixty-five feet high, significant elevation in a scrub brush valley which was otherwise flat as a baking pan. The height appealed to Walter, who had become frustrated arranging tee times at the increasingly popular Tamarisk and El Dorado. "Weekends, I had to wait," he said. "Then once we got out on the course, there were people ahead of me and behind me. They're hitting into you or you into them." The idea of building his own course grew more appealing.[6]

They took the Deutsches to see the property. The mound looked like everyplace else to them. "We're standing in the middle of the desert looking at sand," Ardie recalled. "Anyone might well have said, 'Why here? Why not over there?' But Walter had examined every aspect of the location carefully. Endless study had gone into the choice."[7] Title research showed that in 1913, one Percy Marrow had sold the land to the San Diego Subdivision Company for a $10 gold coin. Four years later, just as the U.S. was entering the First World War, Riverside County tax collector C. R. Stibbins sold the land to the state for nonpayment of taxes amounting to $10.46.[8]

The price had risen considerably by April 1963, when Walter decided to buy. Roger had died the previous August, and he and Lee wanted a change of scene and a project in which to immerse themselves. Wallis had been married for nearly three years. Lee's daughter Diane Katleman was also married. Of the children, that left only Elizabeth Rosenstiel, then fourteen and attending Philadelphia's Shipley School, to come on occasion, though she more often spent holidays with her father.

Walter first bought 197 acres, including the mound, for which he paid $899,500, or $4,500 an acre. In 1967, he spent $238,000 for an additional 69 acres, or $3,450 an acre. A year later, he paid $1.66 million, or $2,525 an acre, for a 658-acre adjacent tract which he kept undeveloped as a protective buffer zone.[9] Overall, he had bought 933 acres, 10 percent more than New York's Central Park. He had paid less than $3 million for what would become some of California's highest-priced real estate in the most desirable area of the Coachella Valley. In later years, the area north of Palm Springs became a vast field of windmills, while Walter's property became the heart of residential Rancho Mirage, where land in 1998 was selling for $100,000 an acre.[10]

To remake his landscape, Walter had thought of everything. Rights to a local water company were available with the property. Walter bought it as well to insure that he would never be short of water for the lakes which irrigate the golf course. (He sold it a few years later when he tired of neighbors calling to complain about water pressure or backed-up pipes.) Because the October 1962 Cuban missile crisis was a recent reminder of Cold War perils, he decided to include a basement bomb shelter. (Thirty-five years after building the house, he admitted that he had never been in the basement.)

After buying the land, the first call the Annenbergs made was to William Haines, a handsome star at Metro-Goldwyn-Mayer in the 1920s, Hollywood's box-office king in 1930 and a star the following year in *Just a Gigolo*. Haines's film career had begun to slip in the mid-thirties.[11] He used his film-industry contacts, fine taste, charm and aristocratic manners to launch a new career, and by the fifties he had become one of California's most sought after interior designers. Haines's style was classical, featuring English and French antiques and lots of light, a change from the gloomy Spanish interiors with heavy, dark furnishings which had prevailed in the 1920s American West. Influenced by Robsjohn Gibbings, the English-born designer who had decorated

Walter's apartment on Rittenhouse Square, Haines had done big houses for stars like Carole Lombard, Norma Shearer, William Powell and studio boss Jack Warner.[12]

In decades of design work, he had come to operate, like Walter, according to a series of maxims. One was "It's not the size, the shape or the location. It's what you do with what you have to work with." Another was that "there's no decorator in the world who can make a house good if the architecture is bad." Haines believed that "the interior decorator, the landscape gardener and the architect should all be consulted in the beginning. The three should be hired as a unit and work together."[13]

The Annenbergs and Haines found instant rapport. They liked his approach, style, concepts and social connections and asked him to assemble a team. Haines brought in his partner and furnishings specialist Ted Graber, golf course designer Dick Wilson and A. Quincy Jones, professor of architecture at the University of Southern California and later dean of its schools of architecture and fine arts.

Haines was responsible for the total concept, but Lee and Walter had their own ideas. "When Walter first took us out into that bare desert and tried to explain to Bill and me what he wanted," said Graber, "we both said, 'It sounds as if you really want an oasis.'"

"That's exactly what I want," Walter replied, "and I don't want to see one grain of sand except in the sand traps."[14]

They wanted a Mayan look for the house, which was Quincy Jones's responsibility. They had never visited the famed ruins at Chichen Itza or Uxmal on the Yucatan peninsula, but they liked pictures they had seen of solid but graceful pyramidal structures with flying facades and flat roofs. "After that, our basic instruction was that we wanted the outside to be inside," Lee explained. "Bring in the light and the view and the gardens."[15]

They said nothing about size. The original plans called for the main house to cover 22,803 square feet, about a half acre, including two bedrooms in the main house and a four-room guest wing. Arcades, loggias, terraces and a porte cochere added another 15,000 square feet. Jones's initial estimate in 1963 for construction of the house was $700,000. By early 1964, the architect had raised the estimate to $1,062,170 with the costs of the main house projected at $40 a square foot. Walter agreed that Haines and Jones could authorize changes of up to $1,000, but that anything more had to come to him for approval. Jones's original idea of having the house elevated an additional twelve

feet was deemed too overwhelming and was dropped. The Annenbergs wanted the building to fit as naturally as possible into the landscape. The estate would be massive, but they were insistent that it not
be intrusive.

Lush plantings helped. The tree and shrubbery list Quincy Jones
provided was exhaustive. Lee and Walter ordered 2,060 eucalyptus
trees, 7,114 oleanders, and 915 tamarisks. At a cost from $25 to $150
each, 850 olive trees were planted: 432 trees eight to ten feet in height,
324 from ten to twelve feet, and 108 from twelve to fifteen feet. Shrubs
and smaller trees included 216 fifteen-gallon, 216 ten-gallon, and 10,089
one-gallon trees. Jones estimated the cost of the trees at $99,274.86 plus
$31,000 for labor to plant and mulch them, a modest $130,000 for a
respectable forest.[16]

"I would like to think about colorful floriculture all over my property that is not going to be taken up by the golf course or my bird sanctuary," Walter wrote to Quincy Jones in early 1964. "I may even want
to get into a unique type of cactus garden or perhaps we might have
elements of cacti worked in on the golf course."[17]

Walter, like his father, loved birds. He enjoyed tramping the property with binoculars and well into his eighties could rattle off the
names of various winged creatures flitting about the property. Some
were attracted to a gigantic birdhouse which he called his "feathered
Hilton" in a garden outside his bedroom. A built-in microphone trans-
mitted the sounds of the birds to a speaker in his dressing room. The
house is surrounded by flowers and gardens: one for varieties of cactus,
a second for sculpture, a third filled with banks of rose bushes.

Building the house took three years, long enough for doubts to set
in. "We'd come out from Philadelphia and think we were building the
most horrible monstrosity," said Lee. "There was this raw desert and
red steel beams, and giant roof and this huge space and not one thing
in it and we thought, *aarrgghh*. We were really scared. Without the furniture it looked like we had done something absolutely insane." The
biggest worry was the sixty-by-fifty-foot living room, which looked like
a hockey rink. Still then in the early days of their art collecting, they
had little to display on their walls.

THEY OPENED Sunnylands in the late fall of 1966, although they spent
little time there, as Walter was reluctant to be gone for long from his
office. When in residence, he kept tabs on breaking news with the help
of an Associated Press teletype printer tucked in a sound-proofed

closet near his two-thousand-square-foot bedroom. Working with his editors by phone was never a problem. Even in Philadelphia, much of his business was conducted by telephone from his office in the *Inquirer* tower to the newsroom or to the editors of *TV Guide*, the *Daily Racing Form*, or sister Enid at *Seventeen*. Nor was getting to and from California or anywhere else a difficulty. He had his own plane, which he regularly upgraded. (In 1997, when he was eighty-nine, Walter paid $40 million for a new, elegantly fitted Gulfstream Five, the Rolls-Royce of private jets.)

The moving cartons were barely unpacked before the first guests arrived, Mamie and Ike Eisenhower. Their stay began a tradition of so many high-level visits to the estate by presidents — current and former — prime ministers, sovereigns, princes and business executives from all over the world that in 1990 the property would be designated a national historic landmark. The Secret Service and other security units loved Sunnylands. Few private homes were better protected. Whatever slings and arrows Walter faced outside this Camelot, he and Lee enjoyed a perfectly controlled environment within. Which, of course, was the point.

Lee not only loved to entertain but was extremely good at it. In the early Sunnylands years, the Annenbergs entertained constantly — cocktail parties, barbecues, formal sit-down dinners and lively dances. There was no better venue for high-level fund-raising for the Eisenhower Medical Center or the Palm Springs Desert Museum and not merely because the host always wrote the biggest check. Food, drink, table settings, flowers and musical groups were always the very best quality. That was the only way Lee and Walter operated. Invitations for golf were much sought after and the Annenbergs were generous in having friends join them.

In later years, determined to preserve their privacy, the Annenbergs narrowed their circle and cut back on mingling with the industrialists and retired millionaires who had moved to the desert to spend winters. They continued, though, to play golf together with friends nearly every day and often met at one another's luxurious homes for dinner. With the exception of the famous New Year's Eve parties and a few formal dinners and dances, which Lee and Walter especially loved, entertaining became more low key. Evenings often featured a cookout — pantsuits for women, blazers for men, staff chefs at the grill — and a private movie screening at the Annenbergs' or the Sinatras', who in 1976 were married at Sunnylands.

Walter once explained to Gerald Ford the sanctuary aspect of Sunnylands. "The ancient Chinese philosophers believed that reverence of the landscape was the highest ideal in life and hence most Chinese paintings majored in some aspect of the landscape," Walter wrote him. "Further, the landscape represented a sanctuary of protection and peaceful comfort. Sunnylands has come to represent just this in my life and as a consequence I try to guard the privacy and the beauty of it with respect and consideration."[18]

After Richard Nixon was elected president in November 1968 and the Republican Governors Association gathered a month later in Palm Springs to celebrate, the Annenbergs welcomed the victorious GOP with a dinner at Sunnylands. "Springs Hits the Big Time in Hospitality," read the headline in the *Desert Sun* marking the arrival of thirty-three governors and their spouses, the president-elect and daughter Tricia, who filled in for the ailing Pat Nixon, and vice president–elect Agnew, whom Walter then did not know.[19] The Nixons stayed at the estate with Nancy and Ronald Reagan, who was finishing his second year as California's governor.

The Nixons and Reagans were not close. Reagan had declared for president late in the 1968 campaign and at the Miami Beach convention tried to team up with the forces of New York governor Nelson Rockefeller — two extremes of the GOP working together — in an effort to deny Nixon a first-ballot victory. It didn't work and Nixon had squeaked by with a plurality of fifty-one of the 1,333 votes cast.[20]

The Nixon-Reagan machinations in Miami had intrigued Lee and Walter, but politics did not alter the fact that both couples were friends. It was logical that both president-elect and governor would stay at Sunnylands, and if being together with them helped smooth over any lingering resentments, so much the better. Sunnylands was no place to nurse a grudge. "Sheer heaven" was how Nancy Reagan described her first stay there, in 1967. "How can you ever bear to tear yourself away?" She praised Lee's seemingly effortless ability to manage the house perfectly and jokingly asked whether she'd run the governor's mansion for her.[21]

WALTER AND LEE had attended the Miami Beach convention in August. Nixon wrote in his memoirs that he and John Mitchell had decided — "tentatively and very privately" — two weeks before it opened that the vice presidency would go to Maryland governor Spiro Agnew. Nixon's rationale was that with Alabama governor George Wallace in the race, he could not sweep the South, so he needed to capture the southern border states. Agnew was a border-state governor who had stood up for law and order during the urban riots that followed the assassination of Martin Luther King Jr. that spring. Given the intra-party turmoil, Agnew was also deemed the candidate least likely to harm to what little party unity was left. But the decision remained reversible and Nixon continued to weigh alternatives.[22]

He asked Walter to determine if William Scranton, the able former governor of Pennsylvania, would be interested. "Offer it to him," Nixon had said. "See what you can get out of him."[23] Scranton was a much respected moderate who had figured heavily in the stop-Goldwater movement four years earlier, but he had also pledged to stay out of elective politics once he stepped down in 1966 as governor. Walter felt him out as requested.

"I appreciate him thinking of me," Scranton replied, "but please tell Dick that I would not be interested in the vice presidency." Scranton gave no reason, but made it clear he did not want anything, not the State Department, not an embassy, and definitely not the vice presidency. Walter regretted the decision because he admired Scranton as a man of decency and ability. "He just couldn't see it, but given what happened [to Nixon and Agnew] his decision turned out to be the biggest mistake of his life," Walter said. "Scranton would have been a hell of a president."[24]

The Agnew selection stunned Walter, who had doubts about him from the start. "I thought he was the bottom of the barrel, a nobody. I was really shocked when he was picked because I had heard that he was a foul ball, a two-dollar thief." He had, however, never mentioned his concern to Nixon. "Good God, no," he exclaimed. "That was his decision." He and Nixon were friends, but not political cronies. For Walter to have said anything about Agnew would have been presumptuous.

When the Republicans came to Palm Springs a month after the election, the Agnews stayed at the Riviera Hotel, site of a celebratory dinner for a thousand supporters on Saturday, December 7. Earlier that day, several senior Republicans came by limousine for golf at Sunny-lands. Nixon and Reagan were already in residence. Joining them were Nelson Rockefeller and congressmen Charles Wilson of California and Gerald Ford of Michigan, then the GOP whip on Capitol Hill. Agnew, deliberately excluded, was the butt of several jokes, including smirks at the recollection of his opening remarks to the governors conference when he expressed pleasure at being in "Palm Beach." They marveled at the exquisite house and complimented Walter repeatedly on the perfection of his golf course. Rockefeller, a serious collector himself, surveyed the paintings to the delight of Walter, who enthusiastically described the provenance of his paintings and objets d'art to all who expressed interest.[25]

Nixon, the most socially awkward of presidents, was comfortable around Walter, especially in the cosseting serenity of Sunnylands. He admired the publisher, whose newspaper, unlike others, had not badgered him editorially about Agnew or the Vietnam War or student protests. Nixon hated the *New York Times* and *Washington Post*, which often savaged him, but he had no cause for concern from Walter, who shared the president-elect's feelings about press coverage. "He has no patience with publishers always looking after the money," Nixon told John Cooney, author of a 1982 biography of the Annenbergs. "He's willing to take a position even when it's going to cost him a few bucks. That's very unusual. Unfortunately most of the publishers and many editors are unwilling to take risks except when they are tilting to the left. They have no guts, but Annenberg has guts."[26]

The two had a surprising amount in common. Like Walter, Nixon was a loner, an outsider in politics and society. Each man's circle of intimates was small. Nixon relaxed almost exclusively with businessmen Bebe Rebozo and Robert Ablanalp. Walter's best friend was Lee, who was also a devoted wife like Pat Nixon, albeit a more equal team partner. Each man had been hit by criticism and was constantly on the alert for the next incoming slight. "Harrassment in life is always just around the corner," Walter maintained. Neither turned his cheek when challenged or disparaged. Each could be expected to strike back. Each man considered his mother a saint. In the company of men, each could be earthy and profane. (Later, White House recordings would reveal that Nixon repeatedly made anti-Semitic remarks, but none ever appeared directed at Walter.) Neither was a blue-blood son of the Establishment. When Nixon said that Walter "wasn't part of the so-called 'social elite,'" he meant it as a compliment. He respected Walter's willingness to stand up for what he believed in, a trait Nixon believed he shared. "What impresses me most is his strong character," Nixon said. "His balls — his cojones as the Latins put it."[27]

Looking at Walter in late 1968, it would have been easy to conclude that the squire of Sunnylands, the by then centimillionaire publisher with the beautiful, refined wife, private jet and staff for every need or whim had everything a man could want. Nixon, of course, knew better. He knew all about Moses, and they had compared notes on Walter's theory that life was a series of tests. One of his favorite reminders to Nixon was that "life is ninety-nine rounds." The president understood. You had to pick yourself up when knocked down by adversity, fight back and move on. Both men had done that, Nixon most notably after the disastrous California governor's race. Only weeks before, Nixon had seen his tenacity rewarded, his struggle for respect vindicated when he was elected president. Nixon understood that Walter had also been on a lifelong crusade for respect, a cause the president-elect could now do something about. Unlike most people he knew, Walter had never asked him for anything. He had always been the giver, of loyal support, of ready refuge and, invariably, of respect. Nixon never had to watch his back around Walter. The time had come to reward the publisher.

After the golf, when the others had left to dress for dinner, he asked Walter to stay outside a moment so they could have a quiet word. "Of course, Mr. President," Walter replied. They walked outside where, without overture, Nixon sprang his offer.

"Walter, I want you to be my ambassador to Great Britain."

Walter was startled. He had not expected any job, certainly not in foreign policy. "I've never been a diplomat," he said, stuttering slightly.

Nixon waved off the objection. Walter hesitated. London was the plum among embassies. The biggest party donors always lusted for London. Being named ambassador to the Court of St. James's would be a high honor, an imprimatur of respect from his country and president. All he had to do was say yes, thank you. He wanted to, but instead took a deep breath and spoke calmly.

"Mr. President, I cannot accept," he said. "You'll have enough trouble with the Eastern Establishment without naming me ambassador. You would be better off selecting someone who will cause you fewer problems."

Nixon told Walter later that he had been surprised. He had never considered a rejection. He had thought Walter was saying no because of a lack of policy experience, but Nixon knew that Walter would not need much. The president-elect was a foreign policy expert. He would not require expertise from his ambassador in Britain. Anything important he or his national security adviser Henry Kissinger would oversee personally. "Listen, Walter, I know your character and ability and I respect you. You can handle that job very easily because you have good judgment."

Walter tried again to dissuade him. His family history worried him. All the terrible stories about his father would be dredged up again. The publicity would be brutal and Senate Democrats would use it to attack the administration during his confirmation hearings.

Nixon would not take no for an answer. "Walter, the hell with that. You're strong enough to stand up to them. You've got to do this for me."

Put that way, he could hardly refuse. "If he was going to gamble on me," said Walter, "I knew that I had to shape up and accept it." He stuck out his hand. "All right." The publisher grinned. "I temporarily accept." When he saw her that evening, Nixon gave a hug and kiss to Lee, who would be an important partner in London. "I know you two are going to be wonderful there," he told her. Nixon left the next day with a jaunty, "See you soon, Mr. Ambassador." Walter and Lee beamed, waved and began their homework.

HAVING CHOSEN WALTER, Nixon was immune to the entreaties of two rich, eager, self-promoting candidates. One was W. Clement Stone, the Chicago insurance magnate best known for his ceaseless promotion of P.M.A., or positive mental attitude, and whose pencil-thin mustache made him look like a mariachi band leader or the Joker in Batman comics. Stone had poured money into Nixon's campaign, but he was never taken seriously as a potential ambassador.

The other was William S. Paley, who had built the Columbia Broadcasting System. Paley's cause was advanced by Walter Thayer, a business associate of John Hay Whitney's, who was Paley's brother-in-law and had been ambassador to Britain during the Eisenhower administration. "Paley was very strongly pushed," said Peter Flanigan, who handled high-level appointments for Nixon. "It was a concerted drive."[28] Nixon, though, wanted no part of Bill Paley and was unmoved by the endorsement of Establishment Republican Jock Whitney. If anything, the new president took delight in flummoxing these men. When Flanigan sent in Paley's name on a list of possible nominees for London, it came back crossed out with a notation, "No, that's for Walter Annenberg."

Paley "was so galled," said a CBS executive, according to Paley biographer Sally Bedell Smith. "He would have been psychologically willing to accept that he didn't get it because he was Jewish. But then that damned Annenberg got it — and he was Jewish."[29]

Nixon had already discussed the appointment with William P. Rogers, who as secretary of state would be Walter's nominal superior. "Walter was completely Nixon's choice," Rogers recalled. "They were real friends and had a genuine fondness for each other. There was nothing fake about it." Rogers made no attempt to talk Nixon out of the appointment because he too liked Walter and believed he had great ability. But he warned Nixon that there could be criticism. "I told him that the foreign service would be against him because Walter had no experience in diplomacy and that there might be confirmation problems." Nixon told Rogers that he knew all that, but he was confident Walter would get through and do fine.[30]

Word of Walter's selection began leaking in January 1969. The appointment "virtually is certain," the *New York Times* reported on January 8. The formal nomination came on February 20. After six weeks of trying to avoid saying anything in public, Walter tore the announcement off his A.P. teletype machine at Sunnylands, had it mounted and gave it to Lee at her fifty-first birthday dinner that evening.

No sooner was the nomination made public than the criticism began. J. William Fulbright of Arkansas, the chairman of the Senate Foreign Relations Committee, which determines whether ambassadorial appointments come to a vote, told the *Washington Post* that Annenberg was "simply not up to the standards we expect of our premier diplomatic post."[31] In an editorial headlined "Money and the Foreign Service," the *New York Times* voiced its dismay. Praising Presidents Kennedy and Johnson for scrapping the tradition of awarding wealthy campaign contributors, it said the Annenberg appointment suggested that the new administration "will revive the discredited old practice."

The paper called Britain "still America's most important single ally" and noted that relations between Nixon, a conservative Republican, and Prime Minister Harold Wilson of the leftist Labour party would require deft diplomacy to avoid friction. "Instead of improved consultation on critical world issues . . . there would be a danger of further deterioration in the quality of consultation if an inexperienced amateur replaced a skilled professional."[32]

Walter accepted the apprehension about his lack of diplomatic expertise. He had expressed those very doubts to Nixon. But the suggestion that he had bought the appointment, after the care he had taken to publish balanced campaign coverage and not to have given money to his friend, made him apoplectic. This cloud over him, these allegations, seemed totally unfair, he lamented. He had lived an exemplary life. He worked hard. He tried to be generous. He concluded that liberals were out to get him as they had been trying to get Nixon. The president agreed.

"I wanted him for the reasons the *Times* opposed him," Nixon told biographer Cooney. "They wanted someone like Paley. The *Times* felt he frankly wasn't in the first rank of the social order to go to the Court of St. James's. They were concerned about what his father had done. To them, Annenberg was too candid at times and not diplomatic . . . not the typical soft-headed diplomat. The *Times* is basically a snobbish paper. I wanted somebody who would go to the mat, somebody who was not part of the social elite, someone who could express himself at times.

"But it was a tough fight," Nixon went on. "There were some in those early days who indicated they didn't want to see the fight through. But I insisted. People on our own staff . . . people who are weak-kneed . . . said he was an embarrassment and word came back he was willing to pull out. But I passed word back that I was going to fight and stand by him."[33]

A SIGNIFICANT FACTOR in the equation was David K. E. Bruce, the ambassador Walter was to replace. Bruce himself caused no trouble for Walter, but as one of the most talented ambassadors in U.S. diplomatic history, he was the toughest possible act to follow. A wealthy Virginian of cultivated tastes who devoted his life to public service, Bruce was a student of American history and politics, had written a book about the early presidents and had been a member of both the Maryland and Virginia legislatures. During World War II, while based in London, he had directed the efforts in France of the Office of Strategic Services, the precursor of the CIA. A good friend of Jean Monnet, the father of the European Community, Bruce in the late 1940s had helped devise the Marshall Plan and had served as ambassador to France, Germany and Britain — the only American to hold all three posts — and would later be the first U.S. envoy to China after Nixon opened relations in 1972 with Mao's communist government.

A connoisseur of exceptional charm and wit, whose erudite cable defending the quality of American wines against those of France was a State Department classic, Bruce had a stylish personal life. His first wife had been Ailsa Mellon, the nation's richest woman, daughter of Andrew Mellon, the longtime Treasury secretary, with whose family he had worked to establish the National Gallery of Art in Washington.[34]

They had divorced, and in 1945 he married Evangeline Bell, the daughter of an American diplomat and an English mother from an old, prominent family. Her grandfather, Brigadier Sir Herbert Conyers Surtees, had been colonel of the Coldstream Guards and a Conservative member of parliament; her great-grandmother, the actress Ruth Herbert, was the favorite model and mistress of Dante Gabriel Rossetti, the English poet and pre-Raphaelite painter. Born in London, Evangeline was a recent graduate of Radcliffe when she went to work in 1940 for two years for Attorney General Francis Biddle, the Roosevelt cabinet officer who just then was obstructing Walter's efforts to secure a parole for his father.

A tall, willowy beauty with dark hair and piercing eyes, she had a history as a sexual temptress. A Philadelphia matron threw her out of the house when she found the visiting Evangeline sleeping with her husband. A Washingtonian grande dame described how as a young woman on a Maine camping trip with her father, brothers and Evangeline, when both were twenty-four, she awoke to find Evangeline in a sleeping bag with her father. Evangeline had a first-rate brain, impeccable style and was a perennial on the best-dressed lists. When she arrived in Britain in 1961 after Kennedy named her husband ambassador, many considered her one of the beauties of her generation and were delighted to be included in her salons.[35]

Bruce performed in stellar fashion for Kennedy and for Lyndon Johnson, who had arrived in the Oval Office with little experience in foreign affairs. By the end of 1968, Bruce's tour had been the longest by an American in London and had encompassed a hectic period in foreign policy, including construction of the Berlin Wall, the Cuban missile crisis, the death of Winston Churchill, the overthrow of Nikita Khrushchev by Leonid Brezhnev, the Profumo sex scandal and the expansion of the war in Vietnam. Bruce was a superb interlocutor between his presidents and prime ministers Harold Macmillan, Sir Alec Douglas-Home and Harold Wilson, and he dealt comfortably and confidently with high-level U.S. visitors and senior British officials. He and Evangeline were hospitable hosts at Winfield House, the ambassador's residence, to politicians, academics, artists, actors and senior journalists. They also maintained a European marriage; each had a lover.

After the Annenberg nomination was announced but before Walter went before the Senate committee for confirmation hearings, Evangeline invited Lee to visit the residence, "as soon as possible to survey the house and make some plans respecting it," as David Bruce noted in his diary.[36] The ambassador also invited Walter to discuss the job with him in Paris, as it would have been inappropriate for him to come to London while the appointment was pending. After consulting the State Department, Walter told Bruce that he would not come to Europe before his confirmation, but that Lee would like to see the residence, a three-story, thirty-five-room mansion on twelve acres of lawns and gardens on the northwest side of Regents Park, once a royal hunting park for King Henry VIII. The estate was the second-largest residence in London; only Buckingham Palace was bigger. U.S. heiress Barbara Hutton had purchased the property after a fire in 1936 destroyed the century-old Regency mansion on the site. She built a red brick Georgian-style residence in its place and named it Winfield House for her grandfather, Frank Winfield Woolworth, founder of the Woolworth store chain, who had died three years earlier and left her $40 million.

Hutton had parquet floors laid, eighteenth-century French paneling installed, marble bathrooms fitted and thousands of trees and shrubs planted, which gave the mansion a feeling of being miles from London in the Hampshire countryside instead of minutes from the city center. When she moved in with her husband, Count Haugwitz-Reventlow, Hutton decorated the house with Louis XV furniture, priceless paintings, including two Canalettos which later went to the National Gallery in Washington, Persian carpets and all manner of porcelains, china and antiques.

In 1939, with World War II erupting along with her marriage to Reventlow, Hutton returned to the United States and turned the house over to the Royal Air Force, which used it to lodge an anti-aircraft unit. Near misses from Luftwaffe bombs and a buzz bomb forced the RAF from the mansion, which later became an American officers' club. A year after the war, Hutton, then married to playboy Porfirio Rubirosa, returned to find the place a maze of buckled floors, dangling wires and broken windows. For token payment of a dollar, she gave the property to the U.S. government for the ambassador's residence, which it became in 1954.[37]

Lee had been warned before she arrived by Peter Skoufis, the embassy's administrative counselor, that the house needed work. The roof leaked, paint and paper on the walls were peeling and the electrical system required updating. But the woman who less than three years before had completed building one of America's most palatial homes was not prepared for what she found. The house was structurally sound but cosmetically decrepit. Floors were scarred. Velvet curtains installed by the Whitneys fifteen years earlier were worn thin. Wallpaper was stained. Dark-paneled walls gave some public rooms a funereal look. Carpets revealed that the Bruces' springer spaniels had not been house-trained. The Bruces, typical of many monied aristocrats who were tight with cash, were used to living in shabby elegance.

"We had a maintenance budget for repairs and painting, but when it came to Winfield House, Ambassador Bruce wouldn't let anybody in," Skoufis explained. "He'd say, 'Pete, don't come in my house. I don't want any painters in, or any of your people in here unless I call on them.'"[38] The extent of the inattention and deterioration startled Lee.

"Walter, I hope you're sitting down because I have quite a shock for you," she told him. "The place is a mess. The roof needs to be replaced. The wiring is gone. The plumbing is not great. The ground floor toilets use old-fashioned water boxes. Everything needs repainting. And there'll hardly be any good furniture when the Bruces leave with theirs." Walter instructed her to make a precise inventory of what was needed as well as a cost estimate. If he was confirmed, he did not care what it cost to fix up Winfield House. Given the honor he was receiving, whatever the total would be money well spent on a showplace for the United States.

Coming up with a precise inventory and estimate was not difficult because Lee had brought along Bill Haines and Ted Graber. They moved into the Ritz Hotel, hired a car and driver, and spent several days going over every square inch of Winfield House. Ambassador Bruce quite liked Haines. "A delightful old boy," he called him after meeting the decorator poised on a stepladder and muttering, "I am too old, too tired and too rich for this kind of thing."[39] Bruce also seemed comfortable with Lee, whom he called "pretty and vivacious." Evangeline, though, after demonstrating considerable grace in inviting Lee to London, suddenly became infuriated.

It was bad enough that her husband was being succeeded by a know-nothing conservative crony of that awful man Nixon, she told friends. But to have this nouveau riche blonde — who was not at all the chunky Jewish matron she had expected — show up with a couple of Hollywood decorators and determine that Winfield House, which had been good enough for the Bruces, was a wreck and not fit for the Annenbergs was too much. With every photo and notation Haines and Graber made and every question Lee asked, Evangeline became angrier. "Vangie could be very jealous and envious," said Fleur Cowles, a friend of Evangeline's and one of the best-known Americans in London. "She had something inside her that drove her to hate and she could not stand the idea that the Annenbergs were going to be in her house and making it nicer."[40]

By the time Lee and the decorators returned home in late February, Evangeline had begun spreading malicious rumors in every direction. How Lee had invited herself to London without waiting for her husband's confirmation. How she had denigrated the house. How she was preparing to rip it apart, build a screening room, pipe in Muzak and paint everything in California pastels. Lee could hardly contain her own anger. After making a gracious gesture, Evangeline had then perverted the good things Lee was trying to do. It wasn't as if Lee were indulging herself with taxpayers' money. All the work would be a gift from the Annenbergs. If Evangeline had not wanted her to come, why had she invited her? Lee wondered. Lee was unaware that Evangeline's friends rarely knew which Vangie they were going to see. They knew that Evangeline considered herself co-ambassador and enjoyed being the center of attention. Yet some also observed that her moods changed quickly and later claimed that Evangeline had a problem with prescription drugs.

Lee knew none of that. To keep control of her own temper, she said, she buried herself in Christian Science readings and the Bible. "It is good to give praise to the Lord and to sing to thy name, O most high, to proclaim thy mercy in the morning and thy faithfulness every night." As she recited the prayer, mantra-like from memory, the knots of tension in her shoulders eased.

Back in the United States, Walter was on edge. He had buried himself for weeks in briefing books about Britain's politics and economy with an intensity he had never shown at Peddie or Wharton. He was confident that he could answer whatever substantive questions the senators on the Foreign Relations Committee might have. It was what they might ask about his father that worried him.

Drew Pearson had given him a taste of what was to come on February 24, four days after the nomination was made official, when his column appeared in the *Washington Post* under the headline "Annenberg Lifts Some British Brows." President Nixon, who that week was visiting Britain on a postinauguration trip to Europe, had "stood British diplomacy on its ear" with the appointment of Annenberg "whose fortune was built up by Chicago gang warfare." Moses Annenberg, the columnist wrote, had been sentenced to four years in prison and was "reported to have paid, according to J. David Stern, former publisher of the *Philadelphia Record*, $1 million a year to Al Capone, czar of the Chicago underworld, to protect his racing wire," which was nonsense, but Pearson was just warming up. The gang warfare, he went on, had started with a circulation battle between the *Chicago Tribune* and Hearst newspapers, "both extremely anti-British," which led, he wrote, to the death of "five or six men and gang warfare in Chicago has continued ever since."

Pearson noted that Walter was divorced and that "the Court of St. James's frowns on divorce," but made no mention of David Bruce being divorced. Nixon's European trip included a stop in France "to patch up relations with de Gaulle," yet his ambassador-designate, Pearson wrote, had waged a crusade which included the purchase of advertising space in newspapers in Canada, London and Brussels to reprint the *Inquirer*'s anti–de Gaulle editorials. Pearson accused Walter of engineering the defeat of Senator Joe Clark, the Pennsylvania Democrat whom Walter had backed for mayor and for a first senate term. The publisher had indeed turned against Clark. The senator, as his staffers acknowledged, had developed a bad drinking problem in Washington which had impaired his effectiveness. Walter, who also opposed Clark's anti-war stance, switched the *Inquirer*'s support to Richard Schweiker, a young, liberal Republican who went on to defeat Clark. Pearson also said that Walter had "waged a vendetta" against Milton Shapp in the governor's race, hounding him with questions about being in a mental hospital and for changing his name until "the continuing vitriol poured out by the *Inquirer*" cost Shapp victory.

At the time, Pearson's column, "Washington Merry-Go-Round," appeared in 650 newspapers. A dedicated and acerbic muckraker who terrorized Washington politicians for four decades, he was the most widely read political columnist in America. He occasionally took shots at Democratic targets, but as his longtime collaborator Jack Anderson acknowledged, Pearson was a "knee-jerk liberal," a zealous New Deal propagandist for the causes he favored and a hatchetman for those he opposed.[41]

Richard Nixon and his friends fit in the latter category. In 1952, Pearson had claimed that he had Nixon's tax returns and charged that the Nixons had falsely sworn they owned property worth less than $10,000 so they could qualify for a $50 veteran's tax exemption. The outraged Nixon insisted it was not true and produced evidence showing that Pearson was citing records of another taxpayer with the same name. The columnist waited until three weeks after the election to print a retraction.[42]

Four years later, Pearson attacked Lewis Strauss, President Eisenhower's nominee to be secretary of commerce, as a puppet of big business. Not content to criticize Strauss in the column, Pearson lobbied the Senate and wrote anti-Strauss speeches for senators. "Since we [he and Pearson] were not beyond tampering with the jury and suborning witnesses," Anderson wrote, "we surely would not stop at helping to pack the prosecution."[43]

His attack on Walter was vintage Pearson, but the February 24 column was so brutal that several news executives wrote to commiserate. Mims Thomason, president of United Press International, called it "in atrocious bad taste."[44] Walter thanked him, saying that, "in the face of hate and resentment, I will continue to practice being dispassionate lest I become infected with those characteristics."[45]

Pearson, though, was not through. On Wednesday, March 5, two days before his scheduled appearance before the Senate Foreign Relations Committee, Walter and Lee arrived in the capital. The following morning, Walter began gasping for breath. Lee thought he was having a heart attack. He had just read another Pearson column in the *Washington Post* that left him clutching his chest and purple in the face. "Senators Wary on Choice of Annenberg," read the headline. Members of the committee were "loathe to tangle with a powerful newspaper publisher," Pearson wrote, particularly one who "has shown every disposition to throw the weight of his publishing empire against anyone who opposes him." The senators "know how vindictive publisher-Ambassador Annenberg can be," he wrote, and that other examples of his revenge "would scare more timid legislators green around the gills." As examples, he cited the *Inquirer* story Walter had ordered about Curtis Publishing's *Holiday* magazine and claimed that the publisher had pursued Charles de Gaulle because "the French consul snubbed Annenberg at a reception." Whether that had happened was unclear — Walter called the allegation "ridiculous" — but there had never been any question about his feelings toward the French leader. Walter had hated him from the moment he laid eyes on him in 1946.

Walter was convinced that the two Pearson columns were part of a strategy to destroy his chances of being confirmed. He was livid about the ad hominem attack and found it especially galling that it had been published by the *Washington Post*, whose success and prosperity he continued to believe he had guaranteed by persuading Colonel McCormick to sell the *Times-Herald* to Phil Graham. When Graham had killed himself in 1963, precisely a year after Roger Annenberg committed suicide, Walter and Lee tried to console his widow, Katharine, whose dignity they had admired as her husband's behavior deteriorated under the weight of his mental illness. They had her as a weekend guest at Inwood and later at Sunnylands and also respected her effort to run the *Post*. They both believed she was doing a better job than her husband. In return, Katharine Graham had liked Walter and was grateful for the kindness and sympathy he had shown her.

But when Walter caught his breath after reading Pearson, his next thought was to call and berate her for allowing the column to run. "Goddamn it, Katharine, what are you trying to do to me?" he bellowed. "This is a vile attack on me and you know it." Mrs. Graham tried to soothe him. She knew Drew could be difficult. His wife, Luvie, was one of her best friends. And she was profoundly grateful for the kindnesses that Walter had shown her, but she had had nothing to do with the column. She had not known it was going to run. The decision to print it or pull it would have been made by Ben Bradlee, her editor, whose judgment she completely trusted.

"That's not the way I run my paper," publisher Annenberg growled.

"But it is the way I run mine," publisher Graham responded.[46]

At ten minutes before 10 A.M. the next day, March 7, Walter arrived outside committee room 4221 in the New Senate Office Building. He had had a miserable night's sleep and was still angry about Pearson, his conversation with Katharine Graham and an unsatisfactory follow-up talk with Bradlee. The hearing room was crowded. The nominations of Jacob Beam, to be ambassador to the Soviet Union, and John Eisenhower, son of the former president, to be ambassador to Belgium were also scheduled for consideration, although there was no doubt they would be confirmed. Walter's was the controversial appointment. The crowd and reporters were there for him.

As is normally the case for nominees, he was introduced by his home-state senators, Hugh Scott and Richard Schweiker, the former congressman from Walter's district who had ousted Joe Clark a year earlier. Both were Republicans whom the *Inquirer* had supported. Scott, a good friend, ran through Walter's résumé, citing several awards from foreign governments which he said attested to "his interest in international affairs," and concluded that the special relationship between the United States and Britain "will be definitely advanced by this appointment." Schweiker cited his philanthropy, his community leadership and how for Walter, "the title of editor is not just an honorary designation."[47]

When the introductions ended, Senator Fulbright opened the questioning. The chairman was the only committee member who really worried Walter. He was a close friend of Joe Clark's, who had served on the Foreign Relations Committee. Walter was convinced that Clark, hating Walter for withdrawing his support in the 1968 race, had urged Fulbright to be tough. Walter had mixed feelings about Fulbright. He admired the senator's creation in 1945 — twenty years after having been a Rhodes scholar — of the Fulbright scholarship program, which sent thousands of U.S. students and teachers on exchange programs around the world. But in other areas, there were too many contradictions in the senator to allow unequivocal judgment. Fulbright was a liberal in Washington, but a conservative when home in Arkansas. He promoted worldwide amity, but had voted against civil rights legislation. He was a sponsor of the 1964 Gulf of Tonkin resolution, which authorized presidential action in Vietnam, yet he was also the foremost critic in Congress of the war.[48]

Fulbright had also had a long string of confrontations with the White House. As a young Democratic senator, Fulbright had been so distressed by the Republican landslide in the 1946 elections that he proposed that President Truman — who had no vice-president at that point — appoint Senator Arthur Vandenberg secretary of state, then resign, making Vandenberg president. Truman thereafter referred to Fulbright as "Halfbright."[49] Fulbright would clash endlessly over Vietnam with Nixon just as he had with Lyndon Johnson. One reason Nixon had selected William Rogers as secretary of state, he wrote in his memoirs, was that "I felt that the almost institutionalized enmity between Senator Fulbright's Foreign Relations Committee and the White House had become damaging to the national interest and I thought Rogers could thaw that freeze."[50]

Fulbright began by asking Walter why he wanted to be ambassador. He responded that the appointment was "about as high an honor as any citizen could be offered" and that if he were confirmed, he would do his best to measure up, and was prepared to serve at least two years. The senator touched lightly on any conflicts of interest Walter might have, his attitude about the current British government, and whether Britain should join the Common Market. Walter responded that he would relinquish editorial control of his publications, turn over his investments to a trustee and resign from directorships he held in several public companies; that he respected the government of Harold Wilson and that he favored anything that would advance alliance solidarity.

"Have you made contributions to political campaigns?" Fulbright asked.

"I have not," Walter replied.

"You have never contributed to a campaign of our president?" the senator asked again, apparently incredulous.

"I have not," Walter said again. "I believe it is unsound for an independent editor to be a financial contributor to any cause which would involve any type of special pleading." His wife, Lee, he said, had given $2,500 to the campaign.

Noting that recent articles alleged that Walter had taken "more than a casual interest in political matters," Fulbright shifted his entire line of questioning to the Pearson columns, which he ordered entered into the record.

Quoting from the February 24 column in the *Washington Post*, Fulbright read, "'Publisher Annenberg has not hesitated to mix politics with news and he, probably more than anyone else, was responsible for the recent defeat of Senator Joe Clark, Pennsylvania Democrat, who for years was Annenberg's pet hate.' Is that an accurate statement?"

"That statement is absolutely untrue," Walter replied. Clark had just thanked him a few weeks before "because I completely abstained from any adverse editorial comment in relation to him in the last campaign. That is the fact, sir."

Fulbright asked why he had opposed Shapp and whether the candidate had been questioned about having been in a mental hospital. Walter said he had no knowledge of the asylum issue, but acknowledged that he opposed Shapp "because I thought that any citizen who would spend almost all his own fortune, $4 to $5 million for the purpose of electing himself governor, would be an irresponsible individual." Shapp, Walter went on, had proposed that every Pennsylvanian should have a free college education, which would have cost the state billions of dollars. Between that recommendation and Shapp's personal spending patterns, Walter had concluded that he "would hardly be a sound individual to have any respect for the fiscal position of the Commonwealth."

When Fulbright asked about his attacks on de Gaulle, Walter admitted that he had written and reprinted anti–de Gaulle editorials. He did so out of the belief that the general was trying to destroy Western unity and had shown "the very essence of ingratitude" after "our country had expended over $8 billion to revive France, a sum far greater than that which was given to any other country."

Walter's worst — and best — moment came after Fulbright turned to the Pearson claim that the source of the Annenberg fortune was in Chicago gang warfare. "I think that should not be left unanswered," said Fulbright.

There was nothing Walter hated more in life than the gangster allegation. He had spent a quarter century denying and trying to overcome the blot on the family's record and here it was again. Millions of Americans who had never known about his father's troubles would now read about it in newspapers, yet not understand the whole story. Having expected the question, at least he could make one important point. He leaned toward his microphone and responded slowly, with every ounce of the conviction that had been driving him all those years.

"Well, that is a — that episode, of course, is a tragedy in the life of the family, and for the past thirty-odd years, I have attempted to operate, and I have actually found the tragedy a great source of inspiration for constructive endeavor, and I have sought at all times to engage in that which is wholesome.

"There is no question that a tragedy of such a magnitude will either destroy you or inspire you to overcome it, and drive you on to deeds of affirmative character."

Walter leaned back in his chair. He was exhausted from the effort. The audience was moved and applause rippled through the hearing room.

Fulbright called the response "very appropriate," but pressed on. What about the accusations of David Stern that the elder Annenberg had paid Al Capone a million dollars a year?

"Absolutely untrue," Walter replied. Stern was "distressed when he found he was not able to compete" with his father's *Inquirer*. Stern's paper folded and, "as a result of his understandable very great bitterness, Mr. Stern, having been an extremely active supporter of the then Democratic party, was able to wreak a vengeance."

There were a few more questions, including whether he was prepared to pay the extra thousands of dollars ambassadors traditionally spent out of pocket over and above the small government allowance to operate the London embassy. "I am not only prepared to do that, but I am desirous of refurbishing the embassy residence, which is in some real need of refurbishing," he replied. Then, showing a sensitivity and diplomatic touch that might have surprised his critics, Walter added, "I hastily want to add that in no sense do I want to be critical of Ambassador Bruce, who has been a tremendously effective representative of our country, but there does come a period when refurbishing is the order of the day." It was through the courtesy of the Bruces, he went on, that Mrs. Annenberg had visited with a team of decorators to assess what might be needed. "I am anxious to do that as a contribution to our government."

"I didn't realize Ambassador Bruce would allow the embassy to deteriorate," Fulbright interjected.

"I don't want to say that," Walter replied. "I want to correct any impression that I may be giving. But as you know, furnishings have a way of deteriorating."

The questions from the rest of the panel were congenial. When Missouri senator Stuart Symington, a candidate for the Democratic party's presidential nomination in 1960, stated how impressed he was "with the high plane on which you have answered these questions," Walter thanked him and settled back in his chair. He could feel sweat in the small of his back, but he knew then that he had made it. He was going to be ambassador. When the hearing ended and congratulations were offered, he was eager to go home, but he was committed to attending a dinner in his honor hosted by none other than Katharine Graham. He did not want to go after the previous day's telephone fight. Lee convinced him that was precisely why they must attend. It was for them, had been set up for weeks and regretting that late would be unconscionably rude.

They went, Walter grumpily and Lee hoping to set things right. Walter was pleased at the turnout of some fifty politicians and leading Washingtonians as well as a number of friends from Philadelphia. Syndicated columnist Rowland Evans was talking to Paul Ignatius when Walter came over during cocktails. Evans, whose column ran in the *Inquirer*, congratulated him and said there had been a lot of talk about other jobs for him.

"Really, what other jobs?" Walter asked.

"I heard you were going to be secretary of the navy," Evans replied.

Walter looked surprised and drew himself up a bit. "What, me an errand boy?" he snorted.

Evans then introduced him to Ignatius, who was then secretary of the navy. Walter recovered with aplomb and the three men laughed good-naturedly.[51]

Soon after, the event began to sour when he spotted Ben Bradlee and the Bruces, who had flown in from London that day and had been a last-minute addition to the dinner. Any hope the evening might be salvaged sank irretrievably a few minutes later. Walter, who even before his ambassadorship was a stickler for protocol, found himself seated not at Mrs. Graham's right, the proper place for the guest of honor, but across the table and between Evangeline Bruce and Lorraine Cooper, wife of Kentucky senator John Sherman Cooper.

Walter had not met Evangeline, but he knew how she had tried to humiliate Lee and was undercutting him at every opportunity. When he tried to engage Mrs. Cooper in conversation, she snootily asked if he could afford to take over the London embassy. It took every ounce of Walter's self-control to restrain his rage and he and Lee left at the earliest moment. That was it for Katharine Graham. She was out of his life, although he remained so angry that he considered commissioning an article or book about Phil Graham and his mental illness, a bad idea which he recognized and dropped.

Mrs. Graham regretted the denouement. She had no second thoughts about the Pearson columns, but had she to do the dinner over again, aware that Evangeline and Mrs. Cooper were amusing themselves at Walter's expense, she would have handled the seating differently. She had had no idea that Walter was so thin-skinned. Simply childish, was her verdict, prone to tantrums and so insistent on having his own way.

The party had been a disagreeable climax to a bittersweet day. But the sting of the insults he had felt was eased a week later when the Senate voted to confirm him by a vote of ninety-nine to one. Fulbright was the lone holdout.

23

ROUGH START

———

WHEN WALTER WAS SWORN IN at the State Department on April 14, 1969, by chief of protocol Emil Mosbacher, with Lee holding the Bible and his sisters and Secretary of State William Rogers looking on, America's newest and least experienced diplomat was a happy and grateful man. "I am extremely proud of this appointment," he declared. He had every right to be. He had come a long way from the dark days when he sat in Judge Wilkerson's courtroom in abject humiliation and terror. For decades the Annenberg name had been tainted by the real and perceived sins of his father. And now, here was the son, affirmed by the president and confirmed by the Congress as a worthy national envoy.

To Walter, it meant that he had been recognized by the highest authorities in the land as an honorable citizen. That was a breakthrough realization. Yet years would pass before the full significance of the appointment became clear: that it was a transforming experience for Walter personally. He had launched magazines which sold billions and earned millions, introduced revolutionary television programming and put his stamp on one of America's biggest metropolitan dailies, but it was this appointment that would make Walter his own man. "The most important development in my life," he called the psychological turbocharger given him by Nixon. No longer just his father's son — "Moe's Boy Walter at the Court of St. James's" was how *Fortune* headlined a feature on his posting — he was about to emerge from Moses's overwhelming shadow.

None of this was apparent at the ceremony. There he was properly modest about his shortcomings to occupy the post held by fellow

Philadelphian Benjamin Franklin, who had represented the American colonies in England, and the five earlier envoys to Britain who had become president.[1] "I do not have a record of performance as a diplomat; therefore I have a record to develop and it is my hope that it will be regarded as affirmative," he told the gathering in the Thomas Jefferson room. "Quite possibly there will be periods when I shall have to remind myself that I no longer have an editorial page in which to affirm, denounce or advocate, but the discipline of remembering that I represent the president will be wholesome and respected."

He told the guests that he was leaving four days later on the eighteenth. "An historic day," according to an old Peddie schoolmate who had called to wish him good luck. "Yes, I may on occasion be on the fringes of history," Walter replied. "Please," said the caller. "I was referring to the anniversary of Paul Revere's ride." Walter chuckled telling the story on himself.

With the remarks complete, the guests moved to a reception in the adjacent John Quincy Adams state drawing room, where Walter fell into discussion with Clement Conger, the White House and State Department curator who had supervised the room's recent restoration. After praising Conger for the fine eighteenth-century furnishings and paintings he had collected from donors, Walter critiqued the Jefferson room they had just left. "That's the most God-awful place I've seen. You've got French and American, eighteenth and twentieth century. Everything's incongruous. You must fix it." Conger, far too skillful a fund-raiser to miss such an opening, pounced. "We hope to change it," he replied, "but first we have to raise the money." Walter pledged $250,000 on the spot. By honoring him, and thus restoring the Annenberg name, his country had done all that he could have ever asked. With John Kennedy's admonition in mind, he was starting to think more about what he could do for his country.

The night before the Annenbergs' departure for London, Lieutenant General Milton Baker, commandant of Valley Forge Military Academy and a friend, arrived at Inwood with six busloads of spit-and-polish cadets. In sashes and plumes, the honor guard played patriotic anthems as they marched back and forth in review across the estate's manicured lawn under the delighted eye of the new ambassador. The next morning, police commissioner Frank Rizzo saw the Annenbergs off at the Philadelphia airport.

After the shoals of Washington, the departure was a triumph for the Annenbergs. They were excited to be off on a grand new adventure to what Walter considered the motherland. He told friends, "I love Britain, everything about it" — language, landscape, traditions, pageantry, bespoke tailoring. Not only did Philadelphia and the Main Line feel a common bond with Britain, but Walter had nurtured a special feeling about England since touring as a teenager with his parents. He had returned in his twenties with his cousin Stanley Rose and on his honeymoon with Lee. On this flight, he spent some time reviewing his arrival remarks — "to do whatever I can to contribute to the relationship of trust and confidence which unites us will be my major objective" — then reminisced to himself about the earlier trips and a 1949 stag dinner in New York at Sherry's on Park Avenue. That evening, when he was the guest of financier Bernard Baruch, an awed Walter had found himself seated next to Winston Churchill.

"About one in the morning, after endless wines and beakers of brandy, I turned to Churchill and said, 'Sir, I hope you don't think me presumptuous, but I must tell you how saddened I was at the electorate in your country rejecting you as they did after you had saved their empire and their way of life.' The wartime leader had looked at Walter for about ten seconds, then put his hand on his shoulder, and said, 'Young Annenberg, look not for reward from others — but hope that you have done your best.'" Churchill spoke a few more moments then again fixed his gaze on him. "Annenberg, I am going to give you my autographed picture upon my departure. Don't tell anyone until I am out of the country because I don't readily hand out my autograph.'"[2]

As Lee dozed and he stared out the window of the airplane, Walter recalled Churchill's remark. He had had the words inscribed under the autographed portrait, which he considered one of his most prized possessions. The icon was in his luggage, ready for display in his London office, where it would inspire him throughout his posting.

Every bit of inspiration was required because, as upbeat as his departure had been, his early days in London were fraught with difficulty. Walter's trouble did not come from the mainstream British press, which for the most part treated the appointment more kindly than had American newspapers. "Ambassadors Don't Often Come As Colourful As This," headlined the *Daily Mail*. "Mr. Nixon has done us proud," said the front-page story. "We are [getting] an American ambassador who owns the country's top racing sheet, has a private army, a private golf course and seven sisters who are all multi-millionairesses. That refutes those people who say Richard Nixon has a flair for being dull."[3] The *Daily Express* wrote a story headlined "Lively Lee About to Put

New Zip in the American Embassy," and called her "one of Philadelphia's finest hostesses."[4]

Yet there was criticism that the president had not replaced Bruce with someone more Bruce-like, although the reaction was less than that which had greeted Franklin Roosevelt's designation of Joseph Kennedy as the first Irish-American ambassador in 1937. The sharpest barbs came from the *New Statesman*, a left-leaning weekly. "If President Nixon had a sense of humor, he might have conceived of the designation of Walter Annenberg to be ambassador in London as a monstrous impractical joke. . . . One can only conclude that the Annenberg appointment is either an expression of despair about America or contempt towards Britain." The opinion journal described Walter as America's "ranking press lord," a man who was "part corporatist, part philanthropist, part political manipulator . . . a complex, self-protective, somewhat desperate character, not unworthy of some admiration for his tycoonery and some sympathy for his hangups," whose qualifications to be ambassador "are few, in fact not more than two: a loud editorial mouth and a great deal of money." It wondered whether the appointment had been a matter of tit for tat. "After all, the British had the bad taste to appoint a sophisticated leftist journalist to their Washington embassy; why not retaliate with an impulsive right-wing publisher?"[5]

The sophisticated leftist journalist serving as Britain's ambassador to the United States was John Freeman, the *New Statesman*'s former editor. Labour prime minister Harold Wilson had misjudged the coming U.S. elections and had appointed Freeman ambassador in the spring of 1968, anticipating that Freeman's old friend Hubert Humphrey would win the presidency in November. Freeman had been a left-wing Labour minister, then editor of the *New Statesman* and high commissioner to India before moving to Washington. As editor he had written that Nixon's record "suggests a man of no principle whatsoever" and that he had "done lasting damage to the conventions of American political life."[6] When Nixon won seven months after Freeman took up his post, Wilson was embarrassed. "With hindsight, one can look on his appointment as a mistake," said then foreign minister George Brown.[7] Wilson's refusal to replace Freeman looked like a bigger mistake.

Nixon was outraged, considered the appointment an insult to the presidency as well as to himself and swore that he would have nothing to do with Freeman, who was busy attempting to make amends. Nixon "has proved by his success," said Freeman immediately after the 1968 election, "and the quite admirable struggle which he has made to achieve it, that he has the qualities of leadership that make him worthy of high office."[8]

The revisionism appeared inadequate and the ambassador's tenure looked doomed. When the president visited London in February 1969, the White House requested that Freeman be removed from the guest list for a dinner at 10 Downing Street. Prime Minister Wilson refused. At the end of a tense meal, it was Nixon's turn to surprise. Standing to propose a toast, he looked at Freeman and said, "Some say there's a new Nixon. And they wonder if there's a new Freeman. I would like to think that that's all behind us. After all, he's the new diplomat and I'm the new statesman, trying to do our best in the world."

"The impact was electric," wrote Henry Kissinger, the president's national security adviser. "Wilson called the toast the most gracious he had heard. . . . The usually imperturbable Freeman was close to tears. Thus was born a mission to Washington that proved a spectacular success. John Freeman was one of the most effective ambassadors I ever dealt with."[9]

Kissinger saw a host of strengths in the Briton. "Freeman eschewed all flattery; he met socially only with those he respected; he made little effort to turn his embassy into a fashionable salon . . . he was a man of superb intelligence and utter integrity. . . . He had a shrewd geopolitical mind and rather shared our philosophy of foreign relations. I thought so highly of Freeman's judgment that I frequently consulted him on matters outside his official purview; on one or two occasions, I let him read early drafts of presidential speeches, tapping his talents as an editor."

Nixon came to so like and trust Freeman that he was the only ambassador invited to the White House socially during Nixon's first term. Kissinger came to consider him "one of my closest friends" and their relationship "one of the greatest rewards of my public service."[10]

All of which ordained that whatever substantive business was to take place between Nixon's White House and Wilson's Downing Street would either be handled directly by the principals or through Freeman in Washington. As ambassador in London, Walter would represent the United States, but would have virtually no policy role. That was fine with everyone, including Walter. "He'd be the first to say he wasn't the policymaker or discusser," said Arthur Hartman, former ambassador to France and the Soviet Union, who was an assistant secretary of state at the time.[11]

Lee Rosenstiel (right) was at a Boca Raton party with her best friend, Harriet Simon, in 1950 when she and Walter met and danced through dinner. He was separated and she was married; but, as Harriet said, "Everyone could see something was happening." (ANNENBERG FAMILY COLLECTION)

After a year's separation and her tumultuous divorce, Lee and Walter were married in September 1951 at Sadie Annenberg's apartment in New York by the headmaster of the Peddie School. (ANNENBERG FAMILY COLLECTION)

Roger (left) and Wallis (right) lived with their mother in Washington, D.C., in the early 1950s but often visited Inwood and Lee's daughters, Diane (center) and Elizabeth (below Lee).
(ANNENBERG FAMILY COLLECTION)

Walter and the Annenberg ladies in all their 1956 glory. Some were difficult, others gracious; all were formidable. From left: sisters Lita, Jan, Polly, Esther, mother Sadie, Lee, sisters Evelyn, Harriet and Enid.
(ANNENBERG FAMILY COLLECTION)

Conventional wisdom had Walter primarily influenced by his father, Moses, but he was even closer to his mother, Sadie. He sometimes addressed her as "Dearest Celestial." (ANNENBERG FAMILY COLLECTION)

Invariably warm and generous, Sadie was the spark for the family's great philanthropy. When financier Bernard Baruch gave her an award as an "outstanding friend of the underprivileged," fifteen hundred people attended the dinner at New York's Waldorf-Astoria hotel.

(ANNENBERG FAMILY COLLECTION)

Seventeen was Walter's first publishing creation, launched in 1944 when he saw that teenage girls had no magazines and that wartime paper quotas were forcing *Vogue* and *Harper's Bazaar* to turn away advertisers. (ANNENBERG FAMILY COLLECTION)

Enid, his closest sister in age and temperament, became *Seventeen*'s most influential editor and publisher. Tough, elegant and with a keen understanding of her audience, she was a stickler for tastefulness and moved the magazine from stories about clothes and kissing to articles about menstruation, drugs and teen marriage. (UPI/CORBIS-BETTMANN)

Walter's only son, Roger, endured multiple operations for a cleft lip as a child and battled schizophrenia as a teen, but was an academic star at Episcopal preparatory school and in 1958 won early admission to Harvard. (ANNENBERG FAMILY COLLECTION)

Lonely in Washington, D.C., after Roger moved back to Philadelphia, Wallis had identity problems at the National Cathedral School but loved Pine Manor Junior College in Massachusetts and graduated with honors. (ANNENBERG FAMILY COLLECTION)

Often considered a dyed-in-the-wool Republican, Walter had high regard for President Harry Truman, and the *Inquirer*'s support for Philadelphia's Democratic mayor Joseph Clark (left) helped oust a GOP machine that had controlled City Hall since 1884.

Walter slept overnight in his office at the *Inquirer* to be on time to meet President Lyndon Johnson and Lady Bird, who came to Philadelphia a week before Johnson's 1964 landslide election to thank the publisher for his support. (AP/WIDE WORLD)

Sadie introduced Lee and Walter to Pat and Richard Nixon, who became close friends and stayed with them in Pennsylvania and California.
(ANNENBERG FAMILY COLLECTION)

Walter gave strong editorial support but no money to Richard Nixon's 1968 presidential campaign. When Nixon won, he nominated Walter to be ambassador to Britain and thus honored the once-disgraced family name.
(OFFICIAL WHITE HOUSE PHOTO)

Walter's April 1969 confirmation hearings, chaired by J. William Fulbright, a strong Nixon critic, were contentious and focused on Moses's racing wire and tax history and Walter's lack of diplomatic experience. Here, anticipating what is to come, he is being introduced by Senator Richard Schweiker of Pennsylvania. (UPI/CORBIS-BETTMANN)

Walter would become the only U.S. envoy knighted by the queen, but when he presented his credentials, he briefly became a laughingstock for his stilted comment that he was living in the embassy subject to "discomfiture as a result of a need for elements of refurbishment."
(ANNENBERG FAMILY COLLECTION)

A gift to the United States from Woolworth heiress Barbara Hutton, Winfield House has housed American ambassadors to Britain since 1954. When the Annenbergs succeeded the Bruces in 1969, the thirty-five-room mansion in Regents Park was cosmetically decrepit. (COURTESY OF DERRY MOORE)

Walter paid $5 million in current dollars from his own pocket, but it was Lee's supervision and exquisite taste that made the renovation of Winfield House such a success and helped to transform public perceptions of the Annenbergs. (PHOTOGRAPH BY CECIL BEATON)

While Winfield House was being restored, Lee and Walter loaned thirty-two Impressionist paintings to London's Tate Gallery, including Renoir's *The Daughters of Catulle Mendès*. Walter paid all expenses for the exhibit, which drew 100,000 visitors and widespread praise for the collection's quality and the Annenbergs' generosity. By 1991, when it was bequeathed to New York's Metropolitan Museum, the collection had grown to fifty-three paintings valued at $1 billion. (ANNENBERG FAMILY COLLECTION)

The Annenbergs loved the Nixons' younger daughter, Julie, but Tricia was another matter. Fascinated by Prince Charles, she was peeved when he failed to attend a 1969 party the Annenbergs hosted for her in London. Walter tried to comfort the woman he had known since her childhood by putting an arm around her shoulder. She called the White House and absurdly accused him of being "overfamiliar." (UPI/CORBIS-BETTMANN)

Raised in California, Lee had legions of friends in the West with whom she and Walter socialized. Walter, though, was basically a loner whose best friend by far was Lee. Some of their happiest times were playing golf alone together on the Sunnylands private course. (ANNENBERG FAMILY COLLECTION)

As chief of protocol, Lee smiles here with former presidents Carter, Nixon and Ford en route to the 1981 funeral of assassinated Egyptian president Anwar Sadat, but she was furious at the White House handling of the trip, which marked the beginning of the end of her abbreviated service. (AP/WIDE WORLD)

When Queen Elizabeth and Prince Philip visited California in 1983, they
paid a rare visit to a private residence—Sunnylands. Walter joked that he
wanted the royals to see "how the average American family lived."
(AP/WIDE WORLD)

Richard Nixon gave him his greatest honor, but Walter was closer to
Ronald Reagan, whom he had known since the 1930s. Both held
strong, uncomplicated core beliefs, chief among them that America
was a great land of opportunity for decent people who worked hard.
(ANNENBERG FAMILY COLLECTION)

Built beginning in 1963 on 240 acres of raw desert near Palm Springs, California, Sunnylands was surrounded by its own golf course, housed the Annenberg art collection, hosted five U.S. presidents and was so luxurious that Prince Charles quipped, "You gave up *this* to move to London?"
(AL SCOTT/WESTERN RESORT PUBLICATIONS)

With much in common except personality, Lee and Nancy Reagan have been friends for decades. In the early 1970s, the Annenbergs introduced Nancy to Prince Charles, who invited the First Lady (and the Annenbergs) to his 1981 wedding to Diana Spencer. Walter, who loves her husband, feels different about Nancy. (ANNENBERG FAMILY COLLECTION)

Wallis Annenberg was Walter's sole surviving child after her brother Roger's 1962 suicide. She had four children, including her youngest, Charles (right), and the eldest, Lauren, shown with her two children, Dorian (top) and Maya. Following her divorce in 1975, she worked for *TV Guide* and became a philanthropist in her own right. (COURTESY OF WALLIS ANNENBERG)

Scholar and educator Vartan Gregorian advised Walter on his philanthropy to schools and universities. The former president of the New York Public Library and Brown University, Gregorian, now president of the Carnegie Corporation in New York, shares Walter's passion for using modern technology to spread knowledge. (COURTESY OF VARTAN GREGORIAN)

In 1990, with President George Bush looking on, United Negro College Fund president Christopher Edley thanks Walter for his $50 million challenge grant to the umbrella organization that supports forty-one private historically black colleges. (AP/BARRY THUNMA)

Decrying violence in schools and convinced that improving education was
the next great national security challenge, Walter announces his 1993 gift of
$500 million to improve U.S. public schools. President Bill Clinton and edu-
cation secretary Richard Riley were as astonished as most Americans by the
extent of his generosity. (AP/WIDE WORLD)

Walter was too pragmatic to mind. He understood that Nixon and Kissinger were probably the most sophisticated foreign policy duo since Thomas Jefferson advised George Washington. They had little need of his unschooled analysis. As a successful executive, Walter also knew that his embassy staff was there to handle the details of substantive issues.

When Kissinger traveled to London he routinely ignored Walter, who would meet him at Heathrow, then watch the security adviser drive away to Downing Street without him. Walter was not the only ambassador Kissinger treated that way. The White House aide once visited Moscow for five days without informing ambassador Jacob Beam, an experienced career diplomat, of his presence until he was leaving for the airport. In London, the foreign office would receive telegrams from Freeman saying, "I had a long talk with Kissinger today and he wanted me to be sure none of this reached the American embassy in Britain. . . ."[12] Although Walter did not aspire to a policy role, such affronts were humiliating. British officials acknowledged that Bruce would not have been so ignored. (Then a bachelor, Kissinger also dodged the Annenbergs in his off-duty hours, staying at Claridges Hotel and spending time with the estranged wife of a British cabinet member.)

"Annenberg never really figured in anything," said William Hyland, Kissinger's deputy on the national security council staff. "It wasn't that he was cut out of anything that dramatic. But there wasn't that much going on with London. The first-rate issues were Vietnam, the Paris peace negotiations, the Russians and Chinese. Nixon and Kissinger wanted to keep those to themselves."[13] Often most of the State Department and Secretary of State William Rogers were also frozen out.

At the outset, there were questions about whether Walter could handle even the ceremonial diplomatic responsibilities. Because of his stutter, he was uncomfortable speaking publicly. Before arriving he had written to David Bruce, as Bruce had noted in his diary, that "he had no desire to make speeches unless it were absolutely necessary."[14] Some, of course, were. His first address as ambassador, on May 28 at the Savoy Hotel, set eyebrows arching. The Pilgrims, a society founded in 1902 to foster Anglo-American relations, had a distinguished membership of government officials, executives and diplomats from both countries. The American ambassador traditionally made his maiden and departure speeches at a Pilgrims dinner, usually emphasizing the strength of the bilateral relationship. Walter promptly abandoned tradition.

At his swearing-in he had said that he would have to remind himself that he no longer had an editorial page, but six weeks later at this dinner his judgment failed. The black-tie audience listened in amazement as Walter bitterly castigated the anti-war demonstrators in the United States, a subject of deep political divisiveness in his own country.

He began what turned into a searing analysis of "academic sickness" in America by noting that the U.S. and Britain shared a respect for the rule of law but that "we find the ideals of freedom and justice threatened by unrest, disorder and turmoil in our colleges and universities." The Berkeley campus of the University of California "has been crippled by revolution." There had also been turbulence at Harvard, Cornell and Swarthmore, the last a small college near Philadelphia which had been shut down by protests during which its "sensitive and brilliant" president, Courtney Smith, a personal friend of Walter's, died of a heart attack as "a direct result" of the disorders. "In almost every case," he said, "the students who caused and participated in the upheavals asked for and were granted amnesty for their actions. They were permitted, for one reason or another, to break the law, participate in the destruction of their institutions without having to face the consequences." It was time "to call an end to giving in to students, an end to making decisions out of expediency, an end to appeasement."[15]

Philip Kaiser was the embassy's deputy chief of mission, Annenberg's second in command. An adviser to three Democratic presidents and an ambassador in Africa before becoming Bruce's deputy, Kaiser had been a Rhodes scholar at Oxford. He knew most of Wilson's cabinet and senior officials in the opposition Conservative party by their first names. "I told him not to make the Pilgrims speech, which was badly received," said Kaiser who was inundated with questions from his British friends about the new ambassador. Liberal Democrat Kaiser considered his new boss a conservative Republican. The press considered the speech bizarre. "A surprising public debut," said the *Daily Telegraph*.[16] The *Sunday Telegraph*, pro-American and staunchly conservative itself, called the speech "inept" and said it demonstrated "all the right-of-the-line prejudices of the rich American."[17]

"Walter didn't want to do a puff-ball, so he didn't do one," said Robert Montgomery Scott. The forty-year-old son of Hope and Edgar Scott, Main Line patricians and great friends of Lee and Walter's,

"Bobby" Scott was a socially acceptable, charming lawyer whom Walter had the State Department hire as his executive assistant, in no small part because of his blue-blood connections. He functioned as Walter's liaison to the staff, de facto social secretary, speechwriter and general jack-of-all-trades. Scott performed very well in every category except for the Pilgrims speech, which he wrote at Walter's direction.

"Not one's best offering, I'm afraid," Scott sighed. "Timely, but not exactly what you do at the Pilgrims."[18] It was received better at the White House. Walter sent the president a copy with a note conceding that "quite possibly the theme I got into about collegiate disorder might be a bit strong."[19] Not at all, Nixon wrote back. He thanked Walter and called the remarks "right on target."[20]

FOUR WEEKS after the Pilgrims speech, the British Broadcasting Corporation televised "The Royal Family," a historic, behind-the-scenes documentary they had been filming and editing for a year. There had been national debate over every aspect of the 105-minute program, including whether there should be one at all, but Queen Elizabeth had accepted her advisers' proposition that a modern monarchy should be seen as less distant. She had allowed the filmmakers unprecedented access to some of her family's daily activities. "We particularly wanted a scene of the queen receiving the credentials of an ambassador, so naturally we waited for the United States ambassador," said Martin Charteris, then the queen's long-serving private secretary.[21]

Walter had actually presented his credentials on April 29, six weeks before the broadcast, in a ceremony that he and Lee had agreed, in her words, "will forever remain the highlight of our lives." They had practiced for days in advance, entering and leaving the room as they would be expected to when they met the queen; Lee perfecting her curtsy, Walter rehearsing his lines. On the appointed morning, the ambassador dressed in white tie, morning coat, silk top hat and medals — his French Legion of Honor medal for fund-raising philanthropy to resistance groups during World War II and decorations from Finland and Italy for supporting their newsprint industries. As four hundred onlookers cheered, the nervous and exhilarated ambassador climbed into one of four gilded state coaches with red-liveried drivers and grooms. The procession left Grosvenor Square and wound a mile through Mayfair to Buckingham Palace, arriving in time for the noon changing of the guard, for which thousands of tourists had gathered. Lee, wearing a champagne-colored suit and riding behind in the embassy limousine, could barely control her excitement. "This procession was the most incredible, most exciting, most thrilling — there aren't enough adjectives to describe it," she wrote in a memorandum later that day.

Met by an equerry, Walter was led up the red-carpeted staircase to the Bow Room, an enormous red-damask-and-gold reception room, where he was given last-minute instructions by a protocol officer: "When the door opens we all take a pace forward with our left foot."

"With our left foot," Walter echoed.

Then the huge mahogany doors opened and in the center of the room stood the queen, wearing a royal blue crepe dress and carrying a black handbag. Flanked by the marshal of the diplomatic corps and the comptroller to the lord chamberlain, Walter took one step forward on the left foot and bowed. Then another step forward on the left foot and bowed. He walked ten more steps toward the queen, who extended her hand. He bowed a third time and formally presented his credentials smoothly with his practiced line: "Your Majesty, I have the honor to present the letter of recall of my predecessor and my own letters of credence."

The queen smiled and said, "Thank you very much, indeed." Then, as the BBC cameras rolled, she began a few minutes of pleasantries. "You aren't living at the embassy at the moment, are you?" she asked.

Walter hesitated for a beat, then in a sepulchral tone replied, "We're in the embassy residence, subject, of course, to some of the discomfiture as a result of a need for, uh, elements of refurbishment and rehabilitation."

The queen cocked her head slightly and looked bemused as she absorbed the polysyllabic response. Apparently uncertain whether he was discomfited, she asked him to present his counselors. Then, moments later, the doors opened again and Lee entered, curtsying, walking, curtsying. Lee was introduced and the two of them chatted with the queen for several minutes before they withdrew and returned to the embassy, as Lee put it, "stimulated, excited and overwhelmed."

It had been a marvelous day. But when the documentary aired six weeks later on twenty-five million British television screens — and ultimately to an overseas audience estimated at four hundred million viewers — Walter's reply to the queen sounded like Peter Sellers playing Inspector Clouseau. The reaction in Britain, and the United States, which quickly heard of the incident, was one long guffaw. "Flustered Envoy Becomes Minor Celebrity," read the *Sunday Times* headline. Newspapers reprinted the phrase and held contests challenging readers to construct a more stilted sentence. In a nation where members of Parliament joust memorably without scripts and linguistic agility is a prerequisite of social grace, the ambassador with the "verbal felicity of W. C. Fields," as a British magazine put it, looked like a made-to-order target.

He was for a while the laughingstock of London. There had already been a flap about his threat to remove the ugly sculptured eagle mounted on the embassy building. Walter had defused that one by declaring that "as long as the eagle does not bother me, I will not bother it." Another mini-contretemps involved his offhand remark that Winfield House lacked finger bowls, which the press escalated into an assault by the new ambassador on the Bruces for maintaining an inferior residence. And many Britons, including intellectuals predisposed to mock a rich American, found terribly amusing Walter's habit of addressing Lee as "Motherrr."

But nothing compared with the presentation of his credentials, which no one would have heard about had the BBC not been filming. "There was hysteria on Fleet Street about this genuine American folk baroque," said Thomas Hughes, who would succeed Kaiser as Walter's deputy. "People were calling it the greatest sentence since Beowulf."[22]

"'Elements of refurbishment' was considered an extremely good joke here," said Peter Carrington, one of the Conservative party's most respected officials, who quoted the phrase without hesitation three decades after Walter first uttered it. "So it was a difficult start for him."[23]

WALTER WAS so embarrassed by the reaction that he called Secretary of State Rogers and, while stopping short of offering to resign, told him that if he or the president considered him a liability, he would leave. (Bill Paley of CBS saw Walter's difficulties as a second chance to win the London post. While attending an affiliates' meeting in California that July, CBS president Frank Stanton was told that Paley had been tapped to replace Annenberg and that he should return to New York and prepare to assume Paley's CEO position. When he arrived back, Stanton said, "Zilch happened. The offer was gone."[24] Hearing Kissinger belittle Annenberg, White House aides had expected that the ambassador would be withdrawn. Nixon, though, understood adversity and had no intention of replacing his friend.) Rogers told Walter not to worry, but to hang in and his situation would surely improve.[25]

Relieved, Walter lowered his profile by refusing to speak to the press for three months. "He wasn't hostile," said Ray Scherer, then London correspondent for the National Broadcasting Corporation, "but he was gun-shy and wary."[26] When he gave his first interview, he was unapologetic about his choice of words. "I could hardly be expected to respond to Her Majesty as if I were attending a barbecue," he told the *Daily Express*. "I chose my words carefully. They meant what I meant to convey."

But he did not explain his lifelong history of stuttering, the speech therapy he had undergone for years and that he always chose every word with particular care. To minimize his stammer, he tried to frame entire sentences before opening his mouth. The result was often circumlocution as phrases poured from his mouth complete with whereases and heretofores. In the presence of the queen he had been determined not to stumble over his words. Sounding stilted in front of the monarch, who had heard all sorts of high-flown utterances, was preferable to embarrassing them both by stuttering.

He often used odd and grandiloquent words. "He'd never use a simple word if he had a complicated word," said deputy Hughes. (In a conversation once with Churchill's grandson Nicholas Soames, Walter remarked, "I had the honor of meeting your mother last week, Mr. Soames, and she is a rose plucked from the herbaceous border of British motherhood." The startled Soames replied, "Yes, she is rather . . . isn't she?")

Walter did not consider long or rarely used words pompous; to him, they were usually more precise. He knew such words because he studied vocabulary as well as elocution twice a day as part of his speech therapy. Precise words tended to sound more formal, and while Walter had a highly developed sense of humor and fun, he considered precision a reflection of character and respect. Formality was a mark of separation from the masses, and thus even more appropriate for use with the queen.

As for "refurbish," not then a word often used in England, he had used it several times during his Senate confirmation hearing. Senator Karl Mundt, uncertain that he had heard the nominee correctly, asked whether Walter had said that he intended to "refurnish" or "refurbish" Winfield House at his own expense. "Refurbish," Walter had specified, "which would also include a certain amount of addition in the way of furnishings."

In explaining what had inspired his response, Walter was forthright. "You must remember, I had never met Her Majesty before. I had never been inside the environment of Buckingham and you must realize the impact of a thousand years of history. You must remember that along with that I'm an inexperienced diplomat. I'm basically a businessman. So if you merge all that together, with white tie and tails and your letters of credence, and your predecessor's recall, what could have had a greater impact on somebody, a neophyte in the arena? I'd never in my life experienced anything like it. I responded in formal terms to a formal occasion. Was I so wrong? I don't reckon so."

He tried to shrug off the criticism by attributing it to envy. "Mine is like the case of the injured pullet in the poultry farm. All the other chickens pick on it. Why has this been?" he asked. "Mind you, I realize there is no small amount of resentment and jealousy of one in my position. Envy inevitably pursues the fortunate and meritorious. Whereas I may not belong to the latter category, I certainly do belong to the former. Fortune has been more than usually beneficent to Walter H. Annenberg."[27]

BUT HE AND LEE were frustrated. What had been briefly amusing had soured into a tedious ongoing humiliation. The perfectionist Lee, who was overseeing the Winfield House renovation as well as trying to carry out all the duties of a prominent ambassador's wife, was under a terrible added strain. On June 14, while at the opera at Glyndebourne with Walter, she was summoned to take a call from her son-in-law Howard Deshong in Rochester, Minnesota. He was crying. Diane, her twenty-seven-year-old daughter, had collapsed and had been rushed to the Mayo Clinic, where a tumor had been discovered in her spinal cord. The doctors were not sure whether she would survive. Lee raced in her evening dress to Heathrow, where a New York–bound plane was held. An embassy driver delivered her Christian Science reading material to the airport. Diane was operated on, underwent radiation treatment and recovered, although three decades later she still wore a neck brace. Lee returned to London emotionally drained. Yet the criticism lingered and left her as exasperated as Walter. "I think my husband carried off a difficult situation extremely well. And yet this remark keeps haunting us. It's so unfair."[28]

Britons began to agree. "A lot of people thought the BBC film was a dirty trick," said Carrington. "So there was this sympathy vote and in a remarkably short space of time, opinion turned around."[29] Letters of support began arriving at the embassy. "These churlish comments in the press do not in fact reflect the views of most of the 'natives' such as myself," Londoner H. H. Williams wrote that July. "May I urge you and your lady not to take any future boorishness too seriously."[30] Thomas Williams wrote that "my wife and I saw the film of the incident and thought it a splendid example of what the English language should sound like."[31] Walter acknowledged every letter with heartfelt thanks. He was surprised at how welcome a boost they gave him and Lee.

The attitude of the royal family also helped. "When we reviewed the film before it was finished, the great refurbishment thing was rather laughable and we debated whether to include it," said Charteris. "We allowed it to remain, but we should not have. As a result, I think the royal family felt a certain sense of guilt about Walter because they allowed a joke to be made about him. In fact, he was honorable and straightforward and Lee was such a splendid character that before very long, he was the most admired ambassador at the Court of St. James's."[32]

THERE WAS a turnaround, but it seemed to Walter and Lee to take far longer for the merciless criticism to subside than the brief interlude suggested by Charteris and Carrington. Some censure was beyond Walter's control and stemmed from antipathy among American and British intellectuals and press to Nixon and his Vietnam policy, which his ambassador was known to support. Contrary to some expectations, the new president's conduct of the war seemed just as aggressive as Lyndon Johnson's futile escalations. Rather than the "peace with honor" that Nixon had pledged, the war seemed headed into an ugly new phase. The greater target Nixon became, the more Walter floundered in the backwash. "President Nixon seems to be developing a weakness for the avoidable blunder," columnist James Reston wrote on June 29 in the *New York Times*. "Not satisfied with the agonies of unavoidable problems, he somehow manages to depart periodically from his normal caution and not only creates but plans unnecessary trouble. He didn't have to appoint Walter Annenberg, of all people, to London, of all places."[33]

Within certain circles of the London diplomatic community, Walter was also subjected to a battering. The *Diplomatist*, a monthly journal published in London and devoted to the corps of foreign envoys, claimed that when he presented his credentials, Walter had brought along his daughter, Wallis, a breach of royal etiquette. The breach was the magazine's. Wallis had been at the embassy but had not gone to the palace.

The *Diplomatist* also complained that Walter was "persona incognita," a nonentity in the corps. "Amongst the leading members of the diplomatic corps in London, there were many who complained about a certain aloofness in His Excellency's predecessor, the Hon. David K. Bruce. This aloofness, they said, was more than compensated by that ambassador's experience and personal charm. The diplomats who complained were looking forward to appreciating the new ambassador's bluff and unpompous attitude. They have been deeply disappointed so far. He has been even more unobtainable than his predecessor," the magazine claimed. "He has failed to attend a great many social functions where he could have been expected to come and so far has refused to mix with the bulk of the diplomatic corps in the same friendly, open and winning way as his opposite number from the other super-power, the Soviet ambassador, Mr. M. Smirnovsky."[34]

To be compared unfavorably with the Soviet ambassador was about as harsh an insult as could have been leveled at Walter. But again, the magazine was wrong. Walter had been meticulous about making every diplomatic call, more than forty in his first three months. He and Lee made every ceremonial function, from trooping the color, which marked the Queen's birthday, to the endless skein of "national day" embassy celebrations.

The *Diplomatist*'s criticism was also off the mark. American ambassadors in major capitals socialize less with other envoys than they do with their host nation contacts. That, after all, is the reason they are there. However high and mighty it may sound, the fact is their social plate is inevitably fuller because they represent the United States, a fact which has been known to antagonize representatives from less influential countries. That Smirnovsky may have mixed more with other envoys reflected his different situation and assignment: fewer British drawing rooms were open to a Russian lobbying for Soviet influence. Still, the misguided comments stung.

WALTER WAS, however, having quite a good time at events he did attend. So good that Bobby Scott feared that he might become indiscreet. One story had made it back to the embassy that at a stag lunch with members of Parliament, Walter had asked that the waitress be withdrawn. The door to the dining room was closed and the guests leaned in to hear what some expected to be inside political information. "Did you hear the one about Gertrude Ederle . . . ?" he began, regaling them in Ronald Reagan fashion with a slightly off-color story about the famed channel swimmer.

One morning, Scott urged that he be careful. "This is a terribly gossipy town. You're one of the major figures here and everything you say is repeated."

"Oh, Bob, you're being silly. They have better things to do."

"Give me five minutes," Scott said. "I will tell you with whom you sat last night at dinner, what the conversation was and I will do it without calling your hostess." He was back in a trice, identified Walter's table partners and what they discussed and pointed out that two notable indiscretions had been made concerning state secrets. "And," said Scott, "I didn't talk to anyone who was even AT the party."[35]

Walter absorbed the lesson. He was always impatient when business subordinates told him anything twice, and neither Scott nor anyone else had to warn him again about people talking behind his back. For a while, in fact, the reverse was true. "He came to London with a degree of insecurity which turned into a considerable case of paranoia," said Phil Kaiser, a partisan Democrat who had been close to David Bruce and did not get along well with Walter during their six months together.[36]

The Annenbergs, who had long been used to dealing with presidents, diplomats and business titans and hosting them at their homes in Philadelphia and California, were foreign policy novices, but as the head of a very successful publishing empire, Walter was by no means as insecure as Kaiser made him out to be. But he and Lee were upset, and properly so, by the behavior of the Bruces and, to a lesser extent, of Kaiser himself.

Tradition called for an outgoing ambassador to stay away from the country where he served for a year after leaving his post to give the new man a fair chance to settle in without feeling second-guessed by his predecessor. The Bruces, however, did not want to leave London. They moved into Albany, a historic apartment building just steps from Piccadilly Circus, and ran a competing court, continuing to entertain officials and socialites just as they had in the embassy. Britons in this circle were friends of the Annenbergs or of the Bruces, but rarely both.

Some people accepted the new ambassador's hospitality, then deliberately did not reciprocate. "It was very awkward for the Annenbergs," said Tom Hughes. "You had the most polished ambassador in decades staying while the least polished was trying to get established."

The Annenbergs never stopped trying, although one result of Walter's decision not to speak with the press was that few people realized how hard he worked those first difficult months. His calendar was filled with meetings with British politicians, businessmen and diplomats and the usual unending stream of visitors from the United States. Winfield House was under construction, but a week rarely passed without Walter's hosting a large working lunch at the chancery or, with Lee, a drinks party or dinner at one of London's better hotels or restaurants. Barbara Castle, minister of labour in the Wilson government, attended an embassy reception because "I felt that I owed it to the poor, harassed ambassador, Annenberg." After arriving, she found that "I enjoyed it enormously, which seldom happens to me at cocktail parties. But there were a lot of trade unionists there," which she had not expected to find at a party given by a wealthy Republican.[37]

The trade unionists were there because, for all his diplomatic problems, Walter's business instincts remained keen. Even during the most painful early days, British and American executives sought him out for his expertise and connections. Both were displayed impressively soon after he arrived.

The issue was a billion-dollar merger proposed in June 1969 between British Petroleum and Sohio (Standard Oil of Ohio) that involved the development of North Slope oilfields and the trans-Alaska pipeline. Partly because BP had earlier acquired refining and marketing properties from Atlantic Richfield, the Justice Department attacked the Sohio merger as a violation of U.S. anti-trust laws. Richard McLaren, the new chief of the Justice's anti-trust division, said such mergers posed a serious threat to competition and that the government would oppose any and all big company mergers whether they be friendly or involuntary. "Sir Eric Drake, the chairman of British Petroleum, came to me and said McLaren wanted to criminally indict all the BP directors and put them in jail," said Walter.[38]

He considered the likelihood of criminal indictments remote, but Drake regarded the threat as serious. One of Britain's most respected and experienced executives, the BP chairman was not frightened easily. As BP's general manager in Iran in 1951, Drake had stood up to

Mohammed Mossadegh when the premier attempted to nationalize the British-controlled oil industry and was threatened with death.[39]

The Justice Department position, Walter believed, was short-sighted and xenophobic. He doubted that the administration had considered the ramifications for U.S. firms wanting to invest in European companies, including the interest of American oil companies in North Sea oil and gas ventures. The U.S. could not have it both ways. The government owned 51 percent of British Petroleum and members of Parliament of both major parties, including inveterate free-traders, told Walter that they would have no compunction about retaliating against American firms if the BP\Sohio merger were stymied. France had already begun to retaliate, rejecting a bid by Westinghouse to purchase 60 percent of Jeumont-Schneider, a leading French producer of generating equipment.

Walter wrote President Nixon, made the case for the merger to proceed, stressing what happened in France, and prevailed. "Whenever it came to matters of business, I listened to what Annenberg said," Nixon explained. "He always knew what he was talking about. He understood business matters better than anyone else."[40] Eric Drake was delighted. And while he could not speak for her, it was Sir Eric's understanding that the queen, a major shareholder in British Petroleum, was pleased as well.

After the relieved BP directors spread the word of Walter's role, U.S. corporate executives began beating a path to his office. Chase Manhattan's David Rockefeller and burger bosses from McDonald's sought his advice on opening London branches, the opening wave of the 1970s push to expand globally. Walter showed a fine sensitivity. When some of his British banking friends complained that the incoming Americans were raiding and overpaying employees, the ambassador put a stop to the rising enmity by persuading the U.S. firms to hire local retirees instead.[41] While the press was still critical in those early days, business executives, many of whom had been startled by his maiden speech to the Pilgrims, were drawing a more sophisticated and positive impression of his skills.

YET, WHENEVER Lee and Walter seemed to be making progress, Evangeline Bruce made the situation worse by openly and viciously disparaging them. "Vangie went to her friends — and she had a lot of them — saying things like 'Don't bother with them,'" said David Metcalfe, an insurance executive and socially well connected Londoner.

"She made it as difficult for the Annenbergs as she could." Upset about the Bruces, Lee and Walter were further annoyed when Phil Kaiser stayed in London as chairman of Encyclopaedia Britannica, a job Walter felt he might have pursued while an embassy officer, although Kaiser denied that he had. With both the former ambassador and deputy there, the situation was almost intolerable.

There was so much tension that the thin-skinned and mercurial Walter could not always restrain himself. One outburst came at a dinner in honor of visiting columnist Walter Lippmann hosted by Fleur Cowles and her husband, Tom Meyer, whose apartment was in Albany, adjacent to that of the Bruces, who had not been invited. The Meyers were far too savvy for that.

Around the table were a dozen prominent government officials, diplomats and journalists. Fleur Cowles, a writer and painter, seated the two Walters on either side of her and opened the general conversation by asking Lippmann to speak about de Gaulle, the subject of his column that morning in the *International Herald Tribune*. A great admirer of the French leader, Lippmann explained how he had not handled the student demonstrations in Paris well, but was otherwise one of the greatest public men he had known.

As Lippmann spoke, Walter began palpably to squirm. Fleur Cowles turned to him and asked if he had read the column.

"Yes, and you ought to be shot," Walter replied, leaning across his hostess to address Lippmann. "How could anyone say one kind thing about Charles de Gaulle?"

"What are you talking about?" asked the columnist.

"Sir, you have completely misunderstood the machinations of an evil man who is a self-declared enemy of the United States. It was a disgrace to write that." Walter was livid. His face was flushed.

A hush descended on the table. The guests looked to Lippmann for his rejoinder. The eighty-year-old columnist merely shook his head. "Fleur, please excuse me, but I'm an old man and I cannot bear to sit here and listen to such drivel." He rose, grabbed his cane and stumbled from the room in search of his coat. Fleur Cowles ran after him.

"Please don't go," she implored.

"I will not stay in the same room with that man," Lippmann said.

At that moment, the first of several dozen more guests invited for after-dinner drinks arrived. Among them was Tom Hughes, Annenberg's new deputy, who had arrived in London only two weeks earlier. Shaking Hughes's hand, Lippmann nodded toward the ambassador and said, "We know why you're here — to take his foot out of his mouth." Hughes peered into the dining room. "The guests were sitting there in shambles, looking like they'd been hit by a train."[42]

Walter's perception was different. He had no sense of having misspoken. He certainly felt no reason to apologize. He and Lippmann each had his own opinion. As a longtime newspaperman, Walter felt that his judgment was as valid as that of the columnist, who was hardly speaking ex cathedra. After all, Walter hired and fired columnists and might well have dropped this one for failing to note the flaws in de Gaulle.

At the time of the Lippmann dinner in mid-October 1969, Walter's three-decade tenure as a newspaper proprietor was coming to an end. When his ambassadorial appointment had been announced in February, there were so many rumors that the *Philadelphia Inquirer* would be sold that he had felt it necessary to publish a denial saying, "These rumors are utterly without foundation in fact. I have no intention whatever of disposing of the *Philadelphia Inquirer* or the *Philadelphia Daily News.*"[43]

Initially, he had planned to keep the papers. After arriving in London, he continued to run them and Triangle publications from an office on the top floor of Winfield House. Punctilious about never conducting private business in the embassy on Grosvenor Square, he would not make or take a personal business phone call or meet at the embassy about anything involving Triangle affairs. When Lewis Van Dusen, a friend and prominent Philadelphia attorney, asked for the name of a Briton he could contact to resolve an insurance dispute, Walter refused on the grounds that in a private, bilateral matter it would be inappropriate for him even to provide a name.[44]

With permission of the State Department, Walter installed a personal phone line in the residence connecting him with the Philadelphia offices and had rooms converted on the top floor for living quarters and an office for a secretary he hired locally to work on Triangle business. Peter Skoufis, the embassy administrative counselor, offered to lend him spare equipment, but Walter declined. "He wouldn't let me put in a desk, a file cabinet or even a typewriter that I had just sitting in a warehouse," said Skoufis. "He said, 'Peter, I'm going to buy everything myself. I don't want to do anything that might embarrass my president.' He was so sensitive about doing anything where he might be accused of doing something improper or unethical."[45] As the ambassador's wife, Lee was entitled to use his official car, but Walter had doubts that the policy was appropriate. He shipped over their Rolls-Royce for her use and hired a chauffeur from the motor pool, paying the driver personally after putting him on unpaid leave to preserve his seniority.

All Triangle business was conducted at the residence before and after embassy hours. In the morning, he dealt with correspondence. Given the five-hour time difference with the East Coast, he waited until evening to talk with his executives — Joe First at Triangle, Merrill Panitt at *TV Guide* and E. Z. Dimitman at the *Inquirer* — and old pals like Frank Rizzo, with whom he often spoke about goings-on in Philadelphia.

Joe First, his longtime mentor, most trusted associate and extremely capable lawyer, was his primary contact. A superb deputy, First understood both details and the big picture and required little supervision, but he was a manager, not an editor. Walter refrained from dictating editorials, as he had promised at his confirmation. But just as Moses had issued instructions by letter from Lewisburg penitentiary based on Walter's advisories, Walter was making every key decision on input from trusted aides with whom he had worked by phone and mail for decades. The only difference was that his phone line was longer and his mail bill higher. In the pre-fax era, he received running counts of circulation and advertising linage and capital and petty expenses, and directed and reviewed personnel issues and strategic planning for all his newspapers, magazines and radio and television stations. "He really loved keeping his hand in the business," said Eric Larson, then *TV Guide*'s ad sales director.[46]

The routine was grueling, though, and the combined demands of London and Philadelphia were taking a toll. A robust sixty-one-year-old, Walter was nonetheless becoming physically and mentally exhausted trying to learn a job under siege, extricate himself from the diplomatic holes he had dug, cope with a residence ripped apart by decorators and contractors, run Triangle and represent the United States. Life, as he had told Nixon, was a series of never-ending tests, some of which, including the fates of his father and son, were cruel and unreasonable. This continuum of challenges in London, though, was proving too much.

The correspondence and calls to and from Philadelphia often took hours each day. *TV Guide, Seventeen* and the *Daily Racing Form* were in good hands, but the *Inquirer* was very difficult to supervise. Joe First could keep tabs on the business side, but the paper's editorial operations posed much bigger problems. After the Harry Karafin shakedown scandal Walter had lost confidence in his editors. He was at least a decade late in coming to that conclusion, and he had only himself to blame. Executive editor Dimitman was seventy-one and a full generation, if not two, out of date as an editor. A warhorse from the twenties, he was still practicing Hearst-style journalism, albeit at Walter's direction. Walter never should have taken him back after he returned from Chicago in the 1950s, but Dimitman had been a loyal editor for his father and during his second stint at the *Inquirer* would be for him too. The managing editor was John Gillen, a handsome Irishman with wavy white hair who *Inquirer* reporters said held the job because he looked the part and was a reliable yes-man for Dimitman and Walter. In non-*Inquirer* ventures, where he had been largely content to be publisher, Walter was a modern thinker, but the daily was stuck like a beetle in prewar amber.

The *Inquirer*'s staff was demoralized, depleted and needed restocking. The plant and presses required modernizing and, dare he say it, refurbishment. Circulation of the daily had been dropping for a decade, from 619,381 in 1958 to 483,182 in September 1969. Ad linage was holding, but as quality slipped, circulation of the morning and Sunday *Inquirer* had each dropped 20,000 in the past year. Sunday circulation stood at 891,810, down from a postwar high of 1.2 million. Unable to dictate editorials, Walter was finding little joy left in the *Inquirer*.

ANOTHER PROBLEM lurked in Milton Shapp, who was still angry that Walter had wrecked his 1966 bid for the governorship of Pennsylvania. Shapp was campaigning again for the office, which he would win in 1970. One of his early moves came in July 1969 when he asked the Federal Communications Commission not to renew WFIL's television license. "Renewal of the Triangle license is not in the public interest," Shapp claimed, "because this company exercises a near news monopoly in the Philadelphia area." In his petition, he called the 1966 coverage of his campaign "a personal vendetta," charged that news had been "censored, omitted, twisted, distorted" and said that the *Inquirer* "and other media controlled by Walter Annenberg are and have been used to poison the political life of Pennsylvania."

Had he still lived in Philadelphia, Walter almost certainly would have fought back. He said he would. But he was an ambassador now, a public figure. He could not train the *Inquirer* guns again on Shapp without causing an uproar. A man who would not use a spare government typewriter out of fear of embarrassing his president could hardly get into a nasty personal battle with an embittered state politician. Although the FCC eventually rejected Shapp's appeal, there appeared a chance that Walter might lose WFIL, the hub of his six-station group, which was more profitable than the *Inquirer.* The FCC had recently denied renewal of a Boston television station license on monopoly grounds and similar challenges had been mounted in other cities.

Walter did not want more distractions or controversies. He was trying to be a good ambassador and was loath to wreck his chances. Too many factors favored selling the *Inquirer.* Eventually he would have to. Roger was gone. Wallis had four small children. His sisters had never pressed him to sell the *Inquirer,* but he continued to feel a strong fiduciary responsibility to them. At a distance and without full hands-on control, he was reluctant to make the major investment he knew was necessary to modernize the paper and its staff.

In September 1969, publisher Samuel Newhouse offered him $55 million for the *Inquirer* and *Daily News* with the sweetener that he could remain publisher for life. Walter knew the price was right and was immediately tempted. But he told Newhouse that years before at the Gridiron Club's annual dinner in Washington, where reporters entertain leading politicians, he had promised first right of refusal to Jack Knight, who had bought the *Miami Tribune* from his father. "I gave him my word as a gentleman," Walter said, "so I must give him the opportunity to match your offer." Walter told Knight that the price was firm, but that he did not have to be named publisher for life. He did want to keep his twelfth-floor office at the *Inquirer,* a ten-year consulting contract at $100,000 a year, and listing on the *Inquirer* masthead as publisher and editor emeritus.

Knight agreed and on October 29, 1969, a joint announcement was carried on page one of the *Inquirer.* "With the passing of my only son, there is no likely possibility of family transference and hence my desire to insure a future ownership in which I have confidence," Walter's statement read. "I have invited John S. Knight and his organization to take on this responsibility because of their consistent record of community service and leadership. I have devoted my best energies to advancing the welfare of our city, state and nation and it is vital to me to see this work continued." Knight was similarly high-minded and noted that Walter's "determination to make the *Inquirer* one of America's leading newspapers has been crowned with unusual success."[47]

Despite the earlier rumors, news of the sale stunned the staff and many Philadelphians who found it difficult to think of the *Inquirer* in other than Annenberg hands, quite a change from 1936, when Moses had bought the paper. The sale went through, but soon both Walter and Knight were having second thoughts. Knight told associates that he had paid too much and his executives were lambasting the new property. "I expected to find a pretty bad operation and I wasn't disappointed," said John McMullan, Knight's first editor, who promptly and wisely fired seventy of the paper's two hundred eighty editorial employees. "It was pretty much held in contempt and deservedly so. It was appalling. Years of cronyism and mismanagement; editors who couldn't edit, reporters who couldn't write. Annenberg had no interest in journalism of quality. To him, the *Inquirer* was an instrument of his bidding, to give him the influence he desired."[48]

McMullan was right, both about the paper and Walter. The paper was understaffed and many of the reporters it had were underskilled. Walter was guilty of using the paper as a personal instrument. His far too cozy relationship with Mayor Frank Rizzo was an indefensible conflict of interest. Edward Barrett, the respected dean of Columbia University's graduate school of journalism from 1956 to 1968, wondered in 1970 whether "perhaps Walter Annenberg never really understood the mission, the obligations or the ethical principles of ethical journalism."[49] What Walter understood was his father's activist, Hearstian model.

The situation might have been different had Walter been content being publisher and had hired a strong, independent editor. But Moses had edited the *Inquirer* and there had never been any question that his son would do less. Walter had conceded that "without the *Inquirer* I'd be just another rich guy feeding the pigeons," and he long relished his bully pulpit. When reports reached him of what Knight's new team was doing to the *Inquirer*, he was infuriated. But because it was difficult to rebut criticism of the paper's editorial problems, Walter charged that Knight was complaining to cover up his own bad business judgment.

"The biggest mistake of my life was living up to my word and selling the *Inquirer* to Jack Knight," Walter complained. "The son of a bitch didn't invest a cent. He borrowed $14 million and gave me a series of notes for the $41 million. When it came to interest, I said, 'Jack, I don't really need the money, just put down prime [the rate banks charge their best customers].' Well, in a year, prime climbed to fifteen percent and he told everybody I robbed him. Who knew prime was going to climb like that? If he had a brain he could have capped it. Jack turned out to be a rat. And then he supported and elected Milton Shapp, that jerk."[50]

Two years later, McMullan returned to Knight headquarters in Miami and was replaced by Eugene Roberts of the *New York Times*. After McMullan, a thorough professional but not one he could tolerate, Walter was delighted to see a respected *Times* man in command. "The honeymoon did not last long," said Roberts, under whose eighteen-year editorial leadership the *Inquirer* won seventeen Pulitzer prizes. "Annenberg was very gracious, but he soon stopped speaking to me. Ultimately, he didn't like the way I ran the paper."[51] Knight's *Inquirer* paid Walter's consulting fee, but never sought out his views. "Whatever I supported," Walter grumped, "they opposed."

The *Inquirer* sale took effect on the first of January 1970. In February, Walter pressed ahead with what would become a long process of dismantling Triangle. He had not originally planned to sell more than the *Inquirer* until Tom Murphy, the head of Capital Cities Broadcasting, heard that the paper was for sale and flew to London to ask whether Walter might unload his television and radio properties. Walter agreed to sell him nine stations for $110 million in cash and notes. A few months later he sold seven more broadcasting properties to two former employees for $16 million. In 1973, three cable television properties and part of a fourth went for $11 million to Harris Cable of Los Angeles.

In the Cap Cities case, Walter gave Murphy twenty-one months to get the deal approved by the Federal Communications Commission — the time their lawyers figured it would take — and orally guaranteed his selling price for the duration. Murphy won approval on the final day. "But during those twenty-one months, broadcasting was booming; the value of his assets had appreciated considerably," Murphy said. "All he had to do was wink at the FCC and the deal would have collapsed and he could have negotiated a higher price. But he's a stand-up guy. He completely stayed with his word and lived up to every part of his offer. I'd rather have Walter Annenberg's handshake on a deal than anyone else's signature."[52]

Walter helped finance the purchase. "He said, 'You look like your balance sheet could use a little help,'" recalled Murphy, laughing. In 1986 he paid $3.6 billion to buy the American Broadcasting Company and ten years later sold Cap Cities/ABC to Disney for $18.9 billion. "I never would have been able to buy ABC if Walter hadn't sold to me," said Murphy. "That deal gave me stations in Hartford, New Haven, Fresno and Philadelphia, the fourth market in the country, and made Cap Cities the biggest ABC affiliate. Everything came from that step." Walter was equally pleased. Eighty-five million dollars of Cap Cities' money was to buy WFIL-TV in Philadelphia, the license he had sought in 1947 against the advice of his executives. "I had no complaints," Walter chuckled. "WFIL only cost me three cents to mail in the license application. That was a pretty good return."[53]

24

SMOOTH FINISH

———

D ESPITE THE DIFFICULTIES they encountered outside the embassy, inside among the staff Walter and Lee were a great hit. They relied on embassy officials more than the Bruces had, involved them in business and social affairs and treated them with courtesy and affection. David Bruce got along with everyone but did not need his staff, who felt almost extraneous. His method had been to hold a staff meeting once a week and give general guidance that would filter down as if from Mount Olympus. "Bruce was not a hands-on person, but stood back, did what he wanted to do and assumed everyone else knew what they were doing," said William Galloway, who served with Bruce and as political counselor for Walter.[1]

Walter was never a micromanager, but he thoroughly understood power and was a more engaged executive. Used to dealing with division heads, he ran the embassy staff of six hundred much as he did Triangle. The management itself was not difficult. Embassies are hierarchical and composed of self-contained units — political, economic, cultural, military, intelligence — each with its own counterparts, locally and in Washington. Walter referred to the division chiefs as his "cabinet," calling them in regularly to keep abreast of what they were doing and to ensure they had whatever they needed.

"Walter certainly knew how to manage and got very good results," said Skoufis. By delegating, he was also able to skip out occasionally when the weather allowed and play golf with Admiral Louis Kirn, the defense attaché who was also Milwaukee-born and had been his schoolmate at Peddie. Periodically, he would grab the embassy agricultural officer for an early-morning expedition to Smithfield Market or Covent Garden, where Walter would inspect meats, press cheeses and talk with vendors as if he were one of them, just as he and his father used to visit the men in the newspaper kiosks.

As was his habit, he went out infrequently for lunch his first year. Never a man who enjoyed lunching with other men, Walter kept to his routine. Shyness was a factor, but Walter's biggest reluctance to lunching was that he considered it a waste of time. He attended lunches with a stated purpose, but otherwise begged off by claiming that he needed extra office time to learn his job. He often ate a sandwich or a cup of soup — always Campbell's because he was a stockholder and former director — alone in his embassy office at the magnificent partner's desk David Bruce had sold him for $10,000.

As at Triangle, he did not need to know every detail as long as he trusted his deputy, the careerist who traditionally ran the embassy. He had four during his posting. Two worked well with him; two did not. His first was Kaiser, his polar opposite. After six months, Tom Hughes arrived. A superb professional with a refined sense of humor, Hughes worked well with Walter. "Shoot your way in, as my father used to say," was Walter's way of inviting Hughes to join the table for a postprandial cognac or, as he called it, "a little dividend." But his wife became ill and they had to return to the U.S. Walter was not pleased with his replacement, a career foreign service officer named Joseph "Jerry" Greene, who Walter believed tried to upstage him by keeping him in the dark.

During the 1973 Middle East war, Greene turned his office into a command center with pins in maps over the walls to no discernible purpose, since a host of U.S. agencies were monitoring the war's progress. "Von Clausewitz is at it again," Walter snorted and set about working around Greene. On the other hand, he retained the services of aides he considered effective and loyal, such as administrative officer Skoufis and consular affairs director Jack Hurfort, by intervening with the State Department to extend their assignments.

He had not built the Triangle empire by being woolly-headed with subordinates. Political counselor Galloway was designated his de facto number two and given simple marching orders. "He told me, 'Make sure I'm always up to date on what I should know; make sure I'm not surprised or caught off base, and make me look good,'" said Galloway. "Run the embassy and always act in the best interests of the United States of America. Those are your instructions."[2]

Given broad authority, welcomed as guests to ambassadorial dinners, participating to an extent they had not been before and aware that Walter both trusted and needed them, the embassy staff worked hard to protect him and deliver well-crafted reports. He read their work promptly and carefully, did not second-guess his advisers, never asked for favors for friends, such as expedited visa approvals, and was such a straight arrow that he made everyone pay their parking tickets instead of hiding behind diplomatic immunity, which he considered freeloading.

His booming "Hello" echoed through embassy offices and brought smiles to the faces of staffers unused to an ambassador striding the halls and inquiring about their welfare. There were many kindnesses. If the Annenbergs were celebrating his birthday at the residence, Lee ensured that cake and wine were served first at Walter's office. As in Philadelphia, if Walter heard that a staffer had a problem, he stepped in. The expenses of an ill secretary were paid quietly out of his own pocket. When Tom Hughes's son needed an eye operation, Walter called on his network of medical specialists to determine who could best treat the young man. After a junior officer was caught in a homosexual incident, Walter had him counseled about the dangers of blackmail, then buried the report so the young man's career was saved. Neither prude, libertine nor moralist, he believed what consenting adults did discreetly and privately on their own time was their own business.[3]

The more they saw of him, the more the embassy officers and staff respected Walter. Bronson Tweedy, the first of his three CIA station chiefs, said, "He didn't know the State Department from the Soil Erosion Corps when he arrived, but he grew and learned. He was the easiest person in the world to work with."[4] Rolfe Kingsley succeeded Tweedy and found Walter to be "a very, very shrewd cookie. He was sharp and very quick to take a briefing. I left considering him one of the best ambassadors I ever served with."[5] Walter's final station chief, Cord Meyer, agreed. "On a scale of one to ten, he was a nine or ten. First-rate. He was attentive, asked good questions and did not try to get into what didn't involve him."[6]

WHAT FINALLY turned the situation around for Lee and Walter was their palpable love of Britain, the skill with which they entertained, their taste and appreciation of beauty and their generosity. "At first he was his own worst enemy, but even those who might have ridiculed him initially came to accept him so that the net impression by the time he left was very positive at every level," said Edward Streator, deputy chief of mission for U.S. ambassadors Kingman Brewster and John Louis in the later 1970s and early 1980s and a longtime expatriate resident of Britain. "He's a generous, thoughtful man with a genuine warmth and a real charm."[7]

The more partisan of Walter's countrymen and embassy subordinates focused on the generosity and maintained that the Annenbergs bought acceptance. "He handled the early days very badly, but he bought his way back," said former deputy Kaiser. According to former deputy Hughes, "There were so many benefactions — books published, chalices and sword replicas donated, swimming pools built — that the criticism was stifled. And the British, no strangers to hypocrisy, would vilify him by day, then by night rush to his dinner table."

Walter did spend millions, although most was given after he left Britain. Just as important, he opened his heart as wide as his wallet. The first indication most Britons had that there was a greater dimension to Walter and Lee than they might have suspected from reading the initial press reports came in September 1969 when the Tate Gallery put on display thirty-two of the Annenbergs' prized Impressionist paintings. To make it easier to share his collection of Monets, Cézannes, van Goghs and Renoirs with the British public, Walter paid all the exhibit's expenses, including transportation, insurance, publication of a catalogue and the entrance fees for the more than 100,000 persons who flocked to the Tate during the six-week show. Even critics admired his generosity and the exceptional quality of the paintings.

Unlike the big and ostentatious collections of some wealthy Americans, Lee and Walter's paintings were relatively few and carefully selected to represent the best works of the nineteenth and twentieth centuries' greatest painters. "Taste as fastidious as it is wide is represented," said the *Daily Telegraph,* citing the collection's "compelling grandeur."[8] According to *Spectator* magazine, "the Annenberg collection illustrates an aspect of American collecting revolving around two factors easily forgotten in the vague era of affluence enveloping such a gathering, namely, taste and imagination."[9]

The collection was more than good; it was intensely personal. Walter's background explained the presence of so many female images by Renoir, Morisot and Monet. Vincent van Gogh's *La Berceuse* showed a masterful portrait of Madame Roulin, wife of his friend the Arles postmaster, sitting before a brilliant floral wallpaper of pink dahlias and holding a slack cord with which she rocks the cradle of her newborn daughter out of sight beyond the picture frame. Painted often by van Gogh, who gave her a choice of five versions, Roulin chose this one, which the painter called his best. A powerful image of motherhood, she suggested the way Sadie Annenberg may have looked while raising her children. Walter, who bought the painting from Daniel Wildenstein for $1.5 million, believed he knew what caused the new mother's nostril to flare. "Look at that expression," he marveled. "It's as if she's smelling limburger cheese. It's vitally humanistic."

Gauguin's *Portrait of Women*, in his interpretation, revealed a mother filled with experience and cynicism who believed in nothing and a daughter whose bovine innocence suggested that she would believe anything. "The psychological combination of those two faces," said Walter, "tells the story of life." The *Daughters of Catulle Mendès* was a monumental Renoir for which Walter had paid $860,000 to Wildenstein. What appears to be a serene and intimate scene of three stunning young women with a piano and viola was actually a tangled family portrait, he related with exuberance, involving illegitimate children, the youngest of whom hated the elder's music, as did Renoir himself. Complexity in relations among sisters, he explained, had a special resonance for him.

WITHIN WEEKS of the Tate show, another event affirmed the taste finding and initiated a reassessment of the Annenbergs. Ironically, it involved the very "elements of refurbishment" which had prompted the worst of Walter's troubles. In early November 1969, Bill Haines and Ted Graber completed their nine-month total restoration of Winfield House.

They had put on a new roof, rewired, redone the plumbing, the ground-floor powder rooms, rebuilt a sweeping, eighteenth-century staircase and restored to their original detail the ceilings, walls and floors of the reception and dining rooms downstairs as well as the family bed-, guest and sitting rooms upstairs. Fluted columns, pilasters, elegant door moldings and a multi-branched crystal-and-gilt brass chandelier from an Indian palace accentuated the elegant forty-foot-long reception hall, which ran the depth of the house and served as the ballroom as well as the gathering place for visitors circulating between rooms. In the center of the hall, on a French tapestry-style carpet made to replace an eighteenth-century original, stood an elegant circular Regency table of dark red stone on an Empire base, the kind of table at which George III might have read America's Declaration of Independence. At the far end of the room, three French doors curtained in gray silk with lush coral fringes led across a broad stone terrace to lawns which swept to Regent's Canal. The tennis court was resurfaced; the indoor swimming pool redone. Scores of old and ailing trees were replaced with conifers brought fully grown from Scotland. A trellised box garden was added outside the dining room.

Inside, where every detail was overseen by Lee, the painting, wall coverings, draperies, fabric and trim — made in California — were flawless. The old French pine-paneled walls were stripped and repainted a pale bluish-green heightened by off-white molding. The eighteenth-century Chinese wallpaper on the fourteen-foot-high walls of the garden room had been removed from a castle in Ireland, flown to New York for drycleaning, to Hong Kong for pressing and fitting on canvas and back to London for installation. The painted birds, butterflies, chrysanthemums and peonies on the wallpaper were complemented by two huge Ch'ing chests, rare 1790 giltwood furniture upholstered in terra-cotta silk. The light streaming through eight French windows overlooking the gardens created an effect of mesmerizing beauty.

The house was also lovingly refurnished. Lee and Walter brought many antiques from Inwood, including elegant Chippendale, which they supplemented with extensive purchases of fine English pieces, plus Louis XV armchairs and an exceptional tulipwood commode, Regency lacquer tables, chinoiserie, and Adam furniture. There was a collection of eighteenth-century Lowestoft English china that they had spent two decades assembling. Walter's interest in birds was reflected in a complete edition of porcelain birds by Dorothy Doughty. Edward Boehm, his favorite porcelain artist, was represented in a collection of delicate floral sculptures.

The pièces de résistance were the paintings which had been moved to Winfield House after their exhibition at the Tate. The walls had been painted in neutral colors with their arrival in mind. Seven hung in the reception hall, including Gaugin's *Still Life with Fruit* and Renoir's *The Children of Catulle Mendès*, the warm oranges and beiges of which set the soft, welcoming tone of the room and subtly commanded attention.

Walter had spent $1.1 million on the renovation, or nearly $5 million in current dollars. The Annenberg Foundation had provided $960,000 of the total, which the U.S. allowed him to charge off as a charitable deduction as a gift to the nation. The improvements had been made to a government structure in which most of the new furnishings and objets d'art would remain. The additional $140,000 came from his own pocket. He was happy to spend every penny. "Since the renovation was necessary, it gave us an opportunity at the beginning of our tour of service to express ourselves," he explained. "It has been done, though, so that the total effect will reflect the character and dignity of our country."[10] Their goal, Lee added, was an informal formality. "This is a formal residence, but we tried to make it like a real home, not a cold impersonal place." She had the family quarters' drawing room painted in shades of gray, white and lemon yellow as a reminder of Sunnylands, and Walter hung the portrait of his pink-clad mother above the fireplace in the Red Room, his upstairs study.

As the spectacular restoration neared completion, rumors about what had been done spread, and anticipation grew in London's social circles. On Thanksgiving eve, the Annenbergs gave their first major party — thirty-six seated for dinner and 450 invited for after-dinner dancing, caviar and vintage champagne. The guests were astonished at the transformation of the once gloomy mansion into an exquisitely tasteful gem. Lee had the house filled with flowers, including red-white-and-blue arrangements suitable for both countries, while the kitchen dazzled, thanks to the Annenbergs' French chef and Walter's extensive cellar of wines, a collection he had assembled with nearly as much care as his paintings and porcelains. Running the residence and entertaining in such fashion, Walter later acknowledged, cost him $250,000 a year, about $1 million in current dollars, on top of his $42,500 government salary.

In New York society columnist Aileen Mehle devoted nearly an entire "Suzy Says" column to the event. "The residence looked glorious with all the fabulous newly acquired antiques and objets arranged to perfection. The 600 [sic] guests, most of them rather hard to impress, were more than impressed — maybe awestruck is the word. Remembering the house in pre-Annenberg days, one guest said 'a miracle has been wrought.' The food was superb. The flowers were divine. There was a heady mixture of people — and everyone had a marvelous time."[11]

Lord Palmerston had not supped with the Annenbergs when he remarked that "dining is the soul of diplomacy," but Lee and Walter were demonstrating that the nineteenth-century prime minister had a point. Their art collection and their taste in restoring Winfield House had Britons wondering if they had perhaps been wrong about the ambassador, that he was not a buffoon after all, but a cultured aesthete. The *Times* of London saluted the "spectacular splendor that justifies Walter Annenberg's sesquipedalian profundity." Talk of their importing movie-set decor from Hollywood abruptly ceased. What had been considered inept became rough-hewn charm. Diplomats who had called Walter aloof decided he was shy and trying to be unobtrusive. Judgments considered blunt — "He has all the qualities of a dog, except loyalty" was a favorite Annenbergism — were seen instead as refreshingly direct. His manner of speaking was considered less foolish or pompous than amusing, original and even touching as more Britons quietly became more aware of his hearing and speech impediments. The *Daily Express* wrote of "this tough, bluff Yank," while the *Evening Standard* also reflected a new sympathy. The ambassador "has impressed independent observers by his sincerity and determination," the newspaper wrote, adding that "perhaps the critics will relent a little when they get to know him better."[12]

WITH THE Winfield House restoration finished, the results and reaction more positive than he had ever anticipated, press commentary turning and the *Inquirer* sale finalized, a weight of life-changing proportions had been lifted from Walter's and Lee's shoulders. He had been an angry man up to this moment. He was wealthy and accomplished, but there had been too many bruises and knockdowns in his "ninety-nine rounds" of life: the frustrating hearing and stuttering problems; the injustice he believed had been done his father; the club turndowns and the barriers to full acceptance in Philadelphia; his troubled first marriage; Roger's death; the attacks on his stewardship of the *Inquirer* and the censure of his appointment as ambassador. Now he was turning the corner.

Just as his appointment would prove to be the turning point in Walter's life, the restoration of Winfield House defined that posting. Everything that had happened since Moses's death nearly thirty years earlier had led to this moment; everything that took place later could be traced back to it. "London changed our lives," said Lee. Until this moment, Walter had still been an outsider. Now, overnight, he and Lee would be insiders. So much for Philadelphia with its Anglophilia-driven pretensions and restrictive social circles. The Annenbergs were about to soar above Philadelphia and on to a higher cruising altitude.

"There was Before Winfield House and After Winfield House. It was a watershed, like the change from B.C. to A.D.," said Caroline Seitz, whose husband, Raymond, served as the talented U.S. ambassador to Britain during the Bush administration. "The sense of acceptance thereafter changed them completely."[13]

Walter wanted Britons to know him better. Political officer Galloway, Bobby Scott and other advisers had urged that he not to try to emulate David Bruce, but be an ambassador of goodwill, moving around the country and making friends. "It was the only thing that any ambassador could do after Bruce and with Nixon and Kissinger running everything," said Galloway.

Walter was eager to plunge in and deal with a broader cross section of the country beyond the lumpen aristocracy. He abandoned the crew cut he arrived with in favor of growing his hair out to match the longer British style. Then, as he and Lee turned Winfield House into the most convivial venue in London — Walter called the more social Lee "Rubber Walls" for her habit of adding extra guests — they began visiting towns all over Britain, including places that had not seen an American ambassador in decades, if ever. "It was quite extraordinary," said James Hanson, chairman of the international conglomerate which bears his name and who considered Walter a business and personal mentor. "Here was this obscure publisher, shy by nature and hesitant of speech, and suddenly he was all over the place, believing he was ambassador to all Britain, not just the West End."[14]

They attended some country weekends on baronial and ducal estates, but because Walter did not shoot and was sensitive from Sunnylands about guests who overstay, he and Lee usually arrived on Saturday rather than the traditional Thursday evening and left Sunday after lunch instead of on Monday. More often they sampled other cities — Manchester and York, Sheffield and Liverpool, Birmingham, Nottingham and Edinburgh, where they met city fathers and industrialists, union leaders, craftsmen, workers, farmers, teachers and nurses. Both were curious and showed a good-humored fascination with whomever they met and whatever they were shown. (Presented with a steel chastity belt during an official visit to Sheffield, Walter was delighted and immediately sent it to Main Line socialite Hope Scott, who modeled it at her next dinner party.)

Often he made a contribution to a local cause: to repair the fire-damaged roof of York cathedral, to excavate Roman artifacts near

Leeds, a Royal Worcester Mayflower bowl to the lord mayor of Plymouth, books for a city library, an early computer to a school space-tracking team in Northamptonshire, and, unfailingly, a donation to the local police society for help in arranging and securing his trip. (Some eminent locals, by no means all British, awaited such visits with the anticipation and forethought usually reserved for Santa Claus. While escorting him around Giverney, the impressionist Claude Monet's retreat outside Paris, Gerald Van Der Kemp, the curator of Versailles, who had restored the Monet gardens, showed Walter where a road bisected the property and shrewdly mentioned his fear that a child might be hit by a car if an underpass were not built. Walter promptly offered $50,000 to finance construction.)[15]

On returning to London, Walter wrote brief but eloquent thank you notes to everyone who had shown him courtesy. After visiting Manchester, Walter wrote the chief constable to ask that the records of the seven officers who helped him — whose ranks and names he had noted — "reflect commendation for their outstanding performance."[16] He always had a special feeling for the police, and with reason.

Scotland Yard took great care to protect him, one of the world's wealthiest Jews living in a nation that had long been a haven for unhappy Arabs. There was high tension involving the Middle East throughout his posting. In 1967, Israel had destroyed Arab forces in the Six Day War, which led to the rise of militant Palestinian groups and terrorist attacks, including one in which hijackers took four planes belonging to Swissair, TWA, Pan Am and BOAC to a remote airstrip in the Jordanian desert and blew them up. Israeli embassy attachés were attacked. Bombs were planted in London and terrorists arrested, part of a pattern of global terror that culminated in Egypt and Syria's attack on Israel in the 1973 Yom Kippur War. When a threat was received that he would be kidnapped while visiting Scotland, Walter told Secretary of State William Rogers that under no circumstances was he to be ransomed if he actually were seized. Rogers was grateful, but called the offer moot. The only one who could afford to ransom Walter, he teased, was Walter.

The political climate placed tremendous demands on Scotland Yard, which also worked hard to protect the embassy throughout countless anti-war demonstrations which began in nearby Hyde Park and inevitably wound up at the embassy, sometimes in violent confrontations. During the Bruce years, a bobby had lost his eye in a battle on Grosvenor Square when demonstrators hurled heated coins and marbles at the police and their horses. The embassy raised two hundred pounds, then about $500, in a collection for the injured cop, which Bruce matched. The demonstrations continued during Walter's early years. One Sunday, the traditional protest day, a policeman and his horse were injured. The bobby's injuries were mild, but those of his horse, Pearl, were serious, which led to extensive play in the national newspapers. Walter, who witnessed the demonstration, led by the activist actress Vanessa Redgrave, suggested that the embassy do something to thank the police. Peter Skoufis told him about the four hundred pounds raised earlier. Walter bellowed to his secretary Anabelle Mitchell, to "bring in the book," and wrote a personal check for five thousand pounds, or $12,000, for the police fund.

"Ambassador, this is a little heavy," Skoufis said.

"Peter, you only go down this road once," Walter replied, a favorite expression. "This is the amount I want to give."[17] Scarcely had the check been sent than the police commissioner called to say he believed that the ambassador had inadvertently added an extra zero. Told that the amount was correct and that Annenberg wanted no publicity, the police could thereafter not do enough for the embassy.

(As for Redgrave, Walter ordered that her next visa application be rejected because she was anti-American. It was, but over the objections of deputy Jerry Greene, who maintained that there were insufficient legal grounds to declare her ineligible for a visa. The actress appealed to Attorney General John Mitchell and won a waiver. Soon after, Greene, who had served only fourteen months in London, told the State Department that he could no longer work with Walter, asked for a transfer and was reassigned to Cairo. If Greene had not pulled the plug himself, Walter was ready to. The two were incapable of working together: Greene wanted a more substantive role; Walter wanted a team player. One way or another, the ambassador would prevail. He did with his fourth and final deputy, the late Earl Sohm. Their relationship was excellent.)[18]

Other gifts were also given quietly, partly to avoid being inundated with requests. When he spotted a tabloid report that a retired British Rail employee had a fatal heart attack after vandals in a northern town destroyed the garden he had spent a lifetime maintaining, Walter ordered Skoufis to have the garden totally restored for the man's widow, adding, "but I don't want anybody to know about it, no newspapers, nobody."[19]

His largesse, often extended discreetly but made public by the recipient, was broad-ranging in scope and magnitude. He spent $7,000 to purchase a portrait of Field Marshal Viscount Montgomery painted by President Eisenhower, which he gave to the British embassy in Washington. St. Paul's Cathedral received $10,000 for restoration; After a 1970 tour of London's National Gallery, Walter told board member Lord Robbins to let him know if the art museum, whose acquisition budget was limited, ever needed help buying something exceptional. Two years later, the gallery could not afford Henri Rousseau's *Tropical Storm with a Tiger,* put up for sale by Pennsylvanian Henry Clifford for $900,000, and took Walter up on his offer. "A great painting," said Walter, who had been negotiating for six months to add the 1891 work to his own collection. He immediately withdrew his offer and made good on his promise, giving $352,500 to the gallery to buy the painting, now worth an estimated $15 million.

After Walter accompanied Richard Nixon on the first presidential visit ever to Chequers, the official country residence for Britain's prime ministers, to meet prime minister Edward Heath and lunch with Queen Elizabeth II, the ambassador gave $100,000 to be spent on "an identifiable and lasting improvement" in honor of the 1970 gathering. During World War II, Roosevelt aide Harry Hopkins had been so cold during a visit to Chequers to see Churchill that he promised impishly that if the allies beat Hitler, he would personally ensure that the American people gave the retreat a central heating system. Thirty years later, Chequers had been heated. The trust which maintains the house and Heath, who swam almost daily in London at the Grosvenor House Hotel, opted to build a fifty-by-twenty-five-foot indoor pool. With the money left over, Walter purchased from a Michigan collector a portrait of Sir Robert Frankland Russell, an eighteenth-century owner of the property, to hang in the residence.

Heath was effusive in his thanks and Walter offered his version of the saying that much was expected from those to whom much was given. "Over the years I have found compensating, the philosophical belief that gifts and services to, or on behalf of others, should at least be in character with your own good fortune in life," he wrote the prime minister. He had a few more ideas in mind but recognized that "there is always the risk that if one undertakes too much, adverse criticism might surface, and perhaps in the scheme of things, even this might have some justification."[20]

Until 1996 when Walter gave $10 million to the British Museum to construct and endow an information center in its Great Court, the gift that had won him widest notice was his commissioning and publishing of a sumptuous volume titled *Westminster Abbey* to commemorate the nine-hundred-year-old church. A great admirer in general of tradition and grandeur, Walter had been captivated by the abbey in 1923 on his first visit to London with his parents. Each time he returned to London he visited the abbey. When the criticism of him was most vocal in 1969, one day he found himself sitting at his desk in the embassy weeping in frustration. Slipping away, he sought comfort in the cool interior of the basilica, the final resting place for many of Britain's greatest heroes. In those early months, the abbey provided "a sanctuary of peace and comfort," he wrote in a dedication. "As I reflected on the difficulties, the trials and the burdens of those whose remains are forever associated with this historic building, I recognized how insignificant were the problems which confronted me."[21] Staring at the vaulted ceiling, the magnificent stained glass and the masterpieces of sculpture, he had felt inspired by the majestic beauty of the building. Browsing through the bookstore, he was surprised to find no high-quality book on the abbey.

When Walter was excited by an idea, as he was this one, he threw himself and his resources into the project to make certain it was done properly. He assembled a team of eminent contributors: Sir John Betjeman, the poet laureate; A. L. Rowse, the Oxford historian and biographer; George Zarnecki, professor of art history at the University of London and a leading scholar of Romanesque art; Sir John Pope-Hennessy, director of the Victoria and Albert Museum and an expert on gothic, baroque and Renaissance sculpture. Eric Abbott, the dean of Westminster, wrote the prologue; the epilogue was written by Lord Clark, who as Kenneth Clark was Britain's best-known art historian and whose program *Civilization* was one of television's most acclaimed series.

Published in 1972 by the Annenberg School Press and the British publishers Weidenfeld and Nicolson, the 264-page coffee-table book contained stunning photos and beautifully written essays on the abbey's history and architecture. It warranted a price of twenty pounds (then $48), but Walter wanted the book to be affordable for the widest number of readers, so he paid for a first edition of ten thousand copies. He donated eight thousand copies to schools and libraries across Britain. The remaining two thousand volumes he gave to the abbey to be priced at ten pounds ($24) and directed that all revenues go to the cathedral. The abbey reciprocated by designing — after discovering that there was no Annenberg coat of arms — and installing a stained-glass panel in his honor. He was overwhelmed by the gesture and ranked the abbey window alongside his nomination as ambassador, his knighthood, his marriage to Lee and being born Moses's son among the best things that ever happened to him. He had been driven all his adult life to earn respect, not just a fortune, and there was no other institution from which he could imagine receiving a more enduring mark of recognition.

America's highest civilian award was the Medal of Freedom. President Reagan awarded him that for his pioneering work in educational television, and while Walter was grateful and honored, all kinds of talented Americans had one of those. In the abbey, he was in the company of kings and queens, statesmen and generals, writers and poets. He would be connected indefinitely to the culture he admired and loved through its greatest landmark. There was no little irony in his being commemorated in the high church of Anglicanism, the WASP equivalent of St. Peter's. That was not something Walter would have acknowledged or perhaps absorbed consciously; subliminally, it could only have sweetened the reward.

AMONG THOSE most struck by his generosity was the queen, who had never joined in the unkind laughter that followed their first meeting. She regretted indirectly subjecting him to ridicule, and as it became more clear how much he loved Britain and was trying hard to do good things for her nation and her own royal causes, she went out of her way to get to know him better and demonstrate her gratitude. There were small touches at first, such as suspending protocol when necessary to ensure that he was seated on her right so he could hear her more easily.[22]

As an affinity slowly developed between the prim and discreet monarch and the combative and outspoken publisher, she praised him to friends for his responsible and imaginative good works, which both thrilled Lee and Walter and led to their greater social acceptance. Such acceptance was important to both Annenbergs. Only interested in the best and the highest quality — whether in art, homes, publications, charities or acquaintances, it was natural that they wanted to be leaders in the world of art and culture, society and philanthropy, business and politics.

They were good citizens who felt responsibility and had the means to make a difference in major ways. They were not looking for publicity and they neither sought nor asked anything from royals, presidents or anyone else. They did, however, want to participate at the highest level with the good and the great. In Britain that group included poets and academics, actors and directors, trade unionists and industrialists, clerics, soldiers and politicians of every stripe — all of whom came to the Annenbergs' table. As did the royals.

Walter developed a particularly close relationship with Queen Elizabeth, the Queen Mother. "I am crazy about that woman," he said.[23] He loved what all Britons loved about the icon they had treasured for more than six decades. Courageous during the war, hardworking and graceful in her unending series of royal engagements, a strong and supportive wife and mother, the very embodiment of what Walter and most Britons believed royalty should be, the Queen Mother was also well informed, had superb instincts, strong conservative convictions, a smile to melt the hardest heart and a great sense of humor. She was only eight years his senior, but in looks, behavior, demeanor and dress, including her hats, purse and white gloves, Walter believed she bore a startling resemblance to his sainted mother. Missing Sadie, who he wished had lived to see what her "Boy" was experiencing, Walter thrived on contact with the Queen Mother. When he was first invited to lunch at 12:45 at her Clarence House residence, the scrupulously protocol conscious envoy nonetheless presented himself at 12:35 P.M.

"Ambassador, you're a bit early," she noted, awaiting an explanation.

"Your Majesty," he replied, "I took the liberty because I was so desirous of visiting alone with you for a few minutes before the rest of the other peasants arrived."

The Queen Mother burst into laughter. "In that case, Ambassador, you can go to the pantry and fix me a martini."

"Your Majesty, I'll make it a double. And with your permission, I'll make myself one as well." Which he did.[24]

The friendship flowered, nurtured by Walter's adulation of her plus his rock-ribbed patriotism and the Queen Mother's instinctive love of the United States, which she first visited in 1936 with her husband, King George VI — who also battled a stutter. They ate hot dogs at a baseball game at Yankee Stadium, stayed with the Roosevelts in the country atmosphere of Hyde Park and developed an affection for America which grew during World War II, when she credited the U.S. with saving Britain from the Nazis. "Without question the Queen Mother and Walter Annenberg 'hit it off,'" said Sir Alastair Aird, her private secretary. "He is not shy and timid with her and the Queen Mother rather enjoys those who are outgoing. His kindness has been absolutely wonderful."[25]

So was his largesse. In some cases, his philanthropy specifically involved her. In 1989, for example, he contributed $250,000 in the Queen Mother's name to Oxford University. In other instances, he gave huge amounts to the major British cultural and educational institutions: more than $10 million to the British Museum, $5 million to the National Gallery, $1 million each to the Tate Gallery and Covent Garden's Royal Opera House and Royal Ballet. Some cynics charged that he was currying favor, that the recipients were all favorites of the Establishment and the royal family. Of course they were. Walter loved and supported the Establishment. And it was natural that he would give to institutions that the royals favored. But all these larger donations were made in the 1990s, well after he had been honored and had built solid ties to the Queen Mother, Queen Elizabeth and the family. They were his way of showing respect and gratitude. The favor of acceptance by then had long since been granted.

Throughout the 1990s, Walter made a special trip to London annually to host a birthday luncheon at Claridges for the Queen Mother and forty of her friends. To his delight, in 1995 the queen attended to mark her mother's ninety-fifth birthday. In 1998, the Queen Mother hosted the luncheon at Clarence House, her home off the Mall. At Sunnylands, Walter devoted an entire wall in his "Room of Memories" to the Queen Mother, a shrine on which he framed and mounted each of the Christmas cards she had sent him annually for a quarter century.

The Annenbergs' hospitality encompassed all members of the royal family. When the queen's uncle, Earl Mountbatten of Burma, was seventy, they gave him a party at Winfield House for which the ballroom was draped in dark blue silk with red and orange stripes, the colors of the Burma Star. Princess Margaret once stayed at Winfield House until four in the morning drinking gin and singing with a pianist and bleary-eyed guests, protocol prescribing that they stay until she left. When Frank Sinatra performed before three thousand fans at Festival Hall, Lee and Walter arranged a small preshow dinner for the princess with the singer. They escorted Prince Charles and Princess Anne around Washington, D.C., in 1970 on the young royals' first visit. Charles, whose relationship with his own parents was distant, developed a friendship with the Annenbergs, who in turn supported his Prince's Charitable Trusts. When he visited Sunnylands, Charles, who was not a golfer, careened down Walter's fairways playing golf-cart polo, his host in delighted pursuit.

Lee and Walter were careful not to betray confidences from their royal friendships, especially with Charles, who sent them long handwritten letters and in later years spoke with them about his troubled marriage. That was long after their inadvertent involvement in Charles's love life.

The first incident involved Tricia Nixon. The president's daughter was twenty-three, and to show her a good time when she came to attend Charles's 1969 investiture as Prince of Wales at Caernarfon Castle, Lee and Walter hosted a ball at Claridges because Winfield House was still under renovation. They flew in thousands of roses in Tricia's favorite pink and invited Charles and Princess Anne. Tricia had made a special request for Charles. She had never met him, but she had developed a crush on the prince, who was two years her junior, and had researched subjects to discuss with him. Anne attended the party, but Charles, who was uninterested in her, did not, bitterly disappointing Tricia, who spent the evening dancing with Prince Michael, a handsome cousin of the queen's but only sixteenth in line of succession.

Tricia was so disturbed about the prince and also about the queen's "failure" to invite her to tea, that when Walter put his arm around her shoulder to console the young woman he and Lee had known since she was a child, she fled to her room, and ordered her secret service agent, Bill Duncan, to call the White House and tell her father that his ambassador was "apparently intoxicated and had put his arm around her shoulder in a most objectionable and familiar fashion."[26] Nixon aide John Ehrlichman took the call, but, used to Tricia's frequent petulance, did not tell the president. Three weeks later, Nixon wrote Walter to thank him for "the magnificent way Lee and you entertained Tricia. . . . She is still on Cloud Nine whenever the word 'London' is mentioned."[27]

(Later, apparently angry at not being pardoned by the president for his role in Watergate, Ehrlichman knocked Walter, a known Nixon friend, by including the unflattering anecdote in a venomous 1982 memoir, *Witness to Power.* Walter loves women. Naturally at ease with them thanks to his upbringing, he enjoys complimenting women, speaking with and listening to them and swirling them around the dance floor, but he has neither loose hands nor a reputation as even a flirt. He was horrified when Ehrlichman published the allegation. He had put his arm on Tricia's shoulder to comfort her, but had not fondled her, as Lee, who was present, attested. Their conclusion was that the

Nixons had a wonderful daughter — named Julie. Peevish sister Tricia did not compare.)

The second incident with Charles involved an actual romance. The twenty-five-year-old prince was serving in the British navy aboard HMS *Jupiter* when it docked in San Diego in March 1974, and he met a tall, stunning, twenty-year-old blonde, Laura Jo Watkins. Charles became besotted with her, asked her to join him at Sunnylands when he left San Diego to visit the Annenbergs, exchanged numerous letters, and invited her to London in June. The smitten Laura Jo, daughter of Admiral James Watkins, who later became chief of naval operations and President George Bush's secretary of energy, flew to Britain, where the Annenbergs arranged a large dinner dance. During the preparations, Charles's great-uncle the duke of Gloucester died, and the royals went into mourning. Charles could not attend the dinner, but instead invited the beauty to attend his debut speech to the House of Lords. "Charles Asks Laura Jo to His Big Day," headlined the *Evening Standard*, sparking a press frenzy.[28]

Laura Jo believed the romance was leading to the altar. Lee sat the young woman down at Winfield House and explained that no matter how much she cared about him, she was an American and a Roman Catholic and Charles would never marry her. She might as well forget it. The press questioned whether the Annenbergs were pushing the comely Californian on the prince. Reporters and photographers staked out Winfield House. Lee and Walter determined that she had to go quickly and quietly. The chief of naval forces in Europe, a friend of Laura Jo's father, arranged delivery of a sailor's uniform. So disguised, Laura Jo was smuggled from Winfield House through Regent's Park to a military base and a flight home. She and Charles rendezvoused again in Bermuda and the Caribbean, and the affair wound down amicably. When the prince married Diana Spencer in 1981, among the guests at St. Paul's were the Annenbergs and several of Charles's former girlfriends, including, famously, Camilla Parker-Bowles, his longtime mistress, and, anonymously, Laura Jo.

WHILE MOST of Walter's service in Britain was more representational than policy-oriented, he did have personal ties to senior political and business figures. When he arrived in 1969, Labour party leader Harold Wilson was prime minister. Their relationship was congenial, but not especially close. Wilson was a wily politician, while Walter, despite his links to the cunning Richard Nixon, was more at home with straightforward people like Ronald Reagan and Margaret Thatcher. Wilson liked to toy with Walter, asking with a twinkle in his eye for a detailed rundown of what he should discuss with the president, or joking that agreement had been reached on his successor.

Although Walter was scrupulously nonpartisan, he was more at ease with Edward Heath, the Conservative party leader who was prime minister during most of his posting, from June 1970 until Wilson returned to office in February 1974. Highly intelligent, with a passion for music and sailing, Heath was an odd man to be a successful politician, except perhaps in Britain, which has long accommodated eccentrics. The son of a lower-class builder, Heath had attended Balliol College, Oxford, on an organ scholarship. He was a socially awkward bachelor, a brittle loner, painfully shy with women and often abrasive and arrogant with men. But he liked Lee and was gracious to Walter, not least because of the swimming pool gift to Chequers, saw them at Winfield House and invited them to his hometown of Broadstairs to watch him conduct the orchestra at the annual Christmas carol charity concert he had directed since 1936. In what was becoming a trademark gesture combining generosity and ensuring acceptance, Walter quickly set up a fund to support the musical series.

Heath realized that the ambassador had little to do with policy, but told Walter to come to 10 Downing Street any time he wished, an offer Walter took up infrequently. "President Nixon always telephoned me direct and we could discuss anything and everything," Heath explained. "I knew that if it came through the ambassador it wasn't important." Walter arrived one day with his deputy and handed the prime minister an envelope with a presidential message. "As I took it out, said Heath, "he said, nodding to his deputy, 'I will ask the minister to explain what it all means.' That really summed up everything."[29]

Their relationship unraveled for two reasons, one substantive, the other personal, both revealing of Walter. First, Heath was a committed European. He led Britain's 1961 application to join the Common Market, and despite France's rejection of the U.K. bid, Heath had tremendous respect and admiration for Charles de Gaulle. That in itself was almost enough to doom his friendship with Walter. What made it worse was that Walter began to see Heath's pro-Europeanism as anti-American. He was not alone. "Paradoxically, while the other European leaders strove to improve their relations with us," Henry Kissinger wrote in his memoirs, "Heath went in the opposite direction."[30]

Heath, who frequently traveled and lectured in the United States after leaving office, denied that he was, but even in his Conservative party he was considered the most anti-American prime minister of the postwar period if not the twentieth century. "Ted was besotted with Europe and thought that to be besotted with Europe you must be anti-American," said Margaret Thatcher, Heath's successor as party leader and the most pro-American prime minister of the postwar period if not of all time.[31] Heath wanted to pool Britain's nuclear deterrent with France's; sided with India against the U.S. and Pakistan in the 1972 subcontinent war which created Bangladesh; mocked (appropriately) Nixon's public relations gambit declaring 1973 the "year of Europe"; and refused during the 1973 Middle East war to allow U.S. warplanes to land in Britain or refuel at British military bases on Cyprus. Walter was indignant each time Heath failed to support the U.S. or knocked Nixon rhetorically.

The final straw came when the prime minister disinvited Walter on the eve of a dinner he was giving for Luis Echeverría Alvarez, the leftist president of Mexico. Ostensibly, the reason was that Mexico was feuding with the U.S. at the time and Heath belatedly realized that the presence of the U.S. ambassador might prove awkward. Furious, though less at being disinvited than by Heath's later insistence that he had never been invited — which in Walter's eyes made Heath a liar and thus dishonorable — Annenberg waited a decade to take revenge. In 1984, Charles Price, the then U.S. ambassador in London, and his wife, Carol, hosted a dinner in honor of their good friends the Annenbergs. Well in advance, Lee and Walter helped put together and approved the guest list, which included Heath, who accepted. Twenty-four hours before the dinner, Walter asked the embassy to deliver to Heath, still an influential member of Parliament, a personal note on Claridges stationery. The letter told him to cancel his acceptance. Heath did and the two men never spoke again.[32]

WHEN WALTER first accepted the ambassadorship, he promised to do the job for two years. Even as he grew to like it, he still intended to serve no longer than one presidential term, believing that he should be back at the helm of Triangle. As a result of the sale of the *Inquirer* and the broadcasting properties, the company's earnings had more than doubled in 1970 over the previous year to $13.19 a share and shot up again in 1971 to $22.61 a share. Fair market share value — determined by the accounting firm Price Waterhouse — was also rising, from $180 in 1971 to $210 a year later. With 4.044 million shares held privately by the family, Triangle was valued at the end of 1972 at $850 million, far too valuable and complex to be managed indefinitely by an absentee proprietor.

Surprises had a way of popping up in publishing, and Walter doubted that he would always be as prepared for trouble as he was in April 1972 when the printers of his *Morning Telegraph* struck in a dispute involving automation and job cutbacks. Walter had anticipated a walkout. The *Telegraph* was an old, hot-type shop that needed updating to the cold-type, computer technology which was so well suited for racing statistics. In 1969, he had bought 7.5 acres in New Jersey near the Peddie school, where he had built a state-of-the-art plant for the *Daily Racing Form*. When the *Telegraph* typesetters struck, Walter had a lock put on the door of that paper's Manhattan offices, announced he was shutting it down, beefed up the *Daily Racing Form* with *Telegraph* copy and within hours had transferred all racing production to New Jersey. To the horror of the International Typographical Union local, the new and improved *Daily Racing Form* never missed a publishing day.

Still, it might not have worked out so well, and Walter was concerned about being away too long. As soon as the *Telegraph* matter was resolved, he began a long process of telling the president that while the appointment "has been the high point of my life," he was ready to leave immediately after the November election. That May, Walter suggested that the tire company executive Leonard Firestone would be an able replacement.

Having asked to leave, wishing no other appointment and no longer owning the *Philadelphia Inquirer*, Walter felt that he was finally free to make a contribution to Nixon's reelection campaign. "What the hell," said Walter, who gave $254,000 in 1972, "I was on my way out and had no editorial voice where I could be accused of influencing opinion. It was the proper moment to say thank you for what he had done for me."[33]

The president, though, did not want Walter to leave. The Chicago insurance mogul W. Clement Stone, who contributed heavily in 1968 and gave more than $1 million in 1972, was back asking for London. Nixon did not want to give it to him. The easiest way to deal with Stone was telling him that Walter was staying put.

A week after Nixon swamped Democratic party challenger George McGovern in November to win a second term, Walter wrote again, "urging that another be given this ambassadorial honor during your second administration."[34] In December, the White House announced that Walter would stay, but behind the scenes he kept pressing to leave. He wrote in July 1973 asking to be relieved after Nixon's upcoming visit to Britain in the fall and again in November to say that "the pressure of personal affairs has now become such that I feel obliged to tender my resignation" by February 1974.[35]

Nixon continued to put him off until December 1973, when, in near desperation, Walter called Rose Mary Woods, the president's secretary, with more suggested replacements, including Robert Anderson, the chairman of Atlantic Richfield, and Phillip Hofmann, chairman of the pharmaceutical firm Johnson and Johnson.[36] By then, the president had to tell Walter that he could not replace him. The Watergate investigation that began with the June 1972 break-in at the Democratic National Committee headquarters had accelerated by the fall of 1973. The scandal that would lead to Nixon's downfall and resignation in August of 1974 had overwhelmed his administration, and the president could get no major appointments through Congress. His envoy would have to stay put.

Walter had difficulty dealing with Watergate. Like many loyal Republicans, he initially considered the scandal an extension of the antipathy liberals had long held for Nixon. As a former publisher, he was furious that the attacks on the president were led by journalists from the paper he had come to loathe, the *Washington Post*. For years, until the progressive release of the Nixon tapes began to convince him that the president had shown what he called "bad judgment" and had been ill-served by Attorney General John Mitchell, Walter contended that Watergate was a journalistic conspiracy. "Deep Throat," he felt, was fabricated by *Post* reporters Bob Woodward and Carl Bernstein, editor Ben Bradlee and publisher Katharine Graham. "I thought Nixon was getting ganged up on, but when I heard what was on the tapes, I was shocked and terribly saddened," he conceded years later, adding, with unintended understatement, "Apparently he had some responsibility."[37]

The president was a friend who had given him his highest honor, but Walter was not an intimate, nothing like businessmen Charles "Bebe" Rebozo and Robert Ablanalp, who were close presidential cronies. He was, however, intensely loyal. Just as he would not tolerate any criticism of his father, Moses, Walter would not hear criticism of Nixon, especially during Watergate. It was not that he was incapable of reassessing a friendship. He had disowned Frank Rizzo in the mid-1970s when the then mayor urged Philadelphians to "vote white," which Walter considered a racist disgrace. And he would drop others if he felt they had betrayed him or broken his code of "quality and decency." But Walter, as several of his friends pointed out, liked presidents — with the exception of Roosevelt. He was willing to forgive a president more easily than someone of lower rank, especially one who had done so much for him personally.

While the scandal was peaking in late 1973, Walter tried not to think about it. When it was impossible to avoid — it was, after all, monopolizing the administration and the news — he told himself that Gordon Liddy, the former FBI agent with links to the White House, had masterminded the break-in and other dirty tricks. He could not believe that Nixon was directly involved. And he had no intention of trying to find out.

FOUR MONTHS before Nixon resigned, while he was still overseeing the magazine from London Walter introduced a new feature in *TV Guide* called "News Watch." Ostensibly, the column's purpose was to monitor the balance of television news, which he believed was weighted against the president. In fact, Walter was single-handedly trying to right the balance. His columnists included Patrick Buchanan, the Nixon speechwriter, Kevin Phillips, conservative author of *The Emerging Republican Majority*, and John Lofton, a former editor of *Monday*, a GOP magazine. They ripped regularly into the "liberal elite" which they and Walter, with reason, believed tilted coverage to the left.

He never, however, discussed Watergate with Nixon. "I felt that he would have disliked my patronizing him," Walter explained. "That would not have been intelligent for me."[38] Nor did he ever discuss the subject with prime ministers Heath or Wilson or any senior British officials. "I think Walter was troubled," said Peter Carrington, a good friend who was then Britain's defense secretary, "but it wasn't mentioned and he kept his head down."[39]

With the exception of the British Petroleum case and his efforts to leave his post, Walter rarely wrote to or called on the president. "He was very careful about that and with me, too," said William Rogers. "The president was the president. I was the secretary of state and he was the ambassador. He never wanted to be seen as presumptuous or taking advantage of his friendship. He never asked for a thing. He just wanted to play by the rules and do a good job for his country."[40]

His primary contact with the White House was Rose Mary Woods. He sent her notes with favorable clippings from the British press for her to pass on to the president; occasionally he telephoned. "Don't let these people get you down," he said in December 1973.[41] Sometimes he offered substantive thoughts which showed that his recent diplomatic experience had not turned him soft. Developing countries which relied on America for assistance but refused to sell the U.S. their goods were a particular peeve. "We have to be tough about it," he asked Woods to tell Nixon in January 1974. "We cannot go on feeding the world and then letting them bleed us to death when they have a commodity we need. If they hold back their oil, copper, tin, etc. — we should just produce an enormous amount of food so we can keep the price down for our own people and then refuse to sell it to the others unless they cooperate with us. We've been Boy Scouts too long."[42]

Knowing how much the president and Kissinger loved the luxury and privacy of Sunnylands, he had issued an open invitation to use the estate. "My house is your house," he offered, a generous gesture that produced complicated results.

Kissinger occasionally called London late in the week to ask an Annenberg aide, "This is a nonconversation. We would like to go to Palm Springs this weekend if they cannot get there." Told that Walter and Lee had commitments or were traveling on the Continent, Kissinger replied, "Good, we will go."[43] Such behavior was not surprising coming from Kissinger, who was brilliant but often said one thing in public and the opposite in private. That he had no professional respect for Walter and denigrated him behind his back, yet was more than willing to accept his hospitality was part of his deeply ingrained tendency toward deceit. (When informed later of the Kissinger exchange, Lee checked the estate's records and determined that the security adviser and secretary of state, while he may have planned on going, never actually stayed at Sunnylands without them.)

Unfortunately, the attitude was more widespread. According to Nixon papers in the national archives, White House chief of staff H. R. "Bob" Haldeman asked an aide to plan a presidential trip to California in February 1973. "Let's see if we can find a discreet way of determining whether Walter Annenberg's place in Palm Springs is available during the 7th to the 18th. Don't do it in such a way as to alert anyone, otherwise we'll end up with Annenberg there."[44]

Haldeman almost always spoke for Nixon. "Don't you come whining to me when he tells you to do something," Nixon instructed his cabinet about Haldeman in 1971. "He will do it because I asked him to and you're to carry it out."[45] The implication of Haldeman's Palm

Springs comment is unavoidable. If he were speaking for the president in this case, his choice of words could call into question the nature of Nixon and Walter's friendship. Was the president accepting the generosity of a staunch backer, and using him, but otherwise avoiding him? That would hardly be uncommon. Politicians spend considerable time dodging donors. Nor is it unusual — if anything, it's closer to the norm — for well-to-do supporters to use their wealth to buy proximity to power. In the political arena, that's often what converging interests are all about. (In May 1972, Haldeman wrote in his diary that "P [the president] told me that he wanted to have Walter Annenberg donate a swimming pool to Blair House." Walter would have been glad to had he been asked, but he was not, so the pool was not built.)

In this instance, it is impossible to be certain whether Haldeman was speaking for himself or the president because the chief of staff died in 1993 and Nixon the following year. But Haldeman's memo appears more likely to be a red herring dragged across the Nixon-Annenberg relationship.

First, Haldeman and Annenberg disliked each other. On one visit, Walter was kept waiting for thirty minutes outside Haldeman's White House office while the chief of staff and an aide joked and traded anecdotes. Convinced Haldeman was toying with him, Walter fought to control his temper and, thereafter, did his best to avoid him. When Haldeman was tried and convicted of perjury for his role in Watergate, Walter declined to support his defense fund.

Second, there was no evidence — from their past history, the president's writing and records, released White House tapes or their own extensive correspondence — that the Nixon-Annenberg relationship was anything but a real friendship, between both the men and their wives, that endured for four decades. According to Julie Nixon Eisenhower, the president's younger daughter, "Haldeman was a very negative person who didn't want anyone close to my father. This [memo] had to be a little power play on his part because my father really liked and admired Walter. He loved that he was such a fighter and he thought Lee was brilliant. Both my parents really liked them. They were super friends."[46]

Which is not to say that Nixon and Annenberg did not also serve one another's purposes, because they did. Nixon relished the publisher's uncritical support, while Walter, having recognized that political power outweighed wealth, was, after Roosevelt, always keen to be close to presidents. He was patriotic and wanted to operate, circulate and be accepted at the highest level, meaning the White House as well as Buckingham Palace, but presidents were also his security blanket.

(As for the February 1973 visit to Sunnylands, it never happened. According to the president's daily diary and Sunnylands records, Nixon was in San Clemente, California, from February 8 to February 12 while Lee and Walter were in London but did not go to the estate. He visited six times while in office. On each occasion the Annenbergs were in residence.)

WHEN TOLD on August 7, 1974, that Nixon would resign the following day, Walter immediately sent him a telegram. "Dear Mr. President," it read in entirety, "I continue to be proud of your record of service to the people of our country and be assured of my continuing faith in you and in the solidarity of our friendship."[47] Three weeks later, Nixon accepted Walter's offer to become a consultant in international diplomacy and economics at the Annenberg School of Communications, which at that point had no university affiliation, but existed at Triangle's headquarters. The five-year contract paid the former president $60,000 a year.[48] Walter also offered him the run of Sunnylands to rest in peace and quiet and flew home to see them when the Nixons accepted. "When you're down, you find out who your *real* friends are," Nixon wrote in the Sunnylands guest book on September 8, 1974, the day he was pardoned by Gerald Ford. "We shall always be grateful for your kindness and your loyal friendship." After suffering a potentially fatal bout of phlebitis in his leg that fall, the former president also spent part of his recuperation at the estate.

Gerald Ford, the Michigan congressman who had replaced the disgraced Spiro Agnew as vice president, had been sworn in on August 9 as the nation's thirty-eighth president. Ford knew Walter well. He had been at Sunnylands nearly six years earlier on the day when Nixon had offered the embassy job to Walter and had been among those urging that he take it. With Nixon gone from Washington, Walter could finally leave London. Ford had barely finished reciting the oath of office when Walter asked if he could leave London by October 31.

There was considerable discussion inside and outside the new Ford administration about who would replace him. Because of the energy crisis and the massive pipeline project in Alaska, Bob Anderson could not leave Atlantic Richfield. President Ford initially offered the post, in what would have been a supreme irony, to Senator J. William Fulbright, who had been rebuffed by Arkansas primary voters in his bid for a sixth term. When Fulbright turned the offer down because of his wife's ill health, Ford appointed Elliott Richardson, a liberal Republican who had held three cabinet posts under Nixon until 1973 when he resigned as attorney general after refusing a White House order to fire Watergate special prosecutor Archibald Cox.

"The cuisine took a big drop when we took over," Richardson joked. "There was no way of following in the Annenberg footsteps."[49] A cartoon by the *Evening Standard*'s star cartoonist, J. A. K., showed two marines cooking hotdogs over a campfire outside Winfield House as Richardson and his wife, Anne, stood at the head of a long reception line of nobles in white tie, duchesses in tiaras and a monocled diplomat asking, "I say, what do you suppose he charges for corkage?"

In a turnabout, the U.S. press gave Walter high marks for his service. "Annenberg Leaving London with Critics Mellowed," read the headline over the *New York Times* story on his departure.[50] The Gene Roberts–led *Philadelphia Inquirer* also saluted its former proprietor with a congratulatory editorial titled "Well done, Mr. Ambassador."[51]

Lee and Walter, having hosted nearly five hundred social events during their five-and-a-half-year posting, were lovingly and lavishly feted as they exited. One of Walter's final stops was his departure address to the Pilgrims. He had been contemplating, he told the assembled guests, what advice he could hand on to his successor. Whether he should tell him, for example, that it was much easier to deal with the British government than with Washington. Or, given that Harold Wilson was back in Downing Street, the always useful advisory to "stay on the ins with the outs."

Finally, he decided to pass on just one suggestion. "If Her Majesty should inquire if he was comfortable in the embassy residence," Walter recommended, the ambassador "should reply, quite simply, Yes, Ma'am. . . ."

25

BACK HOME

—————

W HILE LEE AND WALTER left Britain to resounding praise for their success, they arrived home to a family calamity. A dozen years earlier as they were returning from a trip to Europe, Roger had killed himself. This time, a desperately unhappy Wallis seemed intent on destroying herself. She was not schizophrenic as her brother had been. Nor had she tried consciously to commit suicide. But Walter's only surviving child had become an alcoholic and addicted to drugs. Her fifteen-year marriage to neurosurgeon Seth Weingarten was in ruins. He had accused her of drug abuse, having female lovers and being an unfit mother and was suing for divorce. She faced a custody fight over their four children.

Looking back later, sober and recovering, she attributed many of her troubles then to low self-esteem and having had no idea what to do in 1959 when she left Pine Manor Junior College. She had graduated with honors, but "basically, the program was you have two years in which to find a husband or transfer to another school," she half-jokingly told a Pine Manor audience in 1986 when she came with Walter, Lee and First Lady Nancy Reagan to dedicate the Annenberg Library and Communications Center, for which Walter had contributed a million dollars.[1]

By the time she finished her studies at Pine Manor, Wallis had overcome many of the learning problems she had as a child, including finding algebra and geometry so impenetrable that she had wondered whether something was wrong with her. But she had not found a husband. She had not even had much experience dating. Her one semiserious college boyfriend had been thirty-five and worked for National

Cash Register. She liked him because he took her to Boston's Locke-Ober restaurant for lobster, instead of Howard Johnson's for grilled cheese sandwiches, which was where most boys her age took her friends.

She was interested in studying psychology but frightened off because the major required that she take statistics. She decided to stick with liberal arts and major in philosophy at Columbia, to what purpose she did not know. For a while she toyed with becoming a courtroom reporter. In the late 1950s, Eisenhower was in the White House and the start of the women's movement which began redefining options was still more than a decade away. Columbia would give her two more years to learn and find a husband, after which she expected to do what most women did in those years — have children, raise them and try to be a supportive wife. "The message I got was that a woman's life begins when she gets married, so I figured, what the hell, I'll try it."

Wallis needed to create some kind of framework because at nineteen she felt alone and adrift. Her father lived in Pennsylvania and California with Lee, who had two daughters of her own. Her mother, Ronny, had married a third time and was living in New York and Florida. Her only sibling was having problems at Harvard. She was not close to her cousins. None of the cousins were close, and once Sadie died in 1965, the glue that had held the family together was gone. Wallis did not have many close friends. Named for her father, she was saddled with a distinctly unfeminine name. Jewish by birth, with her maternal grandmother a prominent Canadian Zionist and her uncle an Israeli war hero, but educated at the nation's leading Episcopalian school for young women, she was also wrestling with her own identity.

When she spotted Seth, a tall, crew-cut blond in madras shorts lounging on the Lido beach at Venice soon after graduation, Wallis had fixed him up with a boy-crazy Pine Manor classmate who was traveling with her. They went off to play tennis, but at a tea dance later that day, Seth switched his attention to Wallis. They danced and the next day he called and invited her out for dinner. Lee urged that her stepdaughter go. Seth looked great on paper — a Princeton graduate about to begin medical school at Yale and enjoying his own European present from parents who lived in chic Westport, Connecticut.

Back in school that fall, Wallis spent almost as much time at Yale falling in love as she did studying at Columbia. Seth proposed and on a gloriously sunny day in June 1960, they were married in a gala ceremony at Inwood by Rabbi Bertram Korn. Wallis's mother, Ronny, attended, along with a pride of Dunkelmans from Toronto and a collection of Seth's fellow medical students. Her brother, Roger, was the best man.

With no push from Walter to continue her education, Wallis dropped out of Columbia and moved to New Haven, where she and Seth lived for the next three years. Their eldest child and only daughter, Lauren, was born there. Wallis gave birth to Roger and Gregory while Seth was completing his residency at New York Hospital. Charles, the youngest, was born at Walker Air Force Base in Roswell, New Mexico, where Seth fulfilled his Vietnam War era duty for two years as an Air Force captain.

Having suffered with Seth through medical school — she could not watch television, listen to the radio or read in bed because the light and sound bothered her husband — Wallis loved Roswell. They were part of a close-knit family of a dozen doctors, lived in a tiny cottage surrounded by an awe-inspiring landscape and lived a relatively relaxed existence in a culture where the most ostentatious status symbol was the size of one's camper. She made more friends than she had ever had, learned to play bridge, enjoyed the moments when Seth traveled on "tdy," or temporary duty, and loved it when he returned. "It was the first time in my life when I felt part of a community and a peer system," she said. "I felt connected. Those were happy years."[2]

Lee influenced their decision to move to California when Seth was discharged from the service in 1969. Wallis and Seth were both easterners, but Lee convinced them that sunny California was the best place to raise children, that the state was booming, a good place for a doctor to begin practicing, and that they would be close to Sunnylands. Lee and Harriet Deutsch found them a house in Beverly Hills which Walter paid for, and Seth went to work at UCLA's medical center. "I thought it was a very good marriage," said Lee, "but then it all went wrong."[3]

The 1962 death of Roger, her best friend and only confidant, so devastated Wallis that she never completely recovered. Eighteen months after he died, she gave birth to her first son and named him Roger, a choice which disturbed Walter. He understood that Wallis was trying to commemorate her brother, but for him there was only one Roger and his son's life had involved more sadness than the father could bear. Walter was more troubled than angry, but the situation was reminiscent of Moses's fury when his daughter Enid wanted to name an adopted daughter Diana in honor of his and Sadie's first child, who had died at five.

Then, magnifying the tragedy, young Roger was found to have the same disorder as his namesake. He had seemed fine until kindergarten, when he showed signs of hyperactivity. "Everyone laughed and admired his energy," said Wallis, "but I knew intuitively something was wrong." He attended grammar school in Beverly Hills, but by fifteen Roger Weingarten had been diagnosed as schizophrenic and moved to Santa Barbara to the Devereaux School, which treats physically, emotionally and mentally impaired children and adults.

The trauma of her brother's death, her son's illness and ten years of marriage to a doctor whose career was taking off as her own self-esteem sank took a toll on Wallis. She began drinking heavily. In the early 1970s in Los Angeles, where at certain parties cocaine was more available than cashews, she became an alcoholic and then addicted to drugs.

While this was happening, Walter was supporting the Weingarten family, as he had been from the moment Wallis married. Walter paid for three years of Seth's medical school and the family's expenses through medical residency, the Air Force, and as the children grew. He was happy to do it. Walter wanted his son-in-law to have the best possible training regardless of how long it took without his having to worry about producing an income. After Seth's father died in 1966, it turned out that, despite their smart Westport address, his mother, Dorothy, was soon down to her last $500. Walter sent money to the widow. "Lee and I have been disturbed about the immediate pressures that have been visited upon you materially," Walter wrote, enclosing a $1,000 check. "We will be pleased to sit down with you and to be as helpful as possible. . . . Certainly it is our desire to avail you of as much comfort as we can give."[4]

Moses and Sadie had handed out money to their children like candy. And several of Walter's sisters were extremely extravagant, giving large homes and huge allowances to their offspring. Walter was always more careful. He did not want his daughter to be so well taken care of that she and her family would become complacent, the well-fed house dogs that Moses had derided. He had lectured Wallis and her brother throughout their childhood that discipline and hard work were the keystones to good character. Now Walter began to feel that he too had been overindulgent and that his backing had been counterproductive. He had supported Seth "in a very extravagant manner which, perhaps, was a mistake," he wrote Dorothy Weingarten in 1971 from London. "I say this because not only is my daughter extravagant, but considering the money Seth spends on himself, [it] has I think, gotten the two of them off on an unrealistic basis." He felt sorry for both his daughter and her son, Walter went on, "because with all the material comforts they have, they are both miserably unhappy and this is indeed a great tragedy in my life."[5]

Squabbles over money continued. After Wallis and Seth charged $330.90 in excess-baggage costs for a flight home from Paris to a Triangle Publications credit card reserved for employee use for business expenses, Walter recalled the card. Seth was angry and claimed that Walter was trying to ruin his reputation. The exchange prompted a round of letters between Walter and Seth's mother about gratitude and bitterness. Walter had treated Dorothy to a stay at the La Costa spa for which she had expressed her gratitude. Writing to thank her for her thank you — a typical Walter practice — he enclosed copies of the letters between himself and Seth, made clear their differences and said that he was not looking for lavish thanks from her son. Walter did not tell Dorothy that in general he had low expectations for gratitude. Moses had had a cynical attitude about the subject which he passed on to his heirs. "If you want to see gratitude, look it up in *Webster's*," Moses used to say. "Don't expect it anywhere else."[6] Walter wanted something else. "All I ever seek from good deeds is a measure of respect," Walter wrote, "and I cannot regard this as unreasonable."[7]

Lee and Walter returned from London to spend Christmas and the 1972 New Year's holiday at Sunnylands. The Weingartens joined them for a brief weekend reunion during which they worked out a family budget. To provide what he called "a measure of monetary comfort and peace of mind as well," Walter agreed to pay their projected $7,540 a month family expenses — nearly $30,000 in current dollars — plus $2,700 a month for medical care — mostly psychiatric — and $300 monthly for Seth's mother, who was living on a small teacher's pension. In return, he would notify their bank that he would no longer be responsible for their overdrafts. "Fill out your check stubs," he advised them, signing off "with hope and faith in the capacity of you young adults to carry on, and with deep affection."[8]

The budget, which was to be reviewed annually, provided the stability and discipline Walter had intended. When Seth completed his studies in July 1972 — twelve years after he had begun paying for them — Walter offered some paternal advice from London. "I want to remind you that success in life is based on hard slogging. There will be periods when discouragement is great and upsetting, and the antidote for this is calmness and fortitude and a modest yet firm belief in your competence. Be sure that your priorities are in correct order so that you may proceed in a logical manner . . . [and] be ever mindful that nothing will take the place of persistence." If Seth ever had "a particularly gloomy period," Walter added, "You know I am always around to talk it out."⁹

By the end of the following year, Walter felt better about the prospects for Wallis and her family. He could tell that they had settled well into Beverly Hills. "I want you both to continue to be as constructive as you possibly can. This is not only healthy, but collaterally gives your children a certain stability and standing," he wrote in November 1973. "I should like to add that only catastrophic economic conditions affecting my income could possibly interfere with the kind of support that I have been giving, and propose to continue to give in the years ahead. Accordingly, you adults can stop worrying about the money tap."¹⁰

He still believed they were overly extravagant, buying fancy golf bags and otherwise indulging themselves. They had discussed borrowing money to build equity in a home they would own themselves, but Walter doubted they could carry the finance charges. If they were to take out a loan, he advised that they apply the money to family expenses, not real estate. Walter charged them nothing for their home on North Alpine Drive, which he purchased so that each grandchild would have his own bedroom, part of his determination that the children have "every possible wholesome advantage" and that family unity be fostered.

"I continue to want to see you move into better quarters but I repeat my primary reason for urging this is because of the children, not necessarily to provide the two of you with an elegant main floor suite." The truth was that they would never receive all they wished without hard work. "Remember," he said, repeating his core philosophy, "adversity tests us from time to time and it is inevitable that this testing continues during life. . . . Quite simply, the test of character is having the ability to meet challenges."¹¹

The marriage soon after failed to meet the challenge and Seth sued for divorce. Wallis and her father tried to settle the case quietly but failed. Wallis's mother, Ronny, who had a good relationship with Seth, pleaded with her son-in-law not to litigate. But the neurosurgeon was angry at his wife and at her father, who had done everything for them. Walter was horrified at the prospect of a public scandal, but he never contemplated anything less than an all-out defense of his daughter.

"My father stuck by me every minute no matter what," said Wallis. He hired a blue-ribbon law firm, one which could have negotiated a merger between Ford and Chrysler, but which was out of its depth in the shark-filled waters of a bitter Beverly Hills divorce. "I was dragged into the courtroom and called all sorts of things," Wallis said, sobbing at the memory. "It was a very ugly scene. He accused me of very inappropriate behavior, wild parties, drugs, alcohol. Yes, I did drugs and I did alcohol and I had strange people in my bed, but I was not a bad person. I was sick and my judgment was off."[12]

The divorce was granted and Seth won custody of his fourteen-year-old daughter, Lauren, and joint custody of the three boys. He was awarded child support because Wallis had tangible assets, a $2 million home on Ridgedale Drive in Beverly Hills purchased in her name by Walter after the divorce. The court records were sealed and Walter resolved not to discuss the breakup. Wallis insisted that Seth was not the cause of the breakup and should not be blamed, yet Walter found unforgivable his former son-in-law's insistence on taking the case to court and drawing his grandchildren into the proceedings. Publicly and privately he discounted Seth's claims about her bisexuality, but he was outraged that his son-in-law had spread the allegation in public.

He did not want to know whether it was true. Having had a discussion on the general subject with Eppie Lederer, a family friend better known as Ann Landers, whose column he had published in the *Philadelphia Inquirer* since 1955, Walter believed that whatever relationship Wallis might have was a private lifestyle choice, not a sickness. Like any father, he wanted Wallis to be careful of who she was with and to use good judgment, but otherwise, Walter took a Don't ask, don't tell approach to the whole matter. What was left was pure vitriol for his former son-in-law: twenty years later, mere mention of his name could turn Walter red with rage.

A YEAR AFTER the breakup was formalized, Seth offered to relinquish custody of the children. Although he had not been involved with anyone at the time of the divorce, he had since moved in with the widow of a prominent property developer and had taken the Weingarten children with him. Wallis, who had been undergoing therapy, was happy to have back those willing to come. Certain relationships had been scarred, notably with her daughter, who was fourteen during the divorce proceedings and had testified against Wallis. A beautiful young woman who later graduated from Princeton and did graduate work at MIT, Lauren opted for distance. She moved to Britain, married a professor, painted and sculpted and raised Walter's first great-grandchildren. Lee and Walter visited them on their annual trip to London and Wallis's links with her daughter improved. Roger remained at Devereaux. Wallis wondered every day whether what happened to her and the family in the seventies could have contributed to his disorder. Son Gregory graduated from Stanford, studied painting at Parson's and moved to Paris, where he married and worked as an artist. Youngest son Charles graduated from Duke, earned his master's at the University of Southern California's school of cinema and television, and, the only child to remain nearby, wrote screenplays in Los Angeles.

No schism ever developed with Walter and Lee. They did all they could to help Wallis recover and were overjoyed by her success. "She had a difficult time but she fought very hard and pulled herself together. I love her and we are very proud of her," said Lee.[13] "Tremendously proud," echoed an emotional Walter. "She's a good citizen and I love her dearly."[14]

To get her back on track, Walter flew to Los Angeles and took her by the hand to the mid-Wilshire office of *TV Guide*. "He pushed me through the door and said, 'Here, this is where you're going to work,'" said Wallis. "It was the best thing he ever did for me. There's nothing like taking action to break someone out of self-obsession."[15]

At the time she was terrified. Wallis felt that she had grown up always reacting, rarely showing initiative, often feeling defeated before she started anything. She arrived at *TV Guide* knowing little about the workplace and needing all the help she could find. She had been an early patient at the Betty Ford chemical dependency clinic — later she joined its board — and was an Alcoholics Anonymous regular, but the *TV Guide* job had the biggest influence on her recovery. "Just by showing up on a daily basis I had a feeling of belonging and accomplishment unlike any I had felt before," she said. "In being responsible, I felt responsible and I began to find a positive image for myself."[16]

She worked at *TV Guide* for the next dozen years as an arranger and nonwriting story producer. She offered story ideas, conducted interviews and, very important for her self-esteem, earned a modest $30,000 salary. "Wallis is a nice woman and it worked out great," said David Sendler, a former editor of *TV Guide*. "She knew everybody and could get the big players out to lunch or to meet with us." Once she had some on-the-job journalism training, Sendler went on, "she learned to ask the right questions and became quite knowledgeable and a good scout. She gave us early warning on what projects were starting, what stars and executives were doing, bits of information that could turn into news items. She made a real contribution to what ended up in the magazine. And her parties were terrific."[17]

Bill Bruns, an author who was then *TV Guide*'s Los Angeles bureau chief, was uncertain what to expect when he first saw the owner's elegantly dressed daughter, but pleased by what he found. "She couldn't have been nicer. She didn't lord it over anybody. She wasn't a writer, but she was happy to do anything you asked. She always came to story conferences, knew what was going on, and if we had a visiting VIP or a meeting with a network chief, she'd set up the dinner, flowers, everything. She was great."[18] She was also generous. *TV Guide* writers who came to California from New York or Washington to work on stories found her quick to offer the services of her secretary or driver, private phone numbers for celebrity friends or meetings with her industry contacts.

AFTER THEIR London stint, Walter was thrilled to be back in the United States, especially as a minor celebrity. He was much more comfortable in his own skin. "He mellowed greatly after London," said Martin Hillenbrand, who had been assistant secretary of state for Europe during Walter's posting.[19] "Walter was once quite autocratic," his London friend David Metcalfe said with affection, "but in returning to the States, he mellowed far more, far, far more."[20] James Hanson, a British executive who first met Walter in the late 1950s, initially found him "peremptory. He was not the easiest person to get along with, but he became quite wonderful. He developed. He allowed himself to become confident. When he returned home from Britain, he realized that he was a star on the world scene. Everyone knew him."[21]

He was asked to join the American Philosophical Society, the nation's oldest learned society, founded by Benjamin Franklin in 1743, in which membership is limited to persons and scholars of distinction. But he still could not get into the Philadelphia club, the city's most exclusive, despite the efforts of his former aide Bobby Scott and his father Edgar, who, fearful they would not succeed, had not told Walter they were trying. "It was absolutely infuriating," said the younger Scott. "I tried, my father tried, various other people tried, but nothing worked." The WASPs weren't keeping him out. They liked his Republican politics. Those who opposed him and threatened to blackball his application were a small number of old Jewish members, descendants of those families that arrived in Philadelphia in the early and mid-19th century. Their objections were personal. They hadn't liked Moses, didn't care for his son and would not be budged. Walter, who eventually learned of the failed effort, had not mellowed enough to let the rejection roll off his back. "He was mad," said Scott, "really mad."[22]

But he did not try to get even, as he would have before London. He would show them in another way. Although he would not acknowledge any linkage, he became an even greater contributor to local Jewish causes. "Not so much when he was running the paper, but since he came back from London he's been a huge supporter," said Philadelphia activist Meyer "Pat" Potamkin.[23] "Our biggest contributor," echoed Sylvan Cohen, chairman of the city's United Jewish Appeal.[24] Having already walked in unsolicited to the federation of Jewish agencies after the 1967 Six Day War with a check for $1 million, Walter on his return from London chaired for years the annual "Ambassador's Dinner" for donors of $100,000 and more. "He single-handedly turned around fund-raising in the Jewish community by hosting those dinners," said businessman and activist Ronald Rubin.[25]

(By 1998 — the year he was finally invited to join the Philadelphia Club and graciously accepted — his gifts to Philadelphia's Jewish Federation totaled $9.7 million. In addition, he gave $5.8 million dollars to Yeshiva University and its Albert Einstein College of Medicine. Fifteen million dollars went to Operation Exodus, which relocated thousands of Soviet Jews to Israel. He gave $2 million to Congregation Emanu-El in New York in his mother's name and $2 million more to the United States Holocaust Memorial Museum in Washington. In Israel, he gave $1 million each to the Weizmann Institute of Science and the Technion-Israel Institute of Technology, $2 million to the Jerusalem Foundation and $4.4 million to Hebrew University of Jerusalem. His biggest Jewish-oriented gift was to the former Dropsie College, a nonsectarian institute of Judaic and Near East studies in the shadow of Independence Hall. Dropsie had trained generations of scholars since its 1907 founding, but lost students and funding after a damaging 1984 fire. Walter contributed $30 million to Dropsie, which was renamed the Annenberg Research Institute. Walter objected to the change, but the board, said Judge Arlin Adams, "figured if they had Walter's name on the building, he couldn't walk away if they had financial problems again."[26] Walter made the gift from a conviction that

understanding history was impossible without knowledge of the inter-
action of Judaism, Christianity and Islam. "These are the three great
rivers which nurtured Western civiliation," he said. "Their influence
must be understood.")[27]

DESPITE HAVING once claimed in Britain in a moment of exuberant
honesty that Philadelphia was a "bush-league London," which annoyed a number of Philadelphians, he loved being back at his office.
Most of all, now that he was known, he appreciated having his privacy
back. His staff and friends continued to call him "Ambassador," which
he liked, and he and Lee settled into a routine of spending seven
months a year at Inwood and from December through April at Sunnylands. Out West they often played golf as a twosome, using balls and
golf carts embossed with the house's Mayan symbol, and had quiet
dinners with friends at home or at various country clubs. Occasionally,
they would attend civic dinners and charitable events, perhaps at the
Eisenhower Medical Center in Rancho Mirage, where Walter was a
founding member and donor of more than $11 million, or the Palm
Springs Desert Museum, to which he and Lee gave $2.5 million.

Some of Walter's favorite evenings were spent in the East at meetings of the Benevolent Marching and Philosophical Society, the code
name for his Philadelphia poker and golf group. He played with Campbell Soup chairman Jack Dorrance, Stuart Saunders of the Penn Central, investment broker Howard Butcher, Cummins Catherwood, an
investment manager whose wife, Susan, was also a good friend of both
Annenbergs', and other Main Line worthies. Sometimes they played
for a few thousand dollars a night, but more often for hundreds. Even
at penny-a-point bridge games with the Catherwoods, Walter hated to
lose. But because the poker players all had money and were not out to
take much of someone else's, the monthly gatherings were for camaraderie and the chance to jump in someone's private jet and fly to
Florida to play golf. Walter loved the group, which had only one firm
rule: he kept the books.

Walter liked to gamble, always within limits. "You've got to have
your head examined if you gamble regularly," he said.[28] What others
might consider risk never put him off, but he did limit his high-stakes
gambling to twice a year, with a self-imposed cap of $100,000, 100,000
pounds if he were in London. He occasionally played baccarat, but
roulette was his game, preferably in Europe, where the wheel has a single zero favoring the house. On U.S. equipment, double zeros reduce a

gambler's chances. He won more often than he lost, but when he did drop his stake, he quit. Monte Carlo was his favorite casino, although he enjoyed Baden-Baden and Deauville. He played only once in London while ambassador, afraid that he would be spotted and criticized. When in Las Vegas once to hear Frank Sinatra perform at the Golden Nugget, Walter was invited by Mirage Resorts chairman Steve Wynn to visit his casino. He said he would come if he could play roulette on a European table. Wynn, a creative businessman himself and a serious art collector who considered The Ambassador a role model, agreed and gave Walter — a "modest gambler" by Wynn's standards — a private room with a French wheel and table.[29] Walter lost the $100,000, but gained respect for the business skills of the Mirage boss. "Those high-roller suites are the last word," he said, chuckling.

THEY WERE the opposite of his spartan *TV Guide* offices in Radnor, where Walter moved Triangle after he fell out with the Knights and quit his space in the *Inquirer* tower. The Main Line was not all mansions and country clubs. Like any suburb, it had its shops, car dealers and apartment complexes. The Triangle headquarters was office-block utilitarian. It was spotless, well lit, had adequate parking, offices with windows for *TV Guide* editors and executives and nonwindow cubicles for writers and the lean support staff. Walter, maintaining a proprietor's degree of separation, had a huge corner office on the top floor, one flight above his editorial operations. He never considered moving *TV Guide* or his headquarters to New York, the center of the publishing and television universe. He loved Inwood and the manageability of Philadelphia, where he had lived for nearly forty years. Radnor was only a short drive to the city, but felt more remote in the 1970s. "When I took a taxi there for my job interview, I thought I was riding into the heart of Pennsylvania," said Bill Bruns. "It was astonishing how he ran this empire which shaped TV coverage all over the country from deep in no-man's land."[30]

Seventeen was edited in New York and *Daily Racing Form* headquarters were in New Jersey. Walter had *TV Guide* reporters and stringers, part-time writers, deployed in New York, Washington and Los Angeles, and he could supplement them quickly if needed with writers from Radnor. In his view, there were other good business reasons for the isolation. Building space and overhead costs were more reasonable. Housing and living expenses were cheaper for his editors and staff. Public schools were better. He paid well, but never extravagantly, because he was prudent at work and did not have to match New York salaries.

Such attention to the bottom line was especially necessary when he returned from London to reassume full control of an empire diminished by the sales of the *Inquirer* and the television stations. Triangle stock in 1974 was down to $100 from $210 in 1972, when he began lobbying Nixon to let him come home. He pushed it to $145 a share in 1975, the start of a run-up that by 1985 would see the share price at $525.

One way he managed the growth was by working hard to minimize risk. He borrowed money only when he felt confident that the upside far outweighed the down. When he took out a loan, he borrowed as much as he could get and paid it back as quickly as possible, then repeated the process. He hated taking loans for anything that depreciated easily. He would never, for example, borrow to buy a car or a plane. Money's long-term cost was a constant concern. He paid off mortgages quickly to operate as debt free as possible. He did not carry a credit card, but paid cash in restaurants and shops from a modest stack of folded greenbacks. Large bills were sent to his office. Casinos offered a credit line.

Although he gave subordinates latitude, Walter paid attention to detail. "You had a passion for the details that count," marketing executive Arthur Brener wrote him.[31] He did more than monitor circulation, advertising revenues and overhead. Because accuracy was so important in past performance statistics, which he did not try to follow, Walter called editor Fred Grossman whenever he saw a typo in *Daily Racing Form* editorial copy. If he spotted a misspelled name, Walter made Grossman write a letter of apology to the person.

He was quick to praise good work and knew when to look the other way. He arrived without warning one day at the *Daily Racing Form* office to find the staff playing gin rummy, a scene which recalled Moses's entrance a half century earlier into the newsroom of the *Wisconsin News*. Moses had tried to shut down the game by joining it, raising the stakes and failing. Walter was more successful. He kept walking and let the copyeditors clear away the cards and whiskey bottle before he returned. "It was a classy move," said Grossman. "He knew what the guys were doing and he didn't want to embarrass them."[32]

He settled business bills on time but drove hard bargains with suppliers. "Walter was a very wise purchaser," said Peter Paine, former head of the Great Northern Nekoosa Paper Company, a major newsprint supplier. "He always made sure he was getting a good price. He wasn't going to be taken as a sucker by anyone."[33]

He hewed to Edward Eagle Brown's advice to "sit, sit, sit" and hold on to his properties, but he also had an acute sense of when to fold. In 1966 and 1967, he had tried to buy *Gourmet*. The privately held, upscale cooking magazine was not for sale, so in 1973 from London, Walter launched *Good Food*, a *TV Guide*–sized monthly aimed at the general public and sold on supermarket racks. A hearty eater himself with tastes that ranged from liverwurst and ravioli to caviar and classic French delicacies — which forced him to constantly watch his weight — Walter believed that a magazine devoted to easy-to-prepare healthy food would find an audience. He was right, but off by a decade. After spending several million dollars to sell 300,000 copies to subscribers and another million on newsstands, Walter too hastily shut the magazine down after only eight issues. In 1985, convinced there was broader-based interest and a better advertising climate, he relaunched *Good Food* and saw circulation climb quickly to more than 485,000 copies.[34]

Without the *Inquirer*, he had more time for other projects. In late 1974, shortly after returning to Philadelphia, he was pleased when Thomas Hoving asked to see him. They had met a few years earlier at Winfield House, where Walter gave the Metropolitan Museum director a tour of his paintings. "I was impressed not only by his knowledge, but by his passion for each one," Hoving noted, adding, "I found him direct and earthy in just the right way, and funny to boot."

Back in the United States, Hoving showed how much stature Walter had gained in London by asking him to become a trustee of the Metropolitan, the nation's foremost cultural institution. To be a trustee, said Hoving, "is to gain the apex of the social, intellectual and artistic position in the nation." But, he noted in his memoir, the Met was also a "combination of the Vatican, Versailles, the Sultan's Court and the Cave of Ali Baba, it can be hurly-burly — and dangerous" for trustees and the director.[35] As Walter soon discovered.

First, though, he surprised Hoving by hesitating. "I am honored and touched," he replied, "but I don't want to say yes or no right now. I want to figure out if I can afford the honor."[36] "Touched" was the right word. Walter understood that the trustees set policy, but at a time when the city of New York and the federal government were strapped for funds for the arts, they also paid for almost everything. Not much had changed, he suspected, since the early 1900s, when board president J. P. Morgan announced the deficit at an annual board meeting to trustees who were expected to write checks on the spot to cover the difference.[37]

Walter was honored, and after researching what his commitment would be, was pleased to join the then thirty-five-member board. He also liked Hoving, a brilliant and innovative director as well as a loose cannon. Soon after he joined, Hoving showed him plans for a new orientation room for the museum. Walter was underwhelmed. "Go bigger," he said. "You ought to reach far beyond, to the fine arts of the entire world." Thinking big on this subject was already on his mind. Ever since being captivated in London by Kenneth Clark's television series *Civilization*, he had been pondering an idea — an extension of his *University of the Air* broadcasts — whereby museums using mass communications technology could become education centers for the broad public as well as scholars.

(He was already the nation's leading impresario of scholarly research into mass communications. In 1962 at Penn, he had established an Annenberg School of Communications, which specialized in studying print journalism. A decade later, he added a second school to focus on electronic media at the University of Southern California. Each was named after Moses.)

Walter followed up their discussion by writing Hoving a letter. "Why not have here at the Met a branch of my school of communications — a school with a faculty, students and a curriculum of how to educate the masses and to train the necessary professionals . . . ? What I'm thinking of doing is to record all the works of art in the world — why not be ambitious? — and to create programs on the whole history of art. To me the recording of man's accomplishments through modern communications devices is an essential and fundamental stepping stone into the future. This is technology in the service of humanism and education."[38]

The scope of Walter's vision was huge. With $150,000 seed money from the publisher, Hoving set out to make it happen. He ordered sketches for construction of a school, communications center, editing and cutting rooms, and several theaters which would occupy 75 percent of a hundred-thousand-square-foot wing to be built in Central Park on the southwest corner of the Metropolitan. Much-needed European and contemporary art galleries would fill the remaining space. He outlined a twelve-part television series incorporating hundreds of slides and drafted plans for a variety of other shows, from specialized research to popular series, lectures by great professors and books to accompany the films.

Complex tax considerations had to be resolved. Walter wanted a graduate school which would have a faculty and grant diplomas and which would operate under the aegis of a cultural institution. Governance would be intricate. There would be joint trusteeship with an eight-member board, half each from the Metropolitan and the Annenberg School; staff would be employees of each institution. If Hoving could secure all the necessary approvals, Walter offered to contribute $40 million toward construction of the new wing and the center's operations. And he held out the possibility of much more.

The project also offered a chance for Hoving. In less than a year he was to complete a decade as director. He was bored and tired of the grind. When Walter asked him to run the center-to-be, Hoving leaped at the chance, admitting, "I was in heaven." By declaring in October 1976 that he would resign as Met director at the end of 1977, he was also in a serious conflict of interest. He continued to run the Metropolitan while attempting to shepherd Walter's center through the political and economic labyrinths of the museum and of New York City.

When the *New York Times* broke the story of Walter's pledge for the center on November 11, 1976, a time when the city was fighting for its economic life, the offer seemed like a wonderful opportunity for all involved. Over the next months, however, criticism began to build. For all his many admirers, Hoving had an equal number of detractors. He was blasted from within the museum by trustees troubled by his conflict of interest and from without by city council, parks department and cultural officials worried about the impact of the Annenberg center on the Metropolitan and the city-owned Central Park, where the museum was proposing to expand.

"With characteristic contempt for the principles of public accounting and legal process, Thomas Hoving is maneuvering once again," charged city councilman Carter Burden, "this time to impose the Annenberg Center on the city of New York."[39] A devastating piece by Barbara Goldsmith in *New York* magazine charged that "while the public is being kept in the dark, the Hoving-Annenberg juggernaut is moving toward a fait accompli," involving "the public give-away, free of charge, of priceless city-owned land."[40]

There was concern that the project would shift the museum's focus away from the display and study of original art toward film and mass reproduction. There were misgivings about the semi-autonomous nature of the center, which was to be housed within the museum but not under its control. Others looked at it as a vast personal monument to Annenberg in space that Hoving had earlier claimed was essential for exhibitions, but which would now be largely closed to the public. Alternate sites were suggested, including the nearby French consulate at 79th Street and Fifth Avenue, which was for sale for $2 million, but Walter insisted the school be on the premises for full interaction between the institutions.

Three different city bodies launched investigations. A column by Pete Hamill in the *Daily News* claimed that Annenberg was trying to buy the Metropolitan to atone for the sins of his father. Museum president Douglas Dillon, who initially backed the project, had second thoughts and asked Hoving for an undated letter of resignation. Angry and offended, Walter called Hoving from Sunnylands. "Here I'm trying to give the city a fine facility and all I get is garbage," he growled. Hoving suggested he pull out. Walter hated the thought of giving up, but he sensed the center was dead. He concluded that the climate in New York was destructive and that Hoving had misled him about the project's chances of approval.

On March 14, 1977, the day the Manhattan Borough Board held its first public hearing on the proposed center, Walter bought space in the *New York Times* for an open letter "To the Citizens of New York City" to explain his motives:

"All the fine arts should be recorded and disseminated for the benefit of mankind. . . . When I was a boy, the important set of reference books was The Book of Knowledge, as I grew older, the Encyclopedia Britannica and World Books. Today I regard the ultimate recording of man's accomplishments through modern communication devices to be an essential and fundamental stepping stone into the future, probably in the form of videocassette or disc libraries. This is technology in the service of humanism and education."

Rejecting claims that he was attempting to "stake out a controlling interest in this distinguished museum," he explained that when he joined the board, he had turned down a request that he become a member of the executive committee. Had he even dreamed of controlling the board, he naturally would have accepted the invitation. All he had wanted was to make a gift to do some good, not to take advantage of the city or museum, or to enhance his own prestige. But unless city officials and Met trustees showed "overwhelming approval," he warned, he would drop the project.[41]

When approval was not forthcoming after the public hearing, he made good on his threat the following day. Dillon blamed the debacle on "opposition by a small group of uninformed or misinformed individuals."[42] Hoving was crushed and was gone from the Metropolitan within three months. Walter was bitter. He had had it with civic authorities. Officials from other cities wrote letters pleading that he establish his arts center in their community, but he was uninterested. Around the country, museum directors and curators began wondering what impact the fiasco might have on the ultimate disposition of Walter and Lee's art collection.

26

REAGAN CONNECTION

RICHARD NIXON had named him ambassador, but Walter was always personally closer to Ronald Reagan. They had known each other longer, shared more interests than pure politics, had seen much more of each other socially and were more relaxed in each other's company. Nixon was a geopolitical intellectual, a strategic theoretician, a voracious reader and prolific writer. Walter, a brilliant businessman and a shrewd judge of character and situations, was none of those. More like Reagan, Walter held uncomplicated core beliefs, chief among them that America was a land of opportunity in which every citizen, if he worked hard, had a basic education, lived as a decent person, and refused to be crushed by adversity could, as Reagan put it, "rise as high and as far as his ability will take him."[1] Reagan's description of the United States as the "Shining City on a Hill" was no metaphor for Walter. It was instead a reflection of what he believed was the nation's inherent goodness, which not only allowed but encouraged infinite success and redemption.

Both men were direct in their likes and dislikes. No chameleon, Walter attacked and defended from the front. They shared a tendency to consider issues and people in black or white with few gray distinctions. Each kept his own counsel and maintained a protective barrier around his psyche. Such remoteness kept each from letting anyone but their wives get close. Both professed to love their children, but each kept a distance from his offspring and neither was comfortable hugging them. Yet each was also capable of great charm and puckish good humor.

Playing golf at Sunnylands one day, Bob Hope asked his host if he could clear a lake with an eight-iron. "When [Bing] Crosby was here, he used a nine," Walter replied. Hope put his eight away, pulled out a nine, took a nice swing and landed the ball in the middle of the lake. "That's exactly where Crosby landed," said a grinning Walter.[2]

Like Reagan, he never pretended to be an intellectual, but he was a student. Walter followed political news closely and developments in finance, business and art and set aside time each morning while Lee read her Christian Science lessons to sit quietly and think. Walter enjoyed privacy, read few books and confined most of his writing to one- or two-paragraph letters, many to "Ronnie," who asked Walter to continue addressing him that way after he won the White House in 1980. "I'm sorry," Walter replied, "but you're Mister President now for the rest of your life."

Both men were patriots, traditionalists, anti-communists, opponents of big government and high taxes and were unabashedly sentimental. Like Reagan, Walter cried at movies. Once, while watching *Sayonara* at Inwood, he asked that the projector be stopped while he went for more tissues. His relationship with Nixon was almost entirely political, but Walter had been a Reagan friend since 1938, well before the actor entered politics. He had recommended him for the job as host of *General Electric Theater* that propelled Reagan into politics. In late 1953, the owner of *TV Guide* had called Reginald Jones, a junior executive who would become CEO of General Electric, to propose Reagan as the pitchman for the CBS Sunday evening series. "I told him Ron was a great speaker, that he had been a very effective and respected head of the Screen Actors Guild, that he was a good-looking guy, genial and very able on his feet."[3]

Reagan became the personification of General Electric. He toured the country for ten weeks a year, promoting the company, visiting its 125 plants and speaking — sometimes a dozen times a day — to its quarter million employees, and countless others at Kiwanis and Elks and American Legion Halls from Los Angeles to Portland and Jacksonville to Seattle. While he was the spokesman for one of America's biggest corporations, Reagan's political philosophy evolved from that of a labor union mouthpiece to that of the voice of management. Soon he was speaking out in favor of the free enterprise system and lashing out against government regulation and high taxes. From there, the step to politics was almost foreordained.[4]

"REAGAN RESPECTED WALTER," said Michael Deaver, a longtime associate. "Walter was smart, successful and powerful. He had come through adversity, beat it all and made it on his own, the kind of record Ronald Reagan admired."[5] As two loners, however, it took something extra to bring them closer. The catalyst was a pair of events six months apart: Walter's marriage to Lee in September 1951 and Reagan's to Nancy Davis in March 1952. Each woman would become her husband's closest friend and truest ally. Tireless workers, masters of detail, well informed, exceptional hostesses and fiercely loyal, each would create the right environment and nurture the social and business relationships that would allow their men to succeed on a far higher level than either would have without them. Walter would have been rich and a successful businessman without Lee, but he would not have become an ambassador, an intimate of presidents and royalty, and a man of culture, grace and dignity. Just as Ronald Reagan would not have become president, and probably not governor of California, without Nancy. "I think both of us," Walter wrote Reagan in 1958, "can very well take comfort in the knowledge that our judgment is tops — on the basis of our wives."[6]

Lee and Nancy, who was seventeen months younger, became close. They shared a similar conservative political philosophy, traveled in the same Hollywood circles, lunched with "the girls" from "the group" — Betsy Bloomingdale, Harriet Deutsch, Marion Jorgensen, Jean Smith, Betty Wilson — and shared the same taste in hairdressers and designers, both dress and interior.

Some considered them peas in a pod, and in terms of their extraordinary closeness to their husbands, they were. But Lee and Nancy were not alike. Lee had more wide ranging interests in culture, civic affairs and politics beyond Ronnie. She had deep religious convictions. Unlike Nancy, who was widely, and sometimes accurately, considered a Dragon Lady with a mean streak, there was a natural generosity of spirit in Lee — an "innate sweetness," said her sister, Judith Wolf — that made it difficult for her to speak unkindly of anyone.

Unlike Nancy, Lee read books at every opportunity. She loved pitching in and working on the boards of the Metropolitan and Philadelphia's Academy of Music, and involving herself in the family's charitable efforts. She was closer to her children, whom she called every day wherever she was, and stepchildren, whom she loved, than Nancy was to hers.

Traits in Walter's and Reagan's fathers — Moses's duality and explosiveness and Jack Reagan's alcoholism — may explain why the two younger men referred to their wives respectively as "Mother" and

"Mommy." It was his mother, and later his wife, who provided each man with his stability. But Lee and Nancy shared significant traits far beyond what their men called them. They had had similar early lives. Neither had been raised by her parents. Each had been abandoned by her father. Nancy's mother and father divorced when she was two. She had lived with an aunt for several years until her mother remarried, as Lee had lived with an uncle. Each became a perfectionist and, ultimately, a force in her own right — decisive, determined, ambitious, unwavering in self-discipline and able to perform superbly in public. (At one elegant dinner for thirty in honor of Margaret Thatcher at Sunnylands, Lee handled the introductions of the prime minister and her dinner partner, former president Gerald Ford, as well as the toasts, while Walter looked on, proud and applauding. She also hosted on her own a birthday luncheon for the Queen Mother and the queen in London when Walter was struck by flu.)

Lee and Nancy saw each other often in California throughout the 1960s, either in Los Angeles, where the Annenbergs leased a bungalow at the Beverly Hills Hotel for a month each summer so Lee could keep up with her friends, in the desert in the winters after Sunnylands was built or with mutual friends. When the Deutsches moved into their home above Beverly Hills in 1960, the Annenbergs were the first guests, followed by the Reagans. In the guest book, Reagan wrote, "We have no hesitation, indeed it is with pride we take second billing to Lee and Walter."[7]

Reagan made the cover of *TV Guide* in 1958 and again in 1961 as the host of *General Electric Theater,* but Walter was careful to keep his distance from his friend during the actor's run in 1966 for the governorship of California. Lee, who thought highly of him as "a thinking man," gave $1,000 to the campaign, but Walter, still publisher of the *Inquirer,* wrote Nancy to explain why he had not made a contribution after she had a friend approach him. "Inasmuch as I am a registered Republican and resident of Wynnewood, Pennsylvania, and because I think it would be presumptuous for me, as a California visitor with a resort home in the Desert, to participate in California politics, I declined the solicitation."[8]

Reagan won that November and Walter immediately offered his congratulations. "Your performance had the stamp of *relentless dignity,*" he wrote, adding that "it certainly is a wonderful thing to be buttressed by a dedicated wife."[9] He ordered the *Inquirer* to commend editorially the wisdom of California voters. Reagan was appreciative. "I know defending me, particularly in the East, can get to be quite an assignment," he wrote Walter, "and I'm more grateful than I can say to have you in my corner."[10]

After Reagan took office (he and Nancy refused to move into the decrepit governor's mansion in Sacramento; Walter called it "termite tavern" and contributed to its $1.4 million replacement)[11] the publisher continued to offer advice, personally or through his editorial page. The *Inquirer's* commentary damning student unrest at Berkeley, Reagan noted in 1967, "is so objective and factual, it is like a shining light."[12] Writing to denounce the state's commutation of sentence of a man convicted of three counts of robbery, six of rape and seven of kidnapping, Walter urged Reagan to recommend a statute "that would make life imprisonment without parole eligibility a fact rather than a fancied condition."[13] When Reagan's economic belt-tightening measures prompted a Conrad cartoon in the *Los Angeles Times* depicting the governor sawing off pieces of a crippled child's crutches, Walter urged Reagan to publish a white paper giving more detail on his health care program. "Let us be sympathetic to those who need it and yet let the freeloaders pay."[14]

AFTER THE ANNENBERGS opened the refurbished Winfield House in November 1969, the Reagans were their first stay-over visitors and guests of honor at their first dinner party, for thirty-six. Nancy had not been to Europe since her mother and stepfather had taken her when she was twelve. The governor had only been once, in 1948 when Warner Brothers sent him to London to make *The Hasty Heart.* On this trip, Walter had arranged for him to address the Institute of Directors in Royal Albert Hall. More than five thousand were in the audience, and Reagan met dozens of executives, members of Parliament and a few lesser royals, although not the queen, for whom Nancy had practiced her curtsy.[15]

When the Reagans returned to London in 1972, Walter took Reagan, then midway through his second term as governor, to 10 Downing Street to meet Prime Minister Heath and foreign secretary Sir Alec Douglas-Home. "Stimulating and beneficial," was Reagan's diplomatic assessment.[16]

It was not as stimulating or beneficial as a London one-on-one that Walter arranged after he and Lee had moved back to the United States. On February 20, 1975, Margaret Thatcher formally assumed the leadership of the Tory party and declared all-out war on socialism. The following day Walter wrote and asked her to meet Reagan, who a month earlier had finished his second term. "While the former governor holds no official position at this time, he is indeed a leader of conservative political philosophy in the United States, and it is only natural that he would very much enjoy a meeting with the leader of Britain's Conservative party."[17] Thatcher was happy to and the fifteen-minute drop-by appointment scheduled at her small office of the leader of the opposition in the House of Commons stretched out to an hour and a half.

Thatcher already knew about Reagan. She had noticed him after his 1964 endorsement of Barry Goldwater's campaign — a political difference between Reagan and Walter that never affected their friendship — and she had followed his speeches while he was governor. "I knew he was a great speaker," she said. Her husband, Denis, had attended Reagan's speech to the Institute of Directors and had come away so "remarkably impressed" that she had sought out a copy. Twenty-five years later without text or notes she quoted from the address: "If we should ever lose our freedom, what will we say to our children when they come and say to us, 'Where were you, Father, when freedom was lost, and what did you do about it?'"

When Reagan came to see her in April 1975, "We just sat and talked. He was so modest. Such a lovely man. He saw the big picture. He had beliefs and he was in politics to translate those beliefs into action. He had started in California with the tax cut proposition," just as Thatcher would in 1979 when she became prime minister.[18]

Both believed, as did Walter, in the primacy of individual endeavor, unreconstructed capitalism, and the need for a strong defense against the Soviets. "We found great areas of agreement," Reagan said later.[19] Reagan was confident but courtly, which Thatcher loved. He was also very good-looking, which she also liked. Their personalities were poles apart. She was up at dawn and worked until after midnight. He strolled into his office at the crack of nine and wandered home at 5 P.M. or earlier. She was a stickler for detail and he was a broad-brush executive. But together Ronald Reagan and Margaret Thatcher would form the most reliable and significant political team of the 1980s, a partnership which surely would have developed in any case but had its origins in Walter's initiative.

IN 1976, a year after he met Thatcher, Reagan made a respectable challenge to president Gerald Ford in the Republican party primaries preceding the presidential race. Republicans rarely challenge incumbents of their own party, but Ford had not been elected. He had succeeded the disgraced Spiro Agnew and then moved into the oval office on Nixon's 1974 resignation. Ford shifted to the right during the campaign and held off Reagan in the primaries, and then lost to Democrat Jimmy Carter in November, ending eight years of Republican governance.

That same year, America celebrated its bicentennial and to mark the event, Queen Elizabeth made her first visit to the former U.S. capital where the Declaration of Independence was signed. From the time she stepped ashore at Penn's Landing from the yacht *Britannia*, the minute-by-minute script she followed had been drawn up in close consultation with the Annenbergs. Walter had been involved in its planning while still ambassador. Lee spent six months working with Philadelphia officials, the State Department and Buckingham Palace to resolve every detail of the twenty-four-hour visit, from the shoreside electrical connections for the ship to the banquet seating plan and fireworks display.

At Independence Hall, the queen presented a six-ton bell made in London's Whitechapel foundry, which had cast the original Liberty Bell in 1725, hosted a lunch for fifty aboard *Britannia* — the most sought after invitations in the city for years — and attended a formal dinner for 400 and drinks for an additional 750 guests at the Philadelphia Museum of Art at which Walter escorted the queen, and Lee, Prince Philip. Each attendee — from all walks of Philadelphia life, from baseball stars and museum curators to politicians, executives and symphony conductor Eugene Ormandy — had been approved by Lee Annenberg.

The visit was a triumph for the Annenbergs, capped soon after by the queen's award to Walter of an honorary knighthood, the first — and still only — given to a U.S. ambassador. He and Lee were very proud. More than vindication for their dark, early days in Britain, it was recognition for the recovery he had made through hard work and good works. He considered the knighthood an acknowledgment of respect. His president had named him ambassador to the country he loved second only to his own, and the monarch he most respected had honored him for the manner of his representation. He had been recognized at last as an honorable man who had done honorable work.

There were still some Philadelphians who did not like the Annenbergs, but they were a dwindling number, and the queen's visit, on top of the success they had had in London, made moot the issue of their social acceptance at home. Walter and Lee had vaulted so far over the old obstacles that they had moved into international society's highest stratum. They had outgrown that part of Philadelphia with its narrow aspirations and shortsighted snobbery. They were friends of presidents and heads of state, world-class philanthropists, trustees of great universities and art museums alongside Rockefellers, Whitneys and Sulzbergers. They had nothing left to prove. Philadelphia was lucky to have them.

THE ANNENBERGS kept their primary residence at Inwood both for tax purposes and because Walter preferred the East, where he kept his office, but Lee was always eager to spend more time in California. There she could see her friends and more of her older daughter, Diane, who lived in Beverly Hills and with whom she was particularly close. Triangle was thriving. The *Daily Racing Form* and *Seventeen* remained cash cows and *TV Guide* had become the world's largest-selling weekly — twenty-one million copies, or a billion a year at its peak, the cover of each one still bearing Moses's tiny MLA monogram as Walter's mark of respect. The company's earnings and dividends had more than tripled, from $6.41 a share on their return home in 1974 to $21.39 in 1979. They were loving their privacy, their charity and board work, and the increasing amount of golf they were playing together, especially at Sunnylands.

In 1979, the Annenbergs gave refuge on the estate to the mother and sister of the exiled shah of Iran, who had been chased by Iranian demonstrators from their mansion in Beverly Hills. The hospitality, which extended to the exiles' fourteen dogs, a menagerie of pet birds and a personal veterinarian, was in character.

While Walter was ambassador, he and Lee had made an around-the-world tour with a stop in Tehran, where the shah had entertained them at a lavish dinner. A grandiose man but a charming host, the shah was also an important United States ally. Nixon had visited Tehran in 1972 on his way home from a summit meeting in Moscow to see the shah and stress the strategic significance of Iran. Britain had been the colonial power there, but had withdrawn from east of Suez and had conceded that it was no longer capable of defending Western interests in the Persian Gulf area. In keeping with the Nixon doctrine of supporting local allies with arms sales and other inducements to protect U.S. interests, Iran had become vitally important to Washington's Gulf strategy. Yet when the shah was overthrown by the revolutionary forces of the Ayatollah Khomeini and forced to leave Iran in January 1979, the Carter administration abandoned its former ally. Fearing riots in the United States and a disruption of relations with oil-rich Iran, President Carter refused to grant him asylum. Walter considered the decision outrageous.

He was not alone. Henry Kissinger and David and Nelson Rockefeller took up the shah's plight. Temporary refuge was found in the Bahamas and Panama, but Walter considered it cowardly and immoral to treat the shah as a strategic asset, then abandon him in his hour of need and force him to wander the world like the Flying Dutchman in search of a port of call. He could not influence the Carter administration to allow entry to the shah, but he could do something about the family already in the United States. He called the editor of the Palm Springs newspaper, the *Desert Sun*, and issued a statement:

> "When the government of the United States offers shelter to those seeking protection from radical extremists, the citizens of this country should respond affirmatively if necessary. Accordingly, the outrageous conduct of so-called Iranian students in Beverly Hills earlier this week in threatening the lives of the Shah's elderly mother and his sister in their anarchistic drive to murder them, enraged Americans. My winter residence, Sunnylands, has facilities that enabled me to offer them a temporary haven which they have accepted. I could have done no less as a respectable citizen."[20]

Walter was prepared to welcome the shah as well, although Rancho Mirage officials wanted no part of him, figuring his presence would be a security nightmare for the wealthy town outside the Sunnylands gates. His mother and sister left after occupying one of the Annenbergs' guest cottages for two weeks. The shah never did come. He became ill in October 1979 and the Carter administration offered to allow him into the U.S. for medical treatment. Fury in Tehran at the decision led within days to the overrunning of the U.S. embassy and the capture of fifty-two Americans. President Anwar Sadat gave the shah refuge in Egypt where, heartbroken and ravaged by cancer, he died in April 1980. After 444 days of captivity, the hostages were finally released and flown to freedom on January 20, 1981, minutes after Ronald Reagan was sworn in as president of the United States.

WALTER AND LEE had not seen as much of the Reagans in the previous two years because Ron and Nancy had been on the road campaigning almost constantly. The exception was the Annenbergs' annual New Year's Eve party at Sunnylands. Starting with twenty people and a movie in 1966 after the house was finished, it had since grown to about ninety friends who dined on exquisite Flora Danica china and toasted the New Year with Dom Perignon champagne in Baccarat crystal. The Reagans always made a point of attending. Walter had not contributed financially to the campaign. Lee gave $1,000, the maximum allowed, to the primary campaign in September 1979 and an additional $10,000 in October 1980 to the Republican National Committee for the general campaign. Wallis gave $10,000 for the general and several of Walter's sisters also contributed.[21]

Walter's contribution was a bylined commentary endorsing Reagan three days before the election in the November 1 issue of *TV Guide*. "*TV Guide* has never before taken a position in a presidential election and as head of the company that publishes the magazine I intended that it remain silent in this one. I cannot, however, as a matter of conscience refrain from speaking up when the result of this election is so critical to the future of the nation." He had known Reagan for more than thirty years, he explained in the editorial titled "The Presidency and the People." Television ads created by the Carter campaign, he wrote, were distorting Reagan's record and misleading the public by picturing him "as a warmonger with simplistic, antiquated economic ideas who would divide the country into antagonistic racial, religious and geographical factions."

On the contrary, Walter pointed out, Reagan had surrounded himself with capable men and women and had governed California well. At a time when Americans "see ourselves as a nation in decline," he was confident Reagan would be the strong leader the nation needed. Such a presidency, he wrote, would "restore the self-confidence and the self-respect that until recent years have been the foundation of the American spirit. As we achieve these goals, our friends abroad — and our potential enemies — will respect us too."[22]

Had he shown any interest, Walter could have had a job in the Reagan administration, but he had no intention of seeking or accepting one, as the president was aware. As a courtesy, Reagan asked if he had any desire to return as ambassador to London, but Walter said no. Once was great and had also been enough. He had had the best job that any president could offer and only a greedy man would ask for more. Three years older than the new president, he was two months away from his seventy-third birthday when Reagan took office. He was enjoying his return to private life and the chance to focus on Triangle, his investments and, increasingly, his philanthropy.

Lee, though, was interested in an administration job. Ten years younger than Walter, she loved politics. She followed the news closely, was slightly more conservative than Walter and wanted to be part of the Reagan revolution. Several friends from "the group" were taking jobs: as attorney general, William French Smith, as U.S. Information Agency director, Charles Wick and envoy to the Vatican, William Wilson. The taste, diligence and intelligence that Lee had demonstrated in London and in private life, as well as the sensitivity she had shown in dealing with the State Department and White House about the queen's visit during the Ford administration were evidence of her qualifications to be chief of protocol. Lee also wanted to prove to herself and others that the woman who had been a perfect partner could operate outside Walter's large orbit.

Drugstore mogul Justin Dart and several other members of the Reagan "kitchen cabinet," which included such Annenberg friends as car dealer Holmes Tuttle, oilman Henry Salvatori and steel magnate Earle Jorgensen, urged that she be given the protocol post. Nancy Reagan, who had an influential voice in all senior appointments, was surprised Lee wanted a job, but gave her approval. "It came to my attention that she would like to do it. She was certainly qualified, but I never dreamed of her wanting the job," said Mrs. Reagan. "I think she wanted to show that she could do something, but I knew it was going to be an adjustment for Walter."[23]

The president called Lee at Sunnylands and asked if she would take the post, which manages all visits for heads of state, arranges presidential visits overseas, coordinates ceremonial events for the secretary of state, accredits foreign diplomats and runs Blair House, the official guest residence for visiting dignitaries. If approved, as she was sure to be, Lee too would have the title of ambassador, a seat at every state dinner and on presidential trips and around-the-clock, seven-day-a-week duties. She and Walter discussed the offer at lunch. "Walter said 'I want you to do it. I know you'd be wonderful at it.' He was all for it.

In fact, I think he was more excited about it than I was. I loved what we had done in England. This was a chance for me to serve my country again. And I loved the thought of doing something on my own. Walter said he would move to Washington. So I accepted."[24]

Nominated in early February 1981, Lee went to Washington and discovered that an acting chief had been named and he was not happy to become her deputy. He was Morgan Mason, the son of actor James Mason and his wife, Pamela, a Hollywood heiress and gossip columnist, who were friends of Nancy's. Mason, a twenty-five-year-old man-about-town who enjoyed dating glamorous older women, granting interviews, issuing statements and insisting that he deserved to keep the U.S. Marine driver assigned him during the inauguration festivities, clashed instantly with Lee. Just as quickly, she called Nancy and said she simply could not work with Mason, who was transferred to the White House, where he was happy being named an assistant to the president. Lee hired her own deputy to help run the office's staff of forty-three.

The staff did not know what to expect. They knew she was the wife of one of the nation's richest men, a woman who had never held a job in her life, an international hostess who had closets full of designer suits and gowns, a hundred pairs of shoes, a multimillion dollar jewelry collection and a penchant for occasional lunches with other ladies who wore $3,000 Adolfo and Bill Blass suits. To outsiders, the protocol office sounded glamorous, but the staff knew better. The job involved more hurry-up-and-wait drudgery than parties. The first clue that they might be in for a pleasant surprise came right away. Lee and Walter were huddled with lawyers filling out extensive financial disclosure forms when one staff professional interrupted and was introduced. "Remember, Motherrr," Walter said, "as we learned in London, it's the career people who saved our bacon and made the world go round." Word spread fast. Both Annenbergs seemed approachable, normal and nice.

"She came in so graciously and so low key," said Patrick Daly, a two-decade veteran of the office. "Everyone starts that way, but not everyone middles and ends that way as Lee did. She was endlessly considerate and thoughtful. She was efficient, but she put in whatever hours were needed. If we had to see some foreign minister off on a weekend and she had plans to go to Philadelphia or California, she never dumped the assignment on someone else. She'd rearrange her plans and go see him off herself. She was also very generous in giving praise to people who were doing the work. She never pulled any spoiled acts. She never snapped at anyone. She was always beautifully dressed, but she was very careful not to wear extravagant jewelry or clothes that would draw attention or make others feel uncomfortable. When she came, I had no idea what it was going to be like. Heaven knows it's not always good. But in her attitudes and actions she was very much a noble lady."[25]

Lee plunged in. The first official visitor, Margaret Thatcher, was arriving on February 26, only two weeks after she was nominated. When Lee examined Blair House to make certain it was in perfect shape for the British prime minister, she was horrified by the shoddy condition of the guest house across Pennsylvania Avenue from the White House. Draperies and carpets had not been cleaned. Wallpaper was streaked. Shower curtains, towels, china and furniture were missing. The day after Lee's tour, Blair House manager Carol Benefield was asked to resign. Walter, who had already contributed $70,000 to help Nancy Reagan's effort to fix up the White House family quarters, agreed to help pay for the Blair House refurbishment, the word by then in common use in the United States and Britain. ("We used to just 'do up' our houses," quipped Peter Carrington, "but ever since Walter, we've been refurbishing them.")

On March 30, the president was wounded in an assassination attempt outside the Washington Hilton. Lee was escorting Dutch prime minister Andries van Agt from Boston to Washington when Secret Service agents on the government plane received the initial sketchy reports of the shooting. Learning that European reporters were gathering for his reaction, Lee briefed van Agt and ordered the plane to circle Andrews Air Force Base while they worked together to revise his arrival remarks. "She was in turmoil about the president," said her assistant Gahl Burt, "but she had great compassion for van Agt. His visit had just been wrecked. She took a deep breath, then stayed calm and utterly professional."[26]

Lee did not need her $50,112 salary, but at sixty-three she was excited about making an income for the first time in her life. Rather than spend it on herself, she used the money to set up and pay for a series of small dinners at Blair House. She brought her own china from Inwood and invited foreign diplomats, senators, representatives, cabinet officers and top White House staffers. The gatherings were not designed for the British, German or Japanese ambassadors to meet people. Those envoys had easy access to senior administration and congressional officials. It was the second-tier and Third World ambassadors from places like Chad, Bolivia or Bangladesh that Lee understood would normally never meet White House chief of staff James Baker, secretary of defense Caspar Weinberger or the chairmen of the Senate and House Foreign Relations Committees unless she put them together. The envoys loved her for it. "I just mixed everybody up and we had fun," she said. Jack Valenti, head of the Motion Picture Association, helped execute another idea. She split the diplomatic corps — more than 150 ambassadors plus spouses — into three groups for a buffet and movie at Valenti's private cinema. Soviet ambassador Anatoly Dobrynin, the dean of the diplomatic corps, came each time.

For all her determination to do everything exactly right, there were several problems, although only one of her own making. That happened on April 30, 1981, when she dropped her right knee in a curtsy to Prince Charles when he arrived at Andrews Air Force Base. The gesture prompted a storm of criticism that she had shown subservience and had undercut the entire purpose of the American Revolution. The NBC television network devoted a prime time program to the gaffe. She had planned to go onto the plane to greet the prince, but an aide asked her to wait. The prince liked to collect himself at the end of a flight. Former British ambassador Nicholas Henderson had once observed Charles's predisembarkation routine. Patting himself down, the prince muttered a check-off list: "Spectacles, testicles, wallet and watch."[27]

When he came down the ramp, "I just curtsied without thinking because I had always curtsied in Britain to every member of the royal family. So did the Bruces and everyone else. It's part of the routine. Well, all hell broke loose."[28] Lee was mortified and humiliated by the outcry. When she arrived at the White House with the prince and prepared to take him into the Oval Office, presidential assistant Michael Deaver barred her way. She was crushed at not being allowed to handle the official introduction of the prince, an old personal friend, whom she and Walter had first introduced to the Reagans at Sunnylands seven years earlier.

That evening, the Reagans invited Lee and Walter to a small dinner for the prince in the family quarters. Lee was fascinated to see all the women guests curtsy. As the story had already been on the evening news, she had prepared an apology for the president. Before she could say a word, Reagan held up his hand. "Lee, you did exactly the right thing," he said, reaching out to give her a hug and big kiss. "Forget about it." The next day he told Deaver to apologize for the Oval Office incident. "What character," Walter said. "I love that man."[29]

WALTER'S WARMTH for the president did not extend to the First Lady. He would have walked barefoot on hot coals for Ronald Reagan, but Walter's opinion of Nancy plummeted from the moment she arrived in Washington. "She and the president are very different," he said. "Chalk and cheese. I have very little respect for Mrs. Reagan. There is something about her that is very petty."[30]

Part of the problem was purely the situation. Putting a friend in a staff job rarely works in Washington. Both the principal and the friend often have difficulty adjusting to the new hierarchical circumstances. Lee handled this part well. "I always felt Lee understood her place, three paces behind Nancy," said Deaver, the First Lady's right arm and confidant. Sometimes, though, three steps were not enough. At one south lawn arrival ceremony, Nancy was horrified to discover after the trumpet fanfare that she and Lee were wearing identical Adolfo suits.

Walter's specific complaint was that Nancy was jealous of Lee's success with the diplomatic corps and was trying to keep her at a distance and ultimately force her from Washington. Why, then, had she approved Lee for the job in the first place? Because to bar her would have been too obvious a snub among their many mutual friends. But once Lee had the job and was performing well — with the exception of the brief firestorm over the curtsy — Walter believed that Nancy, through Deaver, began undercutting Lee to compel her resignation. "They were annoying Lee all the time, just determined to cut her down at every opportunity."[31]

Walter maintained that the trouble started on Lee's first day on the job, when she arrived to find Nancy's friend Morgan Mason already in place. The First Lady had solved that problem, and she and the president had hosted Lee's swearing-in as protocol chief at the White House. Three months later, Lee had a second swearing-in at the State Department, for the Senate approval of her ambassadorial rank. Many of Lee's and Walter's friends had flown in for a film premiere and Western-theme party that evening at the Kennedy Center. The Deutsches, Wilsons, Jorgensens, Darts and Hal Wallises had come from California; Carol and Charles Price, who would serve as Reagan's ambassador to Belgium and then Britain, flew from Kansas City. It was the perfect moment to schedule the second swearing-in, with the oath administered by Attorney General William French Smith, an old friend, and a luncheon in honor of Lee. According to sources in the protocol office, a *Washington Post* article and a biography of Nancy Reagan, the First Lady was expected at the luncheon at Les Champs Restaurant in the Watergate Hotel following the ceremony. That would have been natural. Lee and her guests were all her friends too. In California, Nancy shopped with the women, tried things on and then, because she was living on her husband's government salary, one or more of the "girls" would often buy the items for her.

The restaurant was filled with flowers and Secret Service agents with bomb-sniffing dogs had swept the dining room. But the First Lady never arrived. According to the *Post* story and the biography, she lunched alone in the White House with Betsy Bloomingdale.[32] Years later, neither Lee, her friends, Mrs. Reagan or Mrs. Bloomingdale could recall the circumstances of the luncheon, although Nancy said any suggestion that she had accepted and not come was untrue. "Lee is a dear friend," she said, which was how Lee described her. Walter, however, did not share his wife's feelings.

IN JULY, Lee and Walter flew to London for the wedding of Prince Charles and Lady Diana Spencer. The Reagans were also asked, but the president's advisers determined that his first overseas trip should be for something more serious than a royal wedding. He declined, but Nancy, who loved all things royal, was eager to attend. She was invited to the queen's gala prenuptial ball at Buckingham Palace, and Lee made certain that she was included in the smaller, more exclusive gatherings reserved for personal friends of the bridal couple. Although the Annenbergs were naturally invited to those, most of the official VIP guests were not.[33]

Just before attending the wedding, Lee had written a memo to Deaver detailing procedures for presidential trips overseas. On her return, Deaver replied that Joseph Canzeri, one of his deputies and an experienced former advance man for Nelson Rockefeller, would supervise all such travel. Deaver also suggested that Canzeri work directly with the State Department's liaison office with the White House. Lee concluded that Deaver was trying to exclude her from what she had understood to be her responsibility.[34]

What Lee did not understand was that even if her relationship with Nancy had been perfect, the old rules did not apply in the Reagan White House. The chief of protocol worked from the State Department, which was then headed by Alexander Haig. The team in charge at the White House — Nancy Reagan, Deaver, James Baker and chief counsel Edwin Meese — neither liked nor trusted Haig. "Baker saw me as competition for George Bush and they were determined to get rid of me," said Haig.[35] They were determined to maintain total policy and image control in the executive mansion. Lee could handle the small tasks, but not the big ones.

"When the events involved the White House, Nancy would have me involved and we would run the operation," Deaver confirmed.[36] According to Joe Canzeri, White House primacy in protocol had been decided at the outset. "The decision was made by Mike and the Reagans and myself that the best way to handle it was to let protocol do what they do, but when it came to the White House per se, we'd make the final call. There were things we didn't want State involved in; things we didn't want State to know. We'd take the notebooks away from interpreters so they couldn't take their notes back. It had nothing to do with Lee as an individual and everything to do with what we thought was best for the president. It deflated her in some respects, but that's too bad."[37]

The biggest deflation and the beginning of the end for Lee came after the October 6 assassination of Egyptian president Anwar Sadat. Haig headed the prestigious United States delegation to the funeral, but the White House also included former presidents Carter, Ford and Nixon in the traveling party. Lee had researched the protocol and learned that with the secretary of state at the head of the group, the organization was her responsibility. She called Deaver and asked who was going and whether he had special instructions. "You're not in charge. I'm in charge and I'm not certain you're going," he told her. "Mike, I'm going," she replied.

She arrived early at Andrews, boarded the air force jet with her protocol list and saw that Canzeri had already designated the seating. Haig and his aides had the large VIP area. The three presidents were to be crammed around two tables in the work space with Henry Kissinger, who was no longer in government but who had once been Haig's boss. Further back were Jeane Kirkpatrick, the ambassador to the United Nations, and Lee and a host of senators and congressmen. Lee was furious. She told Canzeri he had done it all wrong. He did not care. He was the world's leading funeral director. Canzeri had run the trips for the funerals of Martin Luther King Jr., Bobby Kennedy, Taiwan's Chiang Kai-shek and Saudi Arabia's King Faisal. Because of the rank of the mourners and the egos involved, the Sadat trip was worse than any of those. When Lee told Canzari to change the seating, he told her he had Deaver's authority and threatened to throw her off the plane. Lee kept quiet. She was determined to go. Sadat had been one of Reagan's first official visitors and had brought along his wife and daughters, one of whom had miscarried during the visit. Lee had bonded with the family while sitting with them for hours at the hospital. In Cairo, according to Deaver, Lee had to be told she could not follow the funeral cortege as part of the official delegation as she had insisted, because women were not allowed to participate in the Moslem service. Lee, who sat with Mrs. Sadat, maintained that never happened, but it was plainly a contentious trip.

"When I got home from Cairo I called 'Mommy' to tell her what happened," Canzeri explained later. "Nancy said 'Don't worry. I understand.'"

When Lee told Walter, he had a different reaction. "Walter was very angry," Lee said. "He was certain that Deaver would never have treated me that way without authority from Nancy."[38]

Two weeks after the Cairo trip, Reagan flew to Cancún, Mexico, for a two-day, twenty-two-nation summit about economic cooperation between the rich, industrialized countries of the north and the poor, developing countries of the south. Deaver told Lee she could not attend. The official explanation was that accommodations were tight and staff had to double up. Lee was willing to share a room, but the list was made and she was not on it. "They just humiliated Lee," said Selwa "Lucky" Roosevelt, who succeeded her as protocol chief. "The White House was so unrelenting in having the last say on everything, it was horrendous."[39]

Nor was Walter alone in believing that jealousy on Nancy Reagan's part had also been a factor. "Mrs. Reagan was jealous of the good-lookers, and that included Lee," said Alexander Haig. "There was going to be only one good-looking woman around her White House. There wasn't going to be any glory-sharing. It was awful the way they treated Lee Annenberg, but I never had a single complaint from her."[40]

The Cancún trip clinched it for Walter. "Walter was adamant," said Lee. "He said 'Enough is enough.'"

Despite the strains, she did not want to give up the protocol job. She loved the work. She definitely did not want to quit before the president's trip to Britain in June 1982, when Reagan was to become the first president honored by the queen with a royal dinner and overnight stay at Windsor Castle. Ideally, she wanted to remain through February 1983, when the queen was due to spend nine days touring the West Coast of the United States, including a visit to the Reagans' ranch in the hills above Santa Barbara. But Walter would not hear of it and not just because of Nancy.

He had not brought a secretary to Washington as he had planned. They had leased two adjoining suites on the tenth floor of the Watergate Hotel at a negotiated rate of $2,500 a week instead of the regular $750 daily charge. Walter came from Philadelphia several days a week, but Lee was rarely in the apartment. She bolted for the office at 8:00 A.M., came back just before 6 P.M., changed and was out by 7:30 P.M. most nights for cocktails, a reception, a dinner or all three. She rode the Metroliner north on weekends to join Walter at Inwood. Sometimes he treated her to a helicopter ride back Monday morning, but often she found herself sitting at the Thirtieth Street Station in Philadelphia on Sunday afternoon waiting for the train to Washington and wondering what in the world she was doing there. Walter wanted to spend March and April at Sunnylands, but it was impossible for her to join him there for more than a few days.

When he did come to Washington, he sometimes walked the few blocks to her office in the State Department in search of company. At dinner parties, Lee was the ambassador and sat at the head table; if included at all, former ambassador Walter was usually relegated to the fringes. "I remember when you were an ambassador," German chancellor Helmut Schmidt joshed him before a state dinner, "and now I find you only a consort."[41] Walter told the story on himself and laughed as heartily as Schmidt had, but the truth was, as hard as he tried, he did not enjoy the secondary role. He had not had to play it for a long time, since Moses died.

Walter also demanded a great deal of attention. He had it as a boy and he expected it as an adult, especially from Lee. Most important of all, he was missing her terribly. He loved watching the evening news with her, talking and eating, playing golf and bridge, seeing friends and simply watching her move through the house with that elegant grace. High on his list, he hated not sleeping with her. To ensure he did not have to, in her nongovernment days she would forgo staying over on trips to New York or Los Angeles to see her daughters and friends or attend board meetings to race back at night to join him at Inwood or Sunnylands.

"The handwriting was on the wall," said Lee. She was upset with Walter for failing to fulfill his part of the bargain. He had not moved full-time to Washington as he had promised. Yet there was no question of what she would do. "I fought it as long as I could, but I am a pleasing wife and Walter was my first responsibility. And it was not as if I were going home to some poor, cramped little place." She extended her arm in a gesture to encompass Sunnylands. "This is not so terrible."[42]

Walter did not want to acknowledge, even to himself, how much he wanted Lee home. That might have suggested weakness or selfishness on his part. That was one reason why he placed so much blame on Nancy Reagan. He also recognized that for Lee to continue working for Nancy was a no-win situation for all involved. Allowed to continue, increasing friction might well destroy the couples' thirty-year friendship. The president was unaware of Walter's fury at his wife. Nor did Nancy have any sense that Walter was upset with her, but she knew he was unhappy for other reasons. "Walter wanted her home. It was difficult for him," she said. "After he had been ambassador to the Court of St. James's, it was understandable if his nose was out of joint. And he missed her."[43]

On December 8, Lee submitted her resignation "with profound regret" to Ronald Reagan, to be effective January 1, 1982. "My presence in Washington has necessitated absences from my husband, who has been unable to adjust his schedule to be in Washington with me. This separation has been difficult for us and Walter and I believe it is now time for me to return to my previous life style," she wrote. "Knowing of your loving ties to your family, I am sure that you understand and appreciate my decision."[44]

The president accepted it "with deepest regret," praised her "exceptional grace and wisdom," then scratched off the bottom of the draft letter to write by hand, "There, now I've done what is officially required. You know we'll miss you so don't go too far away. Love, Ron."[45]

The Reagans continued coming to Sunnylands for the New Year's party. After one visit, the president joked at the annual White House correspondents' dinner, "I thought that the Fourth Estate was one of Walter Annenberg's homes."[46] Lee and Nancy Reagan stayed in regular telephone touch. Nancy never forgot Lee's birthday or anniversary.

Walter kept in contact with the president, never asking for anything, but writing to suggest candidates for administration jobs, expressing his concern that the rash of 1980s corporate takeovers was damaging business performance, urging that he invite Russian author Aleksandr Solzhenitsyn for lunch at the White House, lamenting "as a

nonowning shareholder" the cannibalization of AT&T, endorsing —
after undergoing two hip replacements — more arthritic and skeletal
disease research, and giving Reagan a porcelain horse for his seventy-
first birthday.[47]

The Annenbergs even offered a warm welcome to Mike Deaver
when he advanced Queen Elizabeth's February 1983 visit to California
with the Reagans, which included lunch at Sunnylands and a tour of
the property by golf cart in the rain. "I just wanted to show Her
Majesty how the average American lived," Walter joked. (After she
left, the queen told a member of her party that she had noticed that the
Annenbergs had her China pattern, Flora Danica, "Except Walter has
more than I do.") On his advance trip, Deaver had stayed for lunch and
later said, "They could not have been more gracious."[48]

Walter, though, had not forgotten the earlier run-ins. After Reagan
was reelected in a landslide in November 1984, Deaver resigned as
deputy chief of staff the following May and established his own lobbying and public relations firm. Ten months later, he posed for a *Time*
magazine cover on "influence peddling in Washington." He was soon
under investigation for alleged violations of the Ethics in Government
Act laws, which prohibit senior officials from trying to influence former
colleagues for a year after they leave office and forbids lobbying on any
issues they participated in while a government employee. Soon after
he left the White House, Deaver landed in the headlines for lobbying
on behalf of Canada in its dispute with the U.S. government over acid
rain, for Puerto Rico about tax breaks and for meeting the budget
director on behalf of his client Rockwell International to discuss funding of the troubled B-1 bomber.

Deaver was eventually convicted by a federal jury in December
1987 on three counts of perjury for lying under oath about his lobbying
activities. He was given a three-year suspended jail sentence and
ordered to perform fifteen hundred hours of community service. He
did it in exemplary fashion, continued to volunteer for years after completing his mandatory service and was later restored to corporate and
Washington grace. Well before his legal troubles, however, senior
administration officials had privately expressed their concern about his
business methods, claiming that Deaver was trading in unseemly fashion on his near-filial twenty-year relationship with the Reagans.

When Walter got wind in 1986 of what was going on, he ordered a
Triangle aide to compile a dossier of newspaper clippings on the former presidential aide. Noting the scope of the allegations, he became

apoplectic. "When I heard Deaver was off making these contacts, embarrassing the presidency by trading on the president's name, I determined to do something about it."[49] It was not the first time Walter had so acted. In 1981, Richard Allen, the president's first national security adviser, was found to have accepted $1,000 from Japanese journalists who had interviewed Nancy Reagan at the White House. The controversy broadened into a Justice Department investigation of Allen's acceptance of wristwatches from a former business associate, his continued contact with former clients and his financial disclosure errors. Eventually cleared of misconduct, he resigned, which Walter had been urging almost from the moment the allegations surfaced. A president's behavior was one thing, but Walter had zero tolerance for the actions of underlings that could tarnish the presidency. "He was hurting the president," said Walter, "Of course he had to go." Walter called friends at the State Department, where Allen was heartily disliked, and the White House to urge Allen be dismissed. Among those Walter called in 1981 was Mike Deaver.

Five years later, when Deaver materialized in his crosshairs, Walter made another phone call. Deaver was in negotiations at the time to sell his brand-new firm to the British advertising giant Saatchi and Saatchi for $18 million. "It was moving along very nicely when all of a sudden everything stopped," Deaver recounted. He contacted the Saatchi office in New York, which sent two partners to Washington to hem and haw with him about the delay. "Wait a minute, I wasn't born yesterday," Deaver told them. "I can take it. What happened?" They advised him, Deaver went on, that "a very prominent American had called and advised the Saatchis that buying me out would be a bad deal."[50]

Deaver checked around and determined that Walter had scotched the deal. Walter confirmed that he had been the one. "I took the position that Deaver was demeaning the name of Reagan." He told Saatchi's attorney that if the firm planned to expand operations in the United States through Deaver, "they would injure the reputation of President Reagan. The lawyer said, 'Thank you very much.' That was the end of their interest in Deaver. I felt that I owed it to the president, a faithful old friend, to watch out for his interests, and I owed Deaver for abusing my wife. I fixed his wagon."[51] After London, Walter only rarely got mad, but he was still fully capable of getting even.

27

LOOSE ENDS

———

T HE BUSINESS and educational establishment of Los Angeles
were gathered for dinner at the Beverly Hills home of TRW
founder Simon Ramo in 1980 when visiting PBS chairman
Newton Minow was asked to make a few remarks about public broadcasting. Later, he found himself seated next to Walter. Although Minow
had been President Kennedy's chairman of the Federal Communications Commission and had delivered his "vast wasteland" speech in
1961, at the time Walter had *TV Guide* editorializing for better television, the two had never met. "Young man," Walter said to Minow, who
was then nearly a grandfather, "if my wife and I want to see the
Bruegels in Vienna at the Kunsthistorisches, we fly over. Most people
cannot. I would like to make it possible for everyone to have the experience of seeing them."

"Ambassador Annenberg," Minow replied, "the way to do that is
through public television. We now reach every home in America, and
we can take every viewer to see the Bruegels or anything else in the
world."

"In that case," Walter said, "I would like to give PBS five million
dollars to create that opportunity." Minow pushed his chair closer.
Other than his conversations with his family, he could not imagine a
more important one. Public broadcasting was constantly in need of
money, as any viewer was aware from its endless fund-raising appeals.
Congress had created the Corporation for Public Broadcasting in 1967
to develop high-quality, noncommercial educational, cultural and informational television and radio programming. Two years later CPB
launched the Public Broadcasting Service and National Public Radio

in 1970 to produce and distribute national programs. All three were funded by federal tax dollars, but even with specific projects backed by foundation and corporate contributions, public broadcasting had been lurching from one crisis to another, many financial, since its inception. An unsolicited multimillion-dollar offer to fund a fine-arts series was like winning the lottery. Minow was ecstatic.

When dinner ended, they agreed to have their tax advisers discuss the gift, and Minow soon returned home to Chicago, where he was a prominent attorney. Scarcely had he arrived when calls from friends began: from an industrialist, a banker, even Eppie Lederer, the advice columnist. What was he doing with Annenberg? Walter had called them personally, which was his habit, to check out the PBS chief. He liked what he heard and arranged to meet Minow and Robben Fleming, the former president of the University of Michigan and then president of the Corporation for Public Broadcasting, at the Cosmos Club in Washington to discuss his contribution.

Their lunch orders had just been taken when Walter announced that he had changed his mind about the gift. "I'm not going to give you the five million to do an art series," he said, pausing to glance at Lee. Minow turned pale. He felt his stomach drop toward his ankles. Fleming, a distinguished educator, looked bewildered. Walter smiled and ended the suspense. "I want to give you a hundred and fifty million — ten million a year for fifteen years — to do a full university of the air, so people who cannot go to college can get a university education through television." He had in mind a combination of the *University of the Air* that he had instituted in Philadelphia on WFIL in 1950 and the British Broadcasting Corporation's *Open University*, which had a home enrollment of fifty thousand students. Sixty million dollars would be spent on using public television to help students in kindergarten through twelfth grade get a better handle on math and science. "I've made a lot of money in television," he told them. "This is how I want to give it back."[1] (By 1999, the math and science project on the Annenberg/CPB Channel reached into more than twenty-three thousand schools and eleven million U.S. homes.)[2]

GIVING BACK would be the primary theme of the rest of Walter's life, once Lee resigned from the Reagan administration and he resolved what to do with Triangle. Shortly after Queen Elizabeth's 1983 visit to Sunnylands, Walter turned seventy-five, had a second hip replacement and updated planning for his estate, which was then worth $350 million.

Forty million was in cash and marketable securities, $170 million in Triangle shares, $128 million in artworks and $11 million in residential real estate.[3]

It was not the $1 billion he had promised himself that he would make when Moses died and the family was nearly bankrupt. But it was more than enough to show his gratitude for his recognition at home and in Britain. His great-grandmother Leah had lived to be one hundred and four, and Walter fully expected to make it to one hundred himself. With his mother, Sadie's, generosity in mind, he wanted to devote most of the time he had left to philanthropy. Yet there were several reasons he was hesitant to sell out completely.

One was psychological. Giving up Triangle was an acknowledgment of his mortality. It meant the end was approaching, and that was a topic Walter disliked contemplating.

Another was political and economic. From mid-1981 until 1983, the U.S. economy was in its worst recession since the Great Depression which followed the 1929 crash. Inflation was more than 13 percent, unemployment stood at nearly 11 percent, bank loan rates were at 19 percent; housing starts had not been so low since 1946 and automobile sales were at a twenty-year low. Yet, Walter had confidence that Reaganomics, which had cut marginal tax rates by more than half, would spur growth and expansion. And that was what happened starting in 1983.

A third reason for holding on was editorial. In the early 1980s, *TV Guide* was producing some of its best journalism. In 1982, it had published a two-part story titled "Anatomy of a Smear," which charged "inaccuracies, distortions and violations of journalistic standards" in a CBS documentary, *"The Uncounted Enemy: A Vietnam Deception."* The CBS program had suggested that General William Westmoreland had deliberately manipulated figures on enemy troop strength to deceive the government and public about the progress of the war while he commanded U.S. forces. CBS acknowledged lapses in the documentary and Westmoreland sued the network for libel in what would prove to be one of journalism's most renowned libel cases. (In 1985, the two sides settled with no money changing hands and each claiming victory.)

TV Guide was more than the nation's bestselling weekly. With a tiny staff of talented editors and a handful of writers, it was proving itself journalistically. "They were really committed to doing serious reportage about the industry and making an impact," said Sally Bedell

Smith, coauthor of the "Anatomy" series and a veteran writer for *Time* and the *New York Times*.

Walter had published "News Watch" in *TV Guide* and he had endorsed Reagan, but he made the distinction that both had been clearly labeled "commentary." Away from politics, he was more scrupulous about potential conflicts of interest. *TV Guide* never sponsored programs or awards shows. It did not allow its reporters to appear on television. Walter did not try to influence weekly stories.

"I'd heard the stories about Walter at the *Inquirer,* and so it was with some trepidation that I went to Radnor," said John Weisman, *TV Guide*'s Washington bureau chief for most of the 1970s and 1980s, "but never once in my sixteen years did he ever interfere with a piece." When he asked Weisman for an assessment of one of his major interests, public television, on its twenty-fifth anniversary, Walter instructed: "Take as much time as you need; spend what you need. If public television has not lived up to its promise, I want to say so; if it has, I want to say so. But I want it so definitive that no one will challenge us." Weisman spent four months discovering that public TV was in a sorry state. As a major benefactor of public television, Walter was saddened by the finding, but he ran the story as a three-part series and gave Weisman a bonus for his work.[4]

The fourth and final reason for not selling out then was that a direct challenge was keeping Walter at his desk. Despite the better journalism *TV Guide* was showing, there were noticeable gaps in its coverage. Having operated for thirty years as a hugely profitable monopoly which produced 85 percent of Triangle's $200 million annual revenues, *TV Guide* had grown too comfortable and was slow to respond to the growing cable television market. Spotting the opening, Time Inc. launched *TV-Cable Week*, a direct challenge to *TV Guide*. Time Inc. was the dominant power in magazine publishing and America's second-largest cable system operator, two of media's fastest-growing sectors, and also owned HBO, the leading pay television channel. Time had considered buying *TV Guide* in 1981, and had informally offered $1 billion. But, according to Ralph Davidson, the then chairman of Time's board, Walter was looking for $2 billion for the Triangle stable of publications, which was too steep for Time.[5] Hoping to produce another blockbuster like *People* magazine which it started in 1974, Time decided to publish its own guide. Its projected circulation was 10 million copies which, in a revolutionary plan, would be distributed by local cable operators.

When the *TV Guide* staff heard the news, said editor David Sendler, "There was a feeling of, 'Oh my God.' We were intimidated. The ambassador, though, was not."[6] He took the rubber band off his bankroll and immediately made $50 million available to improve cable listings and reviews. He gave Sendler an extra eight pages of editorial space. "Everything was accelerated," said Sendler. "Evolutionary became revolutionary." *TV Guide* publisher Eric Larson, a six-foot-seven, 350-pound brooding Swede with a wicked sense of humor, counterattacked, tracking *TV-Cable Week*'s planned distribution in every market. *TV Guide* beefed up cable coverage in each of the top fifty markets, trumpeting the fact in ads on cable stations and blocking Time's ads.

Time launched "amid fanfares of promises and skyrockets of publicity," explained editor-in-chief Henry Grunwald, "and within weeks the vessel ran aground."[7] Wherever the Time guide went, *TV Guide* was there first. "Walter knew Time was going to throw a lot of money in," said William Henrich, Walter's lawyer who was then president of Triangle, "but he figured we knew a hell of a lot more about a weekly television guide than Time and that they were headed for doomsday."

Walter loved keeping score. Whenever Time announced its magazine's circulation, he crowed to his lieutenants. "You know the numbers? We're at nineteen point five million and they haven't hit six figures yet. We're winning," he'd say to Henrich, slapping his desk. Walter was seventy-five years old, but his competitive juices were flowing.

TV Guide's reaction was a textbook example of how best to respond to a business challenge. It helped that Time did almost everything wrong, in a case study of how not to publish a magazine that Time's own cable operators — the supposed distributors — refused to buy. After five chaotic months, twenty-five issues and a loss the company claimed was $50 million and critics said was double that, Time folded the venture. "The worst magazine flameout in publishing history," wrote *Time*'s Richard Clurman. "It was a laughingstock outside Time, a trauma inside."[8] No one laughed louder at the fall of the arrogant big shots from the big city than the self-proclaimed "country bumpkins" in Radnor. Walter hadn't felt so exuberant or vindicated since his turnaround in London. Beating the heirs of Henry Luce, his old nemesis, was the cherry on his sundae.

TRIANGLE HAD its best year ever in 1986, the midway point of Reagan's second term. The stock was up to $525 a share, a 50 percent increase from the previous year. Dividends and earnings were also up 50 percent, to $31.03. Although never publicly traded, there were 2.96 million shares outstanding worth $1.55 billion. Walter held 502,840 shares in his own name. He was also trustee for an additional 924,000 shares in his father's estate (Moses had held 240 nearly worthless shares when he died) and 251,549 shares held for various nieces and nephews. His sisters had 334,630 shares, while the remaining 947,886 shares supported the Annenberg schools at Penn and the University of Southern California. Yet Walter saw clouds on the horizon.

In November 1986, the Iran-Contra scandal erupted; it sapped the Reagan administration for another year and marked the beginning of the end of the president's effectiveness. By the end of 1987, Triangle stock had slipped to $510 a share. The share value had dropped before — in 1973 and 1974 reflecting the sale of the *Inquirer* and broadcast properties — but this was the first dip for nonextraneous reasons since 1951, when Price Waterhouse had begun determining Triangle's market value. By March 1988, when he turned eighty, all of Walter's instincts told him it was time to sell. Publishing was being segmented. Competition was increasing, and Triangle was not immune.

Walter had built his business in part on the notion of "essentiality." Anyone interested in business had to take the *Wall Street Journal;* in horse racing, the *Daily Racing Form;* in television, *TV Guide.* They were the nation's three essential publishing businesses and Walter owned two of them. By the middle 1980s, though, Walter's publications were no longer required reading. Sunday newspapers and other magazines had boosted coverage of television. Cable sports channels and the proliferation of gambling casinos foreshadowed a sharp drop in racing interest. Dozens of hip young women's magazines were crowding *Seventeen*'s market. "The market was shrinking and our levels couldn't be sustained," said Bill Henrich. "Circulation was dropping. Advertising was getting real soft. All the principal revenue sources were drying up. It was a good time to sell."[9]

On July 6, Walter had Henrich contact New York–based media broker John Veronis. In what would be the most expensive deal in publishing history, Walter would sell Triangle to Rupert Murdoch for $3 billion. The Australian-born press magnate had been a friend for two decades and was the only buyer approached. They had met in London in 1969 soon after Walter arrived and Murdoch had purchased the *Sun* and the *News of the World,* Britain's biggest popular daily and Sunday newspapers.

The two men had much in common and liked each other instinctively. Both were gamblers and risk-takers, political conservatives and outsiders who went their own way according to a set of tenets each had set for himself. Murdoch's father, Sir Keith, had been a successful publisher and radio station magnate who had battled a terrible stutter. An indulgent father, Sir Keith built an Australian media empire and had introduced his only son — there were three Murdoch daughters — to the excitement of news and pressrooms much as Moses had his. Walter had lost his only son; Rupert Murdoch was only twenty-one when his father died. It would be a stretch to claim that Walter and Murdoch, who was then fifty-seven, had a father-son relationship, but there were links that extended beyond business.[10]

When he left London, he kept in contact with Murdoch who, as Walter cut back, continued to expand his global information empire, adding newspapers, television stations, publishing houses, cable systems and satellite networks. Annenberg kept the Australian posted on his thinking. "Rupert, for many years I have been embracing a process of reducing the extent of my operations. Simplicity and streamlining have been my basic thinking," he wrote him in 1975 just as Murdoch moved toward complexity, positioning himself to become the globe's dominant media baron. "You may be certain that I shall ever extend the hand of friendship and support."[11] Murdoch grabbed the hand and asked to meet. "I would particularly value your advice," he replied to Walter.[12]

They stayed in touch throughout the 1970s and 1980s, during which the immigrant Murdoch became a naturalized American citizen and, having shifted his corporate headquarters to New York, took up residence at 2 East Eighty-eighth Street, the same building where Walter's mother, Sadie, had lived. When Rupert and his wife, Anna, visited Sunnylands, both Annenbergs found them very attractive and gracious as well as intelligent. Lee and Walter had high regard for Anna Murdoch and appreciated the handwritten thank you notes each Murdoch wrote after a visit.

Walter also respected the way Murdoch operated. Like the spartan Triangle headquarters at Radnor, his News Corporation offices were functional, not fancy; he had fewer top managers than any major corporation and, like Walter, carried his business plan in his own head. Murdoch had impressed Walter in 1986 when he stunned the British newspaper industry and nearly wiped out the powerful, feather-bedded print unions by moving his publications overnight to a new automated plant at Wapping in East London. The move reminded Walter how he had beaten his union typesetters by abruptly shutting down the *Morning Telegraph*.

On July 7, 1988, media broker Veronis met Murdoch in New York and proposed the sale. Two days later, the two men had lunch at Inwood with Walter and Bill Henrich, who was then president of Triangle. There were no legions of investment bankers or corporate lawyers. "I am honored that you chose to talk to me," Murdoch told him.[13] They reviewed each publication, its content and market. *TV Guide* was the jewel in the crown, not least because Murdoch owned Fox, the nation's fourth network. Not only did the magazine offer computerized summaries of more than 20,000 movies and 150,000 programs, but one of every five magazines sold in the U.S. in 1988 was a *TV Guide*. Weekly circulation had slipped to just below 17 million, published in 106 regional editions, but advertising revenue for the first six months of the year totaled $163 million, on target to match its industry-leading total in 1987 of a third of a billion dollars.

Seventeen's circulation stood at 1.9 million, but it had fallen from thirty-fourth to forty-second in ad revenues. Nonetheless, it would fit well with *Elle*, the glossy fashion magazine Murdoch published with his French partner Hachette. Nearly forty thousand readers paid $2.50 each for the *Daily Racing Form*. "The old brown cow that always gives rich milk," as Walter called it, was still highly profitable sixty-six years after he had carried the packet of money wrapped in newspaper with his father to buy *DRF* from Frank Brunell. Murdoch would also gain Triangle's vast distribution system on which to piggyback his other titles.

The entire negotiation took less than a month. Lawyers joined only in the last ten days. Throughout, Walter stuck to his $3 billion asking price. Murdoch, he said, was "the world's greatest and most dynamic gambler," but years of gambling in the Benevolent Marching and Philosophical Society and business competition had given Walter good insight to negotiating psychology. For a second opinion, he flew to Omaha to consult with his friend Warren Buffett. "Walter, run to the bank," the legendary investor advised. "It's a hell of a deal."

He was getting top dollar at the peak of the market. "The price struck me as very high," said J. Kendrick Noble Jr., media analyst at PaineWebber.[14] Canadian publishing mogul Conrad Black, when asked about the price, replied, "Let me tell you how smart Walter Annenberg is. Rupert Murdoch is one of the smartest men in the world and Walter got him to over-pay by a billion dollars. That's how smart Walter is."[15]

Black was a good friend of Walter's and meant the remark as a compliment, but such talk made Walter bristle because it suggested that he had been money-hungry. "I didn't want to be greedy," he said. "It's a mark of bad character and I've always believed that pigs go to the slaughterhouse."[16] He managed to add pension guarantees, five-year, $500,000 parachutes for six senior managers, and a few other wrinkles, which raised the final purchase price to $3.2 billion.

The base price represented a multiple of 16 on Triangle's annual earnings of $200 million, which was considerably higher than the 11-to-14 multiples for which media companies had been selling. The difference was that Murdoch, who had spent $5.5 billion on acquisitions in the previous three years, wanted the company badly and did not want to haggle rudely with his old friend "the Ambassador."

"These," said Murdoch, "are the most valuable and prized publication properties in the world."[17] Later, after the debt briefly threatened to bankrupt his News Corporation and *TV Guide* circulation and *Daily Racing Form* revenues slid, Murdoch had second thoughts about the price, but not about the purchase. "Maybe I was a bad buyer, too keen," he mused. "I should have beat him down a few hundred million, but he's a hard dealer."[18]

AT THE SAME TIME he was selling Triangle to Murdoch, Walter was involved in more complex negotiations concerning the fate of his art collection, which he had continued to build after London. His single best buy had been the 1983 purchase of his sister Enid Haupt's collection. She had informed Walter that she wanted to raise cash for charitable gifts to Sloan-Kettering and the New York Botanical Garden, projects she wanted completed in her lifetime. "I said, 'Why not sell them to me? I'm your brother.'" Sotheby's established the values, and for $28 million — "a very good price," he said — Walter bought fifteen paintings. They included five Renoirs plus Matisse's *Odalisque with Gray Trousers*, Gauguin's *The Siesta*, and three Cézannes — *Portrait of Uncle Dominique as a Monk, The House with the Cracked Walls*, and *Seated Peasant*. The fifteen were exceptional, among the best of Walter and Lee's total collection.

They continued adding to the collection throughout the 1980s, not always getting what they wanted. When van Gogh's *Sunflowers* sold at auction for $39.9 million in 1987, Walter dropped out when the bidding reached $20 million. "It went by me like a freight train passes a hobo," he said with a laugh.[19] After selling Triangle, Walter had such deep pockets that he could catch and pass any train he wished.

In November 1989, he paid $40.7 million at Sotheby's for *Au Lapin Agile*, the most he ever spent for a piece for his own collection. At that time it was the third-highest price paid for an artwork at auction.[20] He sold stock to buy it "because it's much better to look at than securities in a box." And he loved the story behind the painting, a haunting 1905 self-portrait of Picasso as a harlequin standing next to a woman in an orange dress at the bar of a Paris tavern from which the painting took its name.

"He painted it after his best friend, a Spaniard named Casagemas, killed himself over a tragic love affair involving this very girl, Germaine Pichot, the wife of another of Picasso's friends," Walter explained to a Sunnylands visitor with an enthusiasm that belied the number of times he had told the story. "Casagemas first tried to shoot her, but she was only wounded, so he turned the gun on himself. Naturally, Picasso hated her for being responsible for his friend's death, but years later, when she was old and toothless and sick, he visited her and gave her some money and said, 'Now I forgive you.'" He paused, as if he were absorbing the painting by osmosis, then smiled. "I am attracted to paintings that tell a story."[21]

Although the Annenbergs profess not to have one favorite, *Au Lapin Agile* ranked high, along with Monet's exquisite *Path through the Irises*, which captivated Lee. Another, because they loved flowers, was van Gogh's *Vase of Roses*, which was painted in 1890 and has pride of place over the main fireplace at Sunnylands. A year after they returned from London, they paid $2.5 million for the painting, which depicts a breathtaking, large bouquet of light pink roses against a yellow-green background in a green vase. Formerly owned by philanthropist Mary Lasker, their *Roses* is the fuller, more elegant, vertical companion to the artist's horizontal *White Roses*. That version, which shows fewer flowers in an unglazed earthenware jar, was valued at $60 million when given to the National Gallery in Washington in 1991 by Pamela Harriman to honor her third husband, Averell, who had bought it with his second wife. "Walter's is the male, mine is the female," Pamela said when she saw the two privately side by side at the Gallery.[22]

The overall collection was intensely personal. Many paintings showed flowers, including exquisite roses and lilies by Henri Fantin-Latour. A large Vuillard, *The Album*, painted in 1895, dominated the

Sunnylands dining room. Walter bought it because it contained a portrait of seven women, variations on the wife of Thadée Natanson, the editor and publisher of the lively Parisian journal *La Revue Blanche*. "They reminded me of my seven sisters," said editor and publisher Walter. "They spoiled me and then I spoiled them."

The imagery of other paintings also struck personal chords. Monet's magnificent *Water Lilies*, painted in 1919 at Giverny, shows richly painted flowers and pond water on a three-by-six-and-a-half-foot canvas. "Landscapes of water and reflection have become an obsession," Monet wrote late in life to a friend. Looking at the painting and then through the window toward Sunnylands' banks of flowers, lush grass and perfect ponds, Lee and Walter recognized a symmetry.

There were resounding echoes of family history in the Cézannes. *The House with the Cracked Walls*, painted in 1892, shows a gaping fissure in a side wall, as if the house had been struck by lightning. Yet it stood defiant, surrounded by green trees, rich blue sky and boulders that suggest endurance. "This is a metaphor for a life, or a world, in ruins," wrote critic John Russell.[23] Some saw it as a haunting metaphor for Walter and the Annenbergs, a son and family cracked, but not destroyed, by Moses's fate.

The monumental *Portrait of Uncle Dominique as a Monk*, its paint troweled on with a palette knife, was an image of authority. The monk has massive hands crossed at his chest and a scowling face enveloped by a white cowl from which a small black cross dangles. Painted in 1866, Cézanne's Dominique is a solitary figure confident in his beliefs. In the adjacent "Room of Memories" at Sunnylands, a 1978 portrait of Walter by Andrew Wyeth was displayed. In it Walter wears a cream-colored, monastic robe he ordered from the church garment maker Whipple in London to match those worn by the Ely Cathedral choir. The picture bore a startling resemblance to the noble Dominique. When Lee mentioned to Wyeth that Walter's face seemed too severe, the artist was unapologetic. "There is nothing of the cream puff about Walter."[24]

There was not, but there was something touching about the passion he felt for his art. Each day at Sunnylands, he made a careful tour of the paintings, which shared space with thirty-six pieces of etched Steuben glass, sculpture by Alberto Giacometti, slender and busty marble figures by Jean Arp, Ming jade and an early Ch'ing bullock which Lee nicknamed Walter. "I do adore these paintings. They are family to me," he said, his eyes turning moist. "They are my children."

By 1989, there were fifty-three paintings, relatively few compared with other major collections. They included eight Cézannes, six Monets, six Renoirs and five van Goghs, along with works by Gauguin, Seurat, Manet, Matisse, Degas, Toulouse-Lautrec, Picasso, Braque, Vuillard, Bonnard and Fantin-Latour. *Washington Post* art critic Paul Richard called them "flawlessly picked paintings."[25] John Russell, the art historian and critic, described the collection as "true metal, neither splashy nor outrageous, but the real thing and the solid thing."[26] For National Gallery director J. Carter Brown, the collection was "one of the greatest assemblages of Impressionist and Post-Impressionist art in private hands in the world."[27]

All of which meant that the disposition of the collection was a serious matter. Lee and Walter spent a great deal of time discussing various options. For a while they considered keeping the collection at Sunnylands, where they planned to be buried. That way Walter could ensure that he would always be with his "children." But they soon realized that idea made little sense. The only argument in its favor was that the setting for the paintings was glorious, better than any museum. Otherwise, the scenario flew in the face of his determination that the paintings be as accessible as possible. Few people would see them in the California desert.

Walter also realized that personal museums set up by rich collectors often were silly vanities or unscrupulous tax dodges in which they "donated" artworks to institutions they continued to control. That had been the point of his nine-year effort to pry open the Barnes Foundation. "It was my duty as a citizen to put an end to that tax fraud and make those paintings accessible to the public." He did not want his collection to be displayed in any way that could be perceived as inappropriate. The last thing he wanted to hear was "There goes Annenberg again," or any criticism which lumped him with collectors he did not respect.

Among them were industrialist Daniel Terra's Museum of Contemporary Art in Chicago and the Armand Hammer Museum in Los Angeles, which art critic Robert Hughes called "a $100 million shell with maybe six paintings of quality inside."[28] Walter hated Hammer. "The man was a thief, the most unscrupulous son of a bitch in America and his art was trash," he said. "I wouldn't hang one of his pictures. Can you imagine renaming Leonardo's notebook 'The Codex Hammer'? That shows you the man's lack of character."[29] Such collectors,

he told critic Paul Richard, "are peanut people. So concerned with
their fancied importance. They amount to nothing in the scheme of
things."[30]

He never considered selling his collection, although two Japanese
syndicates tried hard to tempt him in 1987 at the height of the art-
market frenzy. The first group asked to see the paintings at Sunnylands, then startled Walter by offering him $1 billion for them all. He
said he was delighted that they so enjoyed their tour, but that the
paintings were not for sale. The second group bid an additional $100
million. "They thought I was playing a waiting game, trying to jack up
the price. I said, I appreciate your offer, but you're asking me to sell
members of my family. They couldn't believe that I would just give
them away."[31]

Which is what he had decided to do. All museums need new artworks regularly to prevent their permanent collections from stagnat-
ing. The art-market boom of the 1980s had driven prices so high,
however, that even the nation's greatest galleries were having difficulty
replenishing their larders, especially in such a popular and expensive
category as Impressionism. The combination of few worthy collections
and the proliferation of vanity museums meant that competition
among art museums for quality pieces in private hands had become
intense.[32]

There were four obvious candidates for the Annenberg collection — the Philadelphia Museum of Art, the National Gallery in Washington, D.C., the Metropolitan Museum of Art in New York and,
because of his love for and connections to California, the Los Angeles
County Museum of Art. A delicate but ardent stakes race among the
four began unofficially in the spring of 1986 when Anne d'Harnoncourt, director of the Philadelphia Museum of Art, sat next to Walter at
a dinner party. They were old friends. He and Lee were trustees and
Walter was the museum's biggest donor. D'Harnoncourt knew that
Walter did not lend his collection, but decided to ask him anyway. To
her surprised delight, he agreed. She began making arrangements.[33]

The following spring, the Metropolitan trustees held their annual
meeting at the Cloisters, the museum's medieval art branch. Walter
had retired from the board of the Met, but Lee had joined and was an
active member. Two of the museum's top positions had recently
changed. Director Philippe de Montebello, who succeeded Hoving,
remained in place, but six months earlier, former diplomat William
Luers had become president of the Metropolitan, and at the Cloisters

session *New York Times* publisher Arthur Ochs Sulzberger had become chairman of the board. When Luers heard that Walter was coming to pick up Lee, he arranged to speak with the publisher on the ramparts overlooking the Hudson River.

Walter expected Luers to ask him for money. Everyone did. And while some New Yorkers assumed that he had been permanently offended by his experience ten years earlier, Walter never held a grudge against the museum. Two years after the fiasco he had given an unrestricted pledge of $2 million. Luers, though, asked for his collection.

"He did a double take in a way that suggested it was the first time he had ever been asked directly," recalled Luers. He had known the Annenbergs since 1981, when, as U.S. ambassador to Venezuela, he had accompanied its president to Washington and dealt with Lee, then chief of protocol. His wife, Wendy, with Lee in 1986 cofounded the Friends of Art and Preservation in Embassies, a group which raised funds to turn U.S. embassy residences into showpieces of American art and culture.

Quickly, as if thinking out loud, Walter outlined his considerations: the collection had to stay intact; there could be no deaccessioning, meaning no pictures could be sold; he was still considering Sunnylands and the other three museums. Finally, he said he would think about it. In January 1988, National Gallery director Brown sent Walter a proposal of how the collection could be presented in Washington. Director Earl "Rusty" Powell made a bid for the Los Angeles County Museum.

In 1989, three years after his dinner with d'Harnoncourt, the Philadelphia Museum of Art published an elegant catalogue for the collection and mounted a handsome exhibition of the paintings. The *Wall Street Journal* headlined its review "Impressionist Gems in Philadelphia." By the time the show opened, the Annenbergs had agreed to let it travel over the next two years to Washington, Los Angeles and New York.

Although it was widely believed that the tour was a contest, the Annenbergs all along had been leaning toward the Metropolitan. Still, it took Walter four years to make up his mind. He was not stringing them along, but he refused to contemplate dying and turning over his treasures. Walter was eighty-one when the Philadelphia exhibit opened. Not joking when predicting he would live to one hundred, he did not feel pressed for time.

Lee, a practical woman with a keen sense of how far and hard Walter could be pushed, urged that he pick the Met. "We wanted our paintings to be our gift to the world," she said, "and New York City is the center of art in this country. It was the place to go." More visitors toured the Met — 5.5 million in 1998 — than any other U.S. art museum. Immigrants, as Walter's family had been, tourists and city residents streamed through the portals to see the most varied examples of art and learn from the nation's most complete art education programs.

The permanent collections in Philadelphia and Los Angeles were weaker than the Met's. Nor did they have comparable visitor traffic. The National Gallery held a certain allure. Having his collection in the nation's capital appealed to his sense of patriotism. He had also been a trustee of the National Gallery and had great respect for director Carter Brown. But the gallery, he decided, was not a complete museum. It did not have the Met's educational programs or the encyclopedic breadth of its holdings. Many visitors skipped the fine European collection in the main building in favor of exhibits in the new and dramatic East Wing. And finally, although Walter never acknowledged it as a factor, other directors believed he did not want to have his collection in a museum so singly identified with another donor, the Mellon family — father Andrew and son Paul.

Metropolitan officials believed that they would win on the merits. But as years went by after Luers's 1987 request and no commitment was forthcoming, they began to wonder. When they learned that the collection would also be exhibited in Washington and Los Angeles as well as Philadelphia, they worried that it might slip away. Fully aware that Walter had a long memory for bad experiences, Luers, de Montebello and Sulzberger resolved to make Walter comfortable and clinch the gift.

The director decided to redesign the twenty-five-thousand-square-foot area set aside for nineteenth-century European paintings so that the Annenberg collection would hang together in three galleries and be complemented by the museum's holdings in six adjacent galleries. De Montebello then had constructed a six-foot-square scale model of the proposed galleries to demonstrate how Walter's collection would be integrated with the great Impressionist paintings the Met already owned. How the Annenberg 1870s Monets, for example, would eliminate a Met weakness. A small framed photograph of each painting was hung in its proposed space in the model, showing the juxtaposition of the Annenbergs' and Met's artworks. "It was brilliant," said Lee. "I took one look and said, 'Walter, this is it.'"[34]

He agreed and on March 11, 1991, two days before his eighty-third birthday, Walter told the Met it would receive the collection, valued at $1 billion. It constituted the largest single donation to any museum in a half century, more even than the $800 million J. Paul Getty left in his will to the Los Angeles museum bearing his name. "I happen to believe in strength going to strength," said Walter in explaining how he had decided on the Met. In his opinion there were only two complete museums in the world, the Louvre and the Metropolitan, "and I think the Met is the proper repository for the paintings I love with a passion."

In return, the Met proposed to make a half-hour film of the collection in place at Sunnylands with the Annenbergs commenting about their paintings, and agreed to rigorous exhibition terms: the museum could loan a painting to another exhibit in the building, but there were to be no loans outside the Met of individual pictures or of the collection; no paintings could be sold; they could be removed for repair, but not for storage. If they ended up in the basement, Walter warned, "I would get out of my grave and hit the director over the head."[35]

There was jubilation in the New York arts community. Reactions from the rejected museums were mixed. The Los Angeles County Museum of Art took the decision in stride. That was because the day after the New York announcement, Walter gave LACMA $10 million, the largest single cash gift it had ever received. He had been impressed, he told director Rusty Powell, by his "well thought out" proposal.

There was anger, though, at the Philadelphia Museum and the National Gallery, where a number of officials felt teased and exploited. Passions were particularly high at the National Gallery because the *New York Times* broke the story of the gift on the very day that the Gallery was celebrating its fiftieth anniversary. Lee and Walter attended the gala that evening, where several furious trustees refused to speak to him. The Annenbergs were upset themselves. Extremely sensitive to such indignities, they had not been responsible for the timing of the story, which gallery officials believed had been leaked to the newspaper by prideful sources at the Metropolitan out for sport with their Washington, D.C., competitors for the collection. (So sensitive was Sulzberger to Walter's comfort level that he ordered the *Times*'s story about the gift be "devoid of zingers" and written "without cutting off [Walter's] balls.")[36]

One frustrated curator privately accused Walter of using the non–New York shows as leverage to get what he wanted from the

Metropolitan. Walter said that was nonsense. He had made his conditions clear, but had otherwise asked for nothing from any museum, merely loaning his collection in response to their requests. He had already been generous to both galleries. In 1987 he had given two Cézanne sketchbooks valued at $5 million to Philadelphia and over the next two years gave an additional $10 million in cash. In 1989 he had given $5 million to the National Gallery. One museum director predicted that the Met would ultimately break its side of the bargain, either by loaning or by selling works. Walter, though, had full faith in the Met's integrity. His lawyer William Henrich had even greater confidence in the fully executed and detailed legal agreement they had negotiated.

IN SEPTEMBER 1991 the Metropolitan closed its second-floor Impressionist galleries to begin an eighteen-month renovation. The collection would be displayed temporarily each year from May through November when the Annenbergs were away from Sunnylands and permanently after Walter's death. He had no approval rights of the redesign, which allowed viewers to roam through the entire Impressionist collection without being aware — except for a discreet plaque painted to match the exhibit walls — that they were in the Annenberg space. "He was tremendously sensitive not to be seen as seeking recognition," said Luers. Walter was so pleased with the plan that he offered to pay half of the $10 million reconstruction costs.[37]

When the galleries reopened in 1993, Walter marked the event by giving the Metropolitan Vincent van Gogh's *Wheat Field with Cypresses*. He had purchased the 1889 scene of the windswept field under a stormy sky from the family of a Swiss businessman for $57 million, the most he had ever paid for a painting. "It's one of the great van Goghs," Walter said, "and when I heard it might be available, I knew it was something the museum must have."

The City of New York was as delighted as the Metropolitan had been with Walter's generosity. After their original gift of the collection, Lee and Walter were honored and thanked at a museum dinner and at a luncheon hosted by then mayor David Dinkins at Gracie Mansion. Leaving the mayor's residence, Walter had paused to shake hands with his host when he happened to glance up and notice that the paint on the entranceway was peeling. The mayor apologized. The city budget, he shrugged. Walter never missed a beat: "Why don't you let me take care of that."[38]

28

PHILANTHROPIST

―――――――

WITH BILLIONS IN HAND from Rupert Murdoch, Walter focused his attention in the 1990s on investing and philanthropy, pursuing each in monumental fashion. Just as the decade's bull market soared, he poured his Triangle proceeds deep into Wall Street. Deep was the operative word. He preferred to own millions of shares in few companies, rarely more than a half dozen at a time. The 240 nearly worthless shares left in his father's will a half century earlier, he had parlayed into holdings worth $1.5 billion. Contrary to the counsel of most financial advisers, who urge investers to diversify, all his father's estate was invested in a mere six equities, of which in the mid-1990s four were banks: Bank of America, First Union, JP Morgan and Wells Fargo. The other two were General Electric and Spieker properties, whose West Coast holdings he believed would boom in the twenty-first century.

He established the Annenberg Foundation in June 1989 with $1 billion, one-third of the Triangle sale receipts. By early 1999, the foundation's assets had grown to $3 billion. Walter's personal holdings totaled more than $2 billion and he had also made his sisters near billionaires. His sister Evelyn, niece Cynthia Polsky and nephew Ronald Krancer separately used the same words to describe him: financial genius. "He probably should have been an investment banker instead of a publisher," said Lee Annenberg. "He really has the knack."[1]

He traded through two Philadelphia brokers: John McCarthy of Dean Witter and Charles "Chip" Kurtzman of Goldman Sachs. Each knew the other, but theirs was a competitive relationship and they did not share strategy. Walter liked and respected each man and appreciated an extra opinion, but split his holdings so no single person would know too much about what he was doing. When he stayed in hotels, private fax and phone lines were installed so the brokers, each of whom called or faxed material three to six times a day, did not go through the switchboards or front desks.

In addition to speaking with McCarthy and Kurtzman, Walter did his own research, spending hours each day reading business journals. Faith in management remained his prime criterion, but he also followed trends, price and yields. In his early nineties, he could still reel off the previous day's share fluctuations and dividend news, even for some stocks he did not own. "*Feel* is important," he said. "You need balance between caution and being ahead of the pack."[2]

He examined quarterly and annual reports, but did not pore over specialty trade papers, market analyses or long columns of financial indices. Concepts interested him more than numbers. If a company looked appealing, he wanted to speak directly with its chief executive, some of whom were invited to Sunnylands to be assessed. "He would not ask an officer what dividend you were likely to pay," said James Hanson, chairman of the British-American conglomerate Hanson PLC, "but if he thought you were paying too much, Walter's way would be to urge you to reinvest more."[3] And did they listen to his recommendations? "Walter is a very good judge of management, extremely pragmatic and has remarkable intuition," said Richard Rosenberg, chairman of Bank of America through much of the 1990s. "When you have a major shareholder with those skills and he tells you to look harder, you look harder."[4]

Walter's intuition told him to put his Murdoch proceeds heavily into banks. Their price/earnings ratios were as low as four or five and he foresaw widespread consolidation. In the mid-1980s, he told Norman Pearlstine, then managing editor of the *Wall Street Journal*, that he liked Citibank, whose stock was then trading in the teens, and its new chairman John Reed and might "take a flyer." "Walter said it would drop a bit while 'Johnny' straightened things out and then it would move right up," Pearlstine recalled. "Sure enough, it dropped to nine and then went to seventy-one. What an eye for the market."[5] Walter's flyer had been four million shares.

By the mid 1990s, he was comfortable with equity price/earnings ratios between 10 and 20, but wary when they moved higher. There were exceptions: Gillette — "it's a big world and men shave every day"; drugs stocks such as Merck and Johnson and Johnson — "they're the cream in my book"; and General Electric. GE was selling at close to thirty times earnings, but he held the widely admired chairman Jack Welch and GE's varied core businesses in high regard. Buying GE was like buying a half-dozen well-managed firms, including its credit arm, which he considered a well-run investment bank. Americans who wanted to buy foreign stocks or overseas mutual funds would do better to buy General Electric, he advised. Investors were purchasing shares in a firm that operated overseas but were protected from currency and political fluctuations while buying American, which was important for Walter. He liked the company so much he bought five million shares.

Just as he had purchased General Motors and Bank of America shares after meeting Alfred Sloan and A. P. Giannini, sixty years later he remained eager to meet top managers. Walter flew to Bentonville, Arkansas, to meet Wal-Mart founder Sam Walton. They hit it off well, and Walter, who had never been in a Wal-Mart before, was impressed by the quality and prices of the goods as he was guided through the headquarters store by Walton. He did not, however, buy Wal-Mart shares because — General Motors notwithstanding — he was wary of labor-intensive firms. Wal-Mart stores were not unionized, but in Walter's opinion, the possibility that they might be organized after Walton's death made the shares unnecessarily risky. There were too many other good companies that did not present that potential problem.

He did hold some stocks for decades, which was his friend Warren Buffett's strategy for building wealth, but he was not bull-headed about it. "He's not a short-term investor, and he doesn't rattle easily," said broker McCarthy, "but if he thinks something has gone wrong with the stock, he'll change and quickly."

He dumped millions of shares of Bank of America after having lunch once with then CEO A. W. Clausen. "All Clausen talked about was the 'social responsibility' of banks. I sold all my shares the following week."[6] In Walter's view, individuals, governments and religious orders had social responsibility. Corporations had a responsibility to shareholders. When Clausen became president of the World Bank in 1981, Walter resumed buying shares in Bank of America until he had thirty-five million and was, as with General Motors, the bank's largest individual shareholder.

He also bailed out of Philip Morris when he foresaw government moving against tobacco companies. It was a lose-lose situation. If tobacco was truly bad, he wanted no part of it. Nor did he want to fight city hall; in his experience city hall always won.[7]

Usually, he won too, but not always. In the 1990s, because he knew the executives and believed he understood the process, he bought 1.5 million shares of Indigo NV, a technology company with a revolutionary method for printing text and photos on virtually any surface. The share price soared from the teens to $64, then plummeted to $3. He was not fazed. "Ahead of its time," he concluded. Still, that was it for dabbling in technology.

Bonds bored him. There were greater growth opportunities in equities. He did not hedge or take short positions. Mutual funds were for people who wanted others to make their decisions. Market timing was a waste of time. Business cycles he ignored. "Long range, I am very bullish," he said as he approached ninety and began liquidating some equities for treasury bills to simplify his estate planning. He sold most of his bank stocks in early 1998 near their peak, missing the plunge that followed the economic turmoil in Asia, Russia and Latin America. The stocks he continued to like involved satellite communications and DirecTV. "That has tremendous potential. They'll cover the world with satellites and you'll receive hundreds of stations on a six-inch disk. Imagine the variety. Now that's exciting. Think of what we'll be learning."[8]

THE MORE the money rolled in, the more he concentrated his giving on learning. He became so excited about philanthropy that he disliked being away from the Annenberg Foundation offices. Every weekday that he was in the East from May through November, he dressed in a full suit and tie and was driven in a dark green Cadillac from Inwood by Philip Howe, a former Philadelphia police officer, to the elegant but unobtrusive new quarters tucked away on the second floor of a modern office complex in St. Davids, on the Main Line next to Radnor.

Even after he turned ninety, when his net worth neared $6 billion, Walter could scarcely wait to get to work each day. He loved Sunnylands, where he had two secretaries always on call, but once April arrived and Philadelphia emerged from the worst of winter, he became eager to return east. Lee, who was just as anxious to stay longer in California, argued that he could accomplish as much work at Sunnylands.

They were there in 1990 when United Negro College Fund president Christopher Edley came to solicit Walter for a gift for the organization, which supports forty-one private, historically black colleges. Walter had been a donor to the fund since the 1970s, when he had been approached by the late A. Leon Higginbotham, a fellow Penn trustee and one of the first black judges on the U.S. Court of Appeals. "Anyone familiar with eradicating racism in America has to concede that education is the most important passport," said Higginbotham. "The problem is, everyone wants a quick solution. Few recognize that it's a long-term nurturing process. Walter was an exception."[10]

Best known for its slogan, "A mind is a terrible thing to waste," the fund had been in existence since 1944, but it had not been a priority recipient for nonblack philanthropists, and the colleges needed much more help. Many campuses had been built soon after the Civil War and their physical plants desperately needed modernizing. They operated on shoestring budgets, had minimal endowments, charged tuition that was a fraction of that of white schools and were able to offer only limited scholarship money, although many applicants came from below-poverty-level families. For all their handicaps, the black schools were doing a remarkable job of educating students. The UNCF schools accounted for only 18 percent of the nation's black students, but produced one-third of all black graduates. Through discipline and dedication, these colleges delivered.[11]

Their record impressed Walter. So did Higginbotham's argument that the United States might have great museums with wonderful paintings, "but if your life is in jeopardy (from criminals) walking to and from the museum, what does that say about the beauty in society?" Walter had given the fund $100,000 in 1979 in the belief that the colleges could be a force for positive change. Three years later, he set up the Twenty-first Century Scholars Program, a $1.5 million UNCF fund to help outstanding black college students. He gave $2 million dollars to Howard University in Washington, $1 million to Xavier University in New Orleans and $500,000 to Pennsylvania's Lincoln University — all black schools.

Despite Walter's proven track record, Edley was apprehensive when he went to California in 1990, because the fund was about to launch a $200 million capital campaign and he was hoping for a $20 million gift, double what Walter had initially hinted he might donate. Then, just as Newt Minow had been stunned by Walter's gift to public television, it was Edley's turn to be flabbergasted a week later when the philanthropist called. "Twenty million is not enough," Edley heard Walter say. "It's too small. We need a crusade."

The crusade he had in mind went beyond helping black colleges. Walter had decided that the future of the nation was at stake. Unless millions of minority and disadvantaged youths could earn a material stake in society, he feared that the very foundations of the country might crack. "The key to America's future is access to educational opportunity," he said, mindful of what his father, Moses, had missed. "Unless young blacks are brought into the mainstream of economic life, they will continue to be on the curbstone. Unless we do something, we're going to have a great deal of trouble on our hands in ten or twenty years." He wanted to reach that one-third whom he believed were trying to improve themselves. If they could be assimilated as fairly and at as high a level as other immigrants who had made the United States great, "America will become stronger, more resilient and we will all benefit."

Walter pledged $50 million — by far the most ever directed toward black colleges, but he had no intention of merely handing over the money. He offered it as a four-to-one grant. To receive his $50 million, the fund had to raise $200 million. He was leveraging the gift, just as he had since 1927, when he gave Peddie the cinder track so it could charge user fees and build revenue. He was always willing to be the catalyst. "Getting in on the ground floor," as he put it, was his goal on any worthy initiative. But to be successful, any big venture needed partners. The size of the grant was deliberate, to give the fund-raisers confidence, to draw attention to the cause and attract partners. He wanted the whole country — foundations, corporations and private citizens — to join the campaign. "He knew what he was doing," said Edley. "He was putting a whip on our backs to make us function at the level we should be operating on."[11] It took the College Fund seven years to raise the $200 million. "They didn't think they could do it," Walter said, "but by God, they did."

IN JUNE 1993, three years after the UNCF grant, Walter announced the largest single cash contribution to private education in American history: $365 million to four schools — all to be paid immediately. He gave $120 million each to the communications programs at the Universities of Pennsylvania and Southern California, $100 million to Peddie, and $25 million to Harvard. "I'm interested in young people because the character of our country will be shaped by young people. Good heavens, what is more important than that?" he said.[12] "Education is the key to leadership. These things I'm doing are all matters of citizenship and I regard the quality of citizenship as more important than any-thing else."[13]

At Penn, $100 million was to establish a permanent endowment for the Annenberg School for Communication he had founded in 1958, not to produce journalists but to impart information about socially wor-thy policy, such as advising the population about health matters, including why in certain areas young people are underimmunized, and about the impact of television violence on children. The other $20 million was to establish a public policy center to try to improve the democratic process through research into such subjects as privacy and the media, the impact of talk radio and political advertising, on voting patterns and other topics that would change in step with national developments.

(Both the Annenberg School and the public policy institute were headed by Kathleen Hall Jamieson, chair of the Communications Department at the University of Texas when Walter interviewed her in 1989. Widely published and frequently interviewed, Jamieson was a feminist who had just critiqued the successful 1988 presidential adver-tising campaign of George Bush, a good friend of Walter's, as the dirti-est in the modern history of the presidency. She gave him marked portions of her books and television transcripts to make certain he appreciated the extent of their differences, but Walter waved them off. "None of that is any concern to me. You're doing what you think is right based on the standards which you hold. What matters is that I stand for excellence and you're excellent.")[14]

Walter was already Penn's biggest donor. Over the previous thirty years, he had given the university $109 million, initially, much of it anonymously. For the university's fund drives in the 1960s, he had matched personally the amounts by which donors increased their gifts over the previous year.[15] (In 1998, he gave Penn an additional $10 mil-lion to provide scholarships to financially needy students with leader-ship potential. The potential could be shown in academics, athletics, music, or entrepreneurship, but it had to demonstrate a capacity to rise above adversity. That was the characteristic Walter believed defined his life and which most inspired his respect for others.)

At the University of Southern California, the latest $120 million — which was in addition to $57 million he had given over the previous twenty years — was to create the Annenberg Center for Communica-tions. Its mission was to bring together undergraduates, visiting schol-ars and researchers from the Annenberg School of Communications, which was founded in 1971 at USC, with teachers and students from the schools of cinema/television, engineering, journalism and the communication arts and sciences to create a global center for communications study in the twenty-first century.

The grant to Peddie staggered the administrators of the five-hundred-student prep school. "I keep pinching myself to make sure I'm not dreaming," said headmaster Thomas DeGray, whose students put up a sign at the school entrance which read, "Wow! Thanks, Walt." The $100 million, reserved for endowment and need-blind scholarships, was not only the largest gift ever given to a U.S. secondary school, it dwarfed the second-largest gift of $12 million, which had also been given to Peddie by Walter in the 1980s. His overall philanthropy to the school, where he had been a trustee for thirty-five years, totaled $137 million, making it one of the nation's richest schools, seventh in endowment. "When I was fifteen, I went to a football game at a nearby school [Lawrenceville] and I became rather despondent when I saw how much nicer their facilities were," he explained. "Peddie wasn't wealthy, but it had great spirit. So it became a lifelong ambition to do all I could for the old school, my seventy-year program to build it up."

The Hightstown campus had six buildings when Walter first arrived in 1922. His money had built many more on the 280-acre campus, including a high-tech library with computer links that allowed students to read Shakespeare or daily newspapers from their dorm rooms. He attended the library's dedication in May 1993, six weeks before he announced the $100 million gift. "Serve on behalf of others," he told the assembled students and faculty. "Conduct yourself as if it were necessary to be re-elected every day. That is the ballgame in life."[16]

The words sounded like another axiom, but that was still how he talked and the sentiment was heartfelt. He did not tell the students, but every day since his father's death he had felt compelled to prove himself a good citizen. Twice a day, steely discipline forced him to perform his elocution exercises, even after he turned ninety. The unending tests were all part of his ninety-nine rounds. At the time the challenges had felt crushing, but, looking back, he believed they had made him a better person.

THE $25 MILLION GIFT to Harvard was in memory of Roger. He had given $3 million to Episcopal Academy, his son's prep school, and had thought about doing more for his son for a long time, but he had once given a small gift to Harvard and there had been no university follow-up, which had put him off. Then he and Lee met Harvard president Neil Rudenstine and his wife, Angelica, whom they invited to Sunnylands where, unsolicited and out of the blue, Walter made the offer. Ten million dollars was earmarked to fund twenty-five scholarships annually, comprising a rolling undergraduate total of one hundred Roger Annenberg scholarships. Three million endowed a seminar program. And although Walter first told Rudenstine that he did not want to name a building, the final $12 million went to restore Memorial Hall so that all sixteen hundred freshmen could gather for meals together daily. Harvard's upper-class students ate in residential houses, which meant freshman year was the only time they were all together. Some who knew Roger were surprised that Walter had not done something involving music, which had been his son's passion, perhaps building some practice rooms. But Walter saw merit in Rudenstine's portrayal of the hall as an important milieu for integrating freshmen. Given the depth of Roger's problems, it was unlikely that such a space would have eased his own painful social experience at Harvard, but the idea had symbolic value to Walter. "Their all being together appealed to me," he said softly.

FOUR MONTHS LATER, in October 1993, Walter gave $25 million to Northwestern for scholarships and academic programs, which brought the total of his donations to the university in Evanston, Illinois, to $55 million. That included the Annenberg Washington program affiliated with the university since 1987 and where, under the directorship of Newton Minow, and later Kathleen Hall Jamieson, fellows studied public policy in education, politics, foreign policy, financial markets, law and medicine. (Before taking the job, Minow, a Democrat, asked Republican Walter about his goal for the program. "Walter was quiet for a moment, then said, 'I want you to do good in the world.' I said, 'That's it?' He said, 'That's it. Just be sure to always listen to every side.'")[17]

In 1989, Walter had given Northwestern $1.5 million to endow a chair for Minow. The $25 million gift in October 1993 marked the beginning of a five-year hiatus from major donations to higher education. The gifts had been huge and had also involved, with the exception of the challenge grant to the black colleges, great sentimentality and a personal connection with the institutions. He had also come to realize that, for the most part, good students regardless of income could receive a decent college education. States and local communities saw to that. He had begun to worry that if philanthropists kept funding higher education, government might reduce its education funding.

He also decided that he had done his bit for colleges. He had wanted to stir the pot and get others involved, but he feared that too many gifts bearing his name might be counterproductive. When he gave his first $1 million (of $5.2 million) to Pine Manor College, Wallis's school, Walter insisted that it be anonymous. "He knew that some people say, 'Oh, it's Annenberg. Let him do it all,'" said former president Rosemary Ashby. "He wanted us to use his money for leverage while making certain that others took up their responsibilities."[18]

THE MORE Walter thought about how his dollars might best make a difference, the more determined he became to shift focus. "Everybody around the world wants to send their kids to our universities. South America, Asia, Europe, all of them," he said one day to Minow. "But nobody wants to send their kids here to public school. Who would, especially in a big city? Nobody. So we've got to do something. If we don't, our civilization will collapse."[19] His new challenge would be to move down an age level.

He and Lee had been involved for years with grade schools. Some, like Peddie and Episcopal, had received millions. Others had been given more modest gifts. Cielo Vista Elementary, in the California desert, for thirty years had only a single mesquite tree in its schoolyard until Lee visited and funded the planting of twenty-five eucalyptus and carob trees. When dealing with the United Negro College Fund, Walter heard about Piney Woods Country Life School, a small academy near Jackson, Mississippi, which boarded poor, black, inner-city youths from troubled backgrounds. For ten years, he mailed $1,000 annually to Piney Woods, which sent nearly every graduate to college, including the best universities, from which more than 80 percent graduated. Few schools better demonstrated how education could overcome adversity. "Some young people won't be productive unless they turn their lives around completely," said Walter. "Piney Woods does that well."

To other strapped elementary schools he had sent checks to buy math and science books. Certain that the *Encyclopedia Britannica* was the single best source of knowledge, he enjoyed sending sets to needy schools and libraries. But that was retail giving. After giving the $365 million, Walter decided to go wholesale on grammar schools.

On December 17, 1993, one day after he signed the last checks to Penn, USC, Harvard and Peddie, Walter stood in the Roosevelt Room of the White House flanked by President Bill Clinton and Secretary of Education Richard Riley and announced that he was giving $500 million in matching grants to improve education in public schools. Communism had been defeated and he believed that the next big national security challenge was at home. "I kept reading in the papers and seeing on TV about youngsters bringing guns and knives to school. Eleven-year-olds shooting other eleven-year-olds and threatening teachers. Society is breaking down in neighborhoods where this happens. It makes me frightened for the future of my country. Education is the only answer. It's the glue that holds civilization together. Without it, we would go back to the Dark Ages."

He had decided to concentrate on kindergarten through twelfth grade because in those years youngsters grow intellectually and develop character and feelings of compassion and responsibility. "By the time they're old enough for college, it's too late," he said. "We have to attack this problem early." He came up with the $500 million figure the same way he had for the United Negro College Fund donation. "I wanted to startle our leaders and public and get their attention. I wanted to elevate precollegiate education as a national priority. To do that I felt I had to drop a bomb. It is my responsibility as a citizen."

Of the total, $50 million was set aside to rename for Walter and broaden the mission of the new National Institute for School Reform at Brown University under the direction of Theodore Sizer, former dean of Harvard's education school and Andover headmaster, who had established the Coalition of Essential Schools at Brown. Founded in 1984 with twelve schools in four states, the coalition, which has since moved to Oakland, California, became a national network of more than eleven hundred primary, middle and high schools. Its principles include more parental involvement in schooling and greater latitude for teachers and students in the ways they instruct and learn.[20]

"Secondary schools don't work very well in traditional form," said Sizer. "Marching youngsters through grades, each teacher attaching something as they go by — math, social studies — doesn't stand the test of common sense. Yet it persists. If you organize schools in a different way and create a different culture, they can be much more effective." Sizer cited gang violence as one problem area that could be affected by a different approach. Gangs are groups of people who otherwise feel disconnected, he maintained. "Show me a school where there is a focus on each child and where the faculty is accessible and I'll show you a school where violence can be lessened."[21]

A second $50 million went to the New American Schools Development Corporation, an independent, business-backed nonprofit created in 1991 during the Bush presidency, when the United States was shown to have sunk to nearly last among industrialized nations in math and science education. The group's original mandate was to identify visionaries, educators and business executives who would design innovative programs in model schools while honoring local circumstances and encouraging school autonomy. Nonpartisan, the organization was dying from a lack of funds and interest until Walter stepped in. He had earlier given $10 million, in part because he admired the corporation's chairman, David Kearns, the former CEO of Xerox and deputy secretary of education in the Bush administration. His friendship with Kearns helped prompt the subsquent $50 million gift, which in turn drew the Clinton administration to endorse its goals. The Education Commission of the States, a research and policy group founded in 1965 and headquartered in Denver, received $6.4 million to spread the innovative word to states where governors were to provide matching funds to successful models.

The other $385 million of what came to be known as the Annenberg Challenge was to initiate reform in some of the nation's largest and most troubled school districts, where 25 percent of the forty-eight million U.S. schoolchildren reside, and in rural schools, which comprise a third of the nation's schools. Each posed different problems. City schools were plagued by overcrowded classrooms, an often embattled faculty, strident local politics and physical problems from asbestos to leaking roofs. Rural schools were faced with overcoming isolation and marginalization without losing their best qualities. The challenge set aside $50 million for its rural initiative, which focused on five hundred schools stretching from Alabama to Alaska. Walter urged that the urban programs include entire metropolitan districts, not just inner cities. As usual, his rationale was instinctual and pragmatic: he did not believe that "inner city" schools, a euphemism for mostly minority students, were the only urban schools in trouble, and he wanted to attract the broadest community support for reform. The city grants were mostly two-to-one challenges, meaning districts had to produce double his offering from private and some public sources. The federal government endorsed Walter's initiative but was not a participant.

None of the grants were processed through the local boards of education or city authorities. In each case, after consulting with state and municipal authorities, small, separate organizations of community and civic leaders, corporate executives, teachers, school council members and officials from local foundations were established to review proposals from schools for innovative programs. In some cases, the nonprofit groups were already in place. Before they could receive the money — it was to be paid out annually provided they raised the matching funds and complied with the tenets of their five-year contracts, which included keeping overhead costs to less than 10 percent — the schools were also required to form outside partnerships, with a university, a corporation or a community agency and a network with other schools. Walter's objective was unchanged — to leverage the dollars and involve as many partners as possible.

Walter was uninterested in broad theories about education. He had no intention of trying to redesign the nation's public education system. That would be impractical, he believed, and would start an endless war among competing groups of reformers. He wanted ideas that had been shown to work and could be spread around. That was the heart of his communications philosophy and motivation for his philanthropy: learn a worthwhile lesson and pass it on so others can build on the knowledge.

Other than defining the big picture and identifying specific educational problems, Walter had little personal understanding of what precisely had to be done to correct them. He was an executive and a philanthropist, not a professional educator. So he relied on his formula of picking a knowledgeable, trusted lieutenant who would keep him informed and then giving him great latitude. The chief strategist in this case was Vartan Gregorian, whom he had known for twenty years, since serving as a trustee at Penn, where Gregorian was a history professor, dean and, ultimately, provost.

Born in 1934 in an Armenian community in Tabriz in northern Iran, where his grandfather Balabeg had operated a caravansary, Gregorian had attended high school in Beirut. He came to the United States in 1956 when he was accepted as a freshman at Stanford and had to learn English quickly. A stocky bearded man with unruly bushy hair, he charmed Walter as he did most who met him. Warm, ebullient, creative and a stimulating scholar, Gregorian was also a world-class salesman and showman who took on challenges with energy and passion.

Walter liked all those qualities about Gregorian, but there was more to the educator that made him a unique character in the philanthropist's life. He became Walter's closest business friend. In many ways they were an odd couple: the tailored and ever more respectable philanthropist who picked his words with deliberate care and the rumpled intellectual and polyglot scholar who spoke seven languages, most in long, rapid-fire bursts; the billionaire loner and the crowd-pleasing teacher. In other ways, such as donor and fund-raiser, they complemented each other. In still others, they were a perfect match: both were big thinkers, successful, emotional men, humanists and doers who shared a vision of using education to implement that aspect of Wilsonian democracy which sought to maximize hope and reduce inhumanity. Each also was fascinated by using the information and technology revolution to improve education and spread knowledge.

Their friendship was cemented by two more shared experiences: each man had a strong wife and had also been profoundly influenced by the same kind of older woman — Walter by his mother, Sadie, and Gregorian by his grandmother Vosky. "Her influence was tremendous. She had no formal education, but immensely valued it. She lived her life with consummate dignity. She struggled. She coped. She never lost faith, was never cynical. She did not speak ill of others. She insisted that one must do good without expectation of reward."[22] Gregorian was speaking, although Walter could have been.

More important, Walter believed that like himself, Gregorian had risen above adversity to a higher level of achievement. The educator's difficulty had come in 1980 when, despite the overwhelming support of the university deans, faculty, students and several trustees, including Walter, Penn did not select him to replace the university's retiring president, Martin Meyerson. Gregorian, who had been offered the chancellorship of the University of California at Berkeley until he withdrew his name, all but certain that he would get the Penn job, heard on the radio that he had not been named. Devastated, he felt that his dignity had been shredded. Several trustees maintained that Gregorian was rejected because he had bridled when told he had to compete for the post. But Walter blamed the turndown on stuffed-shirt trustees who balked at choosing a rotund Armenian immigrant who spoke with an accent. Few were more sensitive than Walter to slights about being an outsider with a speech problem.

Angry but determined to prove detractors wrong, just like Walter, Gregorian resigned and became president of the New York Public Library. There he led a much-praised restoration of the landmark institution before becoming president of Brown University in 1989. His leadership there also won raves, and in 1997 he left to become president of the Carnegie Corporation, the New York–based foundation.

"He is a magnificent human being," Walter said. "The best all-around executive I know. A man of great character and absolute integrity. The most outstanding human being I know. I love him like a brother."[23]

Young enough to be his son, Gregorian was a soul mate whom Walter was happy to trust with his half-billion dollars. "Walter was born into a generation where he developed a World War I or World War II sense of patriotism," Gregorian said. "He feels that success has its price, that there is an obligation to spread wealth, that philanthropy is not charity, but an investment in our future."[24]

Gregorian, who calls him "a man of few words, but many great deeds," advised Walter on a pro bono basis and was careful never to take advantage of his friendship and ask for money. He did not have to. Walter so appreciated his sensitivity that when he saw an article citing the New York Public Library under Gregorian's leadership as the nation's best-run nonprofit, he sent him, on the first anniversary of his presidency at Brown, an unsolicited $2 million contribution to Brown and a tambourine to bang on to raise more. Gregorian used the funds, a fraction of what Brown received through the Annenberg Challenge, to establish a professorship and fellowships in Walter's name.

Gregorian oversaw everything involved in the Challenge, which by 1998 involved more than two thousand schools with nearly 1.5 million students. He ensured it was nonpartisan; that the ideas considered ranged from community-led reform to change directed by school superintendents; that the voices of diverse educators were heard; that teacher education was included; that collegial exchanges between schools and teachers were encouraged.

There were two things he did not have to worry about: Walter did not second-guess him, nor did Gregorian have to meet specific educational benchmarks, such as dispensing funds on the basis of schools' raising their reading or math levels by certain percentage points. That was a reflection of Walter's trust in him and the philanthropist's vision of the project as a catalyst, not a yardstick. Carping from within the philanthropic and educational worlds that the Challenge was misguided, directed by too many visionaries and not enough detail-conscious specialists, or that after five years it had failed to prompt measurable reform was to Walter so much water off a duck's back. He also ignored criticism from conservatives who charged he was wasting money by directing it through a public school system so encumbered by government bureaucracy that real reform was impossible. "One does not do philanthropic work as the ambassador has for years with a view to the bottom line," said Gail Levin, program director of the Annenberg Foundation. "He is affecting lives and you don't affect lives this way in terms of cost-effectiveness."[25]

Walter hoped that good would come from the process, but his expectations were realistic. He doubted he would ever see any concrete results. For him, that was not the point. And for all its bureaucratic flaws, he was not worried about working within the public school system. Private, parochial and charter schools all should be part of the educational brew, he believed, but because the government had a responsibility to educate its citizens, the nation could not walk away from public schools. There had to be a way to improve them. What he hoped to see was his gift awakening communities and other donors into action.

And he was not disappointed. Five years after he stood in the White House and announced the gift, the Challenge had raised an additional half-billion dollars from businesses, foundations, universities and individuals. Computer manufacturer William Hewlett contributed $25 million to the San Francisco Challenge and, nationally, forty organizations gave at least $1 million. New York, Boston and Chattanooga raised their required matching funds. Philadelphia was 98 percent of the way to its $50 million goal; Detroit and Los Angeles were more than 90 percent complete. That was good news, but Walter and his close supporters remained clear-eyed about long-term prospects. "Some will be big failures," predicted Barbara Rosenberg, a longtime educator, trustee of Brandeis and a friend. "He's prepared for failures, but in the big picture, there'll be an enormously positive impact."[26]

WALTER'S GIFTS became so huge in the 1990s that it was easy to forget that he had given hundreds of other donations which by normal standards would be considered very large — grants of "only" a few hundred thousand or $1 million. An Annenberg Foundation printout of his philanthropy from 1984, when the records were computerized, to 1998, totaled eighty pages, for an aggregate of more than $2 billion. More interesting than the total was where the money went. Institutions, never individuals, were the recipients. And Walter was an equal-opportunity giver. Black, Catholic, coed, single-sex, day, boarding, vocational, public, private, military, civilian, Jewish, Arab institutions — for decades he gave to all. As he explained to one editor: "I made my money from Catholics, Protestants, Jews, whites, blacks, men and women and I give it back the same way."[27]

When Pope John Paul II visited Philadelphia in 1979, Mayor Frank Rizzo announced that city funds would be used to build an altar for an outdoor mass. Walter learned that the local office of the American Civil Liberties Union planned to file suit to halt the use of public tax money and called Cardinal John Krol to ask the cost of the altar. Fifty thousand dollars, the cardinal told him. "You'll have my check on your desk in an hour," Walter said. He would not have the Pope embarrassed in his city.

The following year, impressed by the academic success of Catholic parochial schools, he gave the Philadelphia archdiocese $1 million to make up tuition deficits, then a $2 million challenge grant to support Catholic high schools. "They do a high-quality job efficiently," was his rationale. Notre Dame University received $5 million in honor of former president Reverend Theodore Hesburgh and his deputy the Reverend Edmund Joyce. "First-rate men," in his view. A million each went to Catholic University and Saint Joseph's (Pennsylvania), $1.1 million to La Salle (Pennsylvania) in honor of his lawyer Bill Henrich. Georgetown received $100,000 to endow a scholarship honoring assassinated Egyptian president Anwar Sadat.

While cruising up the Hudson River in 1993 with friends — and declining their suggestion that he visit the Franklin Roosevelt Library at Hyde Park — the party toured the military academy at West Point and lunched with the commandant and cadets. The next morning he told Cummins Catherwood that he had hardly slept. "I was so moved by our visit," he said. "I've decided to make a donation. But I can't overlook the Naval and Air Force Academies, can I?" He sent each $1 million. When he saw news reports of the devastation to Florida caused by Hurricane Andrew in 1992, he sent $1 million to the Red Cross for disaster relief.

General Colin Powell approached him when leading a campaign to build a $500,000 monument at Fort Leavenworth to the Buffalo Soldiers, two black cavalry units which had fought courageously in the Indian wars. Walter said a half-million was not enough. He gave a $250,000 matching grant and urged Powell — whom he encouraged to run for president in 1996 — to raise $1 million. Powell collected $900,000 for a monument, which is a centerpiece at the Kansas fort and a point of pride for more than one race of soldiers. In 1999, Walter gave $1 million to America's Promise, the national campaign chaired by Powell to help disadvantaged children.

To help restore the Statue of Liberty on its centennial, Walter donated $100,000 in the name of his father, who had often described to his children the look of the not-quite-completed statue when he had arrived in New York in 1885. The Library of Congress received $1 million in honor of Daniel Boorstin, the Librarian of Congress and historian who had written extensively about the evolution of American democracy. For colonial Williamsburg, Lee and Walter contributed $25 million in 1993 — in addition to the $6 million he had donated in the 1980s — to build and endow an education center and library adjacent to the eighteenth-century town. It was the most substantial construction project in the old colonial capital since the 1920s, when John D. Rockefeller Jr. had decided to resurrect the town. "The historical importance of Williamsburg must be sustained as a reminder to all our citizens of the challenges our Founding Fathers had to overcome," he said. "This is the fountainhead of Americanism."[28]

Walter had given millions to his hometown, Philadelphia, as well as to its cultural, medical and educational institutions. In 1995 he and Lee gave $10 million to the Avenue of the Arts, a city center cultural development project, to renovate the Academy of Music. Three years later, they contributed another $10 million to revitalize Independence Mall, including $4 million to build a Liberty Bell educational center. "This is where democracy was forged and where the peal of liberty still rings," Walter said, announcing the gift.[29]

The presidents and statesmen he respected benefited from his largesse. A founder of the Eisenhower Medical Center in Rancho Mirage, Walter gave more than $11 million for a training and educational facility at the hospital complex and to support the projects of two friends: the Betty Ford Clinic and Barbara Sinatra's center for abused children. He spent an additional $600,000 on Eisenhower exchange fellowships to promote international understanding by awarding travel and study grants to men and women of high leadership potential. Gerald Ford's presidential library received $350,000; Jimmy Carter received $500,000 because Walter did not want to be seen as partisan and because "Carter's done a lot more good since he's been out of the White House than when he was in it." George Bush received $2 million for his library; Ronald Reagan, $3.5 million for his. "There you go again," Reagan wrote in thanks.[30] Nixon's library and foundation received $8.5 million. "Hell," said Walter, "It was only right that I roll out. He gave me the greatest honor of my life."[31]

There was also $1 million for Somerville College, Oxford, to honor Margaret Thatcher, a 1947 graduate. Another $1 million went to Pennsylvania's Elizabethtown College because science teacher Phares

Hertzog had once been Walter's kindly housemaster at Peddie. Stanford received $3 million in honor of alumna Lee. When Cornell called alumnus William Rogers to thank him for his contribution, the former secretary of state said thanks, but he gave $500 every year and no one had ever called before. "It was fifty thousand," the development officer told him. Rogers, aghast, said there must have been some mistake. Further checking revealed that Walter had made an anonymous contribution in Rogers's name without telling him.[32] After Walter sent $500,000 to the Forum for International Policy, a think tank run by Brent Scowcroft, who had been national security adviser for Presidents Ford and Bush, Scowcroft wrote back that "with one stroke of the pen you have changed the entire character of my operations."[33]

THAT WAS Walter's intention every time he wrote a check. He wanted his investment to encourage the recipient to think bigger and do more. He did not mind having his name linked to giving. He had a healthy ego. The Annenberg Foundation records were also public, which meant that maintaining anonymity was difficult. He also was trying to provoke his fellow billionaires and multimillionaires to step up their own pace of giving. Coincidentally or not, charitable gifts had begun to rise after his 1993 gifts of nearly $1 billion. After stagnating for most of a decade, philanthropy began climbing in 1994 by 10 percent a year to reach $143.5 billion in 1997.[34] Walter understood that the raging bull market had been a major factor in increased giving. He was making money faster than he could give it away. Between 1996 and 1997 he more than made up the $1 billion he had given away in 1993 and 1994.

If his example had helped spur interest in giving, so much the better. He praised the long-term generosity of Paul Mellon ("a superb gentleman"), and the philanthropy of Bill Hewlett, Charles Feeney and George Soros, whose $350 million in charitable contributions made him the biggest single U.S. giver in 1996 — when Walter gave away $128 million. He hoped that the publicity Ted Turner received for pledging $1 billion to the United Nations would encourage more people to give. When he read that a fellow eighty-nine-year-old, Oseola McCarty, gave $150,000, her life savings as a laundrywoman, to establish a scholarship fund for black students at the University of Southern Mississippi, he slammed both hands on his desk and exclaimed, "That's the American spirit." He was thrilled that Microsoft billionaire Bill Gates — who donated $200 million in 1997, $100 million in 1998 to help immunize children in developing countries and in

1999 put $3.3 billion in two of his foundations for future gifts — was demonstrating great interest in philanthropy and not waiting until he turned sixty, as he once said he might.[35]

Generally, though, Walter was reluctant to say much about his peers. "They'll say, 'Who's that son of a bitch think he is, sitting in judgment?'" One exception was political gadfly Ross Perot. It galled Walter that in March 1986 the Texan pledged $2.5 million to the Reagan library, gave $500,000 and then reneged on the remaining two million. Walter urged that the Reagan foundation sue Perot, whose third-party presidential candidacy in 1992 may have cost George Bush a second term. When the foundation opted against legal action, Walter gave another $1 million to help make up the Perot shortfall. "He's a fraud, nothing but cheap talk," Walter concluded.[36]

As for other billionaires, Walter could not resist hoping aloud that they would do more. It discouraged him that Buffett, worth more than $20 billion, had decided to leave his money to be distributed after his death. Walter's strategy was to give away most of his fortune himself. "That way you know where it's going and you don't end up making well-fed house dogs out of those you leave behind."

Although he delegated when making his money, he reserved virtually every decision for himself when it came to giving money away. Mary Anne Meyers, former secretary of the University of Pennsylvania, became president of the Annenberg Foundation in 1990 believing she was going to direct the organization. She left in 1992 when it became clear that Walter ran it himself. "Henry Ford [the second] told me the biggest mistake of his life by far was walking away from the Ford Foundation. That really registered on me," said Walter. "And why shouldn't I do my own [grant] evaluations? I've been through the mill of life. I know about human suffering and aspiration. I don't need people on the sidelines telling me what to do with my money. I think I have the character and intelligence to decide that myself. My record ought to demonstrate that."[37]

He wanted a director who would not second-guess his judgment, yet could manage the $3 billion foundation, which in 1998 ranked twelfth in the nation in assets.[38] He did not have to look far. Gail Levin, Meyer's deputy and successor, was a dedicated administrator with an acute sensitivity to Walter's and Lee's priorities. Her staff totaled six, minuscule compared with foundations of similar size, but lean efficiency had long been a Walter hallmark. Minimum bureaucracy gave him maximum flexibility and control while ensuring that most of the foundation's assets were available for philanthropy and were not drained by overhead. To that end, the foundation produced an application guideline, but not an annual report. "We don't want to tie ourselves down," said Levin. "Just as the ambassador tries to give many of his gifts on an unrestricted basis so the recipients' hands aren't tied, he does not like his own hands tied either. If he chooses to go in another direction, he can do it."[39]

Walter was the sole director, but Lee, Wallis and three of her children were given about $1 million annually to dispense as a group — plus another near $1 million divided among them for projects of personal interest — and met once a year with Levin to plan their giving. Some of Lee's discretionary money went to one of her major interests — the Friends of Art and Preservation in Embassies, which she founded in 1986 with Wendy Luers, Carol Price, wife of Ronald Reagan's ambassador to Britain, and Lee Kimche McGrath, former head of the Art in Embassies program. During the decade Lee chaired it, FAPE raised $8 million in private donations and art contributions to refurbish the public rooms of American embassies in two dozen capitals.

(Hillary Clinton showed up at a 1997 White House reception for the group's major donors wearing a dress identical to Lee's. Unlike Nancy Reagan, who had been upset, Mrs. Clinton grabbed the microphone, pointed out the similarity to the audience and exclaimed with a laugh, "I have finally arrived."[40] Lee's wardrobe was exquisite. She purchased her clothes — mostly by Bill Blass and Oscar de la Renta — with the $1 million annual allowance she received in quarterly allotments from Walter. Jewelry and household expenses he paid for separately. The $1 million was to spend as she wished.)

Walter came for lunch, but he usually skipped the family foundation meetings. He did not want to unduly influence their choices, although they were all aware of his priorities. Lee knew his hopes, fears and expectations better than anyone. Wallis had been hearing what was expected of her since she was a little girl. Walter had kept her on a relatively short leash financially compared with the lavish style in which his sisters kept many of their children. More than a few had been spoiled and their characters destroyed, the overfed lap dogs that he and Moses had disdained. Since Wallis had gone off track in the 1970s, he had been making her prove herself, which she had done with great success. In the 1980s and 1990s, focusing in California on health services, family counseling, and art and music education, the last in memory of her brother, Roger, she had established a considerable reputation as a thoughtful philanthropist in her own right. Walter was tremendously proud of her recovery and delighted with her philanthrophic interests, to which she would one day be able to devote more resources. On her father's death, she stood to inherit close to $200 million, a generation-skipping legacy from her grandfather Moses.

As for the next generation, Wallis's children — Lauren, Gregory and Charles — were instructed in a 1994 letter from Walter how to "appreciate the values of service and sacrifice in the process of 'giving away money.'"

Because the foundation's funds were tax-free, they had to give the money to benefit society. There could be no hint of self-interest. He urged that they avoid scattershot philanthropy, make specific choices about what they wanted to support and let grant seekers know what those areas of interest were. He would not limit their choice, but he hoped they would follow his example and pick projects and areas that were "essential," a reminder that he had built his empire on "essentiality." "I have always tried to support things that are essential, and few things are as essential as education," he wrote. "I am telling you this so that you will understand the basis for my commitment to school reform and, through your own grantmaking, join me in responding to this crisis." Finally, he advised that simply giving money would never be enough because what they could accomplish on their own was limited. For real impact, especially to increase funding for education, they would have to learn to engage the public and private sectors.[41]

THAT WAS Walter's philanthropic philosophy, recorded on a single typed page for his only direct descendants. The outlook and outlay put him in the same category with two other of America's givers — John D. Rockefeller, founder of Standard Oil and the nation's first billionaire, whose personal lifetime philanthropy totaled $520 million or $7.3 billion in current dollars, and steelman Andrew Carnegie, who before his death in 1919 gave $350 million — worth $5.7 billion today — to a vast charitable network of libraries and foundations.[42] In late 1997, *American Benefactor* magazine called Walter "the most beneficent philanthropist in the history of the world." That description was not accurate in constant dollars, but the more than $2 billion — plus $1 billion worth of art — he had given away by 1998, when he turned ninety, plus the $3 billion in his foundation, did qualify him then as the nation's most generous living philanthropist.

During much of his life, critics had claimed that Walter was using his money to buy respect, a charge also leveled at monopolist Rockefeller. But in the decades after returning from London, Walter had not felt that was necessary and he was correct. He had always been more driven to prove himself, to show everyone what he could do, than to atone for what others perceived to be the sins of his father. The massive amounts of his gifts were far more than would ever have been necessary to polish a name. And the institutions which received his philanthropy revealed the breadth and sensitivity of his purpose. A patriot, he had the money, and having done well, he wanted to do good. "Live rich, die poor; never make the mistake of doing it the other way round," was his motto.

Whenever he was asked why he had given away so much, he replied, "My country has been very good to me. I must be good to my country." It was his responsibility, he felt firmly, to share his great fortune with all parts of the society from which it had derived. A vengeful president had destroyed his father, he believed, but he had chosen — with a few notable exceptions — to turn the other cheek. There were elements in his character of Hamlet, the prince of Denmark who was so torn by grief for his dead father that he sought such bloody revenge that all the play's protagonists were killed. Walter sought another kind of vengeance, and got even in his own way. He would be bigger than those who had wronged his family. After his country allowed him to realize his dreams, he would give back more than any of his contemporaries. A passionate man, he had proven himself and become increasingly compassionate. "Grateful and hopeful," he always responded when anyone asked how he was, sometimes abbreviated to "G & H" for friends who understood the reference. Full of thanks; full of hope.

He was full of hope for the future, including that when Americans said the name Annenberg hereafter, it would be with respect. Heaven knows he had tried his best. He was full of thanks for what he had experienced. Good fortune, his own skills, including a steely will and discipline, an opportunity to serve his nation and three other people had contributed to his success. There was not a day when he did not think about Sadie and Moses and feel fortunate to have been their son. He also felt blessed to have found Lee. He would have been a great businessman and supremely wealthy without Lee. Moses had taught him how to make money. Thanks to Sadie, he would have been an exceptional philanthropist as well. That progression was well underway before he met Lee. But he most likely would not have triumphed in life nor gained the respect he had long sought. Lee had smoothed his edges, tempered his anger, channeled his energies and ambitions, loved him and stabilized his world. Individually, they were impressive; as a team, they were extraordinary.

"MOTHERR," his voice boomed across the marble floors of Sunnylands, carried past the Cézanne and the sofa where the embroidered pillow read "It Ain't Easy Being King," and found Lee by the windows. "How about a little fresh air before the guests arrive?" It was early spring 1998. Betty and Jerry Ford were coming for dinner along with Dolores and Bob Hope. Just the neighbors for a simple beef Wellington and a raspberry-and-cream bombe. Everything was ready. Michael Comerford, the superb Irish major domo who had been with them since the London posting, had, as usual, checked every last detail.

They walked out the bedroom and through the cactus garden, Lee in pale yellow silk, Walter in pink slacks and a green blazer which matched the colors of the house and golf course. As the sun dropped behind the San Jacinto peaks, they linked arms and walked down the drive past the lawn where their mausoleum will be built, and toward the first fairway, where Richard Nixon and Ronald Reagan had leaned into their drivers, and the stocked lakes from which Dwight D. Eisenhower and George Bush had pulled fat trout. At dusk like this, Walter sometimes could see his father by the water's edge, fishing pole extended, cork bobbing, as at the original Sunnylands, in the Poconos. On chilly desert nights, the figure looked more like the young Moses trying to catch supper for his family before snow closed in on the lake at Kalvishken. All that, of course, was long ago and far away.

A SELECTED LIST
OF WALTER ANNENBERG'S
PHILANTHROPY

EDUCATION

$500 million	Public School Reform (1993)*
$239 million	University of Pennsylvania (1960–98)
$177 million	University of Southern California (1974–98)
$140 million	Corporation for Public Broadcasting (1981–2003)
$131.6 million	The Peddie School (1927–98)
$55.2 million	Northwestern University (1987–98)
$50 million	United Negro College Fund (1990–99)
$29.5 million	Annenberg Research Institute, Philadelphia (formerly Dropsie College) (1986–98)
$25 million	Harvard University (1993)
$10 million	University of Notre Dame (1990–2001)
$5.8 million	Yeshiva University and Albert Einstein College of Medicine (1989–93)
$5.2 million	Pine Manor College (1983–99)
$5 million	Brandeis University (1996–2002)
$5 million	Temple University (1996–2005)
$4.4 million	Hebrew University of Jerusalem (1976–97)
$3 million	Stanford University (1985–94)
$3 million	Archdiocese of Philadelphia schools (1980–96)
$2.6 million	Episcopal Academy, Merion, Pa. (1991–2002)
$2 million	Howard University (1989)
$2 million	Brown University (1990–91)

Source: Courtesy of the Annenberg Foundation

*The $500 million Public School Challenge total incorporates: Annenberg Institute at Brown University, $50 million; New York City, $25 million; Chicago, $49.2 million; Los Angeles, $53 million; Philadelphia, $50 million; San Francisco Bay Area, $25 million; Rural Initiative (across America), $50 million; Arts in Learning (300 schools in 11 states), $10 million.

$1.35 million	Duke University (1989–93)
$1.35 million	Oxford University, England (1989–95)
$1.3 million	The Chapin School, New York (1990–96)
$1.1 million	Valley Forge Military Academy (1982–94)
$1.1 million	La Salle University, Philadelphia (1994–97)
$1.1 million	Rockefeller University (1991–93)
$1 million	U.S. Military Academy (1993–95)
$1 million	U.S. Naval Academy (1993–95)
$1 million	U.S. Air Force Academy (1993–95)
$1 million	Haverford College (1996–2000)
$1 million	Duke University (1989)
$1 million	St. Joseph's University, Philadelphia (1990–92)
$1 million	Catholic University (1994–98)
$1 million	The Chapin School (1998–2003)
$1 million	Elizabethtown College (1994–98)
$1 million	Xavier University of Louisiana (1990–91)
$1 million	New York University (1991)
$800,000	Winston Churchill Archives, Fellowships and Trust (1989–92)

ARTS AND CULTURE

$1 billion	Metropolitan Museum of Art (1991) (art collection)
$165 million	Metropolitan Museum of Art (1953–99)
$31 million	Colonial Williamsburg (1985–2004)
$12 million	Philadelphia Museum of Art (1988–97)
$12 million	Los Angeles County Museum of Art (1991–92)
$8.4 million	National Gallery of Art, Washington, D.C. (1981–94)
$11.5 million	Academy of Music, Philadelphia (1990–98)
$10.6 million	British Museum (1994–2001)
$10 million	Independence Mall Project, Philadelphia (1998–2000)
$5 million	National Gallery, London (1988–90)
$5 million	Metropolitan Opera (1995)
$5 million	Greater Washington Educational Telecommunications Association (WETA) (1991–95)
$2 million	U.S. Holocaust Museum, Washington, D.C.
$1.5 million	Children's Discovery Museum of the Desert (Coachella Valley, Calif.) (1993)
$1.05 million	KCET Community Television of Southern California (1977–83)
$1 million	Jerusalem Foundation (1989–98)
$1 million	Survivors of the Shoah Visual History Foundation (archive of Holocaust testimonies) (1995–99)
$1 million	Library of Congress
$1 million	White House Endowment Fund (1990–94)

$1 million	Tate Gallery, London (1994–98)
$1 million	Covent Garden and Royal Ballet, London (1997–2001)

MEDICINE

$11.3 million	Eisenhower Medical Research Center, Rancho Mirage, Calif. (1981–91)
$6 million	Mount Sinai Medical Center
$5 million	Pennsylvania Hospital and Thomas Jefferson University (1983–2006)
$3 million	Medical College of Pennsylvania (1990–98)
$1.3 million	Children's Hospital of Pennsylvania (1989–98)
$1 million	Weizmann Institute of Science, Israel (1990)
$1 million	Albert Einstein Medical Center, Philadelphia

COMMUNITY

$15 million	United Jewish Appeal (1990–92)
$9.7 million	Federation of Jewish Agencies of Greater Philadelphia (1963–97)
$4.4 million	United Way of Southeastern Pennsylvania (1984–95)
$2 million	Congregation Emanu-El of New York City (1996–99)
$1 million	United Way of America (1994)
$1 million	American Red Cross (1992)
$1 million	American's Promise — The Alliance for Youth (1999–2003)
$250,000	Philadelphia Zoo (1996–2000)

PRESIDENTIAL LIBRARIES

$8.5 million	Richard Nixon (1985–98)
$3.5 million	Ronald Reagan (1989–99)
$2 million	George Bush (1994–97)
$350,000	Gerald Ford (1979–98)
$500,000	Jimmy Carter (1998–2002)

INTERVIEWS

FAMILY
Leonore Annenberg
Wallis Annenberg
Walter Annenberg
Diane Katleman Deshong
Elizabeth Rosenstiel Kabler
Evelyn Annenberg Hall
Ronald Krancer
Cynthia Hazen Polsky

Antony Acland
Arlin Adams
Alastair Aird
Stephen Ambrose
Cleveland Amory
Jack Anderson
Rosemary Ashby
Ben Bagdikian
Digby Baltzell
Cardinal Anthony Bevilacqua
Peter Binzen
Conrad Black
Jerry Blavat
Betsy Bloomingdale
Irvin Borowsky
Brock Brower
J. Carter Brown
Bill Bruns
David Bull

Gahl Burt
Mabel H. Cabot
Joseph Canzeri
Jill Stern Capron
Richard Carlson
Peter Carrington
Cummins Catherwood
Susan Catherwood
Ray Cave
Hammond Chaffetz
Martin Charteris
Dick Clark
Sylvan Cohen
William Coleman
Ralph Collier
Clement Conger
Geoffrey Cowan
Fleur Cowles
Renee Schine Crown
Lloyd Dahmen
Patrick Daly
Jane Dart
Ralph Davidson
Michael Deaver
Armand Deutsch
Harriet Deutsch
Edwin Diamond
Marion HoeflichDimitman
Lady Drake

Christopher Edley
Julie Nixon Eisenhower
Susan Eisenhower
Rowland Evans
Phyllis Feldkamp
Frederick C. Ferry Jr.
Peter Flanigan
Robben Fleming
Gerald Ford
Ellen Frasco
Joseph Fromm
Murray Fromson
William Galloway
Steve Gelman
George Gerbner
Philip Geyelin
Gene Giancarlo
Joe Goulden
William Green
Robert Greenberg
Joseph N. Greene
Vartan Gregorian
Larry Gross
Fred Grossman
Edward Guthman
Sheldon Hackney
Alexander Haig
James Hanson
Arthur Hartman
Edward Heath
Nicholas Henderson
William J. Henrich Jr.
A. Leon Higginbotham Jr.
Martin Hillenbrand
John Hodges
Thomas Hughes
William Hyland
Kathleen Hall Jamieson
Leo Janos
Marion Jorgensen
Philip M. Kaiser
Shirley Katzander
Nicholas Katzenbach
Rolfe Kingsley
Charles Krause

Irving Kupcinet
Nelson Lankford
Eric Larson
Eppie Lederer
Gail Levin
William Lilley
Thacher Longstreth
William Luers
William McCarter
John McCarthy
John Reagan "Tex" McCrary
Lee Kimche McGrath
John McMullan
David Metcalfe
Cord Meyer
Martin Meyerson
Newton Minow
Tom Montague-Meyer
Acel Moore
Tom Murphy
Philip Olsson
Florenz Ourisman
Mandell Ourisman
George Packard
Peter Paine
Norman Pearlstine
Meyer "Pat" Potamkin
Colin Powell
Earl "Rusty" Powell III
Carol Swanson Price
Charles Price
Nancy Reagan
Donald Regan
Robin Renwick
Nancy Reynolds
Elliott Richardson
Marie Ridder
Anthony Wayne Ridgway
Gene Roberts
Scott Roberts
Judith Rodin
Peter Rodman
William P. Rogers
Selwa "Lucky" Roosevelt
Barbara Rosenberg

Richard Rosenberg
Gene Rosenfeld
Richard Rothman, M.D.
Ronald Rubin
Neil Rudenstine
Philip B. Schaefer
Raymond Scherer
Thea Schilling
Robert Montgomery Scott
Caroline Seitz
Raymond Seitz
David Sendler
Jerome Shestack
Peter Skoufis
Sally Bedell Smith
Jean French Smith
Helmut Sonnenfeldt
Seth Sostrin
Maurice Stans
Frank Stanton
Richard Stolley
Edward Streator

Beverly Sullivan
Margaret Thatcher
Jeremy Thorpe
Harry Toland
Bronson Tweedy
Lewis Van Dusen
Mallory Walker
Barbara Walters
Susan Watters
John Weinberg
Allen Weinstein
John Weisman
J. Robinson West
Rabbi David Wice
Daniel Wildenstein
Morton Wilner
Zelda Wilner
William Wilson
Judith Wolf
Stephen Wynn
Ezra Zilkha

A number of sources spoke with me on the condition that they would not be indentified.

NOTES

INTRODUCTION

1. Elizabeth Northumberland to Leonore Annenberg, 12/1/69, WHA papers.
2. Ginnie Airlie to Leonore Annenberg, 11/26/69, WHA.
3. Helen Adeane to Leonore Annenberg, 11/26/69, WHA.
4. Camilla Nevill to Leonore Annenberg, 11/27/69, WHA.
5. Anthony Wedgwood Benn to Leonore Annenberg, 11/27/69, WHA.
6. Jean Barber to Leonore Annenberg, 11/26/69, WHA.
7. Audrey Elworthy to Leonore Annenberg, 11/26/69, WHA.
8. Pamela Hartwell to Leonore Annenberg, 11/26/69,WHA.
9. Kenneth Harris to Leonore Annenberg, 11/28/69, WHA.
10. Leslie Rouse to Leonore Annenberg, undated, WHA.
11. Denis Greenhill to Walter Annenberg, 11/27/69, WHA.
12. Debo Devonshire to Leonore Annenberg, 11/27/69, WHA.
13. Gillian Rees-Mogg to Leonore Annenberg, undated, WHA.
14. Joan Shawcross to Leonore Annenberg, 11/26/69, WHA.

EAST PRUSSIA

1. Dr. Sebastian Husen, Kulturabteilung, Landsmannschaft Ostpreussen, 11/29/96.
2. Moses L. Annenberg, unpublished notes, WHA papers.
3. Insterburger Brief: *City of Insterburg, 400 Years:* Sept/Oct 1983, p. 177.
4. Hans-Jurgen Kruger, *The Jews in Prussia* (Marburg, 1966), pp. 14–16.
5. Husen, 11/29/96.
6. M. L. Annenberg notes.
7. Ibid.
8. Birmingham, *The Rest of Us*, p. 36.
9. Meltzer, *World of Our Fathers*, p. 195.

10. Meltzer, *Remember the Days*, p. 33.
11. M. L. Annenberg notes.
12. Meltzer, *Remember the Days*, p. 35.
13. Handlin, *The Uprooted*, p. 39.
14. Meltzer, *Remember the Days*, p. 35.
15. Ibid., pp. 35–36.
16. Ibid., p. 37.
17. Ibid.
18. Miller, *City of the Century*, p. 178.
19. Ibid., pp. 179–180.
20. Ibid., p. 181.

CHICAGO

1. Miller, *City of the Century*, p. 131.
2. Trager, *The People's Chronology*, p. 459.
3. William Cronon, *Washington Post*, 8/18/96, p. C2.
4. Smith, *The Colonel*, p. 27.
5. Ibid., p. 28.
6. Miller, p. 16.
7. Miller, p. 188, quoting Lady Duffus Hardy, *Through Cities and Prairielands*, 1881.
8. Morris Dickstein, *Washington Post*, 8/16/96, p. C3.
9. Miller, p. 17.
10. Hirsch and Goler, *A City Comes of Age*, pp. 59–62.
11. M. L. Annenberg unpublished notes, p. 8.
12. Miller, pp. 441–461.
13. Peter Binzen, unpublished interview with Richardson Dilworth, 1971.
14. Smith, p. 137.
15. Rich Cohen, *Tough Jews*, pp. 42–43.
16. Miller, p. 187.
17. Miller, p. 446.

HEARST

1. Wendt, *Chicago Tribune*, p. 11.
2. Smith, *The Colonel*, pp. 71–72.
3. Swanberg, *Citizen Hearst*, p. 195, quoting *Collier's*, 9/29/06.
4. Wendt, p. 352.
5. Murray, *The Madhouse on Madison Street*, p. 3.
6. Lundberg, *Imperial Hearst*, p. 139.
7. Ibid., pp. 141–142.
8. Ibid., p. 140.
9. Murray, p. 12.
10. Ibid., p. 35.

11. Max Annenberg, U.S. Circuit Court of Appeals testimony, 2/18/22, p. 611.
12. *Columbia Encyclopedia*, p. 2343.
13. Miller, *City of the Century*, pp. 198–199.
14. Swanberg, p. 215.
15. Ibid.
16. Cooney, *The Annenbergs*, p. 35.

MILWAUKEE

1. Flynn, *Collier's*, 1/13/40.
2. Moses Annenberg, Dept. of Justice deposition, 4/25/39, p. 38.
3. Walter Annenberg, 5/30/95.
4. Flynn, 1/13/40.
5. Max Annenberg, U.S. Circuit Court of Appeals testimony, 2/21/1922, p. 699.
6. Walter Annenberg, 10/2/95.
7. Cooney, pp. 43–44.
8. Ibid.
9. Evelyn Annenberg Hall, 11/26/96.
10. Ronald Krancer, 9/10/98.
11. Cynthia Hazen Polsky, 3/27/97.
12. Enid Haupt, Orphans Court, Philadelphia, 9/22/80.
13. Walter Annenberg, 10/2/95.
14. Bobrick, *Knotted Tongues*, p. 21.
15. Ibid., p. 23.
16. Ibid.
17. Evelyn Annenberg Hall, 11/26/96.
18. Walter Annenberg, 10/14/95.
19. Ken Smith, *USM at 25*, p. 16.
20. Wells, *This Is Milwaukee*, p. 180.
21. Ibid., p. 106.
22. Ibid., pp. 184–85.
23. *New York Times*, 12/26/36.
24. Boyden Sparkes, interview with Moses Annenberg, 1937.
25. Lewis French, *Milwaukee Journal*, 3/29/36.
26. Walter Annenberg, 5/30/95, Cooney, p. 49.
27. *Wisconsin News*, 11/18/19.
28. Moses Annenberg, Dept. of Justice deposition, 4/25/39.

NEW YORK

1. Great Neck League of Women Voters, *This Is Great Neck*, 1975, pp. 58–59.
2. Ibid.
3. Evelyn Annenberg Hall, 11/26/96.
4. Cooney, *The Annenbergs*, p. 50.

5. Ibid.
6. Zweigenhaft & Domhoff, *Jews in the Protestant Establishment*, p. 9.
7. Ibid.; A. Manners, *Poor Cousins*, p. 63.
8. Ibid.; Baltzell, *The Protestant Establishment*, p. 55.
9. Ibid.; John Higham, *Send These to Me*, p. 144.
10. Ibid.; Baltzell, p. 56.
11. Ibid.; Birmingham, p. 289.
12. Ibid.; Glazer and Moynihan, *Beyond the Melting Pot*, p. 139.
13. Cooney, p. 52.
14. Boyden Sparkes, interview with Moses Annenberg, 1937.
15. Swanberg, *Citizen Hearst*, p. 427.
16. Ibid.
17. Neil Gabler, *Winchell*, p. 203.
18. *New York Times*, obituary, 12/26/36.
19. Irving Dilliard, *Dictionary of American Biography*, 1947, p. 63–64.
20. Boyden Sparkes, interview with Moses Annenberg, 1937.
21. Ibid.
22. Ibid.
23. *Smith v. Annenberg*, Action No. 1, 10/3/27, p. 11.
24. Joe Hirsch, *The First Century*, pp. 1–2.
25. Ibid.
26. Moses Annenberg, Dept. of Justice testimony, 4/25/39, p. 44.
27. Walter Annenberg, 5/30/95.

SPORT OF KINGS

1. Moses Annenberg, Dept. of Justice deposition, 4/25/39, p. 284.
2. Ainslie, *Complete Guide to Thoroughbred Racing*, p. 24.
3. Sasuly, *Bookies and Bettors: 200 Years of Gambling*, p. 107.
4. Moses Annenberg, Dept. of Justice deposition, 4/25/39, pp. 45, 50.
5. Ibid., pp. 132–133.
6. F. B. Warren, *The Nation*, 8/6/1938, p. 124.
7. Moses Annenberg, unpublished notes, p. 11, WHA papers.
8. Hirsch, *The First Century*, p. 34.
9. J. S. Egan, memo to J. Edgar Hoover, 10/3/32, FBI files 62-2392.
10. *Baltimore Brevities*, 11/9/32.
11. Confidential source, interview, 7/3/97.
12. John Flynn, *Collier's*, 1/20/40, p. 54.
13. Sasuly, p. 108.
14. Flynn, 1/20/40, p. 54.
15. Elmer Irey, *The Tax Dodgers*, pp. 218–219.
16. Dimitman, *The Philadelphia Inquirer and the Annenbergs*, 1972.
17. Herbert Asbury, *Gem of the Prairie*, p. 164.
18. Stephen Fox, *Blood and Power*, p. 104.
19. Moses Annnenberg, Dept. of Justice deposition, 4/25/39, p. 59.

20. Walter Annenberg, 5/30/95 and 4/15/96.
21. Walter Annenberg, 10/2/95 and 4/15/96.
22. Sen. John D. Rockefeller IV, 10/27/98.

THE WIRE

1. Trager, *The People's Chronology*, p. 785.
2. Cooney, *The Annenbergs*, p. 65.
3. Moses Annenberg, Dept. of Justice deposition, 4/25/39, p. 61.
4. Flynn, *Collier's*, 1/27/40.
5. FBI case report, 11/7/38, file 60-278.
6. FBI case report, interview with Alfred Kelly, 1/3/39, file 60-195.
7. Flynn, 1/20/40, p. 56.
8. Ibid.
9. *Chicago American*, 12/21/34.
10. Ibid.
11. Irey, *The Tax Dodgers*, p. 220.
12. FBI case report, 11/7/38, file 60-278.
13. Flynn, 1/20/40, p. 56; Fonzi, *Annenberg*, p. 78.
14. Cooney, p. 79.
15. *Chicago American*, 12/21/34.
16. *Chicago Sun*, 5/26/46.
17. *Associated Press*, A115CX, 9/25/46.
18. FBI case report, 3/26/36, file 62-2859.
19. Moses Annenberg to L. Stanley Kahn, 5/11/36, in William J. Campbell's statement of facts, Federal District Court, Chicago, 5/5/40, WHA papers.
20. *Philadelphia Inquirer*, 7/21/42, p. 1.
21. Walter Annenberg, 3/5/96 and 11/22/96.

SCHOOL DAYS

1. Walter Annenberg exercises, WHA papers.
2. Geiger, *The Peddie School's First Century*, pp. 11–12.
3. Ibid., p. 32.
4. Ibid., p. 53.
5. Confidential source.
6. Yearbook, The Peddie School, 1927, p. 40.
7. Walter Annenberg, 7/30/97.
8. Walter Annenberg, 3/6/96.
9. Ibid.
10. Trager, *The People's Chronology*, p. 778.
11. Walter Annenberg, 7/2/96.
12. Ibid.
13. Cooney, *The Annenbergs*, p. 62.
14. Walter Annenberg letter to Lord Snow, 12/6/73. WHA papers.

15. Walter Annenberg, 5/30/95.
16. Cooney, p. 62.
17. Walter Annenberg, 7/2/96.
18. Morton Wilner, 5/19/97.
19. Ibid.
20. Brooks, *Once in Golconda*, pp. 72–73.
21. Galbraith, *The Great Crash*, p. 27.
22. Ibid., p. 79.
23. Ibid., p. 108.
24. Walter Annenberg, 3/5/96.

BOY ABOUT TOWN

1. Moses Annenberg to Thomas McEntegart, 4/9/26, WHA papers.
2. Walter Annenberg, 4/15/96.
3. *Time*, 9/24/45, p. 87.
4. Arnold Kruse, Department of Justice deposition, 4/25/39.
5. Weymouth Kirkland, undated 1939 court brief, p. 53, WHA papers.
6. Walter Annenberg, 10/2/95.
7. Cooney, *The Annenbergs*, p. 73.
8. Brian Dumaine, *Fortune*, 10/12/87, p. 157.
9. Walter Annenberg, 11/1/98.
10. Walter Annenberg, 10/2/95.
11. Walter Annenberg, 11/21/96.
12. *Current Biography*, 1942, p. 724.
13. Damon Runyon to Walter Annenberg, Western Union, 1/22/39, WHA papers.
14. Walter Annenberg, 4/15/96.
15. *Chicago Daily News*, 8/10/39.
16. *Racine Journal-Times*, 4/25/40.
17. Walter Annenberg to Moses Annenberg, 3/3/39, WHA papers.

MIAMI

1. Flynn, *Collier's*, 2/3/40, p. 48.
2. *Chicago Tribune*, 3/18/33.
3. Jeans, *Tropical Disturbance*, 4/4/37.
4. Ibid.
5. Cooney, *The Annenbergs*, p. 86.
6. Muir, *Miami USA*, pp. 208–209.
7. Smiley, *Yesterday's Miami*, p. 132.
8. Walter Annenberg to Victor Miller, 5/23/36, WHA papers.
9. Jeans, pp. 43–47; Smiley, pp. 137–139; Cooney, pp. 87–88.
10. Cooney, pp. 81–82.

11. Hartley testimony to Thompson commission, excerpted in *Philadelphia Record*, "Urban Affairs," 11/4/38, S. Paley Library, Temple University.
12. Jeans, p. 31.
13. Ibid., pp. 45–46.
14. Ibid., p. 50.
15. Ibid., p. 48.
16. Everest Sewell to Anning Prall, 4/21/36, FBI files, 62-31642-43.
17. David Sholtz to J. Edgar Hoover, 4/24/36, FBI files, 62-31642-45.
18. Andrew Kavanaugh to J. Edgar Hoover, 4/28/36, FBI files, 62-31642-48XI.
19. Moses Annenberg to Bessie Bernstein, 9/25/36, WHA papers.
20. *Miami Tribune*, 12/1/37.

PHILADELPHIA

1. Nicholas Wainwright, *The History of the Philadelphia Inquirer, Inquirer* supplement, 9/16/62.
2. Samuel Eliot Morrison, *Oxford History of the American People*, p. 975.
3. Stern, *Memoirs of a Maverick Publisher*, p. 237.
4. Cooney, *The Annenbergs*, p. 106.
5. *Newsweek*, 8/8/36, pp. 30–31.
6. *Time*, 8/10/36, p. 28.
7. *Business Week*, 8/8/36, p. 34.
8. *Time*, 11/11/35, p. 52.
9. *The Nation*, 8/15/36, p. 172.
10. Moses Annenberg cable to Franklin D. Roosevelt, 7/26/33, WHA papers.
11. Moses Annenberg to Arthur Brisbane, 8/13/36, WHA papers.
12. Stern, p. 240.
13. Richardson Dilworth, unpublished interview with Peter Binzen, 1971.
14. Stern, p. 242.
15. Dimitman, *The Philadelphia Inquirer and the Annenbergs*, ch. 3, p. 18.
16. Ibid., p. 7.
17. Cooney, p. 111.
18. Dimitman, pp. 19–23.
19. Shirley Katzander, 5/17/97.
20. Gavreau, *My Last Million Readers*, p. 378.
21. Cooney, p. 113.
22. Ibid., p. 114.
23. Gavreau, p. 403; Cooney, pp. 114–115.
24. Katzander, 5/17/97.
25. Marion Hoeflich Dimitman, 10/16/96.
26. Richardson Dilworth interview, 1971.
27. Enid Annenberg to Walter Annenberg, 1/13/41, WHA papers.
28. Walter Annenberg, 10/2/95.
29. Walter Annenberg, 8/8/96.

30. Moses Annenberg to Sadie Annenberg, 12/7/36, WHA papers.
31. Evelyn Annenberg Hall, 11/26/96.
32. Marion Hoeflich Dimitman, 10/15/96.
33. Richardson Dilworth interview, 1971.
34. Gavreau, p. 402.
35. Ibid., p. 405.
36. Ibid., p. 425.
37. Ibid., pp. 426–428.
38. Dimitman, ch. 4, p. 37.
39. Ibid., p. 29.
40. Ibid.

DONNYBROOK

1. Gavreau, *My Last Million Readers*, p. 424.
2. Samuel Eliot Morison, *The Oxford History of the American People*, p. 968.
3. Ibid., p. 978.
4. *Philadelphia Inquirer,* 5/30/37.
5. *Philadelphia Inquirer,* 12/29/37.
6. *Philadelphia Inquirer,* 12/30/37.
7. *Philadelphia Inquirer,* 1/4/38.
8. Dimitman, *A Great Newspaper Is Reborn,* 1939.
9. Ibid.
10. Gavreau, p. 431.
11. Ibid., p. 433.
12. *New York Times,* 9/22/38.
13. Cooney, *The Annenbergs,* p. 123.
14. Dimitman, ch. 4, p. 15.
15. Stern, p. 242.
16. Ibid., p. 127.
17. Gavreau, p. 434.
18. Fonzi, *Annenberg,* p. 88.
19. James MacGregor Burns, *Roosevelt: The Lion and the Fox,* p. 205.
20. William Manchester, *The Glory and the Dream,* p. 138.
21. Morison, p. 975.
22. Arthur M. Schlesinger Jr., *The Crisis of the Old Order,* pp. 409–410.
23. Ibid.
24. Burns, *Roosevelt: The Lion and the Fox,* p. 317.
25. William J. Small, *Political Power and the Press,* pp. 83–84.
26. *Time,* 5/2/38.
27. *Philadelphia Inquirer,* 4/30/38.
28. Moses Annenberg, Dept. of Justice deposition, 4/25/39, p. 67.
29. Ibid.
30. Harold Ickes, *The Secret Diaries of Harold Ickes, 1933–36,* pp. 631–632.

31. Michael Bradley, *Philadelphia Record*, 11/4/38.
32. *Philadelphia Record*, 10/7/38.
33. Joseph Guffey text, radio station WFIL Philadelphia, 10/6/38. WHA papers.
34. Cooney, p. 128.
35. Burns, *Roosevelt: The Lion and the Fox*, pp. 199–200.
36. Watkins, *Righteous Pilgrim*, pp. 57–58.
37. *Time*, 9/15/41, p. 14.
38. Ickes, p. vi.
39. *Philadelphia Inquirer*, 11/9/38.
40. *Philadelphia Record*, 11/10/38.

INDICTMENT

1. Robert Sherwood, *Roosevelt and Hopkins*, p. 90.
2. John Morton Blum, *From the Morgenthau Diaries*, p. 327.
3. Ibid., p. 329.
4. Harold Ickes, diary, 11/5/38, p. 3028, Ickes papers, Library of Congress.
5. Henry Morgenthau, diary, 10/2/38, p. 195, FDR Library, Hyde Park.
6. Ibid., 12/2/38, p. 154.
7. J. Edgar Hoover to Marvin McIntyre, 12/2/38, FDR Library, Hyde Park, OF 4547.
8. David Burnham, letter to *Washington Post*, 1/26/97.
9. Arthur Schlesinger Jr., *The Coming of the New Deal*, p. 570.
10. Robert A. Caro, *The Path to Power*, pp. 742–753.
11. Ickes diary, 1/1/39, p. 3129.
12. William C. Bullitt, memo for president, 1/11/39, FDR Library, OF 4547.
13. Ibid.
14. Ernest B. Furgurson, "Back Channels," *Washingtonian*, June 1996, p. 58.
15. Ickes, diary, 2/12/39, p. 3225.
16. Morgenthau, diary, 4/11/39, p. 213.
17. Dept. of Justice, tax division, transcript of hearing re tax liability of M. L. Annenberg, 4/25/39, record group 21, records of U.S. district court for the northern district of Illinois, National Archives–Great Lakes Region, p. 106.
18. Ibid., p. 71.
19. Frank Murphy, Morgenthau diary, 4/26/39.
20. E. H. Foley Jr. to Secretary Morgenthau, 4/26/39, FDR Library, Hyde Park.
21. M. L. Annenberg to Secretary Morgenthau, 5/11/39, Morgenthau papers, book 189, reel 50, pp. 278–279, FDR Library.
22. Ibid.
23. Morgenthau diary, 5/12/39, book 189, reel 50, p. 258.
24. Ickes diary, 5/13/39, reel 3, p. 3436.

25. Smith, *The Colonel,* p. 292.
26. Ickes diary, 5/13/39, reel 3, p. 3437.
27. Irey, *The Tax Dodgers,* p. 222.
28. Moses Annenberg, 10/5/39, WHA papers.
29. Richardson Dilworth to Peter Binzen, unpublished interview, 1971.
30. Jane C. Patterson letter to Walter Annenberg, 2/22/83, WHA papers.
31. William Hopewell letter to Walter Annenberg, 3/17/81, WHA papers.
32. Moses Annenberg, *Philadelphia Inquirer,* 10/5/39.
33. *New York Times,* 8/31/39.
34. John Flynn, *Collier's,* 2/3/40, p. 51.
35. Morgenthau diaries, 12/1/39, book 226, reel 60, p. 141.
36. Morgenthau diaries, 12/4/39, pp. 220–221.
37. Gavreau, *My Last Million Readers,* p. 456.
38. Walter Annenberg, 4/15/96.
39. Dimitman, *Philadelphia Inquirer and the Annenbergs,* ch. 5, pp. 8–9.
40. William J. Campbell, memorandum of conversation, 11/15/39, Judge William Campbell papers, National Archives–Great Lakes Region.
41. Richardson Dilworth to Peter Binzen.
42. Draft letter to Samuel O. Clark Jr., undated, but post-1939 indictments, Judge William Campbell papers, National Archives–Great Lakes Region.
43. Richardson Dilworth to Peter Binzen.
44. William Strand, *Chicago Tribune,* 6/7/40.
45. Ibid., 6/12/40.

LEWISBURG

1. Shirley Katzander, 5/17/97.
2. Marion Hoeflich Dimitman, 10/15/96.
3. Stern, *Memoirs of a Maverick Publisher,* p. 243.
4. Gavreau, *My Last Million Readers,* pp. 458–459.
5. Ibid., pp. 446–448.
6. Moses Annenberg, statement, 7/15/40, WHA papers.
7. Sadie Annenberg, letter to Thomas Grover, Lewisburg, 8/6/40, WHA papers.
8. Evelyn Annenberg Hall, 11/26/96.
9. Moses Annenberg, 7/30/40.
10. Ibid., 8/6/40.
11. Moses Annenberg to Walter Annenberg, 1/2/41, WHA papers.
12. Walter Annenberg to Joseph Ottenstein, 12/24/40, WHA papers.
13. Moses left forty-one single-spaced typed pages of personal reminiscences. It was not possible to determine whether he wrote the undated notes — which ended in mid-sentence while describing his 1904 political work in Indiana for Hearst — while at Lewisburg or earlier.
14. Moses Annenberg to Walter Annenberg, 8/9/40, WHA papers.
15. Moses Annenberg to Walter Annenberg, 1/6/41.

16. Walter Annenberg to Moses Annenberg, 11/7/40.
17. Moses Annenberg to Walter Annenberg, 11/7/40.
18. Harold Ickes, diary, 9/22/40, Ickes papers, Library of Congress.
19. Joseph First, handwritten notes, 2/19/41, WHA papers.
20. Walter Annenberg to Moses Annenberg, 7/8/41.
21. Moses Annenberg to Walter Annenberg, 7/14/41.
22. James H. Wilkerson to Franklin D. Roosevelt, 7/31/41.
23. Francis Biddle to Franklin D. Roosevelt, 8/21/41.
24. Walter Annenberg to Moses Annenberg, 10/6/41, WHA papers.
25. Ickes, diary, 1/4/42.
26. Moses Annenberg to Walter Annenberg, 2/12/41, WHA papers.
27. Harold Ickes to Franklin Roosevelt, 12/30/41, Ickes papers, Library of Congress.
28. Franklin Roosevelt to Harold Ickes, 1/2/42, Ickes papers, Library of Congress.
29. Walter Annenberg, notarized affidavit, 3/6/41, WHA papers.
30. Walter Annenberg to Moses Annenberg, 12/26/40, WHA papers.
31. Ickes, diary, 2/22/42.
32. Walter Annenberg to William Smathers, 3/24/42, WHA papers.
33. Moses Annenberg to Walter Annenberg, 4/27/42, WHA papers.
34. Russell Varner, notarized affidavit, 12/2/42, WHA papers.
35. Harriett Ames telegram to Federal Parole Board, 5/16/42, WHA papers.
36. Annenberg family, telegram to Federal Parole Board, 5/16/42, WHA papers.
37. E. C. Rinck to Walter Annenberg, 5/20/42, WHA papers.
38. Walter Annenberg to Dr. E. C. Rinck, 2/8/43, WHA papers.

BOY TO MAN

1. Nathan A. Perilman, transcript, funeral remarks, 7/23/42, WHA papers.
2. Walter Annenberg, 4/16/96.
3. Ronald Krancer, 9/10/98.
4. Evelyn Hall Annenberg, 11/26/96.
5. Marion Hoeflich Dimitman, 10/16/96.
6. Walter Annenberg to Moses Annenberg, 3/12/42, WHA papers.
7. Moses Annenberg to Walter Annenberg, 3/30/42, WHA papers.
8. Walter Annenberg, 7/9/96.
9. Rudyard Kipling, *Gunga Din and Other Favorite Poems*, Dover Thrift Editions, undated.
10. Collected sayings, WHA papers.
11. Fonzi, *Annenberg*, p. 33.
12. Walter Annenberg to Moses Annenberg (Custis quote within), 1/14/42.
13. Walter Annenberg memo to Charles Tyler, 5/15/43, WHA papers.
14. Acel Moore, 7/3/97.
15. Walter Annenberg, 4/15/96.

16. Walter Annenberg to Moses Annenberg (text enclosed), 5/11/42, WHA papers.
17. Walter Annenberg to Martin Tveter, 2/15/43.
18. Cooney, *The Annenbergs*, pp. 175–180.
19. Walter Annenberg, 11/14/95.
20. James O. Bennett to William Hiatt, 3/8/45, WHA papers.
21. Joseph First to Solomon Huberfeld, 7/23/43, WHA papers.
22. Joseph First to Robert Bressler, 5/13/45, WHA papers.
23. Walter Annenberg to J. Edgar Hoover, 3/15/45, WHA papers.
24. Walter Annenberg, 11/14/95.
25. Walter Annenberg, 3/6/96.

MAIN LINE

1. Zelda Dunkelman Wilner, 5/19/97.
2. Cooney, *The Annenbergs*, pp. 116–117.
3. Ben Dunkelman, *Dual Allegiance*, p. 10.
4. Ibid., pp. 6–8.
5. Ibid., p. 11.
6. Zelda Dunkelman Wilner, 5/19/97.
7. Ronny Dunkelman to Walter Annenberg, 4/25/38, WHA papers.
8. Ibid., 5/17/38.
9. Ibid., 6/18/38.
10. Declaration of Trust, 5/28/38, WHA papers.
11. Morton Wilner, 8/15/98.
12. Ronny Dunkelman to Walter Annenberg, 5/20/38, WHA papers.
13. Morton Wilner, 8/15/98.
14. Moses Annenberg to Walter Annenberg, 5/29/38, WHA papers.
15. Ibid., second telegram.
16. Walter Annenberg, 7/9/96.
17. Walter Annenberg to Moses Annenberg, 3/10/41.
18. Moses Annenberg to Walter Annenberg, 3/12/41.
19. Walter Annenberg to Moses Annenberg, 3/13/41.
20. Moses Annenberg to Walter Annenberg, 10/13/41.
21. H. G. Bissinger, "Main Line Madcap," *Vanity Fair*, October 1995.
22. E. Digby Baltzell, *Philadelphia Gentlemen*, p. 31; H. G. Bissinger, p. 170.
23. Robert Montgomery Scott, 11/13/95.
24. *Philadelphia: A 300-Year History*, ed. Russell Weigley, p. 147.
25. Thacher Longstreth, 10/15/96.
26. Sally Bedell Smith, *In All His Glory*, p. 43, citing *Jewish Life in Philadelphia 1830–1840*, ed. Murray Friedman (Philadelphia, 1983), pp. 11–12.
27. Baltzell, interview, 4/10/96.
28. Longstreth, 10/15/96.
29. Zelda Dunkelman Wilner, 5/19/97.

30. Marion Hoeflich Dimitman, 10/15/96.
31. Zelda Dunkelman Wilner, 5/19/97.
32. Cynthia Hazen Polsky, 3/27/97.
33. Ronald Krancer, 9/10/98.
34. Marion Hoeflich Dimitman, 10/15/96.
35. Leonard Howard, testimony to Samuel Klaus, 5/24/39, National Archives–Great Lakes Region; RG200, papers of Judge William Campbell, Skidmore and Annenberg cases, box 3 of 3.
36. Richardson Dilworth to Peter Binzen, unpublished interview, 1971.
37. Walter Annenberg, 4/15/96.
38. Walter Annenberg to Ronny Annenberg, 8/18/41, WHA papers.
39. Ibid., 12/10/40.
40. Ibid., 5/19/42.
41. Secretary to Mr. Annenberg (signed as such) to Ronny Annenberg, 7/21/43.
42. Walter Annenberg to Ronny Annenberg, 2/16/44.
43. Ronny Annenberg to Walter Annenberg, 12/1/41.
44. Walter Annenberg to Ronny Annenberg, 10/21/47.
45. Ibid., 8/4/41.
46. Ibid., 9/17/41.
47. Walter Annenberg to Moses Annenberg, 4/23/42.
48. Wallis Annenberg, 3/4/97.
49. Wallis Annenberg, 3/3/97.
50. *Veronica Annenberg vs. Walter Annenberg*, Bill of Complaint for Divorce, Circuit Court, Dade County, Florida, undated, but 1950, WHA papers.
51. *Veronica Annenberg vs. Walter Annenberg*, Answer and Waiver of Notices, 4/19/50, WHA papers.
52. Joseph First to Morton Wilner, 3/2/50, WHA papers.
53. Mandell Ourisman, 5/25/97.

SEEDS OF EMPIRE

1. Sidney Freiberg, *An Appraisal of the Printing and Publishing Division of the War Production Board, 1942–1945*, published 1946.
2. Walter Annenberg, 4/16/96.
3. David Sendler, 3/26/97.
4. *Newsweek*, 10/30/44, p. 89.
5. Walter Annenberg to Wade Nichols, 12/16/44, WHA papers.
6. Walter Annenberg, 7/8/96.
7. Sadie Annenberg to Walter Annenberg, undated, March 1946, WHA papers.
8. Walter Annenberg, 10/13/95.
9. Helen Valentine to Walter Annenberg, 3/11/48, WHA papers.
10. Walter Annenberg, 11/15/95.

11. Ibid.
12. Cooney, *The Annenbergs*, pp. 247–248.
13. *New York Times*, 4/13/70.
14. Cooney, pp. 248–249.
15. Enid Haupt, *New York Journal American*, 7/21/61.
16. *New York Times*, 9/8/63.
17. Cooney, p. 187.
18. Walter Annenberg to Moses Annenberg, 3/12/42, WHA papers.
19. Cooney, p. 190.
20. Marion Hoeflich Dimitman, 10/16/97.
21. Walter Annenberg to Joe First, 8/3/46, WHA papers.
22. Walter Annenberg to Joe First, 8/5/46, WHA papers.
23. Walter Annenberg to Joe First, 8/19/46, WHA papers.
24. Walter Annenberg to Joe First (second letter), 8/19/46, WHA papers.
25. Walter Annenberg to Joe First, 9/1/46, WHA papers.
26. Walter Annenberg, 11/15/95.
27. Walter Annenberg to Charles J. Mammel, 4/4/69, WHA papers.
28. Peter Binzen, *Philadelphia Inquirer Magazine*, 12/17/89.
29. *Philadelphia Inquirer*, 10/27/49.
30. *Time*, 11/21/49.

LEE

1. Leonore Annenberg, 4/16/96.
2. Harriet Deutsch, 4/18/96.
3. Leonore Annenberg, 4/16/96.
4. Judith Cohn Wolf, 5/30/97.
5. Bob Thomas, *King Cohn: The Life and Times of Harry Cohn*, p. 61.
6. Leonore Annenberg, 4/16/96.
7. Harriet Deutsch, 4/18/96.
8. Walter Annenberg to Leonore Rosenstiel, 4/3/50, WHA papers.
9. Harold Kohn to Walter Annenberg, 10/3/51, WHA papers.
10. Leonore Rosenstiel to Walter Annenberg, 5/13/51, WHA papers.
11. Ibid.
12. Leonore Annenberg, 11/1/98.
13. Evelyn Annenberg Hall, 11/26/96.
14. Leonore Annenberg, 4/16/96.
15. Catherine Barnett, "A Very Private View," *Art and Antiques*, March 1989.
16. Leonore and Walter Annenberg, 2/25/97.
17. Joseph E. Hafner to Walter Annenberg, 10/8/70, WHA papers.
18. Thomas Hoving, *Connoisseur*, May 1983.
19. Joseph E. Hafner to Walter Annenberg, 10/18/70.
20. Clyde H. Farnsworth, *New York Times*, 9/10/73.
21. Daniel Wildenstein, 9/16/98.

TELEVISION

1. Merrill Panitt, *TV Guide: The First 25 Years*, ed. Jay Harris, pp. 15–16.
2. Walter Annenberg, 11/14/96.
3. Ibid.
4. *Newsweek*, 5/19/53, p. 96.
5. Cooney, *The Annenbergs*, pp. 238–239.
6. Irvin J. Borowsky, 11/23/98.
7. Walter Annenberg, 11/15/95.
8. Walter Annenberg, 7/8/96.
9. Walter Annenberg, 11/15/95.
10. Walter Annenberg, 7/11/95.
11. *Newsweek*, 5/18/53.
12. Panitt, p. 17.
13. Walter Annenberg, 7/8/96.
14. Panitt, p.14.
15. James T. Patterson, *Grand Expectations*, p. 348.
16. *Newsweek*, 5/18/53, pp. 96–97.
17. Glenn C. Altschuler and David I. Grossvogel, *Changing Channels*, pp. 8–9.
18. Ibid., pp. 9–10.
19. Ibid., p. 14.
20. *Newsweek*, 9/9/63, p. 58.
21. Altschuler and Grossvogel, p. 7.
22. Walter Annenberg to Maj. Merrill Panitt, 10/15/45, WHA papers.
23. Panitt, p. 17.
24. *Newsweek*, 9/9/63.
25. Altschuler and Grossvogel, p. 19.
26. Panitt, pp. 53–55.
27. Trager, *The People's Chronology*, p. 980.
28. Bill McCarter, 8/19/98.
29. Walter Annenberg, 11/15/95.
30. Fred Hechinger, *New York Herald Tribune*, 1/7/51.
31. Ibid.
32. John A. Jackson, *American Bandstand*, pp. 15–16.
33. Ibid., p. 24.
34. Walter Annenberg, 4/15/96.
35. Dick Clark, 5/19/97.
36. Ibid.

THE CHILDREN

1. Diane Katleman Deshong, 4/18/96.
2. Elizabeth Rosenstiel Kabler, 3/27/97.
3. Walter Annenberg to Doris Staples and Ann Almy, 1/22/46, WHA papers.

4. Wallis Annenberg, 3/3/97.
5. Ibid.
6. Ibid.
7. Zelda Dunkelman Wilner, 5/19/97.
8. Mandell Ourisman, 5/25/97.
9. Florenz Ourisman, 5/26/97.
10. Wallis Annenberg, 3/3/97.
11. Jack Barker, Landon School report, 12/20/50, WHA papers.
12. Ronny Annenberg Ourisman to Walter Annenberg, 7/9/53, WHA papers.
13. Paul M. Oakley, Landon School report, 5/9/54, WHA papers.
14. Mallory Walker, 5/24/97.
15. Ibid.
16. Walter Annenberg to Simeon Maslin, 11/25/87, WHA papers.
17. Jerome Shestack, 9/10/98.
18. Wallis Annenberg, 3/3/97.
19. Landon School report, 5/10/55, WHA papers.
20. Diane Katleman Deshong, 4/18/96.
21. Leonore Annenberg, 11/21/96.
22. Roger Annenberg to Walter Annenberg, 4/29/56, WHA papers.
23. Episcopal Academy report, 1/25/57, WHA papers.
24. Wallis Annenberg, 3/3/97.
25. Walter Annenberg to Wallis Annenberg, 3/30/51, WHA papers.
26. Ibid., 5/21/51.
27. Ibid., 7/22/52.
28. Ibid., 1/5/53.
29. Walter Annenberg to Roger Annenberg, 11/3/53, WHA papers.
30. Walter Annenberg to Wallis Annenberg, 12/1/55, WHA papers.
31. Ibid., 9/19/56.
32. Walter Annenberg to Roger Annenberg, 12/27/55, WHA papers.
33. Wallis Annenberg to Walter Annenberg, 12/29/52, WHA papers.
34. Walter Annenberg to Wallis Annenberg, 5/17/56, WHA papers.
35. Ibid., 9/28/56.
36. Ibid., 9/9/57.
37. Walter Annenberg to Frederick Ferry Jr., 2/5/58, WHA papers.
38. Katharine Lee to Walter Annenberg, 5/15/59, WHA papers.
39. Anthony Wayne Ridgway, 5/26/97.
40. Joseph Hafner to Roger Annenberg, 2/7/58, WHA papers.
41. Episcopal Academy yearbook, 1958, p. 17, WHA papers.
42. Walter Annenberg to Donald Felt, 2/16/59, WHA papers.
43. Walter Annenberg to Roger Annenberg, 2/16/59, WHA papers.
44. Roger Annenberg to Walter Annenberg, 5/30/59, WHA papers.
45. Walter Annenberg to William Slottman, 10/26/59, WHA papers.
46. Lloyd Dahmen, 5/27/97.
47. Philip Olsson, 5/24/97.
48. Burns, *Roosevelt: The Lion and the Fox*, p. 18.

49. Walter Annenberg to Roger Annenberg, 4/11/60, WHA papers.
50. Joseph First to Roger Annenberg, 7/5/60, WHA papers.
51. Jerome Weinberger, M.D., to Walter Annenberg, 1/1/61, WHA papers.
52. O. Spurgeon English, M.D., to Walter Annenberg, 1/23/61, WHA papers.
53. Ibid., 2/17/61.
54. American Medical Association, *Encyclopedia of Medicine*, 1989, p. 884.
55. Roger Annenberg to Lee and Walter Annenberg, 7/20/62, WHA papers.
56. Leonore Annenberg, 11/21/96.
57. Walter Annenberg, 11/10/97.

PRESS LORD

1. *Newsweek*, 11/19/51, p. 64.
2. Walter Annenberg, 11/14/95.
3. Walter Annenberg, 11/21/96.
4. Walter Annenberg to Leonard Bach, 8/18/80, WHA papers.
5. *Time*, 5/21/48, p. 20.
6. Harry J. LaCroix, *Philadelphia Inquirer*, first column, undated, 1952.
7. Walter Annenberg, 2/24/97.
8. Walter Annenberg, 5/30/95.
9. William Coleman, 2/9/96.
10. Confidential source, 9/98.
11. Cooney, *The Annenbergs*, pp. 202–203.
12. Eric Larson, 9/11/98.
13. Walter Annenberg, 4/15/96.
14. *Philadelphia Inquirer*, 4/15/50.
15. Walter Annenberg, 11/15/95.
16. Walter Annenberg, 7/9/96.
17. Confidential source, 6/30/97.
18. Walter Annenberg, 7/9/96.
19. Fonzi, *Annenberg*, p. 139.
20. Nicholas Katzenbach, 10/7/96.
21. Robert Greenberg, 7/3/97.
22. George Widener to Walter Annenberg, 12/14/60, WHA papers.
23. Walter Annenberg to George Widener, 12/16/60, WHA papers.
24. Walter Annenberg, 4/16/96.
25. Stephen Ambrose, *Nixon: The Education of a Politician*, p. 25.
26. Fonzi, p. 164.
27. Katharine Graham, *Personal History*, p. 189.
28. Walter Annenberg, 5/9/97; Richard Norton Smith, *The Colonel*, p. 516.
29. Walter Annenberg, 5/30/97.
30. Carol Felsenthal, *Power, Privilege and the Post*, p. 167.
31. Graham, p. 216.
32. *Time*, 12/23/57, p. 49.
33. Dimitman, *The Philadelphia Inquirer and the Annenbergs*, ch. 6, p. 33.

34. Cooney, p. 252.
35. Richard Nixon to Walter Annenberg, 7/23/90, WHA papers.
36. *Philadelphia Inquirer,* 9/12/60.
37. Ibid., 9/13/60.
38. Walter Annenberg, 7/9/96.
39. Cooney, pp. 264–265.
40. Walter Annenberg, 4/3/96.
41. Mrs. John F. Kennedy to Walter Annenberg, 1/31/62, WHA papers.
42. Walter Annenberg to Mrs. Joseph P. Kennedy, 7/23/63, WHA papers.
43. Joseph Goulden, 11/13/96.
44. Walter Annenberg, 11/21/96.
45. Walter Annenberg to Mrs. Lyndon Baines Johnson, 4/14/64, WHA papers.
46. Mrs. Lyndon Baines Johnson to Walter Annenberg, 4/17/64, WHA papers.
47. Walter Annenberg, 7/9/96.
48. Walter Annenberg to Richard Nixon, 9/21/64, WHA papers.
49. Joseph Goulden, 11/13/96.
50. Walter Annenberg, 11/14/95.
51. Evelyn Annenberg Hall, 11/26/96.
52. Richard Nixon to Walter Annenberg, 7/7/65; Polly Annenberg Levee to Richard Nixon, 8/11/65, WHA papers.
53. "In Memoriam," private printing, Sadie Annenberg service, WHA papers.
54. Sadie C. Annenberg, quoted in *New York Times,* 7/7/65.
55. Paul Hofmann, *New York Times,* 2/8/66.
56. Dick Schaap, *Turned On,* pp. 47–48.
57. Walter Annenberg to Kingsbury Smith, 3/8/66, WHA papers.
58. Walter Annenberg, 7/9/96, 11/22/96.
59. Joseph Daughen and Peter Binzen, *The Wreck of the Penn Central,* pp. 72–75.
60. Associated Press, *The World in 1970: History as We Lived It,* p. 133.
61. Daughen and Binzen, p. 79.
62. A. James Reichley, *Fortune,* June 1970, p. 136.
63. Cooney, p. 291.
64. Raymond Shafer campaign staffer, 7/1/97.
65. Acel Moore, 7/3/97.
66. *Philadelphia Inquirer,* 10/19/66.
67. Robert Coles, *New York Times,* 9/24/74.
68. Ben Bagdikian, 11/10/98.
69. Robert Greenberg, 7/3/97.
70. *Newsweek,* 12/23/57, p. 71.
71. *Editor and Publisher,* 4/9/60, p. 66.
72. Joseph Goulden, 5/11/97.
73. *Time,* 4/21/67.
74. *Philadelphia Inquirer,* 4/16/67; *Philadelphia* magazine, May 1967.
75. Philip B. Schaeffer, 5/20/97.
76. Joseph Goulden, 5/11/97.
77. William Green, 10/8/96.

78. Walter Annenberg to Elmer Bobst, 4/28/64, Richard Nixon Library & Birthplace Collection, Yorba-Linda, Calif., Nixon-Annenberg correspondence, 1959–64.
79. *Philadelphia Inquirer,* 11/14/62.
80. Walter Annenberg, 11/24/97.
81. Joseph Goulden, 5/11/97.
82. Walter Annenberg, 11/24/97.
83. *New York Times,* 8/26/74.

DREAMWORLD

1. Stephen Birmingham, *California Rich,* p. 301.
2. Armand Deutsch, *Me and Bogie,* p. 11.
3. Deutsch, p. 168.
4. *Town and Country,* January 1986, p. 178.
5. Leonore Annenberg, 4/16/96.
6. Walter Annenberg, 4/15/96.
7. Deutsch, p. 171.
8. Illustrated and illuminated manuscript, tracing Riverside County, Calif., property title, presented as a gift to the Annenbergs by Palmer and Charles Ducommun, 9/2/87.
9. Peter Binzen, "Discover," *Philadelphia Sunday Bulletin* magazine, 6/23/74, citing Riverside County, Calif., courthouse records.
10. Wayne Butterfield, Thunderbird Realty, 9/24/98.
11. William J. Mann, *Wisecracker: The Life and Times of William Haines, Hollywood's First Openly Gay Star,* 1998.
12. Tim Street-Porter, *The Los Angeles House,* 1995.
13. William Haines, *Architectural Digest,* September/October 1972, p. 100.
14. Nancy Holmes, *Town and Country,* February 1978, p. 127.
15. Leonore Annenberg, 4/16/96.
16. Quincy Jones, per Harry Saunders to Walter Annenberg, 8/14/64, WHA papers.
17. Walter Annenberg to Quincy Jones, 2/10/64, WHA papers.
18. Walter Annenberg to Gerald Ford, 3/15/74, WHA papers.
19. *Desert Sun,* 12/7/68.
20. Herbert S. Parmet, *Richard Nixon and His America,* p. 509.
21. Nancy Reagan to Lee and Walter Annenberg, 4/15/67, WHA papers.
22. Richard Nixon, *Memoirs,* p. 312.
23. Walter Annenberg, 11/21/96.
24. Walter Annenberg, 10/2/96.
25. Cooney, *The Annenbergs,* p. 12.
26. Ibid.
27. Ibid., p. 14.
28. Peter Flanigan, 7/7/97.
29. Sally Bedell Smith, *In All His Glory,* pp. 472–473.

30. William P. Rogers, 4/4/96.
31. *Time*, 3/21/69, p. 15.
32. *New York Times*, 1/11/69.
33. Cooney, p. 320.
34. Philip M. Kaiser, *Journeying Far and Wide*, pp. 218–219.
35. Nelson D. Lankford, *The Last American Aristocrat*, p. 172.
36. David K. E. Bruce diary, 2/3/69, Bruce papers, Virginia Historial Society.
37. *Winfield House*, official history and guidebook, U.S. Embassy publication, undated.
38. Peter Skoufis, 2/12/96.
39. David K. E. Bruce diary, 2/11/69, Bruce papers, Virginia Historical Society.
40. Fleur Cowles, 5/3/96.
41. Richard Harwood, *Washington Post*, 8/5/97.
42. Stephen E. Ambrose, *Nixon: The Education of a Politician, 1913–1962*, p. 296.
43. Jack Anderson, 1/21/99; Richard Harwood, *Washington Post*, 8/5/97.
44. Mims Thomason to Walter Annenberg, 2/25/69, WHA papers.
45. Walter Annenberg to Mims Thomason, 3/4/69, WHA papers.
46. Cooney, pp. 325–326.
47. Hearing before the Committee on Foreign Relations, 3/7/69, U.S. Government Printing Office, 91st Congress.
48. Roger Rosenblatt, *New York Times Magazine*, 12/31/95, p. 33.
49. David McCullough, *Truman*, p. 523.
50. Nixon, p. 339.
51. Rowland Evans, 5/8/97.

ROUGH START

1. John Adams, James Monroe, John Quincy Adams, Martin Van Buren, James Buchanan.
2. Walter Annenberg, 6/15/95.
3. Peter Younghusband, *Daily Mail*, 2/21/69.
4. *Daily Express*, 2/23/69.
5. Andrew Kopkind, *New Statesman*, 2/28/69.
6. *Time*, 11/22/68, p. 11.
7. George Brown, *In My Way*, p. 131.
8. *Time*, 11/22/68, p. 11.
9. Henry Kissinger, *White House Years*, p. 95.
10. Ibid., p. 96.
11. Arthur Hartman, 5/4/96.
12. Joseph N. Greene, 5/11/97.
13. William Hyland, 3/29/96.
14. David K. E. Bruce diary, 2/28/69, Bruce papers, Virginia Historical Society.
15. Walter Annenberg to the Pilgrims, official United States Information Service text, 5/28/69, WHA papers.
16. *Daily Telegraph*, 5/29/69.

17. *Sunday Telegraph,* 6/1/69.
18. Robert Montgomery Scott, 11/13/95.
19. Walter Annenberg to Rose Mary Woods, 5/30/69, National Archives, President's (Nixon's) Personal File, Nixon-Annenberg correspondence, 1969–71, R. M. Woods, subj. (A), Box 20 (1 of 3 folders).
20. Richard Nixon to Walter Annenberg, 6/7/69, WHA papers.
21. Martin Charteris, 6/6/96.
22. Thomas Hughes, 3/13/95.
23. Peter Carrington, 5/4/96.
24. Frank Stanton, 7/3/97.
25. William P. Rogers, 4/4/96.
26. Raymond Scherer, 6/25/97.
27. Stephen Birmingham, *McCall's,* June 1970, p. 139.
28. Brian Park, *Daily Express,* 10/9/69.
29. Peter Carrington, 5/4/96.
30. H. H. Williams to Walter Annenberg, 7/7/69.
31. Thomas R. Williams to Walter Annenberg, 10/10/69, WHA papers.
32. Martin Charteris, 5/6/96.
33. James Reston, *New York Times,* 5/29/69.
34. *Diplomatist,* July 1969.
35. Robert Montgomery Scott, 11/13/95.
36. Philip M. Kaiser, 9/7/95.
37. Barbara Castle, *The Castle Diaries, 1964–70,* pp. 721–722.
38. Walter Annenberg, 6/5/95.
39. Daniel Yergin, *The Prize,* p. 623.
40. Cooney, *The Annenbergs,* p. 351.
41. Ibid.
42. Thomas Hughes, 3/13/95; Fleur Cowles, 5/3/96; Ronald Steel, *Walter Lippmann and the American Century,* pp. 590–591.
43. *Philadelphia Inquirer,* 2/21/69.
44. Joseph M. First, memorandum, 12/21/70, WHA papers.
45. Peter Skoufis, 2/12/96.
46. Eric Larson, 9/11/98.
47. *Philadelphia Inquirer,* 10/29/69.
48. John McMullan, 7/3/97.
49. Edward W. Barrett, *Columbia Journalism Review,* Spring 1970, p. 55.
50. Walter Annenberg, 4/16/96.
51. Eugene Roberts, 7/1/97.
52. Tom Murphy, 7/2/97.
53. Walter Annenberg, 11/14/96.

SMOOTH FINISH

1. William Galloway, 2/9/96.
2. Ibid.

3. Cooney, *The Annenbergs*, pp. 348–349.
4. Bronson Tweedy, 5/16/97.
5. Rolfe Kingsley, 5/16/97.
6. Cord Meyer, 3/29/96.
7. Edward Streator, 6/4/96.
8. *Daily Telegraph*, 9/4/69.
9. *The Spectator*, 9/20/69.
10. Florence Mouckley, *Christian Science Monitor*, 12/9/69, p. 16.
11. Aileen Mehle, "Suzy Says," *New York Daily News*, 12/1/69.
12. *Evening Standard*, 11/28/69.
13. Caroline Seitz, 6/5/96.
14. James Hanson, 6/4/96.
15. Arthur Hartman, 5/4/96.
16. Walter Annenberg to Chief Constable W. J. Richards, 4/2/70, WHA papers.
17. Peter Skoufis, 2/12/96.
18. Joseph N. Greene, 6/13/97.
19. Skoufis, 2/12/96.
20. Walter Annenberg to Edward Heath, 4/18/71, WHA papers.
21. Walter Annenberg, *Westminster Abbey*, 1972, dedication.
22. Cooney, p. 368.
23. Walter Annenberg, 7/12/95.
24. Ibid.
25. Alastair Aird, 5/7/96.
26. *Daily Mirror*, 1/21/82.
27. Richard Nixon to Walter Annenberg, National Archives, President's (Nixon's) Personal File, Name/Subject (A), 1969–74, Box 5.
28. *Evening Standard*, 5/13/74.
29. Edward Heath, 6/5/96.
30. Henry Kissinger, *Years of Upheaval*, pp. 140–141.
31. Margaret Thatcher, 2/28/97.
32. Walter Annenberg, 6/18/96; Edward Heath, 6/6/96; Carol and Charles Price, 2/25/97.
33. Walter Annenberg, 11/21/96.
34. Walter Annenberg to Richard Nixon, 11/12/72, WHA papers.
35. Walter Annenberg to Richard Nixon, 11/16/73, WHA papers.
36. Walter Annenberg to Rose Mary Woods, 12/7/73, memorandum of phone conversation, National Archives, President's (Nixon's) Personal File, R. M. Woods, Name/Subject (A), 1969–74, Box 3 (folder 3 of 3).
37. Walter Annenberg, 2/24/97.
38. Walter Annenberg, 11/14/95.
39. Peter Carrington, 6/4/96.
40. William P. Rogers, 4/4/96.
41. Walter Annenberg to Rose Mary Woods, 12/7/73, National Archives.
42. Walter Annenberg to Rose Mary Woods, 1/4/74, box, folder, unspecified.

43. Confidential embassy source.
44. H. R. Haldeman to Dave Parker, 1/30/73, National Archives, President's (Nixon's) Personal File, no citation.
45. H. R. Haldeman, *The Haldeman Diaries*, p. 7.
46. Julie Nixon Eisenhower, 11/13/98.
47. Walter Annenberg to Richard Nixon, 8/7/74, telegram, 12:25 P.M., WHA papers.
48. Joseph First to Richard Nixon, 8/28/74 and 9/10/74, WHA papers.
49. Elliott Richardson, 6/18/97.
50. Alvin Shuster, *New York Times*, 10/15/74.
51. *Philadelphia Inquirer*, 10/16/74.

BACK HOME

1. Wallis Annenberg, 5/17/86, Pine Manor College videotape.
2. Wallis Annenberg, 3/4/97.
3. Leonore Annenberg, 2/25/97.
4. Walter Annenberg to Mrs. Charles Weingarten, 9/18/66, WHA papers.
5. Walter Annenberg to Mrs. Charles Weingarten, 8/28/71, WHA papers.
6. Wallis Annenberg, 3/4/97.
7. Walter Annenberg to Mrs. Charles Weingarten, 9/16/71, WHA papers.
8. Walter Annenberg to Wallis and Seth Weingarten, 1/12/72, WHA papers.
9. Walter Annenberg to Seth Weingarten, 9/22/72, WHA papers.
10. Walter Annenberg to Seth Weingarten, 11/23/73, WHA papers.
11. Ibid.
12. Wallis Annenberg, 3/4/97.
13. Leonore Annenberg, 2/25/97.
14. Walter Annenberg, 10/2/95.
15. Wallis Annenberg, 1/15/98.
16. Wallis Annenberg, commencement speech, Pine Manor College, 5/19/91.
17. David Sendler, 3/26/97.
18. Bill Bruns, 3/3/97.
19. Martin Hillenbrand, 10/4/96.
20. David Metcalfe, 5/30/96.
21. James Hanson, 6/5/96.
22. Robert Montgomery Scott, 11/13/95.
23. Meyer Potamkin, 6/30/97.
24. Sylvan Cohen, 10/15/96.
25. Ronald Rubin, 10/14/98.
26. Arlin Adams, 9/10/98.
27. Walter Annenberg, Annenberg Research Institute catalogue, undated.
28. Walter Annenberg, 7/2/96.
29. Stephen Wynn, 11/23/98.
30. Bill Bruns, 3/3/97.
31. Arthur Brener to Walter Annenberg, 11/11/88, WHA papers.

32. Fred Grossman, 5/16/97.
33. Peter Paine, 9/8/97.
34. Philip H. Dougherty, *New York Times*, 3/12/85.
35. Thomas Hoving, *Making the Mummies Dance*, p. 14.
36. Hoving, p. 419.
37. Philip Herrera, *Town and Country*, May 1995, p. 84.
38. Hoving, p. 420.
39. Hoving, p. 427.
40. Barbara Goldsmith, *New York* magazine, 3/7/77, p. 31.
41. Walter Annenberg, *New York Times*, 3/14/77.
42. Grace Glueck, *Art News*, May 1977.

REAGAN CONNECTION

1. Ronald Reagan, 5/21/74, quoted in Lou Cannon, *President Reagan: The Role of a Lifetime*, p. 791.
2. Peter Paine, 7/8/97.
3. Walter Annenberg, 11/14/95.
4. Kitty Kelley, *Nancy Reagan*, p. 104.
5. Michael Deaver, 10/30/96.
6. Walter Annenberg to Ronald Reagan, 11/26/58, WHA papers.
7. Bob Colacello, *Vanity Fair*, July 1998, p. 85.
8. Walter Annenberg to Nancy Reagan, 5/31/66, WHA papers.
9. Walter Annenberg to Ronald Reagan, 11/9/66, WHA papers.
10. Ronald Reagan to Walter Annenberg, 12/7/66, WHA papers.
11. Walter Annenberg to Nancy Reagan, 11/21/66, WHA papers.
12. Ronald Reagan to Walter Annenberg, 2/8/67, WHA papers.
13. Walter Annenberg to Ronald Reagan, 12/30/66, WHA papers.
14. Ibid., 2/7/68.
15. Kelley, p. 182.
16. Ronald Reagan to Walter Annenberg, 8/1/72, WHA papers.
17. Walter Annenberg to Margaret Thatcher, 2/21/75, WHA papers.
18. Margaret Thatcher, 2/28/97.
19. Ronald Reagan, *National Review*, 5/19/89.
20. *Desert Sun*, 1/4/79.
21. Federal Election Commission, selected list of receipts, 1979–80; 10/16/97.
22. *TV Guide*, 11/1/80.
23. Nancy Reagan, 7/10/97.
24. Leonore Annenberg, 2/25/97.
25. Patrick Daly, 5/23/97.
26. Gahl Burt, 1/31/98.
27. Nicholas Henderson, *Mandarin*, p. 394.
28. Leonore Annenberg, 11/21/96.
29. Ibid.
30. Walter Annenberg, 7/8/96.

31. Ibid.
32. Frances Spatz Leighton, *The Search for the Real Nancy Reagan*, p. 243; Stephanie Mansfield, *Washington Post*, 5/28/81, p. D1.
33. Buckingham Palace sources.
34. Michael Deaver to Leonore Annenberg, 8/3/81, Ronald Reagan Library, document control 049820-1130.
35. Alexander Haig, 9/11/98.
36. Michael Deaver, 10/30/96.
37. Joseph Canzeri, 6/25/97.
38. Leonore Annenberg, 11/21/96.
39. Selwa Roosevelt, 9/10/98.
40. Alexander Haig, 9/18/98.
41. *New York Times*, 11/17/81.
42. Leonore Annenberg, 2/25/97.
43. Nancy Reagan, 7/10/97.
44. Leonore Annenberg to Ronald Reagan, 12/8/81, Ronald Reagan Library, document control 048430-FG011-04.
45. Ronald Reagan to Leonore Annenberg, 1/5/82, Ronald Reagan Library, document control 048430-FG011-04.
46. Al Franken, *Rush Limbaugh Is a Big, Fat Idiot*, p. 144.
47. Ronald Reagan to Leonore and Walter Annenberg, 2/10/82; Ronald Reagan to Walter Annenberg, undated; Walter Annenberg to Ronald Reagan, 11/28/?; Walter Annenberg to Edwin Meese, 12/20/84.
48. Michael Deaver, 10/30/96.
49. Walter Annenberg, 4/15/96.
50. Michael Deaver, 10/30/96.
51. Walter Annenberg, 4/15/96.

LOOSE ENDS

1. Newton Minow, 9/12/95.
2. Annenberg/CPB Math and Science Project, 1998 Annual Report.
3. William J. Henrich to Walter Annenberg, 1/24/84, WHA papers.
4. John Weisman, 4/12/96.
5. Ralph Davidson, 11/5/98.
6. David Sendler, 3/26/97.
7. Henry A. Grunwald, *One Man's America*, p. 554.
8. Richard Clurman, *To the End of Time*, p. 74.
9. William Henrich, 10/16/96.
10. William Shawcross, *Murdoch*, p. 269.
11. Walter Annenberg to Rupert Murdoch, 2/12/75, WHA papers.
12. Rupert Murdoch to Walter Annenberg, 4/2/75, WHA papers.
13. Rupert Murdoch to Walter Annenberg, 7/14/88, WHA papers.
14. Neil Barsky, *New York Daily News*, 9/9/88.
15. Conrad Black, 2/28/97; Richard Siklos, *Shades of Black*, p. 284.

16. Walter Annenberg, 3/6/96.
17. *Times of London,* 8/8/88.
18. Shawcross, p. 271.
19. Catherine Barnett, "A Very Private View," *Art & Antiques,* March 1989, p. 99.
20. Rita Reif, *New York Times,* 11/16/89.
21. Walter Annenberg, 4/15/95.
22. David Bull, 9/28/98.
23. John Russell, *New York Times,* 5/22/89.
24. John Russell, *House and Garden,* August 1985.
25. Paul Richard, *Washington Post,* 5/23/89.
26. John Russell, *House and Garden,* August 1985.
27. J. Carter Brown, *New York Times,* 4/28/89.
28. Robert Hughes, *Time,* 3/25/91, p. 61.
29. Walter Annenberg, 5/30/95.
30. Richard, 5/23/89.
31. Walter Annenberg, 5/30/95.
32. Hughes, p. 61.
33. William H. Honan, *New York Times,* 4/1/91.
34. Leonore Annenberg, 2/25/97.
35. Honan, 4/1/91.
36. Max Frankel, *The Times of My Life* (New York: Random House, 1999), p. 517.
37. Glenn Collins, *New York Times,* 9/16/91.
38. Susan Heller Anderson, *New York Times,* 5/2/91.

PHILANTHROPIST

1. Leonore Annenberg, 11/21/96.
2. Walter Annenberg, 2/25/97.
3. James Hanson, 6/5/96.
4. Richard Rosenberg, 7/17/97.
5. Norman Pearlstine, 4/26/96.
6. Walter Annenberg, 4/15/96.
7. John McCarthy, 10/16/96.
8. Walter Annenberg, 5/30/95.
9. A. Leon Higginbotham, 7/9/97.
10. Dan Rottenberg, "The Gift of Knowledge," *Town and Country,* December 1990, p. 156.
11. Christopher Edley, 9/9/98.
12. Deborah Sontag, *New York Times,* 6/20/93.
13. Howard Goodman, *Philadelphia Inquirer,* 6/20/93.
14. Kathleen Hall Jamieson, 4/10/96.
15. Dan Rottenberg, *The American Benefactor,* Fall 1997, p. 44.
16. Goodman, 6/20/93.

17. Newton Minow, 9/12/95.
18. Rosemary Ashby, 7/3/97.
19. Minow, 9/12/95.
20. William Celis 3d, *New York Times*, 12/18/93.
21. Dale Mezzacappa and TaNoah Sterling, *Philadelphia Inquirer*, 12/18/93.
22. Philip Hamburger, *Curious World*, p. 70.
23. Walter Annenberg, 11/15/95.
24. Elizabeth Greene, *The Chronicle of Philanthropy*, 1/11/94.
25. Gail Levin, 4/9/96.
26. Barbara Rosenberg, 7/17/97.
27. David Sendler, 3/26/97.
28. Walter Annenberg, at Williamsburg, 9/28/93.
29. *Philadelphia Inquirer*, 1/13/98.
30. Ronald Reagan to Walter Annenberg, 12/18/93, WHA papers.
31. Walter Annenberg, 4/15/96.
32. William P. Rogers, 4/4/96.
33. Brent Scowcroft to Walter Annenberg, 4/8/94, WHA papers.
34. Ann Kaplan, *American Association of Fund-Raising Counsel*, 9/23/98.
35. *New York Times*, 4/30/95.
36. Ross Perot to Ronald Reagan, 3/6/86, WHA papers; Walter Annenberg to Lodwrick Cook, 7/16/92, WHA papers.
37. *Foundation News*, January/February, 1994, p. 12.
38. *Foundation Center*, Foundation Directory, 1998 edition, in *The Chronicle of Philanthropy*, 3/26/98.
39. Gail Levin, 4/9/96.
40. Hillary Rodham Clinton, 6/18/97.
41. Walter Annenberg to Lauren, Gregory and Charles Weingarten, 10/14/94, WHA papers.
42. Ron Chernow, *Titan*, p. 566.

BIBLIOGRAPHY

Abbot, Dean Eric, et al. *Westminster Abbey.* Radnor, Pa./London: Annenberg School Press, Weidenfeld and Nicolson, 1972.

Aldrich, Nelson W. Jr. *Old Money.* New York: Alfred A. Knopf, 1988.

Altschuler, Glenn C., and David I. Grossvogel. *Changing Channels: America in TV Guide.* Urbana, Ill.: University of Illinois Press, 1992.

Ambrose, Stephen E. *Nixon: The Education of a Politician, 1913–1962.* New York: Simon and Schuster, 1987.

———. *Nixon: The Triumph of a Politician, 1962–1972.* New York: Simon and Schuster, 1989.

———. *Nixon: Ruin and Recovery, 1973–1990.* New York: Simon and Schuster, 1991.

Andrews, Wayne. *Battle for Chicago.* New York: Harcourt, Brace, 1946.

Appel, David H., ed. *An Album for Americans.* New York: Crown, 1983.

Asbury, Herbert. *Gem of the Prairie: An Informal History of the Chicago Underworld.* New York: Alfred A. Knopf, 1940.

Bailey, Colin B., Joseph J. Rishel and Mark Rosenthal. *The Annenberg Collection.* Philadelphia: Philadelphia Museum of Art, 1989.

Baltzell, E. Digby. *Philadelphia Gentlemen: The Making of a National Upper Class.* Glencoe, Ill.: Free Press, 1958.

———. *The Protestant Establisment.* New Haven: Yale Press, 1964.

———. *The Protestant Establishment Revisited.* New Brunswick, N.J.: Transaction Publishers, 1991.

———. *Puritan Boston and Quaker Philadelphia.* New Brunswick, N.J.: Transaction Publishers, 1996.

———. *Judgment and Sensibility: Religion and Stratification.* New Brunswick, N.J.: Transaction Publishers, 1994.

Barnouw, Erik. *Tube of Plenty: The Evolution of American Television.* New York: Oxford University Press, 1990.

Belfield, Richard, Christopher Hird and Sharon Kelly. *Murdoch: The Decline of an Empire*. London: Macdonald, 1991.

Bennett, James V., *Federal Offenders 1940: The Year in Review*. Leavenworth, Kans.: Federal Prison Press, 1941. (also brochure, U.S. Penitentiary, Lewisburg, Pa., 1954.)

Bergreen, Laurence. *Capone: The Man and the Era*. New York: Simon and Schuster, 1994.

Bermant, Chaim. *The Jews*. New York: Times Books, 1977.

Beschloss, Michael R. *Kennedy and Roosevelt: The Uneasy Alliance*. New York: Harper and Row, 1980.

Bessie, Simon Michael. *Jazz Journalism: The Story of the Tabloid Newspapers*. New York: Russell and Russell, 1969.

Binzen, Peter, ed. *Nearly Everybody Read It: Snapshots of the Philadelphia Bulletin*. Philadelphia: Camino Books, 1998.

Birmingham, Stephen. *Our Crowd: The Great Jewish Families of New York*. New York: Harper and Row, 1967.

———. *The Rest of Us: The Rise of America's Eastern European Jews*. Boston: Little, Brown, 1984.

———. *The Grandees: America's Sephardic Elite*. New York: Harper and Row, 1983.

———. *America's Secret Aristocracy*. Boston: Little, Brown, 1987.

———. *California Rich*. New York: Simon and Schuster, 1980.

Bleyer, Willard Grosvenor. *Main Currents in the History of American Journalism*. Boston: Houghton Mifflin, 1927.

Blum, John Morton. *From the Morgenthau Diaries: Years of Crisis, 1928–1938*. Boston: Houghton Mifflin, 1959.

Bobrick, Benson. *Knotted Tongues: Stuttering in History and the Quest for a Cure*. New York: Kodansha America, 1996.

Bremner, Robert H. *American Philanthropy*. Chicago: University of Chicago, 1988.

Brisbane, Arthur. *The Book of Today*. New York: International Magazine Company, 1923.

Brookhiser, Richard. *The Way of the WASP*. New York: Free Press, 1991.

Burnham, David. *A Law Unto Itself: Power, Politics and the IRS*. New York: Random House, 1989.

Burns, James MacGregor. *Roosevelt: The Lion and the Fox*. New York: Konecky and Konecky, 1984.

———. *Roosevelt: The Soldier of Freedom*. New York: Harcourt Brace Jovanovich, 1970.

Burt, Nathaniel. *The Perennial Philadelphians: The Anatomy of an American Aristocracy*. Boston: Little, Brown, 1963.

Byron, Christopher M. *The Fanciest Dive*. New York: W. W. Norton, 1986.

Campbell, John. *Edward Heath: A Biography*. London: Pimlico, 1993.

Carlson, Oliver. *Brisbane: A Candid Biography*. Westport, Conn.: Greenwood Press, 1970.

Caro, Robert. *The Path to Power: The Years of Lyndon Johnson*, vol. 1. New York: Alfred A. Knopf, 1982.

Castle, Barbara. *The Castle Diaries, 1964–1970*. London: Weidenfeld and Nicolson, 1974.

Castleman, Harry, and Walter J. Podrazik. *Watching TV: Four Decades of American Television*. New York: McGraw-Hill, 1982.

Chapman, John. *Tell It to Sweeney: The Informal History of the New York Daily News*. New York: Doubleday, 1961.

Christopher, Robert C. *Crashing the Gates: The De-WASPing of America's Power Elite*. New York: Simon and Schuster, 1989.

Clurman, Richard M. *To the End of Time: The Seduction and Conquest of a Media Empire*. New York: Simon and Schuster, 1992.

Conrad, Will C., Kathleen F. Wilson and Dale Wilson. *The Milwaukee Journal: The First Eighty Years*. Madison, Wis.: University of Wisconsin, 1964.

Cooney, John. *The Annenbergs: The Salvaging of a Tainted Dynasty*. New York: Simon and Schuster, 1982.

Daughen, Joseph R., and Peter Binzen. *The Cop Who Would Be King: Mayor Frank Rizzo*. Boston: Little, Brown, 1977.

———. *The Wreck of the Penn Central*. Boston: Little, Brown, 1971.

Davis, Deborah. *Katharine the Great: Katharine Graham and the Washington Post*. Bethesda, Md.: Zenith, National Press, 1987.

Deaver, Michael K., with Mickey Herskowitz. *Behind the Scenes*. New York: William Morrow, 1987.

Dedmon, Emmett. *Fabulous Chicago*. New York: Atheneum, 1981.

Deutsch, Armand. *Me and Bogie*. New York: G. P. Putnam's, 1991.

Dimitman, E. Z. *The Philadelphia Inquirer and the Annenbergs* (unpublished), 1971.

Dunkelman, Ben. *Dual Allegiance*. New York: Crown, 1976.

Ehlinger, Robert J. *Matt: A Biography of Matthew H. McCloskey*. Philadelphia: Winchell, 1987.

Encyclopaedia Judaica. Jerusalem: MacMillan/Keter Publishing, 1971.

Felsenthal, Carol. *Power, Privilege and the Post: The Katharine Graham Story*. New York: G. P. Putnam's Sons; 1993.

Flynn, John T. "Smart Money." *Collier's*. Four-part series. January 13, 1937–February 3, 1937.

Fonzi, Gaeton. *Annenberg: A Biography of Power*. New York: Weybright and Talley, 1970.

Fox, Stephen. *Blood and Power: Organized Crime in Twentieth Century America*. New York: William Morrow, 1989.

Friedrich, Otto. *Decline and Fall* [of Curtis Publishing]. New York: Harper and Row, 1969.

———. *City of Nets: A Portrait of Hollywood in the 1940s*. New York: Harper and Row, 1986.

Gabler, Neal. *Winchell: Gossip, Power and the Culture of Celebrity*. New York: Vintage, 1995.

———. *An Empire of Their Own: How the Jews Invented Hollywood.* New York: Crown, 1988.

Galbraith, John Kenneth. *The Great Crash.* Boston: Houghton Mifflin, 1961.

Gavreau, Emile. *My Last Million Readers.* New York: E. P. Dutton, 1941.

———. *The Scandal Monger.* New York: Macaulay, 1932.

Geiger, Carl. E. *The Peddie School's First Century.* Valley Forge, Pa.: Judson Press, 1965.

Goodwin, Doris Kearns. *No Ordinary Time: Franklin and Eleanor Roosevelt, The Home Front in World War II.* New York: Simon and Schuster, 1994.

Gosch, Martin A. and Richard Hammer. *The Last Testament of Lucky Luciano.* Boston: Little, Brown, 1975.

Goulden, Joseph C. *Monopoly.* New York: G. P. Putnam's Sons, 1968.

———. *The Best Years, 1945–1950.* New York: Atheneum, 1976.

Graham, Katharine. *Personal History.* New York: Alfred A. Knopf, 1997.

Gunther, John. *Roosevelt in Retrospect.* New York: Harper and Bros., 1946.

Halberstam, David. *The Fifties.* New York: Villard, 1993.

Haldeman, H. R. *The Haldeman Diaries: Inside the Nixon White House.* New York: G. P. Putnam's Sons, 1994.

Handlin, Oscar. *The Uprooted.* Boston: Little, Brown, 1973.

Harris, Jay S., ed. *TV Guide: The First 25 Years.* New York: Simon and Schuster, 1978.

Hirsch, Joe: *The First Century: Daily Racing Form Chronicles, 100 Years of Thoroughbred Racing.* New York: Daily Racing Form Press, 1996.

Hirsch, Susan E., and Robert I. Goler. *A City Comes of Age: Chicago in the 1890s.* Chicago: Chicago Historical Society, 1990.

Holbrook, Stewart H. *The Age of the Moguls.* New York: Doubleday, 1953.

Holli, Melvin G., and Peter d'A. Jones, eds. *Ethnic Chicago: A Multicultural Portrait.* Grand Rapids, Mich.: William B. Eerdmans, 1995.

Hoving, Thomas. *Making the Mummies Dance.* New York: Simon and Schuster, 1993.

Hynds, Ernest C. *American Newspapers in the 1970s.* New York: Hastings House, 1975.

Ickes, Harold L. *The Secret Diary of Harold L. Ickes: The First Thousand Days, 1933–1936.* New York: Simon and Schuster, 1953.

———, ed. *Freedom of the Press Today.* New York: Vanguard, 1941.

———. *America's House of Lords: An Inquiry into the Freedom of the Press.* New York: Harcourt, Brace, 1939.

Irey, Elmer L. *The Tax Dodgers: The Inside Story of the T-Men's War with America's Political and Underworld Hoodlums.* New York: Greenberg, 1948.

Jackson, John A. *American Bandstand: Dick Clark and the Making of a Rock 'N' Roll Empire.* New York: Oxford University Press, 1997.

Jeans, Paul G. *Tropical Disturbance: The Story of the Making of the Miami Tribune.* Miami: Miami Tribune, April 4, 1937.

Johnson, Paul. *Modern Times: The World from the Twenties to the Nineties.* New York: HarperPerennial, 1992.

Josephson, Matthew. *The Robber Barons: The Great American Capitalists, 1861–1901.* New York: Harcourt, Brace, 1934.

Kaiser, Philip M. *Journeying Far and Wide: A Political and Diplomatic Memoir.* New York: Charles Scribner's Sons, 1992.

Kelley, Kitty: *Nancy Reagan: The Unauthorized Biography.* New York: Simon and Schuster, 1991.

———. *The Royals.* New York: Warner Books, 1997.

Kelley, Robert F. *Racing in America, 1937–1959.* (printed privately by the Jockey Club, New York), 1960.

Kessler, Ronald. *The Sins of the Father: Joseph P. Kennedy and the Dynasty He Founded.* New York: Warner, 1996.

Kissinger, Henry. *Diplomacy.* New York: Simon and Schuster, 1994.

———. *White House Years.* Boston: Little, Brown, 1979.

Kogel, Ruth M., Sybil Cohen and Barbara Braunstein. *This Is Great Neck.* New York: League of Women Voters of Great Neck, 1983.

Konolige, Kit. *The Richest Women in the World.* New York: MacMillan, 1985.

Krefetz, Gerald. *Jews and Money: The Myths and the Reality.* New York: Ticknor and Fields, 1982.

Lacey, Robert. *Little Man: Meyer Lansky and the Gangster Life.* Boston: Little, Brown, 1991.

Laing, Margaret. *Edward Heath, Prime Minister.* London: Sidgwick and Jackson, 1972.

Lankford, Nelson D. *The Last American Aristocrat: The Biography of Ambassador David K. E. Bruce.* New York: Little, Brown, 1996.

Lash, Joseph P. *Eleanor and Franklin.* New York: W. W. Norton, 1971.

Learsi, Rufus. *The Jews in America: A History.* Cleveland: World, 1954.

Leighton, Frances Spatz. *The Search for the Real Nancy Reagan.* New York: Macmillan, 1987.

Lewis, Lloyd, and Henry Justin Smith. *Chicago: The History of Its Reputation.* New York: Harcourt, Brace, 1929.

Liebling, A. J. *The Press.* New York: Ballantine, 1972.

Lindberg, Richard. *Chicago Ragtime: Another Look at Chicago, 1880–1920.* South Bend, Ind.: Icarus Press, 1985.

Livingston, Bernard. *Their Turf: America's Horsey Set and Its Princely Dynasties.* New York: Arbor House, 1973.

Longrigg, Roger. *The History of Horse Racing.* New York: Stein and Day, 1972.

Longstreth, W. Thacher, with Dan Rottenberg. *Main Line WASP.* New York: W. W. Norton, 1990.

Lukacs, John. *Philadelphia: Patricians and Philistines, 1900–1950.* New York: Farrar, Straus and Giroux, 1981.

Lundberg, Ferdinand. *Imperial Hearst: A Social Biography.* New York: Equinox Cooperative Press, 1936.

Manchester, William. *The Glory and the Dream: A Narrative History of America, 1932–1972.* New York: Bantam, 1975.

Mazo, Earl, and Stephen Hess. *Nixon.* New York: Harper and Row, 1968.

McCullough, David. *Truman.* New York: Simon and Schuster, 1992.

Meeks, Wayne A., ed. *The HarperCollins Study Bible.* New York: HarperCollins, 1989.

Meites, Hyman L., ed. *History of the Jews of Chicago.* 1924. Reprint, Chicago: Chicago Jewish Historical Society and Wellington, 1990.

Meltzer, Milton. *World of Our Fathers: The Jews of Eastern Europe.* New York: Farrar, Straus and Giroux, 1974.

————. *Remember the Days: A Short History of the Jewish American.* New York: Doubleday/Zenith, 1974.

Messick, Hank. *John Edgar Hoover.* New York: David McKay, 1972.

Miller, Donald L. *City of the Century: The Epic of Chicago and the Making of America.* New York: Simon and Schuster, 1996.

Minow, Newton, and Craig L. Lamay. *Abandoned in the Wasteland: Children, Television and the First Amendment.* New York: Hill and Wang, 1995.

Mosedale, John. *The Men Who Invented Broadway: Damon Runyon, Walter Winchell and Their World.* New York: Richard Mariek, 1981.

Muir, Helen. *Miami, USA.* New York: Henry Holt, 1953.

Murray, George. *The Madhouse on Madison Street.* Chicago: Follett, 1965.

Murray, Ken. *The Golden Days of San Simeon.* Los Angeles: MurMar, 1995.

Nielsen, Waldemar A. *Inside American Philanthropy: The Dramas of Donorship.* Norman, Okla.: University of Oklahoma Press, 1996.

————. *The Golden Donors:* New York: E. P. Dutton, 1983.

Nixon, Richard. *In the Arena: A Memoir of Victory, Defeat and Renewal.* New York: Simon and Schuster, 1990.

————. *The Memoirs of Richard Nixon.* London: Arrow, 1979.

Parmet, Herbert S. *Richard Nixon and His America.* New York: Konecky and Konecky, 1990.

Peirce, Neal R. *The Megastates of America. People, Politics and Power in the Ten Great States.* New York: W. W. Norton, 1972.

Pimlott, Ben. *Harold Wilson.* London: HarperCollins, 1993.

Posner, Gerald. *Citizen Perot.* New York: Random House, 1996.

Pusey, Merlo. *Eugene Meyer.* New York: Alfred A. Knopf, 1974.

Rascoe, Burton. *Before I Forget.* New York: Doubleday, Doran, 1937.

Richardson, Elliot. *Reflections of a Radical Moderate.* New York: Pantheon, 1996.

Robertson, William H. P. *The History of Thoroughbred Racing in America.* Englewood Cliffs, N.J.: Prentice-Hall, 1964.

Roth, Andrew. *Heath and the Heathmen.* London: Routledge, 1974.

————. *Harold Wilson: Yorkshire Walter Mitty.* London: Macdonald and Jane's, 1977.

Sampson, Anthony. *Anatomy of Britain.* London: Hodder and Stoughton, 1962.

Sasuly, Richard. *Bookies and Bettors: Two Hundred Years of Gambling.* New York: Holt, Rinehart and Winston, 1982.

Schaap, Dick. *Turned On.* New York: New American Library, 1966.

Schlesinger, Arthur M. Jr. *The Crisis of the Old Order, 1919–1933.* Boston: Houghton Mifflin, 1957.

————. *The Coming of the New Deal*. Boston: Houghton Mifflin, 1959.

Schmidt, G. W., and Klaus-Peter Steinwender. *Insterburger: Four Hundred Years of the City of Insterburg*, 1983.

Schoenberg, Robert J. *Mr. Capone*. New York: William Morrow, 1992.

Seldes, George. *Lords of the Press*. New York: Julian Messner, 1938.

————. *Freedom of the Press*. New York: Bobbs-Merrill, 1935.

Shawcross, William. *Murdoch: The Making of a Media Empire*. New York: Touchstone, 1997.

Shindler, Colin. *Hollywood in Crisis: Cinema and American Society, 1929–1939*. New York: Routledge, 1996.

Sifakis, Carl. *The Mafia Encyclopedia*. New York: Facts on File, 1987.

Silberman, Charles E. *A Certain People: American Jews and Their Lives Today*. New York: Summit, 1985.

Small, William J. *Political Power and the Press*. New York: W. W. Norton, 1972.

Smiley, Nixon. *Yesterday's Miami*. Miami: E. A. Seemann, 1973.

————. *Knights of the Fourth Estate*. Miami: E. A. Seemann, 1974.

Smith, Ken. *University School of Milwaukee at 25: 138 Years of Tradition*. Milwaukee, 1989.

Smith, Richard Norton. *The Colonel: The Life and Legend of Robert R. McCormick*. New York: Houghton Mifflin, 1997.

Smith, Sally Bedell. *In All His Glory: The Life and Times of William S. Paley and the Birth of Modern Broadcasting*. New York: Touchstone, 1990.

Steel, Ronald. *Walter Lippmann and the American Century*. Boston: Little, Brown, 1980.

Stern, J. David. *Memoirs of a Maverick Publisher*. New York: Simon and Schuster, 1962.

Stone, Irving. *Clarence Darrow: For the Defense*. New York: Doubleday, 1941.

Sullivan, Mark. *Our Times: The United States, 1900–1925*. New York: Charles Scribner's Sons, 1927.

Swanberg, W. A. *Citizen Hearst*. New York: Charles Scribner's Sons, 1961.

————. *Luce and His Empire*. New York: Charles Scribner's Sons, 1972.

Tebbel, John. *An American Dynasty: The Story of the McCormicks, Medills and Pattersons*. New York: Greenwood Press, 1968.

————. *The Life and Good Times of William Randolph Hearst*. London: Victor Gollancz, 1953.

Thomas, Bob. *King Cohn: The Life and Times of Harry Cohn*. New York: G. P. Putnam's Sons, 1967.

————. *Clown Prince of Hollywood: The Antic Life and Times of Jack L. Warner*. New York: McGraw-Hill, 1990.

Tims, Barbara, Meredith Ward and Bettina McNulty. *Winfield House*. London: Abacus, 1987.

Trager, James. *The People's Chronicle*. New York: Henry Holt, 1994.

Waldrop, Frank C. *McCormick of Chicago: An Unconventional Portrait of a Controversial Figure*. New Jersey: Prentice-Hall, 1966.

Warner, Jack L., with Dean Jennings. *My First Hundred Years in Hollywood.* New York: Random House, 1964.

Watkins, T. H. *Righteous Pilgrim: The Life and Times of Harold L. Ickes, 1874–1952.* New York: Henry Holt, 1990.

Weigley, Russell F., ed. *Philadelphia: A 300-Year History.* New York: W. W. Norton, 1982.

Wells, Robert W. *This Is Milwaukee.* Milwaukee: Renaissance Books, 1981.

Wendt, Lloyd. *Chicago Tribune: The Rise of a Great American Newspaper.* Chicago: Rand McNally, 1979.

Werblowsky, R. J. Zwi, and Geoffrey Werblowsky. *The Encyclopedia of the Jewish Religion.* New York: Holt, Rinehart and Winston, 1966.

Whited, Charles. *Knight: A Publisher in the Tumultuous Century.* New York: E. P. Dutton, 1988.

Williams, T. Harry. *Huey Long.* New York: Alfred A. Knopf, 1969.

Wilson, Harold. *The Labour Government, 1964–1970.* London: Weidenfeld and Nicolson and Michael Joseph, 1971.

Wood, James Playsted. *Magazines in the United States.* New York: Ronald Press, 1971.

The World in 1970: History as We Lived It. New York: Associated Press, 1971.

Ziegler, Philip. *Wilson: The Authorized Life of Lord Wilson of Rievaulx.* London: HarperCollins, 1993.

Zito, Anthony, a.k.a. Toney Betts. *Across the Board.* New York: Citadel, 1956.

Zweigenhaft, Richard L., and G. William Domhoff. *Jews in the Protestant Establishment.* New York: Praeger, 1982.

ACKNOWLEDGMENTS

THIS IS an unauthorized biography, but it could not have been written without the complete and unstintingly gracious assistance of Lee and Walter Annenberg. When I inquired in 1994 if he would cooperate in a biography about his family, the ambassador promptly declined. Then eighty-six, he said discussing what had happened to his father was too painful. After an exchange of letters with the dispatch and civility that marks his correspondence, he suggested that I come to Sunnylands to talk. I had met him and Lee once before at a British embassy dinner in Washington, D.C., for Margaret Thatcher, the subject of an earlier biography of mine. While he was serving as the U.S. ambassador to Britain in the early 1970s, I was a correspondent based in London. As it was my first full-time job in journalism, I was too junior to attend the ambassador's functions, but I kept up with what he was doing.

His story, which tracked the rise of the American century, fascinated me. Father Moses fled the pogroms of Eastern Europe and arrived in Chicago a shoeless immigrant. A century later, son Walter had become a multibillionaire and the world's most generous living philanthropist. The ingredients for such a transformation in only two generations were rich and compelling: a tough, brilliant and complex father, a compassionate, socially conscious mother, an only son raised with seven sisters, crime, punishment, tragedies, visionary acumen, engrossing marriages and divorces, presidents, royalty, art, money, redemption and triumph.

While I was at Sunnylands, Ambassador Annenberg changed his mind and agreed to cooperate. Over the next four years, in California and Pennsylvania, he and Lee sat for scores of interviews. No subject was out of bounds, including the investigation and imprisonment of Moses Annenberg, the medical troubles and suicide of his son, Roger, former spouses, children's troubles, details of money and investing. Talk is one thing; records, another. In both areas, the Annenbergs were remarkably forthcoming. The ambassador offered work space in his offices in St. Davids, Pennsylvania, the keys to his storage room and filing cabinets, and told me to help myself. It did not matter if he was there or in California for months at a time. I could delve into any files whenever I wished.

His records were extraordinary. He had kept, it appeared, the original or copy of every letter he had written or received since the 1920s: to and from his parents, sisters, children, schoolmates, teachers, business associates and every president from Herbert Hoover to Bill Clinton. He gave me his father's records, the original books that Treasury agents had pored over, and the forty-five-hundred-page case file of FBI agent reports that he had requested ten years earlier under the terms of the Freedom of Information Act. "Here's something you might find interesting," he said one day, pointing to two thick file boxes. Inside was every letter he and his father had exchanged between 1940 and 1942 while Moses was in Lewisburg penitentiary. He turned over his own stock buy-and-sell slips dating to 1925, computer printouts of his recent equity holdings, medical records, wills, love letters and family photograph albums. In short, although the Annenbergs had no control over the contents of this biography, they could not have been more cooperative nor more generous with their time, hospitality and assistance. Few, if any, biographers have been as fortunate. I am very grateful.

The Annenbergs did check me out before embarking on this venture. Among those with whom they spoke was Eppie Lederer, who has known me nearly forty years, since my newspaper-editor father in Rhode Island and Walter Annenberg in Philadelphia almost simultaneously began carrying her "Ann Landers" column, the world's most widely read. Thanks for the endorsement, Eppie.

After the Annenbergs agreed to participate, other family members followed suit: Thank you, Wallis Annenberg, Diane Deshong, Elizabeth Kabler, Evelyn Hall, Cynthia Polsky and Ronald Krancer. Attorney and former Triangle president William Henrich of Dilworth, Paxson, Kalish and Kauffman of Philadelphia offered valuable insights gathered from four decades of close association with the family. I am grateful to Jack McCarthy of Dean Witter in Philadelphia for helping me understand the ambassador's investing philosophy. A major treat was being introduced to the underpinnings of Walter Annenberg's educational philanthropy by Vartan Gregorian, no mean book subject himself.

The Annenberg staff in the Pennsylvania and California offices and homes are as considerate and helpful as they are highly professional. Thank you Renee Austin Rogen, the delightful and talented executive assistant at St. Davids, Lois Bahm and Mary Baffa. Gail Levin, program director of the Annenberg Foundation, answered quickly and accurately and never complained about my unending questions about the ambassador's philanthropy. At Sunnylands, Julia Dixon and Linda Brooks provided answers with charm and aplomb. Michael Comerford, who supervises domestic operations and staff at both Inwood and Sunnylands, is a marvel. No house functions better or is infused with a more gracious spirit.

Bill Phillips of Little, Brown edited the manuscript with enormous skill. He combines a great eye for context and an ear alert for dissonance with a unique talent for thrilling an author with the prospect of rewrites. Smart, insightful and fun, he's what every writer should hope for in an editor. His assistant, Nicole Hirsh, shepherded manuscript and photographs at every stage with precision and good cheer. My thanks also to publisher Sarah Crichton for her support. I am grateful to Fredi Friedman for helping initiate this endeavor. Thank you, Paul Mahon for your wise and witty counsel, not just for closing the deal, and Heather Kilpatrick for your careful legal review. As always, I was lucky to have Alan Gelfuso in my corner.

Thank you, Betty Power of Little, Brown. What a pleasure to work again with such a fine copyeditor.

Cassie Furgurson once again gave me superb research assistance in Washington, D.C., and at the Franklin D. Roosevelt Library in Hyde Park, N.Y. Also helping me in Washington were my *Time* colleagues Anne Moffett, Lissa August, Mark Thompson, Brian Doyle, Neang Seng and Garry Clifford. Work in London was a pleasure with the help of *Time*'s Jim Jackson, Kate Noble, Mairi Ben Brahim and Michael Brunton. In New York, thank you, Tom Goldstein and Kimberly Brown of Columbia University's School of Journalism and Betty Maset for work in the Roosevelt Library archives.

Lany McDonald and Pat Clark made available the tremendous resources of Time Inc.'s research center. Martin Tuohy made research stress-free at the National Archives–Great Lakes Region facility in Chicago, which houses the documentation of the 1939–40 indictment and trial of Moses Annenberg and the papers of Judge James Wilkerson and District Attorney and Judge William Campbell. Helga Halaki researched German language documents from Kalvishken.

A variety of fortuitously placed friends generously helped dig out other material. Editors Howard Tyner and George De Lama opened up the *Chicago Tribune*'s files on Moses and Max Annenberg. Peter Stothard, editor of the *Times* of London, offered a treasure trove of material from Walter's years as ambassador to Britain. Jane Eisner, editorial-page editor of the *Philadelphia Inquirer*, was instrumental in extracting information from archives of the paper the Annenbergs owned for thirty-six years. The Virginia Historical Society's Nelson Lankford, biographer of David K. E. Bruce and editor of his wartime diaries, delved into those diaries again for Bruce's thoughts about the Annenbergs. Gary Cohen shared an unpublished interview with Moses Annenberg he discovered in his own writing research.

Staff at the Chicago Historical Society, Milwaukee Museum and the Library of Congress were uniformly helpful.

Peter Binzen and Dan Rottenberg, two veteran Philadelphia writers, shared insights on their city and the journalistic, business and social circles with which the Annenbergs dealt. Binzen offered unpublished portions of an interview with Richardson Dilworth in which the former *Philadelphia Inquirer* counsel and mayor spoke at length of dealing with Moses Annenberg. Thanks,

Tex McCrary for your recollections of Moses and your father-in-law, Arthur Brisbane. I did not speak with author John Cooney but found his 1982 biography *The Annenbergs* a helpful guide to the terrain, especially in Pennsylvania.

Marion Hoeflich Dimitman gave me her only copy of an unpublished history of the Annenbergs' *Inquirer* written by her husband, E. Z. Dimitman, hours of reflections and a wonderful meal. Author and former *Inquirer* reporter Joe Goulden typed out pages of detailed recollections and sat for interviews. One of the best times I've had in a city was a tour given me by *American Bandstand* star Jerry Blavat. In Philadelphia, everyone knew the "Geator with the Heater," including the Annenbergs.

Thank you, John Hodges for putting me in touch with Roger Annenberg's Harvard roommates; Mary Paige, and Tom Evans and Phyllis Wyeth for entree to the Delaware Valley; and Margaret Cady for your kind Palm Desert hospitality. Photo research, which can be tedious and frustrating, was easy this time thanks to the generosity of the Annenbergs, who produced the lion's share of *Legacy*'s illustrations from their private collection. Thanks also to Time's James Colburn in Washington and Paul Durrant in London, Robert Brow of the Time Inc. picture collection, Norman Currie of Corbis-Bettmann, and Wide World's Camille Ruggiero.

Jef McAllister, Bruce Nelan and Stanley Karnow read the manuscript and offered excellent editorial advice. So did two Michael Ogdens, my father and son. Margo Carper literally kept me from atrophying at my keyboard.

My editors at *Time* were very supportive, not least for excusing me repeatedly from magazine assignments. Thank you Time Warner chairman Jerry Levin and Time Inc. editor-in-chief Norman Pearlstine — both Haverford graduates and friends of Walter Annenberg's — for your encouragement. I'm grateful also to editors Chris Redman, George Russell, Don Morrison, Charles Alexander, Joe Ferrer, and the late Karsten Prager. You are some Time team! And thank you, Rik Kirkland, my patient editor at *Fortune*. Washington bureau chief Michael Duffy and his assistants Judith Stoler and Sharon Roberts showed me unending courtesies, far beyond the call of collegiality.

My biggest thank you, once again, goes to my wife, Deedy, a painter, and our children, Margaret, who sings and sculpts, and Michael, who writes and sings — my own in-house creative support team. Your love, encouragement and often remarkable substantive insights have bolstered this effort from day one and vastly improved the result. Not to mention the light you bring my life. You are wonderful and I love you dearly.

Washington, D.C.
March 1999

INDEX